1984

Consumer Behavior
Classical and Contemporary Dimensions

M

CONTRIBUTORS

Ralph I. Allison
Rena Bartos
Raymond A. Bauer
James A. Bayton
Russell W. Belk
Carol K. Berning
Louis E. Boone
Francis S. Bourne
Steuart Henderson Britt
Thomas L. Brown
Bobby J. Calder
Hadley Cantril
Richard P. Coleman
Harry L. Davis
George S. Day
Ralph L. Day
Thomas F. Dietvorst
Robert J. Gatchel
Betsy D. Gelb
Donald H. Granbois
Harrison L. Grathwohl
Edward L. Grubb
Sandra H. Hart
Albert H. Hastorf
Jacob Jacoby
Philip Kotler
Lawrence M. Lamont
Paul F. Lazarsfeld

V. Parker Lessig
Pierre Martineau
Carl McDaniel
William A. Mindak
Walter R. Nord
Terrence V. O'Brien
Richard W. Olshavsky
C. Whan Park
J. Paul Peter
Joseph T. Plummer
Saul Sands
Charles D. Schewe
Jerome E. Scott
Donald E. Sexton, Jr.
Terence A. Shimp
Denise T. Smart
David L. Sparks
Brian Sternthal
Gregory P. Stone
Humberto S. Tapia
Edward M. Tauber
W. T. Tucker
Alice M. Tybout
Kenneth P. Uhl
Donald E. Vinson
Paul J. Watson
George W. Wynn
J. Thomas Yokum

Consumer Behavior:
Classical and Contemporary Dimensions

James U. McNeal
Stephen W. McDaniel

Texas A&M University

Little, Brown and Company
Boston   Toronto

Library of Congress Catalog Card No. 81-14652

ISBN 0-316-563102

9 8 7 6 5 4 3 2 1

BP

Published simultaneously in Canada
by Little, Brown & Company (Canada) Limited

Printed in the United States of America

Source Acknowledgments

1. "Behavioral Models for Analyzing Buyers" by Philip Kotler from *Journal of Marketing,* vol. 29 (October 1965), pp. 37–45. Reprinted by permission of the American Marketing Association.

2. "Selected Social Psychological Models for Analyzing Buyers" by Charles D. Schewe from *Journal of Marketing,* vol. 37 (July 1973), pp. 31–39. Reprinted by permission of the American Marketing Association.

3. "Consumer Behavior Models: An Introduction" by George W. Wynn was prepared especially for this book.

4. "What About Disposition?" by Jacob Jacoby, Carol K. Berning, and Thomas F. Dietvorst from *Journal of Marketing,* vol. 41 (April 1977), pp. 22–28. Reprinted by permission of the American Marketing Association.

5. "Situational Variables and Consumer Behavior" by Russell W. Belk from *Journal of Consumer Research,* vol. 2 (December 1975), pp. 157–164. Reprinted by permission from *Journal of Consumer Research,* published by The Journal of Consumer Research, Inc.

6. "Theories of Attitude Structure and Change" by George S. Day in *Consumer Behavior: Theoretical Sources,* editors Scott Ward and Thomas S. Robertson, © 1973, pp. 303–353. Reprinted by permission of Prentice-Hall, Inc., Englewood Cliffs, New Jersey.

7. "Cognitive Consistency and Consumer Behavior" by Bobby J. Calder from *Perspectives in Consumer Behavior,* 2nd ed., edited by Harold H. Kassarjian and Thomas S. Robertson, pp. 247–263. Copyright © 1973 by Scott, Foresman and Company. Reprinted by permission of the author. Figure 1 used by permission of Elsevier North Holland Inc.

8. "The Role of Consumer Knowledge in the Study of Consumer Behavior" by James U. McNeal and Stephen W. McDaniel, pp. 37–41, *Journal of Marketing Education* (Spring 1981). Reprinted by permission of the publisher, Business Research Division, University of Colorado at Boulder.

9. "Applying Learning Principles to Marketing" by Steuart Henderson Britt, pp. 5–12, *MSU Business Topics* (Spring 1975). Reprinted by permission of the publisher, Division of Research, Graduate School of Business Administration, Michigan State University.

10. "How Advertising Can Use Psychology's Rules of Learning" by Steuart Henderson Britt from *Printers' Ink,* vol. 252 (September 23, 1955), pp. 74, 77, 80. Reprinted by permission of Hartford National Bank and Trust Company and of Decker Communications, Inc.

11. "A Behavior Modification Perspective on Marketing" by Walter R. Nord and J. Paul Peter from *Journal of Marketing,* vol. 44 (Spring 1980), pp. 36–47. Reprinted by permission of the American Marketing Association.

12. "Murray's Theory of Human Needs: A Useful Guide to Understanding Consumer Behavior" by James U. McNeal and Stephen W. McDaniel was prepared especially for this book. Illustrative material taken from Henry A. Murray, *Explorations in Personality* (New York: Oxford University Press, 1938) by permission of Oxford University Press.

13. "Motivation, Cognition, Learning—Basic Factors in Consumer Behavior" by James A. Bayton from *Journal of Marketing,* vol. 22 (January 1958), pp. 282–289. Reprinted by permission of the American Marketing Association.

14. "Why Do People Shop?" by Edward M. Tauber from *Journal of Marketing,* vol. 36 (October 1972), pp. 46–49. Reprinted by permission of the American Marketing Association.

15. "They Saw a Game: A Case Study" by Albert H. Hastorf and Hadley Cantril from *Journal of Abnormal and Social Psychology,* vol. 49 (1954), pp. 129–134. Copyright 1954 by The American Psychological Association. Reprinted by permission of the publisher and author. Extracts on page 152 reprinted by permission of *Dartmouth.* Extract on page 157 from *New York Herald Tribune,* Dec. 21, 1951. © 1951 International Herald Tribune. Used by permission.

16. "Brand Identification and Perception" by Ralph I. Allison and Kenneth P. Uhl from *Journal of Marketing Research,* vol. 1 (August 1964), pp. 80–85. Reprinted by permission of the American Marketing Association.

17. "Subliminal Stimulation—Marketing Applications" by Sandra H. Hart and Stephen W. McDaniel was prepared especially for this book.

18. "A Multivariate Analysis of Personality and Product Use" by David L. Sparks and W. T. Tucker from *Journal of Marketing Research,* vol. 8 (February 1971), pp. 67–70. Reprinted by permission of the American Marketing Association.

19. "City Shoppers and Urban Identification: Observations on the Social Psychology of City Life" by Gregory P. Stone reprinted from *The American Journal of Sociology,* vol. 60 (July 1954), pp. 36–45, by permission of The University of Chicago Press. Copyright 1954 by The University of Chicago.

20. "The Concept and Application of Life Style Segmentation" by Joseph T. Plummer from *Journal of Marketing,* vol. 38 (January 1974), pp. 33–37. Reprinted by permission of the American Marketing Association.

21. "Consumer Self-Concept, Symbolism and Market Behavior: A Theoretical Approach" by Edward L. Grubb and Harrison L. Grathwohl from *Journal of Marketing,* vol. 31 (October 1967), pp. 22-27. Reprinted by permission of the American Marketing Association.

22. "The Self-Concept in Buyer Behavior" by Terrence V. O'Brien, Humberto S. Tapia, and Thomas L. Brown from *Business Horizons,* vol. 20 (October, 1977), pp. 65-71. Copyright 1977, by the Foundation for the School of Business at Indiana University. Reprinted by permission.

23. "Decision Making Within the Household" by Harry L. Davis from *Journal of Consumer Research,* vol. 2 (March 1976), 241-260. Reprinted by permission from *Journal of Consumer Research,* published by The Journal of Consumer Research, Inc.

24. "Consumer Decision Making—Fact or Fiction?" by Richard W. Olshavsky and Donald H. Granbois from *Journal of Consumer Research,* vol. 6 (September 1979), pp. 93-100. Reprinted by permission from *Journal of Consumer Research,* published by The Journal of Consumer Research, Inc.

25. "Consumer Behavior as Risk Taking" by Raymond A. Bauer in *Dynamic Marketing for a Changing World,* Robert Hancock, ed. (1960), pp. 389-398, published by the American Marketing Association. Reprinted by permission. Extracts on pages 255-256 reprinted by permission of the publisher from Joseph W. Newman, "Consumer External Search: Amount and Determinants," Chapter 6 in *Consumer and Industrial Buying Behavior* edited by Arch G. Woodside et al. © 1977 by Elsevier North Holland.

26. "Using Information Processing Theory to Design Marketing Strategies" by Alice M. Tybout, Bobby J. Calder, and Brian Sternthal from *Journal of Marketing Research,* vol. 18 (February 1981), pp. 73-79. Reprinted by permission of the American Marketing Association.

27. "Toward a Process Model of Consumer Satisfaction" by Ralph L. Day from *Conceptualization and Measurement of Consumer Satisfaction and Dissatisfaction,* proceedings of conference conducted by Marketing Science Institute and National Science Foundation, M.S.I. Report No. 77-103, H. Keith Hunt, ed. (May 1977), pp. 161-175. Reprinted by permission.

28. "Consumer Satisfaction Research: A Review" by Denise T. Smart was prepared especially for this book.

29. "The Adoption Process" by Francis S. Bourne reprinted from *The Adoption of New Products* published by The Foundation for Research on Human Development (1959), pp. 1-8.

30. "Who Are the Marketing Leaders?" by Paul F. Lazarsfeld from *Tide* (May 9, 1958), pp. 53-57. Reprinted by permission of Hartford National Bank and Trust Company and of Decker Communications, Inc.

31. "The Search for the Consumer Innovator" by Louis E. Boone from *Journal of Business,* vol. 43 (April 1970), pp. 135-140. Reprinted by permission of The University of Chicago Press and the author.

32. "Group Influence in Marketing and Public Relations" by Francis S. Bourne. Reprinted by permission from Rensis Likert and Samuel P. Hayes, Jr. (eds.), *Some Applications of Behavior Research* (Paris: The UNESCO Press, 1957), pp. 208-210, 211-212, 217-224. Figure 1 and Table 1 used by permission of the Center for Social Sciences, Columbia University.

To our parents
MARY & CECIL McNEAL
and
ELIZABETH & WELLS McDANIEL

PREFACE

For more than two decades, the field of consumer behavior has been recognized as a most fascinating and legitimate area of study. As more people realize the central role of the consumer in our economic system, more and more interest has been shown in this field. Of particular significance in recent years has been the adoption of the "marketing concept" by most business firms. The marketing concept has as its central theme that all elements of a business should be oriented around the satisfaction of its customers. A firm operating under this philosophy would therefore wish to find out all it could about its customers—who they are, what they like, why they buy, how they make buying decisions, and so forth—and make the desired products available to these consumers under the desired buying conditions. The assumption is that the business firm that does not do this will, in effect, lose customers to the firm that does. Therefore, a thorough understanding of the consumer behavior process will tend to aid the business person in making these customer-oriented business decisions.

Increased interest in consumer behavior is also occurring in other sectors of our economy. Since the early 1960s, government has taken a very active role in consumer affairs and, in particular, consumer protection. Consumer affairs offices, designed to actively pursue consumer rights, can be found at every level of government. Some of their activities include developing consumer laws, enforcing some of these laws, preparing consumer information literature, handling consumer complaints. Doing a beneficial job in this regard is aided by having a good comprehension of consumers and the entire buying process.

An understanding of consumer behavior has also been found desirable among home economists and others charged with providing individuals with information that might be helpful in efficiently carrying out activities associated with their role as consumers. Having an understanding of why consumers buy specific products and behave in certain ways in a buying situation is virtually a prerequisite for teaching individuals to be more perceptive consumers in the marketplace. Ideally, an informed consumer is going to be the best regulator of business activities, since he or she is more likely to perceive which company's product is indeed the best buy for the money. Therefore, helping individuals to know more about themselves as consumers is very important not only for the individuals but also for our type of economic system.

As interest in consumer behavior has risen in recent years, the amount of research and writing in the area has also increased. The purpose of *Consumer Behavior: Classical and Contemporary Dimensions* is to bring together some of the best work in the field into a unified package that will provide a somewhat comprehensive look at this broad area of consumer behavior. In order to cover the spectrum of interests, a mixture of classic and also more recent articles is organized into four major sections. The first section provides an introduction to the subject of Consumer Behavior and emphasizes that consumer buying activites can be systematically analyzed by taking basic human behavioral research and applying it to a consumer buying situation. Two overriding influences on consumer behavior are then stressed in the next two sections of the book. The consumer, in purchase decision making, is going to be influenced by his or her own psychological makeup and also the sociological effects of society. Each of these broad-based influences is analyzed from the standpoint of some of the most important topics of concern to consumer behaviorists. When analyzing the psychological reasons for behavior, it is important to consider such influences as the attitudes that consumers have toward products and companies, the knowledge they possess about these, how learning takes place, what kind of needs people are trying to satisfy in buying certain products, and what motivates individuals to behave in a certain way. Consumers are also influenced by their perception of certain events and their own particular personality, lifestyle, and self-concept, which consumers possibly extend into the specific product they choose to buy. Also in the psychological realm of influences is the actual decision-making process itself, which will then lead to either satisfaction or dissatisfaction on the part of the consumer.

The sociological aspects of consumer behavior are covered in the third section. These include the influences of other people on the actions of an individual. There are innovators and opinion leaders, whose actions will greatly affect the buying decision a consumer will make. A person's reference groups and social class will serve to set norms of behavior that will apply to the selection of one product over another. And the particular subculture of which a person is a part will tend to help form the value system a person possesses, which will be carried over into the marketplace.

The final section takes a look at some major research techniques employed in analyzing consumer behavior. Of particular interest in this section are some of the motivation research techniques that attempt to discover why individuals behave the way they do in a buying situation. Even though this is considered in a separate section, one should realize that the application of these techniques can be found throughout the entire book. Therefore, this section might be a useful reference for supplemental use with other articles in the book.

In deciding on the articles to be contained in this book, we kept two objectives in mind. First, we attempted to bring together the most comprehensive package of articles available, covering all the essential elements of consumer behavior—therefore making this book appropriate for both graduate and undergraduate courses. However, we also took extreme care to select only those articles that the typical undergraduate student can read and comprehend—therefore avoiding articles that were too complex or too technical in nature. In some cases we found it necessary to provide original papers to fulfill the purposes of the book. We hope that we have achieved these two objectives and that this book not only provides comprehensive coverage of the area but also does so with the best quality articles available, in terms of both content and readability.

It is a rare consumer behavior text that can stand alone and still satisfy the diverse demands of breadth and depth of the many teachers in the field. This book is recognition of this fact. It was developed alongside a consumer behavior text, *Consumer Behavior: An Integrative Approach,* by one of the co-editors, James U. McNeal. The two books should provide a complete package for the consumer behavior teacher. We believe that this book of readings will also work well with most leading consumer behavior texts and provide the instructors using texts with the flexibility they desire for their courses. At the end of the book a grid is provided that indicates the specific readings appropriate for each chapter in several leading consumer behavior textbooks.

Comprehensive subject and author indexes, as well as descriptive introductions to each section of the book, are other features that will facilitate its use. Also, at the end of each reading is a set of questions to encourage the student to reflect on the reading's major points. Finally, we have worked closely with the publisher to ensure that the book's printing style provides the student with an invitation to read.

James U. McNeal
Stephen W. McDaniel

ACKNOWLEDGMENTS

This book would not have been possible without the assistance of certain individuals. We sincerely wish to thank Bernard Palela and Jane Tamplin for their efforts with much of the detail work involved in putting together this book of readings. And to our wives, Monie and Nancy, we extend a very warm thank you for putting up with our long hours while this book was in process.

CONTENTS

SECTION ONE

Introduction to Consumer Behavior

The first section of the book serves two purposes: to familiarize the student of consumer behavior with the interdisciplinary approach that is required in order to adequately examine the buying process and to make the student aware of two aspects of consumer behavior typically ignored in discussions of the buying process. This section contains some of the most well-known behavioral and social psychological models along with their applications to the field of consumer behavior. The modeling approach to analyzing consumer behavior is introduced in order to point out the process used to tie together many of the concepts that have an impact on individual buying behavior. Also in this introductory section product disposition is analyzed and situational variables that have an effect on every buying decision are set forth.

In the initial article, Philip Kotler analyzes five of the behavioral models—the Marshallian economic model, the Pavlovian learning model, the Freudian psychoanalytic model, the Veblenian social-psychological model, and the Hobbesian organizational factors model. These models are presented from the standpoint of their marketing applications. Kotler notes that each can be useful in shedding some light on consumer behavior.

Charles Schewe, in the second article, extends Kotler's analysis but confines his discussion to the consumer behavior implications of five social-psychological models—The McClelland model, stressing the theory of achievement motivation; the Goffman model, emphasizing role theory; the Festinger cognitive model, dealing with consistency theory; and the Riesman model, stressing social character. Both Kotler and Schewe emphasize the need for integration of the several models to form one reliable predictive model for consumer behavior. Much can be learned about consumer behavior by applying these theories to buying situations and analyzing consumer actions within the framework of these models.

The next article in this introductory section provides a look at recent attempts to construct actual models of individual consumer behavior. In "Consumer Behavior Models: An Introduction" George Wynn presents an overview of modeling and also provides a brief comparative analysis of three of the most well-known models of consumer behavior—the Howard-Sheth Model; the Engel, Kollat, and Blackwell Model; and the Nicosia Model.

In the fourth article of this section, Jacob Jacoby, Carol K. Berning, and Thomas F. Dietvorst look at what consumers do with products once they have outlived their usefulness and how this relates to the purchase of replacement products. In "What About Disposition?" the authors offer three general alternatives for dealing with such products—(1) consumers can keep the product, (2) they can permanently dispose of it, or (3) they can temporarily dispose of it. Pursuing disposition in their study, they propose several possible alternatives, including converting for another use, storage, throwing away, giving away, trading, selling, renting, loaning, and so forth. The actual choice will depend on psychological characteristics of the decisionmaker, factors intrinsic to the product, and situational factors extrinsic to the product.

Russell W. Belk, in the final article of this section, presents an excellent summary of a very significant area of influence on the buying behavior process. In "Situational Variables and Consumer Behavior" Belk contends that there are three main influences on consumer behavior—personal characteristics, objects, and situations. However, since personal characteristics and objects tend to be stable over time, often it is the situational characteristics that primarily influence behavior. Belk categorizes situational characteristics into five groups—physical surroundings (sounds, weather, lighting, etc.), social surroundings (i.e., other persons present), temporal perspective (i.e., time dimension), task definition (i.e., purpose of shopping), and antecedent states (i.e., mood or momentary condition of consumer). Although this classification might take in some influences that some might consider psychological or sociological, the point is well made that there are definitely other aspects of the buying situation that need to be considered.

1. Behavioral Models for Analyzing Buyers

Philip Kotler

In times past, management could arrive at a fair understanding of its buyers through the daily experience of selling to them. But the growth in the size of firms and markets has removed many decision-makers from direct contact with buyers. Increasingly, decision-makers have had to turn to summary statistics and to behavioral theory, and are spending more money today than ever before to try to understand their buyers.

Who buys? How do they buy? And why? The first two questions relate to relatively overt aspects of buyer behavior, and can be learned about through direct observation and interviewing.

But uncovering *why* people buy is an extremely difficult task. The answer will tend to vary with the investigator's behavioral frame of reference.

The buyer is subject to many influences which trace a complex course through his psyche and lead eventually to overt purchasing responses. This conception of the buying process is illustrated in Figure 1. Various influences and their modes of transmission are shown at the left. At the right are the buyer's responses in choice of product, brand, dealer, quantities, and frequency. In the center stands the buyer and his mysterious psychological processes. The

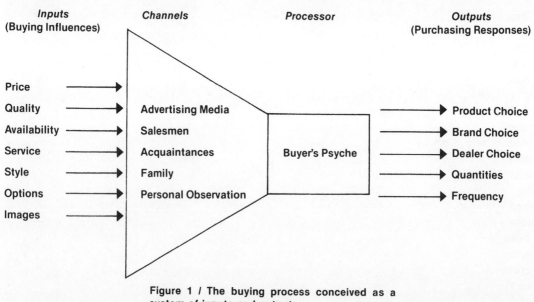

Figure 1 / The buying process conceived as a system of inputs and outputs

buyer's psyche is a "black box" whose workings can be only partially deduced. The marketing strategist's challenge to the behavioral scientist is to construct a more specific model of the mechanism in the black box.

Unfortunately no generally accepted model of the mechanism exists. The human mind, the only entity in nature with deep powers of understanding, still remains the least understood. Scientists can explain planetary motion, genetic determination, and molecular behavior. Yet they have only partial, and often partisan, models of *human* behavior.

Nevertheless, the marketing strategist should recognize the potential interpretative contributions of different partial models for explaining buyer behavior. Depending upon the product, different variables and behavioral mechanisms may assume particular importance. A psychoanalytic behavioral model might throw much light on the factors operating in cigarette demand, while an economic behavioral model might be useful in explaining machine-tool purchasing. Sometimes alternative models may shed light on different demand aspects of the same product.

What are the most useful behavioral models for interpreting the transformation of buying influences into purchasing responses? Five different models of the buyer's "black box" are presented in the present article, along with their respective marketing applications: (1) the Marshallian model, stressing economic motivations; (2) the Pavlovian model, learning; (3) the Freudian model, psychoanalytic motivations; (4) the Veblenian model, social-psychological factors; and (5) the Hobbesian model, organizational factors. These models represent radically different conceptions of the mainsprings of human behavior.

THE MARSHALLIAN ECONOMIC MODEL

Economists were the first professional group to construct a specific theory of buyer behavior. The theory holds that purchasing decisions are the result of largely "rational" and conscious economic calculations. The individual buyer seeks to spend his income on those goods that will deliver the most utility (satisfaction) according to his tastes and relative prices.

The antecedents for this view trace back to the writings of Adam Smith and Jeremy Bentham. Smith set the tone by developing a doctrine of economic growth based on the principle that man is motivated by self-interest in all his actions.[1] Bentham refined this view and saw man as finely calculating and weighing the expected pleasures and pains of every contemplated action.[2]

Bentham's "felicific calculus" was not applied to consumer behavior (as opposed to entrepreneurial behavior) until the late 19th century. Then, the "marginal-utility" theory of value was formulated independently and almost simultaneously by Jevons[3] and Marshall[4] in England, Menger[5] in Austria, and Walras[6] in Switzerland.

Alfred Marshall was the great consolidator of the classical and neoclassical

[1]Adam Smith, *An Inquiry into the Nature and Causes of the Wealth of Nations,* 1776 (New York: The Modern Library, 1937).

[2]Jeremy Bentham, *An Introduction to the Principles of Morals and Legislation,* 1780 (Oxford, England: Clarendon Press, 1907).

[3]William S. Jevons, *The Theory of Political Economy* (New York: The Macmillan Company, 1871).

[4]Alfred Marshall, *Principles of Economics,* 1890 (London: The Macmillan Company, 1927).

[5]Karl Menger, *Principles of Economics,* 1871 (Glencoe, Illinois: Free Press, 1950).

[6]Leon Walras, *Elements of Pure Economics,* 1874 (Homewood, Illinois: Richard D. Irwin, Inc., 1954).

tradition in economics; and his synthesis in the form of demand-supply analysis constitutes the main source of modern microeconomic thought in the English-speaking world. His theoretical work aimed at realism, but his method was to start with simplifying assumptions and to examine the effect of a change in a single variable (say, price) when all other variables were held constant.

He would "reason out" the consequences of the provisional assumptions and in subsequent steps modify his assumptions in the direction of more realism. He employed the "measuring rod of money" as an indicator of the intensity of human psychological desires. Over the years his methods and assumptions have been refined into what is now known as *modern utility theory*: economic man is bent on maximizing his utility, and does this by carefully calculating the "felicific" consequences of any purchase.

> As an example, suppose on a particular evening that John is considering whether to prepare his own dinner or dine out. He estimates that a restaurant meal would cost $2.00 and a home-cooked meal 50 cents. According to the Marshallian model, if John expects less than four times as much satisfaction from the restaurant meal as the home-cooked meal, he will eat at home. The economist typically is not concerned with how these relative preferences are formed by John, or how they may be psychologically modified by new stimuli.
>
> Yet John will not always cook at home. The principle of diminishing marginal utility operates. Within a given time interval—say, a week—the utility of each additional home-cooked meal diminishes. John gets tired of home meals and other products become relatively more attractive.
>
> John's *efficiency* in maximizing his utility depends on the adequacy of his information and his freedom of choice. If he is not perfectly aware of costs, if he misestimates the relative delectability of the two meals, or if he is barred from entering the restaurant,

he will not maximize his potential utility. His choice processes are rational, but the results are inefficient.

Marketing Applications of Marshallian Model

Marketers usually have dismissed the Marshallian model as an absurd figment of ivory-tower imagination. Certainly the behavioral essence of the situation is omitted, in viewing man as calculating the marginal utility of a restaurant meal over a home-cooked meal.

Eva Mueller has reported a study where only one-fourth of the consumers in her sample bought with any substantial degree of deliberation.[7] Yet there are a number of ways to view the model.

From one point of view the Marshallian model is tautological and therefore neither true nor false. The model holds that the buyer acts in the light of his best "interest." But this is not very informative.

A second view is that this is a *normative* rather than a *descriptive* model of behavior. The model provides logical norms for buyers who want to be "rational." Although the consumer is not likely to employ economic analysis to decide between a box of Kleenex and Scotties, he may apply economic analysis in deciding whether to buy a new car. Industrial buyers even more clearly would want an economic calculus for making good decisions.

A third view is that economic factors operate to a greater or lesser extent in all markets, and, therefore, must be included in any comprehensive description of buyer behavior.

---

[7]Eva Mueller, "A Study of Purchase Decisions," Part 2, *Consumer Behavior, The Dynamics of Consumer Reaction,* edited by Lincoln H. Clark (New York: New York University Press, 1954), pp. 36–87.

Furthermore, the model suggests useful behavioral hypotheses such as: (a) The lower the price of the product, the higher the sales. (b) The lower the price of substitute products, the lower the sales of this product; and the lower the price of complementary products, the higher the sales of this product. (c) The higher the real income, the higher the sales of this product, provided that it is not an "inferior" good. (d) The higher the promotional expenditures, the higher the sales.

The validity of these hypotheses does not rest on whether *all* individuals act as economic calculating machines in making their purchasing decisions. For example, some individuals may buy *less* of a product when its price is reduced. They may think that the quality has gone down, or that ownership has less status value. If a majority of buyers view price reductions negatively, then sales may fall, contrary to the first hypothesis.

But for most goods a price reduction increases the relative value of the goods in many buyers' minds and leads to increased sales. This and the other hypotheses are intended to describe average effects.

The impact of economic factors in actual buying situations is studied through experimental design or statistical analyses of past data. Demand equations have been fitted to a wide variety of products—including beer, refrigerators, and chemical fertilizers.[8] More recently, the impact of economic variables on the fortunes of different brands has been pursued with significant results, particularly in the case of coffee, frozen orange juice, and margarine.[9]

But economic factors alone cannot explain all the variations in sales. The Marshallian model ignores the fundamental question of how product and brand preferences are formed. It represents a useful frame of reference for analyzing only one small corner of the "black box."

THE PAVLOVIAN LEARNING MODEL

The designation of a Pavlovian learning model has its origin in the experiments of the Russian psychologist Pavlov, who rang a bell each time before feeding a dog. Soon he was able to induce the dog to salivate by ringing the bell whether or not food was supplied. Pavlov concluded that learning was largely an associative process and that a large component of behavior was conditioned in this way.

Experimental psychologists have continued this mode of research with rats and other animals, including people. Laboratory experiments have been designed to explore such phenomena as learning, forgetting, and the ability to discriminate. The results have been integrated into a stimulus-response model of human behavior, or as someone has "wisecracked," the substitution of a rat psychology for a rational psychology.

The model has been refined over the years, and today is based on four central concepts—those of *drive, cue, response,* and *reinforcement.*[10]

1962), pp. 300–324; and William F. Massy and Ronald E. Frank, "Short Term Price and Dealing Effects in Selected Market Segments," *Journal of Marketing Research,* Vol. 2 (May, 1965), pp. 171–185.

[10]See John Dollard and Neal E. Miller, *Personality and Psychotherapy* (New York: McGraw-Hill Book Company, Inc., 1950), Chapter III.

[8]See Erwin E. Nemmers, *Managerial Economics* (New York: John Wiley & Sons, Inc., 1962), Part II.

[9]See Lester G. Telser, "The Demand for Branded Goods as Estimated from Consumer Panel Data," *Review of Economics and Statistics,* Vol. 44 (August

Drive. Also called needs or motives, drive refers to strong stimuli internal to the individual which impels action. Psychologists draw a distinction between primary physiological drives—such as hunger, thirst, cold, pain, and sex—and learned drives which are derived socially—such as cooperation, fear, and acquisitiveness.

Cue. A drive is very general and impels a particular response only in relation to a particular configuration of cues. Cues are weaker stimuli in the environment and/or in the individual which determine when, where, and how the subject responds. Thus, a coffee advertisement can serve as a cue which stimulates the thirst drive in a housewife. Her response will depend upon this cue and other cues, such as the time of day, the availability of other thirst-quenchers, and the cue's intensity. Often a relative change in a cue's intensity can be more impelling than its absolute level. The housewife may be more motivated by a 2-cents-off sale on a brand of coffee than the fact that this brand's price was low in the first place.

Response. The response is the organism's reaction to the configuration of cues. Yet the same configuration of cues will not necessarily produce the same response in the individual. This depends on the degree to which the experience was rewarding, that is, drive-reducing.

Reinforcement. If the experience is rewarding, a particular response is reinforced; that is, it is strengthened and there is a tendency for it to be repeated when the same configuration of cues appears again. The housewife, for example, will tend to purchase the same brand of coffee each time she goes to her supermarket so long as it is rewarding and the cue configuration does not change. But if a learned response or habit is not reinforced, the strength of the habit diminishes and may be extinguished eventually. Thus, a housewife's preference for a certain coffee may become extinct if she finds the brand out of stock for a number of weeks.

Forgetting, in contrast to extinction, is the tendency for learned associations to weaken, not because of the lack of reinforcement but because of nonuse.

Cue configurations are constantly changing. The housewife sees a new brand of coffee next to her habitual brand, or notes a special price deal on a rival brand. Experimental psychologists have found that the same learned response will be elicited by similar patterns of cues; that is, learned responses are *generalized.* The housewife shifts to a similar brand when her favorite brand is out of stock. This tendency toward generalization over less similar cue configurations is increased in proportion to the strength of the drive. A housewife may buy an inferior coffee if it is the only brand left and if her drive is sufficiently strong.

A counter-tendency to generalization is *discrimination.* When a housewife tries two similar brands and finds one more rewarding, her ability to discriminate between similar cue configurations improves. Discrimination increases the specificity of the cue-response connection, while generalization decreases the specificity.

Marketing Applications of Pavlovian Model

The modern version of the Pavlovian model makes no claim to provide a complete theory of behavior—indeed, such important phenomena as perception, the subconscious, and interpersonal influence are inadequately treated. Yet the model does offer a substantial number of insights about some aspects of behavior of considerable interest to marketers.[11]

An example would be in the problem of introducing a new brand into a highly competitive market. The company's goal is to extinguish existing brand habits and form new habits among consumers for its brand. But the company must first get customers to try its brand; and it has to decide between using weak and strong cues.

Light introductory advertising is a weak cue compared with distributing free samples. Strong cues, although costing more, may be necessary in markets characterized by strong brand loyalties. For example, Folger went into the coffee market by distributing over a million pounds of free coffee.

To build a brand habit, it helps to provide for an extended period of introductory dealing. Furthermore, sufficient quality must be built into the brand so that the experience is reinforcing. Since buyers are more likely to transfer allegiance to similar brands than dissimilar brands (generalization), the company should also investigate what cues in the leading brands have been most effective. Although outright imitation would not necessarily effect the most transference, the question of providing enough similarity should be considered.

The Pavlovian model also provides guide lines in the area of advertising strategy. The American behaviorist, John B. Watson, was a great exponent of repetitive stimuli; in his writings man is viewed as a creature who can be conditioned through repetition and rein-

forcement to respond in particular ways.[12] The Pavlovian model emphasizes the desirability of repetition in advertising. A single exposure is likely to be a very weak cue, hardly able to penetrate the individual's consciousness sufficiently to excite his drives above the threshold level.

Repetition in advertising has two desirable effects. It "fights" forgetting, the tendency for learned responses to weaken in the absence of practice. It provides reinforcement, because after the purchase the consumer becomes selectively exposed to advertisements of the product.

The model also provides guide lines for copy strategy. To be effective as a cue, an advertisement must arouse strong drives in the person. The strongest product-related drives must be identified. For candy bars, it may be hunger; for safety belts, fear; for hair tonics, sex; for automobiles, status. The advertising practitioner must dip into his cue box—words, colors, pictures—and select that configuration of cues that provides the strongest stimulus to these drives.

THE FREUDIAN PSYCHOANALYTIC MODEL

The Freudian model of man is well known, so profound has been its impact on 20th century thought. It is the latest of a series of philosophical "blows" to which man has been exposed in the last 500 years. Copernicus destroyed the idea that man stood at the center of the universe; Darwin tried to refute the idea that man was a special creation; and Freud attacked the idea that man even reigned over his own psyche.

[11]The most consistent application of learning-theory concepts to marketing situations is found in John A. Howard, *Marketing Management: Analysis and Planning* (Homewood, Illinois: Richard D. Irwin, Inc., revised edition, 1963).

[12]John B. Watson, *Behaviorism* (New York: The People's Institute Publishing Company, 1925).

According to Freud, the child enters the world driven by instinctual needs which he cannot gratify by himself. Very quickly and painfully he realizes his separateness from the rest of the world and yet his dependence on it.

He tries to get others to gratify his needs through a variety of blatant means, including intimidation and supplication. Continual frustration leads him to perfect more subtle mechanisms for gratifying his instincts.

As he grows, his psyche becomes increasingly complex. A part of his psyche—the id—remains the reservoir of his strong drives and urges. Another part—the ego—becomes his conscious planning center for finding outlets for his drives. And a third part—his super-ego—channels his instinctive drives into socially approved outlets to avoid the pain of guilt or shame.

The guilt or shame which man feels toward some of his urges—especially his sexual urges—causes him to repress them from his consciousness. Through such defense mechanisms as rationalization and sublimation, these urges are denied or become transmuted into socially approved expressions. Yet these urges are never eliminated or under perfect control; and they emerge, sometimes with a vengeance, in dreams, in slips-of-the-tongue, in neurotic and obsessional behavior, or ultimately in mental breakdown where the ego can no longer maintain the delicate balance between the impulsive power of the id and the oppressive power of the super-ego.

The individual's behavior, therefore, is never simple. His motivational wellsprings are not obvious to a casual observer nor deeply understood by the individual himself. If he is asked why he purchased an expensive foreign sports-car, he may reply that he likes its maneuverability and its looks. At a

deeper level he may have purchased the car to impress others, or to feel young again. At a still deeper level, he may be purchasing the sports-car to achieve substitute gratification for unsatisfied sexual strivings.

Many refinements and changes in emphasis have occurred in this model since the time of Freud. The instinct concept has been replaced by a more careful delineation of basic drives; the three parts of the psyche are regarded now as theoretical concepts rather than actual entities; and the behavioral perspective has been extended to include cultural as well as biological mechanisms.

Instead of the role of the sexual urge in psychic development—Freud's discussion of oral, anal, and genital stages and possible fixations and traumas—Adler[13] emphasized the urge for power and how its thwarting manifests itself in superiority and inferiority complexes; Horney[14] emphasized cultural mechanisms; and Fromm[15] and Erickson[16] emphasized the role of existential crises in personality development. These philosophical divergencies, rather than debilitating the model, have enriched and extended its interpretative value to a wider range of behavioral phenomena.

Marketing Applications of Freudian Model

Perhaps the most important marketing implication of this model is that buyers are motivated by *symbolic* as well as *economic-functional* product concerns. The change of

[13]Alfred Adler, *The Science of Living* (New York: Greenberg, 1929).
[14]Karen Horney, *The Neurotic Personality of Our Time* (New York: W. W. Norton & Co., 1937).
[15]Erich Fromm, *Man For Himself* (New York: Holt, Rinehart & Winston, Inc., 1947).
[16]Erik Erikson, *Childhood and Society* (New York: W. W. Norton & Co., 1949).

a bar of soap from a square to a round shape may be more important in its sexual than its functional connotations. A cake mix that is advertised as involving practically no labor may alienate housewives because the easy life may evoke a sense of guilt.

Motivational research has produced some interesting and occasionally some bizarre hypotheses about what may be in the buyer's mind regarding certain purchases. Thus, it has been suggested at one time or another that

- Many a businessman doesn't fly because of a fear of posthumous guilt—if he crashed, his wife would think of him as stupid for not taking a train.
- Men want their cigars to be odoriferous, in order to prove that they (the men) are masculine.
- A woman is very serious when she bakes a cake because unconsciously she is going through the symbolic act of giving birth.
- A man buys a convertible as a substitute "mistress."
- Consumers prefer vegetable shortening because animal fats stimulate a sense of sin.
- Men who wear suspenders are reacting to an unresolved castration complex.

There are admitted difficulties of proving these assertions. Two prominent motivational researchers, Ernest Dichter and James Vicary, were employed independently by two separate groups in the prune industry to determine why so many people dislike prunes. Dichter found, among other things, that the prune aroused feelings of old age and insecurity in people, whereas Vicary's main finding was that Americans had an emotional block about prunes' laxative qualities.[17] Which is the more valid inter-

pretation? Or if they are both operative, which motive is found with greater statistical frequency in the population?

Unfortunately the usual survey techniques—direct observation and interviewing—can be used to establish the representativeness of more superficial characteristics—age and family size, for example—but are not feasible for establishing the frequency of mental states which are presumed to be deeply "buried" within each individual.

Motivational researchers have to employ time-consuming projective techniques in the hope of throwing individual "egos" off guard. When carefully administered and interpreted, techniques such as word association, sentence completion, picture interpretation, and role-playing can provide some insights into the minds of the small group of examined individuals; but a "leap of faith" is sometimes necessary to generalize these findings to the population.

Nevertheless, motivation research can lead to useful insights and provide inspiration to creative men in the advertising and packaging world. Appeals aimed at the buyer's private world of hopes, dreams, and fears can often be as effective in stimulating purchase as more rationally-directed appeals.

THE VEBLENIAN SOCIAL–PSYCHOLOGICAL MODEL

While most economists have been content to interpret buyer behavior in Marshallian terms. Thorstein Veblen struck out in different directions.

[17]L. Edward Seriven, "Rationality and Irrationality in Motivation Research," in Robert Ferber and Hugh G. Wales, editors, *Motivation and Marketing*

Behavior (Homewood, Illinois: Richard D. Irwin, Inc., 1958), pp. 69–70.

Veblen was trained as an orthodox economist, but evolved into a social thinker greatly influenced by the new science of social anthropology. He saw man as primarily a *social animal*—conforming to the general forms and norms of his larger culture and to the more specific standards of the subcultures and face-to-face groupings to which his life is bound. His wants and behavior are largely molded by his present group-memberships and his aspired group-memberships.

Veblen's best-known example of this is in his description of the leisure class.[18] His hypothesis is that much of economic consumption is motivated not by intrinsic needs or satisfaction so much as by prestige-seeking. He emphasized the strong emulative factors operating in the choice of conspicuous goods like clothes, cars, and houses.

Some of his points, however, seem overstated by today's perspective. The leisure class does not serve as everyone's reference group; many persons aspire to the social patterns of the class immediately above it. And important segments of the affluent class practice conspicuous underconsumption rather than overconsumption. There are many people in all classes who are more anxious to "fit in" than to "stand out." As an example, William H. Whyte found that many families avoided buying air conditioners and other appliances before their neighbors did.[19]

Veblen was not the first nor the only investigator to comment on social influences in behavior; but the incisive quality of his observations did much to stimulate further investigations. Another stimulus came from Karl Marx, who held that each man's world-view was determined largely by his relationship to the "means of production."[20] The early field-work in primitive societies by social anthropologists like Boas[21] and Malinowski[22] and the later field-work in urban societies by men like Park[23] and Thomas[24] contributed much to understanding the influence of society and culture. The research of early Gestalt psychologists—men like Wertheimer,[25] Köhler,[26] and Koffka[27]—into the mechanisms of perception led eventually to investigations of small-group influence on perception.

Marketing Applications of Veblenian Model

The various streams of thought crystallized into the modern social sciences of sociology, cultural anthropology, and social psychology. Basic to them is the view that man's attitudes and behavior are influenced by several levels of society—culture, subcultures, social classes, reference groups, and face-to-face groups. The challenge to the marketer is to determine which of these social levels are the most important in influencing the demand for his product.

[18]Thorstein Veblen, *The Theory of the Leisure Class* (New York: The Macmillan Company, 1899).

[19]William H. Whyte, Jr., "The Web of Word of Mouth," *Fortune*, Vol. 50 (November, 1954), pp. 140 ff.

[20]Karl Marx, *The Communist Manifesto,* 1848 (London: Martin Lawrence, Ltd., 1934).

[21]Franz Boas, *The Mind of Primitive Man* (New York: The Macmillan Company, 1922).

[22]Bronislaw Malinowski, *Sex and Repression in Savage Society* (New York: Meridian Books, 1955).

[23]Robert E. Park, *Human Communities* (Glencoe, Illinois: Free Press, 1952).

[24]William I. Thomas, *The Unadjusted Girl* (Boston: Little, Brown and Company, 1928).

[25]Max Wertheimer, *Productive Thinking* (New York: Harper & Brothers, 1945).

[26]Wolfgang Köhler, *Gestalt Psychology* (New York: Liveright Publishing Co., 1947).

[27]Kurt Koffka, *Principles of Gestalt Psychology* (New York: Harcourt, Brace and Co., 1935).

Culture

The most enduring influences are from culture. Man tends to assimilate his culture's mores and folkways, and to believe in their absolute rightness until deviants appear within his culture or until he confronts members of another culture.

Subcultures

A culture tends to lose its homogeneity as its population increases. When people no longer are able to maintain face-to-face relationships with more than a small proportion of other members of a culture, smaller units or subcultures develop, which help to satisfy the individual's needs for more specific identity.

The subcultures are often regional entities, because the people of a region, as a result of more frequent interactions, tend to think and act alike. But subcultures also take the form of religions, nationalities, fraternal orders, and other institutional complexes which provide a broad identification for people who may otherwise be strangers. The subcultures of a person play a large role in his attitude formation and become another important predictor of certain values he is likely to hold.

Social Class

People become differentiated not only horizontally but also vertically through a division of labor. The society becomes stratified socially on the basis of wealth, skill, and power. Sometimes castes develop in which the members are reared for certain roles, or social classes develop in which the members feel empathy with others sharing similar values and economic circumstances.

Because social class involves different attitudinal configurations, it becomes a useful independent variable for segmenting markets and predicting reactions. Significant differences have been found among different social classes with respect to magazine readership, leisure activities, food imagery, fashion interests, and acceptance of innovations. A sampling of attitudinal differences in class is the following:

Members of the *upper-middle* class place an emphasis on professional competence; indulge in expensive status symbols; and more often than not show a taste, real or otherwise, for theater and the arts. They want their children to show high achievement and precocity and develop into physicists, vice-presidents, and judges. This class likes to deal in ideas and symbols.

Members of the *lower-middle* class cherish respectability, savings, a college education, and good house-keeping. They want their children to show self-control and prepare for careers as accountants, lawyers, and engineers.

Members of the *upper-lower* class try to keep up with the times, if not with the Joneses. They stay in older neighborhoods but buy new kitchen appliances. They spend proportionately less than the middle class on major clothing articles, buying a new suit mainly for an important ceremonial occasion. They also spend proportionately less on services, preferring to do their own plumbing and other work around the house. They tend to raise large families and their children generally enter manual occupations. This class also supplies many local businessmen, politicians, sports stars, and labor-union leaders.

Reference Groups

There are groups in which the individual has no membership but with which he identifies and may aspire to—reference groups. Many young boys identify with big-league baseball players or astronauts, and many young girls identify with Hollywood stars. The activities of these popular heroes are carefully watched and frequently imitated. These reference figures become important transmitters of influence, although more along lines of taste and hobby than basic attitudes.

Face-to-face Groups

Groups that have the most immediate influence on a person's tastes and opinions are face-to-face groups. This includes all the small "societies" with which he comes into frequent contact: his family, close friends, neighbors, fellow workers, fraternal associates, and so forth. His informal group memberships are influenced largely by his occupation, residence, and stage in the life cycle.

The powerful influence of small groups on individual attitudes has been demonstrated in a number of social psychological experiments.[28] There is also evidence that this influence may be growing. David Riesman and his coauthors have pointed to signs which indicate a growing amount of *other-direction,* that is, a tendency for individuals to be increasingly influenced by their peers in the definition of their values rather than by their parents and elders.[29]

For the marketer, this means that brand choice may increasingly be influenced by one's peers. For such products as cigarettes and automobiles, the influence of peers is unmistakable.

The role of face-to-face groups has been recognized in recent industry campaigns attempting to change basic product attitudes. For years the milk industry has been trying to overcome the image of milk as a "sissified" drink by portraying its use in social and active situations. The men's-wear industry is trying to increase male interest in clothes by advertisements indicating that business associates judge a man by how well he dresses.

Of all face-to-face groups, the person's family undoubtedly plays the largest and most enduring role in basic attitude formation. From them he acquires a mental set not only toward religion and politics, but also toward thrift, chastity, food, human relations, and so forth. Although he often rebels against parental values in his teens, he often accepts these values eventually. Their formative influence on his eventual attitudes is undeniably great.

Family members differ in the types of product messages they carry to other family members. Most of what parents know about cereals, candy, and toys comes from their children. The wife stimulates family consideration of household appliances, furniture, and vacations. The husband tends to stimulate the fewest purchase ideas, with the exception of the automobile and perhaps the home.

The marketer must be alert to what attitudinal configurations dominate in different types of families, and also to how these change over time. For example, the parent's conception of the child's rights and privileges has undergone a radical shift in the last 30 years. The child has become the center of attention and orientation in a great

---

[28]See, for example, Solomon E. Asch, "Effects of Group Pressure Upon the Modification & Distortion of Judgments," in Dorwin Cartwright and Alvin Zander, *Group Dynamics* (Evanston, Illinois: Row, Peterson & Co., 1953), pp. 151–162; and Kurt Lewin, "Group Decision and Social Change," in Theodore M. Newcomb and Eugene L. Hartley, editors, *Readings in Social Psychology* (New York: Henry Holt Co., 1952).

[29]David Riesman, Reuel Denney, and Nathan Glazer, *The Lonely Crowd* (New Haven, Connecticut: Yale University Press, 1950).

number of households, leading some writers to label the modern family a "filiarchy." This has important implications not only for how to market to today's family, but also on how to market to tomorrow's family when the indulged child of today becomes the parent.

The Person

Social influences determine much but not all of the behavioral variations in people. Two individuals subject to the same influences are not likely to have identical attitudes, although these attitudes will probably converge at more points than those of two strangers selected at random. Attitudes are really the product of social forces interacting with the individual's unique temperament and abilities.

Furthermore, attitudes do not automatically guarantee certain types of behavior. Attitudes are predispositions felt by buyers before they enter the buying process. The buying process itself is a learning experience and can lead to a change in attitudes.

Alfred Politz noted at one time that women stated a clear preference for G. E. refrigerators over Frigidaire, but that Frigidaire continued to outsell G. E.[30] The answer to this paradox was that preference was only one factor entering into behavior. When the consumer preferring G. E. actually undertook to purchase a new refrigerator, her curiosity led her to examine the other brands. Her perception was sensitized to refrigerator advertisements, sales arguments, and different product features. This led to learning and a change in attitudes.

THE HOBBESIAN ORGANIZATIONAL–FACTORS MODEL

The foregoing models throw light mainly on the behavior of family buyers.

But what of the large number of people who are organizational buyers? They are engaged in the purchase of goods not for the sake of consumption, but for further production or distribution. Their common denominator is the fact that they (1) are paid to make purchases for others and (2) operate within an organizational environment.

How do organizational buyers make their decisions? There seem to be two competing views. Many marketing writers have emphasized the predominance of rational motives in organizational buying.[31] Organizational buyers are represented as being most impressed by cost, quality, dependability, and service factors. They are portrayed as dedicated servants of the organization, seeking to secure the best terms. This view has led to an emphasis on performance and use characteristics in much industrial advertising.

Other writers have emphasized personal motives in organizational buyer behavior. The purchasing agent's interest to do the best for his company is tempered by his interest to do the best for himself. He may be tempted to choose among salesmen according to the extent they entertain or offer gifts. He may choose a particular vendor because this will ingratiate him with certain company officers. He may shortcut his study of alternative suppliers to make his work day easier.

In truth, the buyer is guided by both personal and group goals; and this is the essential point. The political model of Thomas Hobbes comes closest of any model to sug-

[30]Alfred Politz, "Motivation Research—Opportunity or Dilemma?", in Ferber and Wales, same reference as footnote 17, at pp. 57-58.

[31]See Melvin T. Copeland, *Principles of Merchandising* (New York: McGraw-Hill Book Co., Inc., 1924).

gesting the relationship between the two goals.[32] Hobbes held that man is "instinctively" oriented toward preserving and enhancing his own well-being. But this would produce a "war of every man against every man." This fear leads men to unite with others in a corporate body. The corporate man tries to steer a careful course between satisfying his own needs and those of the organization.

Marketing Applications of Hobbesian Model

The import of the Hobbesian model is that organizational buyers can be appealed to on both personal and organizational grounds. The buyer has his private aims, and yet he tries to do a satisfactory job for his corporation. He will respond to persuasive salesmen and he will respond to rational product arguments. However, the best "mix" of the two is not a fixed quantity; it varies with the nature of the product, the type of organization, and the relative strength of the two drives in the particular buyer.

Where there is substantial similarity in what suppliers offer in the way of products, price, and service, the purchasing agent has less basis for rational choice. Since he can satisfy his organizational obligations with any one of a number of suppliers, he can be swayed by personal motives. On the other hand, where there are pronounced differences among the competing vendors' products, the purchasing agent is held more accountable for his choice and probably pays more attention to rational factors. Short-run personal gain becomes less motivating than the long-run gain which comes from serving the organization with distinction.

The marketing strategist must appreciate these goal conflicts of the organizational buyer. Behind all the ferment of purchasing agents to develop standards and employ value analysis lies their desire to avoid being thought of as order-clerks, and to develop better skills in reconciling personal and organizational objectives.[33]

SUMMARY

Think back over the five different behavioral models of how the buyer translates buying influences into purchasing responses.

Marshallian man is concerned chiefly with economic cues—prices and income—and makes a fresh utility calculation before each purchase.

Pavlovian man behaves in a largely habitual rather than thoughtful way; certain configurations of cues will set off the same behavior because of rewarded learning in the past.

Freudian man's choices are influenced strongly by motives and fantasies which take place deep within his private world.

Veblenian man acts in a way which is shaped largely by past and present social groups.

And finally, Hobbesian man seeks to reconcile individual gain with organizational gain.

Thus, it turns out that the "black box" of the buyer is not so black after all. Light is thrown in various corners by these models. Yet no one has succeeded in putting all these pieces of truth together into one coherent instrument for behavioral analysis. This, of course, is the goal of behavioral science.

---

[32]Thomas Hobbes, *Leviathan,* 1651 (London: G. Routledge and Sons, 1887).

[33]For an insightful account, see George Strauss, "Tactics of Lateral Relationship: The Purchasing Agent," *Administrative Science Quarterly,* Vol. 7 (September, 1962), pp. 161–186.

Questions

1. Name the five different behavioral models discussed in this article and briefly describe the consumer behavior applications of each model.
2. Which of the five models seems most practical from a consumer behavior standpoint? Explain your answer.
3. Take each of these five behavioral models and explain each model's potential contribution for analyzing the purchase decision of a college student buying a new automobile.
4. Describe the influence of levels of culture as explained in the Veblenian model.

2. Selected Social Psychological Models for Analyzing Buyers

Charles D. Schewe

Because of its close relationship with the study of human behavior, consumer behavior theory has borrowed heavily from the behavioral sciences. While there is a huge body of literature on the many aspects of human behavior, literature on consumer behavior is almost scarce in comparison. Furthermore, the major behavioral disciplines have contributed to consumer research in varying amounts. While psychologists have been most active, the field of social psychology offers the greatest opportunity to further our understanding of consumer behavior. The consumer rarely acts solely as an individual but rather behaves in the "actual, imagined, or implied presence of others."[1] What is needed, then, is an investigation of different behavioral science theories and an observation of the implications that these theories have for marketing situations.

The purpose of this article is to describe and evaluate four models of behavior that have been developed by social psychologists. The four models presented here represent theories which have substantial practical appeal for marketing management:

[1]Gardner Lindzey and Elliot Aronson, *The Handbook of Social Psychology*, 2nd ed. (Menlo Park, Cal.: Addison-Wesley, 1968), p. 3.

1. The McClelland model, stressing the theory of achievement motivation
2. The Goffman model, role theory
3. The Festinger model, the theory of cognitive dissonance
4. The Riesman model, the inner- versus other-directed individual

THE McCLELLAND MODEL

The theory of achievement motivation is one class of theories which attributes the strength of a motivation (i.e., the active impulse to engage in some activity) to the cognitive expectation that the activity will produce a particular consequence and also to the attractiveness or value of that consequence to the individual.[2] The theory deals only with an important but limited type of behavior—achievement-oriented activity. This type of activity is usually undertaken with the idea that performance will be judged against some standard of excellence. Presumably, any situation which affords a challenge to achieve must also pose the threat of failure. Therefore, achievement-oriented activity is always affected by the conflict between the tendency to achieve success and the tendency to avoid failure. The theory of achievement motivation focuses mainly upon the resolution of these two opposing tendencies, both of which are inherent in any achievement-oriented activity.

The strength of the motivation or tendency to achieve success (T_s) is considered a multiplicative function of the motive or need to achieve success (M_s), the expectancy (or subjective probability) that success will be the consequence of a particular activity (P_s), and the incentive value of success at that par-

[2]David C. McClelland, *The Achieving Society* (Princeton: D. Van Nostrand Company, 1961).

ticular activity (I_s). The value of the incentive is assumed to be the complement of the perceived probability of success ($I_s = 1 - P_s$). The complete equation is represented as follows:

$$T_s = M_s \cdot P_s \cdot I_s$$

The theory underlying the tendency to avoid failure follows the same conceptualization as the tendency to achieve success. A multiplicative equation is again used:

$$T_f = M_{AF} \cdot P_f \cdot I_f$$

This time the incentive to avoid failure (I_f) is set equal to the negative probability of success ($-P_s$). This relationship is based on the assumption that the incentive value of failure becomes more negative as the task becomes easier. Interpretation of the equation indicates that the tendency to avoid failure operates in a way exactly opposite the tendency to achieve success, i.e., it is negative. This tendency to avoid failure must be viewed as an inhibitory tendency—a tendency to avoid performance of an activity which is expected to lead to failure. This tendency tells nothing about which acts will be performed but rather indicates which acts will be resisted.

How can an individual's behavior be predicted when he is confronted with an achievement-oriented task? The behavior will be the result of the conflict between the tendency to achieve success and the tendency to avoid failure. The resultant achievement-oriented tendency is the sum of the two tendencies—$T_s + T_f$, and it can be proven algebraically that the sum will be positive when M_s is greater than M_{AF} and negative when M_{AF} is greater than M_s. When the resultant achievement-oriented tendency is negative, there will be no active impulse to undertake an achievement-oriented activity unless some positive external force compels performance of the undesirable activity.

The theory of achievement motivation is

more complex than implied by the above treatment, since several confounding factors must also be recognized. For instance, it is important to recognize the particular individual's personality. The tendency to achieve success (T_s) depends on certain personality characteristics intrinsic to each individual. In addition, situational variables also must be considered, since the individual does not reside in an isolated environment in which his actions are directed by only *one* achievement motive. In spite of these problems, the theory of achievement motivation offers an interesting motivational approach—with importance for marketing managers.

Marketing Implications of the McClelland Model

Many opportunities exist for research into consumer implications of the theory of need achievement. Little empirical evidence has been collected on the role of need achievement in buyer behavior. Some studies have used various measures of need achievement along with measures of other personality variables to explore differences between Ford and Chevrolet owners,[3] consumer innovators and later adopters,[4] and smokers and non-smokers.[5] Need achievement was not found to explain such behavioral differences. However, these negative findings may be attributable to the measurement instrument.

Other interesting evidence indicates the importance of need achievement in motivating buyer behavior.[6] Men scoring high on need achievement by use of a self-report technique tended to favor products considered virile and masculine, such as boating equipment, straight razors, and skis. Men with low need achievement scores preferred to buy products characterized as meticulous or fastidious, such as mouthwash, deodorant, and automatic dishwashers. No such clear-cut pattern existed for females, suggesting that the need for achievement is more closely associated with the male sex role than with the female sex role. Men are expected to be competitive and aggressive, while women are not—and the study supports this reasoning. For marketers, these findings suggest that certain classes of products have a distinct market segment with a distinct motivation. Stores and manufacturers would do well to learn these motivations and tailor their appeals, stores, and products to each specific group of customers.

In another study, results obtained through use of the Thematic Apperception Technique (TAT) suggest that a large portion of people engaged in active outdoor sports may be high in need for achievement.[7] Manufacturers of active outdoor sports products are most likely to satisfy this group by generating just the right level of perceived risk[8]—neither too high

[3]Franklin B. Evans, "Psychological and Objective Prediction of Brand Choice," *Journal of Business,* Vol. 32 (October 1959), pp. 340–369.

[4]Thomas S. Robertson and James H. Myers, "Personality Correlates of Opinion Leadership and Innovative Buyer Behavior," *Journal of Marketing Research,* Vol. 6 (May 1969), pp. 164–168.

[5]Arthur Koponen, "Personality Characteristics of Purchasers," *Journal of Advertising Research,* Vol. 1 (September 1960), pp. 6–12.

[6]E. Laird Landon, Jr., "A Sex Role Explanation of Purchase Intention Differences of Consumers Who Are High and Low in Need for Achievement," in *Proceedings of the 3rd Annual Conference, Association for Consumer Research,* M. Venkatesan, ed., 1972.

[7]David M. Gardner, "An Exploratory Investigation of Achievement Motivation Effects on Consumer Behavior," in *Proceedings of the 3rd Annual Conference, Association for Consumer Research,* M. Venkatesan, ed., 1972.

[8]See L. W. Littig, "The Effect of Motivation on Probability Preferences and Subjective Probability" (Unpublished Doctoral Dissertation, University of Michigan, Ann Arbor, 1959); and G. H. Litwin, "Motives and Expectancy as Determinants of Preference for Degrees of Risk" (Unpublished Honors Thesis, University of Michigan, Ann Arbor, 1958).

nor too little. In addition, men's clothing manufacturers and clothing departments of department stores appear to serve customers with a high need for achievement.[9] People with high need achievement may be more likely to patronize an institution that uses appeals of excellence,[10] liberal use of positive achievement words,[11] and appropriate shades of color (bluish versus bright tones).[12]

In another study, both the TAT and self-report techniques were used to explore media and product usage.[13] The TAT instrument indicated that individuals high on need achievement were low users of television and high users of magazines and radio. Exactly the reverse was found for individuals scored by the self-report method. Similarly, those measured high on need achievement by the TAT did choose products judged as high achievement products, while those measured high in need achievement by the self-report method did not. More questions than answers result from this empirical research.

The importance of the influence of need achievement on consumer behavior is not yet clear. The greatest problem appears to be determining a valid and reliable measure of the need achievement construct. In addition, it is not reasonable to suggest that an individual's achievement needs will be operating in all purchase situations. This is due to the belief that

(P_s) or (I_s) are often at relatively low levels and, hence, when combined multiplicatively with (M_s), result in low levels of the strength of the motive to achieve (T_s). Further research is necessary in the area of need achievement to uncover its true potential as a determinant of consumer behavior.

THE GOFFMAN MODEL

Borrowed directly from the theater, role theory views persons as actors "playing a role." In the presence of others, the actor is seen to organize his activity in order to express an impression that he wishes to convey.[14] This expression is known as the *role enactment*. The object of the study of role theory is to increase understanding of role enactment of individuals in social settings. The focus is on overt social conduct—there is no place for the study of isolated individuals. Role enactment is the major dependent variable in role theory and is the resultant of the following independent variables.

> *Role expectations.* "Role expectations comprise the rights and privileges, the duties and obligations, of any occupant of a social position in relation to persons occupying other positions in the social structure."[15] Role expectations define the limits or range of tolerated behavior—they induce conformity. This conformity, however, is not a set of rigid directives; instead, it provides limits within which the individual may act.
>
> *Role location.* To properly determine the role that he must perform, the individual must locate himself in the existing social structure. Once given his social location, he may select the role appropriate to the situation.

[9]Same reference as footnote 7.

[10] Same reference as footnote 8.

[11]David McClelland and Alvin M. Liberman, "The Effect of Need for Achievement on Recognition of Need-Related Words," *Journal of Personality,* Vol. 18 (December 1949), pp. 236–251.

[12]Robert H. Knapp, "Need Achievement and Aesthetic Preference," in *Motives in Fantasy, Action and Society,* John W. Atkinson, ed. (Princeton: D. Van Nostrand Company, 1958), pp. 367–372.

[13]William S. Whittaker, "The Relationship Among Individual Difference Variables, Media Usage and Product Usage" (Unpublished Doctoral Dissertation, University of Rochester, 1972).

[14]Erving Goffman, *The Presentation of Self in Everyday Life* (Garden City: Doubleday Anchor Books, 1959).

[15]Same reference as footnote 1, p. 497.

Role demands. Once the location of the social position is obtained, some potentially more restrictive constraints are often imposed on the choice of a role when additional features of the situation are perceived. These restraints reflect the demand for a specific role enactment.

Role skills. A skill generally can be viewed as a physical or psychological ability to perform a task at a given level of competence. "Role skills, then, refer to those characteristics possessed by the individual which result in effective and convincing role enactment: aptitude, appropriate experience, and specific training."[16]

Self-role congruence. The term *self* refers to a person's cognitive structure based on his past experience with other persons and objects; it is the experience of identity arising from an individual's interactions with things, body parts, and other persons. Self-role congruence maintains that role enactment will be more effective and appropriate when self characteristics coincide with role expectations.

The audience. The audience refers to the observers who are present during role enactment. The performance of the actor is "staged" to produce a desired impression on the audience. The effectiveness of this role enactment is deduced from the face-to-face interaction between the individual actor and his audience.

The discussion so far has focused primarily on one single role. As with the theory of achievement motivation, this overview represents a great oversimplification. In reality, individuals are forced into situations where they must choose among alternative roles and where multiple role obligations provide dissonance for the performer. Transferring from one role to another, transition among roles over time, spending time and effort among various roles, and conflict among roles all impose great complexity on role theory. Complex as it may be, however, role theory still provides valuable insights for marketing management.

Marketing Implications of the Goffman Model

The product offering—goods and services—provides the consumer with what Goffman calls the "setting." Products are vehicles for conveying the impression one tries to impose on the audience. Each product conveys a symbolic representation through its perceived appearance. Effective marketers should mold their product into an image that will fit properly into the "setting" surrounding the consumer's perceived role expectations.

To provide the consumer with the proper "props" to perform his role, marketers should be aware of their product's image and should shape that image to match the consumer's self-image. Research has shown that congruence between product image and self-image provides a suitable means for segmenting markets.[17] An automobile owner's perception of his car was found to be essentially congruent with his perception of himself[18] and with his perception of fellow owners.[19] Beer drinkers were found to perceive themselves as more social, extroverted, forward, confident, impulsive, sophisticated, and temperamental than non-beer drinkers.[20] Greater

[17]See Edward L. Grubb, "Consumer Perception of 'Self-Concept' and Its Relationship to Brand Choice of Selected Product Types," in *Marketing and Economic Development,* Peter D. Bennett, ed. (Chicago: American Marketing Association, 1965), pp. 419–424; and Edward L. Grubb and Harrison L. Grathwohl, "Consumer Self-Concept, Symbolism and Market Behavior: A Theoretical Approach," *Journal of Marketing,* Vol. 31 (October 1967), pp. 22–27.

[18]Al E. Birdwell, "A Study of the Influence of Image Congruence on Consumer Choice," *Journal of Business,* Vol. 41 (January 1968), pp. 76–88.

[19]Edward L. Grubb and Greg Hupp, "Perception of Self, Generalized Stereotypes, and Brand Selection," *Journal of Marketing Research,* Vol. 5 (February 1968), pp. 58–63.

[20]Grubb, same reference as footnote 17.

[16]Same reference as footnote 1, p. 514.

similarity exists between one's self-image and the images of preferred brands than the images of least preferred brands.[21]

The store where products are purchased also has an image. Self-image theory suggests that sometimes the consumer expresses his "real self" in purchases, and sometimes he expresses his fantasy or his "ideal self." The ideal self was found more important in the selection of a department store, while the real self was found more influential in the choice of a specialty store.[22] The retailer, in developing his store image, should concentrate on the image he feels most relevant to his particular situation.

Evidence has also indicated that buyers purchase goods in accordance with the expectations of their audience.[23] In certain situations a buyer may select the brand which fits the image that he considers socially acceptable. This finding suggests that brand choice for a product used socially, such as automobiles, clothing, and liquor, may involve social-congruity rather than self-congruity.

Product image also results from the sociopsychological utility afforded by the promotional effort of the marketer. Advertising can build a new image as well as reinforce an already perceived image. Advertisers can employ selective appeals to inform the consumer of a product's position within a role.

The use of role theory by marketers may not be as well defined as stated above. Many products, such as light bulbs, screwdrivers, and faucet washers, are bought strictly for functional reasons and involve no consideration of image. Another consideration is that product image is often decided after the actual purchase[24] and may not motivate initial behavior. A third point is that a particular role may be expressed in a number of ways. A mink coat, a Cadillac car, and an expensive suit all communicate the same role, but the choice of which product to use is outside the control of the marketer. Finally, the same product may have different meanings within different contexts.

THE FESTINGER MODEL

A third explanation of consumer behavior can be derived from a family of concepts called cognitive consistency theories: balance theory,[25] congruity theory,[26] and particularly the theory of cognitive dissonance.[27] Balance theory focuses mainly on an individual's perception of three social elements: (1) the person

[21]Ira J. Dolich, "Congruence Relationships Between Self Images and Product Brands," *Journal of Marketing Research,* Vol. 6 (February 1969), pp. 80–84.

[22]Ronald J. Dornoff and Ronald L. Tatham, "Congruence Between Personal Image and Store Image," *Journal of Marketing Research Society,* Vol. 14 (January 1972), pp. 45–52.

[23]G. David Hughes and José L. Guerrero, "Automobile Self-Congruity Models Reexamined," *Journal of Marketing Research,* Vol. 8 (February 1971), pp. 125–127; and Edward L. Grubb and Bruce L. Stern, "Self-Concept and Significant Others," *Journal of Marketing Research,* Vol. 8 (August 1971), pp. 382–385.

[24]Franklin B. Evans, "Automobiles and Self-Imagery: Comment," *Journal of Business,* Vol. 41 (October 1968), pp. 484–485. Research on this criticism is being performed; see E. Laird Landon, Jr., "The Role of Ideal-Self Concept in Consumer Purchase Intentions" (Working paper, University of Colorado, Business Research Division, March 1973).

[25]Fritz Heider, *The Psychology of Interpersonal Relations* (New York: John Wiley and Sons, 1958).

[26]Charles E. Osgood, George J. Suci, and Percy H. Tannenbaum, *The Measurement of Meaning* (Champaign, Ill.: University of Illinois Press, 1957).

[27]Leon Festinger, *A Theory of Cognitive Dissonance* (Evanston, Ill.: Row, Peterson and Company, 1957); for an excellent review of these three theories and allied research, see Bobby J. Calder, "Cognitive Consistency and Consumer Behavior," in *Perspectives in Consumer Behavior,* Harold H. Kassarjian and Thomas S. Robertson, eds. (Glenview, Ill.: Scott, Foresman and Company, 1973).

himself, (2) some other person, and (3) some event, idea, or object. Two types of beliefs relating these cognitive elements are seen: positive and negative. That is, these elements can be connected by liking (+) or disliking (−) or by favorable (+) or unfavorable (−) feelings. A system is balanced if all three of the system elements possess positive signs or if two signs are negative and one positive. Otherwise, a state of imbalance exists. People, the theory holds, strive to maintain a state of balance with no cognitive stress in the system. People attempt to restore balance to an imbalanced system by changing the signs of the relations.

Congruity theory, developed independently of balance theory, deals with the direction of attitude change. The theory centers on communication sources and objects or concepts which are related by either an associative (likes) or dissociative (dislikes) assertion. A state of congruity exists whenever a source and an object with the same direction of evaluation are associated and whenever a source and object with opposite evaluations are dissociated. As with imbalance, incongruity creates pressure to change both the source and object to a congruent state.

The theory of cognitive dissonance, like balance theory and congruity theory, holds that an individual strives to maintain internal harmony among his opinions, values, attitudes, and knowledge. Dissonance theory, however, deals only with inconsistency which arises *after* a decision is made.

A number of situations can produce dissonance. Dissonance always exists *after* a decision is made between two or more alternatives. Cognitions constituting favorable or positive elements in the rejected alternative are dissonant with the chosen alternative. Likewise, negative dimensions of the chosen alternative foster dissonance within the individual. Dissonance is also created when re-

wards or punishments are posed to obtain behavior (called forced compliance) that is inconsistent with the person's private opinions. If the action is obtained, dissonance arises from discrepancy between the individual's knowledge of his behavior and his opposing internal opinion. If the behavior is not elicited, the individual is dissonant with the knowledge of the reward not obtained or the punishment to be incurred. Accidental or forced exposure to new information may create new cognitions dissonant with existing cognitions. Open expression of group disagreement may effect dissonance within the members. Finally, dissonance may even occur within a large group of people when an event takes place which is forceful enough to produce similar reactions in everyone—such as when an event invalidates a widely held opinion or belief.

How, then, can cognitive dissonance be reduced or eliminated? Two general alternatives for reduction of dissonance are open to the individual: changing existing cognitions or adding new ones. When these considerations are applied to actual situations, the following possible means of reducing dissonance can be identified:

1. Reduction of dissonance can be achieved by psychologically increasing the attractiveness of the chosen alternative and/or by mentally decreasing the attractiveness of the rejected alternative.
2. Postdecision dissonance can be decreased by rationalizing to perceive more identical characteristics between the chosen and unchosen alternatives.
3. Dissonance can be reduced by cognitively decreasing the importance of the decision.
4. If forced compliance has been elicited, dissonance reduction can be effected by changing existing opinion about the forced action to make it more consonant with the behavior or by intensifying the amount of the reward or punishment. On the other hand, if the forced behavior was not elicited, dissonance can be

lessened by strengthening the original opinion or by minimizing the reward or punishment.

5. Dissonance will lead the individual to seek new information which is consonant with existing cognitions. New information likely to increase dissonance will be avoided. Should accidental or forced exposure to new dissonant information be effected, misrepresentation or misperception of the information will likely result to achieve avoidance of increased dissonance.

6. When cognitions about behavior are the cause of dissonance, the behavior can be changed.

7. When dissonance is aroused by disagreement with others, reduction can be obtained by the person changing his own opinion, by influencing others to change their opinions, or by rejecting the opinions of others.

8. Reduction of dissonance can be achieved by seeking the social support of others who already agree with the cognition the person wishes to maintain.

Marketing Implications of the Festinger Model

A considerable amount of empirical evidence has been reported which supports the existence of dissonance theory within the marketing context.[28] When dissonance does occur, its magnitude depends upon a number of factors—greater dissonance occurs with greater commitment or ego-involvement in a product purchase,[29] greater number of alternative brands to choose from,[30] greater dissimilarity between alternatives,[31] greater brand familiarity,[32] decisions involving high conflict situation,[33] and purchases associated with high expectations that are not confirmed.[34]

Postdecision information seeking has also been investigated. While evidence documents the consumer's search for consonant information, he apparently does not avoid discrepant information. Recent purchasers of automobiles read advertisements about the car they have just bought but, contrary to the theory, they also read as many or more ads about the other cars they had considered.[35] Some individuals, apparently high in self-confidence, actually seek out discrepant information in order to refute it and thereby

[28]Lee K. Anderson, James R. Taylor, and Robert J. Holloway, "The Consumer and His Alternatives: An Experimental Approach," *Journal of Marketing Research,* Vol. 3 (February 1966), pp. 66–67; Leonard A. LoSciuto and Robert Perloff, "Influence of Product Preference on Dissonance Reduction," *Journal of Marketing Research,* Vol. 4 (August 1967), pp. 286–290. For an excellent review of existing research, see M. Venkatesan's chapter on cognitive dissonance in *Handbook of Marketing Research,* Robert Ferber, ed. (New York: McGraw-Hill, forthcoming).

[29]James F. Engel and M. Lawrence Light, "The Role of Psychological Commitment in Consumer Behavior: An Evaluation of the Theory of Cognitive Dissonance," in *Applications of the Sciences in Marketing Management,* Frank Bass, Charles King, and Edgar Pessemier, eds. (New York: John Wiley and Sons, 1968).

[30]Jack W. Brehm and Arthur R. Cohen, *Explorations in Cognitive Dissonance* (New York: John Wiley and Sons, 1962).

[31]Same reference as footnote 30.

[32]Jagdish N. Sheth, "Cognitive Dissonance, Brand Preference and Product Familiarity," in *Insights Into Consumer Behavior,* J. Arndt, ed. (Boston: Allyn and Bacon, Inc., 1968); and Joel B. Cohen and Marvin E. Goldberg, "The Dissonance Model in Post-Decision Product Evaluation," *Journal of Marketing Research,* Vol. 7 (August 1970), pp. 315–321.

[33]Jagdish N. Sheth, "Are There Differences in Dissonance Reduction Behavior Between Students and Housewives?" *Journal of Marketing Research,* Vol. 7 (May 1970), pp. 243–245.

[34]Richard N. Cardozo, "An Experimental Study of Consumer Effort, Expectation, and Satisfaction," *Journal of Marketing Research,* Vol. 2 (August 1965), pp. 244–249.

[35]James F. Engel, "The Psychological Consequences of a Major Purchase Decision," in *Marketing in Transition,* W. S. Decker, ed. (Chicago: American Marketing Association, 1963), pp. 462–475; and Danuta Ehrlich, Isaiah Guttman, Peter Schonbach, and Judson Mills, "Post Decision Exposure to Relevant Information," *Journal of Abnormal and Social Psychology,* Vol. 54 (January 1957), pp. 98–102.

reduce dissonance.[36] Others seek *useful* information regardless of its content.[37] The type of information utilized by dissonant consumers appears to be a function of the buyer's confidence in his product choice[38] and the amount of his ego involvement.[39]

Information should be provided to aid the consumer in reducing any dissonance resulting from a product choice. The seller's advertisements can reassure the consumer of the wisdom of his choice. Dissonance reduction, however, may not operate as a strong reinforcer in the case of frequently purchased convenience items. Here, the purchase involves little commitment and will result in marginal postdecision dissonance. On the other hand, expensive specialty goods involving substantial financial outlay may be more susceptible to dissonance and should be followed with sufficient dissonance-reducing advertising.[40] Advertising is not the only means of reducing dissonance. Customers of a retail store who received a post-transaction letter experienced less dissonance and had higher intentions of future purchases than did a control group.[41]

Dissonance theory also has an impact on brand loyalty. Research found that the greater the post-decision dissonance after the first purchase, the greater the probability of buying that brand again. In addition, since dissonance should increase as the number of rejected alternatives increases, brand loyalty for all brands should increase as the number of brands expands.[42]

A standard marketing pricing tactic is the special introductory low-price offer. This pricing approach may have some dissonance-related ill effects, however. Two prices—regular and introductory low price—were tested in two groups of stores. Sales in the low-price stores were higher during the test. However, after the lower price was raised, sales in the low-price stores fell below those in the stores which had the higher price all along. These findings may be explained by the dissonance prediction that the low price would not result in developing commitment and brand loyalty among the initial purchasers.[43]

Consideration of the marketing implications of the theory of cognitive dissonance leads to more questions than answers. It has been said that knowledge "of situations in which dissonance *can* occur is not always useful in determining whether dissonance *does* occur."[44] Moreover, in most situations, consumers find prior experience, personality variables, social support, and other situational factors dominating the arousal of any dissonance. In addition, the value of some

[36]Ehrlich, et al., same reference as footnote 35.

[37]L. K. Cannon, "Self-Confidence and Selective Exposure to Information," in *Conflict, Decision and Dissonance,* Leon Festinger, ed. (Stanford: Stanford University Press, 1964), pp. 83–95; Jonathan L. Freedman, "Confidence, Utility, and Selective Exposure: A Partial Replication," *Journal of Personality and Social Psychology,* Vol. 2 (November 1965), pp. 778–780; Rosemary H. Lowe and Ivan D. Steiner, "Some Effects of the Reversibility and Consequences of Decisions on Postdecision Information Preferences," *Journal of Personality and Social Psychology,* Vol 8 (February 1968), pp. 172–179.

[38]Cannon, same reference as footnote 37.

[39]Sidney Rosen, "Postdecision Affinity for Incompatible Information," *Journal of Abnormal and Social Psychology,* Vol. 63 (July 1961), pp. 188–190.

[40]Sadaomi Oshikawa, "Can Cognitive Dissonance Theory Explain Consumer Behavior?" *Journal of Marketing,* Vol. 33 (October 1969), pp. 44–49.

[41]Shelby D. Hunt, "Post-transaction Communications and Dissonance Reduction," *Journal of Marketing,* Vol. 34 (July 1970), pp. 46–51.

[42]Robert Mittelstaedt, "A Dissonance Approach to Repeat Purchasing Behavior," *Journal of Marketing Research*, Vol. 6 (November 1969), pp. 444–447.

[43]Anthony N. Doob, J. Merrill Carlsmith, Jonathan L. Freedman, Thomas K. Landaner, and Soleng Tom, Jr., "Effect of Initial Selling Price on Subsequent Sales," *Journal of Personality and Social Psychology,* Vol. 11 (November 1969), pp. 345–350.

[44]Elliot Aronson, "Dissonance Theory: Progress and Problems," in *Theories of Cognitive Consistency: A Sourcebook,* Robert P. Abelson, et al., eds. (Chicago: Rand McNally and Company, 1968), p. 9.

empirical research has been reduced by criticism of the measurement of cognitive dissonance[45] and of the experimental designs employed.[46] Marketers, however, should be familiar with the possible consequences of this theory.

THE RIESMAN MODEL

This theory claims that human beings can be grouped into three major types of social character: tradition-direction, inner-direction, and other-direction.[47] By social character, Riesman refers to "ways of behavior" or "modes of conformity to the culture and society" in which the individual is operating. Riesman's thesis is that each society or culture shows one of the three types depending upon its particular phase of development. In each phase, Riesman contends, society enforces conformity and molds social character in a definably different way.

Tradition-direction. This society is characterized by general slowness of change, dependence on familial ties, low social mobility, and a rigid value structure. The important relationships in life are controlled and made stable by intensive socialization of the young by their extended family. In this society, conformity is maintained by the fear of being shamed.

Inner-direction. This society is characterized by increased social mobility, less security for the individual, rapid accumulation of capital, industrialization, and almost constant expansion—expansion of goods, people, ex-

ploration, colonization, and imperialism. The "source of direction for the individual is 'inner' in the sense that it is implanted early in life by the elders and directed toward generalized but nonetheless inescapably destined goals."[48] The inner-directed individual has a feeling of control over his life and sees his goal as striving for a career. While he seems independent, he is actually guided by an "internal gyroscope" based upon the values and principles acquired from his parents. Riches are assembled and consumption is conspicuous, but as a sign of success rather than for his own pleasure. In this society, conformity of behavior is maintained through the fear of guilt.

Other-direction. This society finds a world of social mobility and mechanization such that production is no longer a problem. In this world of abundance, the individual is taught to be a consumer rather than a producer. Other-directed persons behave according to the expectations and preferences of their contemporaries. In this society, the peer group rather than the family provides guidance for both children and parents. Spending is important but should not be conspicuous. The other-directed person is "kept from splurging too much by others' envy and from consuming too little by his own envy of the other."[49] The primary pressure for conformity in this society is the anxiety created by what others think of the individual.

Riesman holds that the United States no longer contains anyone who can be characterized as tradition-directed, but is composed primarily of inner- and other-directed individuals. However, he states that the majority of the population would still have to be considered inner-directed.

For study purposes it is proper to visual-

[45]Oshikawa, same reference as footnote 40.

[46]Sadaomi Oshikawa, "The Measurement of Cognitive Dissonance: Some Experimental Findings," *Journal of Marketing,* Vol. 36 (January 1972), pp. 64–67.

[47]David Riesman, Nathan Glazer, and Reuel Denny, *The Lonely Crowd,* Abridged Edition (New Haven: Yale University Press, 1961).

[48]Same reference as footnote 47, p. 15.

[49]Same reference as footnote 47, p. 79.

ize tradition-direction, inner-direction, and other-direction as having sharply defined differences. It would, however, be a mistake to expect to find such a sharp separation in the real world. In some circumstances, a person could be more motivated by inner-direction; while in others, he could be more motivated by other-direction. The main question concerns the degree to which an individual or social group relies upon one or the other of the available mechanisms. In spite of this drawback to Riesman's theory, some important implications for marketers exist.

Marketing Implications of the Riesman Model

Social character appears useful in segmenting markets. While behavioral concepts used in segmenting markets are not easily operationalized, the application of Riesman's theory is aided by some empirical work which defines the inner- and other-directed individuals in more manageable terms. A valid and reliable instrument for measuring inner- and other-direction has been developed by Waltraud Kassarjian.[50] In a number of studies,[51] inner-directed individuals were found to be foreign-born, reared in small towns, academically interested in the natural sciences, older, wanting jobs such as architect, artist, or librarian, and having more theoretical and aesthetic values. Other-directed persons were from metropolitan areas, interested in education or business

administration in school, younger, wanting other-directed jobs such as salesman or teacher, and having more economic and political values. These and further studies can be helpful in identifying such inner- and other-directed market segments.

This means of market segmentation is particularly helpful when presenting an innovative or new product to the market. The categories of adopters have been fairly well defined.[52] The innovators are described as venturesome and consequently more willing to take risks. They are the opinion leaders who diffuse the innovation through the remaining individuals within their peer group. They appear to be Riesman's inner-directed persons.[53] The other-directed individuals, less willing to accept risk, will adopt the new product upon the word of the inner-directed innovator. Consequently, to gain proper initial acceptance of their product, marketers should initially direct their campaign to the wants and desires of the inner-directed market.

Further studies have found a relationship between advertising appeals and social character.[54] Inner-directed persons favor inner-directed appeals in their advertising while other-

[50]Waltraud M. Kassarjian, "A Study of Riesman's Theory of Social Character," *Sociometry,* Vol. 25 (September 1962), pp. 213–230.

[51]Same reference as footnote 50; Richard Centers, "An Examination of the Riesman Social Character Typology: A Metropolitan Survey," *Sociometry,* Vol. 25 (September 1962), pp. 231–240; and Waltraud M. Kassarjian and Harold H. Kassarjian, "Occupational Interests, Social Values, and Social Character," *Journal of Counseling Psychology,* Vol. 12 (Spring 1965), pp. 48–54.

[52]Everett M. Rogers, *Diffusion of Innovations* (New York: The Free Press, 1962).

[53]James H. Donnelly, Jr., "Social Character and Acceptance of New Products," *Journal of Marketing Research,* Vol. 7 (February 1970), pp. 111–113; Harriet Linton and Elaine Graham, "Personality Correlates of Persuasibility," in *Personality and Persuasibility,* Carl I. Hovland and Irving L. Janis, eds. (New Haven: Yale University Press, 1959), pp. 69–101; and Richard Centers and Miriam Horowitz, "Social Character and Conformity," *Journal of Social Psychology,* Vol. 60 (August 1963), pp. 343–349.

[54]Harold H. Kassarjian, "Social Character and Differential Preference for Mass Communication," *Journal of Marketing Research,* Vol. 2 (May 1965), pp. 146–153; and Arch G. Woodside, "Social Character, Product Use and Advertising Appeal," *Journal of Advertising Research,* Vol. 8 (December 1969), pp. 31–35.

directed individuals prefer other-directed appeals.[55] Although not tested, perhaps this relationship would hold true for message formats as well.[56]

A number of indicators—urbanization, suburbanization, and high mobility—point to the increasing trend toward other-direction within the United States. This increased social interaction permits the more rapid spread of new ideas and product acceptance than ever before. This fact may decrease brand loyalty, since other-directed individuals will receive new and different product needs and be pressured to conform to their peer group's norms. Results of one study indicate that when perceived differences between a new and an old product are small, the new product will be more readily accepted. This is attributed to the lower risk, i.e., less chance of social disapproval, associated with small departures between products.[57] Hence, such new products will diffuse through a social group at a faster rate.

As the population becomes more other-directed, word-of-mouth communication may have a greater impact on consumer buying than advertising. When advertising is used, however, the marketer should emphasize the benefits derived from social approval rather than product characteristics.

[55]Kassarjian, same reference as footnote 54.
[56]Thomas S. Robertson, *Innovative Behavior and Communication* (New York: Holt, Rinehart and Winston, 1971), p. 193.
[57]Donnelly, same reference as footnote 53.

CONCLUSION

The goal of the study of consumer behavior is to properly describe, explain, and ultimately predict human actions in the marketplace. Four social psychological theories have been investigated for their value in understanding why individuals buy. Two recurring problems appear. Some theoretical models resist confirmation because of the lack of a reliable and valid measure of the underlying construct. Perhaps even more problematic, existing theories tend to focus on the individual and do not adequately consider situational variables that intervene and seemingly invalidate the theory.[58] While substantial strides have been taken to provide a comprehensive explanation of consumer behavior,[59] integration of situational factors and reconciliation of measurement problems must receive attention before an encompassing theory of consumer behavior can be expected.

[58]For further amplification of these problems, see Thomas S. Robertson and Scott Ward, "Toward the Development of Consumer Behavior Theory," paper presented at the Fall Conference of the American Marketing Association, Houston, Texas, August 1972.
[59]See John Howard and Jagdish N. Sheth, *The Theory of Consumer Behavior* (New York: John Wiley and Sons, 1959); Francesco M. Nicosia, *Consumer Decision Processes* (Homewood, Ill.: Richard D. Irwin, 1966); James F. Engel, David T. Kollat, and Roger D. Blackwell, *Consumer Behavior* (New York: Holt, Rinehart and Winston, 1968); and Fleming Hansen, *Consumer Choice Behavior* (New York: The Free Press, 1972).

Questions

1. Give a brief description of the underlying theory for each model mentioned in the article.
2. Give a brief description of how each of these models has application to the field of consumer behavior.

3. In what ways have consumers with a high need for achievement been found to differ in their buying behavior from consumers with a low need for achievement?

4. Describe how an "inner-directed" individual might behave differently from an "other-directed" individual in a buying situation.

3. Consumer Behavior Models: An Introduction

George W. Wynn

Kotler (1965) has contrasted five behavioral models and Schewe (1973) has examined four social-psychological models in their pursuit of a better understanding of consumer behavior. In 1972, Hansen cited twenty-eight basic consumer behavior models. Today there are considerably more than that. Even though some of these models are not very comprehensive in their analyses of buyer behavior, this large number does point out the significant role of modeling in this field.

What are the benefits of these general behavior models and specific models of consumer behavior? What are they supposed to accomplish?

This paper is an attempt to offer some answers to these questions. It consists of two parts—(1) a brief explanation of the nature and purposes of models and (2) a summary of three comprehensive models of consumer behavior.

MODELS

Definitions

Models have been described as "the perception or diagramming of a complex or a system" (Lazer 1962: 9) and "a conceptual scheme, depicting in verbal, diagrammatic, or symbolic form some process of interest to the researcher" (Green and Tull 1975: 41). A model has also been defined as a technique that represents or depicts a studied relationship—that is, a model is any structure that purports to represent something else (Rigby 1965).

Types of Models

There are various types of models. The type used depends on the particular situation a researcher wishes to depict. Rigby (1965) has pointed out four general types of models.

1. Iconic—The iconic model has the actual appearance of what it seeks to represent. A statue or a model airplane would be an example of an iconic model. The iconic model does not have to be the actual shape of the item it seeks to represent. A photograph would be a good two-dimensional example of an iconic model.

2. Analog—The analog model does not necessarily look like what it seeks to represent, but it behaves in a similar manner. An example of an analog model would be furniture templates used to plan the layout of furniture in a new home or the familiar blueprint or drawing of a particular building or machine. The figures of the consumer

behavior models shown later in this article are analog models.

3. Symbolic—A symbolic model uses symbols to represent the phenomenon being studied. Symbolic models generally take the form of mathematical equations. An example of a symbolic model would be the McClelland model in the article by Charles Schewe (1973).

4. Verbal—The verbal model relies upon words to represent the ideas or concepts involved. Very often, before we build an iconic, analog, or symbolic model, we may develop a verbal model. Early in the stages of development of new products we do concept testing. In concept testing we describe a product idea that is being considered and ask potential users what they think of the idea. The description we use often is in the form of a verbal model. All five of the models described in "Behavioral Models for Analyzing Buyers" (Kotler 1965) are verbal models, whereas the buying process shown in Figure 1 of that same article is an analog model.

Uses of Models

Models are used primarily to develop a device or medium to analyze or represent relationships among concepts. Lazar (1962), for example, presents the following five uses of marketing models—(1) to provide a frame of reference for solving marketing problems, (2) to play an explanatory role in relationships and reactions, (3) to provide a useful aid in making predictions, (4) to help in the construction of a theory, and (5) to stimulate the creation of hypotheses that can then be validated and tested.

According to Walters (1978), consumer behavior models have two overall purposes: They are "(1) identify[ing] hypotheses and developing new consumer behavior theory, and (2) explaining the present state of consumer behavior theory" (p. 42). Most consumer behavior models approach the first

purpose, since consumer behavior as a science is in its infancy.

COMPREHENSIVE MODELS OF CONSUMER BEHAVIOR

Three of the most often cited comprehensive models of consumer behavior will be analyzed and compared. It should be recognized that other comprehensive models of consumer behavior do exist. These three were selected because of their widespread use and acceptability. These models attempt to explain each stage and show linkages between the stages of consumer buyer behavior from the stimulus, through the purchase, to postpurchase behavior. Thus they are known as comprehensive models. Each of these models approaches consumer buyer behavior from a slightly different perspective. However, each model has some steps or stages in common with the other models.

The Howard-Sheth Model of Buyer Behavior

The Howard-Sheth (H-S) model is a learning model that attempts to explain consumer behavior in the context of brand choice when the buyer is given several brands to choose from (Howard and Sheth 1969). This model in analog form is shown in Figure 1.

The H-S model can be divided roughly into four fundamental parts—(1) stimulus input variables, (2) exogenous variables, (3) sequential output variables, and (4) the "internal state of the buyer." While the inputs and outputs are labeled, the exogenous variables are the seven boxes shown across the top of the model, and the internal state is shown as the central rectangular box in Figure 1.

The inputs of the H-S model consist of

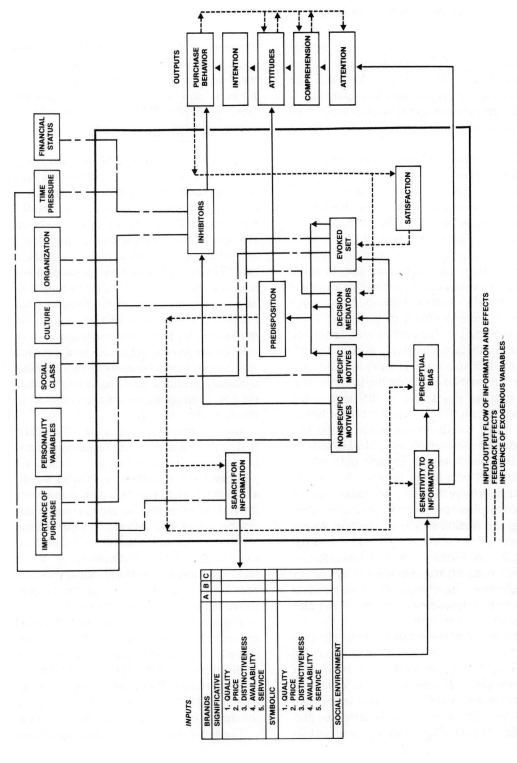

Figure 1 / The Howard-Sheth Model. *Source:* John A. Howard and Jagdish Sheth, *The Theory of Buyer Behavior* (New York: John Wiley and Sons, Inc., 1969), pp. 22–49.

various significative (transmitted by the brand) and symbolic (transmitted by the promotion efforts) dimensions of the brand. The buyer's social environment (including family and reference groups) regarding a purchase decision is the third stimulus input of the H-S model.

The exogenous variables might be likened to the "givens" in a mathematical equation: In other words, they are forces (primarily environmental) over which the buyer has little or no control, at least in the short run. These exogenous variables—importance of purchase, personality variables, social class, culture, organization, time pressure, and financial status—are inputs to the internal state that are not generally situational specific except in the case of the importance of purchase. These variables may be the constraining factors on action or the stimulus to spur action, depending on their strengths. These exogenous variables can and do affect the buying process at all internal stages and at different times, depending on what is important to the buyer.

One of the distinctive items of the H-S model is the form of outputs. Most models include a purchase–no purchase output. The H-S model exhibits five sequential steps—attention, comprehension, attitudes (output determined as a part of predisposition), intention, and finally, purchase behavior. As can be seen from the above explanation and figure, attitude formation generally manifests as expectations of, attitudes toward, or specific images of a certain brand. Purchase results in satisfaction depending on the extent to which expectations were met.

The hypothetical constructs that help form the sequential outputs are perception and learning. Perception consists of (1) search for information, (2) sensitivity to information, and (3) perceptual bias. Together they obtain and process information relative to purchases. The learning construct consists of six

elements—(1) specific and nonspecific motives, (2) evoked set, (3) predisposition (toward brands), (4) decision mediators, (5) inhibitors, and (6) satisfaction. In tandem, these six hypothetical elements provide the consumer with a decision making process that leads to satisfying purchases. Thus, inputs are processed by the perceptual variables; decisions about the inputs are then made by the learning variables, or the decisions result in outputs, including purchase. At any time, the perceptual and learning constructs can be influenced by the seven exogenous variables.

One idea novel to this model is the "evoked set." The evoked set is a partial list of products in a class. It is the total list of brands or alternatives that the buyer will consider when motivated to purchase. (An implication for marketers and promotion managers is to be certain their brands are in the buyer's evoked set.) The H-S model is applicable for branded consumer products and products for which the buyer can secure information that can be placed in the evoked set.

One possible limitation of the H-S model is that it does not account for nonsystematic behavior. A few products, for instance, are purchased only occasionally. In other words, a consumer might purchase a product simply for variety or because buying the same product or brand has become boring (Faison 1977). Another limitation of the H-S model is its nonapplicability to situations in which there is no awareness of individual products within a class of products that can be construed in the mind of the buyer as "brands."

Two major advantages of the H-S model are that (1) it has been partially tested empirically, thus establishing some credibility for the model, and that (2) the model is also a dynamic model. This dynamic feature is accomplished by the learning that occurs due to the change in exogenous variables over time.

The H-S model has made some significant

contributions to the field of consumer behavior. Not only has it made a strong attempt to bring together many variables influencing consumer behavior, but such concepts as the evoked set have influenced the direction of consumer research. As a teaching tool and heuristic model in the field of consumer buyer behavior, it is outstanding.

The Engel-Kollat-Blackwell Model

The Engel-Kollat-Blackwell (EKB) model as shown in Figure 2 is essentially a conscious problem-solving and learning model of consumer behavior. Its focal point is a central control unit that directs information search and processing and acts as a storage facility for the information (Engel, Blackwell, and Kollat 1978).

The information processed in this model is the stimulus. This is comparable to the inputs of the H-S model. Once processed, this stimulus is acted upon by the consumer's decision processes in order to determine a response to it.

The decision process stage of the EKB model can easily be compared to the output stages of the H-S model. The decision stages of the EKB model proceed from problem recognition through search, evaluation, choice, and finally, outcomes. When the decision is based on habit, the decision process moves from problem recognition directly to choice. The environmental influences may act upon any part of the decision processes.

The general motivating influences affect the decision processes, notably problem recognition. These motivational factors can be internal (i.e., hunger) or external (i.e., an advertisement for food, making the consumer feel hungry and thereby initiating behavior).

One of the interesting and important features of the EKB model is the outcomes of the decision process. It may be a satisfactory purchase, or it may be postpurchase dissonance. It is graphically shown in Figure 2 that the satisfied customer stores this information in memory for future purchase decisions. However, the other possible outcome, postpurchase dissonance, is the state in which available alternatives are qualitatively dissimilar and the purchaser is undecided about the advantages of the alternatives not chosen (Engel 1968). This type of behavior is not uncommon, and the purchaser will likely seek additional information to relieve this dissonance and confirm his or her choice. (A twofold implication for marketers is to (1) develop promotions that will reassure dissonant consumers of the wisdom of their choice and (2) develop additional promotions that will create dissonance with the consumer's present competitive product.)

The environmental influences of the EKB model compare directly to the exogenous variables as outlined in the explanation of the H-S model. These environmental influences are changing over time, and the buyer is learning of the changes and applying them to future purchase decisions. Hence, this model is a dynamic learning model, as is the H-S model. These environmental influences can determine whether the customer will continue through the conscious problem-solving and decision-making stages of this model or abort the process before a purchase decision.

The EKB model is a conscious problem-solving model. One of its strong points is that it is a good description of active information-seeking and evaluation processes of the consumer. Apparently, this model has received little empirical testing. However, the relationships and flows appear to be valid and logical.

The authors of the EKB model stated that their initial purpose in developing this model was to produce a systems model that would clarify and extend the understanding of con-

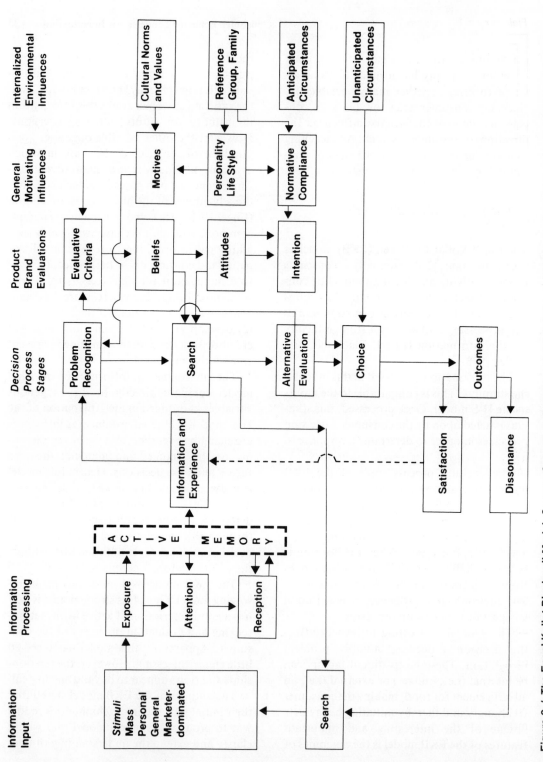

Figure 2 / The Engel-Kollat-Blackwell Model. *Source: Consumer Behavior,* Third Edition, by James F. Engel, Roger D. Blackwell, and David T. Kollat. Copyright © 1978 by the Dryden Press, a division of Holt, Rinehart and Winston. Reprinted by permission of Holt, Rinehart and Winston.

Field 1: From the source of a message to a consumer's attitude

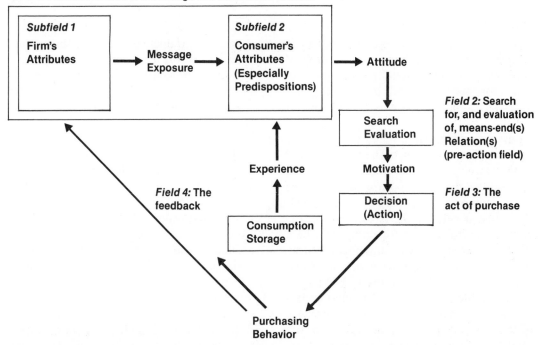

Figure 3 / **The Nicosia Model.** *Source:* Francisco M. Nicosia, *Consumer Decision Processes: Marketing and Advertising Implications* (Englewood Cliffs, N.J.: Prentice-Hall, Inc., 1966), p. 156.

sumer behavior. From a teaching standpoint it accomplishes this.

The Nicosia Model

The Nicosia model of consumer decision processes shown in Figure 3 is actually a simplified version of the total model. The original description of this model shows each field further flowcharted in considerable detail (Nicosia 1966).

Field 1 of the model consists of the output of a message from the firm to the consumer, where it is compared to the consumer's attributes, especially predisposition. The Nicosia model explicitly assumes that the message is about products with which the consumer is not familiar. After the consumer

evaluates the message against his or her attributes, an attitude is formed. This attitude is the input for search and evaluation (Field 2). If motivation to buy the product results from search and evaluation, then this is the input for decision or action (Field 3). This action results in purchasing behavior, which in turn results in (1) use and/or storage of the product, (2) supply of sales results to the business firm, and (3) storage of experience of the purchase in the buyer's memory. These three items above are classified as the feedback (Field 4).

Motivation is specifically included in the Nicosia model. This motivation to action is a result of favorable attitudes toward a firm's product after search and evaluation.

This model is considered a dyadic model

because it allows for the behavior of the firm and the individual as well as their interaction. (Research of message input and how firms reach the consumer should provide implications for marketers and promotion managers.) The Nicosia model is the only one of the three models discussed that explicitly includes the selling firm.

The biggest limitation of the Nicosia model is the extremely limited situation discussed previously—that of exposure to a message and formation of an attitude where no knowledge existed before. The Nicosia model offers no way to account for responses where the consumer has varying amounts of information about or experience of the firm's product prior to the exposure in Field 1.

This model, like the EKB model, apparently has not been empirically tested. Because of the brevity of published description of the model as well as inexact linkages between certain elements, it may never be empirically tested. However, because of the dyadic nature and the complete closure aspect of the model, it was included in this analysis. Complete closure of this model means that the structure is not affected by the choice of a starting point. For instance, we could trace the specific attitude toward a product and trace the feedbacks of this attitude as well as the forward flow resulting from the attitude.

SUMMARY AND CONCLUSIONS

Models indeed have a place in marketing literature. They aid in the teaching and understanding of relationships between consumer behavior concepts, as well as providing a frame of reference that can be used for explaining, making predictions, and solving marketing problems.

This paper gives brief consideration of three current comprehensive models of consumer behavior. The Howard-Sheth model describes variables that affect a consumer's behavior before and during a purchase. It considers the constructs of learning as the primary variables. The information processing of the active memory is the main part of the learning processes on which the Engel-Kollat-Blackwell model is based. The Nicosia model explicitly emphasizes the dyadic relationships between the behavior of the consumer and the behavior of the firm as well as the interaction of these two behaviors. The models outlined in this paper have a number of similarities. Each model (1) revolves around the flow process, (2) portrays the individual as the central component and problem solver with inputs and outputs, and (3) treats the environmental variables as constraints or influences (Walters 1978: 62). All three models have made great contributions to understanding consumer behavior.

Our discussion is not intended to imply that there are only three useful consumer behavior models. Other excellent models exist in the literature, and a study of some of these other models would be beneficial to any student of consumer behavior. The interested reader may wish to review some of the models, such as Andreasen (1965), Markin (1974), McNeal (1973), Kerby (1975), and Hawkin, Coney, and Best (1980).

REFERENCES

Andreasen, Alan R. 1978. "Attitudes and Consumer Behavior: A Decision Model." In *Perspectives in Consumer Behavior,* H. S. Kassarjian and T. S. Robertson, eds., pp. 498–510, Glenview, Ill.: Scott, Foresman, and Company.

Engel, James F. 1968. "The Dissonance Dilemma." *Bulletin of Business Research* XLIII (July): 1–5.

———, Roger D. Blackwell, and David T. Kollat. 1978. *Consumer Behavior.* Third ed. New York: Holt, Rinehart and Winston.

Faison, Edward W. J. 1977. "The Neglected Variety Drive: A Useful Concept in Consumer Behavior," *Journal of Consumer Research* 4: 172–175.

Green, Paul E., and Donald S. Tull. 1975. *Research for Marketing Decisions,* 3rd ed. Englewood Cliffs, N.J.: Prentice-Hall.

Hansen, Flemming, 1972. *Consumer Choice Behavior: A Cognitive Theory.* New York: The Free Press.

Hawkin, Del I., Kenneth A. Coney, and Roger J. Best. 1980. *Consumer Behavior Implication for Marketing Strategy.* Dallas: Business Publications.

Howard, John A., and Jagdish Sheth. 1969. *The Theory of Buyer Behavior.* New York: John Wiley and Sons.

Kerby, Joe Kent. 1975. *Consumer Behavior Conceptual Foundations.* New York: Dun-Donnelly Publishing Corp.

Kotler, Philip. 1965. "Behavior Models for Analyzing Consumers," *Journal of Marketing* XXIX (October): 38–44.

Lazer, William. 1962. "The Role of Models in Marketing," *Journal of Marketing* 26 (April): 9–14.

Markin, Rom J. 1974. *Consumer Behavior: A Cognitive Orientation.* New York: Macmillan.

McNeal, James U. 1973. *An Introduction to Consumer Behavior.* New York: John Wiley and Sons.

Nicosia, Francisco M. 1966. *Consumer Decision Processes: Marketing and Advertising Implications.* Englewood Cliffs, N.J.: Prentice-Hall.

Rigby, Paul. 1965. *Conceptual Foundations of Business Research.* New York: John Wiley and Sons.

Schewe, Charles. 1973. "Selected Social Psychological Models for Analyzing Buyers," *Journal of Marketing* 37 (July): 31–39.

Walters, C. Glenn. 1978. *Consumer Behavior Theory and Practice,* 3rd ed. Homewood, Ill.: Richard D. Irwin.

Questions

1. What is a consumer behavior model? How can these models be useful?

2. In what way is the Nicosia model different from the EKB and H-S models?

3. What idea is novel to the Howard-Sheth model? Explain this concept.

4. From the standpoint of the Engel-Kollat-Blackwell model, explain the possible outcomes of the decision process.

4. What About Disposition?

Jacob Jacoby

Carol K. Berning

Thomas F. Dietvorst

Consumer behavior can be defined as the "acquisition, consumption, and disposition of goods, services, time and ideas by decision making units."[1] As described elsewhere,[2] different disciplines typically focus on different portions of this behavioral process. For example, marketers and advertisers tend to focus attention on acquisition (particularly that form of acquisition called purchasing), whereas home economists and nutritionists are typically more concerned with actual usage or consumption (e.g., in the preparation and consumption of foods).

Examination of the published literature across those behavioral science oriented disciplines studying micro-consumer behavior reveals that, except for a handful of papers dealing with packaging and solid waste disposal, virtually no conceptual or empirical work has been addressed to the general issue of disposition by consumers.[3]

Accordingly, the present investigation was undertaken in the spirit of exploratory research.

We started by developing a conceptual taxonomy to accommodate what we believed to be the major disposition behaviors engaged in by individual consumers. Using the taxonomy as our guide, we next developed an interview schedule designed to probe consumer disposition decisions and behavior vis-a-vis six commonly owned durable products. After pretesting on one sample (n = 60), this questionnaire was administered to a second sample of 134 consumers. The primary purpose of this preliminary study was to determine whether the taxonomy was indeed comprehensive. These developments are described below and are followed by a concluding section in which the findings are discussed, additional issues raised, and directions for future research briefly outlined.

A TAXONOMY FOR DESCRIBING CONSUMER DISPOSITION BEHAVIOR

When a consumer contemplates the disposition of a product, there appear to be three general choices available to him:

1. Keep the product.
2. Permanently dispose of it.
3. Temporarily dispose of it.

If he decides to keep the product, he may either:

a. Continue to use it for its original purpose.
b. Convert it to serve another purpose.
c. Store it, perhaps for later use.

If he decides to get rid of it permanently, he can:

a. Throw it away or abandon it.
b. Give it away.
c. Sell it.
d. Trade it.

Finally, if he decides to dispose of it only temporarily, he can:

a. Loan it.
b. Rent it to someone else.

Exhibit 1 / Disposition Decision Taxonomy

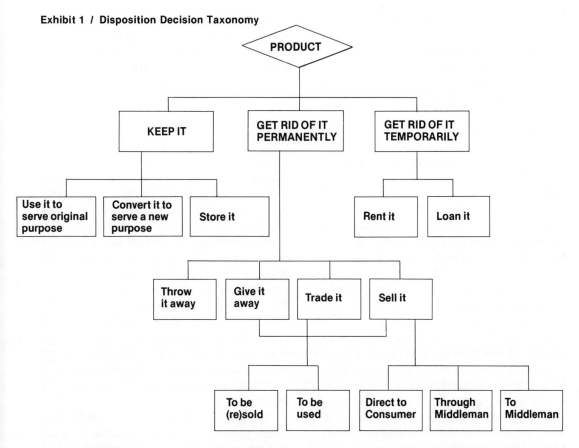

These nine specific alternatives are depicted in Exhibit 1.

This basic taxonomy can be articulated further. For example, the give it away, trade it, and sell it options for "get rid of it permanently" can all be subdivided according to what will happen to the product once this course of action is taken. Will it be used by or be [re-]sold by the recipient or, in what is hopefully a more frequently occurring option, will it be recycled? Especially where the "sell it" option is concerned, one can ask whether this is directly to another consumer, to a middleman (as when selling a used car to a used car lot), or through a middleman (as when using a realtor to sell one's home).

Not withstanding the potential that such speculative articulating has for enriching the taxonomy, it was thought that such conceptual extensions should await at least a preliminary empirical assessment of the basic taxonomy. Accordingly, we now turn to the description of an investigation carried out for this purpose.

EMPIRICALLY EXPLORING THE DISPOSITION TAXONOMY

Methodology

Subjects. The subjects were 134 residents (38% male and 62% female) of the Lafayette/West Lafayette, Indiana metropolitan area. Only one was less than 20 years of age and 17 were older than 60; thus, 88% were between the ages of 20 and 60. Further, 78% were currently married, 13% single, 5% widowed, and 3% divorced. Although the Lafayette area includes a college community, only 5% indicated they, or their spouses, were college students; of those surveyed, 95% indicated they were from Lafayette and the surrounding area, rather than the West Lafayette college community.

Products examined. The products examined were selected to be representative of commonly purchased durable goods. Among the selection criteria employed were price and product turn-over. The six products selected were: stereo amplifier, wrist watch, toothbrush, phonograph record, bicycle, and refrigerator.

Interview schedule. Because of its complexity, the questionnaire was designed as an interview schedule (containing approximately 20 questions per product) and was administered by a trained interviewer. For each product, the core items on the schedule asked the respondent if he now owned the item; and, if yes, whether he had owned another one previously. If the reply to this second question was also yes, the schedule then explored the disposition decision made with respect to the earlier purchased item. That is, did the respondent convert the earlier purchased item to serve another purpose, did he store it, throw it away, give it away, trade it, sell it, rent it or loan it to someone? In the event that this item was still being used by the respondent to serve its original function, the respondent was asked what he thought he would do with it once he decided to no longer use it for this purpose.

Procedure. A pretest was conducted using an independent group of 60 respondents, with a larger proportion of these being associated with the university community. After modifications were made, the main survey was conducted in the downtown business center of Lafayette and in a Lafayette city park during July and August of 1974.

Results

Ownership information for the 134 respondents across the six test products is shown in Exhibit 2. The number of disposition decisions provided by these respondents ranged from a low of 61 for stereo amplifiers to a high of 133 for toothbrushes. (It is of interest to note that one 62 year old respondent reported never having owned a toothbrush.) Rows A, B, and C of Exhibit 2 represent numbers of respondents in each category. Row D represents numbers of disposition decisions. It should be noted that Row B respondents were able to provide data regarding 1 or 2 disposition decisions for the phonograph record category and 144 disposition decisions were obtained from these 79 subjects.

As indicated in line B–1 of Exhibit 2, a small proportion of respondents in each category were still using an earlier acquired product for its original purpose even though they had acquired another one of these products more recently. To a certain extent, this represents the frequency of occurrence of the "decides to use it to serve the original function" disposition option. These respondents were next asked what they thought they would most likely do once they were ready to no longer use this item to satisfy this purpose, and the responses to this question were tallied as disposition decisions.

Thus, by collecting "disposition intentions" data from the respondents actually in the "currently using item to satisfy original function" category and adding these responses to those from respondents who had

Exhibit 2 / Ownership and Disposition Decision Information for the Six Test Products[a]

	Stereo amplifier	Wrist watch	Toothbrush	Phonograph record	Bicycle	Refrigerator
A. Currently own, but have not owned before	48	17	0	29	28	20
B. Owned another before most recent acquisition						
1. Still using product acquired first for original purpose	5	20	6	25	5	8
2. No longer using product for original purpose	43	84	127	54	33	83
C. Owned product at one time but not now	13	4	0	11	26	2
D. Number of disposition decisions for product category (lines B1, B2, & C above)	61	108	133	125[b]	64	93

[a]Rows A, B, and C represent respondents; Row D represents decisions.
[b]Respondents were able to provide more than one disposition decision for Phonograph Records. Thus, the 79 respondents in Row B provided 114 disposition decisions.

already made a decision to dispose, the original nine specific disposition options were reduced to eight.

Combined across all products, the interviews yielded 584 disposition decisions. These are summarized in Exhibit 3. The "other" category includes those items for which the disposition decision was forgotten. For each disposition decision, the subjects were asked whether any other disposition decision was considered. In approximately 80% of the cases, no other disposition was contemplated before the final decision was made.

Given our earlier remarks regarding the increasing necessity to move toward a conservationist ethic, it is noteworthy that the option to discard the item, while only one of the remaining eight alternative means of disposition, is the single most frequent option taken—nearly 40% of the time. Even large and relatively expensive items which most likely have usable parts (e.g., refrigerators and bicycles) are thrown away approximately 1 out of 5 times.

It is also obvious that, while there are some consistencies, the patterns of disposition differ, considerably across the different products. The major consistency across all six products is the relative absence of rental and loan decisions. Temporary disposition appears to be a rarely considered option. Perhaps more interesting, although not unexpected, is the divergence in disposition patterns across products. For example, the single most used option for stereo amplifiers was to sell the item (42.6%). This option was never employed with toothbrushes, where the single most employed decision was to throw the old toothbrush away (79.7%).

Considered by themselves, these data are fairly dull and uninteresting. However, the implications emanating from them and the questions raised are not. After a brief description of the "highlight" findings regarding each individual product, we will return to elaborate upon what we believe are the noteworthy implications of these data.

Stereo amplifiers. Of those people who now own a stereo amplifier and also owned one earlier, 10 (20.8%) kept their old amplifiers. Interestingly, eight of the 10 amplifiers kept by the owners when they acquired a new one were still in working order. The most frequently cited reason for acquiring a new amplifier when the old one was still functioning satisfactorily was the desire for an amplifier of better quality.

Wrist watches. Of those who currently own a wrist watch and also owned another one earlier, 70 (66%) kept their old watches. Of these, 36 (52.2%) were in working order. The reason most often cited for having more than one watch that functions properly is that the other watches were received as gifts. Of all products surveyed, wrist watches were most likely to be stored: 48 of the 70 watches (59.7%) are so stored.

Toothbrushes. Although toothbrushes were the most likely of all products to be thrown away, they were also the product most likely to be used for another purpose, such as a cleaning tool. Despite the fact that they were the least expensive product studied, alternatives to the final disposition decision were more likely to be considered for toothbrushes than any other product.

Phonograph records. If a phonograph record is not thrown away, it is likely that it will be stored—even though the owner very often claims he will probably never play it again. As many as 33% (42) of the disposition decisions for phonograph records were to store a record that the owner would no longer use. Those phonograph records which the owner becomes tired of are more likely to be stored than those that are scratched.

Bicycles. Of all disposition decisions, those for bicycles were most likely to be forgotten. Although directly relevant data were not collected, we speculate that this memory loss resulted from having made the bicycle disposition decision a long time ago, relative to the other products. Of those consumers who presently do not own a bicycle but at one time did, 9

Exhibit 3 / Disposition Decisions for the Six Test Products

	All products		Stereo amplifier		Wrist watch		Toothbrush		Phonograph record		Bicycle		Refrigerator	
	f	%	f	%	f	%	f	%	f	%	f	%	f	%
Converted	46	7.9	1	1.6	2	1.8	23	17.2	12	9.6	1	1.5	7	7.5
Stored	74	12.7	—	—	31	28.7	—	—	41	32.8	2	3.1	—	—
Thrown away	232	39.7	7	11.5	33	30.6	106	79.7	54	43.2	11	17.3	21	22.6
Given away	100	17.1	19	31.1	25	23.1	—	—	12	9.6	26	40.2	18	19.3
Traded	31	5.3	3	4.9	6	5.6	—	—	1	.8	2	3.2	19	20.4
Sold	67	11.5	26	42.6	6	5.6	—	—	—	—	11	17.3	24	25.8
Rented	4	.7	—	—	1	.9	—	—	—	—	—	—	3	3.2
Loaned	2	.3	—	—	—	—	—	—	—	—	1	1.5	1	1.0
Other	28	4.8	5	8.3	4	3.7	4	3.1	5	4.0	10	15.9	—	—
Σ =	584	100	61	100	108	100	133	100	125	100	64	100	93	100

(33.3%) could not recall the disposition decision made.

Refrigerators. Of all the products studied, disposition decisions for refrigerators were most likely to result in re-sale of the product. Refrigerator was the only product category in which the disposition decision was more likely to involve a store rather than family or friends. Consumers were least likely to keep this item when a new one was obtained.

Discussion

As noted above, the present investigation is considered a highly preliminary exploration of relatively unknown terrain. Its primary goals have been: to acquire some familiarity with the phenomenon, to achieve some insight, and to develop hypotheses.

One of the more interesting set of findings concerns data relevant to the question of why people acquire new products when the old ones they possess are still performing satisfactorily. Common responses supplied to this question include either receiving the new product as a gift, or purchasing the new product for oneself, because:

- It had features which the old one did not (e.g., the date or second hand on wrist watches).
- It didn't fit in with the changing environment (e.g., the old refrigerator was the wrong style and color for the new home).
- It no longer corresponded to one's preferences or self-image.

Consumers also reported that they sometimes used the malfunctioning of a small and repairable aspect of a product as an "excuse" to purchase an entirely new product (e.g., scratches on the lens of a watch occasionally provided sufficient cause for the purchase of a new watch). Identifying reasons like these and noting their relative incidence in a product-by-product basis should provide marketing and advertising managers with information useful in developing promotional strategies.

The basic question, however, remains: What factors influence the disposition choice the consumer makes? Consideration of the many varied responses to the interview schedule suggests that these factors can be grouped into three categories:

1. Psychological characteristics of the decision maker: personality, attitudes, emotions, perception, learning, creativity, intelligence, social class, level of risk tolerance, peer pressure, social conscience, etc.
2. Factors intrinsic to the product: condition, age, size, style, value, color, and power source of the product, technological innovations, adaptability, reliability, durability, initial cost, replacement cost, etc.
3. Situational factors extrinsic to the product: finances, storage space, urgency, fashion changes, circumstances of acquisition (gift vs. purchase), functional use, economics (demand and supply), legal considerations (giving to avoid taxes), etc.

The description of these three categories is not meant to imply that they are discrete and non-overlapping, nor does it imply that there is an absence of interaction among them. However, it does assist us in speculating about disposition decisions and behavior; and it does provide us with a framework for developing and structuring hypotheses—the third function of this exploratory study.

For example, given the decision alternatives and the various influence factors, it becomes interesting to speculate about various possibilities. Consider a wrist watch which still runs but is no longer stylish. The consumer is faced with a first level decision: keep it, get rid of it permanently, or get rid of it temporarily. Assume he decides to keep it because of his thriftiness (psychological characteristic). He could have also decided to keep it because, although it was not stylish, it was still very reliable (product characteristic) or because he had no money for another one (situational factor). At some later point in time, the old watch is again brought to mind. He may decide to get rid of it permanently this time because his status needs are no longer met by the watch (psychological characteristic), the band is worn (product characteristic), and/or he has too many old watches in his dresser drawer (situational factor). At the second level, he may decide to give it away to a charitable institution so that he can claim a tax deduction.

The result of such speculations has been the development and collection of a large number of testable hypotheses. For purposes of illustration, several of these are noted here.

Characteristics of the decision maker can be expected to affect product disposition in several ways: high need for achievement will be more strongly related to decisions to convert the product into something else; highly creative persons will be most likely to convert a product, and least likely to throw it away; persons highly involved (in a sentimental or emotional sense) with a product will be more likely to keep it than will other people; persons high in self-esteem will be more likely to convert a product or to sell it directly than will other people.

▶ Product-related factors will affect the disposal decisions in several ways: high value products will be more often sold than disposed of in any other way; products in good condition will be least likely to be thrown away; products in poor condition will be least likely to be sold.

▶ Situational factors will affect disposal decisions: when time is valuable or limited, a product will more often be given away or thrown away. If it is sold, a middleman will be involved.

▶ When the individual is concerned with the financial aspect of the disposal, the item will be sold, more often to another customer than to or through an agent.

▶ As the amount of available storage space increases, the probability that an item will be kept will increase, and the probability that it will be thrown away will decrease.

Given the exploratory nature of this investigation, we believe it appropriate that the data collected be considered simply descriptive and not be employed to "test" hypotheses in any strict or formal sense of the term. However, it is possible to illustrate some of the potential of the approach by returning to the data to informally examine some of these hypotheses.

Consider the following hypotheses: higher value products will be more often sold than disposed of in any other way. The data show that the range of disposition decisions chosen increases as a function of product value. The more expensive the product, the greater variety in disposition decisions made. However, the decision to give a high value product away was more popular than the decision to sell it. It would thus appear that not all of the findings likely to come from disposition research are straightforward and to be expected.

WHERE DO WE GO FROM HERE?

The present investigation has obviously just scratched the surface of an enormous iceberg. Its primary objective has been to call attention to consumer disposition decisions and behavior in the hope that, by so doing, this subject would begin to receive the serious attention it deserves. In our opinion, the study of consumer disposition decisions and behavior merits the status of a major research focus within consumer behavior.

To begin, data must be collected regarding the frequency and rates of disposition decisions and behavior with respect to a variety of consumer products. Such data are necessary both in the sense of establishing benchmarks against which to evaluate possible later changes and also so that cross-product (or product category) generalizations can be made (e.g., temporary disposition appears to be an infrequently utilized option).

Relatedly, the systematic ways in which demographic, psychological, socio-cultural, and economic differences may relate to disposition decisions and behavior should be probed. Important issues here include:

- Do different socio-economic segments engage in different patterns of disposition behavior? If so, how do these patterns relate to subsequent acquisition behavior?
- Under what conditions do consumers retain products longer or convert products to another function?
- How do disposition patterns vary over time?

Given that adequate descriptive data have been collected, the next level of understanding requires that we begin to provide explanations for "why" certain patterns exist. In particular, why (i.e., under what conditions) do consumers dispose of something that is still functioning satisfactorily? Answering this question should also provide better understanding of the acquisition process. Another element within this category of issues is the question: Why do consumers select one type of disposition behavior over another?

Prediction and change become the primary concern at the next level. How and in what beneficial ways can disposition behavior be changed? For example, can the value consumers receive from a product be increased by showing them new ways to use said product once they are no longer using it to satisfy its original function? As one specific illustration, how many consumers know that they can take refrigerators to an automobile body (and paint) shop and have them inexpensively repainted so that they can be made to "fit in" with new decor?

Independent of prolonging the product's value for the individual consumer, can the product's value to society at large be increased by educating consumers to dispose of prod-

ucts they no longer want in ways which satisfy the conservation ethic rather than by simply destroying or discarding said items? What would the impact be of establishing more recycling centers and making consumers aware of the significance of these centers for their own well-being?

We have here touched upon only a few of the many interesting and important aspects of consumer disposition decisions and behavior. It is an area wide-open for meaningful research and one which has the potential of providing answers to assist the consumer, the marketer, the government, and society at large. Hopefully, this article will stimulate some of the needed work.

ENDNOTES

1. Jacob Jacoby, "Consumer Psychology: An Octennium," in Paul Mussen and Mark Rosenzweig, eds., *Annual Review of Psychology,* Vol. 27(1976), pp. 331–58.

2. Jacob Jacoby, "Training Consumer Psychologists: The Purdue University Program," *Professional Psychology,* Vol. 2 (Summer 1971), pp. 300–302; Jacob Jacoby, "Consumer Psychology as a Social Psychological Sphere of Action," *American Psychologist,* Vol. 30 (October 1975), pp. 977–87; and Jacob Jacoby, "Consumer and Industrial Psychology: Prospects for Theory Corroboration and Mutual Contribution," in Marvin D. Dunnette, ed., *The Handbook of Industrial and Organizational Psychology* (Chicago: Rand McNally, 1976), in press

3. Arsen J. Darnay, Jr., "Throwaway Packages—A Mixed Blessing," in David A. Aaker and George S. Day, eds., *Consumerism: Search for the Consumer Interest,* 2nd ed. (New York: Free Press, 1974), pp. 402–14; Raymond A. Marquardt, Anthony F. McGann, and James C. Makens, "Consumer Responses to the Problem of Disposable Containers," in Scott Ward and Peter L. Wright, eds., *Advances in Consumer Research,* Vol. I (Urbana, IL: Association for Consumer Research, 1974), pp. 38–50; and William G. Zikmund and William J. Stanton, "Recycling Solid Wastes: A Channels-of-Distribution Problem," *Journal of Marketing,* Vol. 35 No. 3 (July 1971), pp. 34–39.

Questions

1. Name and briefly describe the three choices available to a consumer for the disposition of goods and services.
2. List and briefly explain the factors that will influence the disposition choice of a consumer.
3. Under what conditions would situational factors have maximum influence on disposition patterns?
4. How useful is this concept to marketing?
5. How does income affect disposition?

5.   Situational Variables and Consumer Behavior

Russell W. Belk

Growing recognition of limitations in the ability of individual consumer characteristics to explain variation in buyer behavior has prompted a number of appeals to examine situational influences on behavior. Ward and Robertson argued that "situational variables may account for considerably more variance than actor-related variables" (1973, p. 26). Lavidge (1966) cautioned that many buyer behaviors may be enacted only under specific conditions and necessitate situational investigations of intra-individual variability. Engel, Kollat, and Blackwell (1969) urged that *both* individual and situational factors must be considered in order to explain consumer choices. Nevertheless, these and other suggestions to include situational variables in research on consumer behavior have gone largely unheeded. The primary obstacle has

been the absence of an adequate conception of the variables which comprise a situation. It is the purpose of the following discussion to explore such concepts and to suggest directions for the study of situational influence in consumer behavior.

CONSUMER SITUATIONS AND RELATED CONCEPTS

Situations, Behavioral Settings, and Environments

As a starting point for a definition, most theoreticians would agree that a situation comprises a point in time and space (Belk, 1975). For students of human behavior, a discrete time and place occupied by one or more persons identifies a situation of potential interest. A somewhat larger alternative unit of analysis would be Barker's (1968) "behavioral setting." A behavioral setting is not only bounded in time and space, but also by a complete sequence of behavior or an "action pattern." For example, a basketball game or a piano lesson is a behavioral setting because each involves an interval in time and space in which certain behaviors can be expected regardless of the particular persons present. But such patterns of behavior require stretching the time and place dimensions to broader and more continuous units than those defining a situation. While a behavioral setting might be a store which is open from 8:00 AM to 6:00 PM (Barker, 1968, p. 19), the current perspective would recognize a number of discrete situations which may occur within this setting.

The concept of an "environment" extends the time, place, and behavioral dimensions still further. Although there is less agreement as to what bounds and defines an environment,[1] it is clear that situations and behavioral settings are subunits within an environment. In one of his early formulations Lewin pointed out that an environment may be thought of as the chief characteristics of a more or less permanent "situation" (Lewin, 1933). In this sense situations represent momentary encounters with those elements of the total environment which are available to the individual at a particular time. Environment is also broader in terms of the geographic area over which it applies. For example, while the "legal environment" may be

described to consist of laws, legal institutions, and interpretive tendencies within a governmental territory, and the behavioral setting may refer to a certain courtroom, the specific experience of individual A being cross-examined by attorney G during trial M in city R at 4:00 on day X, can only be described from a narrower situational perspective. It is this latter view of the conditions for experiences and the effect of these conditions on specific behavioral outcomes which the current perspective seeks to develop.

Situational Versus Non-situational Determinants of Consumer Behavior

A second group of concepts from which situations must be distinguished are the non-situational determinants of a particular consumer behavior. Figure 1 shows a familiar stimulus-organism-response paradigm which has been modified to divide the stimulus into an object and a situation. This split is analogous to the perceptual distinctions between figure and ground or focal and contextual cues (Helson, 1964). That is, because behavior with respect to a product or service object is of primary significance in consumer behavior, the object to which the consumer is directly responding will be regarded as a unique source of behavioral influence. In not including personal and object characteristics within the concept of the situation there is also a purposeful departure from Lewin's (1935) formulation of the life space. The rationale for this more limited view of situation is the greater possibility of operationalizing a construct which has an existence apart from the individual's total consciousness. For there to be a hope of really adding to the ability to ex-

---

[1] A great deal of the effort in the emerging discipline of environmental or ecological psychology has been spent in debating boundaries. See for example Barker (1963), Craik (1970), Proshansky, Ittelson, and Rivlin (1970), Ittelson (1973), and Rivlin (1973).

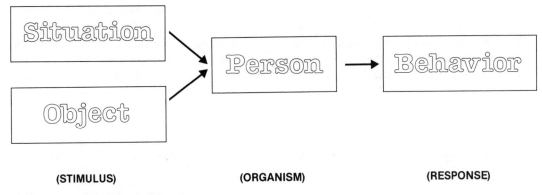

(STIMULUS)   (ORGANISM)   (RESPONSE)

Figure 1 / A revised S-O-R paradigm

plain consumer behavior, this separate existence is essential.[2]

It might seem that a clear distinction may
be made between persons, objects, and situations as separate sources of influence on
behavior, but some potential for confusion
exists in attempting to separate the characteristics of each determinant. R. L. Thorndike's (1947) concept of "lasting and general
characteristics of the individual" is a useful
device in distinguishing personal and situational characteristics. These individual features, including personality, intellect, sex,
and race, are stable over times and places of
observation and may therefore be attributed
consistently to the individual. Where the
feature is more transitory, such as having a
headache, it must be considered to be at least
partly a function of the situation. It is
necessary to impose similar constraints on the
conception of object characteristics in order
to categorize a description such as a brand of
soda being 10¢ less than competing brands. In

cases where the characteristic tends to be a
lasting and general feature of the brand it may
be attributed to the object. Where the characteristic is specific to a time and place (e.g., a
special sale) it should be regarded as a characteristic of the situation.

Characteristics of
Consumer Situations

Consistent with the previous distinctions, a
consumer situation may be viewed as comprising ". . . all those factors particular to a
time and place of observation which do not
follow from a knowledge of personal (intra-
individual) and stimulus (choice alternative)
attributes and which have a demonstrable and
systematic effect on current behavior" (Belk,
1974a). The greatest problem in operationalizing this view lies in defining "all those factors." Several attempts have been made to
develop comprehensive taxonomies of situational characteristics. Using general guidelines suggested by Sherif and Sherif (1956),
Sells (1963) constructed a subjective classification of over 200 situational variables including gravity, temperature, group structure, role requirements, and novelty of the

---

[2] This point is elaborated by Belk (1975). Mausner
(1963) captured the argument in stating that "if one
specifies the stimulus in terms of the nature of the
receiver, lawfulness becomes impossible."

49

situation in relation to prior experiences. Unfortunately, from the point of view of the current conception of situation, Sell's classification also includes some characteristics of the individual (e.g., age, sex, race) and environment (e.g., sources of food, erosion, language), and excludes certain descriptors of the physical locale (e.g., noises, colors, room or area size). Classification attempts by Bellows (1963), Wolf (1966), and Moos (1973), are less complete and suffer from similar drawbacks. Although also incomplete and parochial in its focus, a limited taxonomy by Allen (1965) of the situational factors found to affect conformity highlights several important social dimensions (e.g., public/private, interdependence of participants) and task dimensions (e.g., difficulty, importance) of the situation. These features contrast sharply with the taxonomy of 66 bipolar adjectival scales constructed by Kasmar (1970) to measure situations. From an initial list of 300 characteristics generated through room description protocols obtained from architecture students, scales were developed to describe 13 aspects of the situation; size, volume, scale, mood, color, texture, function, illumination, esthetic quality, climate, color, acoustical quality, and miscellaneous. Such characteristics provide a comprehensive description of the design features of the situation, but they completely neglect the social and task attributes which Allen's review (1965) emphasized. Furthermore a higher order factor analysis of data from Kasmar's scales has shown them to be highly redundant in terms of an underlying affective dimension (Mehrabian and Russell, 1974). Mehrabian and Russell's own (1974) attempt to develop three comprehensive situational descriptors (pleasure, arousal, and dominance) is also not very satisfying to depict the array of possible situational dimensions. However, by selectively combining features suggested in the various taxonomies cited, a skeletal notion of what is meant by "all those factors" comprising a situation may be offered. The following five groups of situational characteristics represent the general features from these taxonomies which are consistent with the current definition of situation.

1. *Physical Surroundings* are the most readily apparent features of a situation. These features include geographical and institutional location, decor, sounds, aromas, lighting, weather, and visible configurations of merchandise or other material surrounding the stimulus object.

2. *Social Surroundings* provide additional depth to a description of a situation. Other persons present, their characteristics, their apparent roles, and interpersonal interactions occurring are potentially relevant examples.

3. *Temporal Perspective* is a dimension of situations which may be specified in units ranging from time of day to season of the year. Time may also be measured relative to some past or future event for the situational participant. This allows conceptions such as time since last purchase, time since or until meals or payday, and time constraints imposed by prior or standing commitments.

4. *Task Definition* features of a situation include an intent or requirement to select, shop for, or obtain information about a general or specific purchase. In addition, task may reflect different buyer and user roles anticipated by the individual. For instance, a person shopping for a small appliance as a wedding gift for a friend is in a different situation than he would be in shopping for a small appliance for personal use.

5. *Antecedent States* make up a final group of features which characterize a situation. These are momentary moods (such as acute anxiety, pleasantness, hostility, and excitation) or momentary conditions (such as cash on hand, fatigue, and illness) rather than chronic individual traits. These conditions are further stipulated to be immediately antecedent to the current situation in order to distinguish states which the individual brings to the situation from states of the in-

dividual which result from the situation. For instance, a person may select a certain motion picture because he feels depressed (an antecedent state and a part of the choice situation), but the fact that the movie causes him to feel happier is a response to the consumption situation.[3] This altered state may then become antecedent for behavior in the next choice situation encountered, such as passing a street vendor on the way out of the theater.

Given a conception of the dimensions characterizing a situation, the final element of the definition of a situation requiring clarification is the requirement that these features have a "demonstrable and systematic effect on current behavior." To a greater extent than the problem of situational dimensions, this is an empirical question which has been the subject of some research. The following section reviews this research and examines the extent to which situational knowledge can be expected to add to our ability to explain consumer behavior.

ASSESSMENTS OF SITUATIONAL EFFECTS ON CONSUMER BEHAVIOR

Inventory Evidence

In the past six or seven years a small but growing number of empirical tests of situational influence in consumer behavior have been conducted using inventories of situational scenarios and choice alternatives. These inventories ask subjects to rate the likelihood that they would choose each of several alternative products or services under each of several sets of situational conditions. Sum-

mary descriptions of seven of these inventories are provided in the Appendix. It may well be argued that the situations investigated in these studies do not constitute random samples of possible situations and do not always reflect the full range of situational dimensions just outlined. Despite the fact that most of the inventories have relied on pretests to generate familiar situations, the argument is undoubtedly valid. Even so, any demonstration that behavior differs widely between the situations specified is evidence that there are important situational determinants for the class of choices considered.

Results comparing the relative influence from persons, products (responses), situations, and their interactions are presented in Table 1 for the six product categories that have been examined.[4] For all inventories the effects explaining the smallest proportions of variance are those which reflect superfluous response styles. For instance, a sizable interaction term for persons by situations would only indicate that some subjects view using any of the products in certain situations as more likely than do other subjects. Similarly, sizable main effects for persons or situations would have little meaning since they do not involve preference differences by product. A more dominant influence is the responses by situations interaction, especially for the meat and beverage inventories. This is the variance component which directly reflects the influence of systematic situational differences in product preferences. Furthermore, the lower contributions from the responses main effect in all inventories except motion pictures, suggest that general product popularity is a

---

[3] Hansen (1972) distinguishes between purchase, consumption, and communication situations. Comments in this paper concentrate primarily on consumer purchase choices.

[4] The research reported generally employed a situations by products by persons repeated measures experimental design. While nearly all main effects and two way interactions yielded significant F-ratios, proportions of variance accounted for by each effect are more revealing (Belk, 1974a).

Table 1 / Analyses of Consumer Behavioral Variance[a]
(percents of total variance)

Source	Response category[b]					
	Beverage products	Meat products	Snack products[a]	Fast foods[c]	Leisure activities[d]	Motion pictures
Persons (P)	0.5%	4.6%	6.7%	8.1%	4.5%	0.9%
Situations (S)	2.7%	5.2%	0.4%	2.2%	2.0%	0.5%
Products (Responses: R)	14.6%	15.0%	6.7%	13.4%	8.8%	16.6%
R × S	39.8%	26.2%	18.7%	15.3%	13.4%	7.0%
P × S	2.7%	2.9%	6.1%	2.2%	4.0%	1.9%
P × R	11.8%	9.7%	22.4%	20.1%	21.2%	33.7%
P × S × R	_e	_e	3.4%	_e	_e	_e
Residual	27.8%[f]	36.4%	35.6%	38.7%	46.1%	39.4%
Total	100.0%	100.0%	100.0%	100.0%	100.0%	100.0%

[a] Components of variance analyses for mixed effects model with subjects random. For computational details, see Gleser, Cronbach, and Rajaratnam (1965) and Endler and Hunt (1966).
[b] Inventories are described in Appendix.
[c] Variance components from this inventory have not previously been presented.
[d] Means of four samples.
[e] Not obtained due to single presentations of each situation-response combination.
[f] Incorrectly reported as entirely P × S × R.

substantially less important determinant of consumer preferences than are situational conditions. For the meat and beverage inventories the small interaction terms for persons by responses reveal that in these categories situational influence also outstrips *individual* product preferences. For other inventories, again excepting motion pictures, the effects of situational and individual influences are jointly dominant. Motion pictures is the only category examined in which situational effects appear to be minimal. In this case individual preferences appear to be the consistent choice determinant with the general popularity of the movies following in importance.

A recent challenge to the validity of these inventory-based findings has been presented by Lutz and Kakkar (1975). They argued that the experimental procedure of having subjects rate the same choice alternatives under all situational conditions may have spuriously inflated the situations by products interaction term. In order to test this possibility they replicated Belk's (1974a) snack product inventory, but exposed each subject to only one level of the situation factor (see Appendix for a description of their experiment). Their analysis obtained a contribution of less than 6 percent for the situations by products interaction, with a residual term which accounted for over 86 percent of the variance.[5] Unfortunately, their analysis assumed an inappropriate completely randomized factorial design rather than the split plot factorial design which was actually employed (Winer, 1971,

[5] Hays's Omega squared statistics (Hays, 1964) was employed to derive these estimates. Since this statistic assumes a completely fixed effects model, results are not strictly comparable to those of the mixed effects components of variance method employed in the other studies reported.

pp. 366–371, Kirk, 1968, pp. 245–318). This problem renders their analysis meaningless and leaves the question of artifactual situational influence open. By altering the numbers of situations or responses by a factor of one half, Belk (1974b) has shown the variance component estimates of this inventory to be relatively stable across the resulting formats. Comparable results have been found by Endler and Hunt (1969) for a similar anxiety inventory. However, since these examinations do not reduce the number of situations to one per subject, the possibility that situational influence has been overestimated by these inventories still exists.

Other Evidence

Evidence of the importance of consumer situations has been found using other approaches which lend additional credence to a conclusion that situational influence is a pervasive factor in consumer behavior. Using multidimensional scaling Green and Rao (1972) found that consumer perceptions of and preferences for various bread and pastry items changed markedly over differing meal and menu situations. In a series of experimental choice simulations Hansen (1972) found that selection of a hairdryer as a gift depended upon characteristics of the supposed recipient, and that information seeking and choices from a fixed menu varied according to the description of the restaurant. Grønhaug (1972) found that buyers of tableware utilized different types and sources of information depending upon whether the purchase was for personal use or for a gift. By having subjects reconstruct word of mouth incidents, Belk (1971) found that one-third of the conversations about a new freeze dried coffee took place where the prior conversation concerned food, and that another third of the conversations began while drinking coffee. Sandell

(1968b) was able to condition choice of specific cigarette brands to either stressful or boring situations and to consumption of a specific brand of beer.

Anecdotal evidence of situational influence abounds as well. For example, in retail settings the mere presence of children (Wells and LoSciuto, 1966), friends (Bell, 1967), and sales personnel (Albaum, 1967) have been observed to alter purchase outcomes; as time since last meal increased so did the total food bill of non-obese supermarket shoppers in a study by Nisbett and Kanouse (1968); Pennington (1965) found appliance sales were most frequent when customer and salesman were similar in their propensity to bargain; and greater risk was found to be perceived in buying the same good by mail than at a retail store (Spence, Engel and Blackwell, 1970).

From the variety of methods employed in these studies it appears that situational effects can be demonstrated both descriptively and experimentally. Although the amount of research specifically focused on situational influence is still quite small, a number of instances have been found in which situations can be shown to affect consumer behavior systematically. There is further encouragement for situational research from the refreshing fact that analyses of the behavioral inventories specifying situations have been able to explain the majority of variance encountered.

SITUATIONAL RESEARCH IN CONSUMER BEHAVIOR

Despite the substantial promise and appeal of research which employs situational variables to explain consumer choice behavior, several basic issues require resolution before this potential can be fully realized. Foremost among the issues which this research must address is the question of the most appropriate means of measuring situations. Two alternative perspectives proposed have been labeled ''psychological'' (Lutz and Kakkar, 1975) and ''objective'' (Belk, 1975) measurements. Psychological measurements of situations rely on the subjects' perceptions of the situation and are an extension of sociological inquiry into the ''situation as defined'' (Thomas, 1927). The premise for such measurements is that the way an individual construes a situation should be more important to behavior than the inherent features of that situation. Objective measurements of situations restrict themselves to features of the situation as it exists before subjects' interpretations. The primary rationale for this perspective is that it removes the idiosyncrasies of perception which may otherwise limit aggregation and manipulation of consumer situations. The possibility has also been raised that some situational influences, such as subtle cueing effects, may operate without the subject's perceptual awareness. Without some sort of hybrid measurement which merges these perspectives, it appears that situational research must utilize both types of measurements.

A related issue concerns the most appropriate means of manipulating situations in experimental research. Both psychologically and objectively defined situations may be manipulated by assigning subjects to different times, places, and conditions, although successful manipulations of psychologically defined situations may need to be more clever or elaborate. However, this sort of research is costly and is best limited to the investigation of one or two situational dimensions at a time. Alternatively, and more commonly, the projective use of situational scenarios may continue to be used. Typically these scenarios have ranged from a one phrase to one paragraph written description of situational conditions. Photographs, motion pictures, and video tapes are possible refinements of stimulus input in this procedure, but these methods favor visual cues and may unnaturally focus attention and control the *rate* of experience. Perhaps the best means of manipulation, short of actually modifying situational conditions, is to couple written descriptions of features such as temporal perspective, task definition, and antecedent states, with visual and auditory input of physical and social surroundings. Comparisons of results using each alternative means of manipulation will be needed to assess their relative adequacy.

Whether the existence of a particular situational effect has been determined under simulated or actual conditions, interpretation of the importance of this effect requires knowledge of the frequency of occurrence of these conditions. Because consumers can selectively seek or avoid many of the situations they encounter and because all unanticipated situations are not equally common, descriptive evidence of the frequency of situational occurrences is needed. A number of time budget studies based on consumer diaries (e.g., Szali, 1973) are available which provide general records of the times and places of consumer activities. But even the most detailed consumer accounts (e.g., Muse, 1946) seldom go beyond ''shopping'' in their descriptions of purchase situations. Nevertheless, activity diaries appear to be a useful approach to gathering relevant data on situational occurrences. In addition to providing data on relevant situational variables, this approach may simultaneously measure individual characteristics and behavioral outcomes which can be cross tabulated with situations to obtain a picture of individual differences in situational exposure and susceptibility to situational influence.

The ultimate problem for all future situational research is the lack of a comprehensive taxonomy of situational characteristics and normal combinations of these characteristics. Hopefully this discussion has made some headway in establishing a general conceptualization of consumer situations, but obviously greater detail is necessary. It is a false hope at this point to expect that we can systematically investigate a complete list of situational characteristics, because no such list exists. Only by continuing to conceptualize and research situational characteristics under a guiding understanding of the scope and criteria for situations can such a summary ever be achieved.

APPENDIX: SUMMARY DETAILS FOR SEVEN SITUATIONAL INVENTORIES

1. *Beverages.* Sandell (1968a) presented 31 student subjects with ten beverages (e.g., coffee, water, beer) which they rated in seven situations (e.g., when alone, feeling sleepy in the afternoon, reading the paper in the morning) using a seven-point scale from "extremely unwilling" to "extremely willing" (to try). Situations and beverages tested were apparently chosen subjectively, although five subjects who did not appear to view the products as alternatives were eliminated.

2. *Leisure Activities.* Bishop and Witt (1970) investigated the effect of ten situations (e.g., returning from studying at a noisy library, relaxing Friday afternoon following a busy week, waking up fresh and rested on a Saturday morning) on the likelihood of engaging in each of 13 leisure activities (e.g., go shopping for clothes, watch televison, visit a friend) using a five-point scale from "almost

certainly" to "I would not feel like" (doing this). Situations were selected based on five alternative theories of leisure behavior, and leisure activities were based on their frequency of occurrence in previous community surveys. Subjects were male and female students at two colleges and totalled 141.

3. *Meat Products.* Belk (1974a) examined choices of 11 different meat products (e.g., hamburger, steak, chicken) in nine different situations (e.g., party for friends, meal on a weekday evening, at a nice restaurant with friends) using five point scales from "extremely likely" to "not at all likely", administered to 100 members of a community. Situations and meat products were chosen from protocols and familiarity pretests.

4. *Motion Pictures.* Belk (1974b) had 100 students rate 12 hypothetical motion pictures (e.g., The Motorcycle Freaks, Summer of Dreams, Only Fools are Sad) described in mock advertisements, in nine situations (e.g., on a weeknight with friends of the same sex, just for something to do, together with spouse or date at their request) on a five-point scale. Situations were selected via protocols and pretests based on familiarity, and motion pictures were structured to parallel currently popular themes.

5. *Snack Products A.* Belk (1974b) varied ten different situations (e.g., while watching television with family, going on a long automobile trip, an urge for a between meal snack) and had 100 student subjects rate the likelihood of choosing each of ten snack products (e.g., potato chips, pastries, ice cream) on two occasions (two weeks apart) using five point scales. Situations and products were chosen as in the meat inventory.

6. *Snack Products B.* Lutz and Kakkar (1975) replicated Belk's snack product inventory except that subjects in each of ten groups of from 24 to 36 students responded within only one of the situations and on only one occasion. Each group rated products in a different situation and a total of 306 subjects were employed.

7. *Fast Foods.* Using data collected by Leo Burnett U.S.A., Belk (1975) analyzed the effect of ten different situations (e.g., too tired

to cook dinner, unexpected dinner guests, having a few friends over for a casual get-together) on responses to a six-point likelihood scale for each of ten (confidential) fast food outlets and related meal choices. Subjects were 98 housewives in a single community.

REFERENCES

Albaum, G. "Exploring Interaction in a Marketing Situation," *Journal of Marketing Research,* 4 (May, 1967), 168–72.

Allen, B. L. "Situational Factors in Conformity," in Leonard Berkowitz, *Advances in Experimental Social Psychology,* Vol. 2, New York: Academic Press, 1965.

Barker, R. G. *The Stream of Behavior.* New York: Appleton-Century-Crofts, 1963.

——. *Ecological Psychology: Concepts and Methods for Studying the Environment of Human Behavior.* Stanford University Press, 1968.

Belk, R. W. "Occurrence of Word of Mouth Buyer Behavior as a Function of Situation and Advertising Stimuli," *Proceedings,* American Marketing Association Fall Conference, 1971, 419–22.

——. "An Exploratory Assessment of Situational Effects in Buyer Behavior," *Journal of Marketing Research,* 11 (May, 1974a), 156–163.

——. "Application and Analysis of the Behavior Differential Inventory for Assessing Situational Effects in Consumer Behavior," in Scott Ward and Peter Wright (eds.), *Advances in Consumer Research,* Vol. 1. Urbana: Association for Consumer Research, 1974b.

——. "The Objective Situation as a Determinant of Consumer Behavior," in Mary Jane Schlinger (ed.), *Advances in Consumer Research,* Vol. 2. Chicago: Association for Consumer Research, 1975.

Bell, G. D. "Self-Confidence and Persuasion in Car Buying," *Journal of Marketing Research,* 4 (February, 1967), 46–52.

Bellows, R. "Toward a Taxonomy of Social Situations," in Stephen B. Sells (ed.), *Stimulus Determinants of Behavior,* New York: Ronald, 1963.

Bishop, D. W. and P. A. Witt, "Sources of Behavioral Variance During Leisure Time," *Journal of Personality and Social Psychology,* 16 (October, 1970), 352–60.

Craik, K. H. "Environment Psychology," in Kenneth H. Craik, et al. *New Directions in Psychology,* Vol. 4, New York: Holt, Rinehart and Winston, 1970.

Endler, N. S. and J. McV. Hunt. "Sources of Behavioral Variance as Measured by the S-R Inventory of Anxiousness," *Psychological Bulletin,* 65 (1966), 336–46.

Engel, J. F., D. T. Kollat, and R. D. Blackwell. "Personality Measures and Market Segmentation," *Business Horizons,* 12 (June 1969), 61–70.

Gleser, G. L., L. J. Cronbach, and N. Rajaratnam. "Generalizability of Scores Influenced by Multiple Sources of Variance," *Psychometrika,* 30 (1965), 395–418.

Green, P. E. and V. R. Rao. "Configural Synthesis in Multidimensional Scaling," *Journal of Marketing Research,* 9 (February, 1972), 65–68.

Grønhaug, K. "Buying Situation and Buyer's Information Behavior," *European Marketing Research Review,* 7 (September, 1972), 33–48.

Hansen, F. *Consumer Choice Behavior.* New York: The Free Press, 1972.

Hays, W. L. *Statistics for Psychologists.* New York: Rinehart and Winston, 1964.

Helson, H. "Current Trends and Issues in Adaptation-Level Theory," *American Psychologist,* 19 (1964), 26–38.

Ittelson, W. H. *Environment and Cognition.* New York: Seminar Press, 1973.

Kasmar, J. V. "The Development of a Usable Lexicon of Environmental Descriptors," *Environment and Behavior,* 2 (1970), 133–169.

Kirk, R. E. *Experimental Design: Procedures for the Behavior Sciences,* Belmont, California: Wadsworth Publishing, 1968.

Lavidge, R. J. "The Cotton Candy Concept: Intra-Individual Variability," in Lee Adler and Irving Crespi, *Attitude Research at Sea,* Chicago: American Marketing Association, 1966, 39–50.

Lewin, K. "Environmental Forces in Child Behavior and Development," in Carl C. Murchison, *Handbook of Child Psychology,* second edition, revised. Worcester, Massachusetts: Clark University Press, 1933, 94–127.

——. *A Dynamic Theory of Personality.* New York: McGraw-Hill, 1935.

Lutz, R. J. and P. K. Kakkar. "The Psychological Situation as a Determinant of Consumer Behavior," in Mary Jane Schlinger (ed.), *Advances in Consumer Research,* Vol. 2. Chicago: Association for Consumer Research, 1975.

Mausner, B. M. "The Specification of the Stimulus Situation in a Social Interaction," in Stephen B. Sells, *Stimulus Determinants of Behavior.* New York: Ronald, 1963.

Mehrabian, A. and J. A. Russell. *An Approach to Environmental Psychology.* Cambridge: M.I.T. Press, 1974.

Moos, R. H. "Conceptualizations of Human Environments," *American Psychologist,* 28 (1973), 652–663.

Muse, M. "Time Expenditures in Homemaking Activities in 183 Vermont Farm Homes," *Vermont Agricultural Experimental Station Bulletin,* No. 530, 1946.

Nisbett, R. E. and D. E. Kanouse. "Obesity, Food Deprivation and Supermarket Shopping Behavior," *Journal of Personality and Social Psychology,* 12 (August, 1969), 289–94.

Pennington, A. L. "Customer-Salesman Bargaining Behavior in Retail Transactions," *Journal of Marketing Research,* 5 (August, 1965), 255–62.

Proshansky, H. M., W. H. Ittelson, and L. G. Rivlin. (eds.) *Environmental Psychology,* New York: Holt, Rinehart and Winston, 1970.

Sandell, R. G. "Effects of Attitudinal and Situational Factors on Reported Choice Behavior," *Journal of Marketing Research,* 4 (August, 1968a), 405–08.

———. "The Effects of Attitude Influence and Representational Conditioning on Choice Behavior," Stockholm: The Economic Research Institute, Stockholm School of Economics, 1968b.

Sells, S. B. "Dimensions of Stimulus Situations Which Account for Behavioral Variance," in Stephen B. Sells (ed.), *Stimulus Determinants of Behavior,* New York: Ronald, 1963.

Sherif, M. and C. W. Sherif. *An Outline of Social Psychology,* Rev. Ed. New York: Harper and Row, 1956.

Spense, H. E., J. F. Engel, and Roger D. Blackwell, "Perceived Risk in Mail-Order and Retail Store Buying," *Journal of Marketing Research,* 7 (August, 1970), 364–69.

Szali, A. et al. (eds.) *The Use of Time.* The Hague: Mouten, 1973.

Thomas, W. I. "The Behavior Pattern and the Situation," *Proceedings,* Twenty-second Annual Meeting, American Sociological Society, 22 (1927), 1–13.

Thorndike, R. L. *Research Problems and Techniques.* Washington: U.S. Government Printing Office, Report No. 3 AAF Aviation Psychology Program, 1947.

Ward, S. and T. S. Robertson. "Consumer Behavior Research: Promise and Prospects," in Scott Ward and Thomas S. Robertson, *Consumer Behavior: Theoretical Sources.* Englewood Cliffs, New Jersey: Prentice-Hall, 1973, 3–42.

Wells, W. D. and A. LoSciuto. "A Direct Observation of Purchasing Behavior," *Journal of Marketing Research,* (August, 1966), 227–33.

Winer, B. J. *Statistical Principles in Experimental Design,* Second Edition. New York: McGraw-Hill, 1971.

Wolf, R. "The Measurement of Environments," in Anne Anastasi (ed.), *Testing Problems in Perspective,* Washington, D.C.: American Council on Education, 1966, 491–503.

Questions

1. What are situational variables, and why are they important in consumer behavior?

2. Name, define, and give examples of the five groups of situational characteristics.

3. In the revised stimulus-organism-response paradigm, the stimulus has been split into object and situation. Explain with an example how the two are different and how together they can influence a certain behavior.

4. Would different people under the same situation and objects behave the same? Explain.

SECTION TWO

Psychological Aspects of Consumer Behavior

In analyzing consumer behavior, one must first realize that the consumer is an individual. That individual is completely different from any other. He or she has different attitudes and knowledge, learns in different ways, and is motivated by needs that may differ in importance between individuals. This person perceives events differently from any other individual and has a unique self-concept that is manifested in certain kinds of behavior. This individual goes about making decisions in a particular way and is personally going to be either satisfied or dissatisfied with the consequences of that decision.

In attempting to gain insight into how this individual thinks and what makes him or her buy one product instead of another, we can draw on the field of psychology. Psychology is essentially the study of individual behavior. We can apply many of the same psychological concepts to the field of consumer behavior in an attempt to find out just what makes this consumer "tick."

The articles in this section discuss eight different topics: attitudes and knowledge; learning; needs and motivation; perception; personality and lifestyle; self-concept; decision making; and satisfaction and dissatisfaction.

PART A: ATTITUDES AND KNOWLEDGE

The first article in Part A gives a very thorough look at *attitudes* and their impact on consumer behavior. In "Theories of Attitude Structures and Change" George Day shows that there are explicit theories of attitude change that can illuminate the problems of the decisionmaker. He distinguishes between formal theories of attitudes and the pragmatic measurement-oriented definitions of what they are. It is emphasized that these attitudes do not exist independently but are linked in complex ways to a hierarchy of increasingly fundamental beliefs and attitudes. Three theoretical approaches of studying attitudes are analyzed—(1) the information-processing approach (which emphasizes the stimulus characteristics of the communication situation); (2) the social judgment approach (which emphasizes the effects of discrepant communications and differential ego involvement); and (3) the functional approach (which says that the same attitudes may be held by different persons for different reasons).

Bobby J. Calder's article, "Cognitive Consistency and Consumer Behavior," reviews three of the major cognitive consistency approaches and some of the more significant research evidence. He uses these findings to demonstrate the relationship between cognitive consistency and consumer behavior. Cognitive consistency is essentially saying that a person will attempt to maintain a state of psychological harmony within the system of attitudes or beliefs about a particular situation—in this case, a buying situation. The three cognitive consistency approaches presented in this article are (1) "balance theory," (2) "congruity theory," and (3) "dissonance theory."

The one article dealing with *knowledge* in this section is written by the co-editors. In "The Role of Consumer Knowledge in the Study of Consumer Behavior" we point out that knowledge is basic to many of the concepts and theories of consumer behavior, and yet an analysis of writings in the field might not give this conclusion. The term knowledge is so intertwined with other terms that it is easy to lose sight of its importance. Consumer knowledge is defined as "acquaintance with and understanding of objects relevant to the consumer role." Knowledge of a product, for example, is the first step in the formation of attitudes toward that product and is very closely associated with other elements in the decision-making process.

PART B: LEARNING

There are three articles on *learning* in Part B, two by the noted behavioralist, Steuart Henderson Britt, and one on behavior modification by Walter Nord and J. Paul Peter. All three articles draw on research in the area of learning theory and make application to the field of consumer behavior.

In his first article, "Applying Learning Principles to Marketing," Britt shows how experimental investigations of learning can be used in order to enhance the learning and retention of promotional messages. Such learning concepts as inhibition and transfer, semantic generation and semantic satiation, overlearning and response extinction, overexposure, incongruity, and other terms are discussed relative to this application for creating more effective marketing communications.

In "How Advertising Can Use Psychology's Rules of Learning" Britt summarizes psychological learning concepts into twenty short rules or principles for advertisers. The rules cited in this classic article essentially stress the importance of proper presentational methods in promotion, the importance of proper timing and scheduling of advertisements, and more effective techniques of structuring messages in advertisements.

Nord and Peter's "A Behavior Modification Perspective on Marketing" is a comprehensive article that presents an overview of the learning concept of behavior modification and investigates its applicability to marketing. Behavior modification sees environmental forces as influencing behavior; therefore, these forces can be manipulated by marketers to influence consumer behavior. Nord and Peter describe four common behavior modification processes—respondent conditioning, operant conditioning, vicarious learning, and ecological design. They observe that many marketing tactics are consistent with a behavior modification perspective. However, these tactics appear to have been derived in an ad hoc manner. The authors see much potential for applying behavior modification concepts to marketing strategy planning and for further understanding the consumer behavior process.

PART C: NEEDS AND MOTIVATION

"Murray's Theory of Human Needs: A Useful Guide to Understanding Consumer Behavior" by James U. McNeal and Stephen W. McDaniel discusses one of the most thorough classifications of human *needs* in the literature. The authors present Murray's list of needs and set forth several related principles that can be useful in the study of consumer behavior. Since needs are so basic in the study of consumer behavior, the student should benefit from an in-depth look at this empirically based set of Murray's propositions.

In his classic article, "Motivation, Cognition, Learning—Basic Factors in Consumer Behavior," James A. Bayton proposes that human behavior can be grouped into three categories—motivation, cognition, and learning. In discussing motivation, Bayton notes that behavior is initiated through needs. And he, like Murray, states that there are essentially two kinds of needs—biogenic and psychogenic. He notes that several needs may be involved in a situation and that identical behaviors may have different motivational backgrounds. In discussing cognition he views the cognitive processes as being purposive in that they serve the individual in attempting to achieve satisfaction of his or her needs. He also points out that cognition is regulatory, since it determines the direction and particular steps taken in a person's attempt to attain satisfaction of the initiating need. According to the author, a person starts with need arousal, continues under the influence of the cognitive processes, and engages in necessary action. The individual then arrives at consumption or utilization of a goal object, and it is only through the use of the goal object that a degree of gratification of the initial need will occur.

In "Why Do People Shop?" Edward M. Tauber looks at shopper motivation. Citing the results of his study on this topic, Tauber first distinguishes between shopping, buying, and consuming. He then emphasizes buying behavior and suggests that a person may shop for many reasons other than his or her need for products or services. He categorizes shopping motives into two broad classes—personal and social. Personal motives include role playing, diversion, self-gratification, learning about new trends, physical activity, and sensory stimulation. Social motives for shopping might include social experience outside the home, communication with others having a similar interest, peer group attraction, status and authority, or just pleasure of bargaining. However, impulse shopping or unplanned shopping may also occur.

PART D: PERCEPTION

In "They Saw a Game: A Case Study," Hastorf and Cantril provide an interesting illustration of selective perception at work. This classic article reports on a study which investigated the differing viewpoints held by students from two colleges, following their schools' participation in a hotly contested football game. Student perceptions of certain events in the game differed greatly depending upon the affiliation of the student.

Ralph I. Allison and Kenneth P. Uhl look at consumer perceptions of brands in their article "Brand Identification and Perception." They report on a blind beer comparison experiment designed to test consumer ability to distinguish among major brands of unlabeled beer. They found that the participants failed to match their evaluation of unidentified beer brands with similar but known brands. From this study, the authors conclude that physical product characteristics alone are insufficient to influence purchase behavior and that an overall marketing effort is necessary to create a perception of product differences.

In their article "Subliminal Stimulation—Marketing Applications" Sandra K. Hart and Stephen W. McDaniel explore the concept of subliminal perception. They present a comprehensive review of studies done on subliminal perception and also point out instances of the use of subliminal advertising in actual marketing situations. Hart and McDaniel show that the use of embeds in advertisements or other techniques designed to stimulate a person below his or her threshold level of perception have been studied extensively and used to some extent. The ability of such techniques to actually affect consumer behavior is still being debated.

PART E: PERSONALITY AND LIFESTYLE

"A Multivariate Analysis of Personality and Product Use" by David L. Sparks and W. T. Tucker reports on a study done to explore the relationship between consumer behavior and *personality*. After analyzing several personality traits of subjects and correlating those with reported use of certain products, the authors conclude that certain individual personality traits may not be correlated with product use. Instead, it is probably the entire personality—in a gestalt fashion—that influences product use.

The next article, "City Shoppers and Urban Identification," by Gregory P. Stone, looks at personalities of city shoppers. Stone discusses results of his study that investigated reasons why consumers choose to shop in the stores they do in a city. Four categories of shoppers are then identified: (1) "economic" shoppers (those people who base their store evaluation on price, quality, and variety of products); (2) "personalizing" shoppers (those people who have a tendency to personalize and individualize the customer role in the store in terms of closeness of relationships between them and the store personnel); (3) "ethical" shoppers (those people who feel a moral obligation to patronize specific types of stores); and (4) "apathetic" shoppers (those people who are not interested in shopping and thus do not discriminate between kinds of stores. He points out in this well-known article that the shoppers belonging to different categories had different characteristic role orientations and social profiles to the others and that each consumer type was characterized by a distinctive pattern of social position and community identification.

In "The Concept and Application of Life Style Segmentation," Joseph T. Plummer emphasizes the importance of considering consumers' *lifestyles* and motivations in the process of market segmentation. He introduces the lifestyle segmentation concept, which combines the concepts of lifestyle patterns and market segmentation. Lifestyle is measured in terms of people's activities—how they spend their time, their interests, their opinions about themselves and the world around them, and some of their basic characteristics. Plummer offers three criteria for selecting a good segmentation approach and explains the lifestyle segmentation. He suggests a two-step analytical procedure of relating the lifestyle segments to a particular market—(1) determining which of the lifestyle segments are best from the standpoint of efficiently producing the greatest number of customers for a brand and (2) defining and describing the target customer. He concludes the article by offering seven possible benefits of lifestyle segmentation.

PART F: SELF-CONCEPT

There are two articles that relate *self-concept* to consumer behavior. In "Consumer Self-Concept, Symbolism and Market Behavior," Grubb and Grathwohl present a partial model of consumer behavior based on self-theory and symbolism. The model stresses that an individual's self-concept and image of the product can override the functional benefits of a product in the individual's evaluation of that product. The authors point out that self-concept is formed through interaction between an individual and others, during which period one learns about the values society places on different products. Individuals then use different goods as tools to communicate meaning about themselves to their references in order to sustain or enhance their self-concept.

O'Brien, Tapia, and Brown, in "The Self-Concept in Buyer Behavior," present another look at self-concept and also report on a study that relates self-concept to consumer perceptions of different products. According to self-theory, the selection and avoidance of products in consumer behavior is a function of what an individual knows and thinks about him- or herself, how one values oneself, and how one wants others to see oneself. The authors point out that a person can see her- or himself in "actuality," as one is "expected" to be, or as an "ideal." Like Grubb and Grathwohl, the authors stress that the development and improvement of the self-concept depends on the individual's interaction with others. This article explores self-concept and relates it to product perception based on four research findings about self-concept: (1) that it is stable, individualistic, and pervasive; (2) that there are various possible models of the self-concept theory; (3) that expectations can affect the present; and (4) that self-concept can actually be observed. The relationship between self-concept and personality needs of achievement, affection, identity, hedonism, and others are shown.

PART G: DECISION MAKING

In "Decision Making Within the Household," Harry L. Davis thoroughly reviews the existing research on household *decision making*. He explores the extent of member involvement, the nature of the decision-making process, family role structures, and decision strategies. He concludes that the extent of family member involvement varies according to whether the good is a household or durable good and whether the decision involves a saving or investment decision. Amount of involvement also varies according to product category and for different families. Davis points out that cultural role expectations, amount and type of resources controlled by either spouse, and the relative investment that each spouse has in a particular decision area all affect family member involvement in household decisions. The author presents a model of alternate decisionmaking strategies under consensus and accomodation and shows how role, budgets, problem solving, persuasion, bargaining, and even procrastination are used as decisionmaking tools in decisionmaking strategies.

In "Consumer Decision Making—Fact or Fiction?" Richard W. Olshavsky and Donald H. Granbois present a different viewpoint on consumer decision-making. Some of their main conclusions are that the manner in which income is allocated across consumer budget categories is largely nondiscretionary; that in many instances consumers have no control over the specific products and services they purchase or consume; that the extent of search and evaluation of stores typically does not precede store patronage; and that brand purchases are made on the basis of some kind of surrogate rather than on the basis of a direct evaluation of the brand's attributes. The authors conclude that a significant proportion of purchase behavior is not actually preceded by any decision process. They contend that much purchase behavior is habitual, with no prepurchase processes occurring at any time, not even on the first purchase. Purchasing occurs out of several uncontrollable causes, including necessity, cultural tendencies, learned behavior, conformity to group norms, imitation of others, recommendations, and at random.

In his classic article, "Consumer Behavior as Risk Taking," Raymond A. Bauer introduces the concept of looking at consumer behavior as an instance of risk taking. He argues that the consumer characteristically develops decision strategies and ways of reducing risk that enable him or her to act with relative confidence and ease in situations where information is inadequate and/or the consequences of his or her actions are in some sense undeterminable. Using examples of brand loyalty, added value, personal and group influence, prepurchase deliberations, and cognitive dissonance, Bauer shows the need for considering risk taking as an important aspect of consumer decisionmaking.

In a recent article on a fairly new topic in consumer behavior, "Using Information Processing Theory to Design Marketing Strategies," Alice M. Tybout, Bobby J. Calder, and Brian Sternthal discuss information-processing theory and provide an experimental study that demonstrates its usefulness in consumer behavior. They test two different strategies based on information-processing theory to combat the impact of an adverse rumor (i.e., that McDonald's hamburgers were made from red worm meat). Their results show that the typical marketing strategy of directly refuting the rumor is ineffective.

PART H: SATISFACTION AND DISSATISFACTION

Ralph Day's "Toward a Process Model of Consumer Satisfaction" emphasizes the importance of information on consumer satisfaction and dissatisfaction. Day also addresses the limitations of existing research in measuring consumer satisfaction. He argues that concentrating on using complaints as a way of measuring satisfaction is misleading. He then proposes a model that considers the purchase, consumption, and evaluation sequence as a process that is related to the actual prior expectations of a consumer. He contends that the degree and extent to which the sequence confirms or disconfirms the expectations constitutes a better framework for relating prepurchase expectations, situational variables, and social factors to the consumption and evaluation process.

In "Should We Be Satisfied or Dissatisfied With Satisfaction-Dissatisfaction Research to Date?" Denise Smart provides a thorough synthesis and evaluation of the major empirical efforts in the field of consumer satisfaction and dissatisfaction. Each of the major studies in this area is summarized in order to give the reader a good overview of the relevant research findings. Several shortcomings in the current state-of-the-art satisfaction-dissatisfaction research are presented.

Part A
ATTITUDES AND KNOWLEDGE

6. Theories of Attitude Structure and Change

George S. Day

The study of attitudes is well-entrenched in marketing theory and practice. The acceptance by theorists is evident in the pivotal role that the concept of attitude plays in the major descriptive models of consumer behavior (Engel, Kollat, and Blackwell, 1968; Howard and Sheth, 1969; Nicosia, 1966). Practitioners have tended to take a more limited view of attitude as an easily measured construct they can use to understand their market, and perhaps to evaluate the effect of a persuasive communication. In reality, most practitioners are inveterate theorists, constantly invoking experimental theories of attitude change to predict changes in purchasing or usage behavior as a consequence of alternative strategies for changing attitudes.

The necessity for such theories can be illustrated by the following problems:

- A farm equipment manufacturer in a developing country wants prospective distributors to adopt a new scheme for financing inventories. First he has to change their presently negative attitudes toward investing in inventories; but how?
- Birth-control-pill manufacturers need to predict the response of pill users to negative

information from a highly credible source, such as a U.S. Senate subcommittee. What proportion of the users are susceptible to change because of lack of conviction and ambivalent attitude?

- Consumers have a strong aversion to "reprocessed" forms of materials such as textiles and plastics. Can these attitudes be changed before the U.S. runs out of raw materials?

In these and literally thousands of other situations each year in the public and private sector, predictions and decisions are made on the basis of implicit or explicit theories of the conditions which lead to attitude change.

THE NATURE OF ATTITUDES

I will distinguish between the formal theories of "how attitudes work," and the pragmatic, measurement-oriented definitions of "what they are." The emphasis on measurement is important, for we are dealing with an underlying construct that can be only imperfectly observed. It is easy to make subtle theoretical distinctions that overtax both the measures and the respondents.

How Do Attitudes Work?

One answer to this question is that attitudes structure the way the consumer perceives his environment and guide the ways in which he responds to it (Lunn, 1970). A more precise definition, that effectively touches most of the interesting theoretical issues, was proposed by Allport (1935) and is still widely accepted. An attitude is: (1) a mental and neural state of readiness to respond (2) organized (3) through experience (4) exerting a directive and/or dynamic influence on behavior. Following McGuire (1969), we shall describe the current thinking related to each of the four definite characteristics.

Mental and Neural State of Readiness to Respond. An attitude is viewed as a mediating (or intervening) construct that has two links with observable reality. One link is with the *antecedent* conditions which lead into it; these might be the stimulus of an advertisement, a move into a new house, and so forth. The second link is with the *consequents* that follow from the attitude, including search and purchase behavior. There is nothing in this definition that says we can directly observe the mediating construct, so researchers who adopt this definition generally feel anxious about the ability of their instruments to accurately infer the presence of an attitude.

The mental and neural distinction suggests that measures can be either verbal reports of introspection (of which I will say more later) or physiological measures of change in the person's autonomic activation level when he sees the object of the attitude. Early enthusiasm for such physiological indices as galvanic skin response (Cook and Selltiz, 1964) and pupil dilation (Hess, 1965) seems to have waned recently as evidence accumulates that these indices can say little about the favorable direction of the attitude.

Organized. In the next section, on the structure of attitudes, I will discuss the extent to which a single attitude is made up of separate components.

Through Experience. There is widespread agreement with this contention, although little longitudinal research has been done (some is reviewed by Smith, 1968) and a person can rarely explain how any of his attitudes were acquired. Among the various processes by which attitudes are thought to be formed are:

1. Integrating a number of similar experiences: direct experience through usage, observation of the outcomes of others' explorations, information about performance, and so forth.

2. Differentiating from general to specific situations. Most narrow, highly focused attitudes are partly derived from broad attitudes already held. This is the basis of consistency theory, which would, for example, predict that attitudes toward women drivers will be consistent with the basic underlying attitude toward the general competency of women.

3. Identification. Attitudes are often initially formed by imitating the attitudes of admired individuals. An individual who can engender imitation in this sense is an effective source in a persuasive communication. If this is so, the three components of source effect, credibility, attractiveness, and power, are useful predictors of the degree of identification. (These concepts are most fully developed by Kelman, 1961.) *Credibility* is the extent to which a source is perceived as knowing the right answer and being willing to communicate it. *Attractiveness* is determined by the receiver's similarity to, familiarity with, or liking of the source. Similarity of economic backgrounds, physical characteristics, and political and other attitudes are important determinants of a successful relationship between a salesman and a customer (Evans, 1963). The last component, *power*, depends on the ability of the source to apply positive and negative sanctions to the recipient and

stay around to observe whether a desired attitude or behavior is achieved.

As we will see later, the above processes by which attitudes are formed by experience are similar to the ways that existing attitudes are changed.

Exerting a Directive and/or Dynamic Influence on Behavior. There is wide agreement that attitudes have at least a directive or preferential influence; they determine the choice of one among a set of alternatives. According to McGuire (1968), it appears that an attitude imposes this preferential influence by determining the *perception* of the various alternatives, rather than by determining which possible *response* will dominate the others. This distinction may not appear too meaningful in the abstract, but it is at the heart of the differences between response-oriented (learning) and perceptual theories of attitude change, as we will see shortly.

There is less agreement among psychologists as to whether attitudes also have a dynamic—or more accurately, energizing—influence. This would imply that they affect the absolute level of an activity, as well as determine the directions in which the activity is channeled. There seems to be no easy answer to this matter, although it is relevant to many issues, including whether the increased favor toward some products as objects of consumption will influence the overall need to consume.

Summary. So far I have established that an attitude is a readiness to respond in a preferential manner. In a marketing context, this usually means the consumer's preference for, and readiness to buy, a brand or product, rather than the available alternatives (Maloney, 1966, p. 3). But these attitudes are not simple likes or dislikes. They are the complex outcomes of many separate judgments about the various attributes of the object, such as styling, convenience, economic value, and so forth. Much of the diagnostic value of attitudes comes from the information about these attributes. In the next section I will look at one attempt to divide attitudes into component parts.

Attitude Structure: Cognitive-Affective-Conative Analysis

The notion that the intervening state between stimulus and behavior is richer than affect (or liking) is widely supported, and for good reason. By having three components to explain and interrelate, we have a richer and more flexible construct. Secondly, there is impressive empirical support from the measurement-of-meaning tradition (Osgood, Suci, and Tannenbaum, 1957) for the validity of this view.

The cognitive or perceptual component represents a person's information about an object. Each piece of information can be broadly classified as either beliefs in the existence of the object, or (evaluative) beliefs *about* the object (Fishbein and Raven, 1962). In the former category of beliefs are the familiar awareness measures, such as aided and unaided recall of brand names and advertising copy claims or awareness of services offered.

Evaluative beliefs provide information about the judgments the consumer makes. In marketing we are usually interested in various comparative judgments of one brand or product versus the alternatives. These may be *attribute judgments* (which one is bigger? which one tastes better? which one is more durable?)[2] or *similarity judgments* (which ask the individual whether he perceives the objects as being similar or different). Similarity judgments are highly generalized and respondents are not told the basis they are to use to make the judgments.

The affective or feeling component deals with the person's overall feelings of liking or disliking a situation, object, person, or concept. It is usually measured on a unidimensional scale. Most theorists regard affect as the core of the attitude concept and derived from the more specific cognitive components. However, there is some controversy over the nature of the cognitive-affective relationship, hinging largely on the distinction between affect (like-dislike) and evaluation (the object is good-bad, disagreeable-agreeable, harmful-beneficial, and so forth).

One group treats affect and evaluation as synonymous. The overall attitude is measured by a scale (or scales) involving general evaluative criteria (such as good-bad: see Osgood et al., 1957). The major implication of the affective-evaluative congruity notion is that overall attitude judgments can be predicted from the various evaluative beliefs.

A competing view holds that the affective component is only partially determined by the evaluative belief components. For example, Bem (1970, p. 15) offers the following "non-syllogism":

> Cigarettes taste terrible, cause cancer, make me cough, and offend others (evaluative beliefs). I dislike terrible tastes, cancer, coughing and offending others. But I still like cigarettes.

Bem argued that "emotional, behavioral and social influences can also play important roles, and cognitive 'reasoning' of the type represented in the syllogism may be absent altogether." Greenberg (1968) brought the evaluative-affective distinction to a marketing context. He contrasted *attribute judgments,* which contain evaluative information, and *preference* (or affective)

judgments, which combine information about product evaluation and the respondent's ideal point. The evaluative judgment is "which is sweeter? or bigger?" while the preference judgment indicates "which sweetness is preferred, or which is the better size." In many instances one prefers that which is highly evaluated, but evaluation and affect are not necessarily synonymous.

The conative or intentions component refers to the person's gross behavioral expectations regarding the object: is he "very, somewhat, or not at all likely" to buy a refrigerator, a foreign car if he buys any kind of car, or vacation on the Galapagos Islands? Usually, intentions are limited to a finite time period that depends on the prospective buyer's repurchase cycle or planning horizon. There is a widespread feeling within marketing that intentions differ from attitudes (as measured of affect) by "combining a consumer's regard for the item with an assessment of its purchase probability" (Wells, 1961, p. 82). A more appropriate position is that intentions are correlated or congruent with attitudes under certain conditions, such as (a) when the alternatives are reasonably close substitutes, as when auto market boundaries are defined by a class of cars (compacts, intermediate station-wagons, or Gran Prix touring cars), but not by all cars; and (b) the market is in equilibrium with respect to the number of brands. It appears that attitudes are less sensitive than intentions to short-run perturbations of demand created by a new entry into an established market (Day, 1970b).

Attitude Specificity

The discussion to this point has presumed that the attitudes are toward specific attributes, objects, or issues. These attitudes do not exist independently but are linked in complex ways to a hierarchy of increasingly fundamental beliefs and attitudes.

Most fundamental are *values,* which are attitudes toward end-states of existence (such as equality and self-fulfillment) or modes of conduct (like honesty and friendship) (Rokeach, 1968). Values are ends, and one controversial view holds that marketing deals with the means of achieving these ends (Bauer and Greyser, 1967). Motivation researchers have traditionally taken the point of view that this is the most productive level in the hierarchy to obtain insights into buying and consumption behavior. Unfortunately, these deep-seated values and attitudes are often unconsciously held and thus are difficult to unambiguously identify with the usual projective and related clinical techniques. Their remoteness from the specific attitudes and behaviors of interest to marketers has further reduced their usefulness for diagnostic purposes.

The relative failure of motivation research has focused research attention on middle-level beliefs and attitudes about buying, consumption patterns, and product requirements. The goal of this research (frequently called psycho-graphics) is to find descriptive classifications, such as bargain seeking, economic orientation, experimentalism, style consciousness, home centeredness, and traditionalism (Lunn, 1966; Heller, 1968), that provide more insights and more clearly delineated market segments than those based on demographic variables. Although this area of research holds a great deal of promise for marketing, the realization of the promise will hinge on (a) improvements in the measuring instruments that will reduce the present cumbersome batteries of questions, (b) more effective utilization of data reduction techniques, and (c) a more precise specification of the scope of the research. This latter step

will help reduce the confusion resulting from including explorations at the very general level of life cycle and life style with the very specific and product-related search for benefit segments within the same classification.

ATTITUDE CHANGE THEORIES

The Information-Processing Approach

This approach explains the response to a persuasive communication in terms of (a) the receiver's initial position, (b) a series of behavioral steps through which he must proceed, and (c) his motivation for accepting the proposed position. These three elements act together so that a person's probability of proceeding from one step to another depends on both initial position and acceptance motivation. (Figure 1.)

Before an individual can be persuaded by a communication he must first have the message *presented* to him via informal or formal media; then the message must get and hold his attention. Attention-getting properties such as novelty, opening rhetoric, and nature of competing stimuli will not necessarily hold attention. The ability of a message to hold attention depends on whether the receiver can *comprehend* the arguments and conclusions. Comprehension is influenced by the complexity and clarity of the message, and "the receiver's intelligence, relevant experience, openmindedness, and 'cognitive tuning set' (readiness to pass the information on, to be entertained, etc.)" (Zimbardo and Ebbesen, 1969, p. 21).

The likelihood of acceptance, or *yielding* to the comprehended message, is theorized

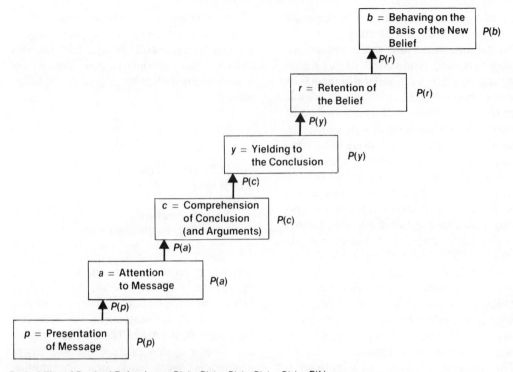

Probability of Desired Behavior = $P(p) \cdot P(a) \cdot P(c) \cdot P(y) \cdot P(r) \cdot P(b)$

Figure 1 / Steps in the response to a communication

to depend on the extent of incentives. The incentives in the message may be in the form of arguments or reasons why the advocated point of view should be accepted in favor of the old attitude, or the arousal of expectations that have reinforcing value. An important expectation, which is enhanced by a highly credible source, is of being right or wrong. Suspicion of someone's manipulative intent is another expectation that will nullify the prospects of acceptance because it is seen as a threat to one's freedom to decide for oneself (see Brehm, 1966). Finally, a communication can lead to the expectation of social approval or disapproval. Social approval is seen as rewarding; thus, anything in the communication that credibly

indicates that acceptance will be socially rewarding will increase acceptability.

If the recipient has taken the fourth step of *yielding* or accepting the message, there is the further question of whether he will *retain* the new position until he has an opportunity to *behave* accordingly. As a rule, the retention of an opinion over time depends on the informational content of the message and the incentives for acceptance.

Each step in the chain is taken with only a certain probability, and its occurrence depends on the probabilities associated with the earlier steps in the chain. The model suggests that the probabilities are multiplicative; so if there were a probability of 0.5 at each step there would be a less than 0.02

probability that purchase behavior would be influenced by the persuasive message. If this were the true situation, it would go far toward explaining the ineffectiveness of most advertising campaigns. However, this analysis is largely speculative in the absence of knowledge about the various probabilities, and uncertainty as to whether a step such as attention is a prerequisite for subsequent yielding. Perhaps, as Krugman (1965) suggests, some attitudes are acquired by a process of incidental learning, without the aid of explicit attention.

Process Models of Behavior

The information-processing approach shares a number of characteristics with other process models of buying behavior. The most familiar of these related models are the "hierarchy of communication effects"—awareness–knowledge–liking–preferences–conviction–purchase (Lavidge and Steiner, 1962)—and the adoption-process model borrowed from rural sociology.

All these models share a view that consumers follow a rational problem-solving approach and base their decisions on the persuasive information provided. Furthermore, as Robertson (1971) notes, these models also share the same shortcomings: (a) The consumer may make decisions in a "non-rational" manner. That is, he may not secure, process, nor carefully evaluate all the available information; "he may make adoption decisions on impulse or to ingratiate himself with other people"; or he may be playing a psychosocial game (Bauer, 1964) rather than solving a problem. (b) There is not a specified *sequence* of stages which must occur. Any such model must make allowances for consumers to "skip" stages. (c) The model must also provide *feedback*

loops, since such a process will not necessarily be linear and unidimensional.

Social Judgment Theory

Attitude Organization. In social judgment theory, an individual's attitude toward an object or a social issue is treated as a range of acceptable positions (an acceptance region) rather than a single point. Operationally, this region is usually defined by the Thurstone-type statements that are considered acceptable or tolerable, including the single most acceptable statement. The rest of the attitude dimension is divided into a rejection region and a noncommitment region. The latter category is generally the residue after the acceptable and objectionable positions have been determined. For people with moderate positions on an issue, there may be two rejection regions—one at each extreme. This accommodates those who cannot tolerate the far left or the far right wing of the political spectrum, for example. This view of attitude structure resembles the familiar brand-attitude scale, which identifies a "consideration" class, a "buying" class, and a "non-consideration" class of brands (Smith, 1965; Day, 1970b). The consideration of acceptable class is also akin to the theoretical notion of an "evoked set" of brands which are within the buyer's reach and are adequate for his needs (Howard and Sheth, 1969).

Contrast and Assimilation. Attitude change in response to a persuasive communication is seen in social judgment theory as a two-step process. First, the recipient makes a judgment that positions the message on a subjective scale of favorability with respect to the issue or object. The amount of attitude change then depends on the judged discrepancy between the message and the recipient's own position. When the message falls within the recipient's acceptance or neutral region, it will be seen as more nearly similar to the recipient's position than it actually is (*assimilation* effect). A persuasive message will be maximally effective when the position advocated by the message falls close to the boundary of the rejection region. However, if the message advocates a position that is *within* the rejection region, a *contrast* effect will occur. Then the judged discrepancy is likely to be exaggerated, the communication will be unfavorably evaluated, and the recipient will resist persuasion. Worse, a very discrepant message is likely to reinforce the recipient's initial attitude and perhaps produce a boomerang effect.

This simple judgment displacement process is highly subject to distortion from the following sources: (a) ambiguity as to the position of the communication (Sherif and Sherif, 1967); (b) limited past experience; (c) situational factors which do not require the respondent to discriminate between attitude positions; and (d) deep involvement in one's position on an issue (Kiesler, Collins, and Miller, 1969, p. 246). Most of the research, however, has focused on the effect of involvement.

Role of Involvement. According to social-judgment theory, the attitude of a person highly involved in his position will be hard to change because that position is strongly anchored within the total belief system. The consequence of increasing involvement is that discrepant communications pose greater threats to one's position and are more likely to fall in the rejection region. This is the reason that involvement is defined operationally by the size of the rejection region. In the early formulations of the theory, it was hypothesized that increas-

ing involvement would lead to a shrinking of the range of acceptable positions. However, the empirical findings have been ambiguous on this matter (Sherif, Sherif, and Nebergall, 1965), and it is now assumed that the acceptance region remains constant for a given stimulus situation.

The involvement level also influences the degree of perceptual distortion of a discrepant message, as well as whether an assimilation or contrast effect will occur. For a communication within the acceptance region, the involved respondent will assimilate the message much more than an uninvolved respondent and consequently will perceive the message as advocating less change. Analogously, when the message is in the rejection region, the involved respondent will displace it further from his own position and find it less credible and less persuasive. Thus, regardless of the level of discrepancy, an involved subject will always be more difficult to persuade.

Functional Theories

The theoretical approaches I have just considered put their stress on the relationship of a person's attitude toward an object and his information, perception, and behavior toward that object. Little attention is given to the motivational underpinnings of this attitude. The crux of the various functional approaches to attitudes (Smith, Bruner, and White, 1958; Katz and Stotland, 1959; Katz, 1960) is that the same attitude may be held by different persons for different reasons and require the employment of different techniques for change.

Utilitarian (Adaptive) Functions. Positive attitudes are developed toward objects or paths that have been instrumental in achieving desirable goals, or avoiding undesirable goals. Similarly, negative attitudes are developed toward objects that thwart desirable goals. These are learned responses that depend on one's past reinforcing experiences with the object (Katz, 1960). Hence this function strongly resembles the behavioristic information-processing approach.

Because utilitarian attitudes toward objects are formed through experience, they are posited to be fairly difficult to change through direct verbal appeals. Also, "the area of freedom for changing utilitarian attitudes is, of course, much greater in dealing with methods of satisfying needs than with the needs themselves. Needs change more slowly than the means for gratifying them, even though one role of the advertiser is to create new needs" (Katz, 1960, p. 178). By a process of exclusion, the most effective means for changing such attitudes are changing the buyer's perception of the ability of the product or brand to satisfy the needs or emphasizing need and better ways of need satisfaction.

Knowledge Functions. Attitudes also function to help the individual cope with a complex world that cannot be grasped in its entirety. Accordingly, people seek stereotypes and broad frames of reference or categories that will provide "a simplified and practical manual of appropriate behavior toward specific objects" (McGuire, 1969, p. 158). Thus, when a new object is placed in an existing category, it becomes the focus of the existing repertory of behaviors which are appropriate to that overall category. This spares the individual the time-consuming and sometimes painful effort of deciding how to relate to the new object. New-product marketers are acutely conscious of this fact and generally avoid

positioning a new product where it defies easy categorization. A better strategy is to demonstrate that the new product fits into several existing categories at the same time and thus delivers additional benefits.

Expressive (Self-Realizing) Functions. Attitudes also function as part of the total belief system to give positive expression to the individual's central values and his self-concept. As such, they reflect and confirm his notion of the kind of person he is. But, conversely, the expression of an attitude can also help the individual define his self-concept. This self-realization function appears to be very similar to the dissonance notion that a person adopts attitudes to bolster or justify his behavior, especially in the face of a difficult decision.

According to Katz (1960, p. 189) "people are much less likely to find their values uncongenial than they are to find some of the attitudes inappropriate to their values." Thus one way to change a specific value expressive attitude is to show that it is inconsistent with a more basic value. Marketers are more likely to take advantage of existing attitudes by portraying their brand as a means of expressing the values and self-concepts of particular market segments. This is particularly true in hard-to-evaluate products such as cosmetics and cigarettes. However, the available research on self-concept as a determinant of brand or product choice has not been particularly successful either because of poor implementation of the strategy, inadequate methodology, or an inapplicable theory. The worth of this approach is still open to question.

Ego-Defensive (Externalization) Function. Some attitudes toward objects or social situations serve primarily to help an individual deal with his inner conflicts and have only the most limited relationship to that object. They may protect him from internal anxieties or from facing up to potential danger, through building defense mechanisms or rationalizing the problem. Of greater interest is the tendency noted by Smith, Bruner, and White (1958) for people to see events or objects in terms of their own concerns, "covert strivings," or "preferred adjustive strategies." Internal problems, which may be unconscious, may well color or bias a person's perception of a social problem. Thus a person who has suffered from a series of problems with product quality or service is especially sensitive to revelations that others are suffering from the same problems. Furthermore, such a person is likely to propose solutions that resemble a successful strategy for dealing with a personal problem. Because ego-defensive attitudes are often irrelevant to the object and may be unconscious, they are probably impervious to conventional informational approaches. Indeed, knowledge of such attitudes may only be useful to marketers insofar as it is possible to avoid communications which elicit them.

Overview. So little research has been devoted to functional theories that their ultimate usefulness cannot be appraised. While their scope is appealing, it appears that many aspects have been subject to more detailed interpretation within the other theories reviewed in this article. The major contribution, and the greatest value for marketing, should come from insights into individual differences. Other theories (such as social-judgment theory) also incorporate individual differences, but predict the main effects of persuasive messages. With functional theories no such prediction can be made without knowing the function the attitude serves for the individual. At present this cannot be determined, for there is virtually no technology for assessing the func-

tion of attitudes. Such a development would be very useful for the design and evaluation of marketing communications.

NOTES

1. This implies that there is a predictive relationship with purchase or choice behavior. For insights into this complex issue, see Day (1970a) and Wicker (1969).

2. I assume that you are familiar with the semantic-differential and Likert ratings, which are usually employed to measure these judgments. If not, see Green and Tull (1970) and Upshaw (1968).

REFERENCES

Allport, G. W. "Attitudes." In *Handbook of Social Psychology,* ed. C. Murchison, Clark University Press (1935), 798–884.

Bauer, R. A. "The Obstinate Audience: The Influence Process from the Point of View of Social Communication." *American Psychologist.* Vol. 19 (1964), 319–328.

———, and S. A. Greyser. "The Dialogue That Never Happens." *Harvard Business Review,* Vol. 45, November-December 1967.

Bem, D. J. "Attitudes as Self-Descriptions: Another Look at the Attitude-Behavior Links." In *Psychological Foundations of Attitudes,* ed. A. G. Greenwald, T. C. Brock, and T. M. Ostrom, Academic Press (1968), 197–215.

Brehm, J. W. *A Theory of Psychological Reactance.* Academic Press, 1966.

Cook, S. W., and C. Selltiz, "A Multiple-Indicator Approach to Attitude Measurement." *Psychological Bulletin,* Vol. 62 (1964), 36–55.

Day, G. S. "Using Attitude Change Measures to Evaluate New Product Introductions." *Journal of Marketing Research,* Vol. 7 (November 1970b), 474–482.

Engel, J. F., D. T. Kollat, and R. D. Blackwell, *Consumer Behavior,* Holt, Rinehart and Winston, 1968.

Evans, F. B. "Psychological and Objective Factors in the Prediction of Brand Choice: Ford versus Chevrolet." *Journal of Business,* Vol. 32 (1959), 340–369.

Fishbein, M., and B. H. Raven. "The A-B-Scales: An Operational Definition of Belief and Attitude." *Human Relations,* Vol. 15 (1962), 35–44.

Greenberg, M. "The Analysis of Preference and Attribute Judgment Data," Unpublished working paper. November 1968.

Heller, H. E. "Defining Target Markets by Their Attitude Profiles." In *Attitude Research on the Rocks,* ed. L. Adler and I. Crespi. American Marketing Association, 1968.

Hess, E. H. "Attitude and Pupil Size." *Scientific American.* Vol. 212 (1965), 46–54.

Hovland, C.I. "Reconciling Conflicting Results Derived from Experimental and Survey Studies of Attitude Change." *American Psychologist,* Vol. 14 (1959), 8–17.

Howard, J.A., and J. N. Sheth. *Theory of Buyer Behavior.* Wiley, 1969.

Katz, D. "The Functional Approach to the Study of Attitudes." *Public Opinion Quarterly,* Vol. 24 (1960), 163–204.

———, and E. Stotland. "A Preliminary Statement to a Theory of Attitude Structure and Change." In *Psychology: A Study of a Science,* Vol. 3, ed. S. Koch. McGraw-Hill, 1959, 423–475.

Katz, F., and P. F. Lazarsfeld. *Personal Influence.* The Free Press. 1955.

Kelman, H.C. "Processes of Opinion Change." *Public Opinion Quarterly,* Vol. 25 (1961). 57–78.

Kiesler, C.A., B. E. Collins, and N. Miller. *Attitude Change: A Critical Analysis of Theoretical Approaches.* Wiley, 1969.

Krugman, H.E. "The Impact of Television Advertising: Learning without Involvement." *Public Opinion Quarterly,* Vol. 29 (Fall 1965), 349–356.

Lavidge, R.C., and G. A. Steiner. "A Model for Predictive Measurements of Advertising Effectiveness." *Journal of Marketing,* Vol. 25 (October 1961), 59–62.

Lunn, J. A. "Attitudes and Behavior in Consumer Behavior—A Reappraisal." Unpublished paper, Research Bureau Limited, 1970.

McGuire, W. J. "The Nature of Attitudes and Attitude Change." In *The Handbook of Social Psychology,* 2nd ed., Vol. 3. ed. G. Lindsay and E. Aronson, Addison-Wesley, 1969, 136–314.

———. "The Current Status of Cognitive Consistency Theories." In *Cognitive Consistency: Motivational Antecedents and Behavioral Consequents,* ed. S. Feldman, Academic Press, 1966.

Maloney, J. C. "Attitude Measurement and Prediction." Paper presented at the Test Market Design and Measurement Workshop, American Marketing Association, Chicago, April 1966.

Nicosia, F.M. *Consumer Decision Processes: Marketing and Advertising Implications.* Prentice-Hall, 1966.

Osgood, C.E., G. I. Suci, and P.H. Tannenbaum. *The Measurement of Meaning.* University of Illinois Press, 1957.

Robertson, T. S. *Innovative Behavior and Communication.* Holt, Rinehart and Winston, 1971.

Rokeach, M. "Attitude Change and Behavior Change." *Public Opinion Quarterly,* Vol. 30 (Winter 1966–67), 529–550.

Sherif, C. W., M. Sherif, and R. E. Nebergall, *Attitude and Attitude Change: The Social Judgment-Involvement Approach.* W. B. Saunders. 1965.

Sherif, M., and C. W. Sherif. "Attitude as the Individuals Own Categories: The Social Judgment-Involvement Approach to Attitude and Attitude Change." In *Attitude, Ego-Involvement and Change,* ed. C. W. Sherif and M. Sherif. Wiley (1967), 105–139.

Smith, G. "How GM Measures Ad Effectiveness." *Printer's Ink.* May 14, 1965.

Smith, M.B. "Attitude Change." In *Encyclopedia of the Social Sciences,* Vol. 1, ed. D. L. Sills, Crowell-Collier and Macmillan (1968), 458–467.

———. J. S. Bruner, and R. W. White. *Opinions and Personality.* Wiley, 1958.

Wells, W. D. "Measuring Readiness to Buy." *Harvard Business Review,* Vol. 39 (July–August 1961). 81–87.

Zimbardo, P.G., and E.B. Ebbesen. "Involvement and Communication Discrepancy as Determinants of Opinion Conformity." *Journal of Abnormal and Social Psychology.* Vol. 60 (1960), 86–94.

Questions

1. Define an "attitude," making sure to include each of the four definite characteristics in your definition.
2. Describe each of the three components of attitude structure.
3. Explain the underlying purpose of "process models" of consumer behavior. What are some of their shortcomings?
4. An attitude is presumed to hold various functions. Looking at attitudes from this "functional" approach, describe each of these four functions.

7. Cognitive Consistency and Consumer Behavior

Bobby J. Calder

In developing psychological models of consumer behavior, a family of concepts called cognitive consistency theories may prove very powerful. These theories postulate, not logical, but psychological operations. In this sense they may provide a valuable supplement to the more rationalistic treatments of consumer behavior. Although consistency theories have received *some* attention with regard to consumer processes, their potential has not been generally recognized. This discussion briefly reviews three of the major consistency approaches and notes some of the more promising relevant research evidence from the social psychology, communication, and marketing literatures. The goal is to establish the relevance of cognitive consistency to consumer behavior and to point out some directions for further research.

Cognitive consistency is perhaps most relevant to consumer behavior in terms of attitude theory. The basic notion behind all of the consistency concepts is that people are motivated to maintain a state of psychological harmony within the system of beliefs and attitudes about a given issue or situation. The various approaches to cognitive consistency differ mostly in the manner in which they attempt to characterize the psychological processes involved in attaining this equilibrium.

BALANCE THEORY

One line of research dealing with cognitive consistency is closely associated with the pioneering work of Fritz Heider. Heider (1946, 1958) was concerned mainly with our perception of the social world. Various perceptual constancies received considerable attention from the early Gestalt psychologists. For instance, most people see the lines below not as a series of eight vertical lines but as a set of four pairs of vertical lines:

| | | | | | | |

It seems that we are biased toward creating such perceptual unity or harmony. Heider's contribution was to extend this thinking to the way people perceive social events.

The social events of principal interest to Heider consisted of three elements in a given person's experience, the person himself (symbolized P), some other person (symbolized O), and some event, idea, or object (symbolized X). (See Figure 1.) Two types of beliefs relating these cognitive elements in the P-O-X system were postulated. Each type may be positive or negative. Sentiment relations refer to beliefs that two elements are connected by liking (+) or disliking (−), favorable feelings (+) or unfavorable (−) feelings, or some other evaluative relation. Unit relations refer to beliefs that two elements belong together (+) or do not belong together (−) in some sense, e.g., P

buys X or O owns X. It was Heider's purpose to explore any systematic tendencies people possess in cognitively organizing a P-O-X system. He proposed that people attempt to maintain a psychological state called balance in which there is no strain or stress in a system. A system is balanced if all three of the signs of the relations between P, O, and X are positive or if any two signs are negative and one is positive. If only one sign is negative and the other two are positive or if all three are negative, a system is imbalanced. Thus, the system P buys X, P admires O, and O buys X is balanced whereas P buys X, P admires O, but O never buys X is imbalanced. Heider postulated that people attempt to restore balance in an imbalanced system by changing the signs of the relations. In the imbalanced system just mentioned, balance could be obtained by changing the perceived relation between P and X so that P never buys X, P admires O, and O never buys X.

Heider's formulation of balance theory has proven valuable in stimulating research.

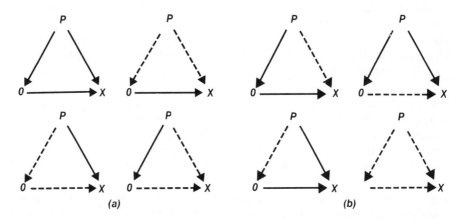

Figure 1 / Examples of balanced and unbalanced states according to Heider's definition of balance. Solid lines represent positive, and broken lines negative, relations. (a) Balanced states. (b) Unbalanced states. *Source:* R. B. Zajonc, "The concepts of balance, congruity, and dissonance," *The Public Opinion Quarterly,* Vol. 24 (Summer 1960), 280–296.

Cartwright and Harary (1956) formalized the theory using mathematical graph theory and extended it to relations between N elements. This work gives a general principle for determining balance: Balance exists if the product of all the signs is positive, imbalance if the product is negative.

Empirical support for the notion of balance has been obtained from two types of studies. The first simply presents a subject with hypothetical relationships and asks him to rate the pleasantness of each one. It is predicted that balanced relationships will be more pleasant. Jordan (1953) gave subjects 64 hypothetical P-O-X situations, half of which were balanced and half unbalanced. In general, balanced relationships were in fact judged more pleasant than imbalanced ones.

The second type of study conducted to test balance theory gives the subject a set of situations and then asks him questions about the relations or requires him to reproduce them. Burnstein (1967) administered a questionnaire to students immediately before the 1964 presidential election containing a series of situations involving hypothetical relations among two people and their feelings about a candidate. Students were then asked which situations were likely to change and how. The results indicated that initially balanced situations were seen as less likely to change. As to what changes would occur, increases in positive relations in excess of the number needed for balance were predicted by the subjects. These predictions also favored changes in interpersonal relations as opposed to feelings about a candidate. Subjects evidently expect balance, positivity, and a preference for interpersonal changes.

Zajone and Burnstein (1965) tested the ability of subjects to learn balanced versus imbalanced situations. If imbalanced relationships are stressful, they should be harder to learn. The relations involved two people and their feelings about either integration (important issue) or *Newsweek* (unimportant issue). For instance, Dick approves of *Newsweek,* Don approves of *Newsweek,* and Dick dislikes Don, or Tom approves of integration, Ted disapproves of integration, and Tom likes Ted. Subjects were presented each relation one at a time and had to remember whether it was positive or negative. Zajone and Burnstein found that unbalanced situations were more difficult to learn but only when the issue was important (integration). In addition, negative relations were more difficult to learn, another positivity finding. Other studies (e.g., Gerard and Fleischer, 1967) indicate the effects of balance may be more complicated still. It seems that perhaps balanced situations may be remembered more easily with long-term memory and imbalanced situations with short-term memory, or even that some situations are intrinsically more interesting and easier to remember because of their imbalance.

Taken together these studies demonstrate that balance does seem to be an important force in social perception, though the principle is not in itself a theory of social perception. The relevance of the basic notion of balance for consumer behavior lies in focusing attention on how the particular sentiment or unit relation linking the consumer and the product fits in with his entire system of beliefs arising in connection with the product. The emphasis of the theory on interpersonal relations might also be fruitful in exploring the effects of social context on product evaluations.

For work in consumer behavior, however, it may be desirable to have a more explicit formulation of balance possessing a greater predictive power. Fortunately Heider's work has directly stimulated research along these lines. Rosenberg (1956, 1960a, 1960b) defines attitudes as pro or con feelings toward objects of affective significance. Attitudes possess a structure composed of an affective component and a cognitive (belief) component. According to Rosenberg there exists a homeostatic tendency to maintain consistency between these components. Because of this tendency, a mathematical index can be calculated for predicting attitudes. Two variables are involved, the importance of the attitude object in leading to or blocking valued states (instrumental relations or beliefs) and the affect felt toward a given value. Figure 2 shows a hypothetical attitude structure concerning "nonphosphate detergents." To compute Rosenberg's index, it is necessary to obtain ratings of the affect associated with each value and the strength of the instrumental relation linking the value and the attitude object. Each value

rating is then multiplied by its instrumentality and these products are summed to form the index of attitude. In our example (see Figure 2), the person's overall attitude, based on the hypothetical ratings given in parentheses, is predicted to be -4.

The affective-cognitive consistency side of this approach was later elaborated more extensively by Rosenberg and Abelson (Abelson, 1959; Abelson and Rosenberg, 1958; Rosenberg and Abelson, 1960). The later version of the theory deals with cognitive elements, the objects of human thought, and the cognitive relations between these elements. Both cognitive elements and relations can be either positive, negative, or null (neutral). No distinction is made between affective or instrumental relations, both are allowed. The conceptual arena refers to the set of all cognitive elements which are relevant to a given attitude object. It may be thought of as a network of cognitive bands, where a band is two cognitive elements connected by a relation. Figure 2 may be interpreted in these terms since each instrumental relation forms a band with an element and the attitude object. Conceptual arenas have the property of being balanced or imbalanced. Balance is achieved when all of the cognitive bands involve either elements of the same sign linked with a positive relation or elements of unlike sign linked with a negative relation. Notice that balance is defined in terms of signs, without reference to any numerical values. As before, balance is associated with a positive product and imbalance a negative product. Note that our example in Figure 2 is imbalanced. Abelson and Rosenberg further posit explicit "psycho-logical" rules which govern how a person thinks about elements in his conceptual arena. One rule states, for instance, that if A is positively related to B and B is negatively related to C,

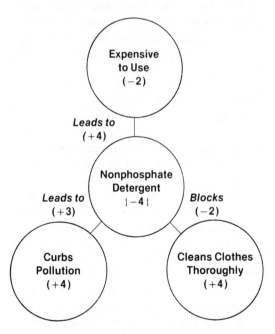

Figure 2 / A hypothetical attitude structure for a product

then A is negatively related to C. A conceptual arena is balanced if no application of these rules leads to the discovery of a negative cognitive band.

A unique feature of Rosenberg and Abelson's theory is that imbalance is predicted to create a pressure toward change only if the individual thinks about the imbalance. Imbalance may be resolved in one of three general ways. A person may change the sign of one or more cognitive elements, change the sign of one or more cognitive relations, or stop thinking about the imbalance. Abelson (1959) specifies four means by which changing the sign of an element or relation may be accomplished: denial, bolstering, transcendence, and differentiation. The affective sign may be simply denied or changed to its opposite. The imbalance in the structure shown in Figure 2 may be resolved by denying that non-phosphate detergent really leads to less pollution. An element in an imbalanced cognitive band may be bolstered by relating it to other elements in a balanced way. If curbing pollution is linked to political fads, increased government spending, etc., imbalance should decrease. Imbalance may be transcended by placing both elements in some superordinate classification. Curbing pollution $(+)$ and nonphosphate detergent $(-)$ may be combined into the larger element "popular gimmick" $(-)$ or "social responsibility" $(+)$, of which only the former would resolve the imbalance in our example. Finally, a very common method of imbalance reduction is to differentiate an element into two different elements which are balanced. Thus our hypothetical person may decide that only air pollution needs curbing $(+)$ while water pollution does not $(-)$ and that nonphosphate detergent $(-)$ leads to $(+)$ that latter, $a -, +, -$ band, but not the former, $a -, -, +$ band.

Attitude change to accomplish imbalance reduction follows one of two sequences: affective change followed by cognitive change or cognitive change followed by affective change. Using posthypnotic suggestions, Rosenberg (1960a) instructed subjects to feel differently about an attitude object. He found that this affective change also produced changes in cognitive instrumental linkages. If, for example, a subject's feeling about blacks living in white neighborhoods was changed, the relations between integrating blacks and various values changed too. Carlson (1956) demonstrated the reverse sequence by convincing students that allowing blacks to move into white neighborhoods leads to values such as equal opportunity, and showing that this cognitive change led to affective change regarding integration.

Another contribution of the Rosenberg and Abelson theory is to hypothesize that imbalance reduction follows the easiest possible path. That is, balance tends to be restored with the fewest number of operations. Support for this contention was gained (Rosenberg and Abelson, 1960) by having subjects play the role of a department store manager where the role was defined by various cognitive bands, e.g., high sales is a positive cognitive element. The total structure represented by these bands was imbalanced in different ways for different subjects. When subjects were asked to evaluate three research reports which had the effect of restoring balance, they favored the report which resolved their particular imbalance in the fewest number of changes. However, these particular experiments also revealed the operation of other factors, a positivity effect and a tendency toward maximizing gain and a minimizing loss (subjects did not reduce imbalance in a way that would reduce sales). This latter factor led Rosenberg and Abelson (1960) to postulate a "dual force conception" which is extremely important for consumer behavior. Balance represents one force on a cognitive band and hedonic satisfaction another. In some cognitive bands these forces may conflict. Rosenberg (1965) provides a valuable discussion of this problem. He argues that imbalance will be less likely to result in change for a hedonic cognitive band than an antihedonic one. For example, the imbalance in "My mother-in-law $(-)$ supports $(+)$ my plan to buy a new car $(+)$" is less stressful than in "The distinguished firm of Schlag and Sons $(+)$ have put on the market $(+)$ a completely worthless sphygmomanometer (Rosenberg, 1965, p. 133)." Rosenberg (1965) also presents experimental data supporting the prediction that hedonic imbalance is less stressful than antihedonic imbalance. It may be possible, however, to account for this hedonic force within balance theory by employing the self as a separate cognitive element. When the self $(+)$ is associated with $(+)$ a motive-frustrating state of affairs $(-)$, imbalance is greater than when it is associated with a rewarding state $(+)$, because another imbalanced band has been added to the structure in the former case (Rosenberg and Abelson, 1960, p. 146). The above example then becomes "My mother-in-law $(-)$ supports $(+)$ my plan to buy a new car $(+)$" and "I $(+)$ am associated $(+)$ with this benefit $(+)$," an imbalanced and a balanced band. The worthless sphygmomanometer band, however, is coupled with an unbeneficial self-association, which creates two imbalances instead of one. It is perhaps worth noting that these authors attribute much of the interest in dissonance theory to the fact that it usually analyzes these doubly stressful antihedonic imbalances involving the self. This entire problem is worth considerable attention from consumer behavior researchers, for many of the important imbalances in this area are of the conflicting hedonic variety. Is "nonphosphate detergent $(-)$ leads to $(+)$ curbing pollution $(+)$" really imbalanced?

To suggest the potential of this research, a study by Insko, Blake, Cialdini, and Mulaik (1970) provides a good example. A survey was administered in which cognitive elements and statements relating these elements to some aspects of birth control were rated, the former on a good-bad scale, the latter on a true-false scale. Respondents were women in a public housing project. The data were analyzed by means of factor analyses to determine differences between users and nonusers of contraceptives. Cognitive consistency seemed to be greater for users than nonusers. The data indicated several requirements for both control campaigns including educating the husband as well as the wife and creating cognitive links between birth control and family goals.

While attitudes are certainly a crucial aspect of consumer behavior, the nature of the relationship between attitudes and behavior is an open question (see Calder and Ross, in press; Fishbein and Ajzen, 1972). Thus, before leaving balance theory, we should describe an extension of Rosenberg and Abelson's theory explicitly incorporating behavior as a variable. Insko and Schopler (1967) present a model treating behavior, an actual goal directed activity, as well as cognitive elements and relations. All three are classified as either positive or negative. Insko and Schopler contend that people try to maintain not only affective-cognitive consistency but triadic consistency too. Consider a person who enjoys smoking (affect) and who smokes two packs of cigarettes a day (behavior). Now suppose he believes (cognition) that he should not be smoking for reasons of health. This triad is composed of a positively evaluated cognitive element, a negative cognitive relation, and a positive behavior. The product of the signs is negative, indicating triadic imbalance. Insko and Schopler predict some change in the triad to restore balance. It follows from this theory that behavior change can produce attitude change as well as that attitude change can cause behavior change. As we shall see, it is important in consumer behavior research for a model to allow for both sequences.

CONGRUITY THEORY

The congruity model of cognitive consistency developed independently of balance theory, though it is certainly similar in spirit. Whereas Heider had been interested in social perception, congruity theory stemmed from Osgood, Suci, and Tannenbaum's (1957) work on the semantic differential as a measure of meaning. One result of this research was to find a general evaluative dimension of meaning which could be equated with attitude. From its inception, the model was oriented toward the changes in attitude produced by source effects (Tannenbaum, 1968, p. 54). Source effects involve a situation where a person has an attitude about a communication source and about an issue. The source then makes an assertion about the issue. How does this assertion affect both the attitude toward the source and the attitude toward the issue?

The theory (Osgood and Tannenbaum, 1955; Osgood, 1960; Tannenbaum, 1967) is stated in terms of communication sources and objects of judgment which are connected by either an associative assertion (e.g., likes, buys, praises) or a dissociative assertion (e.g., dislikes, refuses to buy, criticizes). While assertions have only two values, associative or dissociative, sources and objects can take on values ranging from

+ 3 to − 3 according to their semantic differential ratings. An example of the type of attitude structure we have in mind is diagramed in Figure 3 in a manner introduced by Brown (1962). In this example (see Figure 3a) the source is the magazine *Consumer Reports,* which has been previously evaluated positively (+ 2) by our respondent, and the object of judgment is a certain automobile make previously evaluated as slightly negative (− 1). *Consumer Reports* publishes a story recommending that people buy this automobile, an associative assertion.

According to the theory, a state of congruity exists whenever a source and an object with the same numerical evaluation are associated and whenever a source and an object with opposite evaluations (e.g., + 2 and − 2) are dissociated. The lack of congruity, or incongruity, creates a pressure to change both the source and object attitudes to a congruent state. This pressure, P, is postulated to be different for the source and the object. It equals the amount each one would have to change alone to bring about congruity. In our example (see Figure 3a), the pressure on *Consumer Reports* is − 3, a change of three units in the minus direction would produce congruity. Similarly, the pressure on the automobile attitude is + 3. (If the assertion were dissociative, the pressures would be − 1 and − 1 respectively.) When incongruity exists, both the source (S) and object (O) undergo pressure to change. The theory assumes, however, that the actual change depends on how extreme the attitude value is, a more extreme attitude changes proportionately less. The following equation gives the change for the attitude object:

$$AC_o = \frac{|S|}{|O| + |S|} \, P_o \pm i \pm A$$

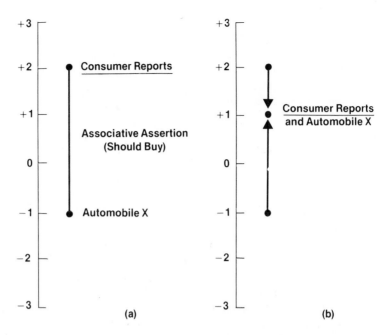

Figure 3 / Attitude change produced by an associative assertion

where AC is the attitude change of the object, S is the absolute numerical value of the source attitude, O is the absolute numerical value of the object attitude, P_o is the pressure toward congruity on the object, and i and A are constants. Similarly, attitude change for the source is given by:

$$AC_s = \frac{|O|}{|O| + |S|} \; P_s \pm i$$

In short, attitudes change a certain proportion of the total distance required to create congruity, this proportion being determined by the relative extremity of the attitude. The two constants are corrections to the equations: i corrects for incredulity, the tendency to disbelieve a highly incongruent assertion (e.g., "the United States government has advocated that people buy Soviet-made automobiles"). The incredulity constant takes the opposite sign as P, thereby reducing the amount of change necessary. The

assertion constant builds in the assumption that the object of an assertion should change more than the source. It is positive for an associative assertion and negative for a dissociative assertion; it is determined empirically. Without bothering with the correction constants, we may calculate that in our example (see Figure 3b), attitude toward *Consumer Reports* should change −1 units and attitudes toward the automobile should change +2 units. These changes would achieve congruity, a similarly evaluated source and object associated by an assertion.

We should note that incongruity need not necessarily lead to attitude change. Tannenbaum, Macaulay, and Norris (1966) have described several alternatives to attitude change as a means of reducing incongruity. A person can deny or distort the association between the source and object (e.g., "a prestige figure was *paid* to endorse a product"). Alternatively a person can bolster his attitude toward the concept by seeking new information or he can alter his attitude toward the source alone and maintain the same attitude toward the concept. Unlike balance theory, these alternatives have not been emphasized.

Although congruity theory focuses on source effects, it can clearly be extended to the same situations as balance by treating more than one object and relation at a time. In fact it appears that balance theory is a subcase of congruity theory in that any situation which is imbalanced is also incongruent, though the converse is not necessary. It should be clear that even with its formalization congruity theory is probably of more narrow interest than balance theory. Notice also that the congruity approach calls for averaging the elements of a cognitive unit whereas Rosenberg's index employs a summation.

Research on congruity theory has yielded mixed results. Osgood and Tannenbaum (1955) found that the equations predicted the direction of attitude change better than the amount of change. Even more troublesome is Kerrick's (1959) finding that like sign attitudes when associated may change to become more extreme than either were separately. Recent research on congruity has tended to discard the mathematics of the theory, concentrating instead on its general implications. Tannenbaum (1966) demonstrated that attitude change toward an object does generalize to a source and to other objects connected to the source as well. In a review of this work, Tannenbaum (1968) explicitly recommends keeping the attitude change through communication aspect of the model separate from its status as a "general model of cognitive interaction." In view of the obvious importance of the source effect situation for consumer behavior, congruity theory could provide a valuable supplement to balance theory in just this connection.

DISSONANCE THEORY

The origins of dissonance theory probably lie in Gestalt psychology via the field theory approach of Kurt Lewin which postulated that changes in a person's life space could occur as a result of psychological tension. Like balance and congruity, dissonance is stated in terms of cognitive elements and relations (Festinger, 1957). Cognitive elements are defined much more loosely though. They may include any knowledge a person has about himself, his behavior, or his world. Cognitive elements may be perceived as related in one of two ways. If the existence of one element x does not follow from another element y (i.e., x implies not-y), the relation is dissonant; otherwise it is consonant. The cognition, "I purchase nonphosphate detergent," is dissonant with the cognition, "nonphosphate detergent does not get clothes clean"; the one does not follow from the other.

Cognitive dissonance is supposed to create a noxious state of psychological tension in the individual. A person is thus motivated to reduce dissonance and to avoid events that would produce dissonance. The intensity of this motivation increases with the relative number of dissonant cognitions and their importance. Dissonance may be reduced by adding new cognitive elements favoring consonance or changing existing cognitions toward consonance. In our example, dissonance may be reduced by adding new cognitions such as "nonphosphate detergents curb pollution" and "nonphosphate detergent makes clothes smell fresh." Alternatively, the person may change his behavior ("I no longer purchase nonphosphate detergent") or his belief about cleaning power ("nonphosphate detergent actually does get clothes clean").

Dissonance theory has not remained static since its introduction. A number of researchers have attempted to modify the theory, usually by specifying the conditions under which dissonance will or will not be aroused. Brehm and Cohen (1962) emphasized the role of commitment and volition in producing dissonance. More recently, Aronson (1968, 1969), Bramel (1968), and Collins (1969) have argued that dissonance is connected with violations of a person's self-concept. Aronson states perhaps the most general form of this argument. He characterizes dissonance as arising most clearly from a violation of strong expectancies. One of the strongest expectancies most people have is that their self-concept will remain positive.

> Thus, at the very heart of dissonance theory, where it makes its clearest and neatest predictions, we are not dealing with any two cognitions; rather, we are usually dealing with the self-concept and predictions about some behavior. If dissonance exists it is because the individual's behavior is inconsistent with his self-concept (Aronson, 1969, p. 27).

Aronson goes on to cite as an example a study by Erlich, Guttman, Schonbach, and Mills (1957) showing that new car owners selectively expose themselves to ads for their car. To have bought a lemon would certainly violate most people's self-concepts.

Recall now our earlier discussion of a similar point in connection with Rosenberg and Abelson's theory: antihedonic imbalance was supposed to be greater than hedonic imbalance. Clearly Aronson is identifying dissonance with antihedonic imbalance. If one considers when either of these cases is likely to arise, it would seem that hedonic imbalance is more prevalent before a behavior is performed and antihedonic imbalance afterward. One does not often intend to do an-

tihedonic things beforehand but may well be trapped by them later. You do not intend to buy a lemon, but you may well find yourself with one. For this reason, it is not surprising that dissonance theory has proven especially powerful in analyzing the effects of having already performed a behavior. It is here that the greatest opportunity for antihedonic violations of self-expectancies exists.

In considering the relationship between attitudes and behavior, there are two possible causal sequences, attitudes may affect behavior or behavior may affect attitudes. It was argued in the above discussion that dissonance theory is more relevant to the effects of behavior on attitudes because of the greater likelihood of antihedonic imbalance. Moreover, dissonance may well produce changes in a person's future behavior (e.g., a person can't deny having smoked for twenty years). For both of these reasons, research has concentrated on how dissonance connected with having performed a behavior affects one's private attitudes.

In this vein Engel and Light have correctly commented on the significance of dissonance theory for consumer behavior:

> Do consumers ever become so committed (for instance, to a brand, a product, or a store) that they will become dissonant if their preference is challenged? The authors are of the opinion that such commitment indeed *does occur* for two different reasons: (1) loyalty to a product or a store can develop because one alternative becomes ego-involved and is, in effect, an extension of the consumer's self-concept; and (2) consumers establish buying routines or habits for the purpose of greater shopping efficiency. Loyalty from this latter source can represent genuine commitment (1968, p. 189).

In terms of the more recent versions of dissonance theory, we might add that loyalty through involvement of the self-concept should be most likely to create the possibility of dissonance.

Although many consumer behaviors might be examined by dissonance theory, perhaps the most salient is the purchase decision. In many cases the act of purchase may be closely identified with consumption itself. One line of dissonance research which is particularly relevant to the effects of purchasing deals with free choice situations. Consider a person wishing to buy a new car who cannot decide between a Pinto and a Vega. Finally he makes a decision, buying, say, the Vega. Dissonance theory predicts that, unless one considers himself a "schnook" (Aronson, 1969, p. 27), once the decision is made the person's evaluation of the Pinto will decrease and the evaluation of the Vega will increase. This revaluation occurs because the positive aspects of the rejected alternative (the Pinto) are now dissonant with the purchase behavior, as are the negative aspects of the chosen alternative (the Vega). Several studies have tested this prediction. Brehm (1956) asked female subjects to evaluate several products such as small appliances. Subjects then chose one of two similarly evaluated products as a gift and were asked to evaluate all the products again. The results indicate that subjects increased their evaluation of the chosen product and decreased their evaluation of the rejected product. This revaluation does not seem to be due to the mere possession of the product. Control subjects who were simply given a product did not change their evaluations. Later studies have improved on the methodology of Brehm's study and have generally supported this finding (e.g., Brock, 1963; Walster, 1964; Deutsch, Krauss, and Rosenau, 1962).

Cohen and Goldberg (1970) conducted an elaborate experimental test of the dissonance account of postdecision product revaluation.

They distinguished between the decision and the actual consumption of a product. As a gift one group of subjects was allowed to choose between a national brand of coffee (prior information) and a larger container of a test brand (no prior information). They were then allowed to inspect but not consume samples of the two brands which, unknown to them, were the same. The results indicated a marginally significant tendency for subjects choosing the national brand to evaluate it more highly than a second group of subjects who had not received either brand as a gift; there was no such tendency for the test brand. As predicted by dissonance, choosing the national brand led to an increased evaluation whereas merely inspecting it did not. The authors tentatively conclude that prior information may affect product revaluation.

Subjects next were allowed to taste the two brands. By mixing an unpleasant additive in a cup of coffee, it was possible to have about half the subjects' choices confirmed (their choice tasted better) and the other subjects' choices disconfirmed. The brands were evaluated again and subjects indicated which they would probably buy. The results revealed that subjects positively revalued their choice if it were confirmed and devalued their choice if it were disconfirmed. The dissonance effect obtained for the first, nonconsumption measure of revaluation approached significance only for the measure of purchase intention. These findings are valuable in that they demonstrate the interactive nature of dissonance effects within a consumer behavior context. Without prior information in the form of brand familiarity, subjects' decisions probably carried little commitment and thus should not have aroused dissonance leading to the revaluation of the test brand. (There is an alternative, methodological interpretation: Subjects who chose the test brand may not have cared about its evaluation—a self-selection problem.) In any event, the weakness of the dissonance effects, especially after the powerful confirmation-disconfirmation manipulation, should not be surprising, for as the authors note the product choice was not ego-involving. Future research along these lines would add considerably to our knowledge of how purchase decisions affect behavior.

In addition to revaluation a purchase decision may lead to other behaviors because of dissonance. Ehrlich et al. (1957), as noted earlier, found that after the purchase of a new car consumers read more ads for the chosen car than for other cars. This study also found, contrary to dissonance theory, that readership of ads for rejected cars was slightly greater than readership of ads for cars not considered in the purchasing decision. The new owners should have found these rejected car ads dissonance provoking. Mills (1965) showed, however, that ratings of product desirability are highly correlated with interest in ads. He argued therefore that the new car owners may have read the rejected car ads because the rejected cars were still more desirable than the other cars. Alternatively the owners may have been seeking faults in the rejected cars. Although Oshikawa (1969) does not find either of these explanations compelling, they do illustrate the myriad possible effects of dissonance. Other investigators have explored reactions to possibly dissonant new product-information (e.g., Carter, Pyszka, and Gerrero, 1969; Straits, 1964). Freedman and Sears (1965), Mills (1965), and Donohew and Palmgreen (1971) provide recent reviews of how people tend to seek consistent information.

An excellent example of how intriguing a dissonance analysis of the effects of purchase behavior can be is presented by Doob, Carlsmith, Freedman, Landauer, and Tom (1969). The "introductory low-price offer" is a standard marketing technique. Conven-

tional wisdom has it that the low price will attract buyers who will continue to purchase the product after the price is raised. Doob et al. advance a dissonance account disputing this conclusion. The higher the price a consumer can be induced to pay for a product, the greater will be his tendency to reduce any possible dissonance by convincing himself of the value of the product. By buying a product at an introductory low price, the consumer is less likely to convince himself it is a good product. To test this hypothesis, Doob et al. conducted several experiments with groups of stores matched on sales and randomly assigned to one of two conditions. One group of stores introduced a product such as mouthwash at a lower price for two weeks and then switched to the regular price while the other group sold the product at the regular price all along. During the first two weeks sales at the lower priced stores were understandably higher. However, after the price was raised, sales fell in these stores to an amount below that of the stores which had the higher price all along. Although other interpretations of the data are possible, these results still support the dissonance prediction that the lower price purchase decisions did not engender as much loyalty as the higher priced ones. Nor is this to say the exposure gained by introductory offers would not raise sales for some products. Even so, in this study a 50% increase in sales from the lower price was insufficient to overcome later the loyalty produced by the higher price.

Research on dissonance theory is voluminous. Our comments have been intended to point out the relevance of the theory to consumer behavior. Although much of the research on dissonance is complex and frequently conflicting, it should be remembered that the theory is intended to function less as a formal model than as a heuristic and language for deriving interesting empirical hypotheses. In fact, an entire style of research has grown up around the theory. While to some "much of the research on dissonance theory has studied behavior in artificial and often trivial situations (Cohen and Goldberg, 1970, p. 316)," in fact much of this research has been ingenious in providing a context for behavior in which dissonance theory predictions could be tested experimentally. The real problem has been in tying down the theory. The very looseness which invites creative derivations renders the theory all but impossible to disprove. As Calder, Ross, and Insko (in press) put it, "At present cognitive dissonance theory is neither very cognitive nor very theoretical." In the face of all its ambiguities, however, dissonance theory remains a novel and creative framework for explaining the effects of behavior.

CONCLUSION

All three of the approaches to cognitive consistency have a place in current consumer behavior research. Balance theory is perhaps most relevant for understanding cognitive structure and predicting behavior where a more formal model is desired. Congruity theory is especially suited for analyzing the effects of communication sources such as the media on consumer product evaluations. Dissonance theory provides a rich framework for predicting the effects of behavior on other consumer processes. Taken together, cognitive consistency theories add a valuable dimension to consumer research.

REFERENCES

Abelson, R. "Modes of Resolution of Belief Dilemmas." *Journal of Conflict Resolution.* Vol. 3 (1959), 343–352.

Abelson, R., and M. Rosenberg. "Symbolic psycho-logic: A Model of Attitudinal Cognition." *Behavioral Science,* Vol. 3 (1958), 1–13.

Aronson, E. "The Theory of Cognitive Dissonance: A Current Perspective." In L. Berkowitz (Ed.), *Advances in experimental social psychology,* Vol. 4. New York: Academic Press, 1969.

Aronson, E. "Dissonance Theory: Progress and Problems." In R. Abelson, E. Aronson, W. McGuire, T. Newcomb, M. Rosenberg, and P. Tannenbaum (Eds.), *Theories of Cognitive Consistency: A Sourcebook.* Chicago: Rand McNally, 1968.

Bramel, D. "Dissonance, Expectation, and the Self." In R. Abelson, E. Aronson, W. McGuire, T. Newcomb, M. Rosenberg, and P. Tannenbaum (Eds.), *Theories of Cognitive Consistency: A Sourcebook.* Chicago: Rand McNally, 1968.

Brehm, J. "Post-Decision Changes in the Desirability of Alternatives." *Journal of Abnormal and Social Psychology,* Vol. 52 (1956), 384–389.

Brehm, J., and A. Cohen, *Explorations in Cognitive Dissonance,* New York: Wiley, 1962.

Brock, T. "Effects of Prior Dishonesty on Postdecision Dissonance." *Journal of Abnormal and Social Psychology,* Vol. 66 (1963), 325–331.

Brown, R. "Models of Attitude Change." In R. Brown, E. Galanter, E. Hess, and G. Mandler (Contributors), *New Directions in Psychology.* New York: Holt, Rinehart, and Winston, 1962.

Burstein, E. "Sources of Cognitive Bias in the Representation of Simple Social Structures." *Journal of Personality and Social Psychology,* Vol. 7 (1967), 36–48.

Calder, B., and M. Ross. *Attitudes and Behavior.* New York: General Learning Press, in press.

Calder, B., M. Ross, and C. Insko. "Attitude Change and Attitude Attribution." *Journal of Personality and Social Psychology.* in press.

Carlson, E. "Attitude Change through Modification of Attitude Structure." *Journal of Abnormal and Social Psychology,* Vol. 52 (1956), 256–261.

Carter, R., R. Pyszka, and J. Guerrero, "Dissonance and Exposure to Aversive Information." *Journalism Quarterly,* Vol. 46 (1969), 37–42.

Cartwright, D., and F. Harary. "Structural Balance: A Generalization of Heider's Theory." *Psychological Review,* Vol. 63 (1956), 277–293.

Cohen, J., and M. Goldberg. "The Dissonance Model in Post-Decision Product Evaluation." *Journal of Marketing Research,* Vol. 7 (1970), 315–321.

Cohen, J., M. Fishbein, and O. Ahtola. "The Nature and Uses of Expectancy x Value Models in Consumer Attitude Research." *Journal of Marketing Research,* Vol. 9 (Nov. 1972), 456–460.

Collins, B. E. "Financial Inducements and Attitude Changes Produced by Role Players." In A. C. Elms (Ed.), *Role Playing, Reward, and Attitude Change.* New York: Van Nostrand, 1969.

Deutsch, M., R. Krauss, and N. Rosenau, "Dissonance or Defensiveness?" *Journal of Personality,* Vol. 30 (1962), 16–28.

Donohew, L., and P. Palmgreen. "A Reappraisal of Dissonance and the Selective Exposure Hypothesis." *Journalism Quarterly,* Vol. 48 (1971), 412–420.

Doob, A., J. Carlsmith, J. Freedman, T. Landauer, and S. Tom. "Effect of Initial Selling Price on Subsequent Sales." *Journal of Personality and Social Psychology,* Vol. 11 (1969), 345–350.

Ehrlich, D., I. Guttman, P. Schonbach, and J. Mills. "Postdecision Exposure to Relevant Information." *Journal of Abnormal and Social Psychology.* Vol. 54 (1957), 98–102.

Engel, J., and L. Light, "The Role of Psychological Commitment in Consumer Behavior: An Evaluation of the Theory of Cognitive Dissonance." In F. Bass, C. King, and E. Pessemier (Eds.), *Applications of the Sciences in Marketing Management.* New York: Wiley, 1968.

Festinger, L. *A Theory of Cognitive Dissonance.* Stanford: Stanford University Press, 1957.

Fishbein, M., and I. Ajzen. "Attitudes and Opinions." *Annual Review of Psychology,* Vol. 23 (1972), 487–544.

Freedman, J., and D. Sears. "Selective Exposure." In L. Berkowitz (Ed.), *Advances in Social Psychology,* Vol. 2. New York: Academic Press, 1965.

Gerard, H., and L. Fleischer. "Recall and Pleasantness of Balanced and Unbalanced Cognitive Structures." *Journal of Personality and Social Psychology,* Vol. 7 (1967), 332–337.

Heider, F. *The Psychology of Interpersonal Relations.* New York: Wiley, 1958.

———. "Attitudes and Cognitive Organization." *Journal of Psychology,* Vol. 21 (1946), 107–112.

Insko, C., and J. Schopler. "Triadic Consistency: A Statement of Affective-Cognitive-Conative Consistency." *Psychological Review.* Vol. 72 (1967), 361–376.

———, R. Blake, R. Cialdini, and S. Mulaik. "Attitude Toward Birth Control and Cognitive Consistency: Theoretical and Practical Implications of Survey Data." *Journal of Personality and Social Psychology,* Vol. 16 (1970), 228–237.

Jordan, N. "Behavioral Forces that are a Function of Attitudes and of Cognitive Organization." *Human Relations,* Vol. 6 (1953), 273–287.

Kerrick, J. "News Pictures, Captions and the Point of Resolution." *Journalism Quarterly.* Vol. 36 (1959), 183–188.

Lambert, R. "An Examination of the Consistency Characteristics of Abelson and Rosenberg's 'Symbolic Psycho-logic.'" *Behavioral Science,* Vol. 11 (1966), 126–130.

Mills, J. "Avoidance of Dissonant Information." *Journal of Personality and Social Psychology,* Vol. 2 (1965), 589–593.

Mills, J. "Interest in Supporting and Discrepant Information." In R. Abelson, E. Aronson, M. Rosenberg, and P. Tannenbaum (Eds.), *Theories of Cognitive Consistency: A Sourcebook.* Chicago: Rand McNally, 1968.

Osgood, C. "Cognitive Dynamics in the Conduct of Human Affairs," *Public Opinion Quarterly,* Vol. 24 (1960), 341–365.

———, and P. Tannenbaum. "The Principle of Congruity in the Prediction of Attitude Change." *Psychological Review,* Vol. 62 (1955), 42–55.

———, G. Suci, and P. Tannenbaum. *The Measurement of Meaning.* Urbana: University of Illinois Press, 1957.

Oshikawa, S. "Can Cognitive Dissonance Theory explain Consumer Behavior?" *Journal of Marketing,* Vol. 33 (1969), 44–49.

Price, K., E. Harburg, and T. Newcomb. "Psychological Balance in Situations of

Negative Interpersonal Attitudes." *Journal of Personality and Social Psychology,* Vol. 3 (1966), 265–270.

Rodrigues, A. "Effects of Balance, Positivity, and Agreement in Triadic Social Relations." *Journal of Personality and Social Psychology,* Vol. 5 (1967), 472–476.

Rosenberg, M. "Some Content Determinants of Intolerance for Attitudinal Inconsistency." In S. Tompkins and C. Izard (Eds.), *Effect, Cognition, and Personality.* New York: Springer, 1965.

———. "An Analysis of Affective-Cognitive Consistency." In C. Hovland and M. Rosenberg (Eds.), *Attitude Organization and Change.* New Haven: Yale University Press, 1960a.

———. "A Structural Theory of Attitude Dynamics." *Public Opinion Quarterly,* Vol. 24 (1960b), 319–340.

———. "Cognitive Structure and Attitudinal Affect." *Journal of Abnormal and Social Psychology.* Vol. 53 (1956), 367–372.

———, and R. Abelson. "An Analysis of Cognitive Balancing." In C. Hovland and M. Rosenberg (Eds.), *Attitude Organization and Change.* New Haven: Yale University Press, 1960.

Runkel, P., and D. Peizer. "The Two-Valued Orientation of Current Equilibrium Theory." *Behavioral Science,* Vol. 13 (1968), 56–65.

Sheth, J., and W. Talarzyk. "Perceived Instrumentality and Value Importance as Determinants of Attitudes." *Journal of Marketing Research,* Vol. 9 (1972), 6–9.

Straits, B. "The Pursuit of the Dissonant Consumer." *Journal of Marketing,* Vol. 28 (1964), 62–66.

Stroebe, W., V. Thompson, C. Insko, and S. Reisman. "Balance and Differentiation in the Evaluation of Linked Attitude Objects." *Journal of Personality and Social Psychology,* Vol. 16 (1970), 38–47.

Tannenbaum, P. "The Congruity Principle: Retrospective Reflections and Recent Research." In R. Abelson, E. Aronson, W. McGuire, T. Newcomb, M. Rosenberg, and P. Tannenbaum (Eds.), *Theories of Cognitive Consistency: A Sourcebook.* Chicago: Rand McNally, 1968.

———. "The Congruity Principle Revisited: Studies in the Reduction, Induction, and Generalization of Persuasion." In L. Berkowitz (Ed.), *Advances in Experimental Social Psychology,* Vol. 3. New York: Academic Press, 1967.

———. "Mediated Generalization of Attitude Change via the Principle of Congruity." *Journal of Personality and Social Psychology,* Vol. 3 (1966), 493–499.

———, J. Macaulay, and E. Norris. "Principle of Congruity and Reduction of Persuasion." *Journal of Personality and Social Psychology,* Vol. 3 (1966), 233–238.

Walster, E. "The Temporal Sequence of Postdecision Processes." In L. Festinger (Ed.), *Conflict, Decision, and Dissonance.* Stanford: University Press, 1964.

Zajonc, R., and E. Burnstein. "The Learning of Balanced and Unbalanced Social Structures." *Journal of Personality,* Vol. 33 (1965), 153–163.

Questions

1. Differentiate between balance theory, congruity theory, and dissonance theory. What commonalities do they have?
2. Explain some of the actions a consumer might take to reduce postpurchase cognitive dissonance.
3. According to dissonance theory, what changes tend to take place in the economic attitude toward a purchased product and the alternative products not purchased?

8. The Role of Consumer Knowledge in the Study of Consumer Behavior

James U. McNeal
Stephen W. McDaniel

We had recent occasion to investigate the marketing literature in an attempt to find information on consumer knowledge and its effect on consumer behavior. However, an examination of the *Journal of Marketing,* the *Journal of Marketing Research,* and the *Journal of Consumer Research* turned up only two articles (Due 1955; Goldman 1977) with the term knowledge in their titles. We were surprised, to say the least, that out of 267 issues of these three journals only two articles would clearly signal the reader that they were about consumer knowledge. We then proceeded to investigate this topic further in an attempt to discover how much was "out there" about consumer knowledge and why this very important topic was not a key word in marketing or consumer behavior literature.

First, before getting involved in the subject of consumer knowledge, let the record show that there are numerous articles related to consumer knowledge in the major marketing journals. However, there are only a few articles, perhaps only two (as of 1980), that employ the term knowledge in their titles. The reasons for this discrepancy—the numerous articles related to the subject of consumer knowledge and the few that use the term in their titles—is not clear and in fact is confusing. Let it also be stated now that the infrequent use of the term knowledge in the titles of marketing articles that concern themselves with consumer knowledge is deceiving to the student of consumer behavior. It suggests a lack of importance of the topic to marketers and consumerologists, when in fact there are few topics of more importance.

WHAT IS KNOWLEDGE AND CONSUMER KNOWLEDGE?

The question, "What is knowledge?" sounds like a title of a narration presented in a coffee house during the 1960s. This is because knowledge is a very general, widely used term. Knowledge is also a common subject of study, usually termed epistemology. It is a focal point of both scientists and philosophers.

We do not want to get entangled in either the science or the philosophy of knowledge. But we do need to put the term in perspective. An objective definition of knowledge is: Knowledge is fact that is verifiable. A subjective definition of knowledge is: Knowledge is acquaintance with and understanding of an object. While presented separately, the two definitions are not mutually exclusive. The objective definition refers mainly to those facts that exist that can be proven, documented, and passed on to others, knowing full well that, for a given time, they cannot be disputed. The statement $2 + 2 = 4$ is an objective unit of knowledge. The subjective definition of knowledge refers to those units of fact that an individual carries in his or her head.

To him they are facts, but they must be verified to be considered knowledge by others. If a person says, "I know where you can buy imported tea," we can verify it. If he can take us to a store that does sell imported tea, we can say that he has some knowledge of imported tea. If a person says, "I know there will be a recession in January," we recognize the statement as something less than fact because we know it cannot be verified—not, at least, until January.

It is the subjective definition that we are mainly concerned with, because we want to know something about what consumers know. We want to know, and be able to verify, what they know about stores, brands, products, prices, and so on. Technically, then, consumer knowledge is acquaintance with and understanding of objects relevant to the consumer role. We assume that the "acquaintance with" can be documented and the "understanding" can be verified. Ultimately, then, marketers are concerned with the units of verifiable facts—knowledge of (acquaintance with) and knowledge about (understanding)—possessed by consumers.

KNOWLEDGE AND OTHER TERMS

The main reason why consumer knowledge is not an apparent topic of marketing journals is that it is hidden in a web of other terms. Without becoming a semantic directory, a few of these terms will be addressed in order to provide some guideposts for exploring the concept of consumer knowledge. However, the introduction of these terms requires saying what they are and are not in relation to knowledge. It is understood that all may not agree entirely with some of these explanations. However, it is hoped that the close rela-tionship of consumer knowledge with each term might at least be recognized.

Some of the main terms under which knowledge may be discussed are (alphabetically):

Attitudes	Information
Attributes	Intentions
Awareness	Interests
Beliefs	Learning
Consciousness	Meanings
Decisions	Perceptions
Expectations	Preferences
Facts	Understanding

Of these sixteen terms, six—attitudes, beliefs, decisions, information, learning, and perceptions—disguise most articles concerned with consumer knowledge. The other ten are employed to a lesser extent. In discussing each of these terms, the less frequently used ten will be addressed first. More consideration will then be given to the six items more commonly related to knowledge in the marketing literature.

Attributes are characteristics of objects or, in the marketing sense, characteristics of products and brands. Marketers are particularly concerned with those attributes of products and brands that are most salient to consumers. For example, today, the salient attributes of cars for many consumers are probably price and gasoline mileage. Consumer knowledge of attributes—acquaintance with and understanding of certain attributes—is frequently discussed in papers on this subject.

Awareness is close in meaning to "acquaintance with." Consumer awareness of new brands, of certain advertisements, and so on is of concern to marketers. If marketers ask consumers, for example, about their awareness of price increases among certain products, they usually are asking them about their knowledge of price increases.

Consciousness is a concept studied by marketers that is very close in meaning to the notion of awareness. For example, researchers might be interested in the degree of price consciousness among consumers. In such a case, researchers will probably want to know the extent to which consumers think about price, how aware they are of price, and how concerned they are about prices. It is likely that knowledge of prices will be a factor in price consciousness.

Expectations about products and their performance are a major concern of marketers who study consumer satisfaction and dissatisfaction. Expectations usually refer to the performance attributes anticipated of a product before it is purchased. In order to have expectations, there must be knowledge of product features and performance. A consumer preparing to purchase a car might expect it to get at least thirty miles per gallon on the road. This expectation is probably based on some knowledge of the car. In fact, the more accurate the knowledge, the more likely the expectations will result.

Facts have already been presented as the essential unit of knowledge. Still, rather than referring to knowledge, researchers may refer to facts about stores or products possessed by consumers. For instance, in investigating consumer behavior of children, we might want to know the facts known by these children about stores and their operations.

Intentions among consumers consist of their planned consumer behavior. Do they intend to buy a microwave oven? If so, when? Studies of consumers' intentions often are concerned also with knowledge of product attributes such as price, finance charges, and various brands and sellers. Thus, we are likely to find information about consumer knowledge in studies of consumers' intentions.

Interests are essentially concerns about consumer objects. We may, for example, study consumers' interests in speculating in precious metals such as gold. We would expect that studies of consumers' interests would automatically display some of their knowledge about the objects of their interests.

Meanings, in terms of consumer behavior, usually refer to the units of information conveyed by an object such as a store name or brand name. A brand name might convey quality, high price, and prestige. Meanings usually, then, are not knowledge per se but do imply acquaintance with an object such as the brand name. If there is no knowledge of the brand name, there will be no meanings associated with it.

Preferences of consumers usually refer to their ranked choices among objects such as stores, brands, and products. Marketers commonly infer from consumer preferences which objects (brands, for example) among a choice of similar objects consumers will buy or want to own. Preferences are not knowledge, but are predicated on one having knowledge of several similar items. Preferences will not exist without knowledge of the objects preferred. Consequently, studies of consumers' preferences should contain some information about consumer knowledge.

Understanding is part of the definition of knowledge. Understanding implies one's interpretation of an object. It is knowledge to the extent it is verifiable. If a consumer has understanding of an advertising message, as an example, his interpretations of the message can be checked for accuracy. Marketers are very concerned with consumer understanding of advertising messages (i.e., did they understand what the advertisement was trying to convey?) and also with consumer understanding of the operation of products (i.e., do they understand how to use a hand-held calculator?). Thus, the term understanding may refer to one's capacity to comprehend a promotional message, or it may refer to one's knowledge of how to do something like solving a problem with the calculator. Consequently, understanding usually means knowledge.

We have shown that the above ten terms are related to knowledge and often mean knowledge. Articles about those topics in marketing journals can be expected to contain information about consumer knowledge. Now let us consider six more terms. It is these six terms that are the topics of many journal articles and also the topics under which we are likely to find substantial material about consumer knowledge.

Attitude

The term attitude is the subject of hundreds of marketing articles. Usually these are concerned with either measurement of attitudes or attitude change. The basic interest among marketing academicians and practitioners in consumer attitudes derives from the belief that attitudes determine much consumer behavior.

Knowledge and attitudes are intimately related in the literature because many consumer researchers subscribe to the notion that knowledge is a part of attitudes. Those theorists who view knowledge as a component of attitudes believe that attitudes consist of three components—knowledge and/or beliefs (the cognitive component); feelings (the affective component); and action tendencies (the conative component). Accordingly, attitudes are predispositions and are made up of three parts, one of which is knowledge.

Since nobody has ever seen an attitude first hand, it makes some sense to hypothesize knowledge as having an integral relationship with attitudes. It is unlikely that a person will

have action tendencies and feelings toward an object without having knowledge of that object, as well. This thinking, however, creates problems. Typically, when a person uses the term attitudes, he means feelings (affect) or action tendencies toward something (conations)—not knowledge. Contrarily, common use of the term knowledge does not include attitudes. Further, when researchers speak of attitude measurement or attitude change, they often do not intend to include knowledge. Thus, there is some conflict between common usage of the terms attitude and knowledge.

If we assume that knowledge is a component of attitude, it would appear that knowledge is the first component to form. As stated above, it is not likely that a person would have feelings or tendencies toward or away from an object until he or she knows something about it. Once a small amount of knowledge of an object is gained, however, we might expect the feelings and action tendencies that develop to determine the nature and extent of any more knowledge that is obtained.

It is regrettable that many consumer behavior theorists subsume knowledge under the concept of attitude, since the two terms often have virtually opposite meanings to the layman. Worse still, some theorists who view knowledge as a component of attitude also use the terms separately and in the same forms as the layman. Research about the concept of knowledge must give consideration to the numerous writings on attitudes.

Belief

The term belief is used in several ways. Often it is a term synonymously substituted for knowledge as a component of attitude. Other times, beliefs are viewed as "near-knowledge" in the sense of believing (or knowing) there is a God. Finally, the term belief is also used to refer to cultural persuasions, such as belief in ghosts of the dead.

The practice of substituting beliefs for knowledge is somewhat common but misleading. The intent is to describe all the judgments we have, such as believing that one brand is better than another or that one store is higher priced than another. These beliefs are knowledge only to the extent that they are verifiable. It would be less confusing to term the unverifiable judgments as attitudes. In any case, we should be aware that knowledge is frequently termed belief and that journal articles employing the term belief in their titles may actually be about knowledge.

Decision

There is a plethora of articles on consumer decisions and decision making. They are concerned with such major matters as the process by which consumer decisions are made, the degree of complexity in decision making, influences on decision making, and the person (husband or wife, for example) who makes consumer decisions.

Within the literature on consumer decisions are many comments and discussions about consumer knowledge. Many of the papers engage in such matters as the amount and kind of knowledge employed in consumer decision making.

Information

The term information is surely the most common term in the marketing literature that includes knowledge. A consumer's information about an object such as a new product, if documented, would embrace both knowledge and attitudes.

The concept of information processing is a major topic in marketing literature that deals with consumer knowledge. The notion of information processing is concerned with the knowledge (often termed cues or attributes) consumers seek, obtain, and store in memory, as well as the knowledge already stored in memory that assists in processing the new knowledge.

The student or teacher of consumer behavior who is interested in consumer knowledge should be alert to those articles about information and information processing. In most cases the term information is synonymous with knowledge.

Learning

A major topic of consumer behavior discussed frequently in the marketing literature is learning. How do consumers learn? How much do they learn? At what specific time do they learn? When do they modify their learning? These are common topics addressed in the literature and in the classroom. A logical object of learning is knowledge. Learning usually is viewed as the acquisition of attitudes and knowledge that cause changes in behavior. Thus, those papers about learning are usually about knowledge.

Perceptions

Perceptions are similar to information, although the term usually implies attitudes more than it does knowledge. A good synonym for perceptions, in addition to information, is meanings. One's perceptions of an object—for example, a brand—might be interpreted as the meanings the object conveys to the person. Thus, a certain brand of camera might convey such perceptions as high quality, high price, extensive warranty, and a camera for professional photographers.

Some of these perceptions may be knowledge, such as price.

KNOWLEDGE UNDERLIES MANY MAJOR THEORIES OF CONSUMER BEHAVIOR

Take practically any consumer behavior theory, strip away its semantic dressing, and you will find the concept of knowledge. That should be apparent from the preceeding remarks. In those we noted sixteen cognitive elements and activities frequently discussed in consumer behavior and marketing literature and showed that knowledge was basic to them all. Those sixteen items make up, or are directly related to, most theories of consumer behavior. At the expense of being redundant, let us amplify this point by mentioning some of the explanatory theories about consumer behavior and the role of knowledge in them.

Perceived Risk

This theory suggests that consumer behavior, mainly purchasing, produces uncertain outcomes and therefore is risky. There is uncertainty, or perceived risk, because the consumer does not have perfect knowledge. Risk can be reduced by increasing one's knowledge prior to a purchase or purchasing that item (among a choice of items) about which knowledge is the greatest.

Cognitive Dissonance

The essence of cognitive dissonance theory says that if a person knows two or more things that are inconsistent, he will experience a mind discomfort (dissonance) and will attempt to remove it. Probably the most common use of this theory has been to explain certain behaviors after a purchase. Because a purchase is usually a choice, a consumer knows something about what he purchased and something about the alternatives that he did not purchase. There may be dissonance (postpurchase cognitive dissonance) if one of the alternatives he did not purchase has an attribute not possessed by the item purchased. An attempt to reduce this postpurchase cognitive dissonance will be made that often takes the form of obtaining more knowledge about the item purchased. Thus, cognitive dissonance arises through conflicts in knowledge and is reduced by obtaining more knowledge.

Social Influence

A variety of social influence theories are intended to show that consumer behavior does not operate in a vacuum, that it is often a function of the influence of others. The influence of others, such as opinion leaders, is usually a function of their knowledge. Consumers who permit the influence of others often do so because of a lack of knowledge about purchase objects.

New Product Adoption

The various theories of new product adoption attempt to explain why and when new products and ideas are accepted. The basic reason why they are accepted is knowledge of their advantages over existing products. When they are accepted is a function of the knowledge a consumer has of the new product. Acceptance will not take place until enough knowledge of the new product has been accumulated to confirm its purchase as a wise choice according to the purchaser's choice criteria.

Self-concept

A person's self-concept consists of the attitudes and knowledge one holds of oneself as an object. It is theorized that much consumer behavior has as its goal the maintenance and enhancement of the self-concept. There are essentially two ways to achieve this goal—(1) to obtain knowledge of those products and brands that match the self-concept and purchase them and (2) to provide knowledge to others of one's self-concept by displaying various new purchases.

Decision Making

The notion of decision making was noted earlier. Theories about consumer decision making usually take two forms—(1) explaining the process of decision making and (2) explaining the factors affecting decision making. The essence of the consumer decision making process does not differ from any other decision making, such as that of a manager. It consists of experiencing a problem (perhaps a need), obtaining information (knowledge) about solutions to the problem, and making a choice. Thus, knowledge is the vehicle for decision making. Often it is noted that consumers do not have to make much effort to make decisions because of the good knowledge they have of purchase alternatives. Thus, much consumer decision making is routine. The factors affecting consumer decision making also are knowledge related—knowledge of the impact of the decision on others, on one's self-concept, and on one's economic and social status.

Attitude Formation and Change

It is theorized that as attitudes form or change, the objects of consumer behavior change. Consequently, marketers are concerned with influencing consumer attitude formation and change in such a way as to benefit themselves. The major means that marketers use to influence consumer attitude

development is information (knowledge). The assumption is that if enough information is presented to a consumer—for example, through advertising—the consumer will "change his mind." This theory can be explained by the following simple model:

Knowledge → Attitude → Behavior

Thus, knowledge (information) presented by the marketer will cause attitude formation or change, which in turn will cause consumer behavior in a direction favorable to the marketer.

Consumerism

Some consumer behaviorists might not view consumerism as a theory of consumer behavior, but as a social movement concerned with consumer welfare. Consumerism is, indeed, a social movement related to the well-being of consumers. But it is predicated, in great part, on the theory that if consumers possess good knowledge, they will make choices that best benefit them and advance their state of being. The current consumerism movement uses as its banner the late President Kennedy's "Consumer Bill of Rights." One of the main elements of the document is the consumer's right to know. Consequently, much consumerism effort is aimed at providing all consumers with more knowledge.

Need to Know

Finally, many consumer behavior theorists pose a need to know, to understand, or to have new experiences. This proposition is based on the theories of such noted behavioral scientists as Abraham Maslow, Henry Murray, David Berlyne, and Salvatore Maddi. The significance of such a theory is that knowledge for knowledge's sake is a major consumer matter. That is, in addition to the functions of knowledge noted in above paragraphs, knowledge is a requirement for total fulfillment. Thus, some consumer behavior, such as shopping ("looking around," "window shopping"), can be explained by the need to know—the need for new knowledge.

CONCLUSIONS

It is an unfortunate fact that the concept of knowledge is not conspicuous in marketing and consumer behavior literature. As shown in this paper, knowledge is a basic underpinning to most explanations of consumer behavior.

There seems to be no logical explanation for the scant use of the term knowledge in marketing writings. Perhaps it stems from the very nature of knowledge itself. It is such a basic, simplistic notion, and simplistic ideas often seem to be avoided in explanations of human behavior.

In any case, knowledge, as a concept, is fundamental to an understanding of consumer behavior. Perhaps this brief exposition of the subject will serve to highlight its significance and interrelationship with many commonly used terms and theories in consumer behavior.

REFERENCES

Due, Jean Mann. 1955 "Consumer Knowledge of Installment Credit Charges," *Journal of Marketing* 20 (October): 162–66.

Goldman, Arieh. 1977 "Consumer Knowledge of Food Prices as an Indicator of Shopping Effectiveness," *Journal of Marketing* 41 (October): 67–75.

Questions

1. Why is the term "knowledge" not prevalent in the titles of articles in the consumer behavior field?
2. Give a definition of knowledge.
3. Explain the relationship of knowledge to each of the following:
   a. Attributes
   b. Expectations
   c. Intentions
   d. Preferences
4. Explain how consumer knowledge is an integral part of each of the following aspects of consumer behavior:
   a. Cognitive dissonance
   b. New product adoption
   c. Decision making
   d. Consumerism

Part B

LEARNING

9. Applying Learning Principles to Marketing

Steuart Henderson Britt

When Vance Packard leveled his charges against "hidden persuaders" he really missed his chance.[1] His discussion of projective techniques and "unconscious" satisfactions implied that advertisers were applying mysterious psychological methods to make consumers mere puppets to be manipulated by string-pulling advertisers and advertising agencies.

Had Packard really wanted to shock his readers, he might have proposed that advertisers eventually could be using such intriguing procedures as *semantic generation* and *vicarious practice*. Then he could have made a dire prediction that such techniques could help promote certain brand names and create a zombie-like rush to the nearest supermarket.

Neither Packard nor most advertisers realize that learning theorists and experimentalists have contributed practical and testable methods of behavior-influence that are relevant to marketing communications. Although learning theories and the results of learning experiments certainly cannot explain all facets of personality and behavior, the contributions of several experimental psychologists have been significant. To concentrate only on motivational research alone, with fashionable discussions of "cognitive dissonance," is a mistake.

The criticism that most experimental investigations of learning are not comparable to real-world situations misses the point. As a significant example, consider the dichotomy between *intentional learning* and *incidental learning*.

This distinction is not simply academic. It has important implications, especially in the promotional aspects of marketing. Intentional learning occurs when an individual is set or "intent" to learn. This is the case when either he is instructed to learn some material, or is told that he will be tested on information that will be presented. Incidental learning is the complement of intentional learning and includes all other learning which occurs without the intention of the individual.

Obviously these two types include all learning. The degree of attention is a most important factor in differentiating intentional from incidental learning.[2] And meaningfulness is the key to intentional learning.[3]

What does this reveal to a business firm in promoting its products and services?

101

Most advertising messages are presented to people who either are doing something or relaxing. Usually the television viewer is relaxing before the screen; the radio listener is doing something else; the outdoor-poster viewer is interested in getting to his destination; the magazine or newspaper reader usually is not primarily searching out the advertisements. Thus, the audience members do not sense the advertisement with an intent to learn.

So, a model of intentional learning apparently does not apply—or does it? In some cases intentional learning *does* apply, regardless of the specific medium in which an advertisement is placed. In other words, a person may watch television passively, but suddenly he or she may begin to pay attention to a commercial for a certain product or service.

This type of situation is likely to occur when a consumer wants to purchase a product which could be classified as a "shopping good." If a person in the process of selection and purchase characteristically compares brands on such bases as suitability, quality, price, and style because he senses a benefit from such comparisons, an advertiser can expect a greater degree of intentional learning than otherwise.

The purchase is the result of price-comparing, store-visiting, and usually reading of relevant advertising. The conditions for intentional learning in experimental situations—that is, instructions or testing—may not be in existence, but the learning certainly is intentional.

SOME LEARNING CONCEPTS FOR MARKETERS

Although some of the concepts dealing with learning may be somewhat familiar to many marketing executives, others may be entirely new concepts.

Retroactive inhibition, proactive inhibition, and *transfer; semantic generation* and *semantic satiation; overlearning* and *response extinction; overexposure; incongruity; covert involvement* and *vicarious practice; predecisional timing; mental completing; reminiscence effect; perseveration;* and *"aha" experiences*—such phrases may sound strange, and perhaps even pedantic. But their applications can aid in creating more effective promotions for the business firm.

Inhibition and Transfer

Retroactive inhibition, proactive inhibition, and *transfer*—all of these learning phenomena deal with the learning and retention of learned associations.

In simple terms, *retroactive inhibition* refers to the loss of retention of the first of two items learned, following the learning of the second item. By learning the second item, an individual may impair his remembering of the first item. Retroactive inhibition occurs as a result of interference. With changes in the interfering messages, differing degrees of retention are found to occur. This interference or intervening activity, then, becomes the independent variable.

In advertising and selling, interference is inescapable; and retroactive inhibition must be considered as an expected effect following the learning of any message conveyed to the typical audience. Given this inevitable occurence of a memory loss due to retroactive inhibition, what suggestions can be given to the communicator in constructing messages to resist this factor?

First of all, this effect can dilute the impact of the campaigns for established brands. The degree to which the established brand does not have a distinctive and unambiguous brand image will affect the amount of retroactive inhibition. The first thing the communicator can strive for in order to alleviate retroactive inhibition is nonsimilarity between his message and other messages to which the audience may be exposed. He can increase emphasis on the most important parts of his message: in television commercials, for example, the emphasis can be on theme music, the product-use illustration, or the announcer's voice, in order to increase the degree of original learning. Repetition within a single message presentation will help to consolidate the remembering of any given point. It will lessen the chance that interfering material will later be confused with the original facts.

Retroactive inhibition has important implications for explaining the differences in promotion strategies for new-product innovations and established-product leaders. Thus, massed practice (number of repetitions per unit of time) represents the best strategy for an innovative product. Massed practice helps consumers to learn the new product concept quickly. If a distributed message strategy were used, consumers would be more vulnerable to retroactive effects.

Proactive inhibition also deals with impairing action involved when learning two items. In this situation, as contrasted with retroactive inhibition, it is the first item that inhibits the remembering of the second.

Either knowledge or attitudes acquired prior to the learning of any new message can be interfering. The presence of a certain amount of information learned in the immediate or distant past can be a negative influence on the degree to which new material may be absorbed. When there are many possible associations and notable similarities between the previously learned material and

the new information, the proactive inhibition will be greatest.

Proactive inhibition affects the reception of marketing communications by the consumer. The consumer's knowledge of standard products will decrease learning before the consumer becomes aware of the difference or differences in a new product. Here, too, massed-practice effects are desirable because promotion to the consumer must take place as rapidly as possible to overcome the confusion caused by proactive inhibition.

"Me-too" advertising—that is, advertising which has the same sales points and similar methods of presentation as the advertising of a competitive product—can be unsuccessful due to effects of proactive inhibition. That is, consumers will not remember a particular advertisement as being associated with a particular brand.

A positive *transfer* effect occurs when a new idea or item requires the same response as an item already familiar to an individual. That is, materials that repeat old stimuli and require essentially the same responses are learned more quickly than new materials.

Positive transfer will aid learning and remembering to the extent that elements being linked are familiar to the individual. The association is effective when it refers to a familiar idea or item, thus increasing the possibility of recalling previous attitudes and similar experiences.

Positive transfer can be used to help facilitate the learning of product characteristics. An advertisement may read, "The new automatic alarm clock is set in the same way as the old one." Similarity is drawn between the old and the new method of operation; the individual does not have to learn any new response to operate the clock.

In television commercials, demonstrations using "subjective camera angles," that is, where the camera shoots from over the demonstrator's shoulder, allow for positive transfer if the skill is familiar. This is especially beneficial if the product is new on the market.

Semantic Generation and Semantic Satiation

A word has meaning when its use as a stimulus evokes an associated response. Continued repetition of a meaningful word, however, sometimes can render the word less meaningful. This phenomenon is called *semantic satiation*.

On the other hand, continued repetition of a meaningless word sometimes generates increased meaning for the word. This process is called *semantic generation,* and implies that people create meanings or associate cognitive responses with meaningless words which are repeated.

To emphasize the contrast, semantic generation refers to the tendency of continued repetition of a word to increase the word's connotative meaning, whereas semantic satiation is the tendency for a word to lose its connotative meaning through repetition.

The more universal the meaning of a word, the more definite and precise is the associated response. For example, the word DOG has a definite cognitive response. The word GRONY has significantly less meaning because it does not evoke a cognitive response, or at least does not evoke a uniform cognitive response for audience members.

However, there is a second dimension to "meaning" of a word. Words can have affective (feeling) meanings which are emotionally rather than cognitively based. The word GRONY has little affective meaning, just as it has little cognitive meaning. As a result, GRONY is not considered a word at all—it is undefined, a nonword.

By contrast, the word LOVE produces an immediate affective (feeling) response. A distinctive and uniform emotional response is associated with the word and evoked when it is used as a stimulus.

"Meaningfulness" does not necessarily imply consistent meaning or the same associational value among different members of an audience. Rather, a word has meaning to each individual if it evokes any affective and/or cognitive response. Semantic generation and semantic satiation refer to changes in the strength and degree of ambiguity of associations to a word when it is a continuously exposed, repeated stimulus.

Obviously, semantic generation and semantic satiation effects are important considerations in the communication process. Since marketers choose words designed to elicit responses from consumers, they need to be aware of the semantic changes possible when certain words are repeated.

Use of a particular emphasized word, especially one coined for a particular campaign, can be subject to semantic generation as consumers are first exposed to the word. Continued exposure, however, may lead to satiation. This effect, in the more general sense of satiation of an entire advertisement, has been reported in one experimental investigation. This study,

> which measured variations in attention or interest, showed that repeated exposures of a TV commercial do generate a true satiation pattern—that is, attention does increase, pass through a maximum, and decline with increased exposure. This effect caused 'unlearning' or a 'subsequent decay' of previously acquired product knowledge. Though product knowledge and attention-interest declined with repeated exposure, studies of DuPont advertising showed no significant decline in product attitudes through satiation.[4]

The clearest implications of the generation-and-satiation phenomena are for any new word or concept created by marketers (1) to elicit a favorable, learned response from consumers; and (2) to have that response positively transferred to the advertised product or service. The word and its favorable meaning should be uniquely representative of the marketable good, or at least perceptibly different.

One example of successful use of semantic generation was an advertising campaign some years ago which involved use of the word "gusto" in talking about Schlitz beer. By repeating the word while making associative responses available to consumers through illustrations and other copy elements, a special meaning was generated; soon, almost everyone could give some definition of his own of what "gusto" meant to him.

Overexposure

Repetition of a message aids in learning and in reinforcing what has been learned. This is so because any single exposure to a message is likely to be too weak a cue, hardly enough to excite an individual's drives above the threshold level. Reinforcing a learned message through repetition is not harmful to the learning process; what is harmful is that increased or increasing repetition eventually can cause boredom, and thus interfere with learning and reinforcing.

Also, the repetition of identical messages beyond some critical point may lead to a negative response. Any message can be repeated too many times and can become overexposed.

The question to be answered, then, is: How many repetitions are appropriate before overexposure occurs? Although there is no simple answer, the answer depends to a considerable extent on whether repetition is being used to teach and improve learning, or to reinforce what already has been learned. The for-

mer situation calls for more repetition than the latter.

If one thinks of a message as a stimulus, learning occurs when the audience associates the stimulating message with a specific response. Repetition of the stimulus somewhat beyond the point of complete learning increases the associative strength of the stimulus, tending to make the response or learned association more resistant to extinction. Thus, overlearning, through repetition, and response extinction are inversely related.

Overlearning and Response Extinction

By overlearning a response, somewhat, an individual decreases the possibilities of that response being extinguished (provided semantic satiation has not resulted). He remembers longer what he learned. The "Wet and Wild" campaign for Seven-Up used the concept of overlearning. Consumers readily could perceive changes in the stimulus, such as different artists performing the theme song, by overlearning the basic "Wet and Wild" theme.

Each time a consumer purchases a brand, the stimulus-response pattern between the need for the product and selection of a particular brand is reinforced. Consumers recognize the product in the store, and they remember the commercials they have learned. With increased trials, the consumer overlearns the response in the process of buying his favorite brand.

Slight Incongruity

Elements of a message which are *slightly incongruous* create emphasis and increase retention. This occurs because elements of the message which do not seem to fit in with surrounding elements create a sort of "cognitive tension" in the audience members. To reduce this tension, they must interact mentally with the stimulus. Thus, incongruity aids both perceiving and learning.

For example, a corporate image promotion for electrical-systems control might include the headline, "The ABC Industry Makes Controls," and at the same time show a picture of an infant in a crib. The incongruous illustration can be explained in the copy, indicating that the controls include individual room thermostats, thus comforting the child. In other words, the reader may be motivated to read the copy and understand it in order to perceive the intended message.

Of course, illustration-incongruity can be misused. Examples are in the advertising of a product in no way related to women, but with the portrayal of a semi-nude female. The illustration may be so incongruous as to interfere with product-perceiving and learning. In such a case, the incongruity mistakenly becomes the focal point of the advertisement, rather than a technique for attracting the reader into a deeper perusal of the advertisement.

The point is that a slightly incongruous illustration or elements of a communication can attract readers, and can cause them to remember the product longer than otherwise.

Covert Involvement and Vicarious Practice

Additional methods of aiding learning and increasing the effectiveness of a promotion are the psychological techniques of *covert involvement* and *vicarious practice.*

Covert involvement has to do with internal responses to a stimulus. The marketer can try to involve the consumer mentally, to create empathy. The consumer may react emotionally to scenes of a beautiful mountain setting, or of an attractive young woman in a sports car. Covert involvement can imply a promise of reward that the individual desires, but which he may never experience in real life.

Closely associated with the concept of covert involvement is that of vicarious practice. An individual is covertly involved with an item to the extent that he vicariously practices its use.

Learning is strengthened by seeing the object in use, with a demonstration or explanation of its special features or benefits. In a TV commercial, for example, the demonstrator should relate to the actual consumer who might want the item.

Special benefits in the use of demonstrated items may be learned best through vicarious practice. This includes those tasks which consist of learning facts that may be observed without movement. A person may not be able actually to learn how to use a new type of razor by watching and imagining its use; but he may be more likely to learn of its greatest efficiency, or some other advantage, through vicarious practice. The point is to involve the consumer in a specific way.

Predecisional Timing

Everyone knows that timing is one of the most important elements in any promotional effort. *Predecisional timing* refers to an individual's probable actions before he has made a decision. He tends to ignore or discount attempts to teach him something which conflicts with his probable decision.

Predecisional timing is an advantage to the communicator who is able to get his message across first, before others do. This learning concept is applicable to marketing strategy, on the theory that the communicator who is able to get his advertising message across first, and in such a manner as to initiate a reaction on the part of the potential consumer, has a distinct advantage—namely, that of placing a mental obstacle in the path of competing strategies. It becomes difficult for some other communicator to get the consumer to learn the conflicting information.

Mental Completing

Mental completing refers to an individual's tendency to remember incomplete patterns better than completed ones. Figures such as the following tend to be perceived and remembered as complete patterns:

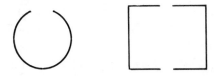

Recall of these figures as complete is known as *mental completing,* involving "mental closure."

Leaving incomplete a message with which the audience is involved can have powerful effects. One psychologist has suggested that

> much German propaganda (during World War II) was more skillful than that of the United States. In German films, hate was built up but the enemy was not killed at the end, while American films showed the happy ending with Nazis or Japanese eliminated—leaving no action to be taken.[5]

In addition to enhancing recall of unfinished tasks and incomplete stimuli, anxiety might account for recall of incomplete stimuli as if they were complete. Just as one "waits for the other shoe to drop," slight anxiety is produced by incomplete stimulus patterns. In an effort to reduce the anxiety, originally incomplete stimulus patterns are remembered as complete.

An outstanding example of advertising that benefited from closure or mental completing was the campaign for Salem cigarettes. Salem radio and television commercials were built around the jingle "You can take Salem out of the country . . . but you can't take the country out of Salem." The jingle was played one and one-half times; but on the second round, the silence following "You can take Salem out of the country, but. . . " invited the listener mentally to complete the message.

Reminiscence Effect

Under certain conditions it is possible that changes in attitude produced by a communication may be greater after a delay than immediately after exposure to the communication. There also is some evidence of a *reminiscence effect*—that is, that after a period of nonpractice of something learned, without intervening overt practice, there may be an actual gain in recall.

If there is sound evidence for the reminiscence effect, then a marketing campaign would be more likely to be more effective if spaced over a period of months, rather than concentrated within one or two weeks.

Certainly the spacing of messages over a longer time, and allowing consumers rest periods where reminiscence might take place after the incomplete learning of previous messages, is well worth consideration.

Perseveration

The word *perseveration* is not to be confused with the word *perseverence. Perseveration* refers to the *re-*emergence of communicated messages to the conscious state after a period of absence. It is seemingly a spontaneous reappearance of the learned material.

Perseveration is concerned with unintentional recall, bringing an idea into consciousness with no apparent stimuli. Thus, perseveration is the tendency for an idea to reoccur spontaneously for some time after its original stimulation.

Promotional campaigns which attempt to gain greater recall through high frequency can be aided if the message occasionally can come into consciousness without the stimulus of any promotion. As to what strategy might help perseveration to occur, there are two possibilities. (1) Perseveration is most likely to occur after an activity which *interested* or *excited* the learner. (2) Perseveration is greater if *relaxation* follows the learning situation.

A brand's musical slogan "running through one's head" might be explained by perseveration; it seems to have been advantageous in musical themes for Coca-Cola, Pepsi, United Airlines, and Salem. Slogans such as "I'd walk a mile for a Camel" also may be placed in this category.

"Aha" Experiences

An *"aha" experience* usually occurs in a problem-solving situation for which there is one correct response. It can be something as simple as the discovery of a phone number—"Now, what was Joe's number? 866–9615? Aha! I just remember—it is 866–6915!" Or, "What is Gregg's wife's name? Tricia? Roberta? Aha! I know it's Joyce!"

The discovery in an "aha" experience is the result of a trial-and-error method in which the person attempting to solve the problem emits the most obvious response. This process continues until he finds the correct solution; and when he does, he feels as though he has "hit upon it."

The "aha" principle may be applied to unplanned purchasing. Consider, for exam-

ple, various concepts of impulse buying.[6] At least two concepts can be associated with an "aha" experience. They are:

- *Reminder impulse buying.* This occurs when a shopper sees an item and remembers that he needs it at home, or remembers information about the product and a previous decision to buy.
- *Suggestion impulse buying.* This occurs when a shopper sees an item for the first time and visualizes a need for it, even though there was no previous knowledge of the item.

An "aha" experience has happened to many people while shopping. Sometimes a person will go shopping with the intention to buy, but without knowing exactly what he is going to buy; this happens with birthday gifts, at Father's Day, Mother's Day, and at Christmas, for example.

Bearing in mind the importance of an "aha" experience, the marketer will do well to structure his messages around a reminder-impulse or suggestion-impulse situation. A woman "discovering" a certain brand as the solution to one of her problems would reflect such an experience.

LEARNING OR PERFORMANCE?

Marketing communications should reflect certain principles of learning if they are to stimulate consumer behavior effectively. For buying behavior to occur, the customer ought to learn the central meaning or benefits of the marketing message.

However, if we test consumers on their ability to recall such facts as slogans or brand names, we may mistakenly be measuring performance rather than learning.

Both recall tests and recognition tests of

various advertisements, campaign themes, slogans, and brand names have been used to show that "learning" has taken place in the minds of consumers. Certainly learning has taken place. But what has been learned —facts about the product? If so, have these facts been learned so well that they can be recalled in situations where they are independent of the advertising message?

In other words, has the message been learned so as to be capable of affecting actual behavior, such as making a purchase? Most consumers are more interested in learning about an actual product or service than in rote memorizing of what advertisers refer to as "copy points."

Much of the psychological literature on learning—especially that dealing with topics such as *vicarious practice, reminiscence,* and *perseveration*—involves testing of improvement in "performance." But performance should not be confused with the concept of learning itself.

ENDNOTES

The basic idea of this article was suggested some time ago by Thomas A. Moore, then a student at Northwestern University and today an account executive at Meldrum and Fewsmith, Inc., Cleveland advertising agency.

1. Vance Packard, *The Hidden Persuaders* (New York: D. McKay Company, 1957).
2. Frank W. Schneider and B. L. Kintz, "An Analysis of the Incidental-Intentional Learning Dichotomy," *Journal of Experimental Psychology,* January 1967, pp. 85–90, at p. 89.
3. Arnold Mechanic, "The Distribution of Recalled Items in Simultaneous, Intentional, and Incidental Learning," *Journal of Experimental Psychology,* June 1962, pp. 593–600, at p. 600.
4. Robert C. Grass, "Satiation Effects of Advertising," speech to the Advertising Research Foundation, 15 October, 1968; published in *14th Annual Conference Proceedings* (New York: Advertising Research Foundation, 1968).
5. Ernest Dichter, *Findings,* vol. 3 (Institute of Motivation Research, August 1967), at p. 3.
6. Hawkins Stern, "The Significance of Impulse Buying Today," *Journal of Marketing,* April 1962, pp. 59–62.

Questions

1. Differentiate between proactive and retroactive inhibition and tell how an advertiser might prevent both from taking place.
2. Would a marketer hope to achieve semantic generation or semantic satiation? Give examples of how both might occur.
3. Explain why a "slightly" incongruous advertisement is probably more likely to get the reader's interest than a "highly" incongruous advertisement.
4. Describe how an advertiser might use each of the following principles in his advertising campaign:
   a. Convert involvements
   b. Mental completing
   c. Reminiscence effect

10. How Advertising Can Use Psychology's Rules of Learning

Steuart Henderson Britt

Most advertising men don't realize it, but their work requires them to use psychological principles of learning. Both advertising men and psychologists want to know more about people's minds.

Every time an advertisement or commercial appears, the objective is to have the reader or viewer *learn* something . . . and *remember* what he learned.

In other words, whether advertising men are aware of it or not, they constantly employ psychological principles. And when psychologists pin down additional facts about learning, they may be making contributions to advertising.

This article presents 20 principles of learning which have been established experimentally by psychologists, and which have practical applications for advertising men. While some of these principles may have been followed by more experienced advertising people, others may be new to them. And all the principles should prove useful to advertising practitioners.

1. Unpleasant things may sometimes be learned as readily as pleasant things, but the most ineffective stimuli are those which arouse little or no emotional response.

The application is that it is better to have rewarding conditions than unpleasant conditions, but either is preferable to learning under neutral conditions. The annoying radio or TV commercial works, but not as well as a message which gives the audience a promise of a rewarding experience.

The closer the actual rewarding experience is to the presentation of the message, the more likely it is to be remembered. Thus, the procedure of giving out samples at the point of purchase is a good one, providing the proper advertising message is used at the time.

2. The capacities of learners are important in determining what can be learned and how long it will take.

The implication of this principle is that *advertisers should know their audience*. Bright people can grasp a complex message that is over the heads of less bright ones. And they grasp the significance of a simple message in less time.

The ability to learn changes with age. For most people, ability to learn reaches a peak around 16 years of age, then begins to decline steadily. Consequently, an advertiser should know his market and be more patient if he is trying to reach an older audience, or one of lower intelligence.

3. Things that are learned and understood tend to be better retained than things learned by rote.

Mere repetition of ads is of no great value unless the message is understood by the people who see and hear it. It must be remembered, however, that extensive drill is still very important in getting facts across. For example, LS/MFT *can* be put across, but only by an enormous expenditure of money. Experimental evidence indicates that understanding contributes more to remembering than merely frequent repetition.

4. Practice distributed over several periods is more economical in learning than the same amount of practice concentrated into a single period.

In planning a campaign, the prospects should usually be exposed to the advertising over a relatively long period. Brief, concentrated, and temporary high pressure campaigns should be avoided, except in exceptional circumstances, such as making a favorable impression on channels of distribution. Thus, a campaign would probably be more effective if spaced over a period of months rather than concentrated in one week.

5. When teaching people to master mechanical skills, it is better to show the performance in the same way that the learner would see it if he were doing the job himself.

For example, in a TV commercial in which a sequence of acts is being demonstrated which you want the viewers to repeat, it may be better to employ "subjective camera angle," that is, place the camera so it is shooting over the demonstrator's shoulder.

In this way the viewers can see the demonstration in the same way they would see it if they were doing it themselves. This is somewhat comparable to writing copy from the "you" attitude.

6. The order of presentation of materials to be learned is very important.

Points presented at the beginning and end of the message are remembered better than those in the middle. Thus, if 4 reasons "why" are given in a series of copy, the 2 most important points should be given first and last.

7. If material to be learned is different, or unique, it will be better remembered.

An outdoor poster may be better recalled if it stands alone than if it is one of a group. If a magazine contained *nothing but* 4-color advertisements, a black-and-white one might get greater attention value than another color one, just because of the uniqueness. Likewise, a TV or radio commercial employing unusual sounds tends to stand out. The "man in the Hathaway shirt" will be long remembered as the first model who wore an eye patch.

8. Showing errors in how to do something can lead to increases in learning.

The effectiveness of a demonstration on television might be increased by showing not only "*what to do*" but "*what not to do.*" Thus, to show how not to use a product and also how to use a product may be very useful. In print advertising, Sanforized has done an outstanding job of showing the shrunken garments that are not Sanforized.

9. Learning situations which are rewarded only occasionally can be more efficient than those where constant reward is employed.

For example, it is more efficient to employ deals or premiums over fairly short periods rather than over extended periods. The reason is that short-time deals are looked upon as some sort of bonus, whereas extended deals come to be expected, and consumers feel cheated if they are cut out. There is likely to be more brand switching away from a product after an extended deal than after a temporary one.

10. It is easier to recognize something than it is to recall it.

The application is obvious. Make the name of your product . . . your package . . . and your sales message easy to recognize. A fine example is the detergent *all* for automatic washing machines. Its distinctive type face stands out in both advertising and packaging.

11. The rate of forgetting tends to be very rapid immediately after learning.

Accordingly, the *continuing repetition of the advertising message is desirable*. It usually takes a lot of advertising in the early weeks of a campaign to overcome rapid forgetting. In fact, it takes a lot of advertising all the time, since the advertising by competitors helps people to forget your product.

12. Messages attributed to persons held in high esteem influence change in opinion more than messages from persons not so well-known, but after several weeks both messages seem equally effective.

The implication for advertising is that it is not essential to employ high-priced, well-known talent in testimonials if you are trying to build a long-range favorable climate for your product. The use of less well-known people should also prove effective and less expensive.

13. Repetition of identical materials is often as effective in getting things remembered as repeating the same story but with variations.

Psychologists term this *identical* vs. *varied* repetition. Using training films, they have failed to find significant differences in learning, after employing a lot of different examples *versus* repeating the same few over again. The implication is that exactly the same advertisements can be run over and over again, with real sales effectiveness each time.

14. In a learning situation, a moderate fear appeal is more effective than a strong fear appeal.

This means that a fear appeal that is too strong is likely to lead to a rejection of the whole sales message.

To take a far-fetched example, it would be poor strategy for a cigarette manufacturer to claim that he now uses treated tobaccos that prevent cancer. The mere association of cancer with smoking may set up a fear that is so strong as to lead to a rejection of the whole sales message.

15. Knowledge of results leads to increases in learning.

If you are interested in teaching a given amount of material to people, knowledge of how well they are doing as they are learning leads to greater learning gains. Advertisers should use this principle, by telling the consumer what specific benefits he will get from the product or service advertised.

16. Learning is aided by active practice rather than passive reception.

This point is of great importance to advertisers. If you can get your audience members to "participate" in your sales message, they are much more likely to remember your brand.

Participation can be accomplished in a number of ways. Get consumers to repeat key phrases, fill in coupons, or even make puns about the brand name. Whatever you do, get the audience to take part in the sales message. Contests with "I like ——— because" tend to put people in a buying mood.

17. A message is more easily learned and accepted if it does not interfere with earlier habits.

Thus, a sales theme which draws upon prior experiences of the audience will help the learning of the sales message. Recent examples are the new uses of aluminum foil, which show how familiar jobs may be done *better* rather than how familiar jobs may be done *differently*.

18. The mere repetition of a situation does not necessarily lead to learning. Two things are necessary—"belongingness," and "satisfiers."

Belongingness means that the elements to be learned must seem to belong together, must show some form of relationship or sequence. As an example, it is easier to learn 2, 4, 6, 8,

10, which seem to belong together, than to learn 2, 1, 4, 7, 43, which do not.

Satisfiers are real or symbolic rewards, as distinguished from annoying consequences that may be present in the learning process. In many learning experiments, it has been demonstrated that merely to say the word "right" when the person is making the correct response is a satisfier and helps to speed up the learning process. To say the word "wrong" is an annoyer or "punishment" and is relatively less effective.

Because of the importance of belongingness and of satisfiers, a good deal of advertising could gain in effectiveness if more attention were paid to the organic unity of the total advertising message (belongingness), and also the element of reward or consumer benefits (satisfiers).

> 19. When two ideas are of equal strength but of unequal age, new repetition increases the strength of the earlier idea more than that of the newer idea.

By the same token, if there are two ideas of the same strength but of unequal age, the older idea will not be forgotten as rapidly as the newer idea.

The application to various brands of merchandise is obvious. For instance, if there are two different brands—one older and one newer—which have equal association with a product, and if both brands are given the same amount of advertising, the older brand will probably benefit more from the advertising than the newer brand. Similarly, the older brand will not be forgotten to as great an extent as the newer brand.

> 20. Learning something new can interfere with the remembering of something learned earlier.

Psychologists refer to this as retroactive inhibition. As a hypothetical case, if you study French for an hour and then study Italian for an hour, your ability to recall the French will probably be less than it would have been had you substituted an hour's interval of rest in place of the hour's study of Italian.

There are many applications of the principles of retroactive inhibition to advertising. Suppose that a person has been looking at a one-hour television show, sponsored by just one advertiser. He is much more likely to remember that sponsor and his advertising message than in the situation where there is multiple sponsorship. The later commercial or commercials tend to interfere with the remembrance of the earlier commercial. The more similar the later commercials are to the earlier ones, the greater is the interference. That is why it is poor practice to have similar products advertised on shows which are too close together.

We should not just blindly apply every one of these principles to the field of advertising. However, we can point out certain applications that these principles suggest to the advertising practitioner.

After all, individuals exposed to advertising and people used in learning experiments are much the same kind of people; and all are reacting to materials that someone wants them to learn.

Questions

1. Describe several of the learning principles cited in the article. Give their implications for advertising.

2. In a certain television advertisement aimed at a middle class female teenage market segment, the advertiser uses a well-known talent to demonstrate the best way of using a new cosmetic. The demonstration follows the sequence of the process with particular repetitions or stresses and stops without showing the final results of using the product. Using some of the learning principles described by Britt, describe how the advertiser could improve the effectiveness of this advertisement.

3. For each of the following, tell whether or not an advertiser should use that technique for his advertising message:

   a. A strong appeal to fear
   b. Repeat key points of the message
   c. Place the key point in the middle of a television ad
   d. Show examples of people using your product incorrectly
   e. Use as spokesman for the ad a person held in high esteem by the audience

11.   A Behavior Modification Perspective on Marketing

Walter R. Nord
J. Paul Peter

Students of marketing have borrowed freely from many areas of psychology. For example, cognitive psychology, need satisfaction models, field theory, psychoanalytic theory, and stimulus-response theory have all provided useful insights for understanding and predicting consumer behavior. However, marketing scholars have given little consideration to one of the most influential perspectives developed in psychology in the last 40 years—the behavior modification approach stimulated by the work of B. F. Skinner[1] (e.g., 1953, 1969). The purpose of this paper is to provide an overview of the Behavior Modification Perspective (BMP) which has evolved from the work of Skinner and others and investigate its applicability to marketing.

FUNDAMENTAL ELEMENTS OF BEHAVIOR MODIFICATION

There is an important basic difference between the BMP and the psychological

[1] Some psychologists consider Skinner and his followers to be S-R theorists. While there are important similarities, the differences are significant enough that leading psychologists consider Skinner's work separately from their treatment of S-R theory (see Hall and Lindzey, 1970).

perspectives which currently dominate the marketing literature: *the BMP focuses on environmental factors which influence behavior.* It takes the prediction and control of behavior as problematic and deliberately shuns speculation about processes which are assumed to occur within the individual such as needs, motives, attitudes, information processing, etc. In fact, the so-called radical behaviorists reject the value of considering these internal processes at all. Our approach is far less radical and more consistent with the social learning theories of Bandura (1978) and Staats (1975). We believe that it is useful and desirable to theorize about and investigate internal, psychological processes which affect behavior. However, we maintain that many marketing objectives can be (and in fact have been) accomplished without such theories by simply studying environmental conditions and manipulating them to influence consumer behavior. The BMP provides the stimulus and technology for systematizing this external focus.

Frequently, treatments of behavior modification are limited to two types of environmental manipulations—those which result in respondent (classical) conditioning and those which produce operant (instrumental) conditioning.[2] This treatment of behavior modification will include these manipulations as well as those which alter behavior through vicarious learning and ecological design.

A review of the literature revealed that these four ways of modifying behavior have been given little systematic attention in marketing. While respondent conditioning has been discussed at length in the marketing

literature in an attempt to explain behavior, it has not been discussed as a method of modifying or controlling behavior. Operant conditioning has been discussed (e.g., Carey et al. 1976; Engel, Kollat, and Blackwell 1973; Kassarjian 1978; Ray 1973) but has not been integrated into the mainstream of marketing thinking. Treatment of vicarious learning and ecological design is almost totally absent.[3] As a result many students of marketing are apt to be unfamiliar with these processes. Therefore, all four will be described in some detail.

Respondent Conditioning

Respondents are a class of behaviors which are under the control of stimuli which precede them. Generally, these behaviors are assumed to be governed by the autonomic nervous system and, therefore, are not susceptible to conscious control by the individual. Pavlov's classical conditioning experiments provide the basic paradigm for this approach.

In general, respondent conditioning can be defined as a process through which a previously neutral stimulus, by being paired with an unconditioned stimulus, comes to elicit a response very similar to the response originally elicited by the unconditioned stimulus. It is well established that a variety of human behaviors including reflexes, glandular responses, and what are often called "emotions" can be modified through the process of respondent conditioning.[4] For example, when a new product for which people have neutral feelings is repeatedly advertised

---

[2] It has been argued that respondent and operant conditioning may not be as separable processes as previously thought. For a discussion of this point, see Miller (1969). However, for present purposes they will be treated as conceptually distinct.

[3] However, Kotler's (1976, p. 324) notion of atmospherics as well as several of Belk's (1974, 1975) situational influences, e.g., physical and social surroundings, are fully consistent with the principles of ecological design (and respondent conditioning).

[4] Miller (1969) has demonstrated that these behaviors can also be conditioned by stimuli which occur after them.

during exciting sports events, it is possible for the product to eventually generate excitement on its own solely through the repeated pairing with the exciting events. Similarly, an unknown political candidate may come to elicit patriotic feelings in voters simply by having patriotic music constantly played in the background of his/her political commercials.

Since it is a process which can account for many of the responses which environmental stimuli elicit from individuals, respondent conditioning has a number of important implications for marketing. Through it, a particular stimulus can come to evoke positive, negative, or neutral feelings. Consequently, respondent conditioning influences whether a wide variety of objects or events are those which an individual will work to obtain, to avoid, or be indifferent to.

At this point, it should be clear that what the BMP views as respondent conditioning can account for many of the reactions to stimuli which have also been accounted for by cognitive or affective models. We are not saying that the BMP view is incompatible with these traditional concerns or that it is a perfect substitute for such models. However, these traditional concerns have led marketing scholars to accept models and to design research in which internal psychological processes are focal and assumed to be "causal." As a result, the role of external events has received insufficient attention. Respondent conditioning and other elements of the BMP focus on the manipulation of external factors and it is clear that consumer behavior can be influenced through this external emphasis without a complete psychology of internal processes.[5]

Consider a product or product-related stimulus. External stimuli which elicit positive emotions can be paired with the product in ways which result in the product itself eliciting positive effect. Consequently, behavior may be triggered which brings the potential consumer into "closer contact" with the product.[6] Similarly, stimuli may be presented which produce certain general emotional responses such as relaxation, excitement, nostalgia, or some other emotion which is likely to increase the probability of some desired response such as product purchase. Note, while it may be useful to obtain verbal reports or physiological measures in deciding what stimuli to employ to elicit such emotions, the BMP bypasses these procedures and focuses directly on ways to modify behavior. While a number of psychological theories could be used to account for these processes, behavior can be modified without such theories. In fact, it seems clear that the actions of practitioners often follow this atheoretical approach.

Consider the following examples. Radio

---

[5] There are three basic ways by which researchers attempt to determine what properties certain stimuli have for people. One way is through verbal reports. A second method may be termed projection whereby the investigator infers the properties from his/her observations of another person's behavior. A third means can be termed empirical. This involves presentation of a stimulus and description of its consequences. Of course, these three are often used in combination. The BMP encourages marketers not to discount the advantages of the empirical approach.

[6] "Closer contact" refers to a general relationship between a person's behavior and a given stimulus (e.g., a product). For example, if a product elicits positive effect, an individual exposed to the product is more apt to move towards it than if negative emotions are elicited. Attending behavior is also apt to be a function of respondently conditioned effect. Stimuli which elicit stronger emotional responses (either positive or negative) are, at least over a considerable range, apt to receive more attention from an individual than are stimuli which are affectively neutral. To the degree that attending behavior is necessary for product purchase or other product-related behavior, respondent conditioning influences product contact.

and television advertisements often use famous sportscasters whose voices have been paired for years with exciting sports events. These voices elicit excitement as a result of this frequent pairing. Repeated pairings of the voices with the advertised product can result, via higher-order respondent conditioning, in feelings of excitement associated with the product. Music, sexy voices and bodies, and other stimuli are used in similar ways. Often these stimuli may influence behavior without this "higher order conditioning" simply by drawing attention to the ad. Of course, the attention generating properties of the stimulus itself are apt to have developed through previous conditioning which occurs "naturally" in society. The use of telephones ringing or sirens in the background of radio and television ads, some legal version of the phrase "news bulletin," and the presence of famous celebrities, are common examples of how stimuli, which are irrelevant to the content of an ad or the function of the product, are used to increase attention to the ad itself. In this sense, one of the major resources that organizations use to market their products is made available through previous respondent conditioning of members of society.

Stimuli at or near the point of purchase also serve the goals of marketers through their ability to elicit respondent behaviors. Christmas music in a toy department is a good example. Although no data are available to support the point, we suspect that Christmas carols are useful in eliciting the emotions labeled as the "Christmas spirit." Once these feelings have been elicited, we suspect (and retailers seem to share our expectations) that people are more apt to purchase a potential gift for a loved one. In other words, Christmas carols are useful in generating emotions which are incompatible with "sales resistance."

These examples can serve as a basis for several generalizations about the role of respondent conditioning as a marketing tool. First, the concept of respondent conditioning directs attention to the presentation of stimuli which, due to previous conditioning, elicit certain feelings in the potential consumer. Sometimes (as with Christmas music) these stimuli trigger certain emotions which are apt to increase the probability of certain desired behaviors or reduce the probability of undesired responses. Second, in many cases the marketer may find it useful to actually condition responses to stimuli. For example, as with the voices of famous sportscasters, it may be desirable to pair the stimuli with the product repeatedly in order to condition the feelings elicited by a particular stimulus to the product. Then, the product itself may stimulate similar reactions. Finally, some of the benefits which can be gained from employing the principles of respondent conditioning have already been used by marketing practitioners in an (apparently) ad hoc manner. While the systematic application of the respondent paradigm is unlikely to result in any new principles, by calling attention to the actual control process being employed, it is apt to yield a number of practical benefits both to advertising and to point of purchase promotion. In particular, stimuli are apt to be arranged in ways which are more effective in eliciting desired emotional responses. Thus, the primary benefit of respondent conditioning, as with other elements of the BMP, is that it encourages the systematic analysis of purchase and purchase-related behaviors and indicates specific techniques for modifying and controlling these behaviors.

Operant Conditioning

Operant conditioning differs from respondent conditioning in at least two important ways. First, whereas respondent conditioning is concerned with involuntary responses, operant conditioning deals with behaviors which are usually assumed to be under the conscious control of the individual. Second, respondent behaviors are elicited by stimuli which occur prior to the response; operants are conditioned by consequences which occur *after* the behavior.

In any given situation, at any given time, there is a certain probability that an individual will emit a particular behavior. If all of the possible behaviors are arranged in descending order of probability of occurrence, the result is a response hierarchy. Operant conditioning has occurred when the probability that an individual will emit one or more behaviors is altered by changing the events or consequences which follow the particular behavior. Some events or consequences increase the frequency that a given behavior is likely to be repeated. For example, a cash rebate given at the time of purchase increases the probability that a shopper will purchase in the same store in the future, other things being equal. In this case, since the cash rebate has the effect of increasing the probability of the preceding behavior, it is referred to as a positive reinforcer. In other cases, the frequency of a given behavior can be increased by removing an aversive stimulus. This is called negative reinforcement. Although there are few examples of negative reinforcement in marketing, one illustration is the situation where a consumer purchases a product primarily to avoid the high pressure tactics of an overzealous salesperson.

Sometimes operant techniques are used to decrease the probability of a response. If the environment is arranged so that the particular response results in neutral consequences, over a period of time that response will diminish in frequency. This process is referred to as extinction. If the response is followed by a noxious or "undesired" result, the frequency of

the response is likely to decrease. The term punishment is usually used to describe this process.[7]

In addition to these general procedures, there are a number of other principles of operant conditioning. (For a rather complete description of these possibilities, Honig 1966 and Staats 1975 are recommended.) However, there are three concepts which deserve specific mention: reinforcement schedules, shaping, and discriminative stimuli.

Reinforcement Schedules. A number of different schedules of reinforcement can be employed. For example, it is possible to arrange conditions where a positive reinforcer is administered after: (1) every desired behavior, (2) every second desired behavior, etc. When every occurrence of the behavior is reinforced, a continuous schedule of reinforcement is being employed. When every second, third, tenth, etc. response is reinforced, a fixed ratio schedule is being used. Similarly, it is possible to have a reinforcer follow a desired consequence on average one-half, one-third, one-fourth, etc. of the time, but not every second time or third time, etc. Such a schedule is called a variable ratio schedule.

The ratio schedules are of particular interest because they produce high rates of behavior which are reasonably resistant to extinction. Gambling devices are good examples. Slot machines are very effective in producing high rates of response, even under conditions which often result in substantial financial losses. This property of the ratio schedule is particularly important for mar-

[7] In this paper, we will focus primarily on the use of positive reinforcement. We are making this choice for two reasons. First, we personally do not believe that aversive consequences should be used to sell products. Second, it is unlikely that the use of aversive consequences to sell products is generally practical in the current socioeconomic system even if organizations were predisposed to use them.

keters because it suggests how a great deal of desired behavior can be developed and maintained for relatively small, infrequent rewards. For example, Deslauriers and Eberett (1977) found that by giving small rewards for riding a bus on a variable ratio schedule, the same amount of bus riding could be obtained as when rewards were given on a continuous schedule. Thus, for approximately one-third the cost of the continuous schedule, the same amounts of behavior were sustained.[8]

Numerous other examples of the use of the variable ratio schedule can be found in marketing practice. Lotteries, door prizes, and other tactics whereby individuals are asked to respond in a certain way to be eligible for a prize are common examples (when the prize is assigned by chance).

Shaping. Another concept from the operant tradition which has important implications for marketing is "shaping." Shaping is important because given an individual's existing response hierarchy, the probability that he/she will make a particular desired response may be very small. In general, shaping involves a process of arranging conditions which change the probabilities of certain behaviors not as ends in themselves, but to increase the probabilities of other behaviors. Usually, shaping involves the positive reinforcement of successive approximations of the desired behavior or of behaviors which must be performed before the desired response can be emitted.

Many firms already employ marketing activities which are roughly analogous to shap-

ing. For example, loss leaders and other special deals are used as rewards for individuals coming to a store. Once customers are in the store, the probability that they will make some other response such as purchasing other full-priced items is much greater than when they are not in the store. Also, shopping centers or auto dealers who put carnivals in their parking lots may be viewed as attempting to shape behavior. Similarly, free trial periods may be employed to make it more likely that the user will have contact with the product so that he/she can experience the product's reinforcing properties.

Discriminative Stimuli. It is important to distinguish between the reinforcement and discriminative functions played by stimuli in the operant model. In our treatment of respondent conditioning, we noted that a stimulus can act as a reinforcer or can function to trigger certain emotions or other behaviors. So far in this section, the focus has been on the reinforcing function. However, the mere presence or absence of a stimulus can serve to change the probabilities of behavior; such stimuli are called discriminative stimuli.

Many marketing stimuli are of a discriminative nature. Store signs (e.g., "50% off sale") and store logos (e.g., K-Mart's big red "K") or distinctive brandmarks (e.g., the Levi tag) are good examples. Previous experiences have perhaps taught the customer that purchase behavior will be rewarded when the distinctive symbol is present and not rewarded when the symbol is absent. Here then is yet another parallel between the principles of behavior modification and common marketing practice.

Vicarious Learning

Vicarious learning (or modeling) refers to a process which attempts to change behavior by having an individual observe the actions of

---

[8] There are a number of other possible reinforcement schedules. However, we will limit our attention to continuous and ratio schedules. Also we will not deal with the consequences that the different schedules have on the pattern, rate, and maintenance of behavior. For a detailed treatment of these effects, Honig (1966) is recommended.

others (i.e., models) and the consequences of those behaviors.

According to Bandura (1969) there are three major types of vicarious learning or modeling influences. First, there are observational learning or modeling effects whereby an observer acquires one or more new response patterns that did not previously exist in his/her behavioral repertoire. Second, there are inhibitory and disinhibitory effects whereby an observer's inhibitory responses are either strengthened or weakened by observation of a model's behavior and its consequences. Third, there is response facilitation whereby the behavior of others ". . . serves merely as discriminative stimuli for the observer in facilitating the occurrence of previously learned responses . . ." (Bandura 1969, p. 120).

Developing New Responses. There are at least three types of new behaviors that marketers often wish to induce in consumers or potential consumers. First, it is often desirable to "educate" consumers in product usage. Second, it may be helpful to induce consumers to shop in certain ways. Finally, by developing certain types of "attending behavior," the sensitivity of a potential customer to advertising information can be increased. Vicarious learning can be very useful in achieving these three goals.

First, modeling can be used to develop behaviors which enable potential consumers to utilize particular products appropriately. The demonstration of ways of using a product may make purchase more probable, particularly if the model(s) appear to be experiencing positive consequences from using the product. Moreover, repurchase or purchase by one's friends may become more probable if the consumer has learned, by watching someone else, to use the product appropriately. This use of modeling is common to both industrial and consumer products salespeople

who are attempting to sell technically complex products. Also, many self-service retail stores now use video cassette machines with taped demonstrations of proper product usage.

Second, models may be very helpful in developing the desired purchasing behaviors. For example, suppose a firm has a product which is currently technically superior to its competitors. It may be important to teach the potential consumer to ask questions about such technical advantages at the point of purchase. Advertisements showing individuals doing just this or behaving in other ways which appear to give a particular product a differential advantage may be useful.

Third, particularly at early stages in the purchase process, it is often necessary to find ways to increase the degree to which potential customers attend to information in advertisements and other messages about a product. Attaining this objective can be facilitated through the application of findings from recent research on factors which influence the attention observers pay to models. For example, attending behavior is influenced by such factors as: incentive conditions, the characteristics of the observers, the characteristics of the model, and the characteristics of the modeling cues themselves.

Advertising practitioners seem to be very sensitive to these factors. Many ads reflect their creators' acute awareness of salient characteristics of the target audience, the characteristics of the users of the product in the ad, and the behaviors exhibited by the model. Moreover, many ads show the models receiving positive social or other reinforcement from the purchase or use of the product.

Inhibiting Undesired Behaviors. Because of the obvious ethical and practical problems involved in attempting to use punishment in marketing, we have given little attention to ways of reducing the frequency of "undesired" responses. However, while these problems exist in the direct use of punishment, they are far less prevalent when aversive consequences are administered to models. Thus, vicarious learning may be one of the few approaches which can be used in marketing to reduce the frequency of unwanted elements in the behavioral repertoire of a potential or present consumer.

It is well known from the modeling literature that, under appropriate conditions, observers who see a model experience aversive outcomes following a particular act, will reduce their tendency to exhibit that behavior. Similarly, vicarious learning can employ an extinction situation to reduce the frequency of behavior.

While most marketing efforts are directed at increasing rather than decreasing behaviors, some ads are directed at reducing such behaviors as smoking, drinking, overeating, wasting energy, polluting and littering, as well as purchasing or using a competitor's product. The effectiveness of messages to achieve these goals may benefit from the use of vicarious negative conditioning.

Response Facilitation. In addition to its role in developing new behaviors and inhibiting "undesired" behaviors, modeling can be used to facilitate the occurrence of desired behaviors which are currently in the individual's repertoire. For example, modeling has been used extensively in advertising not only to illustrate the uses of a product but to show what "types" of people use it and in what settings. Since many of these uses involve behaviors already in the observer's response hierarchy, the function of the model is merely to facilitate these responses by depicting positive consequences for use of the product in a particular way. This technique appears frequently in advertising for high status products. Such ads do not demonstrate any new behaviors, but show the positive consequences of using a particular product. The re-

cent series of Lowenbrau ads stressing the use of this beer for very special occasions is a clear example of this.

It is also possible to influence emotional behavior through a vicarious learning paradigm. Bandura (1969) noted that many emotional behaviors can be acquired through observations of others, as well as through direct respondent conditioning:

> . . . vicarious emotional conditioning results from observing others experience positive or negative emotional effects in conjunction with particular stimulus events. Both direct and vicarious conditioning processes are governed by the same basic principles of associative learning, but they differ in the force of the emotional arousal. In the direct prototype, the learner himself is the recipient of pain- or pleasure-producing stimulation, whereas in vicarious forms somebody else experiences the reinforcing stimulation and his affective expressions, in turn, serve as the arousal stimuli for the observer (p. 167).

To the degree that positive emotions toward a product are desired, vicarious emotional conditioning may be a useful concept for the design of effective advertisements.

In sum, vicarious learning or modeling has a number of current and potential uses in marketing. If a potential consumer has observed appropriate models, then he/she is more likely to know the appropriate behaviors; if the model has been rewarded appropriately, the potential consumer may be more likely to engage in these behaviors. Likewise, if the potential consumer has observed inappropriate models receiving aversive consequences, he/she may be less likely to emit them. Models may be used to develop, inhibit, or facilitate behavior. In short, as with the other components of the BMP, it is clear that this technique for modifying behavior is commonly employed in current television and other advertising messages. In fact, Markin and Narayana (1976,

p. 225) suggest that many of today's most successful products are promoted and advertised on the basis of modeling approaches which show the model receiving positive functional or social benefits from the use of the product. Products they suggest have used this approach include "Coca-Cola," "Pepsi-Cola," "McDonald's," "Kentucky Fried Chicken," "Nyquil," "Absorbine Jr.," "Alka Seltzer," Philip's "Milk of Magnesia," "Pepto Bismol," "Folgers," "Crest," and "Head and Shoulders." However, since the link of current marketing practice to the BMP has not been explicit, research exploring the application of the principles of vicarious learning to marketing settings is lacking. Such research is apt to have both practical importance for marketing and theoretical implications for students of modeling as previous findings are tested in more general, less artificial settings.

Ecological Design

Although knowledge about the role of physical space and other aspects of environmental design is meager, there is considerable evidence that the design of physical situations and the presence or absence of various stimuli have powerful effects on behavior (Barker 1968; Hall 1959, 1966; Sommers 1969). We will use the term ecological design to refer to the deliberate design of environments to modify human behavior.

Ecological design is widely used in marketing. For example, department stores place displays in high traffic areas (e.g., at the end of an escalator) to increase the likelihood that consumers will observe the product on display. Similarly, end aisle displays in supermarkets and the internal arrangements of stores involve efforts to place stimuli in positions which increase the likelihood of consumers making one or more desired re-

sponses. Direct mail is also a means of placing stimuli in the potential consumer's environment to increase the likelihood that the individual will at least be aware of the particular product. Other techniques include the use of sound, odors, lights, and other stimuli to increase attentive behaviors. In fact, store location and external arrangements (e.g., design of malls, arrangement of parking space) are all efforts to alter behavior through environmental design. In a behavioral sense, these are all ways to increase the probability that the individual will make certain responses which increase the likelihood that purchase or some other desired response will follow.

Like shaping, ecological manipulations are frequently employed to modify behavior early in the purchase process. Thus, their major impact is through their role in inducing the potential consumer to come into contact with the product and/or perform product-related behavior. As such, ecological design is best viewed as one part of a comprehensive marketing approach; ecological modifications can be conveniently sequenced with other techniques (e.g., modeling, respondent conditioning, operant conditioning).

As with other elements subsumed under the BMP, ecological designs to modify behavior have received far less attention in the academic literature than they deserve in view of how frequently they are used by marketing practitioners. A major advantage of the BMP is that it encourages the integration of these various techniques to lead to a coherent approach for modifying the entire sequence of behaviors desired of consumers and potential consumers.

SUMMARY OF SOME APPLICATIONS OF THE BMP IN MARKETING

Table 1 provides a framework for considering some applications of the BMP to marketing.

Table 1 / Illustrative Applications of the BMP in Marketing

I. Some Applications of Respondent Conditioning Principles
A. Conditioning responses to new stimuli

Unconditioned or Previously Conditioned Stimulus	Conditioned Stimulus	Examples
Exciting event	A product or theme song	Gillette theme song followed by sports event
Patriotic events or music	A product or person	Patriotic music as background in political commercial

B. Use of familiar stimuli to elicit responses

Conditioned Stimulus	Conditioned Response(s)	Examples
Familiar music	Relaxation, excitement, "good will"	Christmas music in retail store
Familiar voices	Excitement, attention	Famous sportscaster narrating a commercial
Sexy voices, bodies	Excitement, attention, relaxation	Noxema television ads and many others
Familiar social cues	Excitement, attention, anxiety	Sirens sounding or telephones ringing in commercials

II. Some Applications of Operant Conditioning Principles
A. Rewards for desired behavior (continuous schedules)

Desired Behavior	Reward Given Following Behavior
Product purchase	Trading stamps, cash bonus or rebate, prizes, coupons

B. Rewards for desired behavior (partial schedules)

Desired Behavior	Reward Given (sometimes)
Product purchase	Prize for every second, or third, etc. purchase Prize to some fraction of people who purchase

C. Shaping

Approximation of Desired Response	Consequence Following Approximation	Final Response Desired
Opening a charge account	Prizes, etc., for opening account	Expenditure of funds
Trip to point-of-purchase location	Loss leaders, entertainment, or event at the shopping center	Purchase of products
Entry into store	Door prize	Purchase of products
Product trial	Free product and/or some bonus for using	Purchase of product

D. Discriminative Stimuli

Desired Behavior	Reward Signal	Examples
Entry into store	Store signs Store logos	50% off sale K-Mart's big red "K"
Brand purchase	Distinctive brandmarks	Levi tag

Table 1 / *continued*

III. Some Applications of Modeling Principles

Modeling Employed	Desired Response
Instructor, expert, salesperson using product (in ads or at point-of-purchase)	Use of product in technically competent way
Models in ads asking questions at point-of-purchase	Ask questions at point-of-purchase which highlight product advantages
Models in ads receiving positive reinforcement for product purchase or use	Increase product purchase and use
Models in ads receiving no reinforcement or receiving punishment for performing undesired behaviors	Extinction or decrease of undesired behaviors
Individual or group (similar to target) using product in novel, enjoyable way	Use of product in new ways

IV. Some Applications of Ecological Modification Principles

Environmental Design	Specific Example	Intermediate Behavior	Final Desired Behavior
Store layout	End of escalator, end-aisle, other displays	Bring customer into visual contact with product	Product purchase
Purchase locations	Purchase possible from home, store location	Product or store contact	Product purchase
In-store mobility	In-store product directories, information booths	Bring consumer into visual contact with product	Product purchase
Noises, odors, lights	Flashing lights in store window	Bring consumer into visual or other sensory contact with store or product	Product purchase

Each of the four sections of the table outlines the general procedures which would be followed in applying one of the four basic elements of the BMP. The table lists a number of the specific behaviors which marketers may wish to develop and organizes the examples presented in the previous sections of the paper. In reviewing this table, two qualifications should be kept in mind. First, there are many tactics for modifying behavior which are combinations of a number of techniques which do not fit neatly into the simple categories presented in the table. For example, Anheuser-Busch has a series of commercials which begin with a sports trivia question and then give the listener "time to think" while the virtues of a particular brand of beer are discussed. Then, the answer to the question is given. Determination of exactly which principles this approach uses and whether or not the approach can be reduced to principles of behavior modification at all requires a complex analysis of the acquisition and use of language. However, the approach is clearly one of picking a desired behavior (i.e., listening to the commercial) and organizing stimuli to increase the probability of this behavior.

Second, most, if not all of these tactics have already been used by practitioners. While the BMP may lead to some new tactics, its most important value to practitioners will be in systematizing and integrating marketing efforts by focusing attention on the *sequence of specific behaviors* which can be modified to change the probability of product purchase or of some other desired behavior.

POTENTIAL CONTRIBUTIONS OF THE BMP TO MARKETING

As the examples in the previous section illustrate, a number of tactics which are frequently used by marketing practitioners *can be* derived from the BMP. Of course, the fact that they can be derived does not mean that they were so derived or that they could not have been derived from other models. Nevertheless, the fact that such a varied array of tactics can be subsumed under a relatively simple model suggests that the perspective can be a valuable addition to the academic marketing literature. It is in this spirit that we speculate about the potential contributions of the BMP to marketing practice and to the study of consumer behavior.

Marketing Practice

The BMP can make at least two major contributions to marketing practice. First, it can facilitate the development of a comprehensive set of strategies and tactics which encompass those environmental and situational factors which *directly* influence behavior. If the behaviors desired from the potential buyer are specified, it will often be possible to be explicit about a set of actions which should occur in any given situation to move the potential buyer to behave in ways which are more likely to lead to purchase behavior. Marketing tactics developed with this degree of specificity force more careful planning and analysis of exactly what outcomes are sought and are more easily evaluated and refined. It should

be noted here that in other systems where behavior modification has been introduced, it has often been found that there was considerable ambiguity about exactly what results previous methods of organization were really attempting to achieve (Nord 1969; Schneier 1974). We suspect that other than purchase behavior, many students of marketing have never delineated the basic sequence of behaviors that consumers must perform in order to purchase a product.

Second, the BMP can stimulate a closer interchange between academics and practitioners. In this connection it is important to emphasize that while marketing managers are rewarded for developing tactics which generate sales and profits, academics are more apt to be rewarded for attempting to provide theoretical explanations of consumer behavior. The BMP focuses academics on the investigation of behaviors and techniques which produce sales and profits. Moreover, its simplicity and pragmatic emphasis should help academics in their efforts to communicate with practitioners.

Study of Consumer Behavior

There are also two major contributions to the study of consumer behavior. First, the BMP forces explicit recognition that, to the degree that marketing efforts seek to increase sales, marketing is directly concerned with the influence, modification, and control of consumer behavior. Such recognition can have profound effects on consumer behavior research. While research on attitudes and decision processes will not be precluded, valuable empirical research may be conducted without attaching great significance to internal psychological processes. Instead, attention is apt to center on the manipulation of external factors which affect behavior in desired ways. Even in cases where internal psychological processes are the focus of research, the BMP forces explicit recognition that there are a variety of external influences which need to be accounted for in research designs. Several of Belk's (1974, 1975) situational influences as well as a variety of the stimuli discussed in this article could well be affecting both the internal validity (i.e., interpretability) and external validity (i.e., generalizability) of current consumer behavior research findings. The discussions by Snow (1974) and Petrinovich (1979) should be useful for developing research methods to incorporate these external influences.

Second, there is considerable evidence that the behavior of consumers is far more consistent with the principles of the BMP than with traditional explanations. For example Markin (1974) and Markin and Narayana (1976) note that empirical research on consumer decision processes documents that consumers: (1) do not seek extensive amounts of information in relation to purchase and consumption problems; (2) do not process large amounts of information in relation to purchase and consumption problems; and (3) do not appear to engage in extensive problem solving behavior even in relation to big ticket or capital intensive items such as automobiles, houses, and major appliances. Not only does the BMP account for the empirical data better than many other approaches, but it does so with fewer variables. In a word, it is more parsimonious. Further, it has long been recognized that purchase behavior often *precedes* attitudes about the product or brand purchased. Thus, the BMP may well provide insights into predicting and controlling the purchase-consumption process. It is important to emphasize here that the BMP does not nor is it intended to provide theoretical explanations of behavior. However, it is clear that any scientific explanation of the causes of consumer behavior will have to include not only internal psychological processes, but also the external influences embodied in the BMP.

SOME UNRESOLVED ISSUES

Based on our argument, we believe it is reasonable to conclude that a good deal of marketing, at least at the tactical or operational level, is as closely aligned with techniques of behavior modification as with those suggested by more complex, internally-oriented psychological models. To the degree this conclusion is valid, it raises a number of issues about the value of the BMP for marketing.

First, to what extent is the BMP a suitable replacement for more traditional approaches? We believe that it is a useful complement, not a replacement. The BMP focuses on external factors; it stops short of providing adequate explanation of internal processes. Although Skinner (1969) has argued persuasively that the skin is an arbitrary barrier, we do not find the attempts of many radical behaviorists to ignore the internal correlates of external stimuli intellectually satisfying. At the same time, we agree with Bindra (1959) that the efforts of motivational and cognitive psychologists to deal with these internal correlates often are merely classifications of acts, rather than adequate accounts for causes of behavior. Thus, we are driven to a psychological eclecticism which, unlike the current psychological eclecticism in marketing, incorporates an external perspective.

Second, there is the issue of the efficacy of behavior modification techniques. While existing research indicates that the technology exists to modify behavior very effectively, this technology can be used more effectively in controlled environments. While retail stores and shopping malls provide relatively closed environments, they do not permit the type of control which experimenters in hospitals, schools, prisons, and even work organizations may have. Moreover, the degree of control which is possible will vary at different stages in the purchasing process. Empirical research involving applications of behavior modification principles at different stages of the purchasing process would clearly be useful for investigating this issue. It is only at the latter stages that substantial control seems possible.

Third, there are major ethical/moral issues involved in the use of the BMP in marketing. In many areas, the ethical/moral challenges to the application of behavior modification are, at least in the minds of most behavior modifiers, relatively easy to refute. In most areas where behavior modification has been applied (e.g., psychotherapy, education, self-improvement), is is usually possible (although the possibility is often not translated into practice) for subjects of behavior modification to participate in defining the ends and also to what degree they will determine in the means. Thus human freedom and dignity are, to some degree, protected; in such situations, the BMP provides a useful technology for helping human beings achieve the ends they are seeking. However, even in these cases, behavior modification has been challenged on ethical grounds.

We maintain that behavior modification is not, in itself, immoral or unethical, but that valid ethical/moral concerns stem from (1) the ends to which the technology is used and (2) the process by which these ends are determined (see Nord 1976). The application of these techniques in marketing seems ethically vulnerable on both these counts. Efforts to market products rarely include the subject whose behavior is modified as a full participant in determining either the use of the technology or the ends to which it is put. There are, of course, examples of the use of

behavior modification techniques in marketing to achieve purposes which many people believe are socially desirable. For example, certain outcomes such as reduction in littering, reduction in pollution, smoking, and other behaviors can be and are marketed through such techniques. Moreover, much of consumer education involves modifying the purchasing behavior of the uneducated poor to get better economic value for dollars spent. However, there appear to be many other applications which have few redeeming social benefits.

The BMP reveals that these concerns are relevant to the present—not just the future. It is clear that behavior modification techniques, even though they may be called something else, are being currently employed in marketing. Moreover, since it is clear that the type of emotions often labeled "needs" or motives can be developed through conditioning and modeling processes, the defense that marketing satisfies needs is not fully adequate. Thus, while explicit application of the BMP in marketing is apt to trigger ethical concerns, the BMP may be quite useful for viewing ethical problems involved in *current* marketing practice.

Fourth, there are a number of practical issues. In addition to the problem of developing sufficiently controlled environments, there are problems of selecting reinforcers, of designing and implementing effective schedules, and of designing effective ecological structures. Solutions to these problems can benefit from an eclectic research approach. The trial and error approach of the radical behaviorists derived from their research with animals can be useful, but is only one approach. In addition, analysis of historical data on the effectiveness of various marketing tactics in generating desired behaviors and laboratory or field experiments using different types of reinforcers is needed.

Moreover, cognitively-oriented approaches which rely on verbal reports may offer insights into these questions. Of course, the most important practical issue requires cost-benefit analysis. While the bottom line will be the ultimate test, the BMP does lead to the analysis of the sequence of behaviors which is expected to lead to purchase or to other desired behavior. These outcomes can be defined and measured more precisely with current technology than can attitudes, needs, etc. Thus it is likely that research to test the BMP will have a clear action orientation as well as permit measurement of success at a number of intermediate steps.

CONCLUSIONS

This paper has attempted to provide an overview of behavior modification and investigate its applicability to marketing. While it appears that many marketing tactics currently employed are quite consistent with the BMP, these tactics appear to have been derived in an ad hoc manner. A more systematic application of the BMP to marketing may well provide insights for the development of improved tactics and overall strategies and for describing how the purchase-consumption process works. Although marketing academics and practitioners may be reluctant to view marketing as a technology for modifying and controlling consumer behavior, it is clear that marketing tactics which are fully consistent with this perspective will continue to be implemented. In terms of consumer behavior research, it will undoubtedly be some time before researchers actively catalog and sample elements of the external environment given the predilection toward the study of internal processes. In any case, the BMP may provide a clear understanding that one of the major de facto functions of marketing in our society is the modification of behavior.

REFERENCES

Bandura, A. (1969), *Principles of Behavior Modification*. New York: Holt, Rinehart, and Winston.
——— (1978), "The Self System in Reciprocal Determinism," *American Psychologist*, 33 (April), 344–358.
Barker, R. G. (1968), *Ecological Psychology*. Stanford: Stanford University Press.
Belk, Russell W. (1974), "An Exploratory Assessment of Situational Effects in Buyer Behavior," *Journal of Marketing Research*, 11 (May), 156–163.
——— (1975), "Situational Variables and Consumer Behavior," *Journal of Consumer Research*, 2 (December), 157–164.
Bindra, D. (1959), *Motivation: A Systematic Reinterpretation*, New York: Ronald Press.
Carey, R. J., S. H. Clicque, B. A. Leighton, and F. Milton (1976), "A Test of Positive Reinforcement of Customers," *Journal of Marketing*, 40 (October), 98–100.
Deslauriers, B. C. and P. B. Everett (1977). "The Effects of Intermittent and Continuous Token Reinforcement on Bus Ridership," *Journal of Applied Psychology*, 62 (August), 369–375.
Engel, J. F., D. T. Kollat, and R. D. Blackwell (1973), *Consumer Behavior*, 2nd Ed., New York: Holt, Rinehart, and Winston.
Hall, C. S. and G. Lindzey (1970). *Theories of Personality*, 2nd Ed., New York: John Wiley and Sons.
Hall, E. T. (1959), *The Silent Language*, New York: Doubleday.
——— (1966), *The Hidden Dimension*, New York: Doubleday.
Honig, W. K. (1966), *Operant Behavior: Areas of Research and Application*, New York: Appleton-Century-Crofts.
Kassarjian, H. H. (1978), "Presidential Address, 1977: Anthropomorphism and Parsimony," in *Advances in Consumer Research*, Vol. 5, H. K. Hunt, ed., Chicago: Association for Consumer Research, xiii–xiv.
Kotler, Philip (1976), *Marketing Management*,

3rd Ed., Englewood Cliffs, NJ: Prentice-Hall, Inc.

Markin, R. J. (1974), *Consumer Behavior: A Cognitive Approach,* New York: Macmillan, Chapter 17.

————, and C. L. Narayana (1976), "Behavior Control: Are Consumers Beyond Freedom and Dignity?" in *Advances in Consumer Research,* Vol. 3, B. B. Anderson, ed., Chicago: Association for Consumer Research, 222–228.

Miller, N. E. (1969), "Learning of Visceral and Glandular Responses," *Science,* 163 (January), 434–449.

Nord, W. R. (1969), "Beyond the Teaching Machine: The Neglected Area of Operant Conditioning in the Theory and Practice of Management." *Organizational Behavior and Human Performance,* 4 (November), 375–401.

———— (1976), "Behavior Modification Perspective for Humanizing Organizations," in *Humanizing Organizational Behavior,* H. Meltzer and F. D. Wickert, eds., Springfield, IL: Charles E. Thomas, 250–272.

Petrinovich, L. (1979), "Probabilistic Functionalism: A Conception of Research Method," *American Psychologist,* 34 (May), 373–390.

Ray, M. L. (1973), "Psychological Theories and Interpretations of Learning," in *Consumer Behavior: Theoretical Sources,* S. Ward and T. S. Robertson, eds., Englewood Cliffs, NJ: Prentice-Hall, 45–117.

Schneier, C. E. (1974), "Behavior Modification in Management: A Review and Critique," *Academy of Management Journal,* 17 (September), 528–548.

Skinner, B. F. (1953), *Science and Human Behavior,* New York: Macmillan.

———— (1969), *Contingencies of Reinforcement: A Theoretical Analysis,* New York: Appleton-Century-Crofts.

Snow, R. (1974). "Representative and Quasi-Representative Designs for Reseach on Teaching," *Review of Educational Research,* 44 (Summer), 265–291.

Sommers, R. (1969), *Personal Space: The Behavioral Basis for Design.* Englewood Cliffs, NJ: Prentice-Hall, Inc.

Staats, A. W. (1975), *Social Behaviorism,* Homewood IL: The Dorsey Press.

Questions

1. Briefly describe the four ways of modifying behavior.
2. For each technique, cite some of the benefits of applying that technique in a marketing situation.
3. Differentiate between respondent conditioning and operant conditioning.
4. Summarize the main potential contributions of adopting a behavior modification perspective in marketing.

Part C
NEEDS AND MOTIVATION

12. Murray's Theory of Human Needs: A Useful Guide To Understanding Consumer Behavior

James U. McNeal
Stephen W. McDaniel

It is a rare marketing book that does not speak frequently of consumer needs. And an examination of the numerous consumer behavior books will indicate that individual needs are emphasized in all of them. The reason is obvious: Most marketing activities are important only to the extent that they help the firm to satisfy consumer needs.

Yet, there is an irony in marketing writings. While most marketing and consumer behavior books give the concept of needs a focal position, there are very few reports of empirical studies of consumer needs in any of the journals. In fact, the term "need" (or its synonyms) appears in the title of only one article in all the issues of the *Journal of Marketing,* and that article does not discuss consumer needs. Even more amazing is the nonexistence of the term needs in any article titles in the *Journal of Consumer Research.*

How does one interpret this irony? Are consumer needs important topics for conversation, but not investigation? Are consumer

needs so crystalized in the minds of marketing practitioners and academicians that they require little examination? Or are needs so complex and evasive as to be impervious to investigation? Whatever the case, researchers in the field of consumer behavior fail to provide us with any information that would give us a better understanding of consumer needs. We must therefore turn elsewhere for such guidance.

If we look through the eyes of one of the most renowned theorists in the field of human needs—Henry A. Murray—perhaps we can appreciate the fundamental nature of consumer needs. Most importantly, we can gain some understanding of them through his research.

In the early 1930s Murray and twenty-seven of his associates at the Harvard Psychological Clinic set out to "discover some of the principles that govern human behavior" (p. ix). After three years of intensive investigation, often developing their own research tools, such as the Thematic Apperception Test, because adequate methods did not exist, they reported their findings in *Explorations in Personality,* a book that has

This article draws extensively on Henry A. Murray's *Explorations in Personality* (New York: Oxford University Press, Inc., 1938). Page references are given in the text.

now been through ten printings. This un-contested classic describes the most thorough investigation of human needs ever made.

While unfair to this classic work, we can isolate several principles of human needs from it that provide useful guides to an understanding of consumer needs. Let us do this briefly, while encouraging the student of consumer behavior to carefully examine the Murray report first hand.

DEFINITION OF A NEED

A need is a hypothetical construct that stands for a force in the brain region that organizes and directs mind and body behavior so as to maintain the organism in its most desirable state (pp. 123–129).

Murray calls a need a hypothetical construct because it is of a physiochemical nature that is unknown. It resides in the brain and is thus in a position to control all significant behavior. Each person has a most desirable state, physiologically, psychologically, and sociologically. Needs organize and direct thinking and behavior, including consumer behavior, so as to maintain that state.

TYPES OF NEEDS

"Needs may be conveniently divided into: (1) primary (viscerogenic) needs, and (2) secondary (psychogenic) needs. The former are engendered and instilled by characteristic bodily events, whereas the latter have no sub-jectively localizable bodily orgins . . ." (pp. 76–77).

Although Murray's classification into only two types lacks perfection, it is simple and logical. There are bodily needs and other needs. These other needs have to do with men-tal or emotional satisfaction. Both classes of needs are satisfied in the marketplace by con-sumers. (See the complete listing of needs in each category in the Appendix.)

In addition to classifying needs as vis-cerogenic and psychogenic, Murray also classifies them into three other dimensions (pp. 76–85):

1. *Positive or negative needs*—depending upon whether they cause the individual to strive toward or away from an object. (Needs fall-ing under each category are shown in the Ap-pendix.)
2. *Manifest and latent needs*—depending upon whether they manifest themselves as realistic behavior or as imaginative behavior. (The manifest needs are indicated in the Appen-dix.)
3. *Conscious and unconscious*—depending upon whether an individual can give an in-trospective report about them or not.

While Murray recognizes the basicity of bodily needs by terming them primary, he also recognizes that the importance of a need is an individual matter. This is in slight contrast to some need theorists.

CHARACTERISTICS OF NEEDS

Needs have universality and permanency (pp. 56–66).

Murray believes that all people possess the same needs, but he recognizes that the expres-sion of them will differ because of the variety of the behavioral field for each person. He sees needs as permanent because they appear to exist and be the same at all ages. He notes the maturity of needs in the child, implying that needs may be innate and show themselves very early in life. All consumers have the same needs and possess them throughout life. Consumer behavior of individuals differs because of differences in behavioral fields.

There are individual differences with regard to frequency, intensity, and duration of different needs (pp. 78–79).

Needs are a function of the individual as well as of her or his environment. Thus, not all consumers express the same need with the same frequency, intensity, or duration. This is a problem for marketers who want large numbers of people to act the same.

Another point here is that even bodily needs may not be expressed with the same frequency, intensity, and duration among all consumers. Logically, some bodily needs will have the same periodicity among all people, but this will not be true for some other bodily needs. This difference could be a result of differences in bodily structure or conditions.

Some needs, particularly body needs, are characterized by periodicity. They possess a more or less regular rhythm of activity and rest (pp. 85–86).

It is rather obvious that people eat and sleep, for instance, with regularity. What may be less obvious is that psychogenic needs, such as affiliation and achievement, may arise at fairly regular intervals. Consumer needs with a high frequency of occurence explain much consumer behavior. These high frequency needs should be the focus of marketers.

"Certain cultures and sub-cultures to which an individual is exposed may be characterized by a predominance of certain needs" (p. 129).

Due to custom or acceptable practices, consumers will express certain needs more frequently than others in various social settings. Sometimes, according to Murray, these predominant needs simply reflect a desire to be different. It is these predominant needs that help explain "generations" such as the "me generation," the "we generation," the "beat generation," and so on.

A marketer who attempts to sell products nationwide or worldwide must be aware of predominant needs and how they vary culturally. For example, what are strong needs in the United States may not be predominant in Mainland China.

HOW NEEDS ARE AROUSED

A need can be provoked by stimuli, either internal or external stimuli (pp. 115–122).

Consumer needs can be aroused by stimuli presented by marketers just as they can by internal stimuli such as a stomach growl. If the stimuli are positive, the consumer will move toward them; if negative, away from them. Thus, if a marketer knows what is viewed positively by consumers, he can cause a lot of consumers to come his way.

Needs exist in three different states: (1) refractory, in which no incentive will arouse it; (2) inducible, in which a need is inactive but susceptible to excitation; and (3) active, in which the need is determining the behavior of the organism (pp. 85–86).

Some consumer needs cannot be aroused at a given time because it is not in the best interest of the consumer to express them or because they could not be more satisfied. Other needs are inducible and thus are easily aroused. Active needs are those that have been aroused and that the consumer is in the process of satisfying. Clearly, the marketer should focus on inducible needs, but there is no recipe for their determination. Of all marketing activities, personal selling has the best opportunity to determine what needs of a consumer are inducible.

RESULTS OF NEED-SATISFYING BEHAVIOR

"only under rare or abnormal conditions do we find behavior patterns that exist for long without satisfying underlying needs" (p. 100).

Consumers will not buy a product, or a brand of product, or shop in a store for long if such behavior does not satisfy needs. Naturally, consumers make mistakes like buying an undesirable product, but the intent was to buy a need-satisfying product. An undesirable product is unlikely to be purchased again by that consumer. If many consumers feel this way about a product, it will fail.

Any object may satisfy any need. To put it metaphorically, a need may have no inkling of what it needs (p. 68).

Consumers may satisfy different needs with the same purchase. Said another way, two marketers may be selling the same product but satisfying different needs among consumers. This situation can be a function of the marketer's presentation of his product. For example, one marketer of chewing gum may position his product as satisfying the need for clean breath, while another may present his chewing gum as satisfying the need for good flavor. In any case, marketers of a certain product do not have a corner on a certain need. Other marketers can satisfy that same consumer need with other products.

The individual tries to satisfy two or more needs with one act. This practice is called need fusion and represents an example of human efficiency (p. 86).

Consumers are unlikely to buy a product or shop in a store that satisfies only one need. It is not logical. Thus, if we ask a consumer what is the main thing liked about a product or the main reason it is preferred, the answer may

not be very significant. The reason is that there are several reasons (needs), and ranking them may be difficult.

Marketers who offer products with multiple need satisfaction probably practice a good strategy. Naturally, offering a product that satisfies many needs could be viewed by the consumer as confusing or doubtful.

Life activities can be divided into episodes. An episode is a reaction to external or internal environments—an experience. It consists of need arousal and resolution. Each episode leaves traces in the brain that determine future actions of the individual (pp. 42–43).

A consumer's activities are a function of past activities that are recorded in the mind. Thus, consumer behavior is a learning experience. Individuality in consumer behavior is a function of recorded experiences.

Needs can become objectified. "One can observe repeatedly in some people the same directional tendency carried along by the same mode toward the same object." Thus, need-object relationships may develop (pp. 111–112).

Episodes of behavior indicate to consumers those things that are satisfying and those that are not. When objects are repeatedly satisfying, a need–object relationship or habit pattern is formed. In such cases, we may speak of consumers as having product preferences, brand preferences or loyalty, and store preferences or loyalty. The ideal situation for a marketer is to have his offering as a need object.

MANIFESTATION OF NEEDS

"needs organize perception, apperception, intellection, conation, and action. . ." (p. 124).

What consumers perceive, think, tend to want to do, and actually do are determined by needs. The consumer is his or her own master and will think and act according to his needs. He can be fooled, but marketers have no control over his mind activities except what he permits.

Needs manifest themselves as wants, or wishes, and decisions (pp. 64–65).

When consumers say they want something, wish they had something, or make a decision to obtain something, they are expressing needs. Thus, consumer wants are verbal expressions of needs. Different wants of a consumer may reflect different or the same needs. To find out what needs are being expressed through wants requires various research techniques that obtain serious introspection by the consumer.

A marketer is courting failure when he bases his efforts on consumer wants alone. He must know what needs are being expressed in order to know why consumers want his offering. If he does not know the needs, there is a good chance that his promotion efforts will be ineffective.

Attitudes are expressions of needs. Positive needs that move people toward an object are expressed through positive attitudes; negative needs that move people away from an object are expressed through negative attitudes (p. 113).

Consumers possess positive and negative attitudes toward marketers' offerings as a result of the consumers' needs. "I like that" or "I don't like that" are common attitudinal expressions.

While positive attitudes toward an object suggest that the object has need-satisfying potential, they do not suggest that consumers will buy the object. That is because there are many objects toward which a consumer may feel positive that will satisfy the same need. Hence, it is possible for many consumers to have favorable attitudes toward a product or brand of product but not buy it.

Attitudes and wants are not the same. Attitudes in some combination may cause wants. That is, when a need is active, several positive and negative attitudes may come together to cause an expression of a want.

Emotions are excitatory processes in the brain that usually accompany needs. They manifest themselves in autonomic disturbances (tears in the eyes, blushing, nervous perspiration, as examples) and verbal reports ("I feel good," "I feel down"). They may intensify or disorganize behavior and thus facilitate or obstruct the satisfaction of a need (pp. 89–92).

The two most general emotions are pleasure resulting from need satisfaction and displeasure resulting from need dissatisfaction. More specific common emotions are fear, anger, disgust, pity, shame, lust, and elation.

Consumers do not want to experience negative emotions such as fear or anger because they are suggestive of needs to be met or because they make meeting needs more difficult. Objects that elicit negative emotions, and thus negative needs, such as fear appeal advertisements, may be avoided.

Consumers are pleasure seekers—seekers of need satisfaction. Objects in the marketplace that promise need satisfaction promise pleasure and will be sought.

Consumers' emotions are measurable. Verbal reports based on personal introspection can produce measures of emotions. Psychophysiological measures, such as the galvanic skin response (GSR), can also assess emotions.

Personality consists of traces of past experiences of need expression, needs, attitudes, emotions, and bodily conditions that produce uniformity in thinking and behavior (pp. 38–49).

Consumers are frequently involved in purchase decisions and purchases. The personality of each consumer is the final determinant of the uniformity in decisionmaking and purchasing. Thus, an understanding of personality will help marketers to explain consumer behavior.

However, the personality is so complex—contains so many elements intricately organized—that study and understanding of it are difficult. Thus, even though there intuitively is a direct link between personality and behavior, defining it is practically impossible.

Murray felt that personality should be studied in parts because of its complexity. His strategy should also guide the study of the consumer's personality. Personality traits, which are styles of need expression, form a logical focal point for helping to explain the function of personality in consumer behavior patterns. One should keep in mind, though, that one part of the personality will explain only a part of consumer behavior.

APPENDIX: COMPLETE LIST OF MURRAY'S NEEDS

Primary (Viscerogenic) Needs

Air—To intake a life-sustaining mixture of gases (*positive*)
Bodily excretions—To discharge bodily waste material (*negative*)
Coldavoidance—To avoid cold temperatures (*negative*)
Food—To consume edible matter (*positive*)

*Harmavoidance—To avoid physical pain (*negative*)
Heatavoidance—To avoid hot temperatures (*negative*)
Noxavoidance—To avoid noxious stimuli (*negative*)
*Sentience—To seek sensuous gratification (i.e., tasting, touching, etc.) (*positive*)
*Sex—To form and further an erotic relationship (*positive*)
Water—To intake life-sustaining liquids (*positive*)

Secondary (Psychogenic) Needs

*Abasement—To accept blame, injury, criticism (*positive*)
*Achievement—To accomplish something difficult (*positive)*
Acquisition—To gain possessions and property (*positive*)
*Affiliation—To have a cooperative relationship with others (*positive*)
*Aggression—To overcome opposition (*positive*)
*Autonomy—To resist influence or coercion (*negative*)
Blamavoidance—To avoid blame, ostracism, or punishment (*negative*)
Cognizance—To explore, ask questions, seek knowledge (*positive*)
Conservance—To protect things against damage (*positive*)
Construction—To organize and build (*positive*)
Contrarience—To be unique (*negative*)
*Counteraction—To overcome weaknesses (*positive*)
*Defendance—To defend the personality against criticism (*positive*)
*Deference—To admire and support a superior (*positive*)

---

* These twenty needs are what Murray calls the "manifest" needs and were systematically studied by Murray. These are usually referred to as "Murray's list of needs." The other needs mentioned by Murray did not receive empirical study.

*Dominance—To influence and direct behavior of others   (*positive*)

*Exhibition—To make an impression, to be seen or heard   (*positive*)

Exposition—To relate facts, to give information   (*positive*)

*Infavoidance—To avoid failure or embarrassing situations   (*negative*)

*Nurturance—To protect others or express sympathy   (*positive*)

*Order—To maintain organization and neatness   (*positive*)

*Play—To relax or have fun   (*positive*)

Recognition—To seek distinction or social prestige   (*positive*)

*Rejection—To ignore or remain aloof and indifferent   (*negative*)

Retention—To retain possessions, to hoard or be frugal   (*positive*)

Similance—To empathize with another   (*positive*)

*Succorance—To seek aid, protection, or sympathy from others   (*positive*)

*Understanding—To analyze, experience, synthesize ideas   (*positive*)

Questions

1. Murray classifies needs into two categories, using four different dimensions. Name and explain these.
2. According to Murray's theory, in what ways are needs manifested?
3. How does a need lead to a consumer's decision to purchase a specific product?

---

13.   Motivation, Cognition, Learning—Basic Factors in Consumer Behavior

James A. Bayton

The analysis of consumer behavior presented here is derived from diverse concepts of several schools of psychology—from psychoanalysis to reinforcement theory.

Human behavior can be grouped into three categories—motivation, cognition, and learning. Motivation refers to the drives, urges, wishes, or desires which initiate the sequence of events known as "behavior." Cognition is the area in which all of the mental phenomena (perception, memory, judging, thinking, etc.) are grouped. Learning refers to those changes in behavior which occur through time relative to external stimulus conditions.

Each broad area is pertinent to particular

problems of consumer behavior. All three together are pertinent to a comprehensive understanding of consumer behavior.

MOTIVATION

Human Needs

Behavior is initiated through needs. Some psychologists claim that words such as "motives," "needs," "urges," "wishes," and "drives" should not be used as synonyms; others are content to use them interchangeably. There is one virtue in the term "drive" in that it carries the connotation of a force pushing the individual into action.

Motivation arises out of tension systems which create a state of disequilibrium for the individual. This triggers a sequence of psychological events directed toward the selection of a goal which the individual *anticipates* will bring about release from the tensions and the selection of patterns of action which he *anticipates* will bring him to the goal.

One problem in motivation theory is deriving a basic list of the human needs. Psychologists agree that needs fall into two general categories—those arising from tension-systems physiological in nature (biogenic needs such as hunger, thirst, and sex), and those based upon tension-systems existing in the individual's subjective psychological state and in his relations with others (psychogenic needs).

Although there is not much disagreement as to the list of specific biogenic needs, there is considerable difference of opinion as to the list of specific psychogenic needs. However, the various lists of psychogenic needs can be grouped into three broad categories:

1. *Affectional needs*—the needs to form and maintain warm, harmonious, and emotionally satisfying relations with others.
2. *Ego-bolstering needs*—the needs to enhance or promote the personality; to achieve; to gain prestige and recognition; to satisfy the ego through domination of others.
3. *Ego-defensive needs*—the needs to protect the personality to avoid physical and psychological harm; to avoid ridicule and "loss of face"; to prevent loss of prestige; to avoid or to obtain relief from anxiety.

One pitfall in the analysis of motivation is the assumption that a particular situation involves just one specific need. In most instances the individual is driven by a combination of needs. It seems likely that "love" brings into play a combination of affectional, ego-bolstering, and ego-defensive needs as well as biogenic needs. Within the combination some needs will be relatively strong, others relatively weak. The strongest need within the combination can be called the "prepotent" need. A given consumer product can be defined in terms of the specific need-combination involved and the relative strengths of these needs.

Another pitfall is the assumption that identical behaviors have identical motivational backgrounds. This pitfall is present whether we are thinking of two different individuals or the same individual at two different points in time. John and Harry can be different in the motivational patterns leading to the purchase of their suits. Each could have one motivational pattern influencing such a purchase at age twenty and another at age forty.

Ego-Involvement

One important dimension of motivation is the degree of ego-involvement. The various specific need-patterns are not equal in significance to the individual. Some are superficial in meaning; others represent (for the individual) tremendous challenges to the very essence of existence. There is some evidence that one of the positive correlates of degree of ego-involvement is the amount of cognitive activity (judging, thinking, etc.) involved. This means that consumer goods which tap low degrees of ego-involvement will be purchased with a relatively lower degree of conscious decision-making activity than goods which tap higher degrees of ego-involvement. Such a factor must be considered when decisions are made on advertising and marketing tactics.

At times the ego-involvement factor is a source of conflict between client and researcher. This can occur when research reveals that the product taps a low degree of ego-involvement within consumers. The result is difficult for a client to accept; because *he* is ego-involved and, therefore, cognitively active about his product, consumers must certainly be also. It is hard for such a client to believe that consumers simply do not engage in a great deal of cognitive activity when they make purchases within his product class. One way to ease this particular client-researcher conflict would be for the researcher to point out this implication of the ego-involvement dimension.

"True" and Rationalized Motives

A particular difficulty in the study of motivation is the possibility that there can be a difference between "true" motives and rationalized motives. Individuals sometimes are unaware of the exact nature of drives initiating their behavior patterns. When this occurs, they attempt to account for their behavior through "rationalization" by assigning motivations to their behavior which are acceptable to their personality structures. They may do this with no awareness that they are rationalizing. There can be other instances, however, in which individuals are keenly aware of their motivations, but feel it would

be harmful or socially unacceptable to reveal them. When this is the case, they deliberately conceal their motivations.

These possibilities create a problem for the researcher. Must he assume that every behavior pattern is based upon unconscious motivation? If not, what criteria are to be used in deciding whether to be alert to unconscious motivation for this behavior pattern and not that one? What is the relative importance of unconscious motives, if present, and rationalized motives? Should rationalized motives be ignored? After all, rationalized motives have a certain validity for the individual—they are the "real" motives insofar as he is aware of the situation.

The situation is even more complicated than this—what about the dissembler? When the individual actually is dissembling, the researcher must attempt to determine the true motives. But, how shall we determine whether we are faced with a situation where the respondent is rationalizing or dissembling? In a given case, did a projective technique reveal an unconscious motive or the true motive of a dissembler? Conceptually, rationalized motives and dissembled motives are not equal in psychological implication; but it is rare, if ever, that one finds attempts to segregate the two in consumer research directed toward the analysis of motivation. This failure is understandable, to some extent, because of the lack of valid criteria upon which to base the distinction.

COGNITION

Need-Arousal

Motivation, thus, refers to a state of need-arousal—a condition exerting "push" on the individual to engage in those activities which he anticipates will have the highest probability of bringing him gratification of a particular need-pattern. Whether gratification actually will be attained or not is a matter of future events. Central to the psychological activities which now must be considered in the sequence are the complex of "mental"operations and forces known as the cognitive processes. We can view these cognitive processes as being *purposive* in that they serve the individual in his attempts to achieve satisfaction of his needs. These cognitive processes are *regulatory* in that they determine in large measure the direction and particular steps taken in his attempt to attain satisfaction of the initiating needs.

The Ego-Superego Concept

The ego-superego concept is pertinent to a discussion of cognitive activities which have been triggered by needs. Discussions of the ego-superego concept usually come under the heading of motivation as an aspect of personality. It is our feeling that motivation and the consequences of motivation should be kept systematically "clean." In the broadest sense, ego and superego are mental entities in that they involve memory, perceiving, judging, and thinking.

The Ego. The ego is the "executive," determining how the individual shall seek satisfaction of his needs. Through perception, memory, judging, and thinking the ego attempts to integrate the needs, on the one hand, and the conditions of the external world, on the other, in such manner that needs can be satisfied without danger or harm to the individual. Often this means that gratification must be postponed until a situation has developed, or has been encountered, which does not contain harm or danger. The turnpike driver who does not exceed the speed limit because he sees signs saying there are radar checks is under the influence of the ego.

So is the driver who sees no cars on a straight stretch and takes the opportunity to drive at excessive speed.

The Superego. The superego involves the ego-ideal and conscience. The ego-ideal represents the positive standards of ethical and moral conduct the individual has developed for himself. Conscience is, in a sense, the "judge," evaluating the ethics and morality of behavior and, through guilt-feelings, administering punishment when these are violated. If a driver obeys the speed limit because he would feel guilty in doing otherwise, he is under the influence of the superego. (The first driver above is under the influence of the ego because he is avoiding a fine, not guilt feelings.)

Specific Examples

Credit is a form of economic behavior based to some extent upon ego-superego considerations. It is generally felt that one cause of consumer-credit expansion has been a shift away from the superego's role in attitudes toward credit. The past ego-ideal was to build savings; debt was immoral—something to feel guilty about, to avoid, to hide. These two superego influences restrained the use of credit. For some cultural reason, credit and debt have shifted away from superego dominance and are now more under the control of the ego—the primary concern now seems to be how much of it can be used without risking financial danger.

The purchasing of specific consumer goods can be considered from the point of view of these two influences. Certain goods (necessities, perhaps) carry little superego influence, and the individual is psychologically free to try to maximize the probability of obtaining satisfaction of his needs while minimizing the probability of encountering harm in so doing. Other goods, however, tap the superego.

When a product represents an aspect of the ego-ideal there is a strong positive force to possess it. Conversely, when a product involves violation of the conscience, a strong negative force is generated against its purchase.

Let us assume that, when the need-push asserts itself, a variety of goal-objects come into awareness as potential sources of gratification. In consumer behavior these goal-objects may be different brand names. The fact that a particular set of goal-objects come into awareness indicates the generic character of this stage in the cognitive process—a class of goal-objects is seen as containing the possible satisfier. What the class of goal-objects and specific goal-objects within the class "promise" in terms of gratification are known as "expectations."

There are, then, two orders of expectation: generic expectancies, and object-expectancies. Suppose the needs were such that the individual "thought" of brands of frozen orange juice. Some of the generic expectations for frozen orange juice are a certain taste, quality, source of vitamin C, protection against colds, and ease of preparation. The particular brands carry expectations specifically associated with one brand as against another. The expectation might be that brand A has a more refreshing taste than brand B.

In many instances, cognitive competition occurs between two or more generic categories before it does between goal-objects within a generic category. Much consumer-behavior research is directed toward the investigation of generic categories—tires, automobiles, appliances, etc. But perhaps not enough attention has been given to the psychological analysis of cognitive competition between generic categories. An example of a problem being studied is the competition between television viewing, movie going, and magazine reading. For a particular producer,

cognitive competition within the pertinent generic category is usually of more concern than cognitive competition between his generic category and others. The producer usually wants only an intensive analysis of consumer psychology with respect to the particular generic category of which his product is a member.

Let us now assume that under need-push four alternative goal-objects (brands A, B, C, and D) came into awareness. Why these particular brands and not others? Why are brands E and F absent? An obvious reason for brand E's absence might be that the individual had never been exposed to the fact that brand E exists. He had been exposed to brand F, however. Why is it absent? The problem here is one of memory—a key cognitive process. The producers of brands E and F obviously are faced with different problems.

Two sets of circumstances contain the independent variables that determine whether a given item will be remembered. One is the nature of the experience resulting from actual consumption or utilization of the goal-object. This will be discussed later when we come to the reinforcement theory of learning. The other is the circumstances present on what might be called vicarious exposures to the goal-object—vicarious in that at the time of exposure actual consumption or utilization of the goal-object does not occur. The most obvious example would be an advertisement of the goal-object. Of course, the essential purpose of an advertisement is to expose the individual to the goal-object in such a manner that at some subsequent time it will be remembered readily. The search for the most effective methods of doing this by manipulation of the physical aspects of the advertisement and the appeals used in it is a continuing effort in consumer-behavior research. Finally, for many consumers these two sets of circumstances will be jointly operative. Experiences with the goal-object and subsequent vicarious exposures can coalesce to heighten the memory potential for an item.

Making a Choice

With, say, four brands in awareness, the individual must now make a choice. What psychological factors underlie this choice? The four brands could be in awareness due to the memory factor because they are immediately present in the environment; or some because they are in the environment, and the others because of memory.

The first problem is the extent to which the items are differentiated. The various goal-objects have attributes which permit the individual to differentiate between them. The brand name is one attribute; package another; design still another. These differentiating attributes (from the point of view of the consumer's perceptions) can be called signs or cues. All such signs are not equally important in consumer decisions. Certain of them are depended upon much more than others. For example, in a study of how housewives select fresh oranges, the critical or key signs were thickness of skin, color of skin, firmness of the orange, and presence or absence of "spots" on the skin.

The signs have expectancies associated with them. Package (a sign) can carry the expectancy of quality. Thin-skin oranges carry the expectancy of juice; spots carry the expectancy of poor taste quality and insufficient amount of juice. Often sign-expectancies determined through consumer research are irrelevant or invalid. Signs are irrelevant when the do not represent a critical differentiating attribute of a goal-object. Certain discolorations on oranges have nothing to do with their intrinsic quality. Expectancies are invalid when they refer to qualities that do not in fact exist in association with a particular sign.

The different goal-objects in awareness can be assessed in terms of the extent to which they arouse similar expectancies. This phenomenon of similarity of expectations within a set of different goal-objects is known as generalization. One goal-object (brand A, perhaps), because of its associated expectancies, can be assumed to have maximum appeal within the set of alternative goal-objects. The alternates then can be ordered in terms of how their associated expectancies approximate those of brand A. Is this ordering and the psychological distances between the items of the nature of:

Brand A	Brand A
Brand B	
or	
	Brand B
Brand C	Brand C

These differences in ordering and psychological distance are referred to as generalization gradients. In the first case, the expectancies associated with brand B are quite similar to those for brand A, but are not quite as powerful in appeal. Brand C has relatively little of this. In the second case, the generalization gradient is of a different form, showing that brand B offers relatively little psychological competition to brand A. (There will also be generalization gradients with respect to cognitive competition between generic categories.) In addition to the individual producer being concerned about the memory potential of his particular brand, he needs to determine the nature of the generalization gradient for his product and the products of his competitors. Mere ordering is not enough—the "psychological distances" between positions must be determined, also, and the factor determining these distances is similarity of expectancy.

The discussion above was concerned with cognitive processes as they relate to mental representation of goal-objects under the instigation of need-arousal. The items brought into awareness, the differentiating sign-expectancies, and the generalization gradient are the central factors in the particular cognitive field aroused under a given "need-push." One important dimension has not yet been mentioned—instrumental acts. These are acts necessary in obtaining the goal-object and the acts involved in consuming or utilizing it. Examples are: "going downtown" to get to a department store, squeezing the orange to get its juice, ease of entry into service stations, and the operations involved in do-it-yourself house painting.

Instrumental acts can have positive or negative value for the individual. One who makes fewer shopping trips to downtown stores because of traffic and parking conditions displays an instrumental act with negative value. Frozen foods are products for which much of the appeal lies in the area of instrumental acts. The development of automatic transmissions and of power-steering in automobiles are examples of product changes concerned with instrumental acts. The point is that concentration upon cognitive reactions to the goal-object, *per se,* could be masking critical aspects of the situation based upon cognitive reactions to the instrumental acts involved in obtaining or utilizing the goal-object.

LEARNING

Goal-Object

Starting with need-arousal, continuing under the influence of cognitive processes, and engaging in the necessary action, the individual arrives at consumption or utilization of a goal-object. Using our consumer-behavior illustration, let us say that the consumer bought brand A and is now in the process of consuming or utilizing it. We have now arrived at one of the most critical aspects of the entire psychological sequence. It is with use of the goal-object that degree of gratification of the initial needs will occur.

Reinforcement

When consumption or utilization of the goal-object leads to gratification of the initiating needs there is "reinforcement." If at some later date the same needs are aroused, the individual will tend to repeat the process of selecting and getting to the same goal-object. If brand A yields a high degree of gratification, then at some subsequent time, when the same needs arise, the consumer will have an increased tendency to select brand A once again. Each succeeding time that brand A brings gratification, further reinforcement occurs, thus further increasing the likelihood that in the future, with the given needs, brand A will be selected.

This type of behavioral change—increasing likelihood that an act will be repeated—is learning; and reinforcement is necessary for learning to take place. Continued reinforcement will influence the cognitive processes. Memory of the goal-object will be increasingly enhanced; particular sign-expectancies will be more and more firmly established; and the generalization gradient will be changed in that the psychological distance on this gradient between brand A and the competing brands will be increased.

Habit

One of the most important consequences of continued reinforcement is the influence this has on the extent to which cognitive processes enter the picture at the times of subsequent need-arousal. With continued reinforcement, the amount of cognitive activity decreases; the individual engages less and less in decision-making mental activities. This can continue until, upon need-arousal, the goal-obtaining activities are practically automatic. At this stage there is a habit.

Note this use of the term "habit." One frequently hears that a person does certain things by "*force* of habit," that habit is an initiator of behavioral sequences. Actually habits are not initiating forces in themselves; habits are repeated response patterns accompanied by a minimum of cognitive activity. There must be some condition of need-arousal before the habit-type response occurs. This has serious implications in the field of consumer behavior. The promotional and marketing problems faced by a competitor of brand A will be of one type if purchase behavior for brand A is habitual, of another if this is not true. If the purchase is largely a habit, there is little cognitive activity available for the competitor to "work on."

Frequency of repeating a response is not a valid criterion for determining whether or not a habit exists. An act repeated once a week can be just as much a habit as one repeated several times a day. The frequency of a response is but an index of the frequency with which the particular need-patterns are aroused. Frequency of response also is often used as a measure of the *strength* of a habit. The test of the strength of a habit is the extent to which an individual will persist in an act after it has ceased providing need gratification. The greater this persistence, the stronger was the habit in the first place.

PROBLEM-CONCEPT-RESEARCH

The above views integrate concepts in contemporary psychology which seem necessary for a comprehensive explanation of human behavior, and apply these concepts to the analysis of consumer behavior. Each psychological process touched upon contains areas for further analysis and specification.

Some type of comprehensive theory of human behavior is necessary as a *working tool* to avoid a lack of discipline in attacking problems in consumer behavior. Too frequently a client with a practical problem approaches a researcher with an indication that all that is needed is a certain methodology—depth interviewing, scaling, or projective devices for example.

The first step should be to take the practical problem and translate it into its pertinent conceptual entities. This phase of the problem raises the question of motivations. Here is a question involving relevance and validity of sign-expectancies. There is a question dealing with a generalization gradient, etc. Once the pertinent conceptual entities have been identified, and only then, we arrive at the stage of hypothesis formulation. Within each conceptual entity, a relationship between independent and dependent variables is established as a hypothesis to be tested.

Often the relation between conceptual entities must be investigated. For example, what is the effect of continuing reinforcement on a specific generalization gradient? Within the same research project, one psychological entity can be a dependent variable at one phase of the research and an independent variable at another. At one time we might be concerned with establishing the factors associated with differential memory of sign-expectancies. At another time we could be concerned with the influence of remembered sign-expectancies upon subsequent purchase-behavior.

Discipline requires that one turn to methodology only when the pertinent conceptual entities have been identified and the relationships between independent and dependent variables have been expressed in the form of hypotheses. Fundamentally this sequence in the analysis of a problem serves to delimit the methodological possibilities. In any event, the methodologies demanded are those which will produce unambiguous tests of each particular hypothesis put forth. Finally, the results must be translated into the terms of the original practical problem.

We have used the term "discipline" in this phase of our discussion. The researcher must discipline himself to follow the above steps.

Some find this a difficult thing to do and inevitably their data become ambiguous. They must resort to improvisation in order to make sense of the results *after* the project is completed. A research project is truly a work of art when the conceptual analysis, the determination of the hypotheses, and the methodologies have been developed in such an "air-tight" sequence that practically all that is necessary is to let the facts speak for themselves.

Questions

1. Briefly describe the three categories of human behavior analysis.
2. Using an example, describe the psychological factors that will affect the choice of a particular brand.
3. Give a brief definition of each of the following, and tell whether each is a motivation, cognition, or learning-related concept.
   a. Ego involvement
   b. Rationalization
   c. Goal object
   d. Reinforcement
   e. Ego
   f. Superego

14.   Why Do People Shop?

Edward M. Tauber

The field of consumer behavior has experienced a dynamic period of growth over the past 10 years. It is frequently overlooked, however, that this broad area consists of three distinct activities: *shopping, buying,* and *consuming.* Considerable progress has been achieved in identifying the behavioral dimensions of buying, and a number of theories of buying behavior have been postulated. However, less is known about the determinants of consuming and shopping which are also of substantial theoretical and managerial importance.

This article attempts to encourage

behavioral research and theory building concerning shopping behavior by presenting some exploratory research findings on the question of why do people shop?

Numerous writings have been directed to this question. For example, researchers have suggested that shopping is a function of the nature of the product,[1] the degree of perceived risk inherent in the product class,[2] and the level of knowledge or amount of information about alternatives.[3] All of these answers are directed at the question, "Why do people shop in *more* than one store?" (comparison shopping). Other authors have maintained that shopping is a function of location, product assortment, and store image.[4] Again, these are variables which help explain, "Why do people shop *where* they do?" (store patronage).

The question considered in this article is, "Why do people shop?" (i.e., go to a store in the first place). The most obvious answer, "because they need to purchase something," can be a most deceptive one and reflects a marketing myopia which management has been cautioned to avoid—a product orientation. This answer considers only the products which people may purchase and is but a partial and insufficient basis for behavioral explanations. It implicitly assumes that the shopping motive is a simple function of the buying motive.

This article hypothesizes that peoples' motives for shopping are a function of many variables, *some* of which are unrelated to the actual buying of products. It is maintained that an understanding of shopping motives requires the consideration of satisfactions which shopping *activities* provide, as well as the utility obtained from the *merchandise* that may be purchased. If needs other than those associated with particular products motivate people to go to a store, the retailer should incorporate this information into his marketing strategy.

METHODOLOGY

An exploratory study was undertaken to determine some reasons why people shop. Individual in-depth interviews were conducted in the Los Angeles area with a convenience sample of 30 people, divided evenly between men and women. Ages of respondents ranged from 20 to 47. Rather than a direct approach in questioning subjects as to why they shop, respondents were asked to recall their most recent shopping trips (of any type), to discuss their activities while shopping, and what they enjoyed about the trip. After considerable probing along these lines, the discussion narrowed to how various types of shopping differed, the subject's preferences for these different types, and his or her reasons.

From the list of reported shopping activities and satisfactions, the author categorized the responses into a number of hypothesized motives for shopping, classified (ex post) as either personal or social. While exploratory research results can be evaluated only on the basis of face validity, some of these motives for shopping have been identified in previous studies. A number of these motives do not relate to purchasing interest.

[1]Richard H. Holton, "The Distinction Between Convenience Goods, Shopping Goods and Specialty Goods," *Journal of Marketing,* Vol. 22 (July, 1958), p. 56.

[2]Donald F. Cox, ed., *Risk Taking and Information Handling in Consumer Behavior* (Boston: Graduate School of Business Administration, Harvard University, 1967).

[3]John A. Howard and Jagdish N. Sheth, *The Theory of Buyer Behavior* (New York: John Wiley and Sons, 1969), pp. 286–295; and Louis P. Bucklin, "Testing Propensities to Shop," *Journal of Marketing,* Vol. 30 (January, 1966), pp. 22–27.

[4]Louis P. Bucklin, "The Concept of Mass in Intra-Urban Shopping," *Journal of Marketing,* Vol. 31 (October, 1967), pp. 37–42.

HYPOTHESIZED MOTIVES FOR SHOPPING

Personal Motives

Role playing—Many activities are learned behaviors, traditionally expected or accepted as part of a certain position or role in society—mother, housewife, husband, or student. A person internalizes these behaviors as "required" and is motivated to participate in the expected activities. For example, grocery shopping is a customary activity of the house-wife. Attempts to eliminate "food shopping" through home delivery and telephone order have to date been relatively unsuccessful. Apparently, *the process* of grocery shopping has positive utility for a large segment of women who view it as an integral part of their role.

Diversion—Shopping can offer an opportunity for diversion from the routine of daily life and thus represents a form of recreation. It can provide free family entertainment which is available without the necessity of formal dress or preplanning. The common term "browsing" and the phenomenon of masses strolling through shopping centers reinforce the belief that shopping is a national pastime. Indoor shoping malls are in an advantageous position to encourage this activity through exhibits and other traffic-generating attractions that appeal to various family members.

Self-gratification—Different emotional states or moods may be relevant for explaining why (and when) someone goes shopping. For example, a person may go to a store in search of diversion when he is bored or go in search of social contact when he feels lonely. Likewise, he may go to a store to buy "something nice" for himself when he is depressed. Several subjects in this study reported that often they alleviate depression by simply spending money on themselves. In this case, the shopping trip is motivated not by the expected utility of consuming, but by the utility of the buying *process* itself.

Learning About New Trends—Products are intimately entwined in one's daily activities and often serve as symbols reflecting attitudes and life styles. An individual learns about trends and movements and the symbols that support them when he visits a store. Rich and Portis found that among department and discount store shoppers in New York and Cleveland, 30% said "seeing new items and getting new ideas" was the reason they enjoyed shopping.[5] Many people are interested in keeping informed about the latest trends in fashion, styling, or product innovations. While such learning may take place with or without a purchase, a certain segment of shoppers for each product category is more prone to buying new items. Stores which are trend-conscious may appeal to these innovators.[6]

Physical Activity—An urban environment characterized by mass transportation and freeway driving provides little opportunity for individuals to exercise at a leisurely pace. Shopping can provide people with a considerable amount of exercise. Many retailers attempt to minimize the walking distance on their premises believing that shoppers perceive it to be an inconvenience. However, some shoppers apparently welcome the chance to walk in centers and malls that have been designed with internal thruways.

Sensory Stimulation—Retail institutions provide many potential sensory benefits for shoppers. Customers browse through a store looking at the merchandise and at each other; they enjoy handling the merchandise, and are

[5]Stuart V. Rich and Bernard Portis, "Clues for Action from Shopper Preferences," *Harvard Business Review,* Vol. 41 (March–April, 1963), p. 147.
[6]See Thomas S. Robertson, *Innovative Behavior and Communication* (New York: Holt, Rinehart, and Winston, Inc., 1971).

either trying it on or trying it out. Sound can also be important, since a "noisy" environment creates a different image than one which is characterized by silence or soft background music. Even scent may be relevant; for instance, stores may possess a distinctive odor of perfume or of prepared food. Structured surveys that attempt to measure why people shop may not detect such influences since shoppers infrequently recall these stimuli in a top-of-mind response. Nevertheless, the gestalt of the shopping environment may influence a consumer's decision to shop in a specific store or mall.

Social Motives

Social Experiences Outside the Home—The marketplace has traditionally been a center of social activity. In a number of underdeveloped countries, the market still serves as a gathering place for a town's inhabitants. Many parts of the United States still have "market days," "county fairs," and "town squares" that offer a time and place for social interaction. In urban environments contemporary equivalents exist in sidewalk sales, auctions, and swap meets. In general, shopping can provide the opportunity for a social experience outside the home (e.g., seeking new acquaintances or meeting those of the opposite sex). Some shopping trips may result in direct encounters with friends (e.g., neighborhood women at a supermarket); on others the social contact may be more indirect, as exemplified by the pastime of "people watching."

Communication with Others Having a Similar Interest—Common interests are a major link in stimulating communication and association between individuals. Many hobbies center around products or services, such as boating, collecting stamps, car customizing, and home decorating. Stores that offer hobby-related goods serve as a focal point for people with similar interests to interact. People like to talk with others about their interests, and sales personnel are frequently sought to provide special information concerning the activity.

Peer Group Attraction—The patronage of a store sometimes reflects a desire to be with one's peer group or a reference group to which one aspires to belong. For instance, record stores are common "hangouts" for teen-agers. Such stores provide a meeting place where members of a peer group may gather. This "shopping" attraction is not necessarily related to the motive of common interest since the gathering spot tends to change over time; in many cases the shopper may have limited interest in the product category and little intention to make a purchase. However, if group status is associated with one's knowledge of the category and nature of holdings (e.g., size of record collection), then peer group influence may motivate the person to "develop" an interest in the product.

Status and Authority—Many shopping experiences provide the opportunity for an individual to command attention and respect. In few other activities can a person expect to be "waited on" without having to pay for this service. A person can attain a feeling of status and power in this limited "master-servant" relationship. The general concept of a store is an institution which *serves* the public.

Store personnel compete for the buyer's favor, especially in lines of merchandise where comparison shopping is likely (e.g., expensive clothes, durables). In such instances, shopping can be more enjoyable than buying. For some customers the enjoyment of this sense of power may considerably delay a purchase decision since it terminates the attention they are receiving.

Pleasure of Bargaining—For many shoppers, bargaining is a degrading activity; haggling implies that one is "cheap." Others, however, appear to enjoy the process believing that with bargaining goods can be reduced to a more reasonable price.

In addition to this competition between buyer and seller, there also appears to be an implicit competition that occurs between buyers—a type of ego-centered buyer competition. An individual prides himself in his ability to make wise purchases or to obtain bargains.

In a face-to-face exchange with flexible prices, a perceived bargain would result when the buyer believes he has paid less for a product than others will have to pay the seller for the same merchandise. The presence of "fixed" labeled prices prevents the buyer from deriving satisfaction in this manner. To the extent that a person perceives himself as a wise shopper, he will seek bargains in fixed-price situations by looking at relative prices between stores (comparison shopping) or relative prices over time (special sales).

IMPULSE SHOPPING

If the shopping motive is a function of only the buying motive, the decision to shop will occur when a person's need for particular goods becomes sufficiently strong for him to allocate time, money, and effort to visit a store. However, the multiplicity of hypothesized shopping motives suggests that a person may also go shopping when he needs attention, wants to be with peers, desires to meet people with similar interests, feels a need to exercise, or has leisure time. The foregoing discussion indicates that a person experiences a need and recognizes that shopping activities may satisfy that need. Yet, retailers often observe that not all of their customers' behavior is so well planned. In the same way that a person may walk down an aisle viewing

merchandise and buying on impulse, he may also drive or walk down a street viewing stores and deciding to enter on impulse.

The likelihood of going shopping on impulse has probably increased over time with changes in the concept of convenience. Gravitationalists[7] and behaviorists[8] have traditionally evaluated a store's attraction power in terms of the number of potential customers within a given radius of a store, or from the viewpoint of the customer's convenience, distance (or time) traveled from his home to that store. However, Robarts suggests that a number of nonretail spatial attractors may also influence a shopper's store patronage decision: e.g., employment, social, religious, education, club, or recreational activities.[9] Thus, shopping convenience would be determined by "the spatial juxtapositions of the greatest number of retail and non-retail attractors."[10] Since many people spend relatively little time at home, a definition of convenience which uses the home as the focal point may be misleading. The existence of modern transportation and the availability of increasing amounts of discretionary time serve to expose people to many shopping clusters while in transit to their job, or social and recreational activities. This mobility increases exposure to new shopping alternatives and enhances opportunities for impulse shopping. The sight of a store may serve as a reminder to purchase needed items. On the other hand, impulse shopping may be

[7]See P. D. Converse, "New Laws of Retail Gravitation," *Journal of Marketing,* Vol. 14 (October, 1949), pp. 379–384.

[8]See David L. Huff, "Defining and Estimating a Trading Area," *Journal of Marketing,* Vol. 28 (July, 1964), pp. 34–38.

[9]A. O. Robarts, "A Revised Look at Selected Determinants of Consumer Spatial Behavior," in *Proceedings,* Thirteenth Annual Conference, Association of Canadian Schools of Business (Summer, 1969).

[10]Same reference as footnote 9, p. 219.

prompted by one of the motives identified above with no planned purchase intended.

SUMMARY AND IMPLICATIONS

It is important to recognize the distinction between the activities of shopping, buying, and consuming and to understand the behavioral determinants of each. A unified theory of shopper behavior does not presently exist. This exploratory study has sought to advance the development of such a theory by identifying a number of hypotheses concerning why people shop. Future research should attempt to quantify the relative importance of these motives (and others that might be discovered) for different types of shopping trips and within different defined shopper segments. If the findings reported here are verified, there are substantial implications for retail management.

If the shopping process offers benefits other than exposure to products, then retail innovations that attempt to reduce "shopping effort" (vending machines, mail order, or home delivery) may have a dim future for some product categories. Automatic vending of convenience goods, especially confectionary items and cigarettes, has had notable success, but efforts to market presold grocery items in this manner have not been successful.[11] In addition, in-home shopping by telephone or mail has never captured a large percentage of retail sales.

Retailers may find that these hypothesized shopping motives offer additional opportunities for market segmentation and store differentiation. According to Haley, "the benefits which people are seeking in consum-

ing a given product are the basic reasons for the existence of true market segments."[12] Darden and Reynolds found significant differences in customer shopping orientation, verifying Stone's contention that some shoppers are largely concerned with buying (economic shopper), while others are more concerned with socializing (personalizing shopper).[13] Thus, shopper segments may be distinguished by their preferences for the alternative benefits they obtain from shopping.

In the search for differential advantage, product-related store benefits such as quality lines, low prices, and credit can be easily duplicated by the competition. To some extent, even new store locations can be matched by competitors establishing nearby branches. In the future, the ability to gain a distinct differential advantage may depend on catering to shopping motives that are not product related.

Levitt and others have urged firms to broadly define their business from the standpoint of the consumer benefits it provides.[14] Product-oriented retailers would probably define their business as "retail distribution," and emphasize the promotion and distribution of goods. However, the list of shopping motives identified above might suggest that

[11]See Charles R. Goeldner, "Automatic Selling, Will It Work?" *Journal of Retailing,* Vol. 38 (Summer, 1962), pp. 41–46, 51–52.

[12]R. Haley, "Benefit Segmentation: A Decision-oriented Research Tool," *Journal of Marketing,* Vol. 32 (July, 1968), p. 31.

[13]William Darden and Fred Reynolds, "Shopping Orientations and Product Usage Rates," *Journal of Marketing Research,* Vol. VIII (November, 1971), pp. 505–508; and G. Stone, "City Shoppers and Urban Identification: Observations on the Social Psychology of City Life," *The American Journal of Sociology* (July, 1954).

[14]Theodore Levitt, *Innovation in Marketing: New Perspectives for Profit and Growth* (New York: McGraw-Hill Book Company, 1962); and Peter F. Drucker. "What is Business?" in *The Practice of Management* (New York: Harper and Row, Inc., 1954).

many retailers would benefit by defining their business as being part of the social-recreational industry. As businesses which offer social and recreational appeal, retailers must acknowledge that they are competing directly for the consumer's time and money with other alternatives that provide similar benefits.

Questions

1. Would buying motives be any different from shopping motives discussed in this article? Explain.
2. Name and give an example of each of the personal shopping motives.
3. Name and give an example of each of the social shopping motives.

Part D
PERCEPTION

15. They Saw a Game: A Case Study

Albert H. Hastorf

Hadley Cantril

On a brisk Saturday afternoon, November 23, 1951, the Dartmouth football team played Princeton in Princeton's Palmer Stadium. It was the last game of the season for both teams and of rather special significance because the Princeton team had won all its games so far and one of its players, Kazmaier, was receiving All-American mention and had just appeared as the cover man on *Time* magazine, and was playing his last game.

A few minutes after the opening kick-off, it became apparent that the game was going to be a rough one. The referees were kept busy blowing their whistles and penalizing both sides. In the second quarter, Princeton's star left the game with a broken nose. In the third quarter, a Dartmouth player was taken off the field with a broken leg. Tempers flared both during and after the game. The official statistics of the game, which Princeton won, showed that Dartmouth was penalized 70 yards, Princeton 25, not counting more than a few plays in which both sides were penalized.

Needless to say, accusations soon began to fly. The game immediately became a matter of concern to players, students, coaches, and the administrative officials of the two institu-

tions, as well as to alumni and the general public who had not seen the game but had become sensitive to the problem of big-time football through the recent exposures of subsidized players, commercialism, etc. Discussion of the game continued for several weeks.

One of the contributing factors to the extended discussion of the game was the extensive space given to it by both campus and metropolitan newspapers. An indication of the fervor with which the discussions were carried on is shown by a few excerpts from the campus dailies.

For example, on November 27 (four days after the game), the *Daily Princetonian* (Princeton's student newspaper) said:

> This observer has never seen quite such a disgusting exhibition of so-called "sport." Both teams were guilty but the blame must be laid primarily on Dartmouth's doorstep. Princeton, obviously the better team, had no reason to rough up Dartmouth. Looking at the situation rationally, we don't see why the Indians should make a deliberate attempt to cripple Dick Kazmaier or any other Princeton player. The Dartmouth psychology, however, is not rational itself.

151

The November 30th edition of the *Princeton Alumni Weekly* said:

> But certain memories of what occurred will not be easily erased. Into the record books will go in indelible fashion the fact that the last game of Dick Kazmaier's career was cut short by more than half when he was forced out with a broken nose and a mild concussion, sustained from a tackle that came well after he had thrown a pass.
>
> This second-period development was followed by a third quarter outbreak of roughness that was climaxed when a Dartmouth player deliberately kicked Brad Glass in the ribs while the latter was on his back. Throughout the often unpleasant afternoon, there was undeniable evidence that the losers' tactics were the result of an actual style of play, and reports on other games they have played this season substantiate this.

Dartmouth students were "seeing" an entirely different version of the game through the editorial eyes of the *Dartmouth* (Dartmouth's undergraduate newspaper). For example, on November 27 the *Dartmouth* said:

> However, the Dartmouth-Princeton game set the stage for the other type of dirty football. A type which may be termed as an unjustifiable accusation.
>
> Dick Kazmaier was injured early in the game. Kazmaier was the star, an All-American. Other stars have been injured before, but Kazmaier had been built to represent a Princeton idol. When an idol is hurt there is only one recourse—the tag of dirty football. So what did the Tiger Coach Charley Caldwell do? He announced to the world that the Big Green had been out to extinguish the Princeton star. His purpose was achieved.
>
> After this incident, Caldwell instilled the old see-what-they-did-go-get-them attitude into his players. His talk got results. Gene Howard and Jim Miller were both injured. Both had dropped back to pass, had passed, and were standing unprotected in the backfield. Result: one bad leg and one leg broken.
>
> The game was rough and did get a bit out of hand in the third quarter. Yet most of the

roughing penalties were called against Princeton while Dartmouth received more of the illegal-use-of-the-hands variety.

On November 28 the *Dartmouth* said:

> Dick Kazmaier of Princeton admittedly is an unusually able football player. Many Dartmouth men traveled to Princeton, not expecting to win—only hoping to see an All-American in action. Dick Kazmaier was hurt in the second period, and played only a token part in the remainder of the game. For this, spectators were sorry.
>
> But there were no such feelings for Dick Kazmaier's health. Medical authorities have confirmed that as a relatively unprotected passing and running star in a contact sport, he is quite liable to injury. Also, his particular injuries—a broken nose and slight concussion—were no more serious than is experienced almost any day in any football practice, where there is no more serious stake than playing the following Saturday. Up to the Princeton game, Dartmouth players suffered about 10 known nose fractures and face injuries, not to mention several slight concussions.
>
> Did Princeton players feel so badly about losing their star? They shouldn't have. During the past undefeated campaign they stopped several individual stars by a concentrated effort, including such mainstays as Frank Hauff of Navy, Glenn Adams of Pennsylvania and Rocco Calvo of Cornell.
>
> In other words, the same brand of football condemned by the *Prince*—that of stopping the big man—is practiced quite successfully by the Tigers.

Basically, then, there was disagreement as to what had happened during the "game." Hence we took the opportunity presented by the occasion to make a "real life" study of a perceptual problem.[1]

---

[1] We are not concerned here with the problem of guilt or responsibility for infractions, and nothing here implies any judgment as to who was to blame.

PROCEDURE

Two steps were involved in gathering data. The first consisted of answers to a questionnaire designed to get reactions to the game and to learn something of the climate of opinion in each institution. This questionnaire was administered a week after the game to both Dartmouth and Princeton undergraduates who were taking introductory and intermediate psychology courses.

The second step consisted of showing the same motion picture of the game to a sample of undergraduates in each school and having them check on another questionnaire, as they watched the film, any infraction of the rules they saw and whether these infractions were "mild" or "flagrant."[2] At Dartmouth, members of two fraternities were asked to view the film on December 7; at Princeton, members of two undergraduate clubs saw the film early in January.

The answers to both questionnaires were carefully coded and transferred to punch cards.[3]

RESULTS

Table 1 shows the questions which received different replies from the two student populations on the first questionnaire.

Questions asking if the students had friends on the team, if they had ever played football themselves, if they felt they knew the rules of the game well, etc. showed no differences in either school and no relation to

[2] The film shown was kindly loaned for the purpose of the experiment by the Dartmouth College Athletic Council. It should be pointed out that a movie of a football game follows the ball, is thus selective, and omits a good deal of the total action on the field. Also, of course, in viewing only a film of a game, the possibilities of participation as spectator are greatly limited.

[3] We gratefully acknowledge the assistance of Virginia Zerega, Office of Public Opinion Research, and J. L. McCandless, Princeton University, and E. S. Horton, Dartmouth College, in the gathering and collation of the data.

answers given to other questions. This is not surprising since the students in both schools come from essentially the same type of educational, economic, and ethnic background.

Summarizing the data of Tables 1 and 2, we find a marked contrast between the two student groups.

Nearly all *Princeton* students judged the game as "rough and dirty"—not one of them thought it "clean and fair." And almost nine-tenths of them thought the other side started the rough play. By and large they felt that the charges they understood were being made were true; most of them felt the charges were made in order to avoid similar situations in the future.

When Princeton students looked at the movie of the game, they saw the Dartmouth team make over twice as many infractions as their own team made. And they saw the Dartmouth team make over twice as many infractions as were seen by Dartmouth students. When Princeton students judged these infractions as "flagrant" or "mild," the ratio was about two "flagrant" to one "mild" on the Dartmouth team, and about one "flagrant" to three "mild" on the Princeton team.

As for the *Dartmouth* students, while the plurality of answers fell in the "rough and dirty" category, over one-tenth thought the game was "clean and fair" and over a third introduced their own category of "rough and fair" to describe the action. Although a third of the Dartmouth students felt that Dartmouth was to blame for starting the rough play, the majority of Dartmouth students thought both sides were to blame. By and large, Dartmouth men felt that the charges they understood were being made were not true, and most of them thought the reason for the charges was Princeton's concern for its football star.

When Dartmouth students looked at the movie of the game they saw both teams make

Table 1 / Data from First Questionnaire

Question	Dart-mouth students (N = 163) %	Prince-ton students (N = 161) %
1. Did you happen to see the actual game between Dart-mouth and Princeton in Palmer Stadium this year?		
Yes	33	71
No	67	29
2. Have you seen a movie of the game or seen it on television?		
Yes, movie	33	2
Yes, television	0	1
No, neither	67	97
3. (Asked of those who an-swered "yes" to either or both of above questions.) From your observations of what went on at the game, do you believe the game was clean and fairly played, or that it was unnecessarily rough and dirty?		
Clean and fair	6	0
Rough and dirty	24	69
Rough and fair*	25	2
No answer	45	29
4. (Asked of those who answered "no" on both of the first questions.) From what you have heard and read about the game, do you feel it was clean and fairly played, or that it was unnecessarily rough and dirty?		
Clean and fair	7	0
Rough and dirty	18	24
Rough and fair*	14	1
Don't know	6	4
No answer	55	71
(Combined answers to ques-tions 3 and 4 above)		
Clean and fair	13	0
Rough and dirty	42	93
Rough and fair*	39	3
Don't know	6	4

Table 1 / *continued*

Question	Dartmouth Students (N = 163) %	Princeton Students (N = 161) %
5. From what you saw in the game or the movies, or from what you have read, which team do you feel started the rough play?		
Dartmouth started it	36	86
Princeton started it	2	0
Both started it	53	11
Neither	6	1
No answer	3	2
6. What is your understanding of the charges being made?**		
Dartmouth tried to get Kazmaier	71	47
Dartmouth intentionally dirty	52	44
Dartmouth unnecessarily rough	8	35
7. Do you feel there is any truth to these charges?		
Yes	10	55
No	57	4
Partly	29	35
Don't know	4	6
8. Why do you think the charges were made?		
Injury to Princeton star	70	23
To prevent repetition	2	46
No answer	28	31

* This answer was not included on the checklist but was written in by the percentage of students indicated.
** Replies do not add to 100% since more than one charge could be given.

about the same number of infractions. And they saw their own team make only half the number of infractions the Princeton students saw them make. The ratio of "flagrant" to "mild" infractions was about one to one when Dartmouth students judged the Dartmouth team, and about one "flagrant" to two "mild" when Dartmouth students judged infractions made by the Princeton team.

It should be noted that Dartmouth and Princeton students were thinking of different

Table 2 / Data From Second Questionnaire Checked While Seeing Film

| Group | N | Total Number of Infractions Checked Against | | | |
| | | Dartmouth Team | | Princeton Team | |
		Mean	SD	Mean	SD
Dartmouth students	48	4.3*	2.7	4.4	2.8
Princeton students	49	9.8*	5.7	4.2	3.5

* Significant at the .01 level.

charges in judging their validity and in assigning reasons as to why the charges were made. It should also be noted that whether or not students were spectators of the game in the stadium made little difference in their responses.

INTERPRETATION: THE NATURE OF A SOCIAL EVENT[4]

It seems clear that the "game" actually was many different games and that each version of the events that transpired was just as "real" to a particular person as other versions were to other people. A consideration of the experiential phenomena that constitute a "football game" for the spectator may help us both to account for the results obtained and illustrate something of the nature of any social event.

Like any other complex social occurrence, a "football game" consists of a whole host of happenings. Many different events are occurring simultaneously. Furthermore, each happening is a link in a chain of happenings, so that one follows another in sequence. The "football game," as well as other complex social situations, consists of a whole matrix of events. In the game situation, this matrix of events consists of the actions of all the players, together with the behavior of the referees and linesmen, the action on the sidelines, in the grandstands, over the loudspeaker, etc.

Of crucial importance is the fact that an "occurrence" on the football field or in any other social situation does not become an experiential "event" unless and until some significance is given to it: an "occurrence" becomes an "*event*" only when the happening has significance. And a happening generally has significance only if it reactivates learned significances already registered in what we have called a person's assumptive form-world (1).

Hence the particular occurrences that different people experienced in the football game were a limited series of events from the total matrix of events *potentially* available to them. People experienced those occurrences that reactivated significances they brought to the occasion; they failed to experience those occurrences which did not reactivate past significances. We do not need to introduce

[4]The interpretation of the nature of a social event sketched here is in part based on discussions with Adelbert Ames, Jr., and is being elaborated in more detail elsewhere.

"attention" as an "intervening third" (to paraphrase James on memory) to account for the selectivity of the experiential process.

In this particular study, one of the most interesting examples of this phenomenon was a telegram sent to an officer of Dartmouth College by a member of a Dartmouth alumni group in the Midwest. He had viewed the film which had been shipped to his alumni group from Princeton after its use with Princeton students, who saw, as we noted, an average of over nine infractions by Dartmouth players during the game. The alumnus, who couldn't see the infractions he had heard publicized, wired:

> Preview of Princeton movies indicates considerable cutting of important part please wire explanation and possibly air mail missing part before showing scheduled for January 25 we have splicing equipment.

The "same" sensory impingements emanating from the football field, transmitted through the visual mechanism to the brain, also obviously gave rise to different experiences in different people. The significances assumed by different happenings for different people depend in large part on the purposes people bring to the occasion and the assumptions they have of the purposes and probable behavior of other people involved. This was amusingly pointed out by the New York *Herald Tribune*'s sports columnist, Red Smith, in describing a prize fight between Chico Vejar and Carmine Fiore in his column of December 21, 1951. Among other things, he wrote:

> You see, Steve Ellis is the proprietor of Chico Vejar, who is a highly desirable tract of Stamford, Conn., welterweight. Steve is also a radio announcer. Ordinarily there is no conflict between Ellis the Brain and Ellis the Voice because Steve is an uncommonly substantial lump of meat who can support

both halves of a split personality and give away weight on each end without missing it.

This time, though, the two Ellises met head-on, with a sickening, rending crash. Steve the Manager sat at ringside in the guise of Steve the Announcer broadcasting a dispassionate, unbiased, objective report of Chico's adventures in the ring. . . .

Clear as mountain water, his words came through, winning big for Chico. Winning? Hell, Steve was slaughtering poor Fiore.

Watching and listening, you could see what a valiant effort the reporter was making to remain cool and detached. At the same time you had an illustration of the old, established truth that when anybody with a preference watches a fight, he sees only what he prefers to see.

That is always so. That is why, after any fight that doesn't end in a clean knockout, there always are at least a few hoots when the decision is announced. A guy from, say, Billy Graham's neighborhood goes to see Billy fight and he watches Graham all the time. He sees all the punches Billy throws, and hardly any of the punches Billy catches. So it was with Steve.

"Fiore feints with a left," he would say, honestly believing that Fiore hadn't caught Chico full on the chops. "Fiore's knees buckle," he said, "and Chico backs away." Steve didn't see the hook that had driven Chico back. . . .

In brief, the data here indicate that there is no such "thing" as a "game" existing "out there" in its own right which people merely "observe." The "game" "exists" for a person and is experienced by him only in so far as certain happenings have significances in terms of his purpose. Out of all the occurrences going on in the environment, a person selects those that have some significance for him from his own egocentric position in the total matrix.

Obviously in the case of a football game, the value of the experience of watching the game is enhanced if the purpose of "your" team is accomplished, that is, if the happening of the desired consequence is experienced—i.e., if your team wins. But the value attribute of the experience can, of course, be spoiled if the desire to win crowds out behavior we value and have come to call sportsmanlike.

The sharing of significances provides the links except for which a "social" event would not be experienced and would not exist for anyone.

A "football game" would be impossible except for the rules of the game which we bring to the situation and which enable us to share with others the significances of various happenings. These rules make possible a certain repeatability of events such as first downs, touchdowns, etc. If a person is unfamiliar with the rules of the game, the behavior he sees lacks repeatability and consistent significance and hence "doesn't make sense."

And only because there is the possibility of repetition is there the possibility that a happening has a significance. For example, the balls used in games are designed to give a high degree of repeatability. While a football is about the only ball used in games which is not a sphere, the shape of the modern football has apparently evolved in order to achieve a higher degree of accuracy and speed in forward passing than would be obtained with a spherical ball, thus increasing the repeatability of an important phase of the game.

The rules of a football game, like laws, rituals, customs, and mores, are registered and preserved forms of sequential significances enabling people to share the significances of occurrences. The sharing of sequential significances which have value for us provides the links that operationally make social events possible. They are analogous to the forces of attraction that hold parts of an atom together, keeping each part from following its individual, independent course.

From this point of view it is inaccurate and misleading to say that different people have different "attitudes" concerning the same "thing." For the "thing" simply is *not* the same for different people whether the "thing" is a football game, a presidential candidate, Communism, or spinach. We do not simply "react to" a happening or to some impingement from the environment in a determined way (except in behavior that has become reflexive or habitual). We behave according to what we bring to the occasion, and what each of us brings to the occasion is more or less unique. And except for these significances which we bring to the occasion, the happenings around us would be meaningless occurrences, would be "inconsequential."

From the transactional view, an attitude is not a predisposition to react in a certain way to an occurrence or stimulus "out there" that exists in its own right with certain fixed characteristics which we "color" according to our predisposition (Kilpatrick, 1952). That is, a subject does not simply "react to" an "object." An attitude would rather seem to be a complex of registered significances reactivated by some stimulus which assumes its own particular significance for us in terms of our purposes. That is, the object as experienced would not exist for us except for the reactivated aspects of the form-world which provide particular significance to the hieroglyphics of sensory impingements.

REFERENCES

Cantril, H. *The "why" of man's experience.* New York: Macmillan, 1950.
Kilpatrick, F. P. (Ed.) *Human behavior from the transactional point of view.* Hanover, N.H.: Institute for Associated Research, 1952.

Questions

1. Why did the Dartmouth students and the Princeton students differ in response to certain questions on the questionnaire? For what questions was this particularly the case?
2. Explain what the authors mean when they say that "the 'game' actually was many different games."
3. From the transactional view brought out in this article, give a definition of an "attitude."

16. Brand Identification and Perception

Ralph I. Allison

Kenneth P. Uhl

As a company tries to find the factors accounting for strong and weak markets, typical consumer explanations for both tend to be about the physical attributes of the product. That is, the product quality often becomes both the hero and the culprit, like Dr. Jekyll and Mr. Hyde, but with the hideous reversal coming not by night but by market. The experiment presented in this paper was also designed to give rough measurements of the magnitude of the marketing influences. Unidentified and then labeled bottles of beer were delivered to homes of taste testing participants on successive weeks. The drinkers' taste test ratings provided the data for the study.

THE EXPERIMENTAL DESIGN

The principal hypothesis subjected to testing through experimentation[1] was this: "Beer drinkers cannot distinguish among major brands of unlabeled beer either on an overall basis or on selected characteristics." Beer drinkers were identified as males who drank beer at least three times a week.

The test group was composed of 326 drinkers who were randomly selected, agreed to participate in the study, and provided necessary classification data. Each participant in the experiment was given a six-pack of unlabeled beer, identified only by tags bearing the letters A,B,C,D,E,F,G,H,I, or J. The labels had been completely soaked off and the crowns had been wire brushed to remove all brand identification from the 12-oz. brown bottles. Each six-pack contained three brands of beer with individual bottles randomly placed in the pack so no one lettered tag predominated in any one position.[2] There were six different pairs placed among the 326 participants. An effort was made to give each participant a six-pack that contained the brand of beer he said he most often drank. The groups and numbers were placed as follows:

	Place
Group 1 (AB,CD,EF)	53
Group 2 (AB,CD,IJ)	55
Group 3 (AB,CD,GH)	55
Group 4 (AB,EF,IJ)	55
Group 5 (AB,GH,IJ)	54
Group 6 (AB,EF,GH)	54
	326

A and B represented one of the company's beer brands; C and D represented one major regional beer brand; and E and F were one other major brand of regional beer. G and H were one national brand; and I and J were the fifth well-known beer brand used in the experiment. Among these five brands there were some taste differences discernible to expert taste testers.

The lettered tags (one around the collar of each bottle in the six-pack) carried a general rating scale from "1" (poor) through "10" (excellent) on the one side and a list of nine specific characteristics on the reverse side. The specific characteristics, which included after-taste, aroma, bitterness, body, carbonation, foam, lightness, strength, and sweetness, could each be rated as "too much," "just enough," or "not enough." These nine specific characteristics were selected from a much larger field. Their selection was based on both greater agreement on meaning among beer drinkers and on the ability of beer drinkers, in general, to identify and rate them.

One week after the distribution of the unlabeled beer, the empties, nude except for the rating tags, were picked up and new six-packs left behind. This time, however, the bottles were properly labeled with each six-pack containing six different brands of beer (the same five brands plus a sixth brand that

was added for the labeled test). In addition, each deposit bottle was tagged, but these tags were identified by the letters K through P. A week after the second placement the empties and rating tags were picked up.

The experiment produced a number of useful findings. More specifically, evidence was available to answer these questions:

1. Could beer drinkers, in general, distinguish among various beers in a blind test?
2. Could beer drinkers identify "their" brands in a blind test?
3. What influence would brand identification have on consumers' evaluations of various beer brands?
4. What influence would brand identification have on consumers' evaluations of specified beer characteristics?

TASTE DIFFERENCES IN A BLIND TEST

The data produced by the experiment indicated that the beer drinkers, as a group, could not distinguish the taste differences among the brands on an overall basis. Table 1 contains the evidence on these ratings. Basically, there appeared to be no significant

Table 1 / Blind Overall Taste Test—All Participants

Beer brand	Overall rating	Significantly different from other brands[a]
AB	65.0	No
CD	64.1	No
EF	63.3	No
GH	63.4	No
IJ	63.3	No

[a] At the .05 level.
Source: Carling Brewing Company.

Table 2 / Blind Taste Test—Specific Characteristics (All Participants)

Characteristic	Per cent indicating "just right" by beer brands					Significant difference among brands[a]
	AB	CD	EF	GH	IJ	
After-taste	59	52	57	55	55	No
Aroma	64	68	63	62	62	No
Bitterness	58	54	53	54	54	No
Body	53	58	60	53	57	No
Carbonation	64	70	62	62	65	Only CD
Foam	62	66	63	59	66	No
Lightness	68	63	69	64	69	No
Strength	50	51	56	50	53	No
Sweetness	64	61	59	62	66	No

[a] At the .05 level.

Source: Carling Brewing Company.

difference among the various brands at the .05 level.

Beer drinkers when asked to rate the nine characteristics listed in Table 2 as "not enough," "just enough," and "too much," indicated a difference that was significant in "just enough" votes for one characteristic on one beer (carbonation of brand CD). Other than the one case, the reported differences among brands were so minor as to be not significant. A second analysis of the data, in which the "just enough" category was treated as a neutral or a zero and the "too much" and "not enough" positions as + 1 and − 1 respectively, in general, substantiated the percentage findings.[3] In addition, this analysis indicated that four of the characteristics—aroma, body, foam, and strength—were rated rather uniformly among the brands as "not enough" and one characteristic—bitterness—received a clear "too much" rating. Based on the overall taste test and the specified characteristics test, the conclusion was that beer drinkers could not distinguish taste differences among the beer brands presented in unlabeled bottles.

COULD DRINKERS IDENTIFY "THEIR" BRANDS?

The labeled test clearly indicated that beer drinkers would assign "their" brands superior ratings and, accordingly, it was assumed that if participants could identify "their" brands in the blind test that they would respond to them with superior ratings. The general ratings in the nude bottle test, by brand drunk most often, indicated that *none* of the brand groups rated the taste of "their" brand beer superior over all of the other beers (see Table 3). For example, regular drinkers of brand AB, indicated via their ratings that they preferred "their" brand over EF and CD, but they gave virtually similar ratings to brands IJ and GH as they gave to their own brand. Drinkers of the other brands did not rate "their" brands as favorably in the blind comparison tests as did AB drinkers. Drinkers of brand EF rated beer CD significantly above "their" brand. Users of IJ rated all of the comparison brands except CD as equals and CD was rated as poorer tasting. Drinkers of

Table 3 / Users' Loyalty to "Their" Brand (Blind Test)

Brand drunk most often	Taste-test ratings by brand rated					Own brand rated significantly higher than all others[a]
	AB	CD	EF	GH	IJ	
AB	67.0	62.4[b]	57.7[b]	65.0	65.8	No
CD	64.9	65.6	65.4	63.2	63.9	No
EF	68.8	74.5[b]	65.0	62.5	61.4	No
GH	55.4	59.2	68.7[b]	60.0	71.4[b]	No
IJ	68.4	60.5[b]	69.2	62.0	65.6	No

[a] At the .05 level.
[b] Brands significantly different from user's own brand.
Source: Carling Brewing Company.

brand GH must not have drunk the brand because they preferred its flavor—they rated two of the four comparison brands as superior in flavor and the other two as no less than equal to "their" brand. And based on the overall taste ratings, the regular drinkers of brand CD could just as well have drunk any of the other comparison brands—there were no significant differences among the assigned ratings.

Based on the data secured from the experiment, the finding appeared to be that most beer drinkers could *not* identify "their" brands of beer in a blind comparison test.

INFLUENCE OF BRAND IDENTIFICATION ON OVERALL RATINGS

A number of important findings arose out of comparisons of the data from the nude bottle phase with the labeled bottle phase. The overall ratings for all the brands increased considerably with brand identifications. However, there was also much variation in the amount of increase registered among the various brands. And when beer drinkers were categorized according to the brand most frequently drunk, they consistently rated

"their" beer higher than comparison beers in this positive identification taste test. Also, there was much variation in the amounts of increase—some brands received much higher ratings (i.e., overall ratings) from their regular users than did other brands from their regular users. The differences in the ratings were assumed to be due to the presence of labels—the only altered conditions of the experiment.

The data that gave rise to the several statements about the effects of brand identification are examined in more detail below. In the *blind* test, none of the five brands received overall ratings that were sufficiently different from all of the others to be considered statistically significant. However, in the labeled test the differences in all but two of the overall ratings were significant (the ratings assigned to brands EF and IJ were relatively the same). Looking at some of the other figures, brand GH was rated significantly higher than all of the other brands and CD was rated higher than all brands but GH. Other differences that were judged statistically significant can be noted in Table 4. And as can be seen in this table, all five brands in the labeled test were rated significantly higher than the same brands in the blind test. Remember, these were the same brands of

Table 4 / Comparison Taste Test—Blind vs. Labeled (Overall Ratings)

Beer brand	Blind test	Labeled test	Significant difference between blind and labeled test[a]
AB	65.0	70.6	Yes
CD	64.1	72.9	Yes
EF	63.3	67.8	Yes
GH	63.4	76.9	Yes
IJ	63.3	67.0	Yes
Significant differences between brands	None	Yes[b]	

[a] At the .05 level.
[b] All brands were significantly different from all others at the .05 level except EF and IJ relative to each other.
Source: Carling Brewing Company.

beer used in the nude test, but in the labeled test the participants could clearly identify each beer brand.

The loyalty of the participants toward "their" brands increased when positive brand identification was possible (see Table 5). All of the labeled ratings assigned by regular users were significantly higher than the blind test ratings. In the blind test, participants indicated, at best, very little ability to pick "their" beers and set them off with relatively high overall ratings. For example, the regular

drinkers of brand CD in the blind test awarded all of the brands about the same overall rating. However, in the labeled test, the CD drinkers awarded their beer brand an overall rating of 83.6, an 18 point increase over the blind test rating. This change was sufficiently above their overall ratings of all comparison brands to be statistically significant.

The gains in ratings were not uniform from one group to another. In the labeled test, brands GH, CD, and EF picked up more sizable gains than did AB and IJ. Comparison of

Table 5 / Users' Loyalty to "Their" Brand (Label Test)

Brand drunk most often	Taste-test ratings by brand rated					Own brand rated significantly higher[a]	Blind test ratings for own brand
	AB	CD	EF	GH	IJ		
AB	(77.3)	61.1	62.8	73.4	63.1	Yes	(67.0)
CD	66.3	(83.6)	67.4	78.3	63.1	Yes	(65.6)
EF	67.3	71.5	(82.3)	71.9	71.5	Yes	(65.0)
GH	73.1	72.5	77.5	(80.0)	67.5	Only over IJ	(60.0)
IJ	70.3	69.3	67.2	76.7	(73.5)	Only over EF	(65.6)

[a] At the .05 level.
Source: Carling Brewing Company.

the data in Table 5 with that in Table 3 will indicate other important rating changes from the blind to the label test.

INFLUENCE OF BRAND IDENTIFICATION ON SPECIFIED CHARACTERISTICS?

The labeled test also produced some changes in ratings of specified characteristics of beer brands. In the blind test with the "just enough" category assigned a zero value, the participants tended to rate all of the beers as not having enough aroma, body, foam, and strength. All but one of the beers were rated on bitterness as "too much," and accordingly, not sweet enough. In the labeled ratings, "aroma" was greatly improved as was "body," "foam," and "strength." However, the ratings on "bitterness" and "sweetness" remained virtually the same as recorded in the nude test.

CONCLUSIONS

Participants, in general, did not appear to be able to discern the taste differences among the various beer brands, but apparently labels, and their associations, did influence their evaluations. In other words, product distinctions or differences, in the minds of the participants, arose primarily through their receptiveness to the various firms' marketing efforts rather than through perceived physical product differences. Such a finding suggested

that the physical product differences had little to do with the various brands' relative success or failure in the market (assuming the various physical products had been relatively constant.) Furthermore, this elimination of the product variable focused attention on the various firms' marketing efforts, and, more specifically, on the resulting brand images.

This experiment also has helped the Company measure and rank its brand image relative to competitive brand images and has offered base comparison marks for similar experiments, both in the same and other markets at later dates. Such information has helped in Company evaluation and competitive marketing efforts. And to the extent that product images, and their changes, are believed to be a result of advertising (i.e., as other variables can be accounted for or held to be homogeneous among the competitive firms), the ability of firms' advertising programs to influence product images can be more thoroughly examined.

NOTES

1. The experimental design and the findings outlined are from one market area. However, similar experiments were conducted and similar results were obtained in several other markets.

2. Pretesting gave no evidence of a positional or letter bias; i.e., for participants to drink or rate the beer in any particular alphabetical or spatial order.

3. This three-place neutral center scale is in need of further testing and comparison with four-and five-position scales to help determine the amount of bias it induces.

Questions

1. Summarize the results of this study in terms of the subjects' ability to differentiate between brands of beer. What implication does this have for the importance of promotional messages?

2. What other products do you think might yield similar results in the same type of experiment?

3. Do you feel it is ethical for marketers, by means of advertising and their promotion, to try to differentiate products that are not really physically different? Explain.

17. Subliminal Stimulation—Marketing Applications

Sandra H. Hart

Stephen W. McDaniel

Few topics in the field of marketing have been more controversial than the potential for using subliminal stimuli to persuade customers to buy products. Of particular concern has been the possible use of one type of subliminal stimulation—subliminal advertising. This refers to the placement in advertisements of embeds, or hidden messages, designed to register a stimulus at the subject's subconscious or below the threshold of perception. Public concern over the possible use of such techniques has been raised at various times in recent years, going back to Vance Packard's (1957) admonition to beware of the "hidden persuaders" and more recently Wilson Bryan Key's warning that "because the media knows everything about your fantasies, fears, and intimate habits—it knows how to manipulate your buying behavior" (1976: cover). Such accusations of exploitation by advertising have heightened interest in its psychological foundations. Of particular concern has been whether or not consumers do perceive stimuli subliminally and, more importantly, whether or not advertisers can and should take advantage of this means of persuading consumers to buy a particular product.

This paper will address the broad topic of subliminal perception and look specifically at the use of subliminal stimulation in the field of advertising. Also, some additional uses of subliminal stimulation in marketing contexts will be noted. Major questions to be considered include: Does research show conclusive evidence of subliminal perception? To what extent have these studies shown subliminal advertising to be a viable tool for advertisers?

TERMS

In attempting to cover this topic, a good starting place is the definition of some key terms. Although there is no unanimity of opinion on some of the nomenclature in this field, some of the "mainstream" definitions will be presented here. This should give us some guideposts for analyzing research done in the area of subliminal perception. First of all we need to understand exactly what is meant by the term perception. Robertson (1970: 24) defines perception as an individual's "impression of a stimulus object." Thus, an object may not be perceived in the same way by two different individuals, since each person's perception of the object is based on many factors. Robertson states that what an individual sees and how he sees it are dependent upon both the stimulus itself and also the characteristics of the individual. Therefore, the psychological makeup of the individual and his or her past experiences, moods, and personality, as well as the actual physical characteristics of the object, will affect perception.

With this in mind, we consider the term subliminal perception. The term subliminal derives from *sub* (below) and *limen* (threshold or level). Therefore, subliminal perception refers to the registration of a stimulus below the threshold of an individual's perception. There are three different interpretations of perceptual threshold (Hawkins 1970: 322)— (1) registration threshold (the level below which a stimulus is presumed to have no effect on the organism); (2) absolute threshold (the length or intensity of exposure where a stimulus is correctly identified 50 percent of the time); and (3) recognition threshold (the length or intensity of exposure where a stimulus is correctly reported for the first time in a series of exposures of increasing duration or intensity). Recognition threshold is the perceptual threshold most commonly used in current studies.

Dixon (1971: 12) defines six states of subliminal perception, with the first three being most often accepted as being subliminal perception:

1. The subject responds to stimulation the energy or duration of which falls below that at which he ever reported awareness of the stimulus in some previous threshold determination.

2. He responds to a stimulus of which he pleads total unawareness.
3. He reports that he is being stimulated, but denies any awareness (i.e., knowledge) of what the stimulus was.
4. The subject reports awareness of the stimulus (i.e., he could describe it if asked), but denies any awareness of the fact that he responded to it.
5. He reports awareness of the stimulus and of making a response, but professes complete ignorance of any connection between the two.
6. In this, the final case, the subject is aware of responding to a stimulus, but unaware of that aspect of the stimulus that governs his response.

Some researchers question whether these last three levels should technically be considered subliminal perception since they involve a supraliminal stimulus. These three states allow for a message to be unconsciously perceived initially, but later consciously perceived when the subject's attention is drawn to the supposedly "subliminal" stimulus. This stimulus is somehow disguised or hidden and can be detected only when the subject is made aware of it. (Glover 1979: 274). On the other hand, a stimulus involving subliminal perception technically cannot be detected by the subject. Murch (1964: 442) recommends using the term subliminal stimulation as a general term referring to both subliminal and supraliminal perception. It is this approach that will be used for the remainder of this paper.

EXPERIMENTAL STUDIES OF SUBLIMINAL PERCEPTION

Even early philosophers speculated about the effects of subliminal stimuli on man. In his book *Subliminal Perception: The Nature of a Controversy,* Dixon (1971: 6–8) cites findings in this area going back to 400 B.C. For example, Democritus stated that "much is perceptible which is not perceived by us." Plato mentioned that a "gentle and inconsiderable process is imperceptible, but its opposite perceptible," and Aristotle spoke of imperceptibility, the effect of unperceived stimuli on dreams, and implied the existence of various thresholds of perception. Montaigne in 1580 made reference to subliminal perception in the waking state. And two statements by Leibnitz in 1698 also showed early recognition of subliminal perception: "There are also numberless perceptions, little noticed, which are not sufficiently distinguished to be perceived or remembered but which become known through certain consequences"; and, "In a word it is a great source of error to believe that there is no perception in the soul besides those of which it is conscious."

Since these early philosophers introduced the idea, subliminal perception or "behavior without awareness" has received considerable attention. When one looks at the myriad of psychological studies done in this area, it is evident that subliminal perception is a most significant topic for scientific research. In fact, the psychological literature contains several excellent review articles (Coover 1917; Collier 1940; Lazarus and McCleary 1951; Adams 1957; McConnell, Cutler, and McNeil 1958) and two books (Miller 1942; Dixon 1971). Rather than attempting to summarize each of the numerous studies covered in these reviews, we will first highlight some of the common techniques used in these types of studies and then summarize some of the major conclusions drawn from these reviews.

Techniques for Measuring Subliminal Perception

One common technique used to measure subliminal perception is the Muller-Lyer illu-

sion (McConnell, Cutler, and McNeil 1958: 55). This technique involves projecting lines or other objects onto a background that is contrasted by a different hue or brightness. The contrast between the objects and the background is such that the objects cannot be perceived consciously. This technique or a variation of it has been used for numerous experiments of subliminal perception and in determining levels of awareness. Some of these variations have centered on the use of such subliminal figures as angular lines, crossed lines, arrows, letters, and numbers.

Another commonly used technique to test for subliminal perception involves the Poeltz phenomenon (Dixon 1971: 103–52). It uses dreams or free association to determine whether a previously administered stimulus had been perceived by a subject. These stimuli are subliminal or, in some cases, concealed in a picture shown to the subject. The dreams of these subjects are then analyzed, or other free association techniques are used, to determine effect of the subliminal or supraliminal stimulus.

Many subliminal perception articles covered in the literature reviews deal with discrimination or "zero confidence" studies (McConnell, Cutler, and McNeil 1958: 55). These studies investigated the ability of subjects to discriminate such subliminal stimuli as low level electrical current, weights, letters, proper names, dots, dashes, and figures. According to Miller (1939), the earliest study in this area used a subliminal level of electrical stimulation on subjects. This study found that even though subjects were not consciously aware of the stimulus, scores from an esthesiometer—used to measure sense impressions—indicated evidence of the subliminal message's effect.

Physiological conditioning or low level behavior modification has also been studied in connection with subliminal stimuli (Mc-

Connell, Cutler, and McNeil 1958: 56). For example, Bach and Klein (1957) tested whether or not a person's verbal evaluation of a neutral drawing could be influenced by a subliminal message. They exposed subjects to subliminally projected words "happy" or "angry" on a drawing of an expressionless face. Subjects were then requested to evaluate the mood of the expressionless face. Results showed that the subliminal message did influence the subject's evaluation. Other related variables studied, and for which positive results have been found, include pupillary response to a subliminal stimulus of sound; subject's response to a subliminal light; subject's writing after exposure to subliminal printed messages of "don't write" or "write more"; and subject's drawings and descriptions of ambiguous human figures after being exposed to subliminal pictures and symbols of a sexual nature.

Other studies have investigated differences in the subject's ability to perceive subliminal stimuli based on personal factors. These studies have indicated that threshold of perception and susceptibility to a subliminal stimulus may vary by individual. Work in this area has investigated such independent variables as emotional factors, needs, personality, level of hunger drive, level of tension, and mental set (McConnell, Cutler, and McNeil 1958: 56–57).

Conclusions from Subliminal Perception Studies

All of the reviews conclude that the phenomenon of subliminal perception can be validated to some extent. Adams (1957), for example, cites seventy-four experiments dealing with subliminal perception. Of these, fifty obtained results purporting to show evidence of subliminal perception, seventeen did not obtain significant results, and seven

reported alternative explanations for the findings. And in the most recent and most comprehensive review of subliminal perception studies, Dixon (1971: 320) concludes:

> As a result of being tested in eight different contexts, subliminal stimulation has been shown to affect dreams, memory, adaptation level, conscious perception, verbal behavior, emotional responses, drive related behavior, and perceptual thresholds.

From these reviews of experimental studies of subliminal perception, the evidence is fairly supportive of subliminal stimulation's effect on individuals. Does this validation also apply when we move into the area of subliminal advertising? The next section will take a look at some experimental studies that have investigated the possible effect of subliminal advertising.

EXPERIMENTAL STUDIES OF SUBLIMINAL ADVERTISING

Reported studies dealing specifically with subliminal advertising are not nearly as plentiful as those dealing with subliminal perception in general. This may be the result of the relative newness of this area, the difficulty of performing studies with advertising, or the fact that much of the research may have been done for business use and the results therefore not made public. Perhaps businesses did not want it known that they were using an advertising technique that aroused public suspicion.

A limited number of experimental studies have been designed to test subliminal perception in areas affecting advertising. Although limited in number, they do represent controlled studies that appear to be reliable. Some of these will now be reviewed.

Physiological Drives

There have been some studies attempting to test whether or not a person's physiological drives (i.e., hunger, thirst, sex) can be influenced by subliminal advertising. Byrne (1959) had subjects rate their feelings of hunger both before and after exposure to a subliminal message. He found that the subliminally presented word "beef" increased the subject's feeling of hunger. Spence (1964) reported increased hunger ratings after subjects were exposed to the word "cheese."

Hawkins (1970) analyzed four experimental groups, each of which was exposed to a different subliminal message—a subliminally presented nonsense syllable "NYTP"; the subliminally presented nonsense syllable "NYTP" along with "forcing" the subject to recognize and repeat the word "Coke" aloud; the subliminally presented word "Coke"; and the subliminally presented words "Drink Coke." Several conclusions were drawn from this study—(1) that thirst can be aroused by a subliminal stimulus; (2) that a subliminal command was not necessary to increase the influence of the subliminal message; and (3) that a frequently presented, familiar subliminal cue may arouse the thirst drive as effectively as the infrequent supraliminal presentation of the same cue.

Bagley and Dunlap (1979) investigated the interesting question of whether or not a subliminal message of a sexual nature can increase the sexual feelings of subjects. They evaluated subjects' responses to questions pertaining to their "emotional feelings" both before and after exposure to certain magazine advertisements. These ads had been developed by an artist who made minor shadings or line changes to indicate sexual images. Words such as "sex" were also added in very small letters and blended into the background of the ad, so that they could not be consciously perceived by the subject. They concluded that the subliminal embeds did arouse sensual feelings in the subjects. These results support the findings from a similar but unscientific study done earlier by Key (1973: 3, 8). Key's study involved 1000 adult males and females who were exposed to a liquor advertisement with sexually oriented subliminal embeds. He reported that 62 percent of the subjects exhibited a "turn on"—that is, they claimed to have feelings of a sexual nature after exposure to the ad.

Behavioral Change

There have also been some experimental studies investigating whether or not overt behavior can be influenced by a subliminal advertising message. De Fleur and Petranoff (1959) attempted to test the effect of a subliminal message broadcast on television. First an attempt was made to increase viewers for a fifteen-minute news program by subliminally broadcasting "Watch Frank Edwards" during the two hours preceding the television show. The two-week effort to increase viewers was not successful. In fact, an actual decrease in viewers resulted. The second phase of their research involved using television advertisements containing a subliminal message to buy a particular food product. They measured the effects of these subliminal messages by analyzing sales figures from a wholesale distributor. Subliminal ads tested alone showed no measurable effect. When the subliminal ads were used in combination with ordinary advertising, substantial sales increases were shown. However, when the ordinary advertising was used without the subliminal ads, sales increases were even higher. Therefore, essentially negative findings resulted from this study.

Hawkins (1970) also investigated possible behavioral change by exposing subjects to a subliminal advertisement for two different perfumes. The subliminal ad showed the brand name of one perfume superimposed over a seductive picture of a woman. The results showed no influence on selection of perfumes brought about by the subliminal ad.

George and Jennings (1975) tested whether subliminal stimuli from a slide projector and also a movie projector could affect buying behavior. In highly controlled buying situations, the words "Hershey's Chocolate" were subliminally shown to two groups of college students—one group watching a film and the other watching slides. Local sales of the product were measured after each experiment, with the result being that no support was found for subliminal stimulation's effect on buying behavior.

Brand Recall

Kelly (1979) investigated subliminal embeds in magazine advertisements. He took ads that Key (1976) cited as containing subliminal messages and bound them into a "dummy" magazine. Subjects were allowed to look through this magazine and were then tested for their ability to recall the brand or illustration in the ads. He found no evidence for subliminal stimulation affecting either brand or illustration recall.

MARKETING USES OF SUBLIMINAL STIMULATION

Advertising

The actual use of subliminal techniques in advertising has been restricted to a great extent by both ethical and legal concerns. Subliminal advertising per se is not presently illegal, in spite of attempts to make it so. For example, in 1959, Representative Wright of Texas introduced a bill to Congress forbidding the use of devices for subliminal stimulation. However, after an experiment before Congress and the Federal Communication Commission (FCC), the FCC felt it unnecessary to ban the use of subliminal advertising ("Unfair to the Subconscious" 1959). Other similar efforts have been rejected. In spite of the lack of legal restrictions on its use, there are other types of restraints on subliminal advertising. The National Association of Broadcasters (NAB) in its Code for Television specifically prohibited subliminal advertising in 1959. Of course, this deals only with voluntary compliance by members of the NAB. The Federal Communication Commission and the Federal Trade Commission both have regulations affecting advertising (i.e., restrictions on deceptive advertising) that could possibly apply to subliminal advertising. Thus far, no major confrontation has occurred between subliminal advertisers and these government regulatory agencies.

Because of the somewhat restrictive, although not illegal, environment surrounding this controversial subject, it is difficult to evaluate completely the extent and the results of actual commercial use of subliminal advertising. There have no doubt been instances where it has been used, but the facts were not disclosed to the public. There have been only a few instances of the known use of subliminal advertising. Some of these will now be reviewed.

One of the first attempts at commercial use of subliminal advertising was in 1956 when BBC-TV in Great Britain projected the subliminal message, "Pirie Breaks World Record," during a broadcast (Kidd 1958). Viewers were asked if they noticed anything unusual about the program, but the few who responded indicated that the message had been visible to them and not actually subliminal.

The most well-known commercial use of subliminal advertising was a 1957 attempt by James M. Vicary to sell Cokes and popcorn through subliminal stimulation. It was this instance that actually started the uproar over the ethics and legality of using this technique. His experiment involved a New Jersey movie theater in which he used a special apparatus that flashed the words, "Eat popcorn" and "Drink Coca-Cola" onto the screen for 1/3000 of a second every five seconds. Mr. Vicary claimed that these subliminal messages increased the sale of popcorn 57 percent and Coke 17 percent ("Unseen TV Gets Exposure" 1958). This study, however, has drawn some criticisms, since no scientific data were made available to support the findings and no replication of the study with its results has occurred.

The Canadian Broadcasting Corporation tested a subliminal message that told its viewers to "telephone now." Only one viewer responded correctly to the message ("'Phone Now,' Said CBC Subliminally" 1958). A radio station in Seattle tested the effects of three different messages, two of which were subliminal. A supraliminal message encouraged listeners to drink a cup of coffee. One of the subliminal messages whispered to the listeners said "answer the phone" and the other said "someone's at the door." As measured by responses of viewers who telephoned the station, the supraliminal message was somewhat effective in communicating its message, while the subliminal messages were much less effective. Several listeners did report going to the telephone, and one person reported looking up to see if anyone was at the door ("Non-Coffee-Using Housewife Made Fresh Coffee" 1958).

A Bangor, Maine, TV station tried an experiment requesting viewers to write the station. No increase in its mail was reported ("Unfair to the Subconscious" 1959). Nucoa, a division of Best Foods, used subliminal messages in persuasive radio spots. However, no results were reported on the effectiveness of the ads ("Nucoa Uses New Subliminal Twist" 1958).

Other uses in an advertising context have been reported, although the effectiveness of the subliminal messages were not determined. For example, WCCO radio in the Minneapolis–St. Paul area broadcast a subliminal public service message—"Slippery Roads"—during icy weather. Chicago radio station WAAF broadcast the subliminal messages "Drink 7-Up," "buy Oklahoma Oil," and a paid commercial message encouraging listeners to "buy this record at Little Al's Record Shop" (Henderson 1958: 4).

In 1966, Toyota added subliminal flashbacks to a television commercial. Black and white shots of a woman driving a race car were added to a color ad depicting a housewife and her children driving a Toyota. The intent of the advertisement was to feature the higher horsepower of Toyota over its competitor, Volkswagen. The obvious purpose of the subliminal message was to help drive home this point ("Subliminal Cuts Show 'Hot Car' in New Toyota Push" 1966). A similar technique was used in 1973 to promote the game, "Husker-Do." The words "Get it" were added subliminally to a 60-second television ad for the product. When brought to the attention of the National Association of Broadcasters, they ruled that the advertisement violated its code ban on subliminal messages. The firm then deleted the subliminal messages from the ad, and no further action was taken by the NAB ("'Subliminal' Ad Flap Raised" 1973).

Other Marketing Uses

There are a few other reported uses of subliminal stimulation in marketing situations. One of the current proponents of this technique is Dr. Hal C. Becker, who has developed a machine that superimposes subliminal messages over music. This machine, called "Dr. Becker's Black Box," was issued a patent from the U.S. Patent Office in October 1966. Since inventors of patented products are given exclusive control of their work for a period of seventeen years, this means the product will be available to anyone who wishes to use it in October 1983 (Lander 1981: 107). This machine has been used for several different commercial purposes. For instance, a supermarket in New Orleans used this device in its store and reported a drop in theft from $50,000 every six months to $13,000. Cashier shortages were down from $125 to less than $10 weekly. The message subconsciously sent said: "I will not steal. If I steal, I will go to jail" (Maxwell 1980). In Buffalo, New York, real estate salesmen listened to music containing the subliminal messages, "I love my job," and "I am the greatest salesman." Revenue reportedly increased 31 percent even though advertising had been decreased (Maxwell 1980). Dr. Becker's box has also been used in reducing the anxiety of patients awaiting special treatment at McDonagh Medical Clinic in Gladstone, Missouri. Where faintings were once a problem, the hospital reports no faintings since the use of the subliminal messages designed to reduce anxiety (Maxwell 1980). Becker has also used subliminal techniques to aid people in weight reduction. He flashed subliminal background images to obese individuals and found this technique effective in reducing weight by eleven to twenty pounds in 69 percent of the individuals who attended at least half the sessions (Becker 1976).

Subliminal techniques have been used even in athletics. Becker has reportedly been involved with a subliminal program for a National Football League team. Louis Romberg, Becker's former partner (now with his own firm), has used the black box to pep up the Montreal Canadien hockey team with subliminal messages ("Secret Voices" 1979).

CONCLUSIONS

We began this paper by asking whether or not research shows conclusive evidence of subliminal perception and to what extent subliminal advertising has been shown to be a viable tool for marketers. When one steps back and takes a look at the published research and reported commercial use of subliminal stimulation—and in particular, subliminal advertising—some general conclusions can be drawn:

1. It appears that individuals do have the ability to perceive stimuli at a subliminal or unconscious level.
2. Research studies indicate that some types of behavior change might be influenced by subliminal stimulation.
3. Physiological drives such as hunger, thirst, and sex may be aroused by the use of subliminal stimuli.
4. Brand preference and ad recall have not been shown to be affected by subliminal embeds or subliminal messages.
5. There is virtually no research support for the ability of subliminal advertising to affect a person's buying behavior—that is, to purchase a product or take some other action suggested by the subliminal stimulus.

These conclusions are generally supportive of the existence of subliminal perception, but only slightly supportive of the effectiveness of subliminal stimulation within a marketing realm. Of particular significance is the technique's unproven ability to affect consumer purchase behavior. As pointed out by some consumer behaviorists (Engel, Wales, and Warshaw 1975), even if subliminal advertising is perceived, consumers seem to have the ability to use "screening mechanisms" to guard against influences aimed at changing their behavior. This has been referred to as a person's "perceptual defense" or the "ability to avoid unsatisfying and anxiety-arousing stimuli" (McNeal 1982: 152). Along these same lines, Berelson and Steiner (1964: 95), after reviewing research on subliminal stimulation, question whether action can be produced against a person's will. They further question if subliminal stimulation is superior to normal messages. Even Vicary argued from his very first experiment that the fears of subliminal advertising were greatly exaggerated and that it could not persuade a viewer to do something he is not conditioned to do already. Its usefulness was in its role as a "reminder, supplementing the message that already had been delivered through conventional printed ads and broadcast commercials" ("Subliminal Ad Is Transmitted in Test" 1958). Following Vicary's reasoning, Lewis (1958: 56) concludes that subliminal advertising "can encourage, but not convince; it can suggest an idea that the viewer may feel he thought of himself, but it cannot change his mind; it can create a mood but not an attitude."

A significant factor to consider in evaluating the reliability of this technique is that subliminal advertising, like conventional advertising, appears to affect only those people with certain needs or predispositions. It has been found that such individual factors as visual perceptiveness, psychological needs, values, and conflicts may influence the person's receptiveness to subliminal stimulation (Kidd 1958). Along these lines, it is necessary to recognize the possibility that a subliminal stimulus may produce negative results rather than the positive ones expected. Two subliminal perception studies, one at Tulane University (Lewis 1958) and a more recent one at Texas Christian University (Glover 1979), showed negative results among certain individuals.

In looking at the effect of subliminal stimulation, it is evident that a greater understanding of the individual consumer is required. It should be realized that people have different degrees of perception of advertising, making it difficult to determine just what is actually subliminal. Many advertisements that pass through a person's sensing devices never enter into his or her realm of awareness and may in fact function as subliminal messages (Barthol and Goldstein 1968).

Although much research has been done in the area of subliminal perception and subliminal advertising, the lack of conclusive research currently offers little guidance for marketing strategy. The fears of misuse have complicated the problem further. Even if the issue of ethics is resolved, the use of subliminal advertising will probably have to recognize, as Kelly (1979: 23) concluded, that "very probably the total impression of an ad illustration overpowers any stimulus created by suggestive objects. . . ." This would imply that no one aspect alone can become a controlling factor in determining an effective advertisement. There still needs to be a good ad layout, good ad copy, good media placement, and so forth. Therefore, even if subliminal advertising becomes an accepted practice, the subliminal stimulus will be only one of many factors in advertising design that must be considered.

REFERENCES

Adams, Joe K. 1957. "Laboratory Studies of Behavior without Awareness." *Psychological Bulletin* 54 (May): 383–405.

Bach, S., and G. S. Klein. 1957. "Conscious Effects of Prolonged Subliminal Exposures of Words." *American Psychologist* 12: 393.

Bagley, Gerrold S., and B. J. Dunlap. 1979. "Subliminally Embedded Ads: A 'Turn On'?" *Proceedings: Southern Marketing Association,* Robert S. Franz, Robert M. Hopkins, and Alfred G. Toma, (eds.) , pp. 296-298.

Barthol, Richard P., and Michael J. Goldstein. 1968. "Psychology and the Invisible Sell." In Harold H. Kassarjian and Thomas S. Robertson, *Perspectives in Consumer Behavior.* Glenview, Illinois: Scott, Foresman and Company.

Becker, Hal. 1976. "Weight Control Through Behavioral Engineering Using Subliminal Communication." Proceedings of the 29th Annual Conference on Engineering in Medicine and Biology, Boston, Massachusetts.

Berelson, Bernard, and Gary A. Steiner. 1964. *Human Behavior: An Inventory of Scientific Findings.* New York: Harcourt, Brace and World, Inc.

Byrne, Donn. 1959. "The Effect of a Subliminal Food Stimulus on Verbal Responses." *Journal of Applied Psychology* 43 (August): 249-52.

Collier, R.M. 1940. "An Experimental Study of the Effects of Subliminal Stimuli." *Psychological Monographs* 52.

Coover, J.E. 1917. "Experiments in Psychical Research." *Psychical Research Monograph No. 1.* Stanford, California: Stanford University Press.

De Fleur, Melvin L., and Robert M. Petranoff. 1959. "A Televised Test of Subliminal Persuasion." *Public Opinion Quarterly* 23 (Summer): 168-80.

Dixon, Norman F. 1971. *Subliminal Perception: The Nature of a Controversy.* London: McGraw-Hill.

Engel, J. F., H. G. Wales, and M. R. Warshaw. 1975. *Promotional Strategy.* Homewood, Illinois: Irwin.

George, Stephen G., and Luther B. Jennings. 1975. "Effect of Subliminal Stimuli on Consumer Behavior: Negative Evidence." *Perceptual and Motor Skills* 41 (December): 847-54.

Glover, Ed. 1979. "Decreasing Smoking—Behavior Through Subliminal Stimulation Treatments." *Journal of Drug Education* 9: 273-83.

Hattwick, Melvin S. 1950. *How to Use Psychology for Better Advertising.* New York: Prentice-Hall.

Hawkins, Del. 1970. "The Effects of Subliminal Stimulation on Drive Level and Brand Preference." *Journal of Marketing Research* 7 (August): 322-26.

Henderson, Carter. 1958. "'Subliminal' Salesmen Stalk Consumers Via TV, Radio and Movies." *The Wall Street Journal* 21 (March 7): 1, 4.

Hilgard, Ernest R. 1962. "What Becomes of Stimulus?" In *Behavior and Awareness,* ed. Charles Erikson, Durham, North Carolina: Duke University Press. pp. 48-50.

Kelly, J. Steven. 1979. "Subliminal Embeds in Print Advertising: A Challenge to Advertising Ethics." *Journal of Advertising* 8 (Summer): 20-24.

Key, Wilson Bryan. 1973. *Subliminal Seduction.* Englewood Cliffs, New Jersey: Prentice-Hall.

———. 1976. *Media Sexploitation.* Englewood Cliffs, New Jersey: Prentice-Hall.

Kidd, R. M. 1958. "Subliminal Stimuli a 'Monster'? Don't Worry—Mass Public's Individual Differences Blunt Its Power, Says Agency Man." *Advertising Age* 29 (August 11): 56-57.

Klein, G. S., D. P. Spence, R. R. Holt, and S. Gourevitch. 1958. "Cognition without Awareness: Subliminal Influences Upon Conscious Thought." *Journal of Abnormal Social Psychology* 57 (November): 255-66.

Lander, Eric. 1981. "In Through the Out Door." *Omni* 3 (February): 45-48, 107.

Lazarus, Richard S., and Robert A. McCleary. 1951. "Autonomic Discrimination Without Awareness." *Psychological Review* 58 (March): 113-22.

Lewis, Herschell G. 1958. "Admen Hop on Critic of Subliminal Ads; Flay 'Witch Burning'; Urge Further Study." *Advertising Age* 29 (August 11): 56.

Maxwell, Neil. 1980. "Words Whispered to Subconscious Supposedly Deter Thefts, Fainting." *The Wall Street Journal,* November 25, sec. 2, p. 1.

McConnell, James V., Richard L. Cutler, and Elton B. McNeil. 1958. "Subliminal Stimulation: An Overview." *American Psychologist* 13 (May 13): 229-42.

McNeal, James U. 1982. *Consumer Behavior: An*

Integrative Approach. Boston, Massachusetts: Little, Brown and Company.

Miller, James G. 1939. "Discrimination without Awareness." *American Journal of Psychology* 52 (October): 562–78.

———. 1942. *Unconsciousness.* New York: Wiley.

Murch, Gerald M. 1964. "Suggestion for Classification of Terminology in Experiments on Subliminal Stimulation." *Perceptual and Motor Skills* (October): 19, 442.

"Non-Coffee-Using Housewife Made Fresh Coffee After Hint in Subliminal Radio Test." 1958. *Advertising Age* 29 (February 3): 3, 58.

"Nucoa Uses New Subliminal Twist: It's 'Contrapuntal.'" 1958. *Advertising Age* 29 (March 24): 2.

Packard, Vance. 1957. *The Hidden Persuaders.* New York: David McKay Co., Inc.

"'Phone Now,' Said CBC Subliminally—but Nobody Did." 1958. *Advertising Age* 29 (February 10): 8.

Robertson, Thomas S. 1970. *Consumer Behavior.*

Glenview, Illinois: Scott, Foresman and Company.

"Secret Voices." 1979. *Time* 114 (September 10): 71.

Spence, D. P. 1964. "Effects on a Continuously Hashing Subliminal Verbal Food Stimulus on Subjective Hunger Ratings." *Psychological Reports* 15: 993–94.

"'Subliminal' Ad Flap Raised." 1973. *Advertising Age* 44 (December 24): 21.

"Subliminal Ad Is Transmitted in Test but Scores No Popcorn Sales." 1958. *Advertising Age* 29 (January 20): 2, 94.

"Subliminal Cuts Show 'Hot Car' in New Toyota Push." 1966. *Advertising Age* 37 (September 19): 3.

"Subliminal Scenario." 1978. *Time* 111 (May 29): 27.

"Unfair to the Subconscious." 1959. *The Economist,* January 31, p. 416.

"Unseen TV Gets Exposure on Both Coasts." 1958. *Broadcasting* 54 (January 20): 98–99.

Questions

1. Differentiate between subliminal perception and supraliminal perception.
2. From the research done in this area, can it be concluded that subliminal perception does exist? Explain.
3. Does it appear from these studies that subliminal advertising would be an appropriate advertising strategy? Explain.
4. Discuss the ethical as well as the legal aspects of subliminal advertising.

Part E
PERSONALITY AND LIFESTYLE

18. A Multivariate Analysis of Personality and Product Use

David L. Sparks

W.T. Tucker

INTRODUCTION

Despite the general failure of empirical studies over the past ten or more years to locate important relationships between personality and consumptive behavior, there remains among students of marketing this item of faith: behavior in the marketplace is critically reflective of individual personality. The corollary of that belief is that the measuring instruments or statistical techniques (or both) that have been commonly used in empirical work are incapable of giving more than glimpses of the structures and processes involved.

Statistical Techniques

Most of the work attempting to relate personality to consumer behavior has used bivariate inferential techniques or regression including multiple correlation. This implies the view (probably not held by any researcher) of personality as a bundle of discrete and independent traits which either do not interact

or do so only in the simple sense that a number of diverse forces can be resolved into a *single* vector.

A recent study by Kernan notes that canonical analysis, alone or in conjunction with hierarchical grouping, can suggest the existence of molar personality types that are essentially synthesized out of the individual traits of a simple personality test [6]. Since Kernan's data delivered only one significant canonical root (at the .10 level), he could not use that technique to draw inferences about the complexity of personality trait interaction; but a hierarchical clustering of subjects based on choice strategies in a game playing situation posited four synthetic character types in which total personalities rather than specific traits seemed to be the operant variables.

The present study parallels the Kernan research with the intention of using hierarchical grouping in the same way, unless canonical analysis infers several significant roots.

In effect, the statistical techniques used in many previous studies relating personality to consumer behavior [2,3,7,8,9,10] probably constitute a part of the "inadequate theoretical framework" referred to by Brody and Cunningham[1].

Measuring Instruments

Psychologists are no more elated than those in marketing with current personality theory or the attendant measuring instruments. There is no persuasive theoretical basis for preferring one sort of personality test to another, despite a great variety of tests. On one hand, instruments like the Edwards or the California Personality Inventory measure a host of individual traits; on the other, the I-O scale locates everyone at some point on a unidimensional continuum. (Clinical techniques requiring subjective judgments are disregarded here for operational reasons.)

Additionally, instruments may be roughly categorized into two subclasses, those asking largely for: (1) direct reports on thoughts and feelings, and (2) reports of activities, actual or preferred. Preferences for one or the other of these subclasses will in some measure depend upon the way the experimenter regards personality. It is legitimate to think of personality as an intimate aspect of the cognitive and affective organization of the central nervous system (or the total organism). It is equally legitimate to regard it as a verbal construct describing behavioral regularities. When someone is described as anti-intraceptive or rigid, it is the cognitive and affective organization that is the principal reference. To call someone sociable or kleptomaniac is to classify him behaviorally with little regard for central processes. This dichotomy is not rigorous; a number of personality tests, Cohen's CAD for instance [2], ask for cognitive evaluations of behavior or otherwise provide mixed cases.

RESEARCH DESIGN

A sample of 190 college students (173 of whom accurately completed forms) chosen for their availability in introductory marketing classes were used to explore the relationship between consumer behavior and personality. The choice of such a sample (in this case all of the males present in particular classes on a particular day) seems appropriate when the effort is to locate the existence of relationships rather than to describe or define them for particular universes. Beyond this, the sample method was essentially that of Kernan [6] and Tucker and Painter [9]. Both previous studies showed that the frequency distributions on the Gordon Personal Profile [5] and Gordon Personal Inventory [4] for such a sample varied little from those of groups on which the test was normed.

The use of the Gordon tests was based on several considerations: (1) the bias of the authors toward the behaviorally-oriented rather than the cognitively-oriented test as relevant to consumer behavior, (2) the previous and partially successful use of that test [6,9], and (3) the short time required for subjects to complete the tests. The fact that eight traits isolated by the test are not fully independent is of concern but seems of less consequence than the test's demonstrated ability to differentiate people with regard to the kinds of behavior under study.

The instrument to measure the subjects' product use had 17 multiple-choice questions. The products, considered to be typical for this subject group, were: headache remedies, mouthwash, men's cologne, hair spray, shampoo, antacid remedies, *Playboy*, alcoholic beverages, complexion aids, vitamins, cigarettes, coffee, chewing gum, and after-shave lotion. In addition, subjects were asked how often they brushed their teeth and had their hair cut. Another question asked about their adoption of new clothing fashions. Response categories were, generally: never, less than once a week, about once a week, more than once a week but less than once a day, and about once a day. For five of the products, dichotomous or specially worded response categories were required. While these products were not a complete inventory of typical products, they did represent a reasonable number and were considered sufficient for this investigation.

A pretest of the 17-item product-use questionnaire with 62 male undergraduates led to minor changes in the question wording and response categories. A varimax factor analysis of the pretest data showed the 17 questions to be almost completely independent, the last of the 17 factors extracting nearly as much variance as the first. While desirable in one sense, independence as extensive as this raises critical issues which will be discussed later.

FINDINGS

A correlation analysis of the data (Table 1) shows essentially the same weak and spotty relationships between personality traits and particular product use reported previously. It may lead one to conclude that some two percent of the variance in the use of mouthwash may be accounted for by cautiousness or that some six percent of the variance in the use of men's cologne is associated with sociability. The total of 18 significant but low correlations in a matrix where seven would be expected to occur by chance may be persuasive that something is responsible, but the findings seem to be of minimal value.

Canonical analysis provides both a more

persuasive case for the relationship under study and some hints concerning the kinds of personality structures involved. That is far from saying that canonical analysis illuminates the field; it is notoriously difficult to interpret beyond the significance levels of R's associated with particular roots.

Table 2 shows the first three canonical roots with R's of .606, .548, and .413. These have significance levels of .0001, .0002, and .0752 respectively, leaving little doubt that there are significant relationships involved. More interesting, since the basic relationship involved has not really been in doubt, is the nature of the relationship suggested. The meanings of the roots can be crudely approximated by extracting the items with heavy loadings from the predictor and criterion sets, somewhat simplifying the picture. In this case, items with coefficients above .30 are used.

The first root is associated with the use of shampoo, alcoholic beverages, cigarettes, and early fashion adoption. Those involved are best described as sociable, emotionally stable, and irresponsible (minus responsibility). The relationships are intuitively acceptable, although they are certainly not the only ones that would be so. Nevertheless, it makes sense to think that early fashion adopters are those particular sociables who are also emotionally stable (not easily upset) and also somewhat irresponsible (responsibility has previously been associated with modal behavior [9]).

The second root is associated with (again converting signs verbally for ease of expression) the use of headache remedies and mouthwash, late fashion adoption, and infrequent use of after-shave lotion. The personality characteristics are sociability, cautiousness, and emotional instability. At this point there emerges a clear advantage to the methodology. Both early and late fashion

Table 1 / Correlation Matrix: Product Use and Personality Trait

Product	Ascendancy	Responsibility	Emotional stability	Sociability	Cautiousness	Original thinking	Personal relations	Vigor
Headache remedy	.0254	-.1391	-.2104[a]	.1490	-.0073	-.0649	-.0875	-.0907
Mouthwash	.0702	-.0983	-.1308	.1125	.1501[a]	-.0242	.0443	-.1238
Men's cologne	.1473	-.1066	-.1222	.2599[a]	.1247	.0715	-.0459	-.0008
Hair spray	-.0580	-.1241	-.0725	.0388	-.0824	-.0668	-.0664	-.0159
Shampoo	.1735[a]	-.1420	.0729	.1459	-.0449	.0757	.0412	.0116
Antacid remedy	.0217	-.1521[a]	-.2692[a]	.0393	-.1222	-.0974	-.1119	-.0886
Playboy	.1293	-.0218	.0787	.2621[a]	-.1038	.0650	.0169	.1185
Alcoholic beverages	.2001[a]	-.1605[a]	.0159	.1973[a]	-.2861[a]	.0041	-.1436	.0261
Brush teeth	-.1324	-.0418	.0196	-.0624	-.0663	-.1645[a]	.0329	-.1074
Fashion adoption	.2892	-.1647[a]	-.0628	.3858[a]	-.0919	.0924	.0838	.0557
Complexion aids	.0065	-.0591	-.0106	.0845	-.1131	-.0826	-.0667	-.0902
Vitamin capsules	.1384	-.1197	-.1759[a]	.1288	-.0855	.0963	-.0414	.0016
Haircut	-.0587	.0616	.0655	-.0774	-.0670	-.0247	-.0394	-.0311
Cigarettes	.0869	-.1465	-.1213	.0954	-.1313	.1408	-.0376	-.0305
Coffee	-.0413	-.0265	-.1478	-.0185	.0403	-.0781	-.0683	-.0734
Chewing gum	.1645[a]	-.1035	-.1165	.2581[a]	-.1209	-.0447	.0433	-.0446
After-shave lotion	.0506	.1016	.0429	.0751	.0091	.1288	.0168	.0676

[a] Indicates correlation coefficient is significant at the .05 level.

Table 2 / Results of the Canonical Analysis

Variables	Canonical coefficients		
	1	2	3
Criterion set (product use)			
Headache remedy	−.0081	−.4433	.1123
Mouthwash	−.1598	−.4538	.2809
Men's cologne	.2231	−.1935	−.2121
Hair spray	.0664	.0706	.0857
Shampoo	.3784	.1587	−.0063
Antacid remedy	−.1421	−.1746	−.3226
Playboy	.1511	.1591	.5220
Alcoholic beverages	.4639	.3098	−.1329
Brush teeth	−.1879	−.0152	.2341
Fashion adoption	.3226	−.3993	.0856
Complexion aids	−.0243	.0925	.1799
Vitamin capsules	.2870	−.0599	−.4975
Haircut	−.1698	.1855	−.0170
Cigarettes	.4065	.0551	−.2894
Coffee	−.2441	−.2453	.1330
Chewing gum	.2051	−.1320	.1342
After-shave lotion	−.0270	.3022	.0108
Predictor set (personality traits)			
Ascendancy	.0182	−.0517	−.4375
Responsibility	−.5125	.0777	−.1688
Emotional stability	.4309	.6405	.4880
Sociability	.6072	−.3597	.6199
Cautiousness	−.2869	−.5959	.2438
Original thinking	.2377	.1620	−.3076
Personal relations	−.1245	−.0567	.0369
Vigor	.1681	.2592	.0481
Roots	.3671	.3000	.1711
Canonical R	.606	.548	.413
x^1	72.7419	56.7026	29.8417
d.f.	24	22	20
Probability	.0000	.0002	.0752

adoption are related to sociability, but in different personality contexts.

This seems to be exactly the kind of relationship personality theory implies: not a simple connection between sociability and early fashion adoption, but a more complex one in which sociability combined with emotional stability and irresponsibility is oriented toward one sort of action while sociability combined with emotional instability and cautiousness is oriented toward its opposite.

In the third root (with the marginal significance level of .075) sociability again characterizes the individual, but in this context the relationship with fashion adoption is very low and there is an association with light or no use of cigarettes, again a reversal of the variate-to-variate relationship suggested by the first root.

The most obvious explanation for these findings lies in the notion that it is the person in some gestalt in which the entire personality and the entire situation form a particular configuration, who acts, not the individual personality trait. But this view includes the possibility that the most useful approach to the subject is to measure individual personality characteristics and synthesize the molar personality from such measures. The relationships of the above canonical analysis suggest that even a simple model based on trait interaction could prove more predictive than a trait-by-trait approach. Nevertheless, some of the relationships suggested could stem in

large part from nonlinearity. Further, canonical analysis is a linear technique which can only indirectly suggest the presence of certain possible nonlinear associations while leaving others occult.

The present study parallels that of Kernan [6] closely enough that there is some interest in seeing whether a hierarchical clustering of subjects on the basis of their reported product-use behavior approximates the interesting personality profiles that related to particular game playing strategies. Table 3 shows the four clusters Kernan located and the six clusters that seem to best describe the present data. No persuasive case can be made for similarities in grouping, although the imaginative mind can perceive parallels. Nor does the cluster analysis, when compared with

Table 3 / Results of Cluster Analysis

	Cluster					
	1	2	3	4	5	6
Personality trait: Kernan's study[a]						
Ascendancy	81.0	19.0	81.0	43.0		
Responsibility	43.0	11.0	19.0	80.0		
Emotional stability	40.0	15.0	40.0	77.0		
Sociability	77.0	12.0	77.0	39.0		
Cautiousness	54.0	31.0	5.0	69.0		
Original thinking	72.0	31.0	45.0	43.0		
Personal relations	70.0	10.0	54.0	57.0		
Vigor	81.0	13.0	38.0	63.0		
Personality trait: present study[a]						
Ascendancy	66.6	54.9	50.8	52.3	49.4	63.0
Responsibility	44.2	55.2	49.2	47.6	61.7	41.1
Emotional stability	43.7	57.4	54.3	50.7	47.8	44.4
Sociability	63.6	49.1	42.9	37.9	36.4	59.8
Cautiousness	40.2	45.1	46.6	51.5	62.2	33.5
Original thinking	52.2	54.5	53.1	48.3	43.9	51.0
Personal relations	49.4	42.3	45.5	48.7	40.3	39.3
Vigor	49.4	61.2	61.5	54.1	44.3	52.3

[a] Mean percentile scores.

product use, add to the conclusions available through canonical analysis alone in this case. It seems possible that the near-fantasy situation of game playing in relative isolation may give freer play to personality expression than consumption patterns which operate under social, economic, and habitual constraints.

The annoying fragmentation of 17 questions into 17 factors of approximately equal magnitude is not readily explained. It is difficult to conceive that the frequency of use of mouthwash, men's cologne, hair spray, shampoo, and after-shave lotion are essentially independent behaviors not tied together. The problem may lie in the methodology, although it is difficult to understand how the response categories could mask associations when most were used by fairly large numbers of subjects. Yet on both pretest and test the same lack of structure appeared. The kind of post hoc explanations that come to mind do little to reassure one that there are not large areas of dissociated events in consumer behavior that will require explanatory models far more complex or far more numerous than one would wish.

CONCLUSIONS

The association of identical personality traits (within different sets of personality traits) with diverse consumer behavior suggests that trait interactions or nonlinear relationships may compose a significant portion of the personality-behavior relation. This may partially explain the difficulty in empirically demonstrating the commonly accepted hypothesis that personality influences consumer activities. Inferential techniques do not generally lend themselves to the location of the sorts of relationships implied by these findings.

The apparent lack of correlation among product-use patterns suggested by factor analyses of questionnaire responses leads to the conclusion that a general model applicable to all consumer behavior would prove extremely complex. The alternative of exploring personality in connection with particular behavior or particular products seems therefore the only current application to practical marketing problems.

The particular relationships among traits suggested by this study should be considered as merely representative of the sorts of interrelations that can occur. In all probability a study of other subjects, and other products, or other sorts of behavioral differences would show the relevance of different trait combinations.

REFERENCES

1. Brody, Robert P. and Scott M. Cunningham, "Personality Variables and the Consumer Decision Process," *Journal of Marketing Research*, 5 (February 1968), 50–7.
2. Cohen, Joel B. "An Interpersonal Orientation to the Study of Consumer Behavior," *Journal of Marketing Research*, 4 (August 1967), 270–8.
3. Evans, Franklin B. "Psychological and Objective Factors in the Prediction of Brand Choice: Ford Versus Chevrolet," *Journal of Business*, 32 (October 1959), 340–69.
4. Gordon, Leonard V. *Gordon Personal Inventory*. New York: Harcourt, Brace, & World, 1963.
5. _____. *Gordon Personal Profile*. New York: Harcourt, Brace, & World, 1963.
6. Kernan, Jerome B. "Choice Criteria, Decision Behavior, and Personality," *Journal of Marketing Research*, 5 (May 1968), 155–64.
7. Koponen, Arthur. "Personality Characteristics of Purchasers," *Journal of Advertising Research*, 1 (September 1960), 6–12.
8. Pessemier, Edgar A., Philip C. Burger, and Douglas J. Tigert, "Can New Product Buyers be Identified?" *Journal of Marketing Research*, 4 (November 1967), 349–55.
9. Tucker, W. T. and John J. Painter. "Per-

sonality and Product Use," *Journal of Applied Psychology,* 45 (October 1961), 325–9.

10. Westfall, Ralph, "Psychological Factors in

Predicting Product Choice," *Journal of Marketing,* 26 (April 1962), 34–40.

Questions

1. From the results of this study, explain the relationship between sociability and early fashion adoption.
2. Why is it difficult to relate one personality trait to one type of buyer behavior?
3. In studying product use, should consumer behaviorists attempt to investigate personality traits individually or together?

19.   City Shoppers and Urban Identification: Observations on the Social Psychology of City Life

Gregory P. Stone

This article is an attempt to supplement findings on urban life with data on shopping. Few treatises on the sociology of the city fail to designate the market place as the epitome of those "impersonal," "segmentalized," "secondary," "categoric," and "rational" contacts said to characterize human relations in the city. Yet the study reported here points to the possibility that some urbanites, as a consequence of the relationships they establish with the personnel of retail stores, manage to form identifications which bind them to the larger community.

PROCEDURE

Some time ago the writer was engaged by a private research agency to study popular reactions to the establishment of a large chain department store in an outlying business district on Chicago's Northwest Side. One of the techniques was a schedule administered to 150 adult female residents[1] of the area

[1]Because marital status was a variable which might have distorted the findings of the study, 26 single, widowed, or divorced subjects were eliminated from the original 150 informants. Housewives were origin-

surrounding the business district. Their responses to certain questions indicated disparate definitions of shopping situations and markedly different orientations to stores in general. The latter were implicit in the criteria by which the housewives said they evaluated stores in the area and in the expectations they had of store personnel as they encountered them in shopping. Particularly striking, in contrast to customary sociological notions, was their recurrent statement that market relationships were often personal.

This suggested a typology of shopping orientations as a basis for a more intensive analysis of the anomalies. The procedure for its construction and application consisted of four steps: (1) a fourfold classification of the *responses* to one particularly discerning question, called here the "filter" question; (2) a similar classification of *informants* as consumer types on the basis of demonstrated consistencies between their responses to the filter question and a number of other questions termed "indicator" questions; (3) a schematization of the consumer types as *empirical models;* and (4) the construction of *social profiles* based on the patterns of social characteristics associated with the consumer types. These procedures revealed further anomalies which are analyzed in the concluding section of the article.

ORIENTATIONS TO SHOPPING

Responses to the question, "Why would you rather do business with local independent merchants (or large chain stores, depending on a prior choice)?" persistently revealed markedly different orientations to different kinds of stores as well as diverse definitions of shopping. Because of the discriminating power of the question, it was used as a "filtering" device for achieving a preliminary classification of the consumers on the basis of their orientation to shopping.[2]

Replies to the filter question were grouped into five empirical categories of criteria housewives used to evaluate stores: (1) economic, (2) personalizing, (3) ethical, (4) apathetic, and (5) a residual category of unique or indeterminate criteria. As may be seen, some statements did not fall precisely into single categories. When a response included multiple orientations, it was coded for each category.

The Economic Category

Remarks coded in this category clearly indicated that the informant regarded shopping as primarily buying, her behavior being unambiguously directed to the purchase of goods. The criteria applied to the evaluation of stores included: an appraisal of the store's merchandise in terms of price, quality, and variety; a favorable evaluation of store practices that maximize the efficient distribution of goods; conversely, an unfavorable evaluation of practices and relationships with personnel which impede the quick efficient sale of merchandise; and a favorable rating of conditions which maximized independence of

---

ally selected as informants because they do most of the buying, but it seems that this situation is changing.

[2]Merton distinguishes orientation from role: "The social orientation differs from the social role. Role refers to the manner in which the rights and duties inherent in a social position are put into practice; orientation. . . refers to the theme underlying the complex of social roles performed by an individual. It is the (tacit or explicit) theme which finds expression in each of the complex of social roles in which the individual is implicated" (Robert K. Merton, "Patterns of Influence," in Paul F. Lazarsfeld and Frank Stanton [eds.], *Communications Research 1948–1949* [New York: Harper & Bros., 1949], p. 187).

customer choice. The following four responses are typical of this category:

> I prefer large department stores. They give you better service. Their prices are more reasonable. . . . There's a wider selection of goods.

> I prefer big chains. They have cheaper stuff. It's too expensive in small stores. Then, too, I like the idea of helping yourself. Nobody talks you into anything. You can buy what you please.

> I suppose I should help the smaller stores, but I can do best at the chains. Local merchants are too nosey—too personal—and their prices are higher. The prices in chains are good, and you get self-service in chains.

> I like to shop in local independently owned stores. You can get better grade materials and better service there. If anything goes wrong with the material, you always have a chance to go back and make a complaint. They'll make it good for you. They have more time. You're more familiar with that kind of store and can find what you want in a hurry. Some of them allow you stamps on their budget plan, and that saves you a lot of money.

The Personalizing Category

In this category were placed responses defining shopping as fundamentally and positively interpersonal. Such informants expressed a tendency to personalize and individualize the customer role in the store and rated stores in terms of closeness of relationships between the customer and personnel. Consequently, "purely" economic criteria, such as price, quality, selection of merchandise, and highly rationalized retailing techniques were of lesser importance. These four remarks exemplify the category:

> I prefer local merchants. They're friendlier and not quite so big. . . .Although prices are higher in small stores, when you trade with local merchants you have a better chance to be a good customer. They get to know you. People in smaller stores greet you cordially when you come in. They get to know you, and make an effort to please you.

> I'd rather trade at my own store than a public store. That's why I prefer local merchants. They're more personal. They get to know your name. They take more interest in you as a human being.

> Local merchants give you better service. They get so they know you. The chains are impersonal. They don't try so hard to please you. The customer doesn't mean anything to the clerk in the big chain stores, because it's not his business.

> I shop at independents if they have the merchandise. They usually know you by name and try to please you. In the big store no one knows you. . . . Maybe it's because I feel at home in the smaller store. When you're in them, you feel more wanted. You feel lost in a big store.

The Ethical Category

Responses in this category signified that the informants feel a moral obligation to patronize specific types of stores. They perceive shopping in the light of a larger set of values rather than of specific values and more immediately relevant norms. Store patronage was appraised in anticipation of such moral consequences. The following excerpts express it:

> It would be better if they were all neighborhood stores. The chains put people out of work because the people have to wait on themselves. But that's what happens in a machine age. They set up everything like a factory. If there's another depression, the chains will put people out of work, because they are set up on a self-help system. So, if you let the chains run the little business out, they will be wrecking their own chances for jobs, if times get too bad.

> I prefer the local independents. I think that the chain store is taking too much business away from the little fellow.

> I prefer local merchants if they have the variety and a large selection of goods. You know, they're making a living and you want to help them out. The chain stores are making a living too—a damn good one!

You have to give the independent merchant a chance to earn his bread and butter. The chain stores grab it all. The big chain store has no heart or soul.

The Apathetic Category

Included in this category are responses showing that the informant was not interested in shopping and did not discriminate kinds of stores. They emphasize the minimizing of effort in purchasing. Illustrations are:

I don't know. I guess there's not much difference.

Local merchants are O.K. It depends on where you happen to be. Whichever store is the closest is O.K. with me.

It depends on which is the closest.

Chain stores. You can get everything there in one trip. There's nothing particular to like about either kind of store.

Questions on the consumer's image of a good clerk and good store manager, unpleasant and pleasant shopping experiences, and price, quality, and service satisfactions were used as "indicators" to test the consistency with which the orientations elicited by the filter question were maintained. Responses to these questions lent themselves, with some exceptions,[3] to a classification like that set forth above.

After replies to the filter and indicator questions were coded as described, the interviews were again examined, and the coding of answers tabulated for each interview. Informants were placed in exclusive categories when the tabulation of the relevant coded responses demonstrated consistent orienta-

[3]E.g., the questions directed toward the informant's satisfaction with price, quality, and service in stores forced her thinking into an "economic" frame of reference. Thus, these more structured questions were used as indicators only when "economic" and "apathetic" orientations had been signified in response to the "filter" question.

tions to the shopping situation. The essential criterion of consistency in this case was met by the requirement that the *majority* of coded "indicator" responses must coincide with *a* coded "filter" response.

A TYPOLOGY OF CONSUMERS

The final classification of housewives yielded four consumer types: (1) economic, (2) personalizing, (3) ethical, and (4) apathetic. Brief sketches of these types were constructed to summarize the characteristics of each as expressed in clustering and interrelated responses to the "filter" and "indicator" questions. These sketches are *empirical models* of the types; they are not designed as concepts for the formulation of propositions to be directly incorporated into a theoretical system.

The empirical models of the consumer types are presented here with the caveat that probably no single consumer was adequately described by any of the models. The models represent composites of actual consumers and their characteristic role orientations.[4]

The Economic Consumer

Here was the closest approximation to the "economic man" of the classical economist. This type of shopper expressed a sense of

[4]Nevertheless, a *post hoc* attempt to "verify" the typology met with some success. Specifically, a number of items dealing with shopping behavior but not included in the construction of the typology were significantly associated with variations in consumer type in logically compatible directions: number of shopping trips to the downtown central shopping district ($p < .02$; $T = .18$), patronage of women's department stores and specialty shops for women's clothing ($p < .05$; $T = .16$), acquaintance with salesclerks ($p < .01$; $T = .21$), chain store versus independent store patronage ($p < .001$; $T = .35$).

responsibility for her household purchasing duties: she was extremely sensitive to price, quality, and assortment of merchandise, all of which entered into the calculus of her behavior on the market. She was interested in shopping. Clerical personnel and the store were, for her, merely the instruments of her purchase of goods. Thus, efficiency or inefficiency of sales personnel, as well as the relative commensurateness of prices, quality, or the selection of merchandise, were decisive in leaving her with a pleasant or unpleasant impression of the store. The quality she demanded of a "good" clerk was efficiency.

The Personalizing Consumer

This type of consumer shopped "where they know my name." It was important that she shop at her store rather than "public" stores.[5] Strong personal attachments were formed with store personnel, and this personal relationship, often approaching intimacy, was crucial to her patronage of a store. She was highly sensitized to her experiences on the market; obviously they were an important part of her life. It followed that she was responsive to both pleasant and unpleasant experiences in stores. Her conception of a "good" clerk was one who treated her in a personal, relatively intimate manner.

[5]The personal pronouns "I," "me," and "my" found their way frequently into the interviews, one indication of the extent to which they built up strong identifications with the stores they patronized. Therefore, their relationships with store personnel are referred to later as "primary" or "quasi-primary," for the store has become incorporated into the social self of the consumer. As Cooley put it, "The social self is simply any idea, or system of ideas, drawn from the communicative life, that the mind cherishes as its own." Hence the store may be seen as a part of the social self of the personalizing type of consumer (see Charles Horton Cooley, *Human Nature and the Social Order* [New York: Charles Scribner's Sons, 1902], p. 147).

The Ethical Consumer

This type of shopper shopped where she "ought" to. She was willing to sacrifice lower prices or a wider selection of goods "to help the little guy out" or because "the chain store has no heart or soul." Consequently, strong attachments were sometimes formed with personnel and store owners or with "stores" in the abstract. These mediated the impressions she had of stores, left pleasant impressions in her memory, and forced unpleasant impressions out. Since store personnel did not enter in primarily as instrumentalities but rather with reference to other, more ultimate ends, she had no clear conception of a "good" clerk.

The Apathetic Consumer

This type of consumer shopped because she "had" to. Shopping for her was an onerous task. She shopped "to get it over with." Ideally, the criterion of convenient location was crucial to her selection of a store, as opposed to price, quality of goods, relationships with store personnel, or ethics. She was not interested in shopping and minimized her expenditure of effort in purchasing goods. Experiences in stores were not sufficiently important to leave any lasting impression on her. She knew few of the personnel and had no notion of a "good" clerk.

The distribution of these types in the sample is shown in Table 1.

SOCIAL PROFILES OF THE CONSUMER TYPES

As found in writings on urbanism and the mass society, a city—an area characterized by the absence of many traditional controls, a predominance of segmented depersonalized relationships, and the proliferation of alter-

Table 1 / Distribution of Consumer Types

Type of Consumer	Number	Per Cent
Economic	41	33
Personalizing	35	28
Ethical	22	18
Apathetic	21	17
Indeterminate	5	4
Total	124	100

native activities—is a place where the consumption of goods is presumably structured as either a highly rational and rationalized activity, the relationship between the consumer and the sales clerk being instrumental, with minimal emotional involvement on the part of either; or an onerous task performed reluctantly by consumers eager to complete their transaction as easily and quickly as possible. Lynd's observations have emphasized the latter consequence, while Simmel has treated both consequences.[6]

Certainly one cannot deduce from the conventional propositions of urban sociology that buyer-seller relationships would take on quasi-primary characteristics. The ethical type of shopper isolated in this study also presents a paradox. Neither type—the personalizing consumer nor the ethical consumer—fits into the perspective of conventional urban social psychology.[7]

The most obvious and, in the light of conventional urban sociology, the most plausible hypothesis explaining the personalization of market relationships in the city as well as the "moralization" of such relationships is that these processes merely manifest a carry-over of rural or "small-town" shopping habits to the metropolitan market place.[8] We would expect, then, that personalizing and ethical consumers are predominantly housewives who learned to shop in nonurban environments. But the data offered no support for this hypothesis, insofar as the types of consumers studied were not significantly differentiated by place of birth.[9] As a matter of fact, the majority of consumers classified in each type were native-born Chicagoans. Although the types were significantly associated with parental place of birth, this was because ethical consumers—presumably not to be thought of as a characteristically urban type—included proportionately and significantly more *third-generation* Chicagoans than any other type. These data suggest that the orientations to shopping typical of both ethical and

[6]Robert S. Lynd, "The People as Consumers," in the *Report of the President's Research Committee on Social Trends: Recent Social Trends* (New York: McGraw-Hill Book Co., 1933), p. 242; George Simmel, *The Sociology of George Simmel,* trans. with an introduction by Kurt H. Wolff (Glencoe, Ill.: Free Press, 1950), pp. 414–17.

[7]Cf. Tönnies' statement: "In the *Gesellschaft,* as contrasted with the *Gemeinschaft,* we find no actions that can be derived from an *a priori* and necessarily existing unity; no actions, therefore, which manifest the will and the spirit of the unity even if performed by the individual; no actions, which, insofar as they are performed by the individual, take place on behalf of those

united with them" (*op. cit.* p. 74). Yet, in the metropolis, we find the consumer who patronizes a particular store with the best interest of the owner in mind—the ethical consumer—and the consumer who enters the market place with the "will" to build a unity out of her relationship with the seller—the personalizing consumer.

[8]"To a greater or lesser degree, therefore, our social life bears the imprint of an earlier folk society. . . . The population of the city itself is in large measure recruited from the countryside, where a mode of life reminiscent of the earlier form of existence persists" (Louis Wirth, "Urbanism as a Way of Life," *American Journal of Sociology,* XI, IV [July, 1938], p. 3).

[9]The chi-square test was used as a measure of the significance of all associations reported here, and, where necessary, T has been used to determine the degree of association. A probability of .05 or less was used as an acceptable indication that the association between two variables could not be attributed to chance variations.

personalizing consumers did not originate in an atmosphere foreign to metropolitan life but precisely in the context of the metropolitan milieu.

On the basis of this general hypothesis, relationships between specific social and economic variables and variations in consumer type were subjected to statistical tests of significance. Significant associations were found for number of children, membership in voluntary associations, and social class.[10]

Explanations of the above relationships always required taking into account the participation of the consumer in the larger social life of her community and suggested that personal involvements in various phases of the social structure of the Northwest Side also played a part in determining her role orientation in the market. On the assumption that variations in personal involvement could be measured by objective and subjective indexes of community identification, further associations were subjected to statistical tests of significance. The results disclosed significant association between variations in consumer type and locus of last place of residence, residence of friends, and the consumer's desire to remain in or leave the Northwest Side.[11]

---

[10]Social class was determined from the application of the "Index of Status Characteristics" described in W. Lloyd Warner, Marchia Meeker, and Kenneth Eels, *Social Class in America* (Chicago: Science Research Associates, 1949). Other results not accepted as statistically significant included associations with age ($p < .20$); officerships in associations ($p < .95$); religious denomination ($p < .70$); occupational status of head of consumer's household ($p < .20$); education of consumer ($p < .20$); education of head of consumer's household ($p < .10$); and ethnic status ($p < .20$).

[11]Except for homeownership, all the other indexes used—length of residence in current dwelling place, length of residence in the Northwest Side, age moved into the community, and subjective evaluation of the residential area—were associated at more than the .05 level but less than the .10 level. This clustering of com-

A qualitative analysis of the above associations suggested that each consumer type was characterized by a distinctive patterning of social position and community identification. To spell out with statistical precision the entire complex of variables identifying each type and assess their relative weights was, at best, extremely difficult and rendered unfeasible by the small number of cases and the consequent impossibility of holding variables constant. To circumvent these difficulties, a "social profile" was drawn up for each type of shopper, none of which was intended directly to represent the empirical data. Rather they represent *some* social conditions which the clustering of relationships point to as *probably* shaping orientations.

The Economic Consumer

Youth, aspiration, and economic disadvantage, when they described lower-middle class housewives, set the stage for the formulation of an economic orientation to shopping. The physical requirements of the economic role were exacting and could best be performed by the young. Economic consumers were socially mobile and seldom loath to instrumentalize the customer-clerk relationship as the orientation required. Many were just passing through the Northwest Side on their way to more highly esteemed residences farther out on the metropolitan periphery. Their mobility aspirations, however, were seriously qualified by the presence of children who demanded

---

munity identification indexes adumbrates the principal point of this article elaborated in the final section. In the Northwest Side, homeownership was structured in such a way that it had to be rejected as a valid index of community identification. Specifically, there were negative associations with education, length of residence, residence of friends, and previous residence; and positive associations with age when the informant moved into the area. Probably that variable reflected the postwar housing shortage more than anything else.

care and cost money at a period in their married life when funds were already low and by subordinate ethnic status in the local area. These qualifications demanded the exercise of caution on the market and the adoption of an economic definition of shopping. Unattached to the local area and free of encumbering allegiances, the economic consumer was able to participate in the market in a detached, interested, and alert manner.

The Personalizing Consumer

Without access to either formal or informal channels of social participation, because of her lower social status, her very few or very many children, and the fact that she had spent the early years of her married life outside the local area, this type of consumer established quasi-primary relationships with the personnel of local independent retail institutions. In a sense, her selection of local independent merchants coerced her into a personalizing orientation to shopping. For, given her status equality with store personnel and the fact that she was a newcomer, the adoption of a different definition of shopping could have eventuated only in disharmony and friction which would have been difficult to absorb without other available primary relationships to take up the shock. Even so, this coercion was hardly disadvantageous to such a consumer. The quasi-primary relationships she was forced to develop on the market compensated for her larger social losses, for, although she had recently moved into the area leaving most of her old friends behind, she attached positive value to living in the Northwest Side and expressed no desire to leave it.[12]

---

[12]The social characteristics of the personalizing consumer resemble those of the "substitute gratification" readers of the urban community press reported in Morris Janowitz, "The Imagery of the Urban Community Press," *op. cit.,* p. 540.

The Ethical Consumer

Relatively high social status, long residence in the Northwest Side, and an unfavorable response to the "social deterioration" accompanying the rapid business growth of the area were prime requisites for the development of an ethical orientation to the market. The "ethic" is an alignment with the symbols of small business against the big business that menaced the housewives' way of life. Patronage of local independent merchants more concretely realized the alliance. In addition, it maintained social distance between the higher-status customer and the lower-status clerk in a shopping situation where social distance was difficult to maintain but, at the same time, necessary to protect the established status of the customer in the larger community.

The Apathetic Consumer

Characteristically, apathetic consumers sought to minimize effort in shopping, and this characterized the older women. Either downward mobility or a lack of success in attempts at upward mobility[13] constricted the

---

[13]A greater proportion of the husbands of apathetic shoppers had completed their secondary-school education or gone on to college than in any other consumer type. Yet, the husbands of the majority of apathetic consumers belonged to lower social strata. When the social class of the 57 informants whose husbands had either completed high school or attended college was examined, the results showed that 23.8 percent of the 21 apathetic consumers were included in the higher educational group and could be placed in the upper-middle or lower-middle social classes, while 33.7 per cent had been recruited from the upper-lower social class. In contrast, 38.1 per cent of the remaining 98 informants were included in both the higher educational group and the middle social classes, while 11.1 percent had completed their secondary education or attended college and were, at the same time, members of the lower status levels. The significance of these relationships was established by the application of the chi-

aspirations of apathetic consumers and confined them to local neighborhood life. Long residence in the Northwest Side begun at an early age, and a strong positive local identification promoted strong bonds with others in the community. The market, in any case, was too far beyond the horizon of experience of the typical apathetic consumer to warrant much attention or interest.

The four profiles described above permit some speculation about the temporal allocation of shopping orientations. Apparently, economic and personalizing orientations were more often adopted by housewives who had recently moved into the area, and ethical and apathetic orientations by those who had lived in the area for relatively long periods of time. Aspiration, marginality, and success are perhaps the crucial intervening variables. This suggests the hypotheses: (1) the higher the level of aspiration among newcomers to a residential area, the greater the likelihood that they will adopt economic orientations to shopping; (2) the lower the level of aspiration and the greater the marginality of newcomers, the greater the likelihood that they will adopt personalizing orientations; (3) the greater the success long-time residents of a residential area have enjoyed, the greater the likelihood that they will adopt ethical orientations to shopping; and (4), conversely, the less the success, the greater the likelihood of consumer apathy among long-time residents.

What remains to be discussed and explained is the place of the personalizing role orientation in resolving the disparity between the apparent subjective indications of positive identification with the Northwest Side offered by personalizing consumers and the fact that objective indexes of community iden-

tification did not point to the likelihood that they would develop a sense of community belonging. Objectively, personalizing consumers were not integrated with the Northwest Side; subjectively, they were.

URBAN SOLIDARITY AND THE PERSONALIZATION OF MARKET RELATIONSHIPS

Despite the fact that certain objective conditions for community identification were absent among many personalizing consumers,[14] a clear majority of the informants concerned expressed no desire to leave the community and, at the same time, evaluated it favorably. In short, without objective basis, personalizing consumers seemed typically to have identified themselves with the Northwest Side.

A hypothesis was advanced to explain the discrepancy: *Among the 119 housewives subjective identification of some with the area in which they lived was a latent function*[15] *of their personalization of market relations.* These consumers usually implied that strong social bonds tied them to the personnel of the stores they patronized. In the absence of other neighborhood ties, such a bond was apparently strong enough to provide the basis for the consumer's attachment. It follows that, if personalizing consumers, *in contrast to the other types,* identified themselves subjectively

---

square test; thus a significant proportion of the husbands of apathetic consumers had been educated "above" their social status.

[14]Many had lived a short period of time in their current residences and in the community at large; a majority said that most of their friends lived outside the Northwest Side, and most had moved into the area at a relatively late age.

[15]"*Functions* are those observed consequences [of social acts] which make for the adaptation or adjustment of a given system . . . *latent functions* being those which are neither intended or recognized [by the social actor or actors]" (Robert K. Merton, *Social Theory and Social Structure* [Glencoe, Ill.: Free Press, 1949], pp. 50–51).

with the locality when objective indexes of local community identification did not suggest that likelihood, the hypothesis stated above could not be rejected.

To test the hypothesis, all informants who had indicated subjective identification with the community either by expressing a preference for continued residence there or by evaluating the community in positive terms were singled out for analysis. In addition, four objective indexes of local community identification were controlled: (1) length of residence in the Northwest Side; (2) age of the informant when she moved to the Northwest Side; (3) location of last place of residence; and (4) location of most of her friends. Those members of the selected group of "subjectively identified" informants who had lived in the Northwest Side six years or less, moved into the area at twenty-nine years of age or more and into their present residences from outside the Northwest Side, and said that most of their friends lived outside the community, were interpreted as having formed subjective identifications with the Northwest Side with *no apparent basis*. Informants characterized by three of the above criteria were said to have formed subjective attachments with *little apparent basis*. Those to whom two of the criteria applied were regarded as having become identified with *some apparent basis*. Finally, informants for whom only one criterion applied were interpreted as having formed a sense of community belonging with *apparent basis*. If personalizing consumers in the selected group of subjectively identified informants were found to have established community identifications without or with little apparent basis more often than the other consumer types, the hypothesis, it is contended, could not be eliminated.[16] Tables 2 and 3 summarize the results of the test.

Collapsing the first and second rows of Tables 2 and 3 and comparing the personalizing consumers with the other types taken as a whole permitted the application of the chi-square test of significance to the ensuing four-fold distributions. The results allow the conclusion that a *significantly larger proportion of personalizing consumers had established subjective identifications with the Northwest Side without or with little apparent basis than had consumers of the other three types taken*

[16]The data placed severe limitations upon the achievement of any more satisfactory test, largely owing to the fact that the entire range of findings reported here was unanticipated at the inception of the research. For a discussion of the adequacy of the criteria used and the test itself see Stone, *op. cit.*, pp. 124–28.

Table 2 / Basis for the Identification of Consumers Preferring to Live in Chicago's Northwest Side

Objective Basis for Community Iden-tification	Type of Consumers				
	Economic	Person-alizing	Ethical	Apathetic	Total
No apparent basis	2	4	—	—	6
Little apparent basis	3	6	—	2	11
Some apparent basis	4	5	6	5	20
Apparent basis	3	2	2	4	11
Total	12	17	8	11	48

Table 3 / Basis for the Identification of Consumers Favorably Disposed to Chicago's Northwest Side

Objective Basis for Community Iden- tification	Type of Consumers				
	Economic	Personalizing	Ethical	Apathetic	Total
No apparent basis	2	3	. . . . .	. . . . .	5
Little apparent basis	3	6	. . . . .	2	11
Some apparent basis	2	5	7	4	18
Apparent basis	3	2	2	4	11
Total	10	16	9	10	45

together.[17] Consequently, the hypothesis was retained.

The hypothesis has important implications for urban social psychology. That field has perhaps been concerned too long with the disintegrative effects or the dysfunctions of urbanism. Urban sociologists have documented with an admirable meticulousness the difficulties accompanying urban living and the obstacles in the path of achieving moral consensus in the metropolis. But they have failed to explain the obvious fact that people in goodly numbers do manage to live and survive in urban environments and that, among many of them, there is a patent sense of identification with the metropolis.

Durkheim observed long ago that the family was being replaced by occupational groupings as the seat of moral consensus in the organically solidary society.[18] However, it may be more sagacious not to single out any one nexus of human relations and attribute to it the function of generating consensus in the mass society. Instead, one might observe that life in the metropolis is largely routinized and that relationships bearing many of the qualities that Cooley spoke of as primary in nature may be established in any area of life where communication is frequent and regular. Such relationships can have the function of integrating the person with the larger society in which he lives.

[17]The level of significance and degree of association for the two distributions are $(p < .02; T = .36)$ and $(p < .05; T = .32)$ respectively—a relatively high degree of significance and association for such a small number of cases.

[18]Emile Durkheim, *The Division of Labor in Society,* trans. George Simpson (Glencoe, Ill.: Free Press, 1947), Preface to the Second Edition, pp. 1–31.

Questions

1. Name the four types of shoppers and briefly describe the social characteristics of each type.
2. How would a marketer promote store sales to the "apathetic" category of shoppers?
3. Which of the four categories do you consider easiest to reach as a target market? Why?

20. The Concept and Application of Life Style Segmentation

Joseph T. Plummer

A new dimension for segmenting markets has been developed in recent years. This new method, called life style segmentation, has been useful for marketing and advertising planning. The purpose of this article is to describe the theory behind life style segmentation and discuss how it has been and can be applied.

Life style segmentation is the marriage of two concepts into a single system. One of the concepts is life style patterns and the other is market segmentation. In order to discuss the uses of life style segmentation, it is important first to examine briefly each component of the system and then the uses of the total system.

LIFE STYLE PATTERNS

The concept of life style patterns and its relationship to marketing was introduced in 1963 by William Lazer. He defined life style patterns as: "a systems concept. It refers to a distinctive mode of living in its aggregate and broadest sense. . . . It embodies the patterns that develop and emerge from the dynamics of living in a society."[1]

Since 1963, methods of measuring life style patterns and their relationship to consumer behavior have been developed and refined. The most widely used approach to life style measurement has been AIO (Activities, Interests, and Opinions) rating statements.[2] Life style as used in life style segmentation research measures people's activities in terms of (1) how they spend their time; (2) their interests, what they place importance on in their immediate surroundings; (3) their opinions in terms of their view of themselves and the world around them; and (4) some basic characteristics such as their stage in life cycle, income, education, and where they live. Table 1 lists the elements included in each major dimension of life style.

The basic premise of life style research is that the more you know and understand about your customers the more effectively you can communicate and market to them.

Over the years, a number of constructs have been useful in better understanding the customer. The most popular constructs have been demographics, social class, and psychological characteristics. Demographics have received broad acceptance and lend themselves easily to quantification and consumer classification. However, demographics lack richness and often need to be supplemented with other data. Social class adds more depth to demographics, but it, too, often needs to be supplemented in order to ob-

[1]William Lazer, "Life Style Concepts and Marketing," *Toward Scientific Marketing,* Stephen Greyser, ed. (Chicago: American Marketing Assn., 1963), pp. 140–151.

[2]William Wells and Doug Tigert, "Activities, Interests and Opinions," *Journal of Advertising Research,* Vol. 11 August 1971), pp. 27–35, Joseph T. Plummer, "Life Style Patterns: A New Construct for Mass Communications Reseach," *Journal of Broadcasting,* Vol. 16 (Fall-Winter 1972), pp. 79–89; and Joseph T. Plummer, "Life Style Patterns and Commercial Bank Credit Card Usage," *Journal of Marketing,* Vol. 35 (April 1971), pp. 35–42.

Table 1 / Life Style Dimensions

Activities	Interests	Opinions	Demographics
Work	Family	Themselves	Age
Hobbies	Home	Social issues	Education
Social events	Job	Politics	Income
Vacation	Community	Business	Occupation
Entertainment	Recreation	Economics	Family size
Club membership	Fashion	Education	Dwelling
Community	Food	Products	Geography
Shopping	Media	Future	City size
Sports	Achievements	Culture	Stage in life cycle

tain meaningful insights into audiences. Lastly, psychological characteristics are often rich but may lack reliability when applied to mass audiences. In addition, the findings from psychological scales frequently are difficult to implement.

The new construct, life style patterns, combines the virtues of demographics with the richness and dimensionality of psychological characteristics and depth research. Life style deals with everyday, behaviorally oriented facets of people as well as their feelings, attitudes, and opinions. It tells us things about our customers that most researchers did not really attempt to quantify in the past, when the focus was on the product or on widely used measures of classification such as demographics.

Life style attempts to answer questions like: What do women think about the job of housekeeping? Are they interested in contemporary fashions? Do they participate in community activities? Are they optimistic about the future? Do they see themselves as homebodies or swingers? When the answers to questions like these correlate significantly with product usage, magazine readership, television program preferences, or other mass communication variables, a picture emerges that goes beyond flat demographic descriptions, program ratings, or product-specific measures. Life style patterns provide a broader, more three-dimensional view of customers, so that one can think about them more intelligently in terms of the most relevant product positioning, communication, media, and promotion.

MARKET SEGMENTATION

As long as people have been selling products to one another there has been some form of market segmentation. In the early days of marketing, segmentation (i.e., selection of a group or groups with common characteristics out of the total) was based on rather general dimensions such as buyers vs. nonbuyers, men vs. women, and the like. Refinements have been made over the years to adjust to the increasing complexity in the marketplace and the rise of mass marketing. One of these segmented buyers in terms of light users, moderate users, and heavy users. This segmentation basis was adopted when sellers realized that in many product categories, the heavy user segment accounted for as much as two-thirds of the business.[3]

[3]Clark Wilson, "Homemaker Living Patterns and Marketplace Behavior," in *New Ideas for Successful Marketing,* John Wright and Jac Goldstucker, eds. (Chicago: American Marketing Assn., 1966), pp. 305–332.

Whether sophisticated or simple, segmentation exists and has been used for a long time. Marketing management knows that no single population is homogeneous and that there is no "average man." People are different and do things for different reasons. Thus there is a need to identify the differences and group them in such a way that a better understanding of the population under consideration emerges. The focus in segmentation is on the differences between identified groups on certain criteria, such as brand purchasing, brand attitudes, media patterns, and so on.

Segmentation is useful because it moves beyond total scores or averages and reveals important differences that can be acted upon. If, for example, research indicated that a new concept received an overall rating of only 3.2 on a 5-point scale among a hundred people, the concept might be dropped. However, if the sample were segmented into light, medium, and heavy users, and the new ratings developed for the concept were 2.1 among light users, 3.3 among medium users, and 4.7 among heavy users, the evaluation of this concept would be different. In this way, segmentation can reveal important insights that averages often hide. Segmentation is particularly useful in developing marketing objectives because it identifies important subgroups in the population as more efficient marketing targets than others.[4]

All of this discussion leads to the question: "Segmentation of the market is useful, but what concepts are the most useful in segmenting the market?" In order to answer this question, we first need to examine what the various approaches to segmenting the market are and then discuss the criteria to be used in selecting among these approaches.

Historically, there have been two general approaches to market segmentation: "people" oriented and "product" oriented. The people-oriented segmentation approaches have utilized various dimensions along which to measure people and then relate the people segments to the product or service. Those people-oriented segmentation dimensions that have enjoyed widespread usage are demographics, social class, stage in life cycle, product usage, innovativeness, and psychological characteristics. The product-oriented segmentation approaches have been designed to measure product characteristics, either directly or indirectly through consumers, in order to better understand the structure of the market. Those product-oriented segmentation dimensions that have enjoyed broad usage include: product benefits, product usage occasions, value, ingredients or taste, perceived attributes, and advertising appeals.

The criteria that should be employed in selecting a useful segmentation approach to aid in marketing and advertising planning are three-fold:

1. Is the segmentation approach based on theory consistent with the objectives?
2. Does the segmentation reveal significant differences between the defined segments on a usage or purchasing measure?
3. Can these differences be understood and acted upon to improve business?

The most recent trend in market segmentation has been in the direction of more sophisticated procedures and product-oriented segmentations. So often, however, the segments developed from a study on one product category have little or no relevance to another product category. Product-benefit, or attribute, segmentation has been useful to marketers and advertisers and is often the basis for multibrand development. As Wells has

[4]Daniel Yankelovich, "New Criteria for Market Segmentation," *Harvard Business Review,* Vol. 42 (March-April 1964), p. 83; and William Cunningham and William Crissy, "Market Segmentation by Motivation and Attitudes," *Journal of Marketing Research,* Vol. 9 (February 1972), pp. 100–103.

pointed out, however, these measures are still inadequate in their description and analysis of the consumer as a person. It is in this area that life style data—activities, interests, and opinions—have proved their importance as a means of "duplicating" the consumer for the marketing researcher.[5]

LIFE STYLE SEGMENTATION

Life style is used to segment the marketplace because it provides a broad, everyday view of consumers. When combined with the theory of typologies[6] and clustering methods,[7] life style segmentation can generate identifiable whole persons rather than isolated fragments. Life style segmentation begins with people instead of products and classifies them into different life style types, each characterized by a unique style of living based on a wide range of activities, interests, and opinions. The rationale for this approach is that consumers have hundreds of products in their world in an average week. Although the product is most important to the marketer, to the consumer, *he* is most important.

The analytical procedure of relating the life style segments to a particular market is a two-step process. In this two-step process, life style segmentation adds important new dimensions to available information on consumers and other market segmentation approaches.

Step 1

The usual first step in the analysis of life style segmentation information is to determine which of the life style segments are best from the standpoint of efficiently producing the greatest number of customers for a brand. The selection of the important segments is derived by examining several product dimensions: (1) usage of the category; (2) frequency of usage of the category, that is, who the heavy users, moderate users, and light users are; (3) brand usage and brand share (if available); and (4) product attitudes and usage patterns.

Ideally, the key segments selected would have high product penetration and would contain the highest proportions of heavy users, indicating greater volume potential, a healthy position for the brand or brands under consideration, and favorable brand attitudes. This type of ideal situation would make the selection of target segments quite easy. Unfortunately, this ideal situation seldom occurs in reality.

The author's experience with life style segmentation has shown that there tend to be three basic results in relationships between life style segments and the marketing data.

First, two or three life style segments account for 60% or more of the total business in that category. This means that these segments (types of people) are crucial to success or failure in the category. They are the ones who need to be appealed to, reached through the media, and concentrated on in marketing.

Second, a number of segments contain important levels of heavy users of the category, and a few segments are relatively unimportant. Here one needs to go beyond the con-

[5]William D. Wells, "Seven Questions about Life Style and Psychographics," (Paper presented at the 55th International Marketing Congress, New York City, April 1972), p. 4.

[6]William Stephenson, *The Study of Behavior* (Chicago: The University of Chicago Press, 1953); Carl Rogers, *On Becoming a Person* (Boston: Houghton Mifflin Co., 1961); and Joseph T. Plummer, "Audience Research in TV Program Development," *Educational Broadcast Review,* Vol. 2 (June 1968), pp. 23–30.

[7]Richard Johnson, "How Can You Tell if Things Are Really Clustered?" (Paper presented to the American Statistical Association, New York, February 15, 1972.)

sumption data to examine the relative positions of the brands. Where is a brand strong and where is it weak? If a brand profile matches the heavy-user profiles by segments, then the task becomes one of maintaining the current position and perhaps expanding it. It may be that the segments where a brand is weak are different people with different needs, which might suggest a second brand.

If, on the other hand, a brand profile does not match the heavier-using segments very well, there is a need to determine how to capture some business from those segments where competition is doing much better.

Third, there are no significant differences in consumption among the segments, but definite attitude, product function, and life style similarities exist between groups of segments. This type of outcome may be the result of two factors: no one brand has attempted to "segment itself," or the product is such that once a purchase is made the individual no longer contributes to the market. It is in this type of situation where creativity and intuition play an important role in selecting segments on which to focus advertising and marketing efforts just on the basis of attitude, usage pattern, or life style similarities. There are really no guidelines for target selection in this situation. In some instances, one must try another basis for segmenting the market and hope the alternative approach will show significant and more useful differences in consumption patterns.

Step 2

Once the target segments have been selected, one can begin to define and describe the target customer in more depth and with more understanding of "why." At this point, thinking can begin on how to reach and communicate more efficiently and relevantly to the target customers (who are usually a composite of several segments). The insights and knowledge of the key life style segments will aid in determining the product positioning, the advertising, the media strategy, and the promotion strategy.

BENEFITS OF LIFE STYLE SEGMENTATION

Definition of the Key Target

Invariably, life style segmentation provides a redefinition of the key target. Instead of defining the target in demographic terms (i.e., middle-aged housewives with a large family and average income) or in product usage terms (i.e., the frequent user, the price buyer, the vacation traveler, etc.), life style segmentation demonstrates the diversity of those definitions, helps tighten them up, and provides new definitions. In addition to middle-aged white collar or blue collar housewives, life style provides definitions like "housewife role haters," "old-fashioned homebodies," and "active affluent urbanites."

Also, since life style segmentation involves many factors simultaneously, it has shown that certain demographics go together to define targets which, considered independently (i.e., one at a time), might not merge. Life style segmentation provides a richer redefinition of the key target audiences.

Provides a New View of the Market

In the past, it was often difficult to determine the structure of the market in terms of usage patterns. Because life style segmentation provides an overview of the market in a multidimensional sense, one can often learn a good deal about the structure of the market. One such learning experience occurred where there had been a running controversy for years on whether the target was parents or children. Life style segmentation demonstrated that the target was heavy using households where both parents and children consumed more than average.

In another situation with which the author is familiar, where a marketer was involved in three closely allied product categories, life style segmentation showed them to be really three different categories. Although the demographic profiles of the heavy users for each category were well known and not dramatically different, life style segmentation indicated how different in life style and product orientation the key segments for each category were. This finding has helped lead to a different product positioning and product improvements for each category.

Product Positioning

Life style information can be used to complement more commonly used information such as product benefits, unique ingredients, and competitive advantages in positioning a product to customers.

Life style information can be employed to *position* a product based on the inferences drawn from the portrait of the consumer both in terms of his basic needs and how the product fits into his life. If, for example, the person's life style indicates a strong need to be with other people in a variety of settings, it may be that the product can be positioned to help satisfy this social need. Or one might learn how a product fits into a person's life. It may be that the basic function of a product is convenience. But if it is found that the target consumer enjoys cooking and is not convenience oriented, it may be appropriate to position the product as a shortcut in creating more elegant dishes.

Communication

Although there are many ways in which life style can be useful in the creation of advertising,[8] there are four major concepts that one can use in applying the findings for the creation of advertising communication. The most obvious one is that, for the creative person, life style data provide a richer and more lifelike picture of the target consumer than do demographics. This enables the writer or artist to have in his own mind a better idea of the type of person he is trying to communicate with about the product. This picture also gives the creative person clues about what may or may not be appropriate to the life style of the target consumer. This has implications for the setting of the advertising, the type and appearance of the characters, the nature of the music and artwork, whether or not fantasy can be used, and so on.

A second and similar concept that can be used in applying the life style data are the insights into the basic *tone of voice* for the advertising. The creative user can get a sense of whether the tone should be serious or humorous, authoritative or cooperative, contemporary or traditional, from the life style dimensions of the target user portrait.

The third major concept which is helpful in developing advertising from life style information is that of the *rewards* people seek in their activities and interests. Do the target consumers obtain rewards by doing something nice for others, or are their rewards derived from more self-centered activities and interests? If the target consumer obtains rewards through others, then it might be more relevant to portray her as doing the right thing for her family by purchasing the product.

[8]Joseph T. Plummer, "Application of Life Style Research to the Creation of Advertising Campaigns," in *Life Style and Psychographics,* William Wells, ed. (in press).

The final major concept which is useful in developing advertising from life style portraits of consumers is the notion of the number and types of *roles* in which the target consumer sees himself. If the female consumer sees her major role as a housekeeper rather than wife or mother or socialite, then it would seem most appropriate to utilize that role in communicating to her. She would have a difficult time identifying or, perhaps, even believing spokesmen not congruent with that role.

Helps Develop Sounder Overall Marketing and Media Strategies

In addition to providing input into the "who" of a marketing plan, life style segmentation often provides insights into the amount of concentration in a market: how difficult conversion of nonusers might be, the potential role of promotion, and the potential role of new products. For example, in one product category it was quite evident that every brand except one was targeted at the same life style segment. Although important, this segment comprised less than half of the users. Here was an instance where a marketing opportunity existed to target a new brand or reposition an older one at the other, less-concentrated segments.

The author is aware of one situation in which life style segmentation was particularly useful in basic media strategy, when an important segment appeared to be more print-oriented and a light daytime television viewer. Using the demographics of that life style segment, further analysis of other media data suggested that a move to print media for part of the budget would be a good one to reach these important consumers.[9]

Can Suggest New Product Opportunities

Because life style segmentation provides a great deal of information on the different needs of types of people and the potential size of those "types" in the population, one can examine existing products to see how well they are meeting the needs of consumer types. In one situation, several segments had a need for more and better alternatives for their children's "spur of the moment meals." Given these unmet needs, some sense of the potential, and a rich definition of the target segments, it was not too difficult to develop some new products which currently are being tested.

Helps Explain the "Why" of a Product or Brand Situation

Knowledge of each segment's life style, attitudes, and usage patterns enables the marketer in many situations to explain or generate hypotheses on why certain segments use or do not use a particular product or brand very heavily. It is often because of several factors interacting rather than a single factor. Without the holistic view of the segments, it would be difficult to observe these interactions and put them into perspective. These insights are helpful in deciding not to appeal to particular segments when there are several "barriers" to conversion or increased usage. On the more positive side, these insights often can help explain why two rather similar

[9]"How Nestle Uses Psychographics," *Media Decisions,* Vol. 8 (July 1973), pp. 68–71.

brands are both doing well. Frequently, it is because they are used equally for different sets of motivations and reasons by different types of people. Life style segmentation often uncovers this type of situation.

CONCLUSION

Life style segmentation is useful because it provides a unique and important view of the market. It begins with the people—their life styles and motivations—and then determines how various marketing factors fit into their lives. This perspective often provides fresh insights into the market and gives a more three-dimensional view of the target consumers.

This article has described the theory underlying life style segmentation, a two-step analytic process, and uses which have been made of the data. This unique and detailed knowledge of consumers has been a useful input to marketing and advertising planning for many of the companies that have been involved in life style segmentation studies.

Questions

1. What have been the two general approaches to market segmentation?
2. Why is lifestyle segmentation a better approach than using some other basis for segmentation?
3. Explain the two-step process in lifestyle segmentation.

Part F

SELF-CONCEPT

21. Consumer Self-Concept, Symbolism and Market Behavior: A Theoretical Approach

Edward L. Grubb

Harrison L. Grathwohl

Efforts to understand the totality of consumer behavior have taken researchers into related fields, with some of the most fruitful results in terms of both theory and practice coming from the behavioral sciences. Two conceptual areas within the behavioral sciences which promise to yield meaningful information about consumer behavior are self-theory and symbolism. A substantial amount of work has been done in these areas, primarily by psychologists, but marketing researchers and theorists do not seem to have developed the marketing potential of the available theory and substance.[1] Some products, brands, and stores have long been recognized as having psychic values to certain market segments, but little has been done to fabricate formal theories useful in predicting consumer behavior.

This article is an effort to develop a partial theory of consumer behavior by linking the psychological construct of an individual's self-concept with the symbolic value of goods purchased in the marketplace. The authors briefly examine previous research and lay theoretical footings from which a set of hypotheses and a qualitative model of consumer behavior are promulgated.

REVIEW OF RELATED RESEARCH

Personality and Consumer Behavior

A number of researchers have attempted to relate purchases of product types or specific brands to personality traits of the purchasers. These researchers advanced the basic hypothesis that individuals who consume in a certain manner will also manifest certain common personality characteristics, leading to prediction of consumer behavior. Evans conducted empirical investigations to determine

[1]George A. Field, John Douglas, and Lawrence X. Tarpey, *Marketing Management: A Behavioral Systems Approach* (Columbus, Ohio: Charles E. Merrill Books, 1966), p. 106.

if choice of automobile brand reflects the personality of the owner.[2] Applying the Edwards' Personal Preference Schedule, he could find no important personality differences between a limited sample of Chevrolet and Ford owners and, therefore, could not show that psychological testing predicted consumer behavior more accurately than standard marketing research. However, Kuehn submitted the same data to further statistical analysis and concluded that prediction could indeed be based upon two of the measured personality characteristics (dominance and affiliation).[3]

Westfall experimented with automobile owners to determine if the personalities of owners of standard models, of compact models, and of convertible models varied.[4] Using the Thurstone Temperament Schedule as a personality measuring instrument, he found little difference between the owners of compact and standard models, but discovered that convertible owners are more active, vigorous, impulsive, dominant, and social, yet less stable and less reflective than the other two groups of owners.

The results of these and similar studies demonstrate the existence of some relationship between personalities of the consumers and the products they consume.[5] Yet the results indicate as well the limitations of our understanding of this relationship. Because of the limited results produced by these and similar studies, further refinements in the theoretical foundations may be necessary to provide useful insights.

Personality, Product Image, and the Consumption of Goods

A further refinement in the attempt to relate personality and purchases was the advancement of the assumption that consumer buying behavior is determined by the interaction of the buyer's personality and the image of the purchased product. Pierre Martineau, a strong advocate of this position, argued that the product or brand image is a symbol of the buyer's personality.[6] In later work, Walter A. Woods identified various types of consumers and the importance of the symbolic content of the product to the purchase. Woods asserted that where ego-involvement with the product is high, product image is important to the consumer.[7]

Along similar lines, Duesenberry advanced the idea that the act of consumption as symbolic behavior may be more important to the individual than the benefits provided by the functioning of the product purchased.[8] The relationship of product image and personality was further substantiated by a recent study that found a low, but statistically significant, correlation between the

[2]Franklin B. Evans "Psychological and Objective Factors in the Prediction of Brand Choice: Ford vs. Chevrolet," *Journal of Business,* Vol. XXXII (October, 1959), p. 340.

[3]Alfred A. Kuehn, "Demonstration of a Relationship between Psychological Factors and Brand Choice," *Journal of Business,* Vol. XXXVI (April, 1963), p. 237.

[4]Ralph Westfall, "Psychological Factors in Predicting Product Choice," *Journal of Marketing,* Vol. 26 (April, 1962), p. 34.

[5]For a bibliography of similar studies see: *Are There Consumer Types?* (New York: Advertising Research Foundation, 1964), p. 28.

[6]Pierre Martineau, *Motivation in Advertising* (New York: McGraw-Hill Book Company, 1957).

[7]Walter A. Woods, "Psychological Dimensions of Consumer Decision," *Journal of Marketing,* Vol. 24 (January, 1960), pp. 15-19.

[8]James S. Duesenberry, *Income, Savings, and the Theory of Consumer Behavior* (Cambridge: Harvard University Press, 1949). For a discussion of the theory of consumption, see James S. Duesenberry, "A Theory of Consumption," *Marketing: The Firm's Viewpoint,* Schuyler F. Otteson, William Panschar, and James M. Patterson (editors) (New York: The Macmillan Co., 1964), pp. 125-132.

masculinity of cigarette smokers and the perceived masculinity of the brand they consumed.[9]

Though meaningful, the early work has not developed the theoretical relationships between the personality of the individual and the product image. To be useful as a guide to marketing decision-making and research, the variables of the buyer's personality and the image of the purchased products need to be organized into a conceptual totality that will allow relevant material to be systemized, classified, and interrelated. Further, the conceptual interrelationship of these variables should be arranged and developed in such a manner that the *why* of the interrelationship is explained. Exposure of all the elements of the theory to critical evaluation should encourage testing of hypotheses, followed by improvement (retesting of theory) so that more informed judgments can be made relative to the marketing value of the approach.

SELF-THEORY AND CONSUMER BEHAVIOR

A more specific means of developing a theoretical approach to consumer behavior is to link the psychological construct of an individual's self-concept with the symbolic value of the goods purchased in the marketplace. The concept of the self is more restricted than personality, which facilitates measurement and centers on the critical element of how the individual perceives himself.[10] Further, use of self-theory allows appli-

cation of the behavioral concept of symbolic interaction; this provides meaning to the association of an individual's buying behavior with his self-concept.

Self-Theory

Self-theory has been the subject of much psychological and sociological theorizing and empirical research with the accompanying development of a rather large body of assumptions and empirical data.[11] The available knowledge strongly supports the role of the self-concept as a partial determinant of human behavior and, therefore, represents a promising area for marketing research.

Current theory and research places emphasis on the concept of the self as an object which is perceived by the individual. The self is what one is aware of, one's attitudes, feelings, perceptions, and evaluations of oneself as an object.[12] The self represents a totality which becomes a principal value around which life revolves, something to be safeguarded and, if possible, to be made still more valuable.[13] An individual's evaluation of himself will greatly influence his behavior, and thus, the more valued the self, the more organized and consistent becomes his behavior.

The Self and the Interaction Process

The self develops not as a personal, individual process, but it evolves through the process of

[9]Paul C. Vitz and Donald Johnston, "Masculinity of Smokers and the Masculinity of Cigarette Images," *Journal of Applied Psychology,* Vol. XLIX (October, 1965), pp. 155–159.

[10]E. Earl Baughman and George Schlager Welsh, *Personality: A Behavioral Science* (Englewood Cliffs, N.J.: Prentice-Hall, Inc., 1962), p. 339.

[11]See, for example, Ruth Wylie, *The Self-Concept* (Lincoln, Nebraska: The University of Nebraska Press, 1961).

[12]Calvin S. Hall and Gardener Lindsay, *Theories of Personality* (New York: John Wiley and Sons, Inc., 1957), pp. 469–475, or David Krech, Richard S. Crutchfield, and Egerton L. Ballachey, *Individual in Society* (New York: McGraw-Hill Book Company, 1962), pp. 495–496.

[13]Theodore M. Newcomb, *Social Psychology* (New York: The Dryden Press, 1956), p. 319.

social experience. From the reactions of others, man develops his self-perception. According to Rogers:

> A portion of the total perceptual field gradually becomes differentiated as the self. . . as a result of the interaction with the environment, and particularly as a result of evaluational interactions with others, the structure of the self is formed—an organized, fluid, but consistent conceptual pattern of perceptions of characteristics and relationships of the 'I' or the 'me' together with values attached to these concepts.[14]

Since the self-concept grows out of the reactions of parents, peers, teachers, and significant others, self-enhancement will depend upon the reactions of those people. Recognition and reinforcing reactions from these persons will further strengthen the conception the individual has of himself. Thus, the individual will strive to direct his behavior to obtain a positive reaction from his significant references.

Context of the Interaction Process

The interaction process does not take place in a vacuum; the individuals are affected both by the environmental setting and the "personal attire" of each involved individual. Therefore, the individual will strive to control these elements to facilitate proper interpretations of his performance.[15] Items of the environmental setting or the personal attire become the tools or a means of goal accomplishment for individuals in the interaction process.

Goods as Symbols

A more meaningful way of understanding the role of goods as social tools is to regard them as symbols serving as a means of communication between the individual and his significant references. Defined as "things which stand for or express something else," symbols should be thought of as unitary characters composed of signs and their meanings.[16] If a symbol is to convey meaning it must be identified by a group with which the individual is associated whether the group consists of two people or an entire society, and the symbol must communicate similar meaning to all within the group. The nature of goods as symbols has been attested quite adequately by Veblen,[17] Duesenberry,[18] and Benedict.[19]

Symbols and Behavior

If a product is to serve as a symbolic communicative device it must achieve social recognition, and the meaning associated with the product must be clearly established and understood by related segments of society. This process is in reality a classification process where one object is placed in relation to other objects basic to society.

> The necessity for any group to develop a common or shared terminology leads to an important consideration; the direction of activity depends upon the particular way that objects are classified.[20]

---

[14]Hall and Lindsay, same reference as footnote 12, p. 483.

[15]Erving Goffman, *The Presentation of Self in Everyday Life* (Garden City, New York: Doubleday and Co., Inc., 1959), p. 22.

[16]Lloyd Warner, *The Living and the Dead* (New Haven: Yale University Press, 1959), p. 3.

[17]Thorstein Veblen, *The Theory of the Leisure Class* (New York: Mentor Books, 1953).

[18]Same reference as footnote 8.

[19]Ruth Benedict, *Patterns of Culture* (New York: Mentor Books, 1934).

[20]Anselm Strauss, *Mirrors and Masks: The Search for Identity* (Glencoe, Illinois: The Free Press of Glencoe, 1959), p. 9.

Classification systems are society's means of organizing and directing their activities in an orderly and sensible manner.

A prime example of symbolic classification and consumer behavior is fashion. If a particular style becomes popular, behavior of a segment of society will be directed toward the purchase and use of items manifesting this style. As the fashion declines in popularity, the group will discontinue purchase of these items and may reject the use of the remaining portion of previous purchases. Thus, an act of classification not only directs action, but also arouses a set of expectations toward the object classified. Individuals purchase the fashion item because of their feelings about what the item will do for them. The *essence* of the object resides not in the object but in the relation between the object and the individuals classifying the object.

Classification and symbolism become means of communication and of directing or influencing behavior. If a common symbol exists for two or more people, then the symbol should bring forth a similar response in each, and therefore members of a group can use the symbol in their behavior pattern. Further, the symbolic social classification of a good allows the consumer to relate himself directly to it, matching his self-concept with the meaning of the good. In this way self-support and self-enhancement can take place through association with goods which have a desirable social meaning and from the favorable reaction of significant references in the social interaction process.

Goods and Self-enhancement

The purchase and consumption of goods can be self-enhancing in two ways. First, the self-concept of an individual will be sustained and buoyed if he believes the good he has purchased is recognized publicly and classified in a manner that supports and matches his self-concept. While self-enhancement results from a personal, internal, intra-action process, the effect on the individual is ultimately dependent upon the product's being a publicly-recognized symbol. Because of their recognized meaning, public symbols elicit a reaction from the individual that supports his original self-feelings. Self-enhancement can occur as well in the interaction process. Goods as symbols serve the individual, becoming means to cause desired reactions from other individuals.

These two means of self-enhancement are represented in diagrammatic form in Figure 1.

Individual A purchases and uses symbol X which has intrinsic and extrinsic value as a means of self-enhancement. (Symbol X could include a purchase of a certain product type such as a swimming pool; purchase of a specific brand such as a Pontiac GTO; or a purchase from a specific store or distributive outlet.) The intrinsic value is indicated by the double-headed arrow a, while the extrinsic values are indicated by the arrows b, c, and d. By the use of symbol X, an individual is communicating with himself; he is transferring the socially attributed meanings of symbol X to himself. This internal, personal communication process with symbol X becomes a means of enhancing his valued self-concept. An example of this situation is the individual who owns and uses a standard 1300 series Volkswagen. He may perceive himself as being thrifty, economical, and practical; and by using the Volkswagen, which has a strong image of being thrifty, economical, and practical, the individual achieves internal self-enhancement. This private and individual symbolic interpretation is largely dependent on one's understanding of the meaning associated with the product. Though the individual may treat this process in a private manner, he has

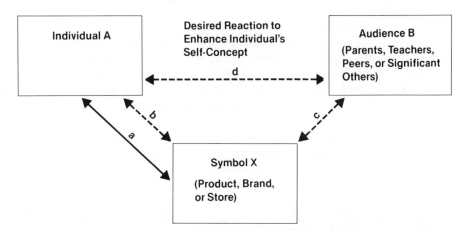

Figure 1 / Relationship of the consumption of goods as symbols to the self-concept

learned the symbolic meaning from public sources.

By presenting Symbol X to Audience B, which may consist of one or more individuals from parents, peers, teachers, or significant others, the individual is communicating with them. Double-headed arrows b and c indicate that in presenting Symbol X to Audience B, Individual A is attributing meaning to it, and that in interpreting Symbol X, the relevant references in Audience B are also attributing meaning to the symbol. If Symbol X has a commonly-understood meaning between Individual A and the references of Audience B, then the desired communication can take place and the interaction process will develop as desired by A. This means the behavior of the significant references will be the desired reaction to Individual A (as shown by arrow d) and, therefore, self-enhancement will take place.

A Model of Consuming Behavior

The following qualitative model is proposed to clarify the systematic relationship be-tween self-theory and goods as symbols in terms of consumer behavior.

Consumption of Symbols: A Means to Self-Enhancement

1 . An individual does have a self-concept of himself.

2 . The self-concept is of value to him.

3 . Because this self-concept is of value to him, an individual's behavior will be directed toward the furtherance and enhancement of his self-concept.

4 . An individual's self-concept is formed through the interaction process with parents, peers, teachers, and significant others.

5 . Goods serve as social symbols and, therefore, are communication devices for the individual.

6 . The use of these good-symbols communicates meaning to the individual himself and to others, causing an impact on the intra-action and/or the interaction processes and, therefore, an effect on the individual's self-concept.

Prediction of the model:

7 . Therefore, the consuming behavior of an individual will be directed toward the fur-thering and enhancing of his self-concept through the consumption of goods as symbols.

This model becomes the theoretical base for a conceptual means to understand consumer behavior. The self-conception approach to understanding consumer behavior is not all-inclusive but does provide a meaningful conceptual framework for the systematic ordering and comprehension of consumer behavior. Of further importance is that this model, although general, can be an aid to the marketing decision-maker and a guide for future research.

Self-Concept Theory of Behavior and Marketing Research

This theoretical model can and should be used as a guide for further research. As Myers and Reynolds state, "We need to know a good deal more about the matching process and the conditions under which it does and does not occur."[21] Opportunity and need exist for both theoretical and applied research.

Further research is needed in terms of specific consumer decision situations to determine to what extent self-enhancement involves a conformity concept or an ideal self-image concept. For example, are consumers, through their consuming behavior and the interaction process, seeking support for their self-concept as they now perceive themselves, or are they seeking reactions that will promote the attainment of a more ideal self? For the average person, self-concept and self-ideal overlap to a large extent, although in specific circumstances one or the other could be the chief motivator of behavior.[22] This information is of central importance to help management evolve promotional efforts that either support the self-concepts of consumers as they now are *or* as they would like to be.

Useful results will be obtained from well-designed research pertaining to the present and desired symbolic content of products, brands, or stores, and how these symbolic meanings can be related to the self-concepts of present and potential users. Success or failure of a product often depends upon the social classification given to the product. Therefore, it is vital that the firm identify those specific products where the symbolic meaning of the product and its relation to the self-concept of the purchaser are active influences in the consumer decision process.

Self-Concept Theory of Behavior and Marketing Management

Firms can and should identify and/or segment their markets in terms of differentiated self-concepts. Recent research had indicated significant differences in self-concepts of different consuming groups both for product classes and for different brands.[23] Identification of self-concept segments may be a key element in the determination of marketing strategy and how, where, and to whom the exact tactics should be directed to achieve the desired goals.

Of real importance to the success of a brand of product is the development of a commonly understood symbolic meaning for the product. This means that management of a firm should carefully control the marketing of a product so that the relevant segments of the market properly classify the product and, therefore, behave toward the product in the manner desired by the marketer. Through product design, pricing, promotion, and distribution the firm must communicate to

[21]James H. Myers and William H. Reynolds, *Consumer Behavior and Marketing Management* (New York: Houghton Mifflin Co., 1967), p. 204.

[22]Same reference as footnote 10, p. 348.

[23]Edward L. Grubb, "Consumer Perception of 'Self-Concept' and Its Relationship to Brand Choice of Selected Product Types," unpublished D.B.A. dissertation, University of Washington, 1965, pp. 120–124.

the market the desired clues for consumer interpretation and, therefore, develop the desired symbolic meaning for the brand.

SUMMARY

From a review of the literature of the behavioral sciences, the authors have developed a more complete theory of consumer behavior based upon self-theory and symbolism. This theory can serve as a theoretical foundation for understanding and predicting consumer market behavior, with particular emphasis on its role as the guide for research and decision making.

The hypothesis presented by the authors stresses the role of the image an individual has of himself as a motivator of human behavior in the marketplace. Because the self-concept is of value and of central importance to the individual, he will direct his behavior to maintain and enhance his self-concept. The self-concept is formed in the interaction process between the individual and others; therefore, the individual will strive for self-enhancement in the interaction process. Of prime importance is the fact that the interaction process will be affected by the "tools" used by individuals and their significant references. Many of these tools are consumer goods, serving as symbolic communication devices. By carefully using goods as symbols, the individual communicates meaning about himself to his references, which causes a desired response and has an impact on the interaction process, thus reenforcing and enhancing his self-concept.

Enhancement of the self-concept can occur through an intra-action process whereby an individual communicates with himself through the medium of goods-symbols, thus supporting his self-concept. This is an internal process which takes place without specific response from others regarding a particular act. However, intra-action self-enhancement is possible only through group classification systems which bestow symbolic value upon certain goods or "tools."

The model of consuming behavior presented here is still in a theoretical state and, therefore, in need of research to refine and further substantiate its predictive value. Research is needed to determine whether and in what circumstances the motivating force is the presently held self-concept or the ideal self-concept. Basic research also is needed to determine what products have symbolic value and how this meaning is related to the consumers' self-concepts.

The advanced hypothesis is an activist theory having real value as a guide for present marketing decision-making. Marketers should consider segmenting their markets on the basis of consumer self-concepts as well as on demographic factors. Further, they must develop and direct their marketing strategy to meet the needs of these specific self-concept segments. Management would be wise to recognize that the success or failure of a product may depend upon the symbolic meaning established for that product. Significant marketing effort should be employed to ensure that the relevant segments of the market properly classify the product which in turn will tend to bring about desired consumer behavior.

Questions

1. Summarize the concept of "self-theory."
2. Briefly describe the systematic relationship between self-theory and goods as symbols, as described in the authors' model of consumer behavior.

3. What is self-enhancement? How can it be used by a firm selling a high-priced fashion good?

4. What do the authors feel is the relationship between the personalities of the consumers and the products they consume?

---

22.   The Self-Concept in Buyer Behavior

Terrence V. O'Brien

Humberto S. Tapia

Thomas L. Brown

An understanding of consumer behavior requires recognition that individuals and groups perceive and react to products differently. Application of self theory to consumer behavior has substantially added to this understanding. Central to the theory are three elements: self-concept, self-enhancement, and symbolic interaction.

The concept of self focuses on how an individual perceives himself. The self-concept consists of what he knows about himself, what he thinks of himself, how he values himself, and how he attempts to enhance or defend himself.[1]

Research indicates that an individual may have more than one self-concept. An actual self-concept (how an individual presently sees himself) has been differentiated from an ideal self-concept (a self-concept to which he aspires—a more valuable one).[2] Related

research has also differentiated an intermediate version of self-concept called the expected self, which implies some developmental position between the actual and ideal.[3] One's self-concept is valuable, and much behavior is directed at protecting or adding to its perceived value.

Self-enhancement, the process of improving one's self-concept over time, like development of the self-concept, is not an individual process but rather one carried out in a social setting. Self-enhancement depends on the reactions of significant others—friends, parents, peers, and coworkers. How these others react to a person's actions in part determines how he reacts to and values himself. Therefore, self-enhancement requires favorable reactions from those persons who are admired.

The social interaction process inherent in the development and enhancement of self

[1] Calvin Hall and Gardner Lindzey, *Theories of Personality* (New York: Wiley, 1957).

[2] E. Laird Landon, Jr., "Self-Concept, Ideal Self-Concept, and Consumer Purchase Intentions," *Journal of Consumer Research 1* (September 1974): 44–51.

[3] Humberto S. Tapia, Terrence V. O'Brien, and George W. Summers, "Self-Concept and Consumer Motivation," *Proceedings,* Fall Conference, American Marketing Association, August, 1975.

takes several forms. A form of particular interest is social interaction through the consumption of products. Products often serve as symbols, like words or pictures, that can be used to communicate meaning to others as well as to the individual. In order to enhance his self-concept, the individual associates himself with, or purchases, those products that will convey the desired meaning to others and to himself. To the extent that the products involved mean the same to the person and the significant others, that person may enhance his self-concept by the selection of certain products and the avoidance of others.

The selection and avoidance of products become a matter of what the person wishes to convey to others and to himself. Thus, his purchase behavior is a function of his image of what kind of person he is and how he wants others to see him. As self-concept changes from one image to some future or expected self-image, then preference for and purchase of products might also change to communicate the new self.

This article investigates the content of self-concept and its relationship to product perception over time. In addition, since self-concept enhancement or development is, like any motivated activity, presumably undertaken to achieve need fulfillment, the relationship of self-concept to need arousal is investigated. Several important and very recent findings on the self-concept are used.[4] First, operation of the self-concept is detectable in marketing situations, although its degree of influence on buying behavior is not yet known. Second, the self-concept is stable, individualistic, and pervasive. Third, there are various modes or versions of the self-concept, such as actual (real, present, current) and

future. And finally, individuals can articulate future self-definitions and are motivated to achieve them.

RESEARCH DESIGN

Forty-six undergraduates in marketing were asked to rank two sets of items in terms of how descriptive each item was of their actual self-concept, their expected self-concept, and their ideal self-concept. The first set, shown in Table 1, listed seventy personality descriptors.[5] The second set, shown in Table 2, listed seventy products and services obtained from colleagues, a current Sears catalogue, and a previously developed set.[6] The items in both lists were ranked, using a modified Q-sort (see box), from 7, most descriptive, to 1, least descriptive. The definitions given for the three self-concept modes were *actual* self-concept—as you honestly see yourself here and now; *expected* self-concept—as you would expect to see yourself if you had left the university and had been working in the job of your choice for a year; and *ideal* self-concept—as you would like yourself to become under ideal circumstances.

In order to illuminate the relationship between self-concept and personality needs, the subjects were also asked to classify the seventy personality descriptors and the seventy products and services according to one (and only one) of the following needs: (1) achievement—need to attain a desired end or goal; (2) affection—need for tender attachment, love; (3) identity—need for unity and stability of personality; (4) hedonism—need for pleasure or avoidance of pain; and (5) none—the item

---

[4] Landon, "Self-Concept, Ideal Self-Concept, and Consumer Purchase Intentions"; and Tapia, O'Brien, and Summers, "Self-Concept and Consumer Motivation."

[5] Jack Block, *The Q-Sort Method in Personality Assessment and Psychiatric Research* (Springfield, Ill.: Bannerstone House, 1961).

[6] Warren S. Martin, "College Students and Product Symbolism," Ph.D. diss., University of Texas, 1972.

Table 1 / Personality Descriptors List

1. Absent-minded	24. Energetic	47. Resentful
2. Affected	25. Fair-minded	48. Reserved, dignified
3. Ambitious	26. Feminine	49. Restless
4. Anxious	27. Frank	50. Sarcastic
5. Bossy	28. Friendly	51. Self-controlled
6. Calm	29. Helpless	52. Self-indulgent
7. Cautious	30. Hostile	53. Selfish
8. Clever	31. Idealistic	54. Self-pitying
9. Competitive	32. Imaginative	55. Sense of humor
10. Confident	33. Impulsive	56. Sentimental
11. Considerate	34. Inadequate	57. Sincere
12. Cooperative	35. Indifferent	58. Sophisticated
13. Cruel	36. Intelligent	59. Stubborn
14. Cunning	37. Introspective	60. Suspicious
15. Defensive	38. Introverted	61. Sympathetic
16. Dependent	39. Jealous	62. Tactless
17. Disorderly	40. Lazy	63. Timid
18. Dissatisfied	41. Likeable	64. Touchy, irritable
19. Dominant	42. Persevering	65. Unconventional
20. Dramatic	43. Personally charming	66. Undecided
21. Dull	44. Poised	67. Unhappy
22. Easily embarrassed	45. Reasonable	68. Versatile
23. Easily hurt	46. Rebellious	69. Warm
		70. Wise

Table 2 / Products and Services List

1. Aquarium	24. Electric shaver	47. Poster
2. Aspirin	25. Flowers	48. Records
3. Automobile	26. Hamburger	49. Roller skates
4. Bath soap	27. Health foods	50. Shoes
5. Beaded belt	28. High-intensity lamp	51. Skis
6. Bible	29. Hot comb	52. Soft drink
7. Bicycle	30. Ice cream	53. Stationery
8. Birthday card	31. Judo lessons	54. Steak dinner
9. Breakfast cereal	32. Life insurance	55. Stereo
10. Camera	33. Magazine subscription	56. Suitcase
11. Camping trip	34. Mini-calculator	57. Sun glasses
12. Candy	35. Mixed drinks	58. Surfboard
13. Check book	36. Movie theater	59. Swim suit
14. Chess set	37. Musical instrument	60. Tea
15. Chewing gum	38. Musk oil	61. Telephone
16. Cigarettes	39. Newspaper	62. Television set
17. Class ring	40. Night club	63. Tennis racket
18. Cologne	41. Novel	64. Toothpaste
19. Credit card	42. Ocean cruise	65. Typewriter
20. Detergent	43. Pen and pencil set	66. Vitamins
21. Double-knit slacks	44. Pet	67. Watch
22. Dry cleaning	45. Pizza	68. Western clothes
23. Easy chair	46. Playing cards	69. Wine
		70. Zoo tickets

MODIFIED Q-SORT PROCEDURE

The Q-sort technique was modified to simplify administration of stimulus materials. In a normal Q-sort procedure subjects are instructed to allocate statements or other reactive items on cards to prespecified categories according to a forced rectangular distribution. For example, a subject begins with a pack of seventy declarative statements and is asked to assign each of them to one of seven piles according to how favorable (or unfavorable) each statement is to the role of women in American society. The final distribution must consist of ten cards in each pile, and piles are numbered and labeled as 1, highly favorable; 2, somewhat favorable; 3, slightly favorable; 4, neither favorable nor unfavorable; 5, slightly unfavorable; 6, somewhat unfavorable; 7, highly unfavorable.

To facilitate mass administration of the Q-sort with subjects using small students' desks, a paper-and-pencil version was devised. "Sort" subjects were each given a list of seventy items alongside a set of seventy blanks labeled by groups of ten; the reactive items and blanks were photo-reduced so that the entire response material fit on one standard-size page but was still easily readable. The response sheet was preceded by an instruction sheet.

Subjects performed a total of eight such sorts, each one taking nearly an hour to administer, and each separated by at least two days. Two item types (personality versus products and services) by three self-concept modes (actual, expected, and ideal) yielded six of the eight sorts. In the seventh sort, assignments were done of each of the seventy items of one type to one of four motivational categories (achievement, affection, hedonism, identity); in the eighth sort the seventy items on the other type (personality or product and service) were similarly assigned. Sequences of the eight sorts were randomized to control for order bias.

does not relate to any of the previously mentioned needs. An example was provided and then subjects were presented with seventy items, either the personality set or the products and services set.

SELF–CONCEPT OVER TIME

Table 3 presents those personality descriptors or products and services that were chosen as important in all three self-concept versions. These items received uniformly extreme classifications—either category 7, most descriptive, or category 1, least descriptive—in all three self-concepts. We conclude that important dimensions of stability and continuity exist across the self-concepts over time. Individuals are able to identify basic personality factors they feel are constant elements of present and future self-definitions, and those that are not. Similarly, some product and service classes are perceived as typifying present and future consumption mixes, and others are not.

Even though there are strong elements of stability among self-concepts, there are also significant differences. In Table 4, for example, fair-minded is judged to be most descriptive for the actual self-concept, but subjects anticipate shedding such objectivity for expected and ideal roles. Table 4 also shows that rankings of product and service items change from the perspective of a present student (hamburger, pizza) through sober establishment member (newspaper, life insurance), to all-out leisure (camera, camping trip, ocean cruise, tennis racket) and avoidance of the mundane (aspirin, detergent).

SELF–CONCEPT AND NEED AROUSAL

A need "produces activity on the part of the organism and maintains this activity until the organism-environment situation has been altered so as to reduce the need."[7] For the purpose of this research, four such needs were ar-

[7] Hall and Lindzey, *Theories of Personality*.

Table 3 / Self-Descriptors Characteristic of All Three Self-Concepts

	Modal classification	
Type of item	Most descriptive	Least descriptive
Personality	Ambitious	Cruel
	Considerate	Dull
	Cooperative	Helpless
	Friendly	Hostile
	Intelligent	Inadequate
		Self-pitying
		Tactless
		Unhappy
Products and services	Automobile	Beaded belt
	Check book	Cigarettes
	Steak dinner	Class ring
	Stereo	Musk oil
		Roller skates
		Western clothes

bitrarily chosen to provide some indication of whether or not self-concept in either the personality or consumption areas is at all sensitive to need arousal.

Perceptions on need distribution of reactive items differed, as indicated in Table 5. For personality items the identity need was prominent. (These results could have been due to these particular subjects, the perception of the personality aura surrounding the seventy items, the composition of the seventy items themselves, the identification of the four particular needs, and so forth. The point is that our interpretations are suggestive and

Table 4 / Self-Descriptors Characteristic of Only One Self-Concept

		Modal classification	
Type of item	Self-concept	Most descriptive	Least descriptive
Personality	Actual	Fair-minded	Dramatic
			Feminine
	Expected	Competitive	—
	Ideal	Confident	—
		Imaginative	
		Versatile	
Products and services	Actual	Hamburger	Aquarium
		Pizza	Musical instrument
	Expected	Newspaper	Bath soap
		Life insurance	
	Ideal	Camera	Aspirin
		Camping trip	Candy
		Ocean cruise	Detergent
		Tennis racket	

Table 5 / Distribution of Personality and Product Service Reactives by Need Category*

Need	Personality	Products and services
Achievement	20%	17%
Affection	15	7
Hedonism	10	29
Identity	32	14
None	23	33
Total	*100%*	*100%*

* Sample size for each column is 3,220, the product of 46 respondents times 70 reactive items. Value of chi-square is 351.36, significant well beyond the .001 level.

not definitive.) About equal portions of both lists were viewed as representing achievement needs, but affection items were more salient for personality description while hedonic items and none (no important need served) were more prominent for products and services.

To gauge the role of needs across the self-concept modes, the three personality items most frequently assigned to the achievement need are shown in Table 6, along with their self-concept ranks and changes in ranks, and similarly for the rest of the need classes in the table. Subjects see themselves as achievement oriented now and in the future, but expect and hope to be somewhat more energetic in achievement activity. Some affection factors (sentimental, sympathetic) face slight reductions (perhaps because they are viewed as weaknesses), but more warmth is desirable. Generally, subjects expect less hedonism and far more identity activity over their adult development. For these subjects, identity development apparently centers on reducing social awkwardness and indecisiveness and moving toward increased dignity, poise, and self-control.

Finally, findings for need factors in products and services are presented in Table 7. In

the achievement category, respondents expect to increase consumption of goods as they succeed in their occupation. A very desirable item is the mini-calculator, evidenced by the three-point discrepancy between present and future descriptiveness of self-concept. Findings on affection items and identity items are mixed. With regard to hedonic and identity items, respondents expect consumption to fall for mixed drinks and double-knit slacks, but the desire for some other items remains stable.

Findings from this study and related studies support the use of a self-concept approach to understanding buyer motivation. The generalizations that can be drawn from these particular results are obviously limited, but the implications are important for comprehensive marketing strategy decisions based on self-concept research tailored to a specific situation. Because a consumer's perception of, preference for, and purchase of products are related to his self-concept, firms should identify their markets in terms of differentiated self-concept groups. Each consumer perceives products as "right" or "wrong" for him; therefore, identifying how consumers perceive a product as being right or wrong for themselves certainly increases the efficiency of the marketing management effort.

The intermediate expected self-concept may be more realistic than the ideal as a target guiding product design and promotion. For example, some individuals might have significant reservations about consuming alcoholic beverages, but they expect to do so in the future. In this case, distillers would have to identify and promote supportive factors in order for persons to discover ways to increase mixed drink consumption. Generally, the self-concept approach permits marketers to understand motivational components of buyer decision making and to view them from the individual consumer's perspective;

Table 6 / Ranks and Rank Changes of Most Important Personality Descriptors for Each Need, Classified by Self-Concept Mode

	Self-concept mode			
Need and descriptors	Actual	Expected	Ideal	Rank change
Achievement				
Ambitious	7*	7	7	0†
Competitive	6	7	6	0
Energetic	5	7	7	+
Affection				
Sentimental	6	5	5	−
Sympathetic	6	5	5	−
Warm	5	5	6	+
Hedonism				
Defensive	6	4	4	−
Self-indulgent	3	3	3	0
Selfish	2	1	1	−
Identity				
Reserved, dignified	3	5	5	+
Poised	4	5	6	+
Self-controlled	5	6	6	+

* Where 7 means "most descriptive of me" and 1 means "least descriptive of me."
† Plus indicates an increase in rank; minus a decrease; zero indicates either no change or a mix of increase and decrease.

Table 7 / Ranks and Rank Changes of Most Important Product and Service Items for Each Need, Classified by Self-Concept Mode

	Self-concept mode			
Need and items	Actual	Expected	Ideal	Rank change
Achievement				
Mini-calculator	2*	5	5	+ †
Credit card	5	7	7	+
Typewriter	5	6	4	0
Affection				
Pet	5	5	5	0
Flowers	3	3	4	+
Birthday card	3	2	2	−
Hedonism				
Movie theater	6	6	6	0
Records	7	6	7	0
Mixed drinks	6	6	5	−
Identity				
Bible	2	2	3	+
Double-knit slacks	6	6	5	−
Western clothes	1	1	1	0

* Where 7 means "most descriptive of me" and 1 means "least descriptive of me."
† Plus indicates an increase in rank, minus a decrease; zero indicates either no change or a mix of increase and decrease.

ideally, both marketing efficiency and customer satisfaction would benefit.

The relationship between self-concept and consumer behavior is not a simple one. This study sought only to explore the content of that relationship. Future research should be directed at more precise measurement of the self-concept construct and its relationship to the various dimensions of consumer behavior. Much more work is needed in exploring self-concept development over time and its impact on buyer motivation.

Questions

1. Name and define the three self-concepts a person may have.
2. Explain why it is important for marketers to study self-concept.
3. Explain how "time" is a consideration in evaluating self-concept and the type of products or services considered most important by that individual.

Part G
DECISION MAKING

23. Decision Making within the Household

Harry L. Davis

INTRODUCTION

The literature on consumer behavior contains a growing number of references to the household as the relevant unit for studying consumer behavior. For example, Ferber (1973b) urged economists to incorporate findings about household decision making into their research on aggregate consumption and savings behavior. Six other papers prepared for that interdisciplinary conference on family economic behavior were published in the same volume (Sheldon, 1973). The first four issues of the *Journal of Consumer Research* included four articles related to family roles in consumer behavior (Davis and Rigaux, 1974; Ferber and Lee, 1974; Granbois and Summers, 1975; Munsinger, Weber, and Hansen, 1975). Academic meetings frequented by consumer researchers are now likely to include at least one session on family or multiperson decision making. The second edition of the largest selling textbook on consumer behavior (Engel, Kollat, and Blackwell, 1973) devotes considerably more space to the family than does the 1968 edition.

This paper attempts to review and evaluate this growing area of research interest. Since no overall theories or well-

defined concepts have guided this literature, the best approach is to consider several related topics in some reasonable order. These are (1) the involvement of family members in economic decisions, (2) the process by which family decisions are made, and (3) the consequences of different family structures and decision-making styles.

Whether, in fact, the family is the appropriate focus in studying consumer behavior is a key issue that deserves comment from the outset. Casual observation would suggest that the family is a critical decision making and consumption unit. Major items of consumer spending such as food, shelter, and transportation are often jointly "consumed." A husband may buy a station wagon, given the reality of having to transport four children, *despite* his strong preference for sports cars. Husbands wear ties, underwear, and socks; yet the purchase of these products is often made by wives. A housewife bases product and brand decisions to some extent on orders or requests from family members and on her judgment of what they like or dislike and what is "good for them." Even preferences for products individually consumed are likely to be influenced by feedback from members of the family—e.g., "Gee, Mom! That dress makes you look fat,'' or ''I like the smell of that pipe tobacco.'' The number of products that an individual always buys for individual consumption must certainly represent a very small proportion of consumer expenditures.

These observations have not escaped some students of marketing. Almost 20 years ago, Converse, Huegy, and Mitchell (1958) dismissed the wife as the principal consumer and described the family as the ''most important business conference in America.'' Alderson (1957) also devoted considerable attention to the family—i.e., the extent of task coordination and compatibility—as a critical aspect of consumer buying.

Two economists have made similar observations. Arrow (1951, p. 134) draws an analogy between the theory of the firm and consumer behavior: ''The unit of the theory of production is not really the individual but the firm, which is an operating organization of individuals. Similarly, the unit of the theory of consumption is really the household, not the individual consumer.'' Samuelson (1956, pp. 8–9) remarks:

> Who after all is the consumer in the theory of consumer's (not consumers') behavior? Is he a bachelor? A spinster? Or is he a ''spending unit'' as defined by statistical pollsters and recorders of budgetary spending? In most of the cultures actually studied by modern economists the fundamental unit on the demand side is clearly the ''family,'' and this consists of a single individual in but a fraction of the total cases.

Despite these observations, most research in this area has been characterized historically by a preoccupation with consumers as individual decision makers. Although various reference groups have been identified and studied, interest is most often focused on whether and how these groups affect individuals' attitudes and behavior. Questionnaires and interviews frequently ask who

''really decided,'' ''had the most to say,'' or ''most often buys'' in a given consumption category. Issues of group decision making are thus avoided by these procedures since they assume that decision responsibility can be attributed to one family member.

Researchers trying to develop and test various theories often link, without apparent concern, individual-based, independent variables to group-based, dependent variables. This approach can be no better observed than in studies using personality traits to predict brand choice. A well-known marketing study by Evans (1959) used husbands' personality to predict family ownership of Ford versus Chevrolet. In all the comments and rejoinders generated by this study, no one bothered to question whether husbands actually made the brand-choice decision. Could it be that Evans included a significant number of ''wrong'' respondents in his analysis?

This same point of view characterizes investigations of brand loyalty and consumer attitudes. Individual characteristics have been used, without much success, to explain differences in brand loyalty measured by panel data (Cunningham, 1956; Farley, 1966; Frank, 1967; Jacoby and Kyner, 1973). Since these data often reflect purchases by several family members as well as their brand preferences, why should one expect the *housewife's* brand attitudes or personality to predict household purchases over time? In a similar fashion, why should one expect an individual's brand attitudes to predict actual purchase behavior if the choice situation involves compromise and other relevant role attitudes, e.g., what a good spouse or parent should do?

By way of overview, this paper will show that recent work on household decision making has not had a noticeable impact in other areas of consumer research. The view of consumers as individual decision makers is still very much alive despite commonsense observations that the family is the relevant decision-making unit and a growing research interest in the field.[1] We further demonstrate that even the relatively simple task of describing which family members are involved in consumer decisions is clouded by a diverse and often noncomparable set of measures and concepts. It is argued that a whole set of group-related constructs, critical to understanding consumer decision making, has been largely ignored. And finally, we describe how researchers have only begun to explore the issue of whether differences in family role structure affect consumer decisions.

INVOLVEMENT OF FAMILY MEMBERS IN ECONOMIC DECISIONS

Categories of Economic Decisions

Research on which family member is involved in various financial decisions can be grouped roughly into three categories. The first two include spending decisions for frequently purchased goods or services and for durables. Almost without exception, data on the former have been collected by the print media with the objective of showing that husbands have a significant influence on household purchase decisions. Studies of family-member involvement in durable goods buying come from more varied sources, including sociologists and marketing researchers in addition to commercial organizations. Typically, these

studies focus on interrelationships among decisions or various determinants of involvement such as social class, life-cycle stages, or the wife's employment status. A third category of economic decisions includes a very small number of published studies about husband-wife involvement in saving and investment decisions, tasks surrounding the family budget, and family planning.

Several examples from each category will be described in the following three sections. This review is not inclusive of all published research on household decision making.[2] Included are studies that sample different decision areas, employ various methodologies, or are frequently cited in the literature.

Frequently Purchased Goods or Services. Three of the earliest studies of male versus female influence were conducted for *True* (*Male vs. Female Influence,* 1948, 1950; Starch, 1958). All were undertaken to dispel that "mythical idea" that 85 percent of every family dollar is spent by women. Products were selected on the basis of the then-current advertisers in *True.*

The first two volumes included information on some 65 product categories, 50 of which were nondurables. In the 1948 survey, questionnaires were returned by 1,376 households in which both husband and wife independently answered questions about "who originally decided on the make or brand" and "who made the most recent purchase." Less than 40 percent of the products studied were mainly husband or wife dominated (defined by 80 percent or more of the respondents in either category). The remainder had substantial proportions in at least two of the categories, i.e., husband, wife, or both. The percentage of respondents reporting "both" was consistently lower in

---

[1] Two papers prepared for this same project point to the fact that group level analyses have been largely ignored in studies of brand-choice behavior (Wind, 1976) and the diffusion of innovation (Rogers, in this issue).

[2] Ferber (1973b), Sheth (1974), and Davis (in press) provide a comprehensive literature review.

response to "who went shopping" than "who decided on the brand."

The report by Daniel Starch and staff (1958) remains one of the most thorough studies of male versus female influence. The reseachers focused on 12 products grouped into eight categories.[3] Among the nondurables studied were beer, liquor, and shaving cream. Using relatively small samples of 100 couples for each product, in-depth interviews were conducted separately with the husband and wife. A wide range of topics were covered, including brand preferences of each spouse, relative involvement of each spouse in brand selection and in shopping, and motivation for involvement. Based on cultural attitudes and patterns of consumption, respondents viewed the three nondurable products as predominantly masculine. In these cases, wives expressed few brand preferences and purchased only those brands that husbands requested. A high level of within-family agreement regarding who influenced the choice of brand was found; i.e., an average of only 8 percent of the couples did not verify each other's answers for the three nondurables.

Undoubtedly, *Life* has sponsored more studies of husband-wife involvement in product decisions than any other publication. Its readership by men *and* women was viewed as attractive to advertisers if it could be demonstrated that brand decisions were frequently made jointly within the family. The products selected, therefore, were frequently purchased items targeted on TV or in print almost exclusively to women.

Two reports prepared for *Life* by Nowland and Company (1964, 1965) were among the earliest efforts to study brand preferences of husbands and wives. In the 1965 study, for ex-

ample, each spouse in 1,134 households was asked to assess his or her preferred brand for 30 different supermarket products. Information was also collected on who went on the last shopping trip as well as brands actually in the home. The data showed that husbands go on 39 percent of supermarket shopping trips—15 percent alone and 24 percent with their wives. Both studies found an association between husband-wife brand consensus and the presence of that brand in the household. There is an advantage, according to the report, "in preselling both the husband and wife of about eight to five over selling the wife alone."

Jaffe Associates (n.d.) conducted a series of pilot studies for *Life* in 301 households. The 11 products studied included coffee, frozen orange juice, toothpaste, pet food, and seven durable goods. For each product, husbands and wives were taken through purchase histories in which they identified the role played by themselves and their spouses. The number of stages in the decision process was found to be less for nondurables than for durables. Yet, even for frequently purchased products, the husband's involvement varied by stage. For example, the percentage of husbands who actually purchased coffee (29 percent) was considerably less than the percentage who initiated the purchase or suggested a particular brand (41 percent). Only 16 percent of husbands initiated the purchase of pet food, while 40 percent of them suggested what brand of pet food to buy.

The Learner Marketing Research and Development report (1968) is an in-depth view of family-member involvement when new or different brands are brought into the home. Housewives, husbands, and teenagers from 706 households were asked to describe "critical incidents" surrounding the purchase of 30 supermarket items. In particular, they tried to recall the overall nature of the incident, who was involved, who initiated the

---

[3] Product groupings included alcoholic beverages, automotive, clothing, insurance, major appliances, men's toiletries, sporting goods, and transportation.

change, and the role of advertising, price, and product dissatisfaction. The overall conclusions reinforced a now-familiar theme. Even though wives did most of the grocery shopping, they did so with an awareness of the products and brands that their families liked. Husbands and teenagers were frequently involved in new or different brand incidents, although the extent of their involvement varied significantly by product category. Interestingly, each family member apparently drew upon a different subsample of incidents (their reality?). Conclusions about who was involved were very sensitive to which respondent in the household was interviewed.

A recent survey sponsored by five magazines (Haley, Overholser and Associates, 1975) carried on the tradition of supplying information to advertisers about the relative influence of husbands and wives in specific product categories. Measures of shopping participation, direct and indirect influence at both product and brand levels, were obtained from 2,373 wives and 1,767 husbands on 87 packaged products.[4] Husband involvement was lowest in actual shopping, with men having made an average of 23 percent of all purchases during the preceding month. At the same time, husbands directly influenced an average of 32 percent of the brand and product decisions. Husbands' indirect influence (taking their preferences into account) was even higher; they accounted for an average frequency of 38 percent of indirect influence for the 87 product and brand decisions.

A study for *Sports Illustrated* (Travel Research International, 1968) examined household decisions for pleasure trips involving airlines. Data from over 500 male respondents showed that husbands played the "predominant" role in mentioning the initial idea to take a trip, suggesting a destination, and selecting an airline.[5] The *decision* (as opposed to suggestion) on where to go was a mutual decision, however, in two-thirds of the households.

The nine commercial studies just reviewed have received relatively little attention by academic researchers. This is unfortunate in light of the large samples generally used and the large number of products represented. Moreover, the studies do dispel some of the conventional wisdom that views the world of supermarket purchases to be the exclusive domain of women. Husbands are involved in actual purchasing, although wives clearly predominate. Husbands are aware of brands in many product categories and express brand preferences on questionnaires.

The commercial studies do seem weak, however, in tracing the extent and nature of the purchase influence of husbands. For example, knowledge that a husband and wife have the same brand preference does not indicate whether brands were discussed or when a discussion took place. It does not even reveal whether a wife is aware of her husband's preferences or vice versa. The husband's response to questions about brand preferences could reflect only awareness under the following logic: "I know what brands my wife buys since I see them on the table," or "I have seen ads for instant coffee on TV and it's good to have preferences when filling out questionnaires." Some of the at-

---

[4] Categories with two or more products included beverages, cereals, desserts, frozen specialties, meats, sauces and dressings, snacks, soups, vegetables, drugs, toiletries, cleaning products, paper products, pet foods, alcoholic beverages, health and personal care, and tobacco products.

[5] This conclusion masks to some extent the amount of variability in the data. According to their husbands, 35 percent of the wives did make the initial suggestion. Moreover, the choices of airline and travel arrangements were made by wives or travel agents in over 40 percent of the cases.

tempts to measure the husband's influence are undoubtedly biased by social desirability. What "good wife" would want to admit that her husband's brand comments were not important to her or that she did not take his preferences into account? Finally, the analyses contained in these commercial studies are very limited: Nothing has been published about interrelationships among products in terms of who shops or influences, and little use has been made of predictor variables to explore differences in husband-wife involvement among families.

Durable Goods. Research on family-member influence in durable goods buying is more abundant than that on frequently purchased items. Even a casual observer would probably agree that important, one-time purchases are likely to involve more than one household member. In contrast to nondurables, purchases of durable goods are often preceded by a progression of interrelated decisions and activities through time. Husbands, wives, and children have more opportunities to become involved at one or more steps in the process. One can presume that family members are also more motivated to participate, since the purchase of an automobile, for example, often precludes other acquisitions, given families' budget constraints.

At one extreme in terms of length of the decision process, amount of deliberation, and financial importance is the housing purchase. A number of studies have shown, not surprisingly, a high degree of joint decision making in buying homes (Bernhardt, 1974; Blood and Wolfe, 1960; Cunningham and Green, 1974; Davis and Rigaux, 1974; Hempel, 1974; Munsinger et al., 1975). Those studies that subdivided the purchase into several interrelated decisions found considerable variability in the relative involvement of husband and wife. Bernhardt (1974) reports that husbands' influence was highest for decisions concerning price range and whether to move, while wives' influence was highest in deciding on the number of bedrooms and other house features.

The automobile purchase has been another popular arena in which to study marital roles (Blood and Wolfe, 1960; Brehl and Callahan Research, 1967; Conway/Milliken Research, 1969; Davis, 1970, 1972a; Green and Cunningham, 1975; Haley et al., 1975; Jaffe Associates, n.d.; Starch, 1958). Some researchers have used overall measures of influence on "deciding about buying a new car." Others have focused on husband-wife influence regarding specific product attributes (e.g., make, model, color, interior, accessories, size, performance features), shopping or use characteristics, and budget considerations (e.g., price or when to buy). In contrast to the housing purchase, all these studies have found husbands' influence to be greater than wives'.

Empirical research has also investigated marital roles in the purchase of home furnishings (Davis 1970; Green and Cunningham, 1975; Jaffe Associates, n.d.; Scott, 1970; Woodside, 1975). Other product categories for which similar data are available include small appliances, major appliances, home entertainment (e.g., TV and stereo), cameras, life insurance, vacation travel, and watches (Green and Cunningham, 1975; Haley et al., 1975; Jaffe Associates, n.d.; Starch, 1958).

Studies of marital roles in durable goods buying represent a very active area of empirical research. Identical measures of purchase influence for the same product categories have been used by different researchers. Even with the small, convenience samples that characterize some of these studies, the results are remarkably consistent. Three studies of automobile buying, for example, all show wives' influence to increase as one moves from the decision on make to that on model and finally on color (i.e., Conway/Milliken Research, 1969; Davis, 1970; Starch, 1958).

These same studies can be criticized, however, on the basis of their rather limited objectives. With few exceptions, researchers have not explored *why* some product categories or subdecisions within product categories are dominated by husbands and others by wives. Since very few studies include more than one product, analyses of roles across product categories within households are rarely made. Little effort has gone into explaining why a single decision usually shows some variability in marital roles among families.

Other Economic Decisions. Although durable and nondurable purchases encompass a multitude of decisions, they have little to do directly with how families manage their overall finances or plan other areas of their life. These areas also require frequent decision making and thus provide opportunities for differing degrees of husband-wife involvement.

Ferber (1973b) has identified and reviewed relevant studies in three related areas of financial management. The first is money management—"an arrangement within the family for the handling of money, payment of bills, budgeting, and keeping accounts" (p. 32). Data from two older studies (Sharp and Mott, 1956; Wolgast, 1958) and a more recent study (Ferber and Lee, 1974) are remarkably consistent in showing considerable variability in the way families handle money and pay bills. These studies reported the percentage of families in which the wife is responsible as 40 percent, 40 percent, and 34 percent, respectively. [6]

A second area identified by Ferber (1973b, p. 33) is saving behavior—"the allocation of available financial resources for a given period between spending and saving, specifically what amount or proportion of these total resources should be allocated to saving and what proportion or amount to spending." Closely related is a third area—asset management. Information about marital roles in both areas is very scarce and generally limited to one question about who takes care of savings or life insurance (e.g., Blood and Wolfe, 1960; Davis and Rigaux, 1974; Green and Cunningham, 1975; Haley et al., 1975; Sharp and Mott, 1956; Wolgast, 1958). More detailed data about marital roles in savings and insurance decisions are contained in the Starch (1958) report and in panel data collected by Ferber and Nicosia (1972).

The reasons why researchers have ignored financial management decisions relative to product-specific decisions are probably numerous. With the exception of financial institutions, there is no consistency for funding such research. The home economics literature has long contained a normative but largely nonempirical discussion of family financial management. It is also true that studies of durable goods buying frequently contain questions relevant to the family budget (e.g., deciding how much to spend and when to make the purchase, handling financing arrangements, or making monthly payments). The view of husband-wife involvement that emerges when these decisions are "piggy-backed" onto product decisions must surely be incomplete, however. Decisions to spend rather than save or to spend money for a new roof instead of a vacation involve "across-product" evaluations that cannot

---

[6] It is interesting to note that the Ferber and Nicosia sample consisted entirely of young marrieds. Since Wells (1959) found increasing specialization of these tasks with length of marriage, it may be that the difference here is due to the sample composition.

possibly be understood if one focuses only on one or two product categories.

A final area that has major economic consequences for the family concerns decisions about the number and spacing of children. Family planning programs generally assume that the wife is the major influence in a household's decision to use birth control practices. As a consequence, these programs are almost always directed toward women, and research is based almost exclusively on samples of women. The reasons for assuming that family planning is the wife's personal decision are numerous and surprisingly reminiscent of the logic encountered in consumer good studies. Consider the following:

1. Many modern birth control methods (e.g., IUD, pill) are used by women. It is convenient to assume that the person who uses a device will be the one who decides whether or not to adopt it.

2. Women are believed to be more receptive to the family planning concept than men. The day-to-day impact of having children falls more heavily on women. Women are also easier to reach since they are the ones who generally visit birth control or family planning clinics. Since children are presumably evidence of men's power and masculinity, it is often assumed that they want large, not small, families. Why promote a "product" to a market segment whose attitudes are basically neutral or even antagonistic?

3. The cost of reaching both spouses within the household must be weighed against the benefits of reaching more women. Program officials, who are typically evaluated on the basis of their activities rather than lowered birth rates, are likely to opt for reaching 10,000 women instead of 5,000 families.

Despite these "commonsense" reasons, recent studies have shown that husbands play an important, perhaps the major, role in family adoption decisions. In one of the earliest studies on the topic (Dubey and Choldin, 1967), the decision to use an IUD was made by the wife alone in only 7 percent of the cases. Husbands were reported to have made the final decision in 44 percent of the families. Other investigations carried out in both developed and underdeveloped countries confirm the husband's considerable influence in contraceptive use (Lam, 1968; Mercado, 1971; Mullen et al., n.d.; Pillai, 1971).

Some Recurring Findings

Three general findings about husband-wife involvement in consumer decisions continue to emerge from the many studies mentioned above.

Variability by Product Category. Husband-wife involvement varies widely by product category. This seemingly obvious conclusion contrasts, nevertheless, with discussions about differences in men versus women as consumers without regard to specific products. Wolff (1958), for example, suggested that women more than men take a long time to make up their minds and are more stubborn about changing them. Women were also described as having a different sense of humor, a tendency toward irrational beliefs, and less desire for achievement, domination, or power. Not only have studies failed to document many of these differences, but when this absolute view of roles is applied to household decision making, the results have also led to curious contradictions. Marketing textbooks in the early sixties (Beckman and Davidson, 1962; Phillips and Duncan, 1964) described both the growing involvement of women in family decisions *and* the growing importance of men as buyers!

Variability within Product Category. Husband-wife involvement within any product category varies by specific decisions and decision stages. Early writings often equated purchasing decisions with actual purchasing activities such that the person who went shopping for a product was assumed to have also made the product and brand decision. This view undoubtedly underlies the folklore that women control 80 percent of every family dollar. According to Converse et al. (1958), this "finding" was based on the rather unbelievable fact that someone once counted shoppers in a city department store and found that 80 percent were women. Manufacturers and advertisers have also found it convenient to look for one dominant spouse in each product category. The studies reported earlier, however, demonstrate again and again that family-member participation varies within each product category depending on what is being done or decided. From any point of view, it is a serious oversimplification to talk about a product category as simply husband dominant, wife dominant, or joint.

The automobile purchase illustrates how variable husband-wife involvement really is. According to the Jaffe report (n.d.), wives were as involved as their husbands in gathering relevant information from people. Davis (1970) found 60 percent of couples classified as husband dominant for the decision about make of automobile but only 25 percent for the decision about color. Couples frequently shop together for the car and use the car equally after purchase.

Family-member involvement also seems to vary systematically at different stages in the decision-making process. In the family planning area, wives are found to be more involved than husbands in information seeking in contrast to initiating search or making the final adoption decision (Lam, 1968; Palmore, 1967). Davis and Rigaux (1974) obtained information about marital roles at each of three decision stages (problem recognition, search for information, and final decision) for 25 household decisions. While no significant dif-

ferences were found in average relative influence across the three stages, the proportion of couples in the "joint" category was significantly less for the information search phase than for either of the other two phases. Similar data were reported by Wilkes (1975). Intercorrelations among relative influence scores in four decision stages (problem recognition, search, final decision, and purchase) were generally low. No significant association was found between "who purchased the major household good" and "who searched for information" (r = .14 for husbands; r = .01 for wives).

Variability among Families. Husband-wife involvement for any consumer decision is likely to show considerable variability among families. Discussions of marital roles frequently understate the variance that is found even in the case of highly specific decisions. To illustrate, the Starch report (1958, p. 59) concludes that "the husband, as the family 'authority' on mechanical matters, decides upon the make of the new family car." This conclusion was drawn from data showing that the husband decides in 61 percent of the families, the wife in 1 percent, and both in 38 percent. In contrast to the quotation, the data indicate that the decision about make of automobile is not actually the exclusive domain of husbands.

Some variability is even present in product categories characterized by a high degree of role specialization. The survey by Haley, Overholser and Associates (1975) reports the percentage of husbands who made purchases of packaged goods during the preceding seven days and the percentage who actually influenced the product and brand selected. In none of the 87 product categories did husbands make less than 10 percent of the purchases.

Marketing studies that show considerable variation in decision roles are paralleled in sociology. The Parsons and Bales (1955) theory, which predicts family role differentiation according to instrumental and socioeconomic functions, has been criticized. Aronoff and Crano (1975), for example, document that contrary to theoretical predictions, women make substantial contributions to subsistence production in over 800 societies.

Some Recurring Problems

At least four problem areas can be identified in the research dealing with family-member involvement in consumer decisions. It is useful to discuss each area in order to highlight future research priorities.

Choosing Decisions and Tasks. The issue raised here, though not unique to the study of household decision making, is fundamental to all the research just reviewed. Before family-member involvement can be measured, the relevant universe of decisions and decision-related tasks must be determined. Researchers (including the present author) typically select decisions on fairly arbitrary grounds and ignore the implications of these choices.[7]

What decisions should be included in order to measure family roles in a single product or expenditure category? What might first seem like an easy task becomes exceedingly complicated on execution. Consider, for example, grocery shopping. In one family, "going shopping" means walking to the store, picking out a "few things that look good for tonight's dinner," and returning home. In another family, "going shopping" includes preparing a detailed list, driving to the store

with two preschool children, cashing a check, looking for store coupons, buying a week's groceries, returning home, and spending a half hour putting things away. Since the meaning of "grocery shopping" differs in the two families, so does the meaning of husband-wife involvement in this activity. It is only possible to interpret answers to such questions once it is clear what *actual* task the respondent is asked to evaluate.

Attempts to specify various stages in the decision-making process are also subject to the same problems. Granbois (1963), as well as Davis and Rigaux (1974), employed traditional formulations of problem-solving behavior—i.e., problem recognition, determination of alternatives via search, and selection from among recognized alternatives. Gredal (1966) divided the purchasing process into a series of four gradual decisions ranging from the initial suggestion to the actual purchase. Specifically, she hypothesized a general purchasing or budgeting decision (how much money can be spent on individual items and how it is to be distributed among these), a concrete purchasing decision (e.g., "Let's buy a new car"), a series of selection decisions (price, quality, brand, store), and finally, a technical purchasing action (placing the order and picking up the product).[8]

---

[7] As an example, it is interesting to note how frequently the Blood and Wolfe (1960) measure of power was used by other researchers simply because the study was widely cited.

[8] Partial support for this typology of decisions and activities is found in a study of husband-wife influence in 12 automobile and furniture purchase decisions (Davis, 1970). Using a clustering technique to group decisions together in terms of their similarities on relative influence, two bases for role differentiation were apparent. The first was the product itself—decision roles in the purchase of an automobile were not related to decision roles in the purchase of furniture. Simply stated, knowing the roles played by a husband and wife in buying a car provides little or no information about who makes furniture purchase decisions in the same family. The study also showed that roles were differentiated on the basis of the type of decision being made. Within each product category, relative influence in "product-selection" decisions (what model, make,

Jaffe and Senft (1966) proposed an even more elaborate framework including information seeking (via people and media), a prepurchase stage (initiating, selecting the type and brand, and budgeting), a buying stage (shopping and purchasing), and finally, a postpurchase stage (using and evaluating). All these formulations suffer from the same problem: They *begin* by assuming that households actually go through these stages. The fact that questionnaires are "correctly" filled out does not justify these questions. Is it any wonder that respondents enjoy answering questions that confirm the logic, rationality, and careful thought given to past decisions?

Studies of household decision making may also want to develop an overall measure of decision-making roles rather than limiting the focus to a single product category. While the objectives of such studies are somewhat different, the problem of specifying relevant decisions is exactly the same as just described. Families in different situations face a different set of decisions and tasks. A low-income household, for example, is not likely to spend much time considering details of a new home purchase. A family with three young children faces an additional set of decisions not present in a childless family. It is of doubtful validity, then, to compare marital roles across families when the universe of actual decisions and tasks is not the same or the weights attached to the same decision are different.

One possible way to deal with this problem is to obtain time budgets within families. An impressive international study (Szalai, 1972), which included about 30,000 time budgets drawn from 12 nations, illustrates the richness of data stemming from this procedure and shows its relevance to household decision making. Patterns of daily life were recorded in nine categories broken down into 96 specific activities. The 24-hour diaries included not only what activities were performed but also time, place, and duration. Secondary activities that occurred simultaneously with the primary activity were also obtained. Data such as these would provide a basis for defining a family's relevant decision and task universe, which could then be used to measure who is involved.

A second approach to solving this problem is found in emerging typologies of household economic decisions. Ferber (1973b) classified financial decisions into four groups—money management, spending behavior, saving behavior, and asset management. Other writers have suggested product typologies that may explain family-member involvement in spending decisions. Gredal (1966) used the dimensions of durable versus nondurable goods and individual versus collective consumption. Individual decision making was hypothesized to be least important for durable goods collectively consumed and most important for nondurables individually consumed. Lovell, Meadows, and Rampley (1968) suggested a longer list of factors affecting the extent of interhousehold influence, including (1) whether the product is jointly or individually consumed, (2) whether it is consumed by children or adults, (3) whether the brand name is clearly visible during use, and (4) whether the product is changed between purchase and use. They hypothesized greater

---

and color to buy) were unrelated to relative influence in "allocation" or "scheduling" decisions (how much to spend and when to buy the car). The decisions labeled as "product selection" seem very close to Gredal's (1966) selection decision. Moreover, the "allocation" decisions are similar to a general purchasing or budgetary decision. It would be interesting to know if additional questions about who made the initial suggestion and who assumed responsibility for shopping would form the two additional clusters suggested by Gredal.

family influence either for durables jointly consumed by husband and wife or for products individually consumed by adults when the brand was visible during use and unchanged by the housewife after purchase. A typology of family consumption by final product is that suggested by Sheth (1974). He classified consumption by individual members (e.g., razor blades for the husband, lipstick for the wife), the family as a whole (e.g., food), and the household unit (i.e., products used indirectly, such as paint or a lawnmower, for maintaining the physical dwelling).

These typologies have been of limited use to date. With few exceptions, they have been developed on an a priori basis. Whether, in fact, the decisions classified together are similar has not been empirically established. Nevertheless, they represent an important first step toward defining the total universe of a household's economic decisions and specifying common decision characteristics that may influence "who is involved."

Specifying the Relevant Decision-Making Unit. The reader is now painfully aware that the "family" in most studies of household decision making is in reality just the husband and wife. While critics of consumer behavior research might argue that this is at least an improvement over research that "forces" decisions into an individual framework, this perspective is still a partial one.

Researchers have probably been guided by intuition in specifying the husband and wife as the relevant decision-making unit for durable goods buying. Measures of influence become exceedingly complicated if more than two people are involved. It is also likely that the desire for comparability of research has tended to focus attention on the husband-wife dyad.

Whatever the reasons, serious problems do exist. The relevant decision-making unit is specified a priori by the research design rather than by the household. Casual observation suggests that some consumer decisions involve other than a husband-wife dyad, e.g., child-wife for cereals or husband-son for sporting equipment. Parents, as well as friends and relatives, can also participate in "family" decisions. It is also possible that the relevant decision-making unit varies throughout the decision-making process. For example, husband and wife decide together about whether to buy a new car or repair the old one; the husband and teenage son decide about what make to buy.

The solution to this problem is not an easy one. Davis (1972a) used information about who talked to whom regarding specific automobile purchase decisions as a method of verifying if the husband and wife were, in fact, the relevant decision-making unit. The results showed differences by families and decisions. (Husbands discussed what make of car to buy with other people as often as they discussed it with their wives.) Perhaps families and/or decisions should be grouped into common decision units *before* the part played by each member is assessed.

Further complicating this issue is the fact that different measures of influence often point toward a different decision unit as being relevant. Turk and Bell (1972) found that children had power—sometimes substantial—when observational measures were used, but they had no power when the same couples were asked to provide self-reports of decision-making power.

Measuring Involvement. The problems of measuring who participates in household decisions are embedded in the two problem areas already described. Several recurring problems should be mentioned, nevertheless.

Relative influence versus total influence. The great majority of studies make use of a scale that measures the relative influence of husband versus wife. This approach has the advantage of being widely used and thus permitting comparisons across studies. Bernhardt (1974) argued that such scales assume an equal amount of influence associated with each decision, which is then partitioned between husband and wife. In reality, a wife may feel that she exerted substantial influence in some decisions and little influence in others quite *independent* of the part played by her husband. Bernhardt proposed an alternative approach whereby each spouse first assesses how much influence he/she had and then how much the spouse had in various decisions. The result is a measure of both total and relative influence. Thus, four housing decisions— choice of house, of community, and of neighborhood, and architectural style—were classified as joint. The latter decision, however, revealed a low level of husband-wife influence in contrast to the other three.

Response categories. Reseachers have utilized various response formats in order to measure purchase influence. Undoubtedly, the most common measure is a 5-point Likert scale ranging from "husband decided" to "wife decided." Some researchers have used a 3-point scale, which has the effect of increasing the expected level of agreement between husbands and wives as well as possibly altering the proportion of families that fall into the "jointly decided" category. Other studies further divide "equal-influence" responses into syncratic (i.e., always decide together) and autonomic (i.e., sometimes one spouse, sometimes the other) in order to obtain a more sensitive measure of the amount of role specialization. Influence has also been measured by asking each spouse to divide 10 points so as to show "share of husband and wife influence" (Haley et al., 1975). More attention should be given to whether these differing response formats yield comparable results.

Number of respondents per family. Two conclusions on how many family members to question can be supported from the literature. If the purpose of a study is limited to describing the relative influence of husband and wife in various decisions, it is sufficient to question only one spouse. Considerable evidence shows that the responses of husbands and wives are very similar when compared on an aggregate basis (Davis, 1970; Granbois and Willett, 1970; Wilkening and Morrison, 1963). If, on the other hand, the researcher wants to use a measure of influence in subsequent analyses (particularly prediction studies), data should be collected from both spouses.

The percentage of couples who agree about the roles played by family members in decision making varies from 30 to 80 percent depending in part on the subject area, the specificity of questions asked, and the skewness of responses. Disagreements are particularly high in areas of communication and decision making—a finding that is worrisome since many studies operationalize the authority relationship between husband and wife in terms of decision-making behavior (Morgan, 1968; Olson, 1969).

A related issue is whether children, particularly adolescents and teenagers, can be used as reporters. An early study by Converse and Crawford (1949) used college students to assess family-member involvement in 19 expenditure categories. Although this study provided no estimate of reliability or validity, Marshall (1963) reported very low intercorrelations when children's and parents' reports about the child's use of money were compared.

Self-reported versus communication measures. A lively controversy surrounds the issue whether influence should be measured by self-reports or interaction analysis. Research has shown that when comparing husbands' and wives' responses, global reports about "who is the boss" or "who makes major decisions" are less valid than product-specific reports (Davis, 1971; Wilkes, 1975). Respondents apparently find it easier to recall decisions about specific choices and activities, particularly if a purchase occurred months or years ago. Even here the level of agreement between spouses in response to very specific decisions is far from perfect.[9] Thus, a more fundamental issue regarding self-reports is whether couples can meaningfully think in terms of decision outcomes or power. As Kenkel (1961, p. 159) has remarked:

> This assumes, of course, that individuals know the relative amount of influence they have, that they are willing to admit it to themselves and others, and that they are able to recall with accuracy how influence was distributed in some past decision-making session.

Olson and Rabunsky (1972) reported that individuals can more accurately report *what* decisions were made than *who* actually made them. It seems likely that respondents, faced with the tasks of answering questions that have little meaning, will respond in terms of what they consider to be the socially desirable role, namely, who should decide.

Interaction-based measures represent another tradition of research on family decision making (Kenkel, 1963; Mishler and Wax-ler, 1968; Strodtbeck, 1951). Power is measured in different ways. Kenkel asked families to decide how they would spend an imaginary gift of $300. A spouse's power was measured by the proportion of items "purchased" that were initially suggested by that person. Strodtbeck also used decision outcomes as a measure of power by noting who won a series of revealed-difference discussions. Other studies have focused on aspects of the interaction itself, e.g., the proportion of instrumental acts initiated or the proportion of interruptions initiated by each person.

As is the case with self-reports, these measures also have limitations. Bales' (1950) Interaction Process Analysis excludes nonverbal communication, which is undoubtedly an important indicator of power in long-lasting groups such as the family. The laboratory certainly has an impact on "normal" family interaction: it is a highly reactive environment. The simulated problems given to families by researchers also reinforce the artificiality of the situation. Zelditch (1971) has argued persuasively that one cannot equate a family's laboratory behavior with the behavior of natural families. On the one hand, experiments remove many "place cues" that impinge on families in normal decision-making situations. On the other hand, since families are more complex than the ad hoc small group, it becomes difficult for researchers to study a single phenomenon isolated from other family processes.

These issues aside, it seems clear that self-reports and interaction measures yield differing assessments of who is involved. Turk and Bell (1972) compared eight different measures of power within the same families. The measures were not highly interrelated. Only two associations (out of 36) were greater than .60; 81 percent were in the range of ± .20. Thus, researchers must deal with the problem that

---

[9] Convergent validity for seven automobile and seven furniture decisions was reported as .66 and .61 by Davis (1971). Wilkes (1975) reported correlations ranging between .59 and .79 for specific stages in the decision process. These data show that the maximum variance explained by comparing both spouses' assessment of the same decision is only 56 percent.

characterizing families in terms of power will differ depending on which commonly used measure is employed.

The solution to these problems does not lie principally in methodological improvements—e.g., using more specific questions, specifying the appropriate referent, reducing the lag between decision and data collection, or asking more members within the same family. More important is how decision making itself is conceptualized. It seems likely that measures of *decision outcome* (e.g., who decided or who won) tap a very different aspect of decision making than do measures of the *decision process* (e.g., who initiated the most instrumental acts or interruptions). In this regard, Turner (1970) has suggested that wives are often able to exercise considerable influence in family decisions while at the same time accepting their husband's superior authority. This is possible because the husband's authority and the wife's centrality in the network may be positively related: the greater the husband's recognized authority is, the fewer will be the direct requests made to him by his children.

As Turner (1970, p. 123) concludes: "An interesting speculation, empirically untested, is the hypothesis that the more unequal the authority of the father in the family, the more powerful the offsetting dominance arising out of the centrality of the mother." Students of consumer behavior have not even begun to consider which orientation (i.e., decision outcome or process) is the most relevant for particular purposes. More attention is given to this issue in the next major section of this paper.

Explaining Variability in Involvement. Researchers have devoted little attention to explaining why, for the same decision, families vary in "who decides." This issue will undoubtedly become more important as efforts are made to "locate" families having

particular role patterns. Although a number of theoretical perspectives are available in the sociological and economics literature, these have not been systematically studied in terms of predicting purchase influence within families. Three general conceptions of how tasks and authority are allocated within families are described here.

Cultural role expectations. A number of sociologists have suggested that power and task responsibility are built into the roles of husband and wife on the basis of cultural norms and controls (Burgess and Locke, 1960; Parsons and Bales, 1955). Similar to French and Raven's (1959) concept of "legitimate power," a spouse's authority is based on the belief that he or she *should* make a decision or carry out a task irrespective of the actual skills or interest that may be present. The source of a spouse's power is thus external to the family: Power resides in the position rather than in the person. A traditional role ideology specifies large authority differences between husband and wife and a highly differentiated division of labor. A husband will decide what make of automobile to buy and his wife what to serve for dinner when guests are invited, simply because these two decisions *should* be made by husbands and wives, respectively. Sharp distinctions are drawn between "things" that are masculine or feminine.

A companionship ideology, in contrast, prescribes a high degree of joint participation in tasks and decisions. Togetherness is viewed as a desirable end in and of itself. A husband may, therefore, help his wife cook and shop because he wants to spend more time with her. His wife may learn how to ski so that they can spend more of their leisure time together. When authority or tasks are delegated, they are done so only on a temporary and often expedient basis.

Measures of cultural role expectations are

either direct or indirect. The direct measures include a large number of scales that ask respondents to agree or disagree about various aspects of the husband's, wife's, and parents' role (e.g., "Marriage is the best career for a woman," "A wife should fit her life to her husband," "I consider the kitchen as the wife's room," or "It is somehow unnatural to place women in positions of authority over men"). Indirect measures attempt to locate categories of families or people that hold a different set of role expectations. Thus, sociologists have found traditional role ideologies more common within families in later stages of the life cycle and among people with no college education, in blue-collar occupations, and with authoritarian personalities.

Comparative resources. A second conceptualization of the allocation of tasks and authority within families views each marital partner as a source of valued resources to the other (Blau, 1964; Blood and Wolfe, 1960; Scanzoni, 1970). Responsibility for decision making is assigned to the husband and wife on the basis of each one's ability to reward or punish, personal attractiveness, or competence. These "resources," possessed in varying degrees by each spouse, are exchanged for the right to make (or not to make) decisions or to participate (or not to participate) in family activities. Unlike cultural role expectations, exchange theory views the determinants of decision roles to be internal to the family itself. If the resources controlled by either spouse change, their decision and task involvement should also change.

Measures of comparative resources have been developed at both general and specific levels. Resources such as the husband's educational and occupational status are an illustration of the first of these levels. Scanzoni (1970, pp. 147–48) provides an explicit rationale for this relationship:

> The more the husband fulfills his economic duties . . . , and thus the more the wife defines her status rights . . . [as] being met, the more she will allow her husband to define the norms for . . . decision-making. . . . She . . . gives him power to shape this dimension of the conjugal unit, in exchange for the economic rewards and status benefits he provides for her vis-à-vis the larger community. She is more motivated to "go along" with him, to "give in" to him, to let him "have his way" to the extent that he provides maximum economic rewards.

If the wife controls resources such as a college education or high occupational status, the husband's "right to govern" is likely to be attenuated. An appropriate measure, therefore, is a score that reflects the difference between the husband's and wife's education or occupational status. Resources also include such specific factors as the time available for decision making. For example, wives have been found to lose influence vis-à-vis their husbands during the child-rearing stage of the family life cycle (Blood and Wolfe, 1960). The reason appears to be the combined effects of having to care for children and of having to give up activities outside the home. Because wives have less time to be involved in decision making and less to contribute in terms of financial resources and information, they become more dependent on their husbands during this period.

Researchers interested in studying the effect of time pressures on household decision making will have to construct indices from sets of background characteristics. In order to construct a measure of the wife's time pressure, one might incorporate the number and ages of children, whether the wife is employed, availability of domestic help, and size of dwelling, among others.

Relative investment. Closely related to the previous conceptualization is the relative investment that each spouse has in a particular decision domain. Typically, the outcomes of a decision do not fall evenly across all family members. These assessments of the costs and/or benefits associated with particular outcomes should influence whether and how each participates in a given choice situation. Two important differences distinguish the relative-investment and the comparative-resources explanations. First, resources define the *potential* to exert influence while investment defines the *motivation* of a family member to exert influence. Second, relative investment leads to predictions about family-member involvement in specific decisions rather than about the general authority structure of the family.

Two economic theories are relevant to this third conceptualization. Coleman (1966) proposed that when individuals face a sequence of decisions, it is possible for them to give up control over those of little interest for more control over those of greater interest. An individual's power is defined as the ability to obtain outcomes that yield the highest utility. If one family member has control over actions that are important to others, he has a valuable resource that can be explained for the purpose of "getting his way" over actions that are more important to him. Coleman develops a precise algebraic expression for the power of an individual in a system of collective decisions.

Becker's (1973, 1974) "Theory of Marriage" represents another attempt to explain family behavior in economic terms. Spouses are assumed to maximize the consumption of household-produced commodities, which leads to optimal strategies regarding mate selection, love and caring, the incidence of polygamy, etc. The theory predicts that high-wage men will marry low-wage women to gain from the division of labor, that high-income persons marry earlier than low-income persons, and that high-income, high-education

people are less likely to divorce than others. Although this framework has not yet been specifically applied to predict family-member participation in decision making and tasks, the extension could certainly be made.

These three conceptualizations need to be tested together as predictors of marital roles. They are probably complementary rather than alternative explanations. French and Raven (1959, p. 155) have drawn attention to the several bases of power in small groups:

> It is rare that we can say with certainty that a given empirical case of power is limited to one source. Normally, the relation between O [a person, role, norm, or group] and P [a person] will be characterized by several qualitatively different variables which are bases of power.

They may or may not reinforce each other. In traditional societies, a traditional family ideology is reinforced by the distribution of resources between husband and wife (e.g., women are denied occupational opportunities or family property rights). In modern societies, the stage is often set for conflict since comparative investment or resources may not be consistent with cultural role expectations. Finally, the predictive power of each conceptualization may differ by family and/or product category. Role expectations are likely to be a more important determinant of marital roles during the early years of marriage and less important during the later years. In the same way, role expectations may do a good job of explaining the general division of labor within the household (i.e., whether the wife is employed), while relative investment is a better predictor of involvement in specific product categories.

This discussion should also underline the fact that current efforts to explain this variability are not likely to be successful. Long lists of conventional demographic, attitudinal, or personality variables mechanically regressed against purchase influence reflect neither the appropriate form of the variables (e.g., difference measures between husband versus wife) nor the correct variables themselves (e.g., time pressure or one's stake in the decision).

PROCESS OF DECISION MAKING WITHIN FAMILIES

The problem areas just described are symptomatic of underlying problems with the research to date. Prescribed roles of husband and wife are probably good predictors of "who decides" in stable societies. However, in developed Western societies norms of shared interest, give and take, and companionship are likely to exist. In this situation it is difficult to predict who will win or decide.

Many of the studies already reviewed focus on the outcomes of decision making rather than on the process that has led to these outcomes. The result is that little has been learned about how families actually reach decisions. To use an analogy suggested by Sprey (1971), it is as though one has tried to understand the game of chess by looking only at the outcomes of each game, ignoring entirely the strategies used by each player.

This section describes some issues related to how families make decisions. It is argued that group decision making differs in some important respects from individual decision making. First, group members may not necessarily agree about goals, and agreement is not necessary to reach decisions. Second, families as groups have characteristics that differ from problem-solving groups in organizations or in the laboratory. Third, a repertoire of decision-making strategies is available, with their use depending on what is appropriate to the situation.

There is little research that is relevant to group decision-making processes.[10] The emphasis is still very much on the individual. No theory of household decision making will emerge, nor will research findings build on one another, until the nature of these processes is made explicit.

Decision Making as Consensual versus Accommodative

Using an analogy from organization theory (Thompson and Tuden, 1959), two "ideal" representations of a group making a purchase decision can be proposed. If decision making is consensual, there is either unanimity about what value—i.e., desired outcome—is relevant in the decision or no conflict among group members in the case where several values are relevant. The satisficing criterion (Simon, 1955) would predict that the group will engage in problem solving and will continue to search for alternatives until one is found that satisfies the minimum level of expectations of all members with respect to the value or values perceived as being relevant. If differences between members arise during the search process, the discussion will center only around questions of fact, i.e., whether a particular alternative will really satisfy the value in question. Relying on the judgment of all or a majority of group members, a choice will be made to which all will give equal consent without holding private reservations or resentments about the outcome.

A second "ideal" type of group decision is accommodative rather than consensual; that is, through discussion or observation, group members realize that priorities and prefer-

---

[10] An exception is a paper by Sheth (1974) that applies a modified Howard-Sheth model to family decision making.

ences are irreconcilable. Even if the group can agree about the likely consequences of each choice, there will be no way that one alternative can be satisfying to all. Bargaining, coercion, and other means may be used to reach an acceptable solution. If the group is successful in this process, the commitment of each person to the solution will be conditional on others carrying out the terms of the compromise. The whole decision area can be reopened for further discussion when, for example, one member perceives that the resulting purchase is not entirely in accord with the agreed-on solution.

While the research evidence is limited, some authors suggest that groups, and particularly families, quite often bargain, compromise, and coerce rather than problem-solve in arriving at decisions. Blood (1960) argues that the involuntary and diffuse character of family relationships and the family's small size and changing developmental tasks lead to a high degree of conflict. Sprey (1969) maintains that treating the family as though the normal state were one of agreement and stability is inadequate, since decisions are frequently an on-going confrontation between members having interests in a common situation. It is important, according to Sprey, to understand how conflict management is possible through a set of mutually agreed-on rules. Weick (1971, p. 26) maintains that groups often form around common ends (means interdependencies) rather than common objectives: "In any potential collectivity, members have different interests, capabilities, preferences, and so forth. They want to accomplish different things. However, to achieve some of these diverse ends, concerted, interdependent actions are required."

It is significant to note that it is not necessary for a husband and wife to agree about objectives in order for them to exchange behaviors viewed as mutually re-warding. Weick continues by suggesting that the relationship between means and ends is continuous—i.e., common means will, over time, promote common objectives. One of the initial common objectives is preserving the group itself via the statement and articulation of norms, role specialization, and communication regularity. By preserving the group, members can continue to pursue diverse ends.

Three marketing studies have compared the goals or perceptions of husbands and wives. Project Home (Raymond Loewy/William Snaith, 1967) compared husbands' and wives' "motivations" in home buying within several segments of the market (e.g., first house, upgrade, retiree, two-family home). Substantial disagreements were found between males and females in the upgrade market based on the criteria of privacy, investment, children, and socializing. An apt summary of the differences in the orientation of men and women is as follows: "A man tolerates buying a house for the sake of the woman, while she tolerates the man for the sake of the home" (p. 15). One of the criteria—convenience—was even defined differently by husbands and wives. To women its meaning was functional convenience; men viewed convenience more personally—close to work and/or suitable for relaxation.

Doyle and Hutchinson (1973) presented the results of a multidimensional analysis of automobiles. Although the perceptual spaces were similar, men and women tended to weigh the two dimensions of size and quality (or luxury) differently. Finally, Cox (1975) found a curvilinear relationship between length of marriage and the amount of spousal agreement in preference for new automobile makes. The level of agreement was highest for couples in the intermediate stages of the life cycle.

In the area of family planning, a study by

Poffenberger (1969) revealed marked differences in attitudes between husbands and wives regarding low fertility. Husbands emphasized the positive effects of low fertility on living costs and children's educational opportunities. Wives, in contrast, viewed low fertility as an advantage in terms of reducing their work load.

These results suggest that a goal-oriented, problem-solving approach is likely to characterize only a portion of a household's economic decisions. Future research needs to consider the relative frequency of consensual versus accommodative decision making within families. Moreover, little is known about the extent of goal agreement as a function of product category or such family characteristics as social class, race, or the wife's employment status. The accommodative model also points out that each spouse can engage in the same consumption behavior for different reasons. The diversity of ends that can support the same behavior within families needs to be explored.

Group Decision Making versus Family Decision Making

A number of writers have suggested that families, more than other groups, are likely to be "poor" decision makers. This is owing, in part, to the environment in which families decide, the nontask needs that impinge on all decisions, and the interrelatedness of family decisions. Each of these reasons is briefly considered here.

The Environment of Family Decision Making. Laboratory groups are studied under "ideal" environmental conditions. Members are rested, and meetings take place in rooms with good lighting, comfortable temperatures, and seating arrangements that encourage group interaction. Distractions are

at a minimum. How does this environment compare with the typical family decision-making session? In the first place, families are often together when energy levels are low—early in the morning or late in the day. Little research has been conducted about decision making under conditions of fatigue although there is a good deal of folklore about the decisions of people "who can't get started in the morning" or "who are too tired to think in the evening." Second, family decision making is undoubtedly subject to distraction. In the morning, the demands of preparing breakfast, or the pressure to leave for work, interfere with concentrated problem solving. The evening contains many of the same distractions—dinner, TV, outside activities. Young children not only make constant demands on their parents throughout the day but also frequently interrupt the parents' conversations.

Although no research on the effects of distraction has been done using families, a laboratory study by Wright (1974) is instructive. He found that distraction (a taped radio program at different volume levels) had the effect of increasing the salience of negative evidence and lowering the number of dimensions on which alternatives were evaluated. It does appear, therefore, that the environment can alter strategies used for making decisions.

The Maintenance Needs of Families. Because of the long-lasting nature of family relationships, actions are frequently taken that assure continuance of the group. This contrasts with the ad hoc laboratory group that exists for a very short period of time. In contrast to a committee or task force, problem situations may be viewed as a threat to the stability of the family, particularly if they are novel or have no obvious solution. One manner of dealing with this situation is to avoid the issue itself and focus instead on group maintenance by minimizing expressions of conflicts and the number of alternatives considered. Aldous (1971, p. 267) suggests that the emphasis within families "tends to be one of reducing the tension-laden situations to an innocuous level rather than submitting the problem to rigorous analysis and assessing the consequences of possible alternative strategies." Legitimate roles can be used to reduce conflict, and this can also have the effect of lowering the quality of decisions. It may be that in the interests of reducing conflict and reaffirming legitimate power (French and Raven, 1959), decisions may be made by a person with less expertise. Weick (1971, pp. 5–6) described this intentional masking of expert power as a "delicate problem of balancing legitimacy with expertness in problem solving procedures" and one that differentiates the family from other decision-making groups.

Results from a series of focus-group interviews (Davis, 1972b) showed that consumers are very much aware of group-maintenance needs in describing their own family decisions. Conflict in at least three areas was described—who should make various purchase decisions, how the decisions should be made (amount of search, reliance on advertising, personal recommendations), and who should implement the decision. Since product-choice situations provide one context in which disagreements arise about appropriate roles in decision making, it is easy for family members to confuse the source of conflict. To the extent that they are confused about the reasons for disagreement, attempts to resolve conflict are likely to be unsuccessful. It is also difficult for the researcher to separate truly product-related disagreements from those relating to family-maintenance needs.

The Interrelatedness of Family Decisions. The typical problem dealt with by committees or laboratory groups is defined and worked on in isolation from other problems. This bypasses a number of questions relevant to the dynamics of family problem solving. Weick (1971, p. 9) succinctly describes the differences as follows:

> They [laboratory groups] bypass such questions as how one comes to know that a problem exists, what it does to solution adequacy to be working on several different things *concurrently* with problem solving, what it's like to go about solving a felt, intuited problem rather than an explicitly stated consensually validated problem which was made visible to all members at a specific point in time.

Families face several problems concurrently. It is likely that among this set the most unambiguous and identifiable problems are solved first. This suggested to Aldous (1971) that the problems which families actually solve are likely to be the unimportant ones. More far-reaching problems may remain undefined or unresolved. This is true for at least two reasons. First, a husband and wife may fixate on different aspects of the problem. A husband, for example, may see the automobile "problem" as uncertainty about getting to work on time or the cost of repairs. His wife, on the other hand, might define the "problem" as the extra burden of monthly payments or her husband's infatuation with cars. Because they do not define the "problem" similarly, it may be dropped and not resolved. A second reason that can delay decisions is the impact which each spouse's solution has on the other spouse, either in the same problem area or in different problem areas. Faced with a limited budget, a new car purchase, for example, precludes new carpeting.

Support for these hypotheses is found in at least two studies. Foote (1974) analyzed data from a three-generation study (Hill, 1970) based on 120 grandparent, 120 parent, and 120 young married families. He found both a high proportion of purchases that were not preceded by plans and a high proportion of planned purchases that were not fulfilled. In fact, in all generations unfulfilled plans and unplanned actions predominated over fulfilled plans and planned actions. The reasons for the discrepancies between plans and actions were numerous and often related to uncontrollable problems and immediate opportunities. This finding is in accord with Weick (1971) and Aldous (1971), who both asserted that families may be more solution oriented than problem oriented. According to Weick, it is the appearance of a solution that really precipitates choice, since family members often have only a vague sense of problems. Families frequently describe disagreements about whether a given purchase was legitimate. They disagree about such things as the timing of a purchase, whether it was *really* necessary, and whether other solutions for satisfying the same need might have existed (Davis, 1972b).

Existing research has tended to focus on "go-ahead" decisions as a means of understanding family decision processes; that is, having made or being about to make a purchase, families are queried about how this came about. Equally important, if not more so, are actions taken to abort or postpone consumer purchases given the interrelatedness of family decisions. Much could be learned about a household's priority patterns and the influence of different family members by recording not only whose purchase suggestions were realized but also whose suggestions were denied or tabled and for what reasons.

Alternative Decision-Making Strategies. Table 1 summarizes various decision-making strategies under the two models of consensus and accommodation. A brief description of each strategy is presented here.[11]

Role structure. The role-structure strategy serves to lessen or even eliminate the need for discussion by making one person (or sometimes two) responsible for the decision. Frequently, family members come to accept one person as a "specialist" in a particular sphere of activity, thus making legitimate his or her right to decide without interference. Often, this expertise is maintained by developing a specialized jargon, by creating an air of mystery about how to perform the task, or by ridiculing the performance of others when they try to perform the same task.

Budgets. In the budget strategy, which is a second form of bureaucracy, decision responsibility is "controlled" by an impersonal arbitrator. Instead of nightly or morning crises, conflict can be restricted to once-a-week meetings at which time criteria of fairness and equity may receive more attention. Rules also serve to "institutionalize" power or coercion. Parents who believe that children should eat everything on their plates can establish a household rule. Thus, when children object, the mother can respond, "That's the rule—now eat!" If a wife has exceeded the clothing allowance set up by her husband, she may place the blame on the budget itself rather than on her husband for having set up such a small allowance. As Blood (1960, p. 215) concludes, "The process of agreeing on a budget is still liable to plenty of conflict, but, once formulated, a budget tends to divert attention from the hostile antagonist to the operational code."

Problem solving. When agreement exists about which goals are desirable, problem-solving behavior is likely. "Experts," both within and outside the family, can be relied on to provide "proof" of the merit of one alter-

---

[11] A more detailed description of each strategy is contained in Davis (1972b). Sheth and Cosmas (1975) have also studied four alternative decision strategies in the purchase of automobiles and furniture—problem solving, persuasion, bargaining, and politicking.

Table 1 / Alternative Decision-Making Strategies

Goals	Strategy	Ways of implementing
"Consensus" (Family members agree about goals)	Role structure	"The Specialist"
	Budgets	"The Controller"
	Problem solving	"The Expert" "The Better Solution" "The Multiple Purchase"
"Accommodation" (Family members disagree about goals)	Persuasion	"The Irresponsible Critic" "Feminine Intuition" "Shopping Together" "Coercion" "Coalitions"
	Bargaining	"The Next Purchase" "The Impulse Purchase" "The Procrastinator"

native versus others. Family discussion can produce a "better solution" than that originally put forth by any of the members individually. Although there have been few studies of problem-solving effectiveness in families, research on other small groups suggests some factors that may be applicable. Groups, for example, can ask more questions and get more information than any individual could alone. In this case, more alternatives will be generated and more complete information obtained about the likely consequences of each alternative.

An example, perhaps, of a better solution is the "multiple purchase." As a way of resolving conflict or trying to avoid it, two or more brands can be purchased instead of one. Instead of a color TV, two black and white sets can be bought for the same outlay. The family vacation can be divided into two separate two-week segments if members are unable to agree on one site. Blood (1960, pp. 214–15) has observed that "the current trends to a second car, a second television set, and a second telephone result not only in increased

profits for the corresponding manufacturers but in decreased tension for family personnel who can now use parallel facilities simultaneously instead of having to compete for control of single channels."

Persuasion strategies. When family members do not agree about goals, strategies of persuasion and bargaining are likely. The distinction between these two strategies is not a sharp one. Persuasion can be viewed as a way of forcing someone to make a decision that he would not otherwise make. Bargaining, on the other hand, leads to willing agreement since by doing so both parties tend to gain.

Typically, the person who has the authority to make a particular decision also gets the credit or blame for how the decision turns out. Those who are freed from this responsibility can try to seize on certain of the advantages of being dominated. Thus, the "irresponsible critic" can put forth ideas freely without having to worry how realistic they might be. The "nagging wife," for example, can criticize her husband freely. If it turns out that he was right, she has nothing to lose; if he was wrong, she can adopt the self-satisfying stance of "I told you so." In the extreme case, the husband may become so tired of hearing his wife begin the same tirade that he prefers to concede to her regardless of the decision area.

When a wife is dominated by her husband, she may have to resort to a strategy referred to in folklore as "feminine intuition"; that is, she learns to identify the moods in which he is most susceptible to new ideas or persuasion. She may also find types of appeals to which he is especially weak. Television programs in the U.S. are filled with stories of wives "plotting" against their husbands to get a new fur coat, living-room furniture, or the like. The presence of this facility (to the extent that it actually exists) may have some basis in fact. As Turner (1970, p. 189) reasons:

> Under the long-standing subordination of women to men, learning to detect and interpret the subtle gestures of the opposite sex accurately has been more adaptive for the woman than for the man. Such learning comes partly from individual discovery during the socialization process, partly from the accumulation of a woman's repertoire of folk techniques for understanding and dealing with men, and partly from the selective direction of attention during interaction.

An interesting persuasion strategy is to take another family member along when shopping for a product. "Shopping together" has the effect of securing a commitment from the other person. Having said "Yes," it is more difficult for that person to back out of the decision at a later time.

"Coercion" is the most extreme form of persuasion since it implies unwilling agreement. The use of this strategy within the family is probably common when there are large authority differences among family members and no cultural norms exist against its use.

"Coalitions" can be formed within the family for the purpose of forcing the lone individual or minority to join with the majority. In cohesive groups, such as the family, the success of appeals designed to bring dissenters into line is probably high.

Bargaining Strategies. Unlike the persuasion strategies just mentioned, which represent relatively short-run efforts to win a specific decision, bargaining involves longer-term considerations. Thus, a wife may be willing to lose a given encounter on the grounds that she will "get her way" in a later decision. Given the long-run and diffuse nature of most family relationships, this situation poses difficult problems for researchers interested in understanding the decision process for one specific consumer good at one point in time. Explicit or tacit agreements may exist as a result of a decision made in a quite different area at an earlier time that will affect the outcome of a current choice.

Waiting for the "next purchase" is an obvious approach if one feels that one will lose or "use up" goodwill by forcing a showdown on a contested decision. The husband can say, for example, "O.K., you buy the fur coat but I'm going to take the two-week fishing vacation with the boys."

The timing of a purchase itself can be used as a strategy. An "impulse purchase" is similar to the first move in a game of strategy. A husband can choose to drive home a new car that he has just purchased without any prior discussion with his wife. The wife may view the decision as already having been made. Moreover, having seen the car, she may conclude that she really likes it.

"Procrastinating" is another way of continuing the bargaining process after a choice has been made. If the wife delays making a purchase that has been agreed on, new information may develop or the situation can change such that the original choice can be changed. In this case, she can easily assign the blame to an outside party, thereby concealing her own delaying tactics—e.g., "By the time I got to the travel agent, the tour was completely full," or "The store didn't have any more."

From this discussion of how decisions are made within families, we can see that the approach is much broader than simply determining who is involved in various decisions and tasks. Research should be directed to these alternative decision strategies—to specifying the circumstances under which each will be used in the same family and how their use differs among families.

CONSEQUENCES OF HUSBAND-WIFE INVOLVEMENT AND DECISION STRATEGIES

In discussing the Ferber (1973b) review paper, Hill and Klein (1973, p. 372) presented Guy Orcutt's comments on the lack of evidence about whether family decision roles make any difference. "I would like to have seen some evidence pointing up the implications of different role-playing allocations, and different budgeting procedures for the economic behavior and well-being of families."

It remains true that very little effort has been directed to the effects of different family structures, even though this is a critical issue. The usual justification of family research in marketing relates to better targeting of marketing activities. Studies of husband-wife influence have been justified in (1) selecting the proper respondent in consumer research surveys, (2) determining the content of advertising messages, (3) selecting advertising media, (4) guiding product designers to include features that appeal to those who are most influential in the purchase decision, and (5) assisting in the location of retail outlets. Although these reasons are legitimate, they represent only a small part of the justification for studying family-member involvement in consumer decisions.

At least two writers have speculated about the effects of household structure on purchase behavior. Alderson (1957) suggested two concepts that form a typology of households—compatibility of attitudes/preferences and coordination of goal-directed activities. Families can be classified into one of the following four "ideal" types: coordinated and compatible, coordinated and incompatible, uncoordinated and compatible, and uncoordinated and incompatible. Family purchase behavior is hypothesized to differ for each type. To illustrate, the coordinated but incompatible family is likely to be "especially price-conscious, immune to emotional appeal, and hard bargainers in the effort to get their money's worth" (Alderson, 1957, p. 179). In contrast, the uncoordinated but compatible family is hypothesized to be especially susceptible to persuasive efforts such as personal selling.

Scanzoni (1966) hypothesized unique consumption behaviors in families as a function of the aspiration and expectation level of the husband vis-à-vis his wife. If, for example, a husband's aspirations *and* expectations exceeded those of his wife, one would expect him to be the motivating force behind an improved life style. His wife would be more likely to "go along" with his desires for increased consumption to the extent that his income level was high and his education substantially greater than hers. In another pattern, the husband could hope for a higher life style than his wife but actually have lower expectations about what was realistic. Unlike the previous pattern, the wife would probably be the major force behind a higher standard of living for the family and for that specific reason might want to work. According to Scanzoni, this pattern is likely to be present for many working-class families in the United States.

Beyond these speculations are a few empirical studies suggesting that family decision roles do indeed make a difference. Ferber and Lee (1974) found that when husbands were the "family financial officer," a higher proportion of income was saved, more assets were in variable dollar form (i.e., real estate, securities), and automobile purchases were less frequent. Granbois and Summers (1975) reported better estimates of total planned expenditures when interviews were conducted with both spouses together rather than with either the husband or the wife individually.

Considerable research has accumulated showing effective contraceptive use in families characterized by equalitarian roles, high within-family communication, and low extra-familial communication. Rogers (1973) described a family planning effort in Pakistan whose high success was attributed in part to the use of male-female teams as opposed to female workers only.

Finally, the Nowland studies (1964, 1965) found significant differences in purchase behavior depending on whether husbands and wives had the same brand preferences. When brand consensus existed, the preferred brand was usually the brand in the household inventory. When husband and wife did not agree, the wife's preferred brand rather than the husband's was more likely to be purchased.

These studies have just begun to examine the impact of the household on consumer behavior. An important research priority is to extend these tentative findings to many other areas of consumer choice.

CONCLUDING COMMENTS

Three brief summary comments capture the essence of this review.

1. The study of household decision and consumption behavior is not simply another "fashionable" topic for consumer researchers. Rather, the focus on consumers as a group acting collectively suggests a reorientation of many existing theories and methodologies. Research on household decision making will be judged on the extent to which it influences thinking about other areas such as family counseling, information dissemination, and marketing research.

2. Much of the work to date has taken an overly restrictive view of family-member roles. Most of the emphasis has been on who shops and decides within specific product categories. Studies of family decision making have in reality been studies of husband-wife decision making. Little is known about household roles (including children) in information gathering and storage, product use, and post decision evaluation or about family-member roles across product domains. Hill and Klein (1973, p. 373) have suggested that "scanty attention has been paid even to the descriptive questions of how and to what extent feed-back of information from past experience influences family decisions, who evaluates the family experience, who 'stores' the information for future use, and who draws on this information storage when the need arises."

3. A third and final research priority is the need to explore *how* families make decisions rather than simply who is involved. In the final analysis, a theory of household decision making will not emerge by focusing solely on decision outcomes such as who decided or who won. This approach has been described by Sprey (1972) both as "in no way sufficient" and as "highly unsuitable." The ongoing nature of family relationships, the interrelatedness of their consumer choices, and the financial and time constraints faced by the family define a unique decision environment.

The impact of this environment on how households manage consumption and savings is an important question for future research.

REFERENCES

Alderson, W. *Marketing Behavior and Executive Action: A Functionalist Approach to Marketing Theory.* Homewood, Ill.: Irwin, 1957.

Aldous, J. "A Framework for the Analysis of Family Problem Solving," in J. Aldous, T. Condon, R. Hill, M. Straus, and I. Tallman, eds., *Family Problem Solving: A Symposium on Theoretical, Methodological, and Substantive Concerns.* Hinsdale, Ill.: Dryden Press, 1971, 265–81.

Aronoff, J., and W. D. Crano. "A Re-Examination of the Cross-Cultural Principles of Task Segregation and Sex Role Differentiation in the Family," *American Sociological Review,* 40 (February 1975), 12–20.

Arrow, K. J. "Mathematical Models in the Social Sciences," in D. Lerner and H. D. Lasswell, eds., *The Policy Sciences: Recent Developments in Scope and Method.* Stanford, Calif.: Stanford University Press, 1951, 129–54.

Bales, R. F. *Interaction Process Analysis: A Method for the Study of Small Groups.* Cambridge, Mass.: Addison-Wesley, 1950.

Becker, G. S. "A Theory of Marriage: Part I," *Journal of Political Economy.* 81 (July/August 1973), 813–46.

_____. "A Theory of Marriage: Part II," *Journal of Political Economy,* 82 (March/April 1974), Part II, S11–S26.

Beckman, T. N. and W. R. Davidson, *Marketing.* (7th ed.) New York: Ronald Press, 1962.

Bernhardt, K. L. "Husband-Wife Influence in the Purchase Decision Process for Houses," Unpublished doctoral dissertation, University of Michigan, 1974.

Blau, P. M. *Exchange and Power in Social Life.* New York: Wiley, 1964.

Blood, R. O., Jr. "Resolving Family Conflicts," *The Journal of Conflict Resolution,* 4 (June 1960), 209–19.

Blood, R. O., Jr., and D. M. Wolfe. *Husbands and Wives: The Dynamics of Married Living.* Glencoe, Ill.: Free Press, 1960.

Brehl and Callahan Research. *Family Decision Making.* Time Marketing Information Research Report 1428, 1967.

Burgess, E. W. and H. J. Locke. *The Family: From Institution to Companionship.* (2nd ed.) New York: American Book Co., 1960.

Buskirk, R. H. *Principles of Marketing: The Management View.* New York: Holt, Rinehart & Winston, 1961.

Coleman, J. S. "Foundations for a Theory of Collective Decisions," *American Journal of Sociology,* 71 (May 1966), 615–27.

Converse, P. D. and M. Crawford. "Family Buying: Who Does It? Who Influences It?" *Current Economic Comment,* 11 (November 1949), 38–50.

Converse, P. D., H. W. Huegy, and R. V. Mitchell. *Elements of Marketing.* (6th ed.) Englewood Cliffs, N.J.: Prentice-Hall, 1958.

Conway/Milliken Research Corporation. *Report of the First Buyers of Automobiles.* A report prepared for Playboy Market Research, 1969.

Cox, E. P. "Family Purchase Decision Making and the Process of Adjustment," *Journal of Marketing Research,* 12 (May 1975), 189–95.

Cunningham, I. C. M. and R. T. Green. "Purchasing Roles in the U. S. Family, 1955 and 1973," *Journal of Marketing,* 38 (October 1974), 61–64.

Cunningham, R. M. "Brand Loyalty—What, Where, How Much?" *Harvard Business Review,* 34 (January/February 1956), 116–28.

Davis, H. L. "Dimensions of Marital Roles in Consumer Decision Making," *Journal of Marketing Research,* 7 (May 1970), 168–77.

_____. "Measurement of Husband-Wife Influence in Consumer Purchase Decisions," *Journal of Marketing Research,* 8 (August 1971), 305–12.

_____. "Determinants of Marital Roles in a Consumer Purchase Decision." Working Paper 72-14. European Institute for Advanced Studies in Management, Brussels, April 1972a.

_____. "Household Decision Making." Working Paper 72-41. European Institute for Advanced Studies in Management, Brussels, November 1972b.

_____. *Consumer Behavior in the Family.* New York: Free Press, in press.

Davis, H. L. and B. P. Rigaux, "Perception of Marital Roles in Decision Processes," *Journal of Consumer Research,* 1 (June 1974), 51–62.

Doyle, P. and P. Hutchinson, "Individual Differences in Family Decision Making," *Journal of the Market Research Society,* 15 (October 1973), 193–206.

Dubey, D. C. and H. M. Choldin. "Communication and Diffusion of the IUCD: A Case Study in Urban India," *Demography,* 4 (no. 2, 1967), 601–14.

Engel, J. F., D. T. Kollat, and R. D. Blackwell. *Consumer Behavior.* (2nd ed.) New York: Holt, Rinehart & Winston, 1973.

Evans, F. B. "Psychological and Objective Factors in the Prediction of Brand Choice, Ford versus Chevrolet," *The Journal of Business,* 32 (October 1959), 340–69.

Farley, J. U. "A Test of the Loyalty Proneness Hypothesis," *Commentary,* 8 (January 1966), 35–42.

Ferber, R. "Consumer Economics, A Survey," *Journal of Economic Literature,* 11 (December 1973a), 1303–42.

_____. "Family Decision Making and Economic Behavior: A Review," in E. B. Sheldon, ed., *Family Economic Behavior: Problems and Prospects.* Philadelphia: Lippincott, 1973b, 29–61.

Ferber, R. and L. C. Lee. "Husband-Wife Influence in Family Purchasing Behavior," *Journal of Consumer Research*, 1 (June 1974), 43–50.

Ferber, R. and F. Nicosia, "Newly Married Couples and Their Asset Accumulation Decisions," in B. Strumpel, J. N. Morgan, and E. Zahn, eds., *Human Behavior in Economic Affairs: Essays in Honor of George Katona.* San Francisco: Jossey-Bass; Amsterdam: Elsevier, 1972, 161–87.

Foote, N. "Unfulfilled Plans and Unplanned Actions," in S. Ward and P. Wright, eds., *Advances in Consumer Research.* Vol. 1. Proceedings of the 4th Annual Conference of the Association for Consumer Research, 1973. Urbana, Ill.: Association for Consumer Research, 1974, 529–31.

Frank, R. E. "Is Brand Loyalty a Useful Basis for Market Segmentation?" *Journal of Advertising Research,* 7 (June 1967), 27–33.

French, J. R. P. and B. Raven. "The Bases of Social Power," in D. Cartwright, ed., *Studies in Social Power.* Ann Arbor: Research Center for Group Dynamics, Institute for Social Research, University of Michigan, 1959, 150–67.

Granbois, D. H. "A Study of the Family Decision-Making Process in the Purchase of Major Durable Household Goods." Unpublished doctoral dissertation, Indiana University, 1963.

Granbois, D. H. and J. O. Summers. "Primary and Secondary Validity of Consumer Purchase Probabilities," *Journal of Consumer Research,* 1 (March 1975), 31–38.

Granbois, D. H. and R. P. Willett. "Equivalence of Family Role Measures Based on Husband and Wife Data," *Journal of Marriage and the Family,* 32 (February 1970), 68–72.

Gredal, K. "Purchasing Behavior in Households," in M. Kjaer-Hansen, ed., *Readings in Danish Theory of Marketing.* Amsterdam: North-Holland, 1966, 84–100.

Green, R. T. and I. C. M. Cunningham. "Feminine Role Perception and Family Purchasing Decisions," *Journal of Marketing Research,* 12 (August 1975), 325–32.

Haley, Overholser and Associates, Inc. *Purchase Influence: Measures of Husband/Wife Influence on Buying Decisions,* 1975.

Hempel, D. J. "Family Buying Decisions: A Cross-Cultural Perspective," *Journal of Marketing Research,* 11 (August 1974), 295–302.

Hill, R. *Family Development in Three Generations.* Cambridge, Mass.: Schenkman, 1970.

Hill, R. and D. M. Klein. "Toward a Research Agenda and Theoretical Synthesis," in E. B. Sheldon, ed., *Family Economic Behavior: Problems and Prospects.* Philadelphia: Lippincott, 1973, 371–404.

Jacoby, J., and D. B. Kyner. "Brand Loyalty vs. Repeat Buying Behavior," *Journal of Marketing Research,* 10 (February 1973), 1–9.

Jaffe Associates, Inc. *A Pilot Study of the Roles of Husbands and Wives in Purchasing Decisions,* n.d.

Jaffe, L. J. and H. Senft. "The Roles of Husbands and Wives in Purchasing Decisions," in L. Adler and I. Crespi, eds., *Attitude Research at Sea.* Chicago: American Marketing Association, 1966, 95–110.

Kenkel, W. F. "Family Interaction in Decision Making on Spending," in N. N. Foote, ed., *Household Decision-Making.* Consumer Behavior, Vol. IV. New York: New York University Press, 1961, 140–64.

————. "Observational Studies of Husband-Wife Interaction in Family Decision Making," in M. Sussman, ed., *Sourcebook in Marriage and the Family.* (2nd ed.) Boston: Houghton Mifflin, 1963, 144–56.

Lam, P. "Experiences in the Use of Communication Methods in Promoting Family Planning in Hong Kong," in *Report of the Working Group on Communication Aspects of Family Planning Programmes and Selected Papers.* Asian Population Studies Series 3. Bangkok: ECAFE, 1968.

Learner Marketing Research and Development. *New Brand Purchasing Dynamics: An In-Depth Examination of the Critical Incidents and Factors Involved in a New or Different Brand Coming into the Home.* Conducted for *Life* Magazine, December, 1968.

Raymond Loewy/William Snaith, Inc. *Project Home: The Motivations Towards Homes and Housing.* Report prepared for the Project Home Committee, 1967.

Lovell, R. C., R. Meadows, and B. Rampley. "Inter-Household Influence on Housewife Purchases." London: The Thompson Organization, 1968, 7–49.

Male vs. Female Influence in Buying and in Brand Selection, New York: Fawcett Publications, 1948.

Male vs. Female Influence in Buying and in Brand Selection, Vol. II. New York: Fawcett Publications, 1950.

Marshall, H. R. "Differences in Parent and Child Reports of the Child's Experience in the Use of Money," *Journal of Educational Psychology,* 54 (June 1963), 132–37.

Mercado, C. M. "Target Audiences in Family Planning." Paper presented at the IPPF-SEAOR Workshop on Information and Education, Kuala Lumpur, Malaysia, 1971.

Mishler, E. G. and N. E. Waxler. *Interaction in the Family.* New York: Wiley, 1968.

Morgan, J. N. "Some Pilot Studies of Communication and Consensus in the Family," *Public Opinion Quarterly,* (Spring 1968), 113–21.

Mullen, P., R. Reynolds, P. Cignetta, and D.

Dornan. "In Favor of Vasectomy—A Survey of Men and Women in Hayward, California." Unpublished working paper, Berkeley, California, n.d.

Munsinger, G. M., J. E. Weber, and R. W. Hansen. "Joint Home Purchasing Decisions by Husbands and Wives," *Journal of Consumer Research,* 1 (March 1975), 60–66.

Nowland and Company, Inc. *Family Participation and Influence in Shopping and Brand Selection: Phase I.* A report prepared for *Life* Magazine, 1964.

————. *Family Participation and Influence in Shopping and Brand Selection: Phase II.* A report prepared for *Life* Magazine, 1965.

Olson, D. H. "The Measurement of Family Power by Self-Report and Behavioral Methods," *Journal of Marriage and the Family,* 31 (August 1969), 545–50.

Olson, D. H. and C. Rabunsky. "Validity of Four Measures of Family Power," *Journal of Marriage and the Family,* 34 (May 1972), 224–34.

Palmore, J. "The Chicago Snowball: A Study of the Flow and Diffusion of Family Planning Information," in D. J. Bogue, ed., *Sociological Contributions to Family Planning Research.* Chicago: Community and Family Planning Center, University of Chicago, 1967, 272–363.

Parsons, T. and R. F. Bales. *Family, Socialization and Interaction Process.* Glencoe, Ill.: Free Press, 1955.

Phillips, C. F. and D. J. Duncan. *Marketing: Principles and Methods.* (5th ed.) Homewood, Ill.: Irwin, 1964.

Pillai, K. M. "Study of the Decision Process in Adopting Family Planning Methods," *Bulletin of the Gandhigram Institute of Rural Health and Family Planning,* 6 (1971), 1–55.

Poffenberger, T. *Husband-Wife Communication and Motivational Aspects of Population Control in an Indian Village.* Green Park, New Delhi: Central Family Planning Institute, 1969.

Rogers, E. M. *Communication Strategies for Family Planning.* New York: Free Press, 1973.

Samuelson, P. A. "Social Indifference Curves," *The Quarterly Journal of Economics,* 70 (February 1956), 1–22.

Scanzoni, J. H. "The Conjugal Family and Consumption Behavior." Occasional Paper Series #1. Bryn Mawr, Penn.: McCahan Foundation, 1966.

_____. *Opportunity and the Family*. New York: Free Press, 1970.

Scott, R. A. "Husband-Wife Interaction in a Household Purchase Decision," *Southern Journal of Business*, 5 (July 1970), 218-25.

Sharp, H. and P. Mott, "Consumer Decisions in the Metropolitan Family," *Journal of Marketing*, 21 (October 1956), 149-56.

Sheldon, E. B., ed. *Family Economic Behavior: Problems and Prospects*. Philadelphia: Lippincott, 1973.

Sheth, J. N. "A Theory of Family Buying Decisions," in J. N. Sheth, ed., *Models of Buyer Behavior: Conceptual, Quantitative, and Empirical*. New York: Harper & Row, 1974, 17-33.

Sheth, J. N. and S. Cosmas. "Tactics of Conflict Resolution in Family Buying Behavior." Paper presented at the meetings of American Psychological Association, Chicago, September, 1975.

Simon, H. A. "A Behavioral Model of Rational Choice," *The Quarterly Journal of Economics*, 69 (February 1955), 99-118.

Sprey, J. "The Family as a System in Conflict," *Journal of Marriage and the Family*, 31 (November 1969), 699-706.

_____. "On the Management of Conflict in Families," *Journal of Marriage and the Family*, 33 (November 1971), 722-31.

_____. "Family Power Structure: A Critical Comment," *Journal of Marriage and the Family*, 34 (May 1972), 235-38.

Starch, D. and staff. *Male vs. Female Influence on the Purchase of Selected Products*. A report prepared for *True* Magazine, 1958.

Strodtbeck, F. L. "Husband-Wife Interaction over Revealed Differences," *American Sociological Review*, 16 (August 1951), 468-73.

Szalai, A., ed. *The Use of Time: Daily Activities of Urban and Suburban Populations in Twelve Countries*. The Hague: Mouton, 1972.

Thompson, J. D. and A. Tuden. "Strategies, Structures, and Processes of Organizational Decision," in J. D. Thompson, P. B. Hammond, R. W. Hawkes, B. H. Junker, and A. Truden, eds., *Comparative Studies in Administration*. Pittsburgh: University of Pittsburgh Press, 1959, 195-216.

Travel Research International, Inc. *A Study of the Role of Husband and Wife in Air Travel Decisions*. Conducted for *Sports Illustrated*, September, 1968.

Turk, J. L. and N. W. Bell. "Measuring Power in Families," *Journal of Marriage and the Family*, 34 (May 1972), 215-22.

Turner, R. H. *Family Interaction*. New York: Wiley, 1970.

Weick, K. E. "Group Processes, Family Processes, and Problem Solving," in J. Aldous, T. Condon, R. Hill, M. Straus, and I. Tallman, eds., *Family Problem Solving: A Symposium on Theoretical, Methodological, and Substantive Concerns*. Hinsdale, Ill.: Dryden Press, 1971, 3-32.

Wells, H. L. "Financial Management Practices of Young Families," *Journal of Home Economics*, 51 (June 1959), 439-44.

Wilkening, E. A. and D. E. Morrison. "A Comparison of Husband and Wife Responses Concerning Who Makes Farm and Home Decisions," *Marriage and Family Living*, 25 (August 1963), 349-51.

Wilkes, R. E. "Husband-Wife Influence in Purchase Decisions—A Confirmation and Extension," *Journal of Marketing Research*, 7 (May 1975), 224-27.

Wind, Y. "Brand Choice," in R. Ferber, ed., *A Synthesis of Selected Aspects of Consumer Behavior*. Washington, D. C.: National Science Foundation, 1976.

Wolff, J. L. *What Makes Women Buy: A Guide to Understanding and Influencing the New Woman of Today*. New York: McGraw-Hill, 1958.

Wolgast, E. H. "Do Husbands or Wives Make the Purchasing Decisions?" *Journal of Marketing*, 23 (October 1958), 151-58.

Woodside, A. G. "Effects of Prior Decision-Making, Demographics, and Psychographics on Marital Roles for Purchasing Durables," in M. J. Schlinger, ed., *Advances in Consumer Research*. Vol. 2. Proceedings of the 5th Annual Conference of the Association for Consumer Research, 1974. Chicago: Association for Consumer Research, 1975, 81-91.

Wright, P. L. "The Harassed Decision Maker: Time Pressures, Distractions, and the Use of

Evidence, *Journal of Applied Psychology,* 59 (October 1974), 555–61.

Zelditch, M., Jr. "Experimental Family Sociology," in J. Aldous, T. Condon, R. Hill, M. Strauss, and I. Tollman, eds., *Fam-* *ily Problem Solving: A Symposium on Theoretical, Methodological, and Substantive Concerns.* Hinsdale, Ill.: Dryden Press, 1971, 55–72.

Questions

1. Do you agree with the author about the importance of research on the household decision making? Why or why not?
2. Briefly explain three decision making strategies using an example in each case to clarify your point.
3. How does the economy affect decision making in the household?

24. Consumer Decision Making— Fact or Fiction?

Richard W. Olshavsky

Donald H. Granbois

The most pervasive and influential assumption in consumer behavior research is that purchases are preceded by a decision process. Writers who have suggested models of this process have used varying terminology, but all seem to agree that:

1. Two or more alternative actions exist and, therefore, *choice* must occur.
2. Evaluative criteria facilitate the forecasting of each alternative's consequences for the consumer's goals or objectives.
3. The chosen alternative is determined by a decision rule or evaluative procedure.
4. Information sought from external sources and/or retrieved from memory is processed in the application of the decision rule or evaluation procedure.

Virtually every text on consumer behavior includes a verbal or flow chart model of consumer decision processes. Engel, Blackwell, and Kollat (1978) base an elaborate stage model on five steps (problem recognition, search, alternative evaluation, choice, and outcomes) suggested 70 years ago by John Dewey. Howard's (1977) refinement of the concept of routinized response behavior, advanced in Howard and Sheth (1969, p. 9), assumes that even simplified, habitual behavior reflects the earlier application of choice criteria to alternative brands. When situational constraints block the repetition of an earlier choice, a reduced-form evaluation process follows, in which dichotomized criteria are applied to a small evoked set of brands (Howard 1977, pp. 27–30).

Research on decision making currently takes several forms. Multidimensional scaling and conjoint measurement are widely applied measurement tools whose relevance grows out of the "multi-attribute nature of consumer decisions" (Green and Wind 1973, p. 5). Different processing rules, such as compensatory, disjunctive, conjunctive, lexicographic, and various hybrid procedures decision makers might use in multi-attribute problems are being tested in studies where subjects verbalize or report on their thought processes as they perform choice tasks. (Bettman and Zins 1977; Lussier and Olshavsky 1974; Payne 1976; Russ 1971). Investigators in other studies observe or photograph the sequence and extent of information utilization by subjects provided with brochures, display boards, labelled packages, etc., containing attribute information for several brands from which a choice must be made (Bettman and Kakkar 1977; Jacoby, Szybillo, and Busato-Schach 1977; Russo and Rosen 1975; van Raaij 1977). Other approaches to the study of decision processes include correlational methods (Scott and Wright 1976) and information integration techniques (Bettman, Capon, and Lutz 1975).

In his presidential address to the Association for Consumer Research, Kassarjian (1978) raised the possibility that we may be attributing choice processes to consumers when no choice processes occur. Kassarjian was not simply saying that decision processes often are routinized or habitual rather than extended (as Howard and Sheth have already pointed out), but that in some cases no prepurchase process exists. This is a very bold

charge, for it implies that much empirical research and theorizing on consumer decision making is less broadly applicable than has been assumed.

Assessing the Evidence

Kassarjian only raised the issue; he presented no supporting evidence. The validity of his position can be assessed in two ways. Applying an evaluation procedure to various alternatives on two or more evaluative criteria requires considerable information, sometimes more than is readily available in memory. Evidence of the circumstances of purchasing behavior occurring in the *absence* of external search, then, helps to establish the *maximum* scope of the nondecision behavior postulated by Kassarjian. Information processing of the sort assumed in alternative evaluation and choice can, of course, be performed with previously acquired and stored information alone. Therefore, the second condition leading to purchase without prior decision process is insufficiency of stored information suitable for alternative evaluation or nonuse of relevant stored information. While the nature of internal processing (or lack of processing) can be studied only indirectly, a convincing case can be made that internal information is frequently either not available, not relevant, or not consulted.[1]

There are several comprehensive reviews of research on consumer prepurchase behavior that provide considerable evidence of external prepurchase information search. These reviews have encompassed surveys in which consumers were asked to describe their

---

[1] Certain "process tracing" techniques, in particular protocol analysis, do permit direct monitoring of internal processing, although to a limited extent. However, when this technique is used, subjects are instructed, implicitly or explicitly, to engage in decision making.

prepurchase behavior retrospectively for a recent purchase, or their "usual" behavior, as well as studies of consumers in real-life purchasing situations during which some type of observational method was used to measure the decision process appearing to precede purchase.

It must be recognized that consumer researchers using observation and retrospective questionnaire techniques have probably been influenced by the assumption of decision process behavior, so that their results may reflect a subtle bias overstating the prevalence of decision-making behavior. To some extent, research instruments measure what their designers expect to find. Consumers, too, may overstate the extent of prepurchase deliberation and choice-making behavior, because this may appear desirable as well as expected behavior. What this means, then, is that the research to be cited probably *overstates* the extent of prepurchase behavior for which the decision model is appropriate.

Objectives and Method

The primary purpose of this paper is to assess, through a synthesis of the review articles just mentioned, the apparent scope of consumer behavior not preceded by external search. Additional objectives, secondary only in that less substantial evidence is available for evaluation, include:

- identifying circumstances in which external environmental and situational constraints limit consumers to a single alternative; and
- identifying research in which purchase has been observed to occur without reference to relevant stored information.

Each of the four sections of the paper represents one element of the comprehensive classification of consumer behavior offered

by Gredal (1966). These are renamed slightly here, and include (1) budget allocation (savings/spending and allocation across broad expenditure categories); (2) generic allocation (expenditures for specific products and services); (3) store patronage (shopping and purchasing at specific shopping centers, stores, etc.); and (4) brand purchase.

In each section, conclusions from review articles on prepurchase behavior are cited. Discussion is then directed to why the behavior involved may be subject to influences and constraints precluding an internal evaluation of alternative actions. The principal review articles drawn upon include Ferber (1973) and Ölander and Siepel (1970) on budget allocation, Ferber (1973) on generic allocation, Granbois (1977) on store patronage, and Newman (1977) on brand purchases.

BUDGET ALLOCATION

Saving Versus Spending

How does the allocation of income between saving and spending come about? In his report of a wide ranging review of research on family economic behavior, Ferber (1973) concluded:

> Despite its basic importance for the understanding of consumer financial behavior, the role of financial planning within the family—in the sense of explicit consideration of the allocation of expected financial resources between saving and spending—seems to have received very little attention in empirical work, and would seem to be a prime area for future research (p. 34).

Since Ferber's review, there appears to have been no empirical studies of consumer's information-seeking relative to savings. There are, however, a few studies of consumers' information about alternative forms of savings and their self-assessment of the degree to which "planning" precedes savings. In his review, Ferber reported substantial proportions of households (up to 87 percent) without a "financial plan," although the meaning of "financial plan" was often not clearly defined (Ferber 1973, p. 35).

A review by Ölander and Seipel (1970) also evaluated consumers' knowledge of financial matters, e.g., interest rates, where stocks can be purchased, and tax regulations. One study reviewed reported: "The respondents' knowledge of tax regulations was good in many respects but often did not appear to influence behavior in the direction of using savings and investment forms which were more advantageous from the tax point of view" (p. 68). Further discussion by these reviewers suggests that individual characteristics, such as low achievement motivation, perceived inability to control one's own financial destiny, and very short future time orientation and planning horizon may inhibit planning. Other evidence on the extent of deliberation preceding savings behavior comes from four studies that found the proportion of self-identified systematic savers to be 15 percent, 27 percent, 28 percent, and 40 percent, respectively (p. 31). In another study, 36 percent of respondents predicted very accurately the extent of savings accumulated six months later (p. 33).

Thus, perhaps one-fourth to one-third of all consumers show evidence of some systematic planning and decision making regarding saving; the majority, however, may not be classified as deliberate choosers. An exception may be newlywed couples; Ferber and Nicosia found that half of the couples they interviewed three to six months after marriage reported a definite plan for saving (Ferber 1973, p. 51).

Allocation of Income Across Expenditure Categories

What, if any, type of decision process precedes the allocation of income across the various categories of goods and services, i.e., food/beverage, housing, household furnishings, etc.? We could find no studies of prepurchase behavior relative to household allocation behavior. Clearly, however, purchases within certain categories are nondiscretionary. Income must be allocated to the categories of food/beverage, housing, clothing, and medical care.

Products within certain other categories are not necessary for survival, yet they are essentially nondiscretionary. Certain items of personal care, recreation, and education are very strongly compelled by social pressure. Moreover, purchase of one product or service is often interlocked with other products or services. The purchase of an automobile, for instance, dictates the purchase of gasoline, repair services, and insurance.

Still other expenditures are compelled by consumers' strong preference for a culturally-mandated life style, usually acquired early in life. Most household furnishings, for example, are discretionary, yet 99.9 percent of the electrically wired homes in the United States have a refrigerator. Presumably this is because few American consumers will tolerate the type of life style implied by living without a refrigerator. Many products in the transportation, personal care, household furnishings, and household operations categories are nondiscretionary in this sense; they constitute what Riesman and Roseborough (1955) termed the "standard package," a set of products uniformly represented throughout American society.

Even allocations to categories that seem

purely discretionary may not reflect true choice behavior. Tobacco expenditures, for example, are by no means universal: cigarette smoking, the dominant form of tobacco usage, occurs in only 35 percent of United States households [*Adult Use of Tobacco-1975* (1976)]. Studies reveal that smoking behavior is acquired largely in the preteen and teen-age years *(Teenage Smoking 1976)*, primarily as a result of such "psychosocial factors" as curiosity, imitation, identification with adult roles, status striving, and rebellion (Lawton 1962). Striving for these goals is socially motivated and strongly influenced by the behavior of peers, siblings, and parents. Processes such as identification and imitation perhaps explain expenditures in this category better than does the notion of individual choice (Wohlford 1970).[2]

All this suggests that the manner in which income is allocated across categories is largely nondiscretionary. This is not to say, however, that consumers make no decisions regarding this type of allocation. Clearly, choices could be made concerning the priorities by which needs will be satisfied and the proportion of income spent within each category. One way to estimate the extent of such decision making in household budget allocation is to ask if a plan exists within the household for distributing income. A unique survey of 300 Minnesota families representing three generations found that only seven percent of grandparents, 21 percent of parents, and 24 percent of married children reported such plans, and similar proportions claimed to use procedures

---

[2] Following experimental smoking during the "transition phase," those going on to become regular smokers (the "maintenance phase") apparently do so because they develop physiological and/or psychological dependence on cigarettes, and discontinuance becomes very difficult or impossible for most smokers.

for estimating expenses and setting specific amounts aside (Hill 1963, pp. 127–37).

The relatively few empirical studies of household budget allocation have sought to discover the comparative roles of family members (Ferber 1973) rather than the nature, incidence, and extent of the process itself. If joint participation by husband and wife, rather than control over the allocation by one spouse, is more likely to indicate conscious deliberation over alternatives, then evidence presented by Ferber and Lee (1974) that the "family financial officer" role tends to shift from joint to individual performance with increasing length of marriage seems to support the hypothesis advanced earlier by Kyrk (1953) that deliberation over household budgets declines over the life cycle.

GENERIC ALLOCATION

What, if any, type of decision process precedes the allocation of income within expenditure categories? Ferber summarizes studies showing that from 20 to 25 percent of durable goods and clothing purchases appear to be "impulsive," in that urgency or a special purchase opportunity displaced deliberation and prepurchase planning, or that satisfaction with the product being replaced reduced family discussion and planning (Ferber 1973, pp. 44–5). Up to 50 percent of supermarket purchases and 33 percent of transactions in variety stores and drugstores are "impulsive purchases." in that shoppers do not state intentions to buy these items in store-entrance interviews (Engel, Blackwell, and Kollat 1978, p. 483). Evidence from other studies (e.g., Wells and LoSciuto 1966) suggests that for certain grocery products decision processes do not occur in the store either.

Additional evidence relating to the existence of prepurchase processes within expenditure category comes from studies of the adoption and diffusion of innovations. A general finding from this research is that substantial differences exist across consumers in the amount of prepurchase deliberation that occurs. Rogers and Shoemaker's (1971) review shows that 12 of 14 studies of information seeking found that early adopters sought more information about the innovation than did later adopters (p. 374). Their review also shows considerable evidence that early adopters have significantly greater exposure to change agents, mass media, and interpersonal communication channels (pp. 371–4). This declining intensity of decision making is explained, at least in part, by the "diffusion effect," the increasing social pressure on nonadopters to adopt the innovation as the percentage of adopters increases. Further, Rogers and Shoemaker (1971, p. 122) and Robertson (1971, p. 61) acknowledge that evidence for the existence of "stages" in the adoption decision may be artifactual: both cite evidence that when unstructured questionnaires are used, certain stages are skipped or in some cases no decision process occurs.

Contemporary consumer researchers often overlook differences in the cognitive and motivational patterns associated with the many products and services involved in consumption. An early attempt to categorize these differences recognized products that are primarily hedonic (appealing to the senses), those with important symbolic meaning (ego-involving), and a third category valued primarily in terms of their functional performance (Woods 1961). While many generic products have two or even all three dimensions, prepurchase choice processes are most likely when functional performance dominates.

Sensory preferences are often well established in early childhood, although these may change somewhat with maturation, e.g., increasing preferences for salty and sharp flavors as children enter the teen years (Reynolds and Wells 1977, p. 83). Likes and dislikes for certain tastes, because of their early origins, may be reflected in consumption patterns without deliberation or even awareness by the consumer. Symbolic aspects of products are also often learned in childhood. Moore (1957) points out that eating, like other physiological activities, is especially prone to symbolic elaboration, perhaps because these activities "reach back into infancy, and are complexly patterned long before there is any autonomous intelligence or maturity with which to perceive the difference between the act itself and its accompanying feelings, social circumstances, contradictions, and coincidental motives" (Moore 1957, p. 77). One study of five-, seven-, and nine-year-olds found:

> Children apparently begin assigning social values to goods around age seven, particularly to elaborate toys. Nine-year-olds also are slightly fashion conscious in the sense that they may express a desire for certain articles of clothing being worn by other children, for example, tennis shoes and skirts . . . Children involve themselves considerably with some durable goods. In discussing automobiles with them, it was found that practically all of them have preferences for certain autos. . .
> (McNeal 1969, pp. 263, 265).

These examples suggest that better understanding of the processes leading to early childhood acquisition of taste preferences and symbolic interpretations of products may be more relevant for understanding preferences for "hedonic" and "symbolic" products than research structured on models of choice and decision.

Finally, in many instances consumers have no control over the specific products and services they purchase or consume. In the extreme case, consumers who are institutionalized (e.g., in hospitals, rest homes, or military institutions) typically have little or no control over the type of food, clothing, or furnishings they use. College students who live in dormitories and fraternities are similarly constrained. Apartment dwellers, and in many cases even home buyers, have little control over such items as fixtures, appliances, and floor coverings.

STORE PATRONAGE

Analysis of the spatial environment within which most consumers obtain goods and services reveals the potential relevance of choice models in portraying shopping and store patronage behavior. Consumers often find desired products and services to be available in two or more cities or towns within reasonable driving distance, or in numerous local shopping centers or areas, scattered retail outlets, and so forth. Catalogs, mail order, door-to-door sales organizations, telephone ordering services, etc., further expand the range of possible sources. A review of studies on shopping and patronage suggests, however, that extended search and evaluation typically does not precede store patronage (Granbois 1977).

Use of Nonstore Sources

While nonstore shopping sources are important in most product categories, studies of their use have revealed considerable city-to-city variation. One study found high users of mail order also to be high telephone order users; another found heavy in-home buyers also to be active store shoppers. Several studies have found distinctive socioeconomic characteristics associated with heavy use of these modes (Granbois 1977, p. 270). All the

findings suggest that a significant subset of all consumers may not even consider sources other than the conventional retail outlets.

Patronage of Urban Areas/Shopping Centers

Patronage of shopping areas tends to vary directly with assortment size and inversely with distance or effort involved in reaching them. Studies of patronage have firmly established the broad predictive usefulness of simple formal models establishing these relationships. Recent research, however, points to exceptions to, and constraints on, the patterns predicted by these models. For example, attention has been given to the impact of physical barriers, differential behavior of consumers with varying socioeconomic characteristics, and the impact of differing levels of promotion and price differences (Granbois 1977). The existence of limitations on the range of alternative shopping areas is further supported by the findings of "outshopping" studies, seeking determinants of shopping trips to nearby cities. Two studies found distinctive profiles of outshoppers with regard to variables such as income, age, race, sex, and beliefs, suggesting this pattern to be limited to certain market segments (Granbois 1977, p. 287).

Patronage Among and Within Store Types

Studies of shopping activity preceding major durable goods purchases have typically found a high incidence of purchases occurring after a single store visit, despite the fact that the high dollar value, physical complexity, relatively low purchase frequency, and the presence of a significant proportion of first-time purchasers in the samples would seem to indicate more extensive consideration of alternative outlets. The following data illustrate this finding (Granbois 1977, p. 264):

Type of purchase	Percent of buyers reporting a single store visit
Black and white television	39
Color television	50
Furniture	22
Carpet	27

Similar studies of soft goods purchases reveal that 75–80 percent of all purchases are made after visiting a single store (Granbois 1977, p. 266).

Deliberation and true choice might be expected to be at a maximum among residents new to an area. Nevertheless, such studies have consistently found that convenience and past loyalty to chains in the previous area are important criteria in making selections, and that new patterns are established quickly—supermarkets selected within three weeks, several other store types picked within five weeks (Granbois 1977, p. 272). These and other results indicate a less-than-full evaluation of alternatives. One study of supermarket shoppers using retrospective accounts of store selection found that nine percent of the sample reported to have made no choice; patronage occurred instead on bases such as personal recommendations or preferences acquired in early childhood (Olshavsky and MacKay 1978).

As in the case of generic product preferences, store preferences developed at an early age may serve as constraints on the range of choice alternatives considered by adults. Evidence of this pattern was also found by McNeal, who writes: "Starting as early as age five children show likes and dislikes for certain stores as well as specific types of stores" (McNeal 1969, p. 263).

BRAND PURCHASE

How does brand purchase occur? In his review of research on prepurchase information seeking, Newman (1977) found little evidence of extensive search and some evidence that no search or evaluation occurred in many instances. On sources of information, Newman reports that:

One survey found that one-third of the buyers of major appliances received information from only one source . . . A more recent survey found that 15 percent of the buyers of major appliances and automobiles consulted no external source before buying . . . In both surveys source referred to a type or category such as friends and neighbors; books, pamphlets and articles; advertising; and retail outlets . . . A survey of small electrical appliance buyers found that 10 percent of them could not recall obtaining helpful information in any way other than by visiting a retail store (p. 80).

On number of alternatives considered, Newman writes:

Several studies have shown that many consumers limit their attention to few alternatives. Forty-six percent of the buyers of major household appliances considered only one price range . . . appliance buyers who examined only one brand ranged from 41 percent for refrigerators to 71 percent for vacuum cleaners . . . of the buyers of household appliances and cars, 47 percent considered mainly a single brand at the outset of the decision process . . . These findings are consistent with other evidence that the buyer's "evoked set" of brands . . . is typically small (p. 81).

Finally, with respect to results based on studies that developed a comprehensive index of information seeking, Newman states:

Using a scale ranging from one for no information seeking to six for very active search, Katona and Mueller reported that 40 percent of the buyers of major appliances had scale values of one or two while 10 percent had values of five or six. . . The results led Katona and Mueller to conclude that 'Any notion that careful planning and choosing, thorough consideration of alternatives, and information seeking accompanied every major purchase was contradicted by the data . . . Rather, it appeared . . . that many purchases were made in a state of ignorance or at least indifference.' In another study of major appliances and automobiles, on a 20-point scale representing out-of-store search (zero meaning none), 49 percent had scores of 5 or less; 38 percent scored from 6 to 11; and 13 percent had scores of 12 to 20 (p. 82).

There are only a few direct studies of the brand choice process, each with strong limitations. Wells and LoSciuto (1966) using an in-store, on-the-spot technique, observed 1,500 supermarket shoppers. Only representative data for cereals, candy, and detergent were presented. In 55 percent of the cases for cereals, 38 percent for candy, and 72 percent for detergent, there was no visible evidence of an in-store prepurchase choice process, such as inspecting two or more packages. In 15 percent of the cases for cereal, 44 percent candy, and 12 percent for detergent, no purchase occurred. Hence, according to these data, in only 30 percent of the cereal, 18 percent of the candy, and 12 percent of the detergent purchases was there even the possibility that an in-store prepurchase process occurred. Unfortunately, the technique used could not observe the mental processes; strong conclusions about the choice process, therefore, cannot be drawn from this study.

In another study of supermarket shoppers (Bettman 1970), a "process tracing" technique was used, which was more likely to reveal any choice processes that occurred. For a period of six to eight weeks, Bettman observed the shopping behavior of two homemakers and asked them to think aloud as they made their purchases. He analyzed these protocol data to obtain insights about the evaluative criteria and evaluation processes used. A similar study of women's ready-to-wear clothing was performed by Alexis, Haines, and Simon (1968).

While these and other studies using process tracing techniques generally find evidence for prepurchase process, the techniques are inherently biased; as Bettman and Zins (1977) point out:

> A second bias in the protocols occurs because the consumer is asked to give protocols for choices where in many cases a great deal of learning has already occurred . . . the consumer may have bought the same brand many times, and may not really think much about this type of choice while it is being made. The request from the experimenter to keep talking may then lead to retrospection about why the particular brand was bought in the first place, although such reasoning is not relevant now (p. 82).

In another study of in-store behavior, Olshavsky (1973) analyzed tape recorded conversations between customer and salesman for major appliance transactions, without the customer being aware of the recording. This study provided clear evidence of at least a limited amount of prepurchase processes. At the same time, however, in some cases customers relied entirely upon the salesman's recommendation.

Other studies provide more direct evidence concerning the way brand purchases occur without prior consideration of alternatives. Several studies document that consumers make purchases on the basis of recommendations from either personal or nonpersonal sources. Feldman and Spencer (1965) reported that 75 percent of newcomers to a community selected a physician solely on the basis of a recommendation. Some studies have indicated that brand purchase behavior represents conformity to group norms; this occurs particularly for highly conspicuous products. Venkatesan (1968) demonstrated in a laboratory study the influence of group pressure on selection of men's suits. Also, some evidence suggests that brand preferences are acquired early in life, as part of the general acculturation process (Ward 1974). It has even been found that brand purchases are influenced by such superficial factors as shelf height and shelf facings (Frank and Massy 1970).

Finally, there is some evidence that brand purchases are made on the basis of surrogates or indices of quality, rather than on the basis of a direct evaluation of the brands' attributes. Price, manufacturer's reputation, and packaging are but a few of the indices studied (Monroe 1973; Gardner 1971; McConnell 1968; Brown 1958).

CONCLUSIONS AND IMPLICATIONS

Our review of studies that provide some evidence, direct or indirect, for the existence of prepurchase processes and our analysis of the constraints and influences on purchasing behavior suggest that Kassarjian is right. A significant proportion of purchases may not be preceded by a decision process. This conclusion does not simply restate the familiar observation that purchase behavior rapidly becomes habitual, with little or no prepurchase processes occurring after the first few purchases. We conclude that for many purchases a decision process never occurs, not even on the first purchase.

How then does purchasing occur if not as a result of some type of decision process? This review identified a number of different ways: Purchases can occur out of necessity; they can be derived from culturally-mandated lifestyles or from interlocked purchases; they can reflect preferences acquired in early childhood; they can result from simple conformity to group norms or from imitation of others; purchases can be made exclusively on recommendations from personal or nonpersonal sources; they can be made on the basis of surrogates of various types; or they can even occur on a random or superficial basis. Further research, free of the prepurchase decision assumption, may identify still other ways.

Another conclusion we draw from this review is that even when purchase behavior is preceded by a choice process, it is likely to be very limited. It typically involves the evaluation of few alternatives, little external search, few evaluative criteria, and simple evaluation process models. There is little evidence that consumers engage in the very extended type of search and evaluation a product testing organization like Consumers Union performs routinely.[3]

It would be an oversimplification, however, to characterize purchasing behavior as either involving predecision processes or not. While this may be an accurate characterization of some purchases, in general, we should allow for combination or "hybrid" strategies whereby choice and nonchoice are used; e.g., personal recommendations can be combined in various ways with limited search and evaluation. Indeed, future research may reveal that such hybrid strategies are the most common type of prepurchase behavior.

These conclusions have important implications for theories of consumer behavior. Certainly any theory whose central thesis is that purchases are preceded by a decision process (Engel, Blackwell, and Kollat 1978; Howard and Sheth 1969) can provide an adequate explanation of only certain types of consumer

---

[3] This is not to imply that consumers who use *Consumer Reports* could not engage in extensive evaluation of the data presented, but that they do not gather such data themselves. Indeed, in most cases, this cannot be done by the typical consumer because of the time, effort, expense, or expertise involved.

purchasing behaviors. Theory needs to be developed along at least two separate lines. Wright has argued that a process he calls "affect referral" often describes purchases. Global measures of affect, not attribute-specific information, provide the basis for choice, where either the "best" or the "first acceptable" option thought of is selected (Wright 1976). This first line of development will be particularly fruitful if it entails low involvement learning as part of an ongoing socialization process.

The second line of development is suggested by the work of Lussier and Olshavsky (1974), Payne (1976), and others who have argued for a contingent processing view of decision making. Payne, for example, points out that the various choice strategies (e.g., additive difference, conjunctive, and elimination-by-aspects) are not competing, but complementary.

> In that regard, the four decision processes discussed in this paper might be conceptualized as different sub-routines in a general choice program. The control conditions under which one of these sets of processes might be called would then seem to depend, at least in part, on the characteristics of the decision problem. In that respect, the less cognitively demanding decision procedures, conjunctive and elimination-by-aspects, might be called early in the decision process as a way of simplifying the decision task by quickly eliminating alternatives until only a few alternatives remained as choice possibilities. The subject might then employ one of the cognitively demanding choice procedures, e.g., additive difference model, to make the final evaluation and choice (Payne 1976, p. 385).

This contingent processing concept needs to be broadened to incorporate other purchasing heuristics of the type identified here, e.g., conformity, imitation, recommendations.

In view of the tremendous interest in consumer purchasing behavior it is surprising, to say the least, that there have been so few studies of prepurchase processes that involve actual consumers in actual settings using methodologies that permit observation of behaviors contrary to those predicted by models of choice and decision processes. Such research is fraught with difficulties that must be overcome if we are to have a secure empirical foundation for theory construction and testing.

These conclusions also have implications for private and public policy. Clearly, if some purchases are not preceded by any type of prior search and evaluation, then recommendations based on research that incorporates the assumption that they are may be inappropriate. The issue of "information overload," for instance, which has occupied so many pages in marketing journals recently, must be interpreted quite differently if a significant percentage of consumers of particular products or services do not engage in prepurchase activities.

REFERENCES

Adult Use of Tobacco-1975 (1976), U. S. Department of Health, Education, and Welfare, Public Health Service, Center for Disease Control, National Clearinghouse for Smoking and Health.

Alexis, Marcus, Haines, George H., and Simon, Leonard (1968), "Consumer Information Processing: The Case of Women's Clothing," in *Proceedings,* Chicago: American Marketing Association, pp. 197–205.

Bettman, James R. (1970), "Information Processing Models of Consumer Behavior," *Journal of Marketing Research,* 7, 370–6.

———. Capon, Noel, and Lutz, Richard (1975), "Cognitive Algebra in Multiattribute Attitude Models," *Journal of Marketing Research,* 12, 151–164.

———, and Kakkar, Pradeep (1977), "Effects of Information Presentation Format on Consumer Information Acquisition Strategy," *Journal of Consumer Research,* 3, 233–40.

———, and Zins, Michel A. (1977), "Constructive Process in Consumer Choice," *Journal of Consumer Research,* 4, 75–85.

Brown, Robert L. (1958), "Wrapper Influence on the Perception of Freshness in Bread," *Journal of Applied Psychology,* 42, 257–60.

Engel, James F., Blackwell, Roger D., and Kollat, David T. (1978), *Consumer Behavior,* Hinsdale, IL: The Dryden Press.

Feldman, Sidney P., and Spencer, Merlin C., (1965), "The Effect of Personal Influence in the Selection of Consumer Services," in *Marketing and Economic Development,* ed. Peter Bennett, Chicago: American Marketing Association, pp. 440–52.

Ferber, Robert (1973), "Family Decision Making and Economic Behavior: A Review." in *Family Economic Behavior: Problems and Prospects,* ed. Eleanor B. Sheldon, Philadelphia: Lippincott, pp. 29–61.

———, and Lee, Lucy Chao (1974), "Husband-Wife Influence in Family Purchasing Behavior," *Journal of Consumer Research,* 1, 43–50.

Frank, Ronald E., and Massy, William F. (1970), "Shelf Position and Space Effects," *Journal of Marketing Research,* 7, 59–66.

Gardner, David M. (1971). "Is There a Generalized Price-Quality Relationship?" *Journal of Marketing Research,* 8, 241–3.

Granbois, Donald H. (1977). "Shopping Behavior and Preferences," in *Selected Aspects of Consumer Behavior—A Summary from the Perspective of Different Disciplines,* Washington, D.C.: U.S. Government Printing Office, pp. 259–98.

Gredal, Karen (1966). "Purchasing Behavior in Households," in *Readings in Danish Theory of Marketing,* ed. Max Kjaer-Hansen, Copenhagen: Einar Harcks Forlag, pp. 84–100.

Green, Paul E., and Wind, Yoram (1973), *Multiattribute Decisions in Marketing,* Hinsdale, IL: The Dryden Press.

Hill, Reuben (1963). "Judgment and Consumership in the Management of Family Resources." *Sociology and Social Research,* 47, 460–6.

Howard, John A. (1977), *Consumer Behavior: Application of Theory,* New York: McGraw-Hill Book Company.

———, and Sheth, Jagdish N. (1969). *The Theory of Buyer Behavior,* New York: John Wiley & Sons, Inc.

Jacoby, Jacob, Szybillo, George J., and Busato-Schach. Jacqueline (1977). "Information Acquisition Behavior in Brand Choice Situations." *Journal of Consumer Research,* 3, 209–16.

Kassarjian, Harold H. (1978). "Presidential Address, 1977: Anthropomorphism and Parsimony." in *Advances in Consumer Research, Vol. 5,* ed. H. Keith Hunt, Ann Arbor, MI: Association for Consumer Research, pp. xii–xiv.

Kollat, David T., and Willett, Ronald P. (1967), "Customer Impulse Purchasing Behavior," *Journal of Marketing Research,* 21–31.

Kyrk, Hazel (1953). *The Family in the American Economy,* Chicago: University of Chicago Press.

Lawton, M. P. (1962). "Psychosocial Aspects of Cigarette Smoking," *Journal of Health and Human Behavior,* 3, 163–70.

Lussier, Denis A., and Olshavsky, Richard W. (1974), "An Information Processing Approach to Individual Brand Choice Behavior," paper presented at the ORSA/TIMS Joint National Meeting, San Juan, Puerto Rico.

McConnell, J. Douglas (1968), "The Development of Brand Loyalty: An Experimental Study," *Journal of Marketing Research,* 5, 13–9.

McNeal, James U. (1969). "An Exploratory Study of the Consumer Behavior of Children," in *Dimensions of Consumer Behavior,* ed. James U. McNeal, New York: Appleton-Century-Crofts, 255–75.

Monroe, Kent B. (1973), "Buyers' Subjective Perceptions of Price," *Journal of Marketing Research,* 10, 70–80.

Moore, Harriet (1957), "The Meaning of Foods," *The American Journal of Clinical Nutrition,* 5, 77–82.

Newman, Joseph W. (1977). "Consumer External Search: Amount and Determinants," in *Consumer and Industrial Buying Behavior,* eds. Arch G. Woodside, Jagdish N. Sheth, and Peter D. Bennett, New York: North-Holland Publishing Co.

Ölander, Folke, and Seipel, Carl-Magnus (1970), *Psychological Approaches to the Study of Saving,* Urbana, IL: Bureau of Economics and Business Research, University of Illinois.

Olshavsky, Richard W. (1973). "Customer-Salesman Interaction in Appliance Retailing,'' *Journal of Marketing Research,* 10. 208–12.

————, and MacKay, David B. (1978). ''An Empirical Test of Four Alternative Supermarket Choice Models,'' unpublished working paper, Indiana University, Department of Marketing.

Payne, John W. (1976). ''Task Complexity and Contingent Processing in Decision Making: An Information Search and Protocol Analysis.'' *Organizational Behavior and Human Performance,* 16, 366–87.

van Raaij, W. Fred (1977). ''Consumer Information Processing for Different Information Structures and Formats,'' in *Advances in Consumer Research, Vol. 4,* ed. William O. Perreault, pp. 176–84.

Reynolds, Fred D., and Wells, William D. (1977). *Consumer Behavior,* New York: McGraw-Hill.

Riesman, David, and Roseborough, Howard (1955), ''Careers and Consumer Behavior,'' in *The Life Cycle and Consumer Behavior, Vol. 2,* ed. Lincoln Clark, New York: New York University Press, pp. 1–18.

Robertson, Thomas S. (1971), *Innovative Behavior and Communication,* New York: Holt, Rinehart, and Winston.

Rogers, Everett M., and Shoemaker, F. Floyd (1971), *Communication of Innovations,* New York: The Free Press.

Russ, Frederick A. (1971). ''Evaluation Process Models and the Prediction of Preference,'' in *Proceedings,* Association for Consumer Research, ed. David M. Gardner, pp. 256–61.

Russo, Edward J., and Rosen, Larry D. (1975), ''An Eye Fixation Analysis of Multi-Attribute Choice,'' *Memory and Cognition,* 3, 267–76.

Scott, Jerome E. and Peter Wright (1976), ''Modeling an Organizational Buyer's Product Evaluation Strategy: Validity and Procedural Considerations.'' *Journal of Marketing Research,* 13, 211–24.

Teenage Smoking, National Patterns of Cigarette Smoking, Ages 12 through 18, in 1972 and 1974, (1976), U.S. Department of Health, Education, and Welfare, Public Health Service, National Institute of Health.

Venkatesan, M. (1966), ''Experimental Study of Consumer Behavior Conformity and Independence,'' *Journal of Marketing Research,* 3, 384–7.

Ward, Scott (1974), ''Consumer Socialization,'' *Journal of Consumer Research,* 1, September, 1–14.

Wells, William, and LoSciuto, Leonard A. (1966), ''Direct Observation of Purchasing Behavior,'' *Journal of Marketing Research,* 3, 227–33.

Wohlford, Paul (1970), ''Initiation of Cigarette Smoking: Is it Related to Parental Smoking Behavior?'' *Journal of Consulting and Clinical Psychology,* 34, 148–51.

Woods, Walter A. (1960), ''Psychological Dimensions of Consumer Decision,'' *Journal of Marketing,* 24, 15–9.

Wright, Peter (1976), ''An Adaptive Consumer's View of Attitudes and Other Choice Mechanisms, as Viewed by an Equally Adaptive Advertiser,'' in *Attitude Research at Bay,* eds. Deborah Johnson and William D. Wells, Chicago: American Marketing Association, pp. 113–31.

Questions

1. The authors have concluded that a large proportion of purchases are not preceded by any type of prior search and evaluation. Do you agree? Why or why not?

2. If indeed there is no prepurchase search and evaluation, what is your opinion about the importance of advertising those particular products?

3. Under what circumstances is a consumer limited to only a single alternative in the search and evaluation of products?

25. Consumer Behavior as Risk Taking

Raymond A. Bauer

One of the fads in discussions of marketing research is to say that the field of marketing research has been marked by fads. Thus, we have become accustomed to the statement: "Last year it was Motivation Research; this year it's Operations Research; I wonder what it will be next year." Seldom is any such new emphasis a radical departure from the past. At least there is always a handful of protesting orthodox practitioners to exclaim: "-but we've been doing it all along." Operations Research, properly speaking, probably should be considered as concerned with simulation as much as with experimentation. But most of the operations research work I have seen in market research uses experimentation rather than simulation, and in this is continuous with traditional, albeit rare, well-executed experiments in marketing research. These new approaches are characterized by a distinctive concentration of attention on particular variables, concepts or techniques. After their potential has been pretty well explored and developed they get absorbed into the general body of research knowledge and technique, usually after having generated a few healthy antibodies.

I make these general remarks about fads in marketing research because I am about to make a modest effort to start a new one. However, if I am to be as modest as my effort I should also state that I have neither confidence nor anxiety that my proposal will cause any major stir. At most, it is to be hoped that it will attract the attention of a few researchers and practitioners and at least survive through infancy. The proposal is that we look at consumer behavior as an instance of risk taking.

We are accustomed to use the term "consumer decision making." Yet, there has been little concentration of research on the element of risk taking that is as characteristic of consumer behavior as it is of all decision-making. A conspicuous exception is the work of Katona and Mueller on prepurchase deliberation. They found, when buying durable goods, that middle-income people deliberated more than either lower- or upper-income people. When buying sport shirts, lower-income people deliberated most.

Consumer behavior involves risk in the sense that any action of a consumer will produce consequences which he cannot anticipate with anything approximating certainty, and some of which at least are likely to be unpleasant. At the very least, any one purchase competes for the consumer's financial resources with a vast array of alternate uses of that money. The man who buys a pint of whiskey today does not know to what degree he prejudices his son's college education 20 years hence. But, he risks more than alternate purchases. Unfortunate consumer decisions have cost men frustration and blisters, their self-esteem and the esteem of others, their wives, their jobs, and even their lives. Nor is the problem of calculation of consequences a trivial one. It is inconceivable that the consumer can consider more than a few of the possible consequences of his actions, and it is seldom that he can anticipate even these few consequences with a high degree of certainty. When it comes to the purchase of large ticket items the perception of the risk can become traumatic. Paul Lazarsfeld tells me that certain unpublished data show that the prospective automobile buyer often goes into a state of virtual panic as he reaches the point of decision, and rushes into his purchase as an escape from the enormity of the problem.

If I may now anticipate what is on your minds, I suspect that about at this point you are saying to yourselves that I have painted an unrealistic picture of the consumer. He simply does not in most instances stand about trying to calculate probabilities and consequences nor is he overtaken by anxiety. True, these things happen on occasion, and particularly on big ticket items, but only in rare instances does the consumer appear to tackle these problems as "'risk taking."

If these objections are on your mind, I agree with them. The consumer who consistently tried to act like the classical "rational man" would quickly sink into inaction. This, in fact, is precisely what I would like to stress. Consumers characteristically develop decision strategies and ways of reducing risk that enable them to act with relative confidence and ease in situations where their information is inadequate and the consequences of their actions are in some meaningful sense incalculable. (When I say "in some meaningful sense incalculable," I mean that not only can the outcomes not be anticipated reliably, but the consequences may be drastic.)

Up to now, what I have had to say has been abstract and general. Therefore, for the next few minutes I would like to move back to familiar ground and argue that many of the phenomena with which we habitually deal have a strong bearing on the problem of "risk taking." I am not going to contend that risk taking is the only thing involved in these phenomena, but rather that it is a common thread which runs through them and is worth pulling out for inspection.

One of our traditional problems is that of brand loyalty. Brand loyalty may involve a number of considerations. In recent years we have heard stressed the compatibility of the brand image with one's self-image, or with the norms of one's reference group. Brand loyalty is also seen as a means of economizing of decision effort by substituting habit for repeated, deliberate, decisions. Without for a moment minimizing such considerations, I would like to reintroduce the old-fashioned concept of "reliability." Much brand loyalty is a device for reducing the risks of consumer decisions. I am told that sugar is one product for which it has traditionally been difficult to develop brand loyalty. But my friend Edward Bursk tells me that when he was a salesman in Lancaster, Pennsylvania, there was a strong loyalty to a particular brand of sugar. The Pennsylvania Dutch housewives of that area are avid and proud bakers and there is more risk involved in making a cake than in sweetening a cup of coffee or a bowl of cereal. Suppose we were to limit ourselves to small ticket items, and to interview a sample of housewives as to the risks—that is a combination of uncertainty plus seriousness of outcome involved—associated with each category of product. I would predict a strong correlation between degree of risk and brand loyalty.

The recently popular phrase that advertising gives "added value" to a product also bears on the question of risk taking. The "added value" of advertising has usually been discussed in terms of the satisfaction of consumer motives that extend beyond the primary function of the product. It is perhaps worth recalling that one of the customer's motives is to have a feeling of confidence in the product he buys. Some, but not all, consumers are willing to pay added money for added confidence. Others prefer to read "Consumer Reports" in the hope that some obscure, unadvertised, low-priced brand will be rated a best buy. And, it is worth recalling, there are still other consumers in whom advertising does not generate confidence but rather the suspicion that it is added, worthless cost.

Now, relating the questions of brand loyalty and the "added value" of advertising to risk taking, or its reciprocal "confidence," is scarcely a radical departure from tradition. This must be the working assumption of every competent marketing practitioner. It is instructive, however, to note how little this relationship has been exploited as a research problem. We know that some people are inclined to favor advertised brands in some categories, and that other people will consistently buy the cheapest product in these same categories. This is about the level on which our knowledge rests. It is my suspicion that our recent concern with the prestige element of advertising and well known brands has deflected our attention from the problem of risk taking even when it was right under our nose.

Another recently popular area of concern where the problem of risk taking has been obscured is the phenomenon known as "personal influence." There are exceptions to what I am about to say, but *in general* discussions of personal influence on consumer behavior have been couched in terms that suggest only that opinion leaders are followed because they are style setters and that the follower wants to accrue to himself the prestige of behaving like the pace setters. Seldom is the fact made explicit that one of the very important functions of opinion leaders is to reduce the perceived risk of the behavior in question.

The work of Katz, Menzel, and Coleman on physicians' adoption of a new drug is very pertinent. They found that the doctors they studied tended to follow the lead of respected colleagues *early* in the life history of the drug

when adequate information was lacking. Once the drug became sufficiently well established, personal influence no longer played a role. The period of risk was passed.

I have seen data on related products that reenforce the notion that the Katz, Menzel, Coleman findings are related to risk taking. We studied two types of products in the same general product category. We were interested in whether the probability of trial of a product and subsequent preference for that product, was influenced by preference for one or another of the companies, or by preference for the salesmen of the various companies. For these particular types of products we confirmed the findings of the drug studies. Both company and salesman preference were more strongly correlated with product trial and preference in the newer products in the general line. That is to say, apparently both company *and* salesmen preference had more influence when product was new and relatively unknown.

However, if I may be permitted some freedom of assumptions and inference, and a certain amount of liberty in filtering out the noise in the data, there were some findings that bore in a more interesting fashion on the problem of personal influence and risk taking. Let me start with some assumptions about the difference between company preference and salesman preference. Relative to each other, company preference is more associated with risk reduction, and salesman preference more with personal influence in the sense of "compliance," of one person "going along" with someone whom he likes. The company is a relatively impersonal entity, and the main function of its reputation is in this instance to guarantee the quality of the product. The salesman, to some extent, also guarantees quality. However, he also exploits his strictly personal relationships to the buyer. Thus we have personal influence operating in two ways, to produce compliance, and to reduce risk. Compliance is relatively more associated with salesman preference, and risk reduction with company preference.

If you accept the above assumptions as reasonable, then certain findings are quite interesting. You will remember that I said we studied two product types. These product types differed as to the degree of risk associated with them. Product type A was by common consent risky. Product type B was safe. In the case of product type A, the risky type of product, the relationship of company preference to product preference was twice as strong as the "effect" (in quotes) of salesman preference. In the case of product type B, the "effect" of company and salesman preference was just about equal. My interpretation of these findings is that when risk was high, the risk relevant factor of company image was the dominant source of influence, and that when risk was low, "personal influence" in the sense of compliance played a relatively more prominent role.

In addition to "personal influence" we have recently been concerned with the effect of "group influence" on consumer behavior. We have heard a great deal in the past few years about the fact that consumers judge their behavior by the standards of groups with whom they identify themselves, or—although this is seldom dealt with—from whom they dissociate themselves. This has been treated predominantly like the classical "keeping up with the Jones." The consumer looks to his reference groups for cues as to the type of consumption that is valued by people whose esteem he in turn values. "But, dahling, everybody, but everybody, knows Wente Brothers' chablis is the best California chablis!"

In his recent work, "Sociological Reflection on Business," Lazarsfeld suggests that group influence will be stronger in those instances in which the wisdom of one's decision is difficult to assess. Interpreted in one way, this suggestion could lead us to the popular notion that when the primary functions of a product are hard to assess, or when all products in a category work equally well, then "secondary attributes" such as group approval come to the fore. Under this interpretation the influence of the group is to get the consumer to pay attention to different attributes of the product. It is equally plausible that in many instances the function of group influence is to reduce perceived risk by confirming the wisdom of the choice. That is to say, the individual may already share the values of his group and agree on the desirability of a given type of purchase but look to the group for guidance as to what is a wise purchase. By a "wise" purchase, I mean one that is likely to satisfy the values for which it is made. In other words, we not only look to our reference groups for standards of values, but on occasion we also use the judgment of the people around us as an informal "Consumer Report." This is what the psychological student of cognition would call "consensual validation." Lacking any sound basis of judgment, we accept the judgment of others.

A final traditional problem worth considering in terms of risk taking is impulse buying, or perhaps we might prefer the label of "prepurchase deliberation." A simple economic approach to impulse buying would suggest that it should increase as a function of the discretionary funds available to the consumer. This would be consistent with Katona and Mueller's finding that the amount of deliberation involved in buying sport shirts was inverse to the consumer's income. Yet, a number of studies show that in many instances the middle-class consumer is more given to deliberation than is the lower-class consumer. When we compare the middle- and lower-class consumers something more than economics simply considered seems to be involved. We speak of the tendency of the middle-class person to plan over a longer period and of various other aspects of middle-class and lower-class culture. Not for a moment would I want to underplay the importance of such cultural factors. However, it is worthwhile to think of the fact that the middle-class person has both a greater possibility of planning and a greater reason to plan. He has more of an investment in career, reputation, and accumulated property to risk if he gets into serious financial difficulty. The lower-class person has less to risk in terms of such long-run investments. Perhaps more pertinently it is more difficult for him to calculate the consequences of his actions because among other things he is likely to have less information. He is also less likely to have time for deliberation, because, as Katona and Mueller found with respect to durable goods, people of lower income are more likely to make a purchase in a situation where the product to be replaced has already broken down.

So that I may not seem to be arguing against a cultural interpretation, let me say simply that the lower-class consumer seems more prone to a decision strategy based on the assumption that the consequences of one's behavior are essentially incalculable in any event, so one may as well take a plunge and do what seems immediately desirable.

My argument to this point has been that the issue of risk taking is readily seen as an integral part of many familiar phenomena of consumer behavior. This is by no means surprising, and is probably novel only in the degree that I have stressed the fact of risk taking. What will be of more interest will be to understand with more elaboration the devices

through which consumers handle the problem of risk. In effect I have suggested mainly one device, namely reliance on some outside source for guidance, whether that outside source be the reputation of the manufacturer or product, an opinion leader or a reference group. This can scarcely exhaust the means that consumers employ to reduce perceived risk, nor does it tell us how the consumer decides where to place his confidence. The discussion of lower- *v.* middle-class deliberation in purchases of durable goods suggests an additional mechanism of reducing perceived risk, namely, to suppress the possible consequences from consciousness and rush through the process with rapidity. This is no more than a caricature of what we all do at times.

It should be noted that I have carefully said "perceived risk" whenever I referred to risk reduction. This is because the individual can respond to and deal with risk only as he perceives it subjectively. If risk exists in the "real world" and the individual does not perceive it, he cannot be influenced by it. On the other hand, he may reduce "perceived risk" by means which have no effect on affairs in the real world. Thus, if he reads advertisements favoring an automobile he has just bought, he may console himself on the wisdom of his action, but he does not reduce the objective probability of the muffler falling off.

Close study will probably reveal a wide range of decision rules which consumers invoke with regularity to reduce the perceived uncertainty involved in the outcome of their decisions. We are not totally oblivious to the existence of such rules. For example, there is a dying race of Americans who abide by the decision rule of not buying anything for which they cannot pay cash. A recent study shows that this is still a dominant decision rule for eating in restaurants. A majority of respondents thought it was improper to use credit cards for eating out, because "you should not eat out when you cannot afford it."[1] Other persons will buy products with plain and sensible design, fearing that surface aesthetics are designed to cover up bad workmanship and material. Some others will buy the most expensive product, and still others the cheapest product when both have equal amounts of money at their disposal. Such persons, for reasons about which we can only speculate, vary in the extent to which they are willing to pay money to minimize the risk of being disappointed in a product. There may be others who expect a certain rate of product failure as assurance that they are not wasting money on overly-engineered and con-structed products. It is doubtful that they will be joyful over the failure of any individual product, but they may persist in patronizing an outlet that features low prices and poor ser-vice. The shabbyness of the store and the rudeness of sales personnel may give further reassurance that one is not paying too much for what he buys.

A long list of such decision rules could probably be produced by the reader. However, I suspect that as ingenious as we all are, it is still worth turning to actual con-sumers to find out from them what their operating decision rules are. We may be in for some surprises. It is of course difficult for a consumer to articulate a notion such as a "decision rule." In an effort to get at such difficult-to-articulate notions, Donald Cox, one of our doctoral students, interviewed two consumers at very great length—an hour or two a week for several months—on their shopping habits. Many of the decision rules reported by these respondents were ones familiar to us. The following two, I suspect,

are not entirely familiar. One of the respondents favored shopping in small shops because she saw the proprietor or buyer as having reduced her range of decision by hav-ing reduced the number of brands among which she had to choose, and also as having weeded out the least preferable lines. The same consumer would look about to see if a store carried advertised brands. She used this as a means of legitimizing *the store*. Once hav-ing satisfied herself on this score, she was will-ing to buy off-brands from this same store. The novelty of individual decision rules is not so important as the fact that the decision rules of each of these subjects appeared to form coherent but contrasting strategies for stabilizing the uncertain world of shopping. Both of these young women could be charac-terized as highly conscious of the risk involved in shopping. But one regularly relied on exter-nal sources of reassurance, while the other was extremely energetic in seeking out infor-mation and attempting to achieve the guise of rationality. We plan to continue such ex-ploratory work with consumers. But in the meantime the problem of decision-making has been tackled in other quarters.

There has been a good deal of research on decision-making under conditions of uncer-tainty, but not much of this work can at this point be translated into terms useful for students of consumer behavior. The students of statistical decision theory have concen-trated on how decisions *ought* to be made. That is to say that the decision theorists have been concerned with the calculation of an op-timum decision within the framework of an explicitly defined limited set of conditions, rather than with how people habitually *do* make decisions in the real world. Experimen-tal psychological research on decision-mak-ing, on the other hand, has studied how peo-ple *do* make restricted types of decisions in a laboratory situation. Such research shows

[1] Study by Benson and Benson reported in *Wall Street Journal,* May 12, 1960.

minimally that problems of risk and uncertainty are handled variously by different people and under different conditions. Even though it is doubtful that any of these findings are directly applicable in the field of marketing, they have an important general implication for us by demonstrating that people do in fact evolve preferred decision rules even in situations much less complicated than that faced by the consumer on a day-to-day basis.

One body of work deserves our attention. Most of it is reported in Leon Festinger's book called *A Theory of Cognitive Dissonance.* Festinger and his associates have concentrated on the ways in which people reduce perceived risk *after* decisions are made. People will seek out information that confirms the wisdom of their decisions. Thus, people who have just bought an automobile tend preferentially to read ads in favor of the automobile they have bought. People will also perceive information in a way to reenforce their decision; smokers are less likely than non-smokers to believe that cigarettes cause lung cancer, and this relationship holds even after those people who stopped smoking,

because they believed in this relationship, were eliminated from the sample. People, finally, change their own attitudes to bolster their perception of the desirability of their actions. They have more favorable attitudes toward products after they have selected them than before they made the decision. Festinger has amassed considerable data to demonstrate that people do employ devices to reduce the perceived risk associated with consumer-type behavior.

Certain psychological research on problems of cognition also promises to be helpful. The book of Bruner, Goodnow, and Austin, *A Study of Thinking,* for example, deals with the way in which people develop decision strategies in handling situations of incomplete information.

The major reason for my remarks on the importance of the risk taking in consumer decision making is my conviction, frankly still in a somewhat less clear state than I would wish, that this is a fruitful area of research. It is my hope that others will suggest leads of which I am ignorant.

Questions

1. What does the author say is the relationship between consumer actions and perceived risk?
2. Define risk as it applies to consumer behavior.
3. How can a marketer assist in minimizing this risk?

26. Using Information Processing Theory to Design Marketing Strategies

Alice M. Tybout

Bobby J. Calder

Brian Sternthal

A common criticism of consumer behavior theories is that they have failed to make much impact on marketing practice. Perhaps this is because inquiry has focused on demonstrating the integrity of various theories rather than on their applicability in designing marketing strategies. As a result, theory is viewed as adding little insight not already provided by the marketer's intuitions about consumer behavior. A new approach, generally termed information processing theory, promises to be more useful to marketers. The research we report shows how information processing theory leads to strategies that go beyond those suggested by previous theory and marketing practitioners' intuition.

The purpose of our research is not to test information processing theory, but to demonstrate its usefulness. The former objective would require a rigorous attempt to falsify the predictions of the theory. The latter requires an evaluation of strategies designed on the basis of the theory. (See Calder, Phillips, and Tybout, forthcoming, for detailed elaboration of this distinction). Showing that the strategies evaluated are ineffective would not necessarily constitute evidence against the theory, for many other factors might be at work. Showing that the strategies evaluated are effective, however, would indicate the utility of the theory as a basis for strategy design. The logic of our research is thus to evaluate the effectiveness of two strategies based on information processing theory. To increase the strength of the evaluation, the strategies are compared with a more theoretically traditional and intuitive strategy.

THE MARKETING PROBLEM

The evaluation of marketing strategies presupposes a marketing problem. To increase the strength of our evaluation, we address a problem that has been intractable in marketing practice—rumors associating products with undesirable, and even bizarre, characteristics. In what is perhaps the best known case, the McDonald's fast food chain was rumored to be using red worm meat in its hamburgers. Although this rumor was not substantiated by fact, McDonald's sales were down by as much as 30% in the areas where the rumor circulated.[1]

To combat the worm rumor, McDonald's tried to refute it. Store managers posted a letter from the Secretary of Agriculture stating that "hamburger produced by these [McDon-

[1] The description of the rumor that McDonald's uses worms is adapted from Bob Greene's columns appearing in the *Chicago Tribune* in December 1978. Statements attributed to the Secretary of Agriculture and McDonald's personnel were originally quoted in Greene's column.

ald's] establishments is wholesome, properly identified, and in compliance with standards prescribed by Food Safety and Quality Service regulations." Television and print advertisements emphasizing "100% pure beef" were intensified. Public relations statements by McDonald's personnel noted, "It doesn't make sense, even from a financial viewpoint. Red worms cost between $5 and $8 a pound. Hamburger meat costs just over a dollar a pound. You'd have to be nuts to put worms in your hamburgers. You just couldn't afford it."

McDonald's strategy for combating the worm rumor was less than effective. As the advertising manager for McDonald's System of Ohio Incorporated observed, "It's [the refutation] not doing any good. The calls are still coming in. Business is still not back." The use of credible spokespeople and compelling evidence was not sufficient to dispel the worm rumor. McDonald's refutation may not have reached persons adversely affected by the worm rumor, or perhaps reached them but did not significantly affect their reaction to McDonald's. Regardless of the specific reason, refutation was unsuccessful in reversing the rumor effect.

McDonald's experience is no isolated phenomenon. A growing number of firms are faced with rumors linking their product to some undesirable attribute. During the last few years, for example, Gillette hairdryers were rumored to be made with asbestos, a carcinogen. Rumors have also circulated that Poprocks, a General Foods candy filled with carbon dioxide, caused children to explode when they consumed it in combination with soft drinks. These stories bear a striking resemblance to the McDonald's rumor. Although the rumors were not based on fact, they were threatening to sales.

Guidance in developing strategies to dispel rumors might be expected to emerge from the attitude change literature (e.g., Fishbein and Ajzen 1975). Fundamental to traditional attitude theory is the notion that attitude change is produced by a persuasive message which changes the beliefs a person holds. The theory identifies several variables, such as source credibility, that ought to cause persuasion. Yet this theory leads to just the strategy that seems ineffective in the McDonald's case. Presenting consumers with persuasive messages contradicting the belief produced by a rumor (in the case of McDonald's, that their hamburgers contain worms) does not seem to change their attitude. This ineffectiveness is particularly striking in that the beliefs being contradicted are not likely to be very strong. In theory, it should not be very difficult to persuade someone that hamburgers do not contain worms. The belief is so incredible to begin with that a credible communication and spokesperson should be able to change it easily.[2]

The failure of the persuasive refutation strategy also runs counter to common sense. Rumors of the McDonald's type seem intuitively implausible. McDonald's strategy was undoubtedly based on the common sense insight that it should be possible to change people's minds about the plausibility of worms, thereby restoring the former appeal of McDonald's.

THE INFORMATION PROCESSING STRATEGIES

Information processing theory explains consumer behavior in terms of cognitive opera-

[2] One might also look for guidance from the literature on rumors. Indeed, the number of investigations on rumors is substantial (see Rosnow and Fine 1976). However, these studies typically have a sociological perspective, and describe the genesis and circulation of rumors but not how to counteract them.

tions. Unlike previous theories, it is not limited to postulating subjective states (traits, attitudes, etc.) as causes of behavior. Information processing theory seeks a more mechanistic account. Behavior is a consequence of not only what people think about but how they think about it. According to the information processing view, incoming information is represented more or less faithfully in active memory. This information may stimulate the activation (called retrieval) of object-relevant thoughts that have been processed earlier. Because active memory is limited in capacity, information represented in active memory requires long-term storage if it is to be available for later use. Both incoming information and previously processed information represented in active memory can be stored by a process of rehearsal. Rehearsal involves the active association of attributes with an object. Storage of information is thought to be systematic. Information about a particular object is stored as associations with that object in one or more memory locations or addresses (see Bettman 1979 for a more detailed description of the theory).

Consider the marketing problem posed by the McDonald's rumor in terms of information processing theory. Individuals exposed to a rumor linking the object, McDonald's, to an attribute, worms, store this association in memory. Subsequent evaluation of the object requires retrieval of object-relevant thoughts from memory. Among the thoughts retrieved is the one produced by the rumor and possibly others related to the attribute specified by the rumor. Because these thoughts are less positive than those that would have been retrieved in the absence of the rumor, the evaluation of the object is less favorable. Consumers are affected because they process the rumor, not because they necessarily believe it.

The theory thus accounts for why the rumor has an impact even though it is so implausible. It also accounts for why a persuasive refutation strategy may be ineffective. Refutation increases rehearsal of the rumor and strengthens the stored association. Even if the refutation were completely persuasive, so that consumers retrieve the thought, "McDonald's hamburgers don't really contain worms," this thought is still less positive than other thoughts that might be retrieved in the absence of the refutation.

The critical aspect of the information processing view for our purposes, however, is that it readily suggests two strategies that might be effective. One can be referred to as a *storage strategy*. It requires introducing a second object at the time rumor information is stored. The presence of the second object is intended to foster the association of the rumor attribute with that object rather than with the object (McDonald's) initially specified in the rumor. Moreover, if the second object is positively evaluated by rumor recipients, some of this effect is likely to become associated with the rumor attribute (worms), making it less negative. Hence, even if the rumor attribute is still associated with the initial object (McDonald's), it will not have as adverse an effect on that object's evaluation as would be the case in the absence of the storage strategy.

The second strategy can be referred to as a *retrieval strategy*. It requires affecting information retrieval. The strategy is based on the notion that judicious choice of a stimulus will direct retrieval of thoughts in memory away from rumor-stimulated associations. Even if the new stimulus does not completely inhibit the retrieval of object-rumor attribute associations, it is likely to dilute these associations with other thoughts in active memory.

We evaluated the storage and retrieval

strategies in a laboratory setting, which enabled us to implement them in as pure a form as possible without interference from uncontrolled communication factors. Personal communication was used instead of media communication to reduce noise. Though this implementation of the strategies could not be used directly in marketing practice, it provides a strong test of whether the strategies work. In a more practically oriented evaluation, the strategies might fail for many reasons (e.g., insufficient exposure to an advertising message). In our test, the strategies can fail only because they are fundamentally unsound.

To provide a strong test of the strategies, we made considerable effort to simulate the rumor marketing problem in the laboratory. The setting was designed to produce the same effects experienced by McDonald's. In addition, a persuasive refutation strategy paralleling the one employed by McDonald's was included for comparison. To be successful, the storage and retrieval strategies had to be effective in negating the worm rumor and perform better than the refutation strategy.

METHOD

Procedure

Sixty-four subjects were recruited from several graduate classes to participate in a study that ostensibly involved the evaluation of television programs and commercials. The participants arrived at the laboratory in groups of four to six, and were introduced to the three members of the research team who jointly administered the experiment. Unknown to research participants, a fourth member of the team served as a research subject. This confederate was present at all experimental sessions.

Videotaped instructions featuring one of the experimenters were played first. These instructions presented the experimental guise and the required tasks. Participants were informed that they would see a television program that recently had been identified as among the most violent on television and that their task would be to evaluate the program. They were also told that commercials were interspersed throughout the program to simulate actual viewing conditions. Because these commercials might affect their program evaluations, subjects were informed that they would also be asked to evaluate the products they saw advertised. Subjects were asked to watch the program as they normally would, but there was to be no talking.

After viewing the instructions, the subjects watched a one-hour episode from the *Hawaii 5-0* series. Twelve commercials were shown during the program at the same intervals that would be used if the program were aired on prime time network television. Three of the commercials were for McDonald's. They were inserted near the beginning, middle, and end of the program and were always preceded and followed by commercials for other products. In experimental treatments requiring the circulation of the rumor, the confederate introduced the rumor at the end of the last McDonald's commercial.

After subjects had seen the program, they were administered a series of scaled questions pertaining to the program. Then they were asked to rate eating at McDonald's on three scales, after which they were sworn to secrecy and dismissed. Two days after the last experimental session, they were asked to complete an additional scale pertaining to the truth of the worm rumor. Subjects were then debriefed about the experimental purpose and procedures. No subjects indicated suspicion about the experimental guise or the confederate.

Independent Variables

For purposes of analysis, the six treatments used were conceived of as a 2 × 2 factorial design with two additional contrasts. The 2 × 2 factorial design was employed to assess the effect of the worm rumor and the retrieval strategy. It entailed two levels of worm rumor (present, absent) and two levels of retrieval cue (present, absent). In the rumor-present condition, the rumor that McDonald's used worms was introduced by the confederate who was ostensibly a research participant. At the close of the third McDonald's commercial, she stated the rumor: "You know these McDonald's commercials remind me of that rumor about worms and McDonald's—you know, that McDonald's uses worm meat in their hamburgers." The experimenter responded by reminding the confederate that there was to be no talking. In the rumor-absent control condition, the confederate simply watched the program with the research participants.

The retrieval cue was manipulated by the presence or absence of a series of questions. After subjects in the retrieval cue condition had completed their evaluation of the program, but before they evaluated eating at McDonald's, they were administered questions asking them to indicate the location of the McDonald's they frequent most often, how often they visit it per year, and whether or not it had indoor seating. This induction was intended to stimulate retrieval of thoughts about McDonald's other than ones related to the worm rumor. In the no retrieval cue condition, subjects completed the evaluation of eating at McDonald's immediately after the program evaluation. Information processing

theory suggests there will be significant rumor by retrieval cue interaction such that the evaluation of eating at McDonald's will be less positive in the worm rumor/no retrieval cue condition than it will be in the other three cells.

Two additional treatments were included. One was designed to emulate the "worming-out" refutational strategy used by McDonald's. Refutation was introduced by having the experimenter respond to the confederate's rumor statement by saying: "That's just not true. If nothing else, worms are too expensive—$8 a pound! Besides the FDA did a study and they found that McDonald's uses 100% pure beef. Now, no more talking." On the basis of information processing theory, the refutation strategy is expected to result in less positive evaluations of eating at McDonald's than would be observed in the rumor absent/no retrieval cue condition.

The other treatment involved the operationalization of the storage strategy by a device we termed "the French connection." Subjects in this treatment heard the experimenter respond to the confederate's rumor statement by saying: "That may sound funny to you, but last week my mother-in-law was in town and we took her to Chez Paul and had a really good sauce that was made out of worms. Now, no more talking." The storage strategy condition was intended to minimize the chance that the worm rumor would be stored with McDonald's. The temporal proximity of the rumor and the French connection was anticipated to help achieve this aim. Even if the worm rumor were stored at the McDonald's address in memory, its association with an affectively positive object. French food, should minimize any adverse rumor effect. Thus we expected on the basis of the information processing view that the storage strategy would induce more positive evaluations of eating at McDonald's than would be observed in the rumor present/no retrieval cue/no storage cue condition.

Dependent Measures

Three rating scales that were likely to be sensitive to the presence and absence of the rumor induction served as the dependent measure of evaluation of McDonald's. They required subjects to rate eating at McDonald's with respect to "good quality food/bad quality food," "completely fits my needs/does not fit my needs at all," and "certain to eat at McDonald's/certain not to eat at McDonald's." Subjects' responses on these seven-point rating scales were summed to derive an evaluative index. Use of the Cronbach α statistic showed this index to be highly reliable ($\alpha = .78$). In addition, 47 of the research participants completed the scale pertaining to the truth of the worm rumor two days after the experiment. It stated, "It's been mentioned that McDonald's hamburgers

have worms. How likely is this to be true?" Responses were on a seven-point scale ranging from "very likely to be true" (scored 1) to "very unlikely to be true" (scored 7).

RESULTS

The means and standard deviations for the evaluative index are shown in Table 1. Figure 1 depicts the experimental results. The effects of the rumor and retrieval cue were assessed through a 2×2 analysis of variance. A significant rumor $\times$ retrieval cue interaction was found ($F = 5.92$, d.f. $= 1,39$, $p < .02$).[4] A comparison of the rumor present/no retrieval cue and rumor absent/no retrieval cue conditions indicated that the rumor induction was successful in causing a less favorable evaluation toward eating at McDonald's ($t = 2.32$, d.f. $= 1, 19$, $p < .01$).[5] This effect emerged despite the fact that subjects' postexperimental responses to the assertion that

Table 1 / Means and Standard Deviations for the Evaluation of Eating at McDonald's Index Categorized by the Independent Variables

	Cell size	$\bar{X}$	S.D.
Rumor absent, no retrieval cue	12	10.75[a]	3.73
Rumor present, no retrieval cue	9	14.89	4.44
Rumor absent, retrieval cue	11	11.46	2.12
Rumor present, retrieval cue	11	10.64	3.83
Rumor present, refutation	10	14.50	3.56
Rumor present, storage cue	11	10.09	4.23

[a] Higher numbers reflect a more negative evaluation.

[3] Attrition in the number of post-experimental respondents was similar for the various experimental treatments and ranged from one to three people.

[4] Analyses of experimental effects are based on a sum scale composed of the three dependent measures. However, the same effects were observed when the scales were analyzed individually.

[5] The F-tests were protected by the significant rumor $\times$ retrieval cue interaction.

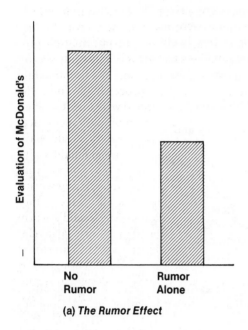

(a) *The Rumor Effect*

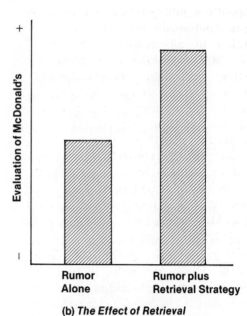

(b) *The Effect of Retrieval Strategy on the Rumor Impact*

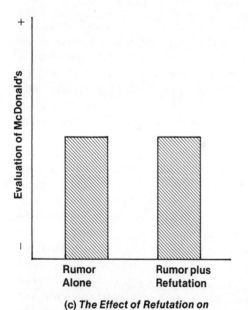

(c) *The Effect of Refutation on Rumor Impact*

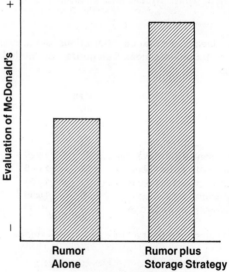

(d) *The Effect of Storage Strategy on Rumor Impact*

Figure 1

McDonald's hamburgers were made with worm meat indicated a strong disbelief of this contention in all treatments $\overline{X} = 6.53$, S.D. $= .78$, $F< 1$). Moreover, a comparison of the rumor present/no retrieval cue and the rumor present/retrieval cue conditions indicated that the retrieval strategy was successful in combating the rumor effect ($t = 2.31$, d.f. $= 1, 18, p< .01$).

The effect of the refutation strategy was assessed by contrasting it to the rumor absent/no retrieval cue condition. The refutation induced a less positive evaluation of eating at McDonald's ($F = 8.13$, d.f. $= 1, 20, p< .01$), thus echoing the result obtained by McDonald's when it employed a similar strategy in natural settings. In contrast, the French connection storage strategy was effective in dispelling the rumor effect. A comparison of this storage strategy and rumor present/no retrieval cue conditions indicated a significantly more favorable evaluation of eating at McDonald's when French connection was employed ($F = 6.11$, d.f. $= 1, 18, p< .02$).

DISCUSSION

The simulation of the worm rumor in the laboratory was successful. Evaluation of McDonald's was less positive in the presence of the worm comment than in its absence. Producing this effect provided the necessary condition for determining strategy effectiveness. The evaluation indicated that the storage and retrieval strategies based on information processing theory were effective. Both increased evaluation of McDonald's to no-rumor levels. The two strategies also were effective in comparison with the refutation strategy.

In addition to demonstrating the effectiveness of the information processing strategies, the results have two important implications. One is the need for further elaboration and testing of information processing theory. The focus of our study was on evaluating strategies, not on disentangling different types of processing. Thus the specific strategies selected were ones expected to be effective on multiple theoretical grounds. The storage strategy could have disrupted the association of McDonald's with worms or it could simply have made that association more positive (by relating worms to French food). The retrieval strategy either blocked the activation of McDonald's worm associations or inhibited their retrieval in relation to other thoughts individuals had stored about eating at McDonald's. Though it is useful in practical terms to design strategies that have multiple bases for effectiveness, such strategies do not allow identification of the specific mechanism at work. Further research is needed to determine the specific processes involved in storage and retrieval.

A similar issue arises with respect to the refutation strategy. Its ineffectiveness may be due to any one of three causes. First, subjects may not have processed the refutation. This possibility seems unlikely because all the other experimental inductions (i.e., the worm rumor, the storage strategy, and the retrieval strategy) were presented in a similar manner and were processed. More difficult to rule out is the possibility that the particular operationalization of the refutation strategy was ineffective, whereas other operationalizations would have been effective. Finally, as predicted by the information processing view, the refutation may have stimulated the retrieval of the McDonald's-worm association. In our study, and in McDonald's implementation of the refutation strategy, there is no way to disentangle these alternative explanations. Nonetheless, investigations employing a "debriefing paradigm" do suggest that refutation can operate in the way depicted by information processing theory (Ross, Lepper, and Hubbard 1975; Walster et al. 1967).

In the Ross study, subjects were initially given false feedback about their ability to distinguish real and fictitious suicide notes. Those assigned to the outcome debriefing treatment were told that the feedback they had received was predetermined and random. Despite this debriefing, subjects persevered in holding the impressions about their ability they had formed on the basis of the false feedback. Apparently, discrediting an object-attribute association did not eradicate beliefs caused by the feedback. They were still retrieved for evaluation. In contrast, those subjects whose debriefing included an explicit and detailed discussion of the psychological process being investigated did not exhibit this perseverance. Our interpretation is that this debriefing procedure cued beliefs other than those formed on the basis of the initial false feedback.

These findings suggest a second implication of our results—that the worm rumor problem may be only one instance of a much more pervasive problem. Specifically, our study and the one done by Ross and his colleagues imply that even when an association is disbelieved, it may stored in memory and may influence evaluation. Although these studies examine a disbelieved association that is negative, disbelieved associations could also be positive. As Maloney (1962, 1963) noted some time ago, presenting a communication that directs people to certain product attributes can create a more favorable attitude, even when people do not believe the communication (e.g., it is too good to be true).

If the disbelief phenomenon is as general as the results indicate, the suggested storage and retrieval strategies should have wide applicability. As a practical matter, ways must be found to implement the strategies through marketing communications. In principle this undertaking should be no more difficult than developing an execution for any other strategy.

Beyond any specific marketing strategies, our research illustrates the value of information processing theory in guiding managerial practice. Everyday insight into consumer behavior may not be sufficient. Strategies should be designed on the basis of theoretical understanding of the psychological processes underlying consumer behavior. Information processing theory offers great promise of providing this understanding.

REFERENCES

Bettman, James (1979), "Memory Factors in Consumer Choice: A Review," *Journal of Marketing,* 43 (Spring), 37–53.

Calder, Bobby, Lynn Phillips, and Alice Tybout (forthcoming), "Designing Research for Application," *Journal of Consumer Research.*

Fishbein, Martin and Icek Ajzen (1975), *Belief, Attitude, Intention and Behavior: An Introduction to Theory and Research.* Reading, Massachusetts: Addison-Wesley Publishing Company.

Maloney, John (1962), "Curiosity vs. Disbelief in Advertising," *Journal of Advertising Research,* 2 (June), 2–8.

—— (1963), "Is Advertising Believability Really Important?" *Journal of Marketing,* 27 (October), 1–8.

Rosnow, Ralph and Gary Fine (1976), *Rumor and Gossip: The Social Psychology of Hearsay.* New York: Elsevier.

Ross, Lee, Mark Lepper, and Michael Hubbard (1975), "Biased Attributional Processes in the Debriefing Paradigm," *Journal of Personality and Social Psychology,* 32 (November), 880–92.

Walster, Elaine, Ellen Berscheid, D'Arcy Abrahams, and Vera Aronson (1967), "Effectiveness of Debriefing Following Deception Experiments," *Journal of Personality and Social Psychology,* 6 (March), 371–80.

Questions

1. Describe what is meant by information-processing theory, and explain how it is different from traditional theories of consumer behavior.

2. According to information-processing theory, explain why the strategy of directly refuting the rumor was not as effective as the storage strategy.

3. According to information-processing theory, explain why the retrieval strategy was effective in producing a positive evaluation of McDonald's by the subjects in the experiment.

Part H

SATISFACTION AND DISSATISFACTION

27. Toward a Process Model of Consumer Satisfaction

Ralph L. Day

The limited amount of experimental research on consumer satisfaction in the consumer behavior literature (Cardozo 1965; Olshavsky and Miller 1972; Anderson 1973) has dealt with satisfaction primarily in terms of the confirmation of expectations. The focus has been on the individual consumer dealing with a single isolated consumption experience, with his evaluation focused on particular attributes or qualities of a specific item, and his response taking place immediately after the experience. A similar orientation is reflected in the definition of satisfaction in the Howard and Sheth model of buyer behavior: "Satisfaction is defined as the buyer's cognitive state of being adequately or inadequately rewarded in a buying situation for the sacrifice he has undergone. The adequacy is a consequence of matching actual past consumption and purchase experience with the reward that was expected from the brand" (Howard and Sheth 1969). The notion that "sacrifices" or costs influence the evaluative response in addition to actual product features is apparent in the Howard and Sheth

definition and was implemented as the effort expended in connection with the consumption experience in the Cardozo study (Cardozo 1965).

None of the three experimental studies cited above actually measured postexperience satisfaction as such. Rather, the measurements in each case were evaluations of the quality of the various attributes and/or the overall quality of performance. Most of the nonexperimental field studies of consumer satisfaction have used a unidimensional scale with categorical responses reflecting a general feeling of satisfaction with the overall product and/or some set of its attributes without a specific criterion for evaluation (Miller 1973; Pfaff 1972).

In order to keep the task at a manageable level, the present effort to establish a more complete conceptual framework for studying consumer satisfaction will focus on the single individual and on a single isolated purchase/use situation. The basic structure of the confirmation/disconfirmation of expectations paradigm will be retained, but an effort will be made to deal with expectations, purchase/use, and postpurchase evaluation as stages in a continuous process and to treat them in more detail than did past conceptualizations. No effort will be made to achieve a high level of rigor or to offer a highly structured theory. In the spirit of the Workshop, the objective is to offer some tentative thoughts for discussion and interaction.

FORMATION OF EXPECTATIONS

In thinking about the task of measuring satisfaction under real-world conditions in the confirmation of expectations framework, it is clear that many factors other than the availability of information on specific product attributes are involved in the formation of expectations. For present purposes, expectations will be broken down into three categories: (1) expectations about the nature and performance of the product or service in question (the anticipated benefits to be derived directly from the product or service itself); (2) expectations about the costs and efforts that will have been expended prior to obtaining the direct benefits of the product or service (the anticipated total costs); and (3) expectations of the social benefits or costs that will accrue to the individual as a consequence of the purchase (the anticipated impact of the purchase on significant others). Each of these will be discussed briefly below.

Nature of the Product

In general, expectations about the nature and performance of the product will be based on previous experiences with that particular item. The consumer who has a lot of experience with a product or service can be expected to have well-formed expectations about the item which have been learned over time. A part of this learning experience will usually be the identification of the salient attributes of the item and the development of expectations about them. The experienced user of the product or service will typically be aware of a number of alternative types or brands and will have specific expectations about the attributes and overall performance of particular brands, depending on the amount and recency of his experience. In addition to his own personal experience, the veteran user of a product develops attitudes that influence his expectations as the result of advertising and personal influences.

The new or inexperienced user will have relatively illformed expectations of the performance of a product or service. He will have to rely on advertising, sales presentations, and the advice of others more than the highly experienced consumer will; his expectations may tend to be more incomplete and less stable than those of the experienced user. The inexperienced consumer is more likely to have unsatisfactory experiences, since his unfamiliarity with types or brands of a product might lead to inappropriate choices. On the other hand, the inexperienced consumer is likely to be less sure of himself and may attribute unsatisfactory experiences to his own incompetence as a consumer. In addition to the experience factor, various personality and situational factors may affect both the expectations of the consumer and how he reacts to their confirmation or disconfirmation in the consumption experience. The consumer's expectations with respect to product features and performance are a key factor in determining whether or not a consumption experience is judged to be satisfactory or unsatisfactory and seem to be an essential part of any predictive model of satisfaction.

Costs and Shopping Efforts

The price paid for an item can have a rather complex effect on the consumer's evaluative reaction. Price is often interpreted as an index of the quality of an item, so that a high price tends to create high expectations for performance and a low price tends to lead to low expectations of performance. Whereas the highly experienced consumer might interpret a higher than expected price as an overcharge and a lower price as a bargain, the inexperienced consumer is likely to adjust expectations in response to the price. Price also tends to serve as an index of the importance of a purchase to a consumer, so that evaluative reactions to relatively expensive items can be expected to be more critical than when the item is inexpensive and thus does not constitute a substantial part of the consumer's budget. To the extent that price is an index of the importance of the purchase to the consumer, the expected cost of an item can have an influence on the prepurchase information seeking and shopping behavior and thus may lead to better-formed expectations and to the expenditure of additional effort in shopping.

Consumers incur costs other than the expenditure for the item itself when they purchase and consume products and services. The most obvious of these is the time and expense involved in making a trip to a shopping district and the time and effort spent in shopping. Some consumers may spend a considerable amount of time in gathering and evaluating information before making a purchase. Such activities tend to increase the importance of the purchase and would seem likely to amplify either a positive or negative experience after the purchase has been made. Except for the work of Cardozo, there apparently has been no effort in consumer behavior and marketing to study the effect of high levels of shopping effort on consumer satisfaction. Cardozo's finding was that subjects in his high-effort condition tended to give the product higher ratings than those in the low-effort condition (Cardozo 1965: 248–249).

Social Benefits of Purchase/Use

For many products there are benefits of purchase and consumption that are independent of the attributes of the product or service itself. These are the benefits to the actual purchaser resulting from the effects of his purchase or consumption of the product on other people. These are especially important for status products, such as the purchase of a membership in a country club, a luxury automobile, or a bottle of an especially fine wine. Although the purchaser's expectations for product quality and his awareness of the costs may have an important bearing on his reaction to the products after purchase, the extent to which his expectations about the reactions of others to his purchase are confirmed or disconfirmed may also have an important bearing on his satisfaction or dissatisfaction. The desire for the approval of family and friends is not limited to the purchasers of luxury cars and Chateau Mouton Rothschild. A wide range of products that are jointly consumed with others or are publicly consumed may have sufficient social significance that the purchaser will have well-formed expectations about the reactions of others whose approval is important to him. Although the consumer's expectations of the reactions of other people may not be as important as his own expectations of performance, they seem sufficiently important for enough products that they should not be overlooked.

The division of the aspects of purchase and

use into the product itself, the costs involved in acquiring the product, and the social effects of the product may seem arbitrary. In fact, one could argue that these should all be considered attributes of the product in a broad sense. However, there do seem to be some advantages in treating these aspects separately. The functional attributes of the product are established by the manufacturer, and expectations about them can be manipulated to some extent by him. The costs to the consumer are less directly under the manufacturer's control and may depend to a considerable extent upon local and personal factors. The social factors are even more individual and personal and less subject to control by the manufacturer. Conceptualizing these aspects separately should help in dealing with individual differences when the measurement stage is reached.

USE AND EVALUATION

In the simplest of all possible purchase and use situations, the product is purchased and consumed independently of other items, consumption begins immediately and is completed in a short time, and there are no circumstantial or environmental factors that have an important influence on the consumer's evaluation of the product. In such a case, the evaluation focuses on the functional attributes of the product; comparison of perceived performance with the consumer's expectations can proceed in a straightforward way; and the process of evaluation can be completed rather quickly. This is basically the scenario which has been reflected in the experimental studies of consumer satisfaction in the consumer behavior literature, but it is hardly typical of all consumption experiences.

The Simple Product or Service

Under the simplest imaginable circumstances, the consumer's evaluation of his consumption experiences is a poorly understood process and is undoubtedly complex. The confirmation/disconfirmation of expectations paradigm suggests some sort of direct comparison process in which the consumer evaluates the extent to which his *a priori* expectations of performance are met or exceeded by the actual performance of the item in the consumption experience. This evaluation process is fundamentally multidimensional in nature; even the simplest of products and services has more than one attribute or feature which can influence the level of satisfaction of the user. This suggests that the evaluative process involves some method either of choosing one particular aspect on which to base the evaluation or of combining the attribute-by-attribute evaluations into an overall evaluation of the product or service.

Just how this process takes place is undoubtedly a function of many factors which may vary over individuals and according to the nature of the attribute structure and complexity of the product or service. Some of the possible ways in which the evaluation process might take place are as follows:

1. A single dominant attribute is identified as the basis of evaluation. The confirmation or disconfirmation of expectations on this attribute leads to satisfaction or dissatisfaction with the product or service. If the consumer's evaluation of the major attribute should be inconclusive, the next most important attribute might be considered.

2. A number of salient attributes of the product or service are identified and evaluated against expectations. Satisfaction occurs only if expectations are confirmed for all salient attributes.

3. A number of salient attributes of the product

or service are identified and evaluated against expectations. Overall satisfaction occurs even when expectations are disconfirmed on some of the attributes, provided that expectations are met or exceeded on a sufficient number of attributes to compensate for the unsatisfactory attributes.

These particular ways of evaluating the consumption experience reflect the structure of lexicographic, disjunctive, and compensatory choice models, respectively. The compensatory model seems to be the intuitive choice among those doing research on consumer satisfaction.

The consideration of alternative ways in which consumers evaluate and react to consumption experiences should not lead us to think that the consumer is a constantly vigilant and precise evaluator of every product and service he uses or that he consciously goes about evaluating his consumption experiences with respect to his prior expectations. It might be more plausible to assume that the consumer enters the typical consumption experience without consciously evaluating anything at all and completes most of his consumption experiences without even thinking about whether or not he was satisfied or dissatisfied. In general, something out of the ordinary must occur either prior to the purchase, during the purchase process, or during the consumption phase to alert the consumer or call his attention to some aspect of the purchase situation. Otherwise, the typical consumer is unlikely to make any effort to evaluate his experiences or even think about whether he is experiencing satisfaction or dissatisfaction.

This suggests that a very important factor in the study of consumer satisfaction is the identification of the triggering cues that initiate an awareness or sensitivity to the purchase/consumption process and lead to conscious feelings about being satisfied or dissatisfied. Some of the circumstances that might trigger the evaluative process are as follows:

1. The nature of the item and/or the occasion for its purchase has some special significance for the individual.
2. The social context in which the purchase is made or the item is consumed calls attention to the product and the purchaser.
3. The consumer has had previous experiences with the product or service which cause him to be conscious of the current experience.
4. The consumer has been exposed to warnings about the product or service by friends, consumer organizations, or consumer protection agencies.
5. The consumer is inexperienced and poorly informed about the purchase and use of the product and is therefore more conscious of all aspects of the purchase/use situation than he would normally be.

In addition to these circumstances which may cause the consumer to be in an "evaluation mode" from the beginning of the purchase process, the following may happen during the purchase or consumption process:

6. The consumer discovers something that suggests caution, such as a shopworn appearance or information or advice from a salesperson which is in conflict with prior beliefs.
7. The consumer discovers after purchase that the product does not have all of the expected features, fails to perform as expected, or is defective or flawed in some way.
8. The consumer discovers after purchase that the product has qualities or features much better than previously thought or otherwise performs at a much higher level than expected.

The above circumstances or any other aspect of a simple product or service that breaks the routine and calls attention to the situation can trigger an evaluative response from a consumer and lead to feelings of satisfaction or dissatisfaction.

More Complex Products and Services

The foregoing discussion focused on relatively simple products that are purchased routinely and are normally consumed soon after purchase. With such products it seems reasonable to consider the process of evaluation as the action of an individual who compares his personal expectations with respect to a small number of product attributes to the perceived performance of the product. A great variety of consumer nondurable products fall into this category. However, there are many purchase and use situations that are considerably more complex in a number of ways that make the consumer's evaluative task more difficult. A set of complicating factors related to the product itself will be considered next. Then aspects of the consumption process apart from the actual features of the product or service will be considered.

Following are some of the factors that contribute complexity to the consumer's evaluation of the products and services he purchases:

1. The time span of use. When a product is purchased for use over a considerable period of time, a satisfaction measure based on the comparison of prepurchase expectations against an evaluation of the product's attributes made soon after the purchase does not seem adequate. A product that is judged highly satisfactory soon after purchase might be rated highly unsatisfactory one year later and possibly satisfactory again three years later. Some periodic monitoring of satisfaction over time or some measure of satisfaction over the life of the product would seem more appropriate.

2. The complexity of the product. When products consist of an assembly or collection of related components, subassemblies, and services, the measurement of satisfaction becomes extremely complex. When the complex product is also a durable, the evaluation of satisfaction over time is made even more difficult by breakdowns and the need for repairs and maintenance services.

3. Commonly consumed products. When products such as houses, cars, and pleasure boats are used in common by a family or other group, additional difficulties are introduced. In addition to the difficulties of evaluating joint satisfaction over a group is the fact that the individual's dissatisfaction or satisfaction with other members of the group will be confounded with his satisfaction with the product.

4. Complementary products. When related products are purchased in different transactions but are used together as a unit (e.g., skis, boots, poles, clothing), the performances of the various items will interact with each other and influence the degree of satisfaction felt with each item.

5. Prestige products. When products are purchased primarily for the effect the owner's possession of the product will have on others, the basis for judging the degree of satisfaction with the product shifts from evaluating the product to evaluating the reactions of significant others.

6. Professional services and intangible products. When the item is a nonproduct consisting primarily of advice or when the benefits are to be obtained in the distant future, evaluation may be focused on the qualifications of the individual or institution involved rather than on specific attributes of the service or intangible.

7. Repair and maintenance services. When services and replacement parts for a durable item are purchased as a separate transaction, three possible sources of satisfaction or dissatisfaction are mixed together. The breakdown requiring repairs may generate dissatisfaction toward the original item, the cost and performance of replacement parts will be the object of evaluation, and the personal skills and abilities of the workmen performing the services will also be the subject of evaluation. The prime example for this category is automobile repairs, which have been at the top of complaint lists for years.

Although the above categories are neither mutually exclusive nor exhaustive, they illustrate the more complex problems of evaluation facing the consumer. Unlike relatively simple products that are purchased and used in routine ways, a purchase occasion for one of these complex products may of itself trigger the consumer's evaluative process and lead to an assessment of satisfaction or dissatisfaction without any additional stimulus.

Circumstances of Purchase and Consumption

Although interest in consumer satisfaction and dissatisfaction has tended to focus on the performance of products and services, publicly expressed concerns of consumers and data on specific consumer complaints reflect a considerable amount of dissatisfaction with aspects of the purchase and use situation apart from the performance of the actual product. A recent study of the complaints received by a consumer hot line reported that approximately 57% of those in a sample of calls received were primarily concerned with some aspect of the prepurchase and purchase situations, while only 43% expressed primary concern with aspects of product quality, service, and repairs (Diamond, Ward, and Faber 1976). Although it seems unlikely that those calling a particular hot line are representative of the entire population, the results seem adequate support for a suggestion that attention should not be focused entirely on product performance and postpurchase service and repairs.

Some of the other circumstances of the prepurchase and purchase situations that appear to influence consumer satisfaction and dissatisfaction are as follows:

1. Prepurchase circumstances. Dissatisfaction which is at least partially directed at particular products and services frequently results from advertising that consumers feel

is either misleading or offensive, potentially misleading displays in stores, and overly aggressive or misleading sales presentations.

2. Purchase transaction. Dissatisfactions are sometimes generated in the purchase transaction by circumstances such as an out-of-stock condition for a desired item or procedural matters such as a refusal to accept a check or grant credit.

3. Delivery of purchased items. Problems with delivery frequently show up in data on consumer complaints (Diamond, Ward, and Faber 1976). These include failure to deliver the purchased item, delivering a damaged item, late delivery, and excessive charges for delivery.

4. Warranty problems. Problems with warranties also appear frequently in complaint data and include deceptive or incomplete warranties and failure to honor a warranty.

5. Credit and collection problems. Aspects of the granting of credit, the rates of interest charged, and procedures for collection are frequently mentioned as sources of consumer dissatisfaction.

While the major focus in the study of consumer satisfaction should be on the performance of products and services, it is clear that marketing practices also have a considerable influence on consumers and the extent to which they experience satisfaction in the purchase and consumption of goods and services.

PERSONAL FACTORS AND THE EVALUATIVE RESPONSE

The way in which the individual consumer responds to the various aspects of the purchase/use situation and experiences feelings of satisfaction or dissatisfaction undoubtedly varies widely from individual to individual. Different experiences in the past, different motivations for purchase, and variations in the circumstances of use are certain to generate different prior expectations. These and other factors can affect the evaluation of the consumer's actual experience and influence the way in which he responds to this comparison of expectations with perceived performance. The particular aspects of the individual that will be considered here are his expertise as a consumer, his degree of sensitivity to consumer problems, and his action tendencies. These can be briefly described as follows:

1. Expertise as a consumer. The poorly informed or careless consumer is more likely to make inappropriate purchases, misuse the items he buys, or have unreasonable expectations of performance. Hence, he is much more likely to have an unsatisfactory experience. He is also more likely to fail to recognize substandard preference. Being an expert consumer involves a willingness to invest the time and effort in acquiring knowledge about products and suppliers. The knowledgeable consumer is much more likely to experience satisfaction with his purchase and is better able to obtain redress when he does have an unsatisfactory experience.

2. Sensitivity to consumer problems. Especially with respect to the more routine kind of purchase, there appear to be many "unconscious consumers" who respond mechanically to the need for products and give little thought to evaluating the products they consume. A recent study of grocery products found that for 45% of the cases in which actual defects were found in products, the respondents reported that they simply ignored the defect (A. C. Nielsen 1976). At the opposite extreme are the "hyperconsumers" who consider every transaction a potential ripoff and frequently become highly dissatisfied with items which most consumers would regard as satisfactory.

3. Willingness to express concerns. Just as there are differences among consumers with regard to the recognition of either high or low levels of performance, there are differences among individuals with regard to the communication of their satisfaction or dissatisfaction after they become aware of it themselves. An effort has been made elsewhere to identify differences over individuals with regard to their "propensity to complain" (Day and Landon 1976).

These factors are indicative of the kinds of interpersonal differences that can influence reported levels of satisfaction or dissatisfaction with products and services. Better understanding of the consumer's abilities, attitudes, and action tendencies seems essential to the future study of consumer satisfactions and dissatisfactions.

REFERENCES

A. C. Nielsen Company. "Caveat Venditor." *The Nielsen Researcher,* 6 (1976), 2–3.

Anderson, Ralph E. "Consumer Dissatisfaction: The Effect of Disconfirmed Expectancy on Perceived Product Performance." *Journal of Marketing Research* (February 1973), 38–44.

Cardozo, Richard N. "An Experimental Study of Customer Effort, Expectation, and Satisfaction." *Journal of Marketing Research* 2 (August 1965), 244–249.

Day, Ralph L., and E. Laird Landon, Jr. "Toward a Theory of Consumer Complaining Behavior." Paper presented at Symposium on Consumer and Industrial Buying Behavior, University of South Carolina, (March 26, 1976).

Diamond, Steven L., Scott Ward, and Ronald Faber. "Consumer Problems and Consumerism: Analysis of Calls to a Consumer Hot Line." *Journal of Marketing* 40 (January 1976), 58–62.

Howard, John A., and Jagdish N. Sheth. *The Theory of Buyer Behavior.* New York: Wiley, 1969.

Miller, John A. "Who Is the Discontented Consumer?" *Combined Proceedings.* American Marketing Association Conference (1973), pp. 486–490.

Olshavsky, Richard W., and John A. Miller. "Consumer Expectations, Product Performance, and Perceived Product Quality." *Journal of Marketing Research* 9 (February 1972), 19–21.

Pfaff, Anita B. "An Index of Consumer Satisfaction." *Proceedings.* Association for Consumer Research (1972), pp. 713–737.

Questions

1. Define consumer satisfaction. Why is the use of complaints data not a good way of measuring consumer dissatisfaction?
2. Summarize some of the factors that affect product evaluation by a consumer.
3. Briefly describe the two possible ways of measuring an individual's level of satisfaction.
4. The author offers three factors that can affect the evaluation of the consumer's actual experience and influence the way in which he responds. Can you think of some more?

28.   Consumer Satisfaction Research: A Review

Denise T. Smart

The growth of interest in the area of consumer satisfaction and dissatisfaction has been impressive during the decade of the 1970s. This growth is a natural result of a number of factors that include a more vocal and organized consumer movement, increased government monitoring of business policies, inflation and the consumer's felt need for more value per dollar spent, and a general concern for improving the image of the business community. The amount of empirical research on consumer satisfaction and dissatisfaction is steadily growing, but still remains fairly limited. The impact of this research is very great, however, in terms of both business strategy and government policy decision making. Because of the importance of this area to marketers, it seems to be an appropriate time to step back in order to synthesize and evaluate many of the empirical efforts that have been published in the marketing area to date.

This paper will be an attempt to briefly review a number of studies in the satisfaction-dissatisfaction area as related to consumer behavior. The following dimensions will be considered—the measurement instrument, sample size and characteristics, measurement time, type of product or service involved in the study, measurement focus, and the major results. Research that focuses mainly on complaints will be excluded, while studies that partially, but not primarily, deal with this area will be included. For a review of consumer complaint behavior, see Robinson (1979).

Another distinction made here is between the more general, global conceptualizations of consumer satisfaction and the more situational, specific measures. The focus in this paper is with the latter. Research in the former area is also attaining a growing body of knowledge, which ranges from an index of consumer satisfaction (Pfaff 1977) to a quality of life indicator (Leavitt 1976; Winter and Morris 1979).

GENERAL GENERALIZATIONS

Although the problem has been acknowledged many times before (Anderson 1973; McNeal 1977; Plummer 1977; Westbrook 1977b, McNeal and Lamb 1979), it would be negligent to start a review without a brief mention of the definitional status of the satisfaction-dissatisfaction concept. Unfortunately, the concept still manages to elude precise definition. A variety of definitions can be found, some framed in terms of satisfaction and others in terms of the lack thereof, or dissatisfaction. The following sample will give the reader a cursory view of the current status of the definition:

> the consumer's perceived or felt attitudinal level of satisfaction or dissatisfaction toward a purchased object. (Ortinau 1979: 35)

> dissatisfaction is said to occur when perceived product performance falls short of remembered expectations for its performance, while satisfaction is said to occur when perceived product performance equals or exceeds remembered expectations. (Richins 1979: 31)

> Consumer dissatisfaction . . . the gap or distance between consumer's "ideal" attribute combination for a particular product or service and the attribute combination of the product or service offered in the marketplace which comes closest to this ideal. (Handy 1977: 217)

> the extent to which a purchase resolves a bothersome mental state and allows the consumer to return to a position of being ready to deal with other life matters. (McNeal 1977: 18)

> the relative "goodness" of the subjective experiences accompanying an individual's consumer behavior. (Westbrook 1977b: 142)

It is evident that most of these descriptions of satisfaction or dissatisfaction are very general. This makes the job of trying to operationalize the concept in terms that will aid measurement extremely difficult. (Andreasen 1977).

A related issue concerns the debate over whether satisfaction and dissatisfaction should be viewed as opposites residing on the same continuum or whether, more correctly, they should be seen as separate, parallel dimensions. Most of the initial work in the area that considered satisfaction in terms of a continuum was related to attainment of expectations. Swan and Combs (1976) have posited a different approach based on the separation of instrumental performance and expressive performance dimensions. The former refers to performance of the physical product, while expressive performance incorporates the psychological aspects of satisfaction. Based on this framework, the authors concluded from their study that satisfaction and dissatisfaction were linked to different types of outcomes that bring with them the suggestion that parallel continua are a distinct possibility. As with the definitional state, this debate remains to be settled (Aiello, Czepiel, and Rosenberg 1977).

These areas of disagreement are further compounded by the fact that there are various levels of satisfaction to take into consideration. Czepiel and Rosenberg (1976) provide a conceptualization of three levels of satisfaction:

1. System satisfaction, which deals with total benefits obtained from the operations of the institutional marketing system.
2. Enterprise satisfaction, which focuses on the complex product-service organizations, such as a retail store.
3. Product-service satisfaction, which is based on consumer evaluation of the benefits received from consumption or use of a particular product or service.

Once the level of satisfaction has been established in terms of research pursuit, decisions about the appropriate salient dimensions and time of measurement become the next issue. Day (1977) provides a process orientation that highlights the necessity to think of satisfaction in terms of the prepurchase-purchase-use-evaluation sequence. Expectations at these levels can be further classified according to the performance, the costs and efforts expended obtaining the benefits, and social effects that accrue to the user of a particular product or service. The combinations are endless. Each product may produce a unique set of expectations and feelings of satisfaction or dissatisfaction at the prepurchase, purchase, usage, and post-usage evaluation stages; this is compounded with multiple products and situation-specific dimensions of each stage. The extension of interest into the complaint behavior and quality of life areas indicates the growing perception of importance that the type of individual, in more general terms, plays in the conceptualization of satisfaction.

Even this elementary look at a few of the most basic issues facing satisfaction researchers points out the complex, multidimensional nature of the area. One must also keep in mind the relative recentness of interest in the area as it is applied to the area of consumer behavior. With these basic limitations in the overall state of the art in mind, let us look at some generalities about recent empirical investigations.

SUMMARY OF STUDIES

In an effort to condense the essence of the major research studies on consumer satisfaction (to 1980) into a form that will facilitate easy reference and comparison, two classification tables are provided. Table I outlines those

studies that have been experimental, and Table II outlines those of a field survey type. Note that the results of each study are only very briefly outlined; for further information regarding full findings, one should refer to the original study reports cited in the references.

COMMENTS ABOUT THE EXPERIMENTAL STUDIES

The experimental (laboratory) studies summarized in Table I mainly viewed satisfaction in terms of cognitive processes and the confirmation or disconfirmation of expectations. Of the five studies included here, only the two most recent measured both pre- and postpurchase perceptions of the product. In addition, the manipulation of different aspects of the buying process makes generalization more difficult. The Cardozo study (1965), for example, incorporated the manipulation of shopping effort along with product expectations, while the others were basically concerned with actual product differences and levels of information that the respondent received. A common thread among the studies is the use of student subjects. Naturally, this is a fine starting point, with advantages of cost minimization and convenience, but it possesses the accompanying disadvantages that are present in the absence of a random sample. The range of products tested also limits the depth of findings and their generalizability. Cardozo (1965) and Anderson (1973) used ballpoint pens in their experiments and did not consider actual product usage, while Cohen and Goldberg (1970) used instant coffee and included actual tasting of the product. Olshavsky and Miller (1972) and Oliver (1977) used more complex, less frequently purchased products (reel type tape recorders and a recently introduced automobile, respectively). The importance of each of these products would certainly vary con-

Table I / Experiments

Author	Year	Measurement instrument	Sample size characteristics	Measurement; time product/service	Measurement focus	Major results
Cardozo	1965	Questionnaire	n = 107 students, University of Minnesota	Postpurchase Ballpoint pens	Product and shopping	Subjects expending shopping effort evaluated the product more favorably than those who expended less; subjects feeling that the product lived up to expectations rated the product more favorably than those feeling that it did not
Cohen and Goldberg	1970	Questionnaire	n = 28 undergraduate students, both sexes, University of Illinois	Postpurchase Instant coffee	Product evaluations; product choice after exposure to confirmation/disconfirmation experience	Postdecision cognitive re-evaluation was primarily influenced by confirmation/disconfirmation experience with the product
Olshavsky and Miller	1972	Questionnaire	n = 100 undergraduate students, all male*	Postpurchase Reel type tape recorder	Product attribute rating after exposure to high and low product expectation information	Evaluations of performance were in the direction of manipulated expectations
Anderson	1973	Questionnaire	n = 144 undergraduate students*	Pre- and post purchase Ballpoint pens	Expectations; product ratings on visual features and performance characteristics; overall rating	Evaluations or perceptions of the product differed depending upon the level of expectations
Oliver	1977	Questionnaire	n = 243 students, 57% male, midwestern university	Pre- and post-purchase Recently introduced automobiles	Overall quality and car attribute perceptions; overall affect and intentions to buy	Expectation level related to postexposure judgments; disconfirmation experience may have an independent and equally significant effect

*Location not specified.

Table II / Field Studies

Author	Year	Measurement instrument	Sample size characteristics	Measurement; time product/ service	Measurement focus	Major results
Pickle and Bruce	1972	Personal interview with questionnaire	$n = 173$ females; two-stage area sample; Columbus, Georgia	Prepurchase; postpurchase (purchased product within one-year period) Major appliances, automobiles, small appliances, food, furniture, wearing apparel	Category of products purchased and leading to dissatisfaction; household member who made purchase was dissatisfied, attempted corrective action, decided to repurchase; factors that influenced purchase decisions; corrective action received	Joint purchasing decision between man and wife produced highest levels of dissatisfaction; automobile and appliances account for most dissatisfaction with products; no differences between races, but younger and more educated (excepting college educated) are more dissatisfied
Mason and Himes, Jr.	1973	Telephone interview	$n = 126$, random sample, female head of household, southeastern community of 70,000	Postpurchase (purchased product within one-year period) Major and small appliances (22 categories)	Types of appliances that produced most frequent dissatisfaction; corrective actions taken; types of outlets sought to seek satisfaction for complaints	Most dissatisfaction from performance (89.2 %, while less than 6% resulted from installation, shipping, and service life); of those who complained, most satisfied after one complaint; 80% started complaint process at retail store; higher income levels, older, and larger number in household felt more dissatisfaction; level of education and marital status not significant

	Year	Method	Sample	Purchase Stage / Product	Variables Measured	Findings
Wotruba and Duncan	1975	Personal interview with questionnaire	n = 430; 2-stage area sample of females; San Diego	Prepurchase and postpurchase / Washing machines	Information about present washing machine and usage; attribute expectations of washing machine performance	Respondents had lower expectations for a new machine than for present one; expectations for new one differed from average actual longevity, performance, and repairs required; low correlations between expectations and demographic variables
Swan and Combs	1976	Semistructured questionnaire	n = 60 undergraduate students (46 male, 14 female)*	Postpurchase / Clothing items from past experiences	Recall of clothing that had been satisfactory and unsatisfactory; the events surrounding that dissatisfaction	Satisfaction and dissatisfaction may be linked to different kinds of instrumental and expressive outcomes; satisfaction associated with performance that fulfills expectations, dissatisfaction with performance not fulfilling expectations
Aiello, Czepiel, and Rosenberg	1977	Questionnaire	n = 315 customers of a retail trading stamp redemption center*	Postexperience / Retail trading stamp redemption experiences	Satisfaction, belief, and importance of experience at the system, enterprise, and product levels	Type of scale used for measurement had a distinct effect on satisfaction measures
Darden and Rao	1977	Interviews	n = 200 households*	Postrepair / Repair work done under warranty for major appliances	Satisfaction with repair work done under warranty, number of years of operation for appliance, price, number of repairs under warranty	Lower levels of satisfaction with repair work done under warranty may lead to increased importance of warranties

(continued)

Table II / Field Studies (*continued*)

Author	Year	Measurement instrument	Sample size characteristics	Measurement; time product/ service	Measurement focus	Major results
Day and Bodur	1977	Drop-off, pick-up questionnaire	n = 600 random sample in midwestern city	Postpurchase (1 year for nondurables; 2 for services; 3 for durables) 73 services categories	Purchases in 200 product categories; use, importance, satisfaction-dissatisfaction with products; complaining behavior	Wide variations in dissatisfaction with different types of services; weak relationship between socioeconomic information and satisfacation
Handy	1977	Questionnaire	n = 1831 households; national random sample for 1974 survey; number not reported for 1976 survey	Postexperience Overall food marketing system; seven major food categories	Expressed satisfaction with products and services; importance of each product attribute; expressions of dissatisfaction	Dissatisfaction with food products from the 1974 and 1976 survey
Hempel	1977	Questionnaire; one interviewer administered; two self-administered	n = 514 households, both men and women, Connecticut and northwestern New England	Postpurchase Housing	Housing satisfaction with 5 different scales, including separate index for husband and wife satisfaction	Locational and social dimensions of housing satisfaction may be more complex than physical requirements
Hughes	1977	Mail questionnaire	n = 928, large midwestern city	Postpurchase 52 general merchandise items	When, where, amount, spent for purchase of 52 items; overall satisfaction with products	Willingness of consumer to express dissatisfaction with general merchandise was not found related to cost of purchase; age was most closely associated with satisfaction

Author	Year	Method	Context/Product	Sample	Variables	Findings
Leavitt	1977	Questionnaire	Postpurchase Bread, electric toasters, spray deoderant, tennis shoes	n = 373 students, Ohio State University	Evaluation of products, price, advertising, and place of purchase	Intrinsic factors and measure of satisfaction and extrinsic factors and measure of dissatisfaction were not found to be highly correlated
Maddox	1977	Questionnaire	Postexperience Grocery shopping	Number not reported, female shoppers, St. Louis; convenience sample	Evaluations of satisfaction of grocery store-related items	6 of 30 factors found to contribute to overall satisfaction; not included were location, parking, price
Mason and Wilkinson	1977	Telephone interview	Postshopping (within last 6 months) Unavailability of advertised food product	n = 187 food shoppers, multistage area sample; n = 219 respondents, random sample, southeastern SMSA; n = 245 food shoppers, random sample, midwestern SMSA	Experience with unavailability of advertised food product; knowledge of FTC rule on product availability; use of rain checks	56% had experienced at least one instance of food product unavailability in last 6 months; were generally not taking action when confronted with this situation; were generally aware of the FTC ruling
Morris	1977	Interviews	Postdecision Housing	n = 455 stratified random sample, all female, small Iowa town	Satisfaction and saliency of housing characteristics, propensity to move, renter status, cultural, structural type deficit	Cultural deficits were shown to be as effective at predicting satisfaction and mobility propensity as family deficits

(continued)

Table II / Field Studies *(continued)*

Author	Year	Measurement instrument	Sample size characteristics	Measurement; time product/ service	Measurement focus	Major results
Swan	1977	Personal and telephone interviews	n = 167 convenience sample of attendees of shopping center opening, southwest	Pre- and post-satisfaction Shopping at new mall	Expectations, fulfillment, and satisfaction regarding shopping at new mall	Satisfaction positively related to fulfillment of expectations, shopper's confidence and level of initial expectations, and purchase of item during shopping trip
Valle and Wallendorf	1977	Open-ended questionnaire	n = 54 MBA students at the University of Pittsburgh	Postpurchase Product was self-designated	Respondents were asked to recall a product with which they were dissatisfied and satisfied and to describe the causes of dissatisfaction or satisfaction and any action taken if dissatisfied	Frequent references were found between prepurchase expectations and actual product performance; attributions were classified on the basis of psychological distance
Westbrook	1977a	Telephone interview	n = 269 major appliance owners, Detroit	Postownership major appliances: washer, dryer, refrigerator, freezer, range/oven, and dishwasher	Satisfaction with ownership; personal competence; prior product experience; working condition of product; status of replacement purchase decision	Satisfaction varied by product; generally high levels of satisfaction reported; personal competence and intent to replace product related to satisfaction; a curvilinear relationship between satisfaction and prior experience; socioeconomic factors not strongly related to satisfaction

Westbrook	1977b	Telephone interviews	n = 158, 80% married female, 6% single female, judgment sample, suburban Detroit	Prepurchase Automatic washer, dryer, range/oven, refrigerator, freezer, dishwasher	Feelings and expectations regarding prepurchase decision activity; previous ownership and purchasing experience, information sought, timing of purchase decision	Dissatisfaction with prepurchase period was limited; some reported dissatisfaction with ability to judge optional features; some requested more product information; those who expected to spend more search time were more dissatisfied than those who expected little or moderate amounts
Sproles and Geistfeld	1978	Mail questionnaire	n = 989 female, head of household, Indiana, stratified random sample	Prepurchase and postpurchase (1 year period) Textiles and clothing; woman's outerwear	Satisfaction with current fashions, shopping; dissatisfaction with clothing and textiles; indicators of priorities for consumer satisfaction or dissatisfaction; problems with clothing; importance of selected criteria in purchases of outerwear	Few were very satisfied with current fashions; most pleased with shopping experiences for clothing; general dissatisfaction with changing fashions and related social pressure; comfort and quality more important than style and price in judging satisfaction; construction and quality were problem areas; styling, performance, and price also influential

(continued)

Table II / Field Studies (continued)

Author	Year	Measurement instrument	Sample size characteristics	Measurement; time product/ service	Measurement focus	Major results
Westbrook and Newman	1978	Telephone interview	n = 236 buyers of major appliances, n = 158 prospective buyers, Detroit area, 86% female	Pre- and post-purchase (planning to buy in next 8 weeks or had bought in last 8 weeks) Appliances including washer, dryer, refrigerator, range, dish-washer	Feelings and experiences during prepurchase period	Expressed dissatisfac-tion with purchase decision process was a function of shopper characteristics; personal competence, previous ownership experiences, plans for information search activity
Aiello and Czepiel	1979	Questionnaire	n = 315, trading stamp re-demption store cus-tomers; n = 84 mail order redemption customers, randomly selected*	Postmeasure Trading stamp redemption store centers (mail versus in store)	Store attribute per-ceptions including products, price, ser-vice, convenience, atmosphere, adver-tising	Mail order and redemp-tion center customers were equally satis-fied with the system; mail order customers were somewhat more satisfied with the process and the merchandise

Study	Year	Method	Sample	Focus	Results
Berkowitz Walton, and Walker	1979	Mailed questionnaire	Postmeasure In-home food and traditional shoppers; $n = 797$ (93% women), consumers receiving orders from in-home food retailer; $n = 266$ (92% women), regular food shoppers, midwest metro, random sample	Satisfaction with services offered by own grocery store; attitudes toward factors in shopping, price sensitivity	Neither in-home nor traditional shopper expressed a high level of dissatisfaction; attitude differences between groups found toward factors most important in shopping
Hagar and Handy	1979	Questionnaire	Postpurchase Beef; $n = 358$ households (data taken from USDA 1976 survey), 300–400 surveyed in this category	Degree of overall satisfaction with product and attributes (price, taste, freshness, etc.)	Product satisfaction significantly associated with taste and price of product; more respondents were satisfied with taste than price; tenderness, freshness, value received, and selection also associated with satisfaction
Krishnan and Mills	1979	Telephone survey	Postmeasure Retail stores; $n = 999$, from two southeastern cities, random digit dialing	Problems encountered at retail stores and the effect on shopping behavior; store images	Price-related problems were correlated with repatronage in 3/4 of stores; price-related problems had lower frequency of mentions rather than service, merchandise, or layout-related problems

(continued)

Table II / Field Studies (*continued*)

Author	Year	Measurement instrument	Sample size characteristics	Measurement; time product/ service	Measurement focus	Major results
Madden and Franz	1979	Questionnaire	$n = 100$ students, midwestern city	Pre- and post-expectations University attributes	Evaluation of expectation of and previous experience with university environment attributes	The interchangeability of evaluations and expectations as longitudinal measures was supported
Madden, Little, and Dolich	1979	Questionnaire	$n = 25$ students, University of Nebraska, utilizing off-campus televised courses	Pre-, during, and postmeasures Course, off-campus	Course attributes in regard to benefit and cost	Including the cost elements with benefit and importance provided additional understanding of the underlying relationships
Oliver	1979	Mailed questionnaire	$n = 291$ residents, south-central city; $n = 162$ university students, random sample from telephone and registration data	Pre- and post-purchase Swine flu shots	Expectations regarding consequences of swine flue shot; perceived problems, benefits, overall attitude toward shot; postexposure attitudes and intentions	Expectations and disconfirmation appeared to affect postusage reactions in an additive manner
Swan and Trawick	1979	Telephone survey	$n = 244$, random sample from telephone directory of two southwestern SMSAs	Postpurchase (bread and meat, same day; movie, 1 year) Bread, meat, movies	Whether consumers had consciously evaluated the product after usage	87% of moviegoers reported evaluating the movie, while only 40% for meat, 29% for bread

| Oliver | 1980 | Questionnaire | $n = 356$, randomly selected residents, south-central city; $n = 248$ randomly selected students | Postmeasure Swine flue shots | Measure of behavior, disconfirmation, attitude, and future intentions | Postusage satisfaction appeared to be a function of expectations or prior attitude and disconfirmation |
| Westbrook | 1980 | Questionnaire | $n = 194$, University of Arizona | Postpurchase (current ownership of car); purchase of footwear in last 4 months Automobiles and footwear | Satisfaction with ownership of product and optimism, pessimism, life satisfaction, generalized consumer discontent, mood; affective/attitudinal variables; expectancy realization | Life satisfaction and consumer dicontent were only two variables that helped explain the variance in auto satisfaction; expectancy realization was only significant measure for footwear with other variables held constant |

* Location not specified.

siderably both within a relatively homogeneous student group and between the various products. Given the minimal number of studies of the experimental type that have been done along with their wide range of focus, there appears to be a great deal of room for further experimentation.

Although the first reported study in the consumer satisfaction area was a laboratory study, few others have followed from this lead. The main advantage of a laboratory study is the possibility of better control over extraneous variables, which may have an effect on the interpretation of the outcomes; the major disadvantage stems from the simulated environment, which reduces external validity. With an area as complex as satisfaction-dissatisfaction, it may be advantageous to back up and consider returning to the laboratory again. The objectivity and control that are afforded the researcher in the laboratory may be well worth the trade-off at this particular time. Since the body of knowledge to date is not overwhelming either in scope or consistency, the possibility of establishing a firmer foundation on which to build in the future may be better achieved by retreating to a more controllable situation. Although the laboratory may not be conducive to studies of great scope, it may be that we have gone too quickly to the field without a firm basis on which to expand our knowledge.

The laboratory also provides the opportunity to make use of mechanical equipment. The studies to date have not made any attempt to incorporate people's physiological measures into information gathering. The validity of such measures remains to be seen. However, it seems reasonable to postulate that dissatisfaction, being an unpleasant state of mind, would tend to produce some type of measurable physiological response (Watson and Gatchel 1979). The galvanic skin response test, for example, seems like an appropriate tool to begin tests in this area, especially with products that require some active involvement such as foods. This procedure would offer an opportunity to measure satisfaction-dissatisfaction during product or service use. Since little effort has been made to expand the measurement of satisfaction during product or service use, a physiological measure may be just the place to start.

COMMENTS ABOUT FIELD STUDIES

Although consumer satisfaction research of a field study nature is much more plentiful than that of an experimental type, the same diversity and inconsistency can also be found here. Even a cursory look at the available research produces enough questions to make generalizations, and consequently the extension to a well-found base of knowledge, inappropriate at the present time.

One questionable matter can be found in the nature of the samples. Although several studies do not provide a breakdown of men and women respondents, nine of the thirty studies reviewed report that women comprised at least 80 percent of the sample. This seems to indicate that a sizable number of field studies in this area may be using a disproportionate share of women subjects. Of note is one study (Hempel 1977) that specifically uses separate measurements of both husband and wife satisfaction levels with housing. Another study (Pickle 1972) also considers the joint decision making (husband and wife) aspects of product purchases but only surveys the wives for measure of satisfaction. The point is that although women may still be the predominant purchasers of many products, the growth in importance of male purchasers has been notable (Miller 1980). The need to more fully explore the attributes and importance of various products and services that lead to satisfaction or dissatisfaction among males becomes increasingly logical given the increase in male shoppers.

As far as sample location, most studies are city specific. Only two of the studies use a national sample, and this data was initially collected by a government agency. Only three additional studies use more than one city as sites for sample selection. The remaining twenty-five studies focus on single cities, many of which are described in general locational terms such as "southwest." Region-specific anomalies may have greatly affected some of the research results thus far. Though costly, an analysis of differences that occur by region, city size, and rural versus urban classifications may be useful. For example, one study by Samli and Uhr (1974) shows many consumers in small towns being dissatisfied and going to big cities to shop.

Sample size in the field studies varies from 25 to over 1800, with most studies being of substantial size. Over half of the studies selected respondents on a random basis, with two-stage area and random digit dialing being used occasionally. These attempts to insure randomness are commendable and should be continued and encouraged in future work. The lack of evidence of national sampling suggests a possible limitation of past studies that should be treated in some future studies.

Another dimension that could benefit from further exploration is the area of family measures of satisfaction. The impact of children's feelings of satisfaction for products primarily consumed by children but purchased by adults may produce some interesting configurations. The combinations of products, purchasers, users, number of family, and stage of usage present a plethora of areas that could be fruitfully explored.

In regard to the time of measurement, the vast majority of studies have used only a postpurchase experience (as in the case of shopping satisfaction) measure. Twenty-one studies can be so classified. While this is certainly an important time and may even be the most appropriate time to measure satisfaction, the additional insight that is afforded by considerations of prepurchase experience measures may be substantial. In addition, very few studies deal with measurement of satisfaction during actual product or service use. Naturally, these feelings may differ from the time of repurchase, but they too may provide some insight and direction to the development of the satisfaction concept.

The related issue of length of time between measurement and initial product purchase is also of importance. Some studies qualify the time since purchase (e.g., purchase of the product during the past year, six months, or same day), while others make ownership of the product the only basis for inclusion in the sample. The variations in time of ownership make combination, comparison, and extrapolation in findings difficult even for studies done with the same product category. For example, major appliances were qualified by Pickle (1972) for purchase within the last year, by Day and Bodur (1977) within the last three years, by Westbrook and Newman (1978) during the last eight weeks, and by Wotruba and Duncan (1975) as simply ownership. Although the desire for knowledge during each of these stages is understood, we may further our overall understanding by concentrating our research using some basic time breakdown, such as five-year, one-year, six-month, or one-month intervals. This would afford some measure of standardization and help to provide at least one common point of focus. When a greater number of studies had been done within each of these time frames, the opportunity would still be there to fill other time intervals.

Other sources of variation are the types of

products under consideration and the length of time under which dissatisfaction may have occurred. Some studies measure dissatisfaction with specific products. The most frequent choices for study are large and small appliances, automobiles, clothing, food products, and housing. Another method used by Valle and Wallendorf (1977) is to ask the respondent to designate a recently purchased product that has caused dissatisfaction. By asking the respondent to recall a source of dissatisfaction, the "power of suggestion" is minimized. This method is worthy of further use. Comparisons between a group given a large set of preselected products to evaluate and another group that is asked general, open-ended questions would provide a measure of the extent to which the prior suggestion of products has an effect on perceived satisfaction-dissatisfaction.

SOME GENERAL RESEARCH DIRECTIONS FOR THE FUTURE

After a look at both the experimental and the field studies, a few general comments seem in order. In many cases, relatively high overall levels of satisfaction were found. For example, Westbrook (1977) found this to be the case with major appliances. Sproles and Geistfeld (1978) found high levels of satisfaction with shopping experiences for clothing, and Berkowitz, Walton, and Walker (1979) had similar results with food shopping from both in-home and traditional shoppers. In view of these findings, the strong trend toward study of dissatisfaction, as evidenced by the increasing number of studies on complaints and complaining behavior, may be somewhat misdirected. While it is important to understand dissatisfaction in order to take appropriate corrective actions and ultimately

prevent dissatisfaction from occurring, maybe we could arrive at the same final point by focusing more effort on trying to understand satisfaction. This would also be following in the tradition of the marketing concept. By isolating dimensions that contribute to satisfaction, the net result should be the reduction in number of complaints. Thinking in terms of trying to increase satisfaction instead of decreasing dissatisfaction may be a more positive approach to the issue.

Another area that Day (1977) alludes to and where little follow-up is evidenced is the "indifferent" consumer. This issue was tangentially addressed in the study by Swan and Trawick (1979) that sought to measure whether consumers actually consciously evaluated products after usage. Moviegoers reported a high rate of postevaluation (87 percent), while meat users reported less (40 percent) and bread users still less (29 percent). This type of study is one dimension of importance in trying to assess levels of indifference. However, as Day points out,

> Among those who do evaluate their consumption experiences it seems likely that there are many who complete the evaluation in a state of indifference, feeling neither satisfied nor dissatisfied by the experience. If either type of indifferent consumer is common for a particular class of product, a research method which forces a satisfied/dissatisfied dichotomy would not be desirable. (Day 1977: 154)

Most measurement instruments do allow for a middle response between satisfied and dissatisfied, but does this middle response mean the same as indifferent? It seems plausible to assume that one may feel either highly satisfied or dissatisfied while still being indifferent with respect to a particular product. Research in this area may offer the marketer some insights into whole categories of products where indifference is more the rule than the exception; this would have some interesting implications in the areas of product research and development and of advertising in particular.

Generally, there has been more emphasis given to satisfaction-dissatisfaction with goods and relatively little focus on services. With the growth in types and numbers of services available, continued interest here is warranted. Frequently used consumer services such as hair care, medical, and physical fitness center services may evoke altogether new dimensions of satisfaction-producing attributes that could also be incorporated into the categories of products more commonly used to measure satisfaction. The not for profit area is also open for investigation.

Another dimension of interest is the difference in satisfaction that may result from a product purchased by the individual and one that was either given to that person or belongs to another person, such as a roommate or another family member. Does one have lower or higher expectations of a gift than for the same product when purchased? Does more or less disconfirmation need to take place to produce similar levels of dissatisfaction?

Another troublesome spot occurs due to actual product performance. When measuring satisfaction of products that people own, there may be a wide variation in the actual performance of different brands, sizes, ages, and number of features of particular products. There seems to be little control for these aspects in most studies. This is another reason why retreating to the laboratory for an interim period may be appropriate at the moment. Number of times the product has actually been used also seems like a relevant factor. While these variables may have been measured in some of the studies, none placed a major focus on them.

Generally, much room for future work remains. The area of satisfaction-dissatisfaction is an extremely complex, multifaceted

area, and research efforts to date have looked at a variety of issues in a variety of ways. Before we get too far afield without a solid anchor, it may be time to consider some steps that can be taken to foster better understanding of the concept and aid in such research efforts. Thought should be given to more experimental work that would help generate a larger, more stable base on which to build. A few common dimensions that would put some of the research efforts on a comparable level and would enable better building blocks to be developed should be investigated. Length of time of ownership would be an easy place to begin standardization. For field studies, national samples would be desirable. All in all, it is an exciting time for expansion of work in the area of satisfaction. With satisfaction being a major goal of marketers and a major desire for consumers, the possibilities are endless.

REFERENCES

Aiello, Albert Jr., and John A. Czepiel. "Customer Satisfaction in a Catalog Type Retail Outlet: Exploring the Effect of Product, Price and Attributes." In *New Dimensions of Consumer Satisfaction and Complaining Behavior,* eds., Ralph L. Day and H. Keith Hunt, pp. 129–35. Bloomington: School of Business: Indiana University, 1979.

————, and Larry J. Rosenberg. "Scaling the Heights of Consumer Satisfaction: An Evaluation of Alternative Measures." In *Consumer Satisfaction, Dissatisfaction and Complaining Behavior,* ed., Ralph L. Day, pp. 43–50. Bloomington: School of Business, Indiana University, 1977.

Anderson, Rolph E. "Consumer Dissatisfaction: The Effect of Disconfirmed Expectancy on Perceived Product Performance." *Journal of Marketing Research* 10 (February 1973): 38–44.

Andreasen, Alan R. "A Taxonomy of Satisfaction/Dissatisfaction Measures." *The Journal of Consumer Affairs* (Summer 1977): 11–24.

Berkowitz, Eric N., John R. Walton, and Orville C. Walker, Jr. "Consumer Interaction with the Micro-Marketing System: Empirical Support of a Satisfaction Model." In *New Dimensions of Consumer Satisfaction and Complaining Behavior,* eds. Ralph L. Day and H. Keith Hunt, pp. 136–39. Bloomington: School of Business, Indiana University, 1979.

Cardozo, Richard N. "Customer Satisfaction: Laboratory Study and Marketing Action." In *Reflections on Progress in Marketing,* pp. 283–89. Chicago: American Marketing Association, 1965.

Cohen, Joel B., and Marvin E. Goldberg. "The Dissonance Model in Post-Decision Product Evaluation." *Journal of Marketing Research* (August 1970): 315–21.

Czepiel, John A., and Larry J. Rosenberg. "Consumer Satisfaction: Toward an Integrative Framework." In *Proceedings of the Southern Marketing Association,* H.W. Nash and D. P. Robin, eds., 169–71. Mississippi State University, Southern Marketing Association, 1976.

Darden, William R., and C.P. Rao. "Satisfaction with Repairs Under Warranty and Perceived Importance of Warranties for Appliances." In *Consumer Satisfaction, Dissatisfaction and Complaining Behavior,* ed., Ralph L. Day, pp. 167–70. Bloomington: School of Business, Indiana University, 1977.

Day, Ralph L. "Extending the Concept of Consumer Satisfaction." In *Advances in Consumer Research,* Vol. IV, ed. William D. Perreault, Jr., pp. 149–54. Atlanta: Association for Consumer Research, 1977.

———, and Muzaffer Bodur. "A Comprehensive Study of Satisfaction with Consumer Services." In *Consumer Satisfaction, Dissatisfaction and Complaining Behavior,* ed., Ralph L. Day, pp. 64–74. Bloomington: School of Business, Indiana University, 1977.

Hagar, Christine J., and Charles R. Handy. "Consumer Satisfaction and Price." In *New Dimensions of Consumer Satisfaction and Complaining Behavior,* eds., Ralph L. Day and H. Keith Hunt, pp. 72–73. Bloomington: School of Business, Indiana University, 1979.

Handy, Charles R. "Monitoring Consumer Satisfaction with Food Products." In *Conceptualization and Measurement of Consumer Satisfaction and Dissatisfaction,* ed., H. Keith Hunt, pp. 215–39. Cambridge, Mass.: Marketing Science Institute, 1977.

Hempel, Donald J. "Consumer Satisfaction with the Home Buying Process: Conceptualization and Measurement." In *Conceptualization and Measurement of Consumer Satisfaction and Dissatisfaction,* ed., H. Keith Hunt, Cambridge, Mass.: pp. 275–99. Marketing Science Institute, 1977.

Hughes, Donald A. "An Investigation of the Relation of Selected Factors to Consumer Satisfaction." In *Conceptualization and Measurement of Consumer Satisfaction and Dissatisfaction,* ed., H. Keith Hunt, Cambridge, Mass.: pp. 300–32. Marketing Science Institute, 1977.

Krishnan, S., and Michael K. Mills. "Dissatisfaction with Retail Stores and Repatronage Behavior." In *New Dimensions of Consumer Satisfaction and Complaining Behavior,* eds., Ralph L. Day and H. Keith Hunt, pp. 124–28. Bloomington: School of Business, Indiana University, 1979.

Leavitt, Clark. "Consumer Satisfaction as the Ultimate Life Force." In *Proceedings of the Association for Consumer Research, Advances in Consumer Research,* vol. III, ed., Beverlee B. Anderson, pp. 252–58. Cincinnati: Association for Consumer Research, 1976.

———. "Consumer Satisfaction and Dissatisfaction: Bi-Polar or Independent?" *Conceptualization and Measurement of Consumer Satisfaction and Dissatisfaction,* ed., H. Keith Hunt, pp. 132–49. Bloomington: School of Business, Marketing Science Institute, Indiana University, 1977.

McNeal, James U. "The Concept of Consumer Satisfaction." In *Management Bibliographies and Reviews,* vol. 3, ed., David Ashton, pp. 231–40. Bradford, England: MCB Publications, 1977.

———, and Charles W. Lamb, Jr. "Consumer Satisfaction as a Measure of Marketing Effectiveness." *Akron Business and Economic Review* (Summer 1979): 41–45.

Madden, Charles Stanley, Eldon L. Little, and Ira J. Dolich. "A Temporal Model of Consumer Satisfaction/Dissatisfaction Concepts as Net Expectations and Performance Evaluations." In *New Dimensions of Consumer Satisfaction and Complaining Behavior,* eds., Ralph L. Day and H. Keith Hunt, pp. 79–82. Bloomington: School of Business, Indiana University, 1979.

Madden, Charles Stanley, and Lori Sharp Franz. "Evaluation as a Surrogate Measure of Expectancy: An Empirical Investigation of Measurement Effect for Longitudinal Models." In *American Marketing Association Educators Conference Proceedings,* pp. 45–48. Chicago: American Marketing Association, 1979.

Maddox, R. Neil. "Consumers' Satisfaction with Supermarkets: A Factor Analytic Study." In *Consumer Satisfaction, Dissatisfaction and Complaining Behavior,* ed., Ralph L. Day, pp. 163–66. Bloomington: School of Business, Indiana University, 1977.

Mason, Joseph Barry, and Samuel H. Himes, Jr. "An Exploratory Behavioral and Socio-Economic Profile of Consumer Action About Dissatisfaction with Selected Household Appliances." *The Journal of Consumer Affairs* (Winter 1973): 121–27.

Mason, Joseph Barry, and J.B. Wilkinson. "Supermarket Product Unavailability and the Consumer Response." In *Consumer Satisfaction, Dissatisfaction and Complaining Behavior,* ed., Ralph L. Day, pp. 153–58. Bloomington: School of Business, Indiana University, 1977.

Miller, Gay Sands. "More Food Advertisers Woo the Male Shopper as He Shares the Load." *Wall Street Journal,* August 26, 1980, p. 1.

Morris, Earl W. "A Normative Deficit Approach to Consumer Satisfaction." In *Conceptualization and Measurement of Consumer Satisfaction and Dissatisfaction,* ed., H. Keith Hunt, pp. 240–72. Cambridge, Mass.: Marketing Science Institute, 1977.

Oliver, Richard L. "A Theoretical Reinterpretation of Expectation and Disconfirmation Effects on Postexposure Product Evaluations: Experience in the Field." In *Consumer Satisfaction, Dissatisfaction and Complaining Behavior,"* ed., Ralph L. Day, pp. 2–9. Bloomington: School of Business, Indiana University, 1977.

———. "Product Satisfaction as a Function of Prior Expectation and Subsequent Disconfirmation: New Evidence." In *New Dimensions of Consumer Satisfaction and Complaining Behavior,* eds., Ralph L. Day and H. Keith Hunt, pp. 66–71. Bloomington: School of Business, Indiana University, 1979.

———. "A Cognitive Model of the Antecedents and Consequences of Satisfaction Decisions." *Journal of Marketing Research* (November 1980): 460–69.

Olshavsky, Richard W., and John A. Miller. "Consumer Expectations, Product Performance, and Perceived Product Quality." *Journal of Marketing Research* (February 1972): 19–21.

Ortinau, David J. "A Conceptual Model of Consumer's Post Purchase Satisfaction/Dissatisfaction Decision Process." In *New Dimensions of Consumer Satisfaction and Complaining Behavior,* eds., Ralph L. Day and H. Keith Hunt, pp. 36–71. Bloomington: School of Business, Indiana University, 1979.

Pfaff, Martin. "The Index of Consumer Satisfaction: Measurement Problems and Opportunities." In *Conceptualization and Measurement of Consumer Satisfaction and Dissatisfaction,* ed., H. Keith Hunt, pp. 36–71. Cambridge, Mass.: Marketing Science Institute, 1977.

Pickle, Hal B., and Ray Bruce. "Consumerism, Product Satisfaction-Dissatisfaction, An Empirical Investigation." *The Southern Journal of Business* (November 1972): 87–100.

Plummer, Joseph T. "Life Style, Social, and Economic Trends Influencing Consumer Satisfaction." In *Conceptualization and Measurement of Consumer Satisfaction and Complaining Behavior,* eds., Ralph L. Day and H. Keith Hunt, pp. 382–408. Bloomington: School of Business, Indiana University, 1977.

Richins, Marsha L. "Consumer Complaining Processes: A Comprehensive Model." In *New Dimensions of Consumer Satisfaction and Complaining Behavior,* eds., Ralph L. Day and H. Keith Hunt, pp. 30–34. Bloomington: School of Business, Indiana University, 1979.

Robinson, Larry M. "Consumer Complaint Behavior: A Review with Implications for Further Research." In *New Dimensions of Consumer Satisfaction and Complaining Behavior,* eds., Ralph L. Day and H. Keith Hunt, pp. 41–50. Bloomington: School of Business, Indiana University, 1979.

Samli, A. Coskun, and Earnest B. Uhr. "The Outshopping Spectrum: Key for Analyzing Intermarket Leakages." *Journal of Retailing* (Summer 1974): 70–78.

Sproles, George B., and Loren V. Geistfeld. "Issues in Analyzing Consumer Satisfaction/Dissatisfaction with Clothing and Textiles." In *Advances in Consumer Research,* Vol. V, ed., H. Keith Hunt, pp. 383–91. Ann Arbor: Association for Consumer Research, 1978.

Swan, John E., and Linda Jones Combs. "Product Performance and Consumer Satisfaction: A New Concept." *Journal of Marketing* (April 1976): 25–33.

Swan, John E. "Consumer Satisfaction with a Retail Store Related to the Fulfillment of Expectations on an Initial Shopping Trip." In *Consumer Satisfaction, Dissatisfaction and Complaining Behavior,* ed., Ralph L. Day, pp. 10–17. Bloomington: School of Business, Indiana University, 1977.

Swan, John E., and I. Fredrick Trawick. "Testing An Extended Concept of Consumer Satisfaction." In *New Dimensions of Consumer Satisfaction and Complaining Behavior,* eds., Ralph L. Day and H. Keith Hunt, pp. 56–61. Bloomington: School of Business, Indiana University, 1979.

Valle, Valerie, and Melanie Wallendorf. "Consumers' Attributions of the Cause of Their Product Satisfaction and Dissatisfaction." In *Consumer Satisfaction, Dissatisfaction and Complaining Behavior,* ed., Ralph L. Day, pp. 26–30. Bloomington: School of Business, Indiana University, 1977.

Watson, Paul J., and Robert J. Gatchel. "Autonomic Measures of Advertising." *Journal of Advertising Research* (June 1979): 15–24.

Westbrook, Robert A. "Correlates of Post Purchase Satisfaction with Major Household Appliances." *Consumer Satisfaction, Dissatisfaction and Complaining Behavior,* ed., Ralph L. Day, pp. 85–90. Bloomington: School of Business, Indiana University, 1977a.

———. "A Study of Consumer Dissatisfaction Before Purchase." In *Advances in Consumer Research,* vol. IV, ed., William D. Perreault, Jr., pp. 142–48. Atlanta: Association for Consumer Research, 1977.

———. "Intra-personal Affective Influence on Consumer Satisfaction with Products." *Journal of Consumer Research* (June 1980): 49–54.

Westbrook, Robert A., and Joseph W. Newman. "An Analysis of Shopper Dissatisfaction for Major Household Appliances." *Journal of Marketing Research* (August 1978): 456–66.

Winter, Mary, and Earl W. Morris. "Satisfaction as an Intervening Variable." In *New Dimensions of Consumer Satisfaction and Complaining Behavior,* eds., Ralph L. Day and H. Keith Hunt, pp. 15–25. Bloomington: School of Business, Indiana University, 1979.

Wotruba, Thomas R., and Patricia L. Duncan. "Are Consumers Really Satisfied?" *Business Horizons* (February 1975): 85–90.

Questions

1. Explain the significance of the length of time between measurement of consumer satisfaction-dissatisfaction and product purchase. Why would this be a potential problem in measurement?

2. Are satisfaction and dissatisfaction opposites on the same continuum, or are they separate dimensions? Justify your answer.

3. Should a marketer attempt to increase satisfaction or decrease dissatisfaction? Explain.

SECTION THREE

Sociological Aspects of Consumer Behavior

In spite of the individuality possessed by everyone, all persons are members of one or more groups. It is for this reason that some behavioral scientists state that all behavior is social in nature. What they mean is that no matter how isolated one seems to be, his or her behavior is still influenced by others. Even the youngster who sneaks away to his "secret hideout" cannot ignore the influence of parents and, perhaps, other people.

As a group member, each person possesses some behavioral patterns that are similar to those of other members of the group. If he or she is a member of ten groups—and this would probably be a small number—then this person will display some behavioral patterns that are like those of the members of each of the ten groups. Thus, an individual will behave somewhat like work associates, other members of the family, social class, ethnic group, and community. It is because of this fact that we often expect the consumer behavior patterns of members of a group to be alike. In such a case, we call the group a market.

The study of groups and of the interaction of their members is essentially the task of sociology. Like the discipline of psychology, sociology consists of many subdisciplines. Usually the subdisciplines have developed to study the behavior of specific groups. For instance, the fields of urban, rural, and industrial sociology study the behavior of their respective groups. There is also a sub-discipline termed sociometry that is concerned with the measurement of social phenomena. Many of the areas of sociology have made direct and indirect contributions to the study of the consumer role. Most of the consumer behavior information in this section has been derived through the use of sociological concepts.

In order to assist in the understanding of these sociological aspects of consumer behavior, this section has been divided into four subsections. Each subsection will deal with a particular type of group influence on the consumer.

PART A: INNOVATORS AND OPINION LEADERS

This section opens with the landmark article by Francis S. Bourne, "The Adoption Process." It was this 1959 article that provided the impetus for much of the subsequent research on product diffusion and product adoption. Bourne sets forth the process by which individuals in a population tend to adopt a new product: The innovators are the pioneers who first try the product; the early adopters wait to see the innovators' results with the product; the early majority are then influenced by the early adopters; the late majority follow; and the laggards adopt the product last.

In the next article, Paul F. Lazarsfeld explains the effects of opinion leaders on various consumer activities in "Who Are the Marketing Leaders?" A number of characteristics for identifying the opinion leaders in a group are set forth in this classic article. Lazarsfeld points out that opinion leaders are an important element for influencing the purchase decisions of products. Therefore, advertising should be directed toward these opinion leaders. Once identification of the leaders has been made, it can help in the choice of the media and planning of ad copy. He notes that opinion leaders are difficult to identify but that three factors tend to distinguish opinion leaders from nonleaders—position on social economic ladder, position in the life cycle, and degree of social integration (gregariousness).

The third article, "The Search for the Consumer Innovator," by Louis E. Boone, explores the personality and socioeconomic characteristics of consumer innovators. In his study of cable television subscribers, Boone found that the consumer innovator possesses most of the same distinguishing socioeconomic characteristics as the first adopter of product goods and services: The innovator has more education, has a higher income, is professional or managerially employed, is married, has position in social and civic organizations, and is occupationally mobile. However, the innovator has leadership ability, is more ascendant, possesses more self-confidence, has a greater acceptance of newness, has higher achievement levels, and initiates change.

PART B: REFERENCE GROUP

In Francis Bourne's classic article, "Group Influence in Marketing and Public Relations," the author shows how reference groups influence the operational level and behavior patterns of individuals. He identifies four types of reference groups against which individuals evaluate themselves—(1) the membership group; (2) the group in which one automatically belongs; (3) the anticipatory group; and (4) the negative, dissociative reference group that an individual would choose to avoid. On the application of the reference group concept, Bourne offers three important considerations for marketers—determine the influence of the reference group, identify the group, and communicate with the group.

In the next article, V. Parker Lessig and C. Whan Park examine the role of reference groups and promotional appeals in satisfying consumer motivation. In "Promotional Perspectives of Reference Group Influence: Advertising Implications," the authors point out three motivational functions—informational, utilitarian, and value-expressive—carried out by reference groups. A study is presented that illustrates several motivational factors that influence an individual and shows that group influence varies for different individuals and products.

PART C: SOCIAL CLASS

In his well-known article, "Social Classes and Spending Behavior," Pierre Martineau introduces the idea that income and occupation are not as significant in the determination of consumption patterns as is social class. He confirms the existence of social classes in metropolitan areas and shows how people, aware of their social positions, tend to conform to their respective class characteristics. He also explains that there are some psychological differences in the various social classes that affect buying behavior. He concludes that consumption patterns operate as prestige symbols for defining social class membership and that a person's social class is a more significant determinant of economic behavior than mere income.

In "The Significance of Social Stratification in Selling," Richard P. Coleman attempts to clarify when and in what ways social class concepts are significant in selling and when they are not relevant. He provides excellent descriptions of Warner's social classes and discusses the relationship between social class, income, and buying behavior. The article makes a substantial contribution to explaining the role of income in social class behavior.

In Terence A. Shimp and J. Thomas Yokum's recent article, "Extensions of the Basic Social Class Model Employed in Consumer Research," the authors present a critical analysis of the manner in which social class has been treated in consumer behavior writings. They point out the flaws of such traditional approaches as measuring only the husband's social class and assuming that the other family members will behave accordingly. They recommend a method that takes into account both husband's and wife's social class. The authors also contend that current behavior is not just a function of the individual's present social class standing, but also of his or her past social class.

PART D: SUBCULTURES AND VALUES

In "Black Buyer Behavior" Donald E. Sexton, Jr., deals with the consumer behavior of one specific subculture. Some conclusions are also drawn on comparing the black and white market segments. Sexton points out that there are distinct differences in consumption habits and attitudes between blacks and whites. However, most of these differences are due to income and/or motivation differences. Sexton also notes that blacks' selection of goods and services is believed to be limited in scope, lower in quality, and higher in price than that of whites. However, he says, the black market itself can be divided into two segments, one with the general middle class lifestyle and the other with the subsistance income level lifestyle. These differences can be observed in store shopping behavior and in product and brand buying behavior.

The next article, "What Every Marketer Should Know About Women," by Rena Bartos, looks at women as a separate market. Bartos indicates that there has been a dramatic increase in the number and change of social values of American working women in the past twenty-five years. She also advances several reasons for the increase in the number of working women and summarizes these reasons as being either economically or attitudinally oriented. Bartos points out that most of these working women are also housewives, though not full time. Four distinct segments in the women's market are presented—the "stay at home housewife," the "plan to work" group, the "casual working woman," and the "career woman." These groups differ demographically and qualitatively, and hence they have different consumer behavior patterns.

In "Children as Consumers: A Review," James U. McNeal describes the child's involvement in the consumer role from a behavioral and cognitive point of view. He argues that yes, indeed, most children are consumers to some extent from age four. In fact, parents encourage them to participate in the consumer role, and by the age of nine, the child is an experienced consumer. Children's consumer behavior in relation to their money expenditure patterns, store choice, and information source are discussed, as well as their cognitive status as consumers.

The next article concerns yet another special group or subculture—the age sixty-five and over consumer. In "Exploring the Gray Market Segment," Betsy D. Gelb studies this elderly market based on four criteria—identity, accessibility, responsiveness, and significance. She concludes from her study that while the market may meet the first three tests as a market segment, it may not, for most marketers, meet the fourth test—enough profits to merit an economic market segment. She volunteers, however, some suggestions on product planning, promotion, pricing, and store location and staffing for those interested in the gray market or those whose products are specifically for this market.

In the final article, "The Role of Personal Values in Marketing and Consumer Behavior," Vinson, Scott, and Lamont note that values are a sociocultural process and that different values lead to differences in consumer behavior. They confirm this proposition in a study among subjects from two culturally distinct regions of the United States. They also discuss personal values in three dimensions—the global or generalized level, the domain specific values, and the evaluation of specific beliefs. As pointed out, however, all three are integrated, affecting the perception of product attributes. These values also provide the basis for individual goal setting as well as helping plan the means to achieve these goals. They suggest that there is a great potential for using the role of personal values in market analysis and segmentation, product planning, promotional strategy, and public policy.

Part A

INNOVATORS AND OPINION LEADERS

29. The Adoption Process

Francis S. Bourne

For many products, the process of adoption follows a rather uniform pattern, from the time the new product is developed until it is widely accepted by the ultimate consumers. More is known about the adoption of agricultural products and practices than about others. Rural sociologists have been concerned with the introduction of new practices and with new product adoption in agriculture for a number of years, and they have systematically studied the process by which change takes place. In addition, some studies have been made of other kinds of innovation, including the adoption by doctors of new wonder drugs for treatment,[1] the adoption of new educational practices by school systems[2] and the adoption of color television.[3] The process of adoption in all these cases has been quite similar. There are exceptions to the pattern; for example, black and white television. The general pattern appears so widely, however, that it is the central theme of this report.

Researchers have charted the course of a new product by determining *when* people adopt it. The curve which results is a simple one, the well known probability curve, in cumulative form.[4] A few people adopt a product at first, then a few more, followed by a rather sharp increase and finally a leveling off when most of the potential consumers have adopted the product.

Such a curve is presented in general form in Figure 1. No scale is given for the time dimension, because this differs from product to product. A number of studies indicate, however, the *form* of the curve remains constant, and therefore that knowledge of the time required for a first relatively small group to adopt a new product will, by establishing the time scale for that product, make possible fairly accurate prediction of the rate of adoption by the rest of the applicable universe.

[1] E. Katz, "The Two-step Flow of Communication: an Up-to-date Report on an Hypothesis," *Public Opinion Quarterly* (1957), pp. 61–78; and H. Menzel and E. Katz, "Social Relations and Innovation in the Medical Profession: The Epidemiology of a New Drug," *Public Opinion Quarterly* (1955–56), 337–352.

[2] R. Mort and T. M. Pierce, *A Time Scale for Measuring the Adaptability of School Systems* (New York: Metropolitan School Study Council, 1947).

[3] Batton, Barton, Durstine and Osborn, *Colortown.*

[4] North Central Rural Sociology Committee, *The Diffusion Process* (Ames: Agricultural Extension Service, Iowa State College, Special Report No. 18, 1957).

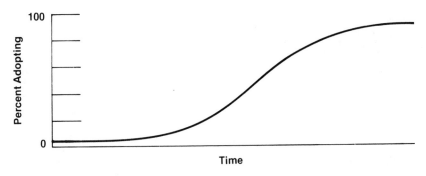

Figure 1

THE KIND OF CHANGE

The time it takes from introduction to wide-spread acceptance depends, in part at least, on the kind of change involved. The adoption of a new product can be viewed as a special case of attitude change. Almost by definition, such a change encounters resistance. The new product or method usually alters or replaces something which is already part of the individual's pattern of thought. If the change under consideration is a really major one, it is quite likely that the attitudes and feelings associated with the old way are strongly held and will account for a great deal of resistance. On the other hand, if the change is trivial, the associated attitudes may be taken on easily. (They may also be cast off easily, of course.) Most new products or practices probably encounter resistance somewhere between these two extremes.

When new products are being adopted, there are different levels of *complexity* of change. The greater the complexity, the more resistance is aroused, and the longer the period required for adoption. Researchers have listed four levels of complexity in the changes usually confronting farmers who are adopting new products or practices.[5] Least

complex is a simple change in materials or equipment. Such a change might be the decision to try another brand of fertilizer or to increase the amount already being used. A change in technique is slightly more complex. The farmer must learn to use the new method and this may involve more risk. An example might be applying fertilizer along planted rows, instead of broadcast over the field. The third level involves both a change in materials and a change in technique. A farmer who has never used fertilizer faces such a change. He must adopt the new material, acquire the equipment to apply it, and learn how to use the equipment. The most complex change is a change of enterprise; for example, a change from cotton growing to dairying.

Obviously there are shadings in complexity among these four types of change, and other kinds of new products may involve a wider range of complexities than do farming practices. However, the level of complexity is an important factor in determining the time it takes for a new product to be adopted. Fifteen years elapsed between the introduction of hybrid seed corn and its adoption by almost 98 per cent of the farmers.[6] Other changes

---

[5] E. A. Wilkening, "The Role of Communicating Agents in Technological Change in Agriculture," *Social Forces* (1956), pp. 361–367.

[6] B. Ryan and N. C. Gross, "The Diffusion of Hybrid Seed Corn in Two Iowa Communities," *Rural Sociology* (1943), pp. 15–24; and B. Ryan and N. C. Gross, *Acceptance and Diffusion of Hybrid Seed Corn*

take longer. The adoption of new educational practices by school systems took 50 years.[7] Some changes take place quickly.

It is not always easy to tell how complex a change is involved in a new product. Hybrid corn is one example. Initially, this seemed like a simple change in materials. Actually, it was a far more complex change. Farmers feared the total reliance on commercial sources for seed corn, something they had previously produced for themselves. Furthermore, many farmers took pride in their ability to select good seed corn from their own crop, and they were accorded status for this skill. The new hybrid corn not only made the farmer feel more dependent, it also did away with an important source of prestige. A large majority of farmers had probably adopted hybrid corn within five years of the initial distribution, but it took fifteen years before almost all farmers were using it. Now, when a new hybrid variety of anything is introduced, it is adopted much more quickly. Examples are hybrid chickens and hybrid hogs.

The complexity of the change is also one important factor in determining the time required for adoption. There are others. For instance, *cost* is important. The more costly the item, the longer it takes before it is widely adopted. *Rate of return* and *visibility of return* are also important. A change which has rapid and obvious results is adopted more quickly than a change with slower, less visible results. In the long run, of course, the change which produces slower results may return more, but it still is not adopted as quickly. A new fertilizer is likely to be adopted more quickly, for example, than soil conservation practices.

---

in Two Iowa Communities (Ames: Iowa Agricultural Experiment Station, Research Bulletin 372, 1950).

[7] P. R. Mort and T. M. Pierce, *op. cit.*

THE INDIVIDUAL ADOPTION PROCESS

The decision to adopt a new product is not simply a "yes" or "no" decision, nor is it something that happens all at once. When an individual is confronted with the possibility of change, he goes through several mental stages before he finally makes up his mind to adopt or not to adopt. Five stages in the decision-making process may be distinguished. Farmers readily recognized these stages when questioned regarding their decisions to make changes and adopt new products.

Awareness comes first. At this point, the farmer learns about the new product. He knows it exists, but he has only general information about it. The *interest or information* stage follows. If interested, the farmer begins to collect more specific information about the new product. If his interest continues to grow, he wants to know the potentialities of the new product for him; whether or not it will increase his income or contribute to other ends considered by him to be important. The next step is the *mental application or evaluation* stage. The farmer goes through the change mentally and asks himself, "How would I do it? Can I do it? If I do it, will I be better off?" The final stage before adoption is the *trial* stage. At this point the farmer tries the product out on a small scale if this is possible. Many farmers purchased a small can of weed spray and used it on their gardens before they used it on their crops on a large scale. A great many farmers planted six acres of hybrid seed corn the first year, the acreage one bushel of the new seed would sow. Some products cannot be tried out on a small scale, and it seems quite reasonable to expect such products to require a longer adoption time. However, people seem to be quite ingenious at finding ways to try new ideas. Some housewives prepared small amounts of food for freezing, and either rented locker space or used a neighbor's freezer before they gave up traditional canning methods and bought the necessary equipment for themselves. Marketing people have been aware of the value of free trials for many years. The trial stage appears to play a crucial role in the decision-making process. However, the other stages are important too, and probably give meaning to this final step before adoption. They should not be ignored.

The last stage is the *adoption* stage. At this point the farmer decides to adopt the new product and begins using it on a full scale. Presumably he is a "satisfied customer," at least until some other product comes along to replace it and the adoption process starts again.

ADOPTER CATEGORIES

Obviously, not all people adopt a new product at the same time. The adoption curve illustrates this point and suggests that some people arrive at a decision more quickly than others. Some people adopt very quickly. Others wait a long time before they take up the new product, and still others never adopt. There has been a great deal of interest in these individual differences and a great deal of speculation about "innovators," those who are first in a community to adopt a new product. To explore these individual differences, the Iowa State researchers took the data from a number of independent studies of new product adoption by farmers. They divided people into groups according to time of adoption,[8] and

[8] For convenience in making comparative studies, researchers used standard deviations of a normal distribution to establish the percentage breaks between categories. People who fall within one standard deviation above the mean are considered in the early majority; people who are between one and two standard deviations above the mean are early adopters. Similarly, people within one standard deviation below the mean are late majority, etc.

then studied each group. Significant differences appeared among them. These were the groups they distinguished and studied:

People adopting		Cumulative total adopting	
First	2.5%	Innovators	2.5%
Next	13.5%	Early adopters	16.0%
Next	34.0%	Early majority	50.0%
Next	34.0%	Late majority	84.0%
Last	16.0%	Laggards	100.0%

"Innovators" are arbitrarily defined here as the first 2.5 per cent to adopt the new product. Based on the data compiled, these generalizations appear for farm innovators.[9]

They have larger than average farms, are well educated and usually come from well established families. They usually have a relatively high net worth and—probably more important—a large amount of risk capital. They can afford and do take calculated risks on new products. They are respected for being successful, but ordinarily do not enjoy the highest prestige in the community. Because innovators adopt new ideas so much sooner than the average farmer, they are sometimes ridiculed by their conservative neighbors. This neighborhood group pressure is largely ignored by the innovators, however. The innovators are watched by their neighbors, but they are not followed immediately in new practices.

The activities of innovators often transcend local community boundaries. Rural innovators frequently belong to formal organizations at the county, regional, state, or national level. In addition, they are likely to have many informal contacts outside the community; they may visit with others many miles away who are also trying a new technique or product, or who are technical experts.

[9] North Central Rural Sociology Committee, *How Farm People Accept New Ideas* (Ames: Iowa Agricultural Extension Service, Iowa State College, Special Report No. 15, 1955); and E. M. Rogers, "Categorizing the Adopters of Agricultural Practices," *Rural Sociology* (1943), pp. 15–21.

The "early adopters" are defined as the next 13.5 per cent of the people who adopt the new product. According to the researchers, early adopter farmers have the following characteristics.

They are younger than the average farmer, but not necessarily younger than the innovators. They also have a higher than average education, and participate more in the formal activities of the community through such organizations as churches, the PTA, and farm organizations. They participate more than the average in agricultural cooperatives and in government agency programs in the community (such as Extension Service or Soil Conservation). In fact, there is some evidence that this group furnishes a disproportionate amount of the formal leadership (elected officers) in the community. The early adopters are also respected as good sources of new farm information by their neighbors.

The third category of adopters is the "early majority," the 34 per cent of people who bring the total adoption to 50 per cent. The number of adoptions increases rapidly after this group begins to adopt.

The early majority are slightly above average in age, education, and farming experience. They have medium high social and economic status. They are less active in formal groups than innovators or early adopters, but more active than those who adopt later. In many cases they are not formal leaders in the community organizations, but they are active members in these organizations. They also attend Extension meetings and farm demonstrations.
    The people in this category are most likely to be informal rather than elected leaders. They have a following insofar as people respect their opinions, their "high morality and sound judgment." They are "just like their following, only more so." They must be sure an idea will work before they adopt it. If the informal leader fails two or three times, his following looks elsewhere for information and guidance. Because the informal leader has more limited resources than the early adopters

and innovators, he cannot afford to make poor decisions; the social and economic costs are too high.
    These people tend to associate mainly in their own community. When people in the community are asked to name neighbors and friends with whom they talk over ideas, these early majority are named disproportionally frequently. On their part, they value highly the opinions their neighbors and friends hold about them, for this is their main source of status and prestige. The early majority may look to the early adopters for their new farm information.

The "late majority" are the fourth category. These are the 34 percent of farmers who have adopted the new product after the average farmer is already using it.

Those in this group have less education and are older than the average farmer. While they participate less actively in formal groups, they probably form the bulk of the membership in these formal organizations. Individually they belong to fewer organizations, are less active in organizational work, and take fewer leadership roles than the earlier adopters. They do not participate in as many activities outside the community as do people who adopt earlier.

The last category, the final 16 per cent of those who adopt a new idea, are the "laggards." This group may include the "nonadopters" as well if the new product is not used by everyone.

They have the least education and are the oldest. They participate least in formal organizations, cooperatives, and government agency programs. They have the smallest farms and the least capital. Many are suspicious of county Extension agents and agricultural salesmen.

These are some of the important differences among the adopter categories. They may provide useful guidelines for further exploration. For example, each of these categories plays an important role for the others in the adoption process. Innovators are the pioneers, and early adopters wait to see the innovators' results before trying the new product themselves. The early adopters, in turn, often influence the early majority. In addition, each of these categories seems to rely on different sources of information and influence, other than the sources already described.

Questions

1. Explain the five stages in Bourne's "decision-making process."
2. Explain the stages in the adoption process and differentiate between each stage.
3. How can knowledge of the adoption process be useful to the marketer?

30. Who Are the Marketing Leaders?

Paul F. Lazarsfeld

According to Paul Lazarsfeld, the key to economic and efficient marketing lies in locating and reaching the opinion leaders who through personal contact with small groups, notably family, friends and neighbors, influence the purchasing decisions of the majority of consumers. A number of studies conducted by other experts reinforce this theory.

William H. Whyte, Jr., in his study of air conditioner ownership in a Philadelphia community, records a very high degree of interpersonal influence in the purchase of the units. In addition, his study shows that the direction of the flow of interpersonal influence is directly correlated with social contact, namely the friendship patterns of the housewives and children of the community.

In other words, Whyte discovered that sheer location of a house can play a major role in opinion leadership. He contends that marketing influence tends to flow up and down streets and across narrow alleys—where there is the greatest chance for casual everyday contact, rather than across the street—where there is apt to be less casual neighboring among the people who live on the two sides.

The importance of opinion leadership and social contact is even more clear in a recent Columbia study of the pattern of adoption of a new ethical drug by a group of doctors.

Opinion leaders were located by having the doctors name the three colleagues whom they see most often socially, the three with whom they most often discuss their cases and the three of whom they usually go for professional information and advice.

Significantly, the study found that the doctors' willingness to try the drug is directly related to their degree of social integration or gregariousness. On the average, the doctors named by many of their colleagues started using the drug earlier than those who were mentioned by few or none of their associates.

The study also charts the acceptance pattern of the drug, thus how buying influence spread through four different groups of doctors: first, of course, the socially integrated "innovators" who took the lead, but whose action did not immediately result in a rush to follow suit; the drug was adopted next by the "influentials"; their action was followed shortly by the largest group, the "followers"; finally, the remaining small groups, the "diehards," who are the least socially integrated of all, adopted the drug.

Thus, from these studies it's clear that there exist certain specific marketing leaders who exert significant influence on the purchasing decisions of their fellow consumers. What practical value does the theory of marketing leadership have for advertisers?

For one thing, it suggests that a radical reappraisal of advertising strategies may be in order. The mere knowledge that most consumers take their purchasing leads from a smaller select group seems to indicate a more specialized selling approach.

Second, the studies indicate the grave importance of aggressive advertising and selling in the initial stages of a campaign, particularly in the case of new products. For example, in his studies Whyte finds that in close-knit communities the earliest buyers of appliances (who are comparable to the "innovators" in the drug study) are generally subject to "raised eyebrows." However, once the proportion of appliance ownership has spread sufficiently to include the marketing leaders, the biggest group of consumers—the followers—jump on the bandwagon and tend to "punish" those who lag behind.

Thirdly, an awareness of the existence of marketing leaders could be an invaluable weapon in the planning of ad copy and the buying of media. Once the advertiser knows who the marketing leaders are, he can direct his advertising to this select group that will eventually, through its influence, establish the buying pattern of his total market.

Who, then, is this marketing leader? Locating him is probably the toughest problem of all. In the first place, since his "leadership" is of the casual, everyday face-to-face variety, it is usually so invisible and inconspicuous that it would actually be more accurate to call it "guidance." It's the very unobtrusiveness of his leadership or guidance that makes the marketing leader exceedingly difficult to pin down.

Lazarsfeld has one suggestion for locating marketing leaders on a local level. Since opinion leadership of any sort is directly related to social integration or gregariousness, marketing leaders in specific communities could be pinpointed through the membership rolls of organized groups such as clubs, civic associations or the PTA.

According to Lazarsfeld, this technique could be a boon for advertisers who work through local dealers and for those who distribute trial samples of products or use direct mail.

On a broader or national level, locating marketing leaders is not quite so simple. Lazarsfeld goes about it by isolating the specific characteristics that seem to distinguish opinion leaders from non-leaders. As benchmarks he uses three factors: position on the social and economic ladder, position in the life-cycle, the degree of social integration or gregariousness.

In studying the relationship of marketing leadership to status Lazarsfeld finds, contrary to traditional sociological thinking, that influence does not emanate from the highest status group and trickle down to the lower levels.

Instead, in what he terms a "horizontal pattern" of influence, each status group has its own corps of leaders who generally influence only the members of their own group.

In the relatively rare instances when marketing influence does exist among people of different status groups, says Lazarsfeld, this influence is just as likely to emanate from the low status group and move upward as it is to start from the top and flow down the status ladder. Again contrary to popular opinion, Lazarsfeld finds that the highest status group does not account for a great preponderance of opinion leaders. As his study of 800 women in Decatur, Ill., shows, marketing leaders are found in almost equal numbers on all status levels (see chart A).

Lazarsfeld concludes that if women consumers in the highest status group do seem a

little more likely to emerge as marketing leaders than women of the lowest group it is because of two things: their ability to afford more household help leaves them more time for socializing; the sheer prestige of their high status position might make them appear more highly qualified as marketing leaders (although, according to Lazarsfeld, there is absolutely no evidence that they are actually any more skilled in marketing than any other women).

Lazarsfeld says there are two sound reasons for the tendency to status-bound, horizontal marketing leadership. Obviously, women of like status have similar budgetary problems and limitations. Therefore, it seems only natural that they should look to members of their own group for marketing advice.

Second, Lazarsfeld maintains that today's stores and shopping centers tend to cater somewhat to women of one particular status

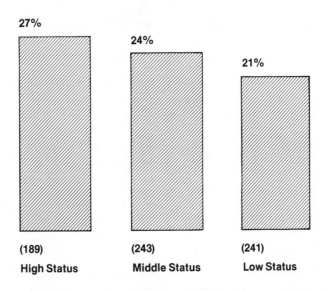

Chart A / Marketing leaders are found in almost equal numbers on all three status levels. *Note:* Numbers in parentheses under each bar represent the total number of cases on which the percentage of opinion leadership is based. Thus 27% of the 189 high status women in our sample are marketing leaders. This procedure is used in all subsequent charts.

group. Therefore, in the course of shopping, when immediate marketing advice is needed, the women on hand to provide it are likely to be of similar status.

In short, with marketing leaders existing on all three status levels, it's obvious that a single advertising campaign is not the most effective way to reach the total market. Clearly, advertisers must use separate and appropriate approaches to appeal to the marketing leaders on each of the three levels, who in turn influence the marketing decisions on the other members of their group.

The second criterion that Lazarsfeld uses to determine the characteristics of opinion leaders is position in the life-cycle (age, marital status, number of children and their ages). He works on the premise that holding a particular position in the life-cycle naturally inclines a person to some special interests rather than others. It is these interests, he says, that characterize her as either a leader or a follower.

Although position on the status ladder seems to have little relevance to marketing leadership, position in the life-cycle is a different story. Lazarsfeld's studies find that among women one particular group—large family wives (two or more children)—emerge strongly as marketing leaders. In fact, according to the Decatur study, large family wives are almost twice as likely to be marketing leaders as women of any other life-cycle type (see chart B).

This concentration of marketing leaders among the large family wives clearly indicates this: the most important factor in marketing leadership is the intensive, everyday "ex-

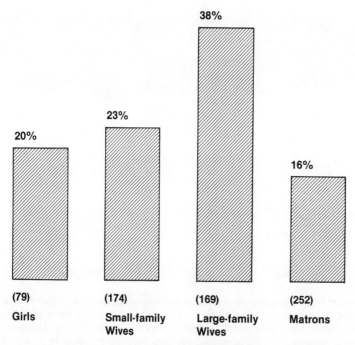

Chart B / The large family wives are the marketing leaders

periencing" of marketing problems, characteristic of a woman with a large or growing family.

Interestingly, Lazarsfeld's studies indicate that the matron (over 45 years of age) with all her years of experience in managing households, is no more likely to emerge as a marketing leader than unmarried girls or small family wives (one or no children). In other words, "experiencing" is far more vital to marketing leadership than "experience—the symbol of the matron and her years."

The fact that the greatest concentration of marketing leaders is found among large family wives raises two important questions:

Do large family wives influence the marketing decisions of the majority of all women?

Or is their marketing leadership of the horizontal variety, and confined to other large family wives?

Lazarsfeld concedes that a good case can be made for both wives.

On the first score, he says it's possible that large-family wives are much more concerned with marketing problems than are women in other positions in the life-cycle.

They are the women who seek advice most. Therefore, out of necessity they generate the greatest number of marketing leaders to provide this advice.

On the other hand, it's just as possible that marketing activities are about the same among all women. This would mean that advice-seeking is distributed about evenly throughout the population.

If such is the case, then the concentration of marketing leaders among large family wives can mean only one thing: women of all life-cycle types turn to the large family wives for marketing advice.

Unfortunately, there are no studies directly corroborating either of the two alternatives. Lazarsfeld approaches the problem by ana-lyzing the ages of both people involved in specific advice-giving marketing situations.

Using this method he finds that large family wives are the prime marketing advisors for women of all other life-cycle types as well as their fellow large family wives. His conclusions are based on the following research findings:

About half of advice-seeking women consult other women of about their own age.

Of the 50% who seek advice from women either younger or older than they, the greatest number seem to turn to women in the 25–44 age group. In other words, both the younger and older women seek market leadership from the group classified as "wives."

When these "wives" themselves seek advice outside their own life-cycle group, they tend to consult older women somewhat more than younger ones.

Furthermore, younger women are far more inclined to consult their seniors on marketing problems than are older women apt to seek advice from their juniors.

William Whyte also notes a high degree of interpersonal advice-giving among young white-collar consumers. He attributes it to two factors: today's young consumers face many more marketing decisions regarding purchasing than did any of their counterparts in the past. Sometimes, they have far less contact with tradition than did their parents and grandparents. Therefore, they depend upon the opinions of their contemporaries to guide them in the "delicate job of keeping in tune with the life style of the moment."

In addition, Whyte's studies find that the more similar the houses in the neighborhood or block, the more important the minor differences become to the people living there. That's why, according to Whyte, marginal purchases are the key ones.

Clearly, then, with marketing leadership concentrated in young consumers, partic-

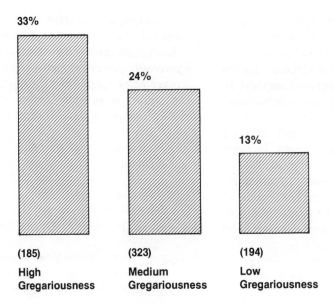

33%

24%

13%

(185)
High
Gregariousness

(323)
Medium
Gregariousness

(194)
Low
Gregariousness

ularly large family wives, advertisers would do well, advises Paul Lazarsfeld, to make their biggest pitch to the young (under 45) housewife with two or more children.

Of the three factors used to locate the opinion leader, Lazarsfeld finds the greatest correlation between market leadership and gregariousness. From the findings of his Decatur study he concludes that the greater the extent of a woman's social contacts, the greater are her chances of emerging as a marketing leader (see chart C).

The correlation between gregariousness and marketing leadership holds true for each life-cycle type. However, says he, among the large family wives, even the least gregarious women have a better chance of becoming marketing leaders than the most gregarious members of the other life-cycle groups.

It's Lazarsfeld's opinion that the combined factors of life-cycle and gregariousness "tell the marketing leadership story." He

points out that the slightly higher incidence of marketing leaders among high status women is merely a result of their greater opportunity for social contact. In fact, according to the findings of the Decatur study, a highly gregarious low status woman is four times as likely to be a marketing leader than a nongregarious woman of high status.

Obviously, the marketing leaders get the information they disseminate from somewhere. Do they get it from other opinion leaders or from sources such as mass media?

Lazarsfeld says that "ideas often flow from air media and print media to the opinion leaders and from them to the less active sections of the population" in what he calls a "two-step flow of influence."

In writing of Lazarsfeld's studies, University of Georgia assistant marketing professor Robert C. Brooks says that opinion leaders are sought out because of their knowledge acquired through media exposure. He also believes that because the leaders are sought out, they feel an obligation to keep informed.

Yet despite the fact that marketing leaders have more contact with media than consumers in general, studies indicate that their own buying decisions are not especially influenced by media advertising.

Lazarsfeld theorizes that marketing leaders, much like the nonleaders, base their decisions primarily on information obtained through personal contact—perhaps with other marketing leaders, and use media only as a supplementary device.

Questions

1. Differentiate between innovators and opinion leaders.
2. According to the author, how do opinion leaders base their decisions? Based on this information, how would a marketer reach them?
3. What three criteria does the author suggest for determining the characteristics of opinion leaders?
4. What practical value does the theory of marketing leadership have for advertisers?

31. The Search for The Consumer Innovator

Louis E. Boone

The acceptance of newness by the members of a particular society or culture is a subject of major interest to anthropologists, sociologists, and businessmen. How are new ideas, practices, and products diffused from one individual or group to another? Are there some groups or individuals who are more receptive to newness than others?

Successful innovation is the key to business success. Yet new-product failure rates are estimated as high as 95 percent.[1] New-product introductions appear to be not only the most important undertaking in marketing but also the most difficult.

Within the past ten years businessmen have discovered that for a number of years the

[1] S. J. Shaw, "Behavioral Science Offers Fresh Insights of New Product Acceptance," *Journal of Marketing* (January 1965), p. 9.

related disciplines of anthropology and sociology have been conducting significant research relating to the diffusion of innovations. Their findings appear to be applicable to the marketing problems involved in introducing new products.

RELATED RESEARCH

Anthropological Studies

Since the nineteenth century anthropologists have been studying the spread of ideas and practices among widely separated cultures. Although some anthropologists have discussed the speed of diffusion,[2] they have generally been more interested in the spreading of ideas and practices between societies than within a particular society. An important exception is H. G. Barnett, who has theorized that certain members of a society are predisposed to accept new ideas or practices and that these individuals possess identifiable biographical (socioeconomic) characteristics.[3]

Sociology

Sociologists have been writing on the subject of diffusion for over sixty years. Tarde was the first to point out that the process of diffusion takes the shape of the normal curve.[4] A few innovators adopt the practice first; then the majority of the community follow the lead of the innovators and adopt; finally, the remaining members accept the innovation. Tarde was also the first to note the

presence of cosmopolitism (intersocietal orientation) in the innovators.

The classic drug study[5] isolated a number of characteristics of the physician-innovator: younger age, larger number of medical journal subscriptions, greater attachment to medical institutions outside the community. It was also discovered that doctors who were mentioned by a number of other physicians as sources of advice and information used the new drug earlier than those doctors mentioned by few or none of their colleagues, indicating a definite relationship between opinion leadership and innovativeness.

Rural Sociology

The largest number of diffusion studies has been conducted by the rural sociologists. Their research studies, frequently financed by funds from the U.S. Department of Agriculture, number over 1,000.[6] Studies such as the investigation of the diffusion of hybrid seed corn[7] have isolated the following characteristics of the farmer innovator: (1) higher income, (2) larger farm, (3) higher educational levels, (4) younger age, (5) community prestige, (6) frequent trips to the nearest metropolitan center (cosmopolitism), and (7) use of farm information sources.

Two sociologists, Rogers and Straus, have mentioned the possibility of relating personality traits and innovativeness.[8] Rogers feels

[2] C. Wissler, *Man and Culture* (New York: Thomas Crowell Co., 1923), pp. 115–16.

[3] H. G. Barnett, *Innovation: The Basis of Cultural Change* (New York: McGraw-Hill Book Co., 1953), pp. 329–410.

[4] G. Tarde, *The Laws of Imitation* (New York: Henry Holt & Co., 1903), pp. 87–88.

[5] J. Coleman, E. Katz, and H. Menzel, "The Diffusion of an Innovation among Physicians," *Sociometry* (December 1957), pp. 253–70.

[6] See E. M. Rogers, *Bibliography on the Diffusion of Innovations* (East Lansing: Department of Communications, Michigan State University, 1967).

[7] B. Ryan and N. Gross, "The Diffusion of Hybrid Seed Corn in Two Iowa Communities," *Rural Sociology* (March 1943), pp. 15–24.

[8] E. M. Rogers, "Personality Correlates of the Adoption of Technological Practices," *Rural Sociology* (September 1957), pp. 267–68: M. A. Straus, "Personality Testing the Farm Population, *Rural Sociology* (June 1956), pp. 293–94.

that mental rigidity and change orientation (dogmatism) may be significantly related to farm-practice adoption. Straus hypothesizes that such traits as ascendancy and sociability are likely to be related to innovativeness.

Marketing Studies

Of the more than 900 research studies on file in the Diffusion Documents Center at Michigan State University, less than 5 percent can be classified as marketing studies.

The first diffusion research in marketing was conducted in 1959 by Opinion Research Corporation (ORC).[9] After interviewing 105 household heads regarding their first use of a number of consumer products, ORC concluded that approximately 27 percent of the population could be classified as "high mobiles"—and that these individuals constituted the leadership elite in the United States. They characterized this group by occupational mobility, continued education, higher incomes, gregariousness, and more frequent travel than the remainder of the population.

A second marketing study revealed that first purchasers of color television and stereophonic equipment had high family incomes, were highly educated, and were concentrated in the professions and in managerial occupations.[10]

Gorman appears to have been the first to apply the model of the rural sociologists to the diffusion of a consumer good.[11] His conclu-

sions regarding the first purchasers of color television receivers were identical with those of Bell.

A recent attempt to relate personality traits to innovativeness was unsuccessful. The investigators were unable to distinguish between purchasers and nonpurchasers of consumer goods on the basis of respondents' scores on a personality inventory.[12]

THE CATV STUDY

Although several marketing investigations had verified the possibility of identifying first adopters of consumer goods on the basis of income, education, and occupation, no empirical research had obtained more probing behavioral characteristics from all adopters over a period of years following the introduction of the innovation. Also, many of the studies have relied entirely upon subject recall of date of first adoption. The authors of the drug study discovered that people would consistently state that they had adopted the drug much earlier than they actually had.

Finally, only one investigation has been conducted to search for common personality characteristics among early adopters of new producer or consumer goods.[13] This study also suffered from the previously mentioned limitation and compared only housewives identifying themselves as innovators and others considered as nonadopters.

The Innovation

The five-year-old community antenna television system (CATV) in Laurel, Mississippi, was selected as the innovation subject. Laurel

---

[9] *America's Tastemakers* (Princeton, N.J.: Opinion Research Corp., 1959).

[10] W. E. Bell, "Consumer Innovators: A Market for Newness," in *Toward Scientific Marketing,* ed. S. A. Greyser (Chicago: American Marketing Association, 1964).

[11] W. P. Gorman, "Market Acceptance of a Consumer Durable Good Innovation: A Socioeconomic Analysis of First and Second Buying Households of Color Television Receivers in Tuscaloosa, Alabama" (Ph.D. diss., University of Alabama, 1966).

[12] T. R. Robertson and J. G. Myers, "Personality Correlates of Opinion Leadership and Innovative Buying Behavior," *Journal of Marketing Research* (May 1969), pp. 164–68.

[13] Ibid.

television viewers received strong signals from the local station and weak signals from the Meridian station with the aid of an outside antenna. The cable provided clear reception from stations in Meridian, Jackson, Mobile, Biloxi, and New Orleans and broadcast continuous local weather reports and FM music to subscribers at a cost of $5.00 per month. To facilitate the diffusion of the innovation and to reduce the perceived risk of potential adopters, the franchisee made an initial offer of free installation of the service and has periodically repeated the offer of free installation.

Methodology

Identification of all adopters and adoption dates were available from the files of the local franchise. Since the franchisee provided the only CATV service in the city, the problem of determining relative dates of adoption was avoided.

A 10 percent systematic sample was selected containing fifty-two Consumer Innovators (persons who subscribed within three months following the initial offering) and fifty-five Consumer Followers (persons first subscribing at least six months following the first offering). Personal interviews were conducted, and relevant socioeconomic characteristics were recorded.

The California Psychological Inventory (CPI) was then administered to the fifty Consumer Innovators and forty-eight Consumer Followers who agreed to participate. The CPI, unlike many other personality inventories, is designed primarily for "normal" subjects. Its eighteen scales provide a comprehensive portrait of the individual.[14]

[14] H. G. Gough, *Manual for the California Psychological Inventory* (Palo Alto, Calif.: Consulting Psychologists Press, 1964).

FINDINGS

Socioeconomic Characteristics

More than 92 percent of the Consumer Innovators were married, as compared with 81 percent of the Consumer Followers. The differences were significant at the .05 level. Both groups showed a much larger percentage of married households than the 66.8 percent reported for Laurel by the 1960 Census Bureau reports.[15]

Findings regarding income, occupation, and educational levels of the Consumer Innovators coincided with those of Bell and Gorman. Fifty-five percent of the Consumer Innovators were employed in professional, managerial, or proprietorial occupations, as compared with 41 percent of the later adopters and 22 percent of all Laurel household heads.

Employment in nonsalaried occupations would possibly expose the Innovator to more risk than those household heads in other occupational categories. All consumer behavior involves risk in that the consumer's actions will produce uncertain, and possibly unpleasant, consequences. Therefore consumers tend to develop decison strategies so that they can act with relative confidence when faced with risk-filled situations.[16] It is possible that certain risk-filled occupations provide the individual with additional experience and additional confidence when making decisions where considerable risk is involved.

Median household income for the first

[15] U.S. Bureau of the Census, *United States Census of Population: Mississippi, 1960* (Washington, D.C.: Government Printing Office, 1961), pp. 26–42, 125.

[16] See R. A. Bauer, "Consumer Behavior as Risk Taking," in *Proceedings of the 43rd National Conference of the American Marketing Association,* ed. R. S. Hancock (Chicago: American Marketing Association, 1960), pp. 389–98.

adopters was $12,000, as compared with $7,900 for the Consumer Followers. Twenty-five percent of the Consumer Innovators earned $20,000 or more, while only 3.6 percent of the later adopters reported incomes as high as this.

Since the Innovator is first to adopt, he must take risks that can be avoided by later adopters. Some of these new untried products are likely to prove unsatisfactory. Thus the Innovator must be willing to absorb the loss from the occasional failures. And the wealthy individual risks proportionately less than does the less affluent individual in making the first purchase of the innovation.

Occupational mobility of the household head was significantly greater for the Consumer Innovators than for the later adopters. Nearly 25 percent of the first adopters had changed jobs at least once between 1964 and 1968, as compared with 16 percent of the Consumer Followers. In this respect the Consumer Innovators appear to resemble the "high mobiles" of the Opinion Research Corporation study. Occupational mobility proved an important means of distinguishing the "high mobiles" in the ORC study.

The first adopters also differed significantly from the Consumer Followers in the number of memberships in social and civic clubs, professional associations, and organized church groups. Consumer Innovators averaged 4.7 club memberships—almost twice as many as the 2.4 average for Consumer Followers. Over 10 percent of the Consumer Innovators belonged to eleven or more organizations.

The Innovators also held an average of 1.4 offices in local and area clubs and organizations—2.5 times as many as the Consumer Followers, who averaged 0.6 offices per household. More than 15 percent of the first adopters held four or more offices, while only

3.6 percent of the Consumer Follower households held four offices or more.

The sizable difference in the number of offices held by the two innovator categories strongly suggests the presence of opinion leadership among Consumer Innovator households. Over fifteen studies by rural sociologists have shown that farmer innovators have more opinion leadership than do later adopters.[17]

Neither age nor number of visits with friends, neighbors, and relatives was statistically significant. Although the differences were not statistically significant, the first adopters did subscribe to an average of 4.5 magazines, as compared with 3.4 for the Consumer Followers. They also averaged 3.4 distant trips per month, compared with 2.5 for the later adopters, suggesting a slightly larger number of impersonal sources of information and slightly greater cosmopolitism.

Personality Traits of CATV Adopters

The Consumer Innovators scored significantly higher than the later adopters on ten of the eighteen scales of the California Psychological Inventory: Dominance, Capacity for Status, Sociability, Social Presence, Self-Acceptance, Sense of Well-Being, Tolerance, Achievement via Conformance, Achievement via Independence, and Intellectual Efficiency (see table 1).

The Dominance scale measures leadership ability and initiative. The high scores by the Consumer Innovators on this scale appear to reflect an important aspect of their personality. They are also consistent with the leadership ability displayed by the disproportion-

[17] See E. M. Rogers, *Diffusion of Innovations* (New York: Free Press, 1962), p. 184.

Table 1 / Mean Scores of Low-Income Innovators, Consumer Innovators, and Consumer Followers on the California Psychological Inventory

Scale	Low-Income Consumer (N = 10)	Consumer Innovators (N = 50)	Consumer Followers (N = 48)
Dominance	30.10	29.72	24.64
Capacity for status	19.10	18.97	15.73
Sociability	27.10	24.97	20.16
Social presence	32.90	31.82	26.76
Self-acceptance	22.30	21.46	18.78
Sense of well-being	41.00	38.15	34.69
Tolerance	24.00	22.13	18.62
Achievement via conformance	28.90	28.18	25.33
Achievement via independence	19.20	18.74	16.78
Intellectual efficiency	38.80	37.28	32.84

ately larger number of offices held in the organized groups and clubs.

The Capacity for Status scale indicates persons who are ambitious, active, and forceful; who are ascendant and self-seeking; who are effective in communication; and who possess a breadth of interests.

High scorers on the Sociability scale tend to be opinion leaders; low scorers are likely to be submissive and overly influenced by the opinions of others. These findings add further validity to the association of opinion leadership and innovativeness.

The Social Presence scale assesses factors of poise and self-confidence in personal and social interaction. Low scorers tend to be more deliberate and uncertain in their decisions, less original in their thinking, than are higher scorers.

Persons with higher scores on the Self-Acceptance scale are usually aggressive and possess more self-confidence and self-assurance than others. Cognitive dissonance is typically present at the purchase of some new

untried product or service, and confidence in one's ability to make wise decisions would likely be present more often in the Consumer Innovator.

Consumer Innovators scored an average of 10 percent higher than did the later adopters on the Sense of Well-Being scale, indicating persons with the necessary ambition and self-confidence to make innovative purchases without having to rely upon the experience of others.

The Tolerance scale identifies individuals with accepting, nonjudgmental attitudes. High scorers tend to be more open-minded about differing beliefs and values and commonly possess broad and varied interests themselves. The presence of a tolerant personality appears to be an important prerequisite for innovative behavior.

The Consumer Innovators scored significantly higher than the later adopters on all three measures of achievement potential and intellectual efficiency. Likely explanations are the higher educational levels, predominance of household heads employed in the professions or as managers or proprietors, and the larger number of magazine subscriptions possessed by households in this adopter category.

Some writers have pointed out that many of the characteristics commonly associated with early adopters, such as value of house and lot and number of pieces of entertainment equipment, can be related to household income and that income might be the common denominator in identifying potential innovators.[18] But several of the Consumer Innovators in the CATV study earned smaller annual incomes than did some of the later adopters. An examination of the personality traits of the first adopters with the lowest reported annual incomes revealed that they had scored higher than the remaining Consumer Innovators on all of the personality scales. Their scores on the Tolerance scale, for example, were almost 10 percent higher than those of the remainder of the first adopters. Apparently several combinations of affluence and personality are possible in determining innovativeness. Higher scores on particular per-

[18] See, for example, P. E. Rockwood, "Comments on the Diffusion of Color Television Sets into a Metropolitan Fringe Area Market," *Southern Journal of Business* (July 1968), pp. 58–64.

sonality traits may be sufficient in overcoming income deficiencies which otherwise would have prevented individual innovativeness.

DISCUSSION

The CATV study has shown that the Consumer Innovator possesses most of the same distinguishing socioeconomic characteristics as his counterpart who first adopts producer goods and services. He is more highly educated, earns a larger annual income, and is more likely to be employed in the professional, managerial, and proprietorial occupations than others in the community. He is more likely to be married, change jobs more often, and belong to, and hold offices in, social and civic clubs, professional associations, and organized church groups than are later adopters of the innovation.

The Consumer Innovator also possesses different personality traits which may distinguish him from the later adopter. He exhibits more leadership ability, is more ascendant, and possesses more self-confidence, a greater acceptance of newness, and higher achievement levels than does the later adopter. He welcomes and initiates change.

Questions

1. Explain why it is important for a marketer to be able to identify innovators in the population.
2. According to the results of Boone's study, describe the socioeconomic characteristics of an innovator.
3. According to the results of this study, describe the personality traits of an innovator.

Part B

REFERENCE GROUP

32. Group Influence in Marketing and Public Relations

Francis S. Bourne

THE CONCEPT OF REFERENCE–GROUP INFLUENCE

Basically, the concept [of reference-group] is a very simple one, and it has been recognized both by social scientists and, on a common-sense basis, by practical men for as long as people have been concerned with human behavior.

On the common-sense level, the concept says in effect that man's behaviour is influenced by different ways and in varying degrees by other people. Comparing one's own success with that of others is a frequent source of satisfaction or disappointment. Similarly, before making a decision one often considers what such and such a person of such and such a group (whose opinion one has *some* reason to follow) would do in these circumstances, or what they would think of one for making a certain decision rather than another. Put in these ways, of course, reference-group influence represents an unanalysed truism which has long been recognized. The problem to which social scientists have been addressing themselves intensively only for the last two decades, however, concerns the refinement of this common-sense notion to the end that it might be effectively applied to concrete situations.

The real problems are those of determining which kinds of groups are likely to be referred to by which kinds of individuals under which kinds of circumstances in the process of making which decisions, and of measuring the extent of this reference-group influence. Towards this end, empirical researches have been conducted in recent years which have at least made a start in the process of refining the reference-group concept.

Reference-group theory, as it has developed, has become broad enough to cover a wide range of social phenomena, both with respect to the relation of the individual to the group and with respect to the type of influence exerted upon the individual by the group in question.

Reference groups against which an individual evaluates his own status and behavior may be of several kinds:

1. They may be membership groups to which a person actually belongs and may involve either: (a) Small face-to-face groups in which actual association is the rule, such as families or organizations, whether business, social, religious, or political, or (b) groups in which actual membership is held but in which personal association is absent. (For example, membership in a political party, none of whose meetings are personally attended.) These groups may be of the same kinds as the former but differ only in the lack of face-to-face association with other members.

2. They may be groups or categories to which a person automatically belongs by virtue of age, sex, education, marital status and so on. This sort of reference-group relationship involves the concept of role. For example, before taking a certain action an individual might consider whether this action would be regarded as appropriate in his role as a man or husband or educated person or older person or a combination of all these roles. What is involved here is an individual's perception of what society—either in general or that part of it with which he has any contact—expects people of his age, sex, education or marital status to do in given circumstances.

3. They may be anticipatory rather than actual membership groups. Thus a person who aspires to membership in a group to which he does *not* belong may be more likely to refer to it or compare himself with its standards when making a decision than he is to refer to the standards of the group in which he actually belongs but would like to leave. This involves the concept of upward mobility. When such upward mobility is sought in the social or business world, it is ordinarily accompanied by a sensitivity to the attitudes of those in the groups to which one aspires, whether it involves the attitudes of country-club members in the eyes of the aspiring non-member or the attitudes of management in the eyes of the ambitious wage-earner or junior executive.

4. They may be negative, dissociative reference-groups. These constitute the opposite side of the coin from the anticipatory membership groups. Thus an individual sometimes avoids a certain action because it is associated with a group (to which the individual may or may not in fact belong) from which he would like to dissociate himself.

Reference-groups influence behavior in two main ways. First, they influence *aspiration levels,* and thus play a part in producing satisfaction or frustration. If the other members of one's reference-group (for example, the neighbours) are wealthier, more famous, better gardeners, etc., one may be dissatisfied with one's own achievements and may strive to do as well as the others.

Secondly, reference-groups influence *kinds* of behaviour. They establish approved patterns of using one's wealth, of wearing one's fame, of designing one's garden. They also lay down taboos, and may have the power to apply actual sanctions (for example, exclusion from the group). They thus produce *conformity* as well as *contentment* (or discontent).

These two kinds of influence have, however, a good deal in common. Both imply certain perceptions on the part of the individual, who attributes to the reference-group characteristics it may or may not actually have. Both involve psychological rewards and punishment.

THE PRACTICAL VALUE OF THE REFERENCE–GROUP CONCEPT IN MARKETING AND PUBLIC RELATIONS

In applying the reference-group concept to practical problems in marketing and public relations, three basic questions arise:

Reference-group relevance. How do you determine whether and to what extent reference-group influence is operating in a given situation? The reference-group is, after all, only one of many influences in decision-making, varying greatly in prominence from situation to situation.

Reference-group identification. How do you identify the particular reference-group or groups, or individuals, who are most relevant in influencing decisions under given circumstances? This is perhaps the most difficult question to answer in many cases, particularly where multiple reference-groups are involved.

Reference-group identification and effective communication. Once having identified the nature of the group-influence operating in a given situation, how do you then most effectively *communicate* with the groups or individuals you desire to influence?

This, of course, is the crux of the matter, since the answers to the first two questions are of value only to the extent that they can be translated into more pertinent and effective communication, designed to influence purchasing behaviour or the attitudes of various publics towards a firm or industry.

Experimental evidence is now available which sheds light on each of these three questions. From this evidence, and from the general advancement in the methodology of social research in recent years, there have emerged some very tentative generalizations. These can be applied only with the most careful attention to the special circumstances operating in individual instances, and serve more as guides to fruitful ways of examining problems as they arise than as simple answers to problems.

Marketing and Reference-Group Relevance

As already suggested, the reference-group constitutes only one of the many influences in buying-decisions, and this influence varies from product to product. How then does one determine whether reference-group influence is likely to be a factor in buying-behaviour in connection with a given product or brand? Research has been conducted on the various factors that influence buying-behaviour with reference to several products, and out of this have emerged some general ideas about how reference-group influences may enter into purchasing.

Buying may be a completely individualistic activity or very much socially conditioned. Consumers are often influenced by what others buy, especially those persons with whom they compare themselves or use as reference-groups.

The conspicuousness of a product is perhaps the most general attribute bearing on its susceptibility to reference-group influence. There are two aspects to conspicuousness in this particular context that help to determine reference-group influence. First, the article must be conspicuous in the most obvious sense that it can be seen and identified by others. Secondly, it must be conspicuous in the sense of standing out and being noticed. In other words, no matter how visible a product is, if virtually everyone owns it, it is not conspicuous in the second sense of the word. This leads to a further distinction: reference-groups may influence either (a) the purchase of a product, or (b) the choice of a particular brand or type, or (c) both.

The possible susceptibility of various product and brand-buying to reference-group influence is suggested in Figure 1.

According to this classification, a particular item might be susceptible to reference-group influence in its purchase in three different ways, corresponding to three of the four cells in the figure on p. 333. Reference group influence may operate with respect to brand or type but not with respect to product (Brand + Product −) as in the upper left cell, or it may operate both with respect to brand and product (Brand + Product +) as in the upper right cell, or it may operate with respect to product but not brand (Brand − Product +) as in the lower right cell.

¹The classification of all products marked with an asterisk (*) is based on actual experimental evidence. Other products in this table are classified speculatively on the basis of generalizations derived from the sum of research in this area and confirmed by the judgment of seminar participants.

Figure 1 / Products and brands of consumer-goods may be classified by extent to which reference groups influence their purchase. [*Source:* Bureau of Applied Social Research, Columbia University (Glock, unpublished).]

Only the "minus-minus" items of the kind illustrated (Brand − Product −) in the lower left cell are not likely to involve any significant reference-group influence in their purchase *at the present time*.

What are some of the characteristics that place an item in a given category, and what significance do such placements have for marketing and advertising policy?

"Product Plus, Brand Plus" Items. Cars are a case in which both the product and the brand are socially conspicuous. Whether or not a person buys a car, and also what particular brand he buys, is likely to be influenced by what others do. This also holds true for cigarettes and drugs (decisions made by M.D.'s as to what to prescribe) and for beer with respect to type (premium versus regular) as opposed to brand. Cigarettes and drugs,

however, qualify as "plus-plus" items in a manner different from cars.

For example, while the car belongs to a class of products where brand differentiation is based at least substantially on real differences in attributes, the cigarette belongs to a class of product in which it is hard to differentiate one brand from another by attributes: hence attributes are ascribed largely through reference-group appeal built up by advertising. Popular images of the kinds of people who smoke various brands have been created at great cost, and in some cases additional images are being created to broaden a particular brand's market. In the case of drugs, it was found that the reference-group influencing *whether* the product was used was different from that influencing the particular *brand* selected. Reference-group influence was found to be prominent in determining whether or not beer was purchased at all, and also in determining whether regular or premium beer was selected. It did not appear strongly to influence choice of a particular brand.

"Product Plus, Brand Minus" Items. Instant coffee is one of the best examples of this class of item. Whether it is served in a household depends in considerable part on whether the housewife, in view of her own reference-groups and the image she has of their attitudes toward this product, considers it appropriate to serve it. The brand itself, in this instance, is not conspicuous or socially important and is a matter largely for individual choice. In the case of air-conditioners, it was found that little prestige is attached to the particular brand used, and reference-group influence related largely to the idea of purchasing the product itself. Analysis in one city revealed that the purchase of this often "visible from the outside" product was concentrated in small areas. Clusters of conditioners were frequently located in certain rows and blocks. In many cases, clusters did not even cross streets. Immediate neighbours apparently served as a powerfully influential reference-group in the purchase of these appliances. In this general class may also be found the black and white TV set, with its antenna often visible from outside the house. As the saturation point in black and white TV set ownership rapidly approaches, however, the influence of reference-groups may soon become unimportant, and the product can then be put in the "brand minus, product minus" quadrant, beside refrigerators. Colour TV may remain in the "brand plus, product minus" quadrant, with type (colour) rather than brand *per se* as the element strongly related to reference-groups.

"Product Minus, Brand Plus" Items. This group is essentially made up of products that all people or at least a very high proportion of people use, although differing as to type or brand.

Perhaps the leading example in this field is clothing. There could hardly be a more socially visible product than this, but the fact that everyone in our society wears clothing takes the *product* out of the area of reference-group influence. The *type* of clothing purchased is, however, very heavily influenced by reference-groups, with each sub-culture in the population (teenagers, zoot-suiters, Ivy League Collegians, Western Collegians, workers, bankers, advertising men, etc.) setting its own standards and often prescribing, within fairly narrow limits, what those who feel related to these groups can wear. Similarly, though not quite as dramatically, articles like furniture, magazines, refrigerators and toilet soap are seen in almost all homes, causing their purchase in general to fall outside the orbit of reference-group influence. The visibility of these items, however, coupled with the wide variety of styles and types among them, makes the selection of particular kinds highly susceptible to reference-group influence.

"Product Minus, Brand Minus" Items. Purchasing behaviour in this class of items is governed by product attributes rather than by the nature of the presumed users. In this group, neither the products nor the brands tend to be socially conspicuous. This is not to say that personal influence cannot operate with respect to purchasing the kind of items included in this group. As with all products, some people tend to exert personal influence and others tend to be influenced by individual persons. Reference-groups as such, however, exert relatively little influence on buying behaviour in this class of items, examples of which are salt, canned peaches, laundry soap and radios. It is apparent that placement in this category is not *necessarily* inherent in the

product itself and hence is not a static placement. Items can move in and out of this category.

While it is true that items which are essentially socially inconspicuous, like salt and laundry soap, are natural candidates for this category, it is not entirely impossible that, through large-scale advertising and other promotional efforts, images of the kind of people who use certain brands of salt or laundry soap could be built up so as to bring reference-group influence into play on such items, much as in the case of cigarettes. The task would be more difficult, however, since the cigarette is already socially visible. On the other hand, items such as radios and refrigerators, which are conspicuously visible and whose purchase was once subject to considerable reference-group influence, have now slipped into this category through near-saturation in ownership.

IMPLICATIONS OF STRONG AND WEAK REFERENCE-GROUP INFLUENCE FOR ADVERTISING AND MARKETING

It should be stressed again that this scheme of analysis is introduced to show how reference-group influence might enter into purchasing behaviour in certain cases. It cannot be regarded as generally applicable to marketing problems on all levels. There is still a need to know more precisely where many different products or brands fit into this scheme. Attempts to fit products and brands into the preceding classification suggest that research needs to be done in order to obtain more relevant information about each product.

Assuming, however, that a product or brand has been correctly placed with respect to the part played by reference-groups in in-

fluencing its purchase, how can this help in marketing the product in question?

1. Where neither product nor brand appear to be associated strongly with reference-group influence, advertising should emphasize the product's attributes, intrinsic qualities, price, and advantages over competing products.

2. Where reference-group influence is operative, the advertiser should stress the kinds of people who buy the product, reinforcing and broadening where possible the existing stereotypes of users. The strategy of the advertiser should involve learning what the stereotypes are and what specific reference-groups enter into the picture, so that appeals can be "tailored" to each main group reached by the different media employed.

Although it is important to see that the "right" kind of people use a product, a crucial problem is to make sure that the popular image of the product's users is as broad as possible without alienating any important part of the product's present or potential market in the process. Mistakes have been made in creating or reinforcing a stereotype of consumers which was too small and exclusive for a mass-produced item; this strategy excluded a significant portion of the potential market. On the other hand, some attempts to appeal to new groups through advertising in mass media have resulted in the loss of existing groups of purchasers whose previous (favourable) image of the product-user was adversely affected. A possible strategy for increasing the base of the market for a product by enlarging the image of its users is to use separate advertising media through which a new group can be reached without reducing the product's appeal to the original group of users. Another method might be to appeal to a new group through co-operative advertising by a number of companies producing the product, possibly through a trade association. This would minimize the risk to an individual producer who, trying to reach a new group of users through his own advertising (women as opposed to men or wealthy as opposed to average people, for example), might antagonize people who had a strong need to identify with the *original* image of the product's kind of user.

Product Attributes versus Reference-Group Influence

A technique which could serve to assess the relative influence of reference-groups, as compared with product attributes, on the purchase of a given product was employed in research on a food product which will be referred to as product "X".

A cross-section of "X" users was asked several questions relating to particular attributes of "X", such as whether it was more harmful or beneficial to one's health, whether or not it was considered fattening, whether it was considered extravagant or economical, whether or not it tasted good, and so on. These same people were also asked a reference-group-oriented question about "X", to determine whether or not "X" was popular with most of their friends. It was found that there was usually more "X" eating among people who reacted negatively to the attributes of "X" but admitted to its popularity among most of their friends, than among those who reacted positively to the attributes of "X" but indicated that it was not popular with their friends.

These relationships are shown in Table 1 below. In this table the scores in parentheses are those of people whose replies showed both attribute influence and reference-group influence exerting pressure in the same direction.

Special attention should be directed toward the other scores. These represent situations in which people are under cross-pressures. For each of the four attributes considered, the reference-group influence is stronger than the attribute influence, in the use of "X". This is brought out by the arrows, which point toward the cross-pressure situations where the reference-group influence is negative. In all these, consumption frequency is less than where attribute influence alone is negative. Or, put another way, positive perception of reference-group behaviour with respect to the food product ("X" is very popular) coupled with negative perception of its actual attribute ("X" does more harm than good, is fattening, etc.) leads to more consumption than negative perception of reference-group behaviour ("X" not very popular) coupled with positive perception of actual attribute value ("X" does more good than harm, not fattening, economical).

As can be seen from the comparisons indicated by the arrows, reference-group influence is markedly stronger than attribute influence for three of the four attributes. Only for "taste" does the attribute influence come close to competing with reference-group influence in determining consumption of "X".

One implication of this finding would be that advertising by the "X" industry might stress the *social* aspects of the product, and the extent to which it is enjoyed by many groups of people like the audience being appealed to, rather than basing its advertising on the *actual attributes* of the product.

In a study of a beverage, it was found that, of those who drank the beverage in question, 95 per cent claimed that their friends also drank it, while of those who did not drink this beverage 85 per cent also claimed that their friends did *not* drink it.

Some products, then, must be sold to whole social groups rather than primarily to individuals.

Table 1 / Relation Between Reference-group and Attribute Influence
in Use of Food Product "X"

	Index of frequency of eating "X"[1]	
	+ Reference-group −	
	With most of respondent's friends "X" is:	
Product attribute	Very popular	Not very popular
Effect of "X" on health		
+ More good than harm	(.41)	−.10
− More harm than good	.08	(−.51)
+ Do not avoid fattening food and/or feel "X" is not really or a little fattening	(.30)	−.21
− Try to avoid fattening food and feel "X" is really or a little fattening	.14	(−.29)
Economic value judgment		
+ Fairly economical	(.29)	−.20
− Sort of an extravagance	.11	(−.33)
Taste judgment		
+ Tastes good	(.42)	.05
− No reference to good taste[2]	.09	(−.38)

[1] All scores in the above table constitute an index of the frequency of "X" eating among respondents falling into the given cell. The scoring procedure used was: frequent "X" users − score +1; medium "X" users − score 0; occasional "X" users − score −1.

The final score is derived by subtracting the number of occasional "X" users in a given cell from the number of frequent users and dividing the remainder by the total number of respondents in the cell. For example, the index score .41 was obtained as follows: 329 respondents felt that a moderate amount of "X" does more good than harm AND report that "X" is very popular with most of their friends. Of these 329 respondents 178 are frequent "X" users, 97 are medium "X" users and 43 are occasional "X" users.

The score: $178 - 43 = 135$ The *Index* value: $135/329 = +.41$

[2] "Tastes good" represents the selection of this phrase from a word list of various attributes that might be applied to "X". "No reference to good taste" refers to those respondents who did not select "Tastes good" from the word list.

Source: Bureau of Applied Social Research, Columbia University.

Questions

1. What are the three basic considerations in the application of the reference group concept in marketing? Explain their importance.

2. The author suggests two ways in which reference groups influence behavior. Briefly describe these.

3. Beer is shown to have been placed in the "product plus" and "brand plus" category of the reference group influence grid. What are the marketing implications of this placement?

33. Promotional Perspectives of Reference Group Influence: Advertising Implications

V. Parker Lessig

C. Whan Park

The objective of this paper is to examine the promotional implications of a theory of reference group influence. Specifically, given the relevance of motivational functions for a number of products, scores are presented which indicate the extent to which various types of reference groups and promotional appeals are appropriate in satisfying the consumer's underlying motivational forces.

A reference group is broadly defined in this study as an actual or imaginary institution, individual or group conceived of as having significant relevance upon an individual's evaluations, aspirations, or behavior. An important point is that the relationship between an individual and a reference group should be motivationally and psychologically significant. Thus, three different reference group influences are identified and examined from the perspective of the individual's motivational functions.

MOTIVATIONAL REFERENCE GROUP FUNCTIONS

The three motivational reference group functions (RGFs) examined in this paper are informational, utilitarian, and value-expressive.

Informational Reference Group Function

An informational reference group imposes no norms on the individual. Instead, an influence is internalized if it is perceived as enhancing the individual's knowledge about his environment and/or his ability to cope with some aspect of it (5). Thus, the likelihood that an individual will accept information from this reference group as evidence of reality increases if he feels uncertainty associated with the purchase and/or lacks relevant purchase related experience.

Informational reference groups can appear in several different modes. One mode is when a consumer actively searches for information from opinion leaders or a group with the appropriate expertise. For example, information on product characteristics could be obtained directly from a retailer or from knowledgeable friends who have relevant product related experience. Based upon attribution theory, two other modes can be identified (2,4,3). One of these modes is to make inferences based upon the observation of others' behavior. For example, an individual may decide to purchase a given brand of automobile tires because this is the brand used by his state's highway patrol. Here, the individual may infer that the tire is durable and rugged because these are surely important characteristics to the highway patrol in their selection process. The other mode is where an individual makes inferences relating to such things as the brand's quality by observing an individual's or group's endorsement (like the American Dental Association's endorsement of a brand of toothpaste).

338

Utilitarian Reference Group Function

The utilitarian reference group function can be described using Kelman's compliance process (5). That is, an individual who is motivated to realize a reward or to avoid punishment mediated by some other individual or group is expected to conform to the other's influence. This compliance occurs only if the individual feels that his actions are visible or will be known.

The utilitarian reference group function suggests that in a product purchasing situation an individual is expected to comply with the preferences or expectations of others who are viewed as being mediators of significant rewards or punishment. The marketing applications of this function are numerous. For example, advertisers often create expectations concerning appropriate product and brand selection behavior, e.g., the appropriate role for housewives or the type of beer which others expect one to drink or serve to guests.

Value–Expressive Reference Group Function

Kelman's identification process is useful in describing the value-expressive reference group function (5). An individual motivated to enhance or support his self-concept would be expected to associate himself with positive referents and/or dissociate himself from negative referents. In other words, an individual utilizes a value-expressive reference group for the purpose of expressing himself and/or bolstering his ego to an outside world. The degree of cohesiveness or norm specificity of the reference group is irrelevant for this function. What is important is the psychological image associated with the group whether the group is real or imaginary.

A number of well-known cases exist in which attempts have been made to use the value-expressive reference group function in promotions. Consider the following examples: the "young generation" promoted by Pepsi, the "seaman image" promoted by Schlitz, the "sophisticated and liberated woman" concept promoted by Virginia Slim cigarettes.

ANALYSIS AND DISCUSSION

Relevance of Reference Group Function

Through intensive interviews with students and housewives, the 14 statements listed in Table 1 were developed as manifestations of the three types of reference group influence. Each statement is specific enough to reflect only one motivational function yet general enough to encompass different manifestations of behavior or feelings. The validity of these statements was verified through two independent pretests and through the application of the Campbell and Fiske convergent and discriminant validation procedure (1). A sample of 100 housewives living in Topeka, Kansas, completed a questionnaire in which they indicated the extent to which the situation described by a particular statement (Table 1) is relevant to a consumer's brand (or alternative) selection decision for each of 20 products. There were four possible responses which were: highly relevant (coded 4), medium relevance (coded 3), low relevance (coded 2), and not relevant (coded 1).

Informational, utilitarian, and value-expressive reference group function scores (RGF scores) for each of the 20 products were calculated by averaging across subjects the highest relevance response (from the ap-

Table 1 / Reference Group Influence Manifestation Statements

Informational function reference group statements

1. The individual seeks information about various brands of the product from an association of professionals or independent group of experts.
2. The individual seeks information from those who work with the product as a profession.
3. The individual seeks brand related knowledge and experience (such as how brand A's performance compares to brand B's) from those friends, neighbors, relatives, or work associates who have reliable information about the brands.
4. The brand which the individual selects is influenced by observing a seal of approval of an independent testing agency (such as Good Housekeeping).
5. The individual's observation of what experts do influences his choice of a brand (such as observing the type of car which police drive or the brand of TV which TV repairmen buy).

Utilitarian function reference group statements

1. To satisfy the expectations of fellow work associates, the individual's decision to purchase a particular brand is influenced by their preferences.
2. The individual's decision to purchase a particular brand is influenced by the preferences of people with whom he has social interaction.
3. The individual's decision to purchase a particular brand is influenced by the preferences of family members.
4. The desire to satisfy the expectations which others have of him has an impact on the individual's brand choice.

Value-expressive reference group statements

1. The individual feels that the purchase or use of a particular brand will enhance the image which others have of him.
2. The individual feels that those who purchase or use a particular brand possess the characteristics which he would like to have.
3. The individual sometimes feels that it would be nice to be like the type of person which advertisements show using a particular brand.
4. The individual feels that the people who purchase a particular brand are admired or respected by others.
5. The individual feels that the purchase of a particular brand helps him show others what he is, or would like to be (such as an athlete, successful businessman, good mother, etc.).

propriate set of reference group function manifestation statements) which each subject assigned to the specific product. These scores are presented in Table 2. Scores of three or more are indicative of medium to high reference group influence whereas scores less than 3 reflect a relatively low reference group influence. The values in parentheses to the immediate right of the RGF scores are the rankings of the products according to reference group influence (1 indicates the product most influenced).

An examination of the RGF scores in Table 2 provides an advertiser with useful information regarding the type of reference group function(s) which should be incorporated in brand promotions. Consider the following examples. The high values of the RGF scores for color television indicate that all three types of reference group influence are extremely relevant. Of the three influences, the informational function is by far the most important. Thus, if only one type of influence is to be emphasized, it should be this one. However, a

Table 2 / Reference Group Function Scores (Values in Parentheses Indicate Rank by Influence)

Product	Informational function	Utilitarian function	Value-expressive function
Headache remedy	3.38 (9)	2.98 (13)	2.42 (16–17)
Beer	2.60 (17)	3.08 (11)	2.71 (11)
Color television	3.84 (2)	3.51 (4)	3.43 (4)
Clothing	3.45 (8)	3.59 (2–3)	3.61 (2)
Laundry soap	2.99 (12)	2.53 (18)	2.42 (16–17)
Hamburger substitute	2.56 (18)	2.33 (20)	1.93 (20)
Automobile	3.85 (1)	3.70 (1)	3.65 (1)
Furniture	3.51 (7)	3.59 (2–3)	3.52 (3)
Facial soap	2.89 (14)	2.94 (14)	2.85 (10)
Home air conditioner	3.75 (3)	3.21 (10)	3.14 (6–7)
Insurance	3.71 (5)	3.38 (6)	3.08 (8–9)
Mouthwash	2.92 (13)	3.02 (12)	2.57 (14)
Coffee	2.88 (15–16)	3.28 (8)	2.58 (13)
Refrigerator	3.70 (6)	3.23 (9)	3.14 (6–7)
Physician selection	3.72 (4)	3.50 (5)	3.18 (5)
Canned peaches	2.49 (19–20)	2.54 (17)	1.99 (19)
Transistor radio	3.16 (10)	2.79 (15)	2.64 (12)
Low Phosphate detergent	2.88 (15–16)	2.35 (19)	2.17 (18)
Magazine or book selection	3.00 (11)	3.36 (7)	3.08 (8–9)
Cigarettes	2.49 (19–20)	2.68 (16)	2.51 (15)

consumer's acceptance of a given brand would be greatly enhanced by also stressing utilitarian and value-expressive functions. On the other hand, for a product such as canned peaches, the values of all three reference group functions are so low that it would be difficult to justify the incorporation of any of these influences in brand promotions. Between extreme products such as color television and canned peaches are products such as coffee for which a subset of the reference groups are relevant. Looking at the RGF scores for coffee, it appears that the utilitarian RGF is the only function of medium to high relevance. Thus, in promoting brands of coffee the advertiser should relate the brand to the norms or behavior of those groups or types of individuals whose ex-

pectations the consumer feels compelled to follow.

Source of Reference Group Influence

Given that a reference group function is relevant in the selection of brands for a particular product, the next immediate issue concerns the means through which this influence is brought to the consumer. Specifically, this information could lead to the identification of (a) the information source which consumers utilize (in conjunction with the informational RGF), (b) the significant others (i.e., reference group) with whose preferences and demands the individual complies (in the case of the utilitarian RGF), and (c) the specific image or means of ego enhancement (for the value-expressive function).

For each product, the mean values across the 100 respondents for the five informational, the four utilitarian, and the five value-expressive RGF manifestation statements are presented in Table 3. Each mean value reflects the degree of relevance of the characterized behavior for brand evaluations of the particular product. A careful examination of informational RGF manifestation statements reveals several interesting contrasts. Consider, for example, a headache remedy and its underlying structure. Statement 1 (information seeking from an association of professionals or independent group of experts) is the most relevant of the five statements. On the other hand, for clothing, whose informational RGF score is very similar to that for the product headache remedy (Table 2), the most relevant statements are statements 2 (information seeking from those who work with the product as a profession) and 3 (seeking related knowledge and experience from those friends, neighbors, relatives, and work associates who have reliable information about the brands). Other informational RGF contrasts can be found between the products clothing and furniture, insurance and refrigerators, and radio and magazine selection.

According to the mean values for the four utilitarian function manifestation statements (Table 3), the relevance score for the third statement (a family member's influence on the selection of a brand) is consistently high for those products whose utilitarian reference group score (Table 2) is also high. Furthermore, for products such as beer, home air conditioners, insurance, and physician selection, statement 2 (the influence of those with whom an individual has social interaction) is also highly relevant. Several interesting contrasts are, however, noted. For example, the utilitarian reference group scores (Table 2) for insurance and magazine selection are very similar. Yet, a substantial difference exists between these two products in terms of the average score across the four utilitarian statements. The main factor responsible for this difference is the different distribution of relevance scores for these four statements. In the case of insurance, statement 3 (the influence of family members) is primarily responsible for the high relevance of the utilitarian RGF. However, for magazine selection, all four statements are highly relevant. This difference in the relevance of the utilitarian function manifestation statements is crucial in the formulation of promotional strategies in that the specific utilitarian reference group utilized in promoting one product may be inappropriate in promoting brands of the other product. Other utilitarian RGF contrasts of this nature are also found, e.g., clothing and furniture, and color television and physician selection.

The mean values across the 100 respondents for each of the five value-expressive manifestation statements (Table 3) reveal three interesting sets of products. The first set consists of color television, home air conditioners, insurance, and refrigerators. These products have very similar distributions of mean values across the five value-expressive statements. The second set of products is made up of clothing, automobiles, and furniture. Statement 1 (enhancement of the image which others have of him) is the most relevant statement for these products. The third set consists of physician selection and magazine selection. Here the most relevant statement is statement 5 (helping an individual show others what he is or would like to be).

Another interesting observation regarding the value-expressive statements is that insurance and magazine selection have identical

Table 3 / Mean Values on Informational, Utilitarian, and Value Expressive Reference Group Function Manifestation Statements

Product	Informational RGF manifestation statement					Utilitarian RGF manifestation statement				Value-expressive RGF manifestation statement				
	1	2	3	4	5	1	2	3	4	1	2	3	4	5
Headache remedy	2.71	2.43	2.60	2.39	2.03	1.70	1.90	2.88	1.43	1.27	1.29	1.76	1.42	1.56
Beer	1.88	1.82	2.01	1.65	1.72	2.04	2.41	2.72	1.97	1.94	1.90	2.15	1.77	1.89
Color television	3.47	3.42	3.34	2.77	2.95	2.42	2.69	3.19	2.34	2.40	2.46	2.25	2.37	2.46
Clothing	2.43	2.87	2.75	2.46	2.41	2.89	2.92	3.04	2.99	3.31	2.98	2.89	2.91	2.95
Laundry soap	2.24	2.00	2.27	2.33	1.89	1.43	1.62	2.23	1.50	1.41	1.32	1.84	1.36	1.63
Hamburger substitute	1.80	1.66	1.74	1.95	1.47	1.24	1.51	2.07	1.34	1.24	1.17	1.54	1.32	1.40
Automobile	3.34	3.55	3.38	2.67	2.89	2.66	2.94	3.37	2.74	3.31	2.93	2.79	2.97	2.92
Furniture	2.71	3.07	2.68	2.59	2.45	2.38	2.71	3.09	2.66	3.00	2.74	2.51	2.73	2.71
Facial soap	2.21	1.93	2.14	2.29	1.92	1.67	1.91	2.66	1.79	1.53	1.72	2.57	1.61	1.89
Home air conditioner	3.23	3.27	3.13	2.65	2.76	2.07	2.42	2.81	2.03	2.05	1.95	2.06	2.08	2.19
Insurance	3.33	3.37	3.00	2.25	2.51	2.18	2.48	2.87	1.92	1.95	2.07	1.91	2.08	2.16
Mouthwash	2.12	1.91	2.11	2.33	1.74	1.86	2.03	2.78	1.94	1.89	1.76	2.13	1.83	1.86
Coffee	2.14	2.07	2.36	2.24	1.88	2.01	2.21	3.02	2.10	1.77	1.66	2.03	1.94	1.96
Refrigerator	3.12	3.28	2.98	2.74	2.66	2.12	2.34	2.85	2.14	2.20	2.00	2.10	2.05	2.32
Physician selection	3.27	3.23	3.11	2.18	2.45	2.44	2.66	3.16	2.06	2.24	2.21	1.62	2.13	2.42
Canned peaches	1.83	1.63	1.94	2.18	1.48	1.40	1.51	2.40	1.52	1.37	1.30	1.66	1.46	1.55
Transistor radio	2.61	2.55	2.40	2.32	2.13	1.81	1.94	2.51	1.76	1.70	1.71	1.87	1.84	1.79
Low phosphate detergent	2.08	1.91	2.17	2.35	1.68	1.40	1.60	2.08	1.44	1.23	1.35	1.70	1.36	1.53
Magazine or book selection	1.98	2.22	2.49	2.04	2.10	2.41	2.49	2.88	2.44	2.35	2.45	1.98	2.44	2.77
Cigarettes	1.87	1.79	1.87	1.81	1.60	1.93	1.86	2.20	1.72	1.72	1.75	2.18	1.66	1.69

value-expressive reference group influence scores of 3.08, indicating a medium influence (Table 2). Yet, these products differ considerably in terms of each product's average score across the five value-expressive manifestation statements; for insurance this score is 2.03 and for magazine or book selection it is 2.40. An examination of the distribution of the mean values across the five manifestation statements shows that these values are relatively low for insurance but high for magazine selection. Thus, although the value-expressive reference group influence is the same for these two products, there was little agreement among the respondents concerning the relevance of specific value-expressive influences upon insurance selection but high agreement on the specific influences for magazine selection. Therefore, in trying to utilize the value-expressive functional influence in promotions, advertisements aimed at influencing magazine selection would be much more efficient than insurance advertisements. Similar circumstances are noted for clothing and furniture and for color television and furniture.

SUMMARY AND CONCLUSIONS

It may be useful at this point to consolidate and to categorize the information presented. Referring to Table 2, if the value 3 is used to discriminate between products for which an RGF is relevant and those products for which the function is not of practical relevance, then the 20 products can be divided into three sets. The first set consists of laundry soap, hamburger substitute, facial soap, canned peaches, low phosphate detergent and, surprisingly, cigarettes. Each of these product's RGF score was less than three for each of the reference group functions. Thus, although

there were exceptions among individual respondents, these are products for which there appears to be no strongly relevant reference group function among the housewives studied. Promotions which attempt to incorporate a reference group appeal for these products are running a high risk that the strategy will be of marginal value. (The degree of risk increases as the RGF score decreases.) The following five products define the second set: headache remedy, beer, mouthwash, coffee, and transistor radios. For each of these products, only one RGF appears to be relevant, i.e., has an RGF score greater than or equal to three. The third set of products consists of: color televison, automobiles, home air conditioner, insurance, refrigerator, physician selection, magazines or books, clothing, and furniture. Each of these products has an RGF score equal to or greater than three on all three of the reference group functions.

Several questions must be raised concerning the products in sets two and three. First, for a given product, what reference group function(s) should be stressed in promotions? Second, given the function(s) to be stressed, what type of cues or sources would be most effective? Tables 2 and 3 provide information useful in answering these questions.

The purpose of this study was to suggest various theoretical and practical promotional implications based upon empirical tests of reference group influence. Specifically, the results of this study suggest the following: (1) The type of function which reference groups perform for an individual can take on three different motivational forms which are informational, utilitarian, and value-expressive. Therefore, whether or not an individual's behavior toward a product is subject to reference group influence should be determined on the basis of these motivational functions. (2) The underlying factors which motivate an individual need not be derived from only one motivational function. Instead, for several products, individuals may be motivated by a combination of functions such as in the case of automobiles or clothing. (3) Given the relevance of a particular reference group function, the means through which that function is expressed varies across products.

REFERENCES

[1] Campbell, Donald T. and Donald W. Fiske, "Convergent and Discriminant Validation by the Multi-Trait-Multimethod Matrix," *Psy-chological Bulletin,* Vol. 56, 1959, pp. 81–105.

[2] Heider, F. *The Psychology of Interpersonal Relations.* New York: Wiley, 1958.

[3] Jones, E. E., D. E. Kanouse, H. H. Kelley, R. E. Misbett, S. Valins, and B. Weiner, *Attribution: Perceiving the Causes of Behavior.* Morristown, N.J.: General Learning Press, 1972.

[4] Kelley, H. H. "Attribution Theory in Social Psychology," In D. Levine (Ed.), *Nebraska Symposium on Motivation, 1967.* Lincoln, Nebraska: University of Nebraska Press, 1967.

[5] Kelman, H. C. "Processes of Opinion Change." *Public Opinion Quarterly,* Vol. 25, 1961, pp. 57–78.

Questions

1. Define "reference group."
2. Name and describe each of the three motivational reference group functions.
3. For each of these three functions, name several products, according to this study, for which the reference group function has the most relevance.

Part C
SOCIAL CLASS

34. Social Classes and Spending Behavior

Pierre Martineau

All societies place emphasis on some one structure which gives form to the total society and integrates all the other structures such as the family, the clique, voluntary association, caste, age, and sex groupings into a social unity.

Social stratification means any system of ranked statuses by which all the members of a society are placed in some kind of a superordinate and subordinate hierarchy. While money and occupation are important in the ranking process, there are many more factors, and these two alone do not establish social position. The concept of social class was designed to include this process of ranking people in superior and inferior social position by any and all factors.

CLASS SYSTEM

It has been argued that there cannot be a class system existent in America when most individuals do not have the slightest idea of its formal structure. Yet in actuality every individual senses that he is more at home with and more acceptable to certain groups than to others. In a study of department stores and

shopping behavior, it was found that the Lower-Status woman is completely aware that, if she goes into High-Status department stores, the clerks and the other customers in the store will punish her in various subtle ways.

"The clerks treat you like a crumb," one woman expressed it. After trying vainly to be waited on, another woman bitterly complained that she was loftily told, "We thought you were a clerk."

The woman who is socially mobile gives considerable thought to the external symbols of status, and she frequently tests her status by shopping in department stores which she thinks are commensurate with her changing position. She knows that, if she does not dress correctly, if she does not behave in a certain manner to the clerks, if she is awkward about the proper cues, then the other customers and the clerks will make it very clear that she does not belong.

In another study, very different attitudes in the purchase of furniture and appliances involving this matter of status were found. Middle-class people had no hesitancy in buying refrigerators and other appliances in discount houses and bargain stores because they felt that they could not "go wrong" with the nationally advertised names. But taste in furniture is much more elusive and subtle because the brand names are not known; and, therefore, one's taste is on trial. Rather than commit a glaring error in taste which would exhibit an ignorance of the correct status symbols, the same individual who buys appliances in a discount house generally retreats to a status store for buying furniture. She needs the support of the store's taste.

In a very real sense, every one of us in his consumption patterns and style of life shows an awareness that there is some kind of a superiority-inferiority system operating, and that we must observe the symbolic patterns of our own class.

Lloyd Warner and Paul Lunt have described a six-class system: the Upper-Upper, or old families; Lower-Upper, or the newly arrived; Upper-Middle, mostly the professionals and successful businessmen; Lower-Middle, or the white collar salaried class; Upper-Lower, or the wage earner, skilled worker group; and Lower-Lower, or the unskilled labor group.[1] For practical purposes, in order to determine the individual's class position, Warner and his associates worked out a rating index, not based on amount of income but rather on type of income, type of occupation, house type, and place of residence.

Although the Warner thesis has been widely used in sociology, it has not generally been employed in marketing. As a matter of fact, some critics in the social sciences have held that, since Warner's thesis rested essentially on studies of smaller cities in the 10,000–25,000 class, this same system might

[1] W. Lloyd Warner and Paul Lunt, *The Social Life of a Modern Community* (New Haven: Yale University Press, 1950). Also, W. Lloyd Warner, Marchia Meeker, and Kenneth Eells, *Social Class in America* (Chicago: Science Research Associates, 1949).

not exist in the more complex metropolitan centers, or might not be unravelled by the same techniques. Furthermore, many marketers did not see the application of this dimension to the individual's economic behavior, since the studies of Warner and his associates had mostly been concerned with the differences in the broad patterns of living, the moral codes, etc.

SOCIAL CLASS IN CHICAGO

Under Warner's guidance, the *Chicago Tribune* has undertaken several extensive studies exploring social class in a metropolitan city, and its manifestations specifically in family buying patterns. The problem was to determine if such a social-class system did exist in metropolitan Chicago, if the dimensions and the relationships were at all similar to the smaller cities which were studied before the far-reaching social changes of the past fifteen years. The studies were undertaken to see if there were any class significances in the individual family's spending-saving patterns, retail store loyalties, and their expressions of taste in typical areas such as automobiles, apparel, furniture, and house types.

It seems that many an economist overlooks the possibility of any psychological differences between individuals resulting from different class membership. It is assumed that a rich man is simply a poor man with more money and that, given the same income, the poor man would behave exactly like the rich man. The *Chicago Tribune* studies crystallize a wealth of evidence from other sources that this is just not so, and that the Lower-Status person is profoundly different in his mode of thinking and his way of handling the world from the Middle-Class individual. Where he buys and what he buys will differ not only by economics but in symbolic value.

Etheridge
Etheridge

It should be understood, of course, that there are no hard and fast lines between the classes. Implicit in the notion of social class in America is the possibility of movement from one class to another. The "office boy-to-president" saga is a cherished part of the American dream. Bobo Rockefeller illustrates the female counterpart: from coal miner's daughter to socialite. As a corollary of the explorations in class, the study also tried to be definitive about the phenomenon of social mobility—the movement from one class to another.

There are numerous studies of vertical mobility from the level of sociological analysis, mostly by comparing the individual's occupational status to that of his father. There are also studies at the level of psychological analysis. This study attempted to combine the two levels, to observe the individual's progress and also to understand something of the dynamics of the mobile person as compared to the stable individual. The attempt was to look both backward and forward: tracing such factors as occupation, place of residence, and religion back to parents and grandparents, and then where the family expected to be in the next five or ten years, what were the educational plans for each son, each daughter, a discussion of future goals.

Because this article is confined primarily to social class, this section may be concluded by saying that the studies show a very clear relationship between spend-saving aspirations and the factors of mobility-stability.

FRAMEWORK OF STUDY

Following are Warner's hypotheses and assumptions for the study:

I. *Assumptions about symbols and values and about saving of money and accumulation of objects.*

Our society is acquisitive and pecuniary. On the one hand, the values and beliefs of Americans are pulled toward the pole of the accumulation of money by increasing the amount of money income and reducing its outgo. On the other hand, American values emphasize the accumulation of objects and products of technology for display and consumption. The self-regard and self-esteem of a person and his family, as well as the public esteem and respect of a valued social world around the accumulator, are increased or not by such symbols of accumulation and consumption.

The two sets of values, the accumulation of product symbols and the accumulation (saving) of money, may be, and usually are, in opposition.

General working hypotheses stemming from these assumptions were: (1) People are distributed along a range according to the two-value components, running from proportionately high savings, through mixed categories, to proportionately high accumulation of objects. (2) These value variations conform to social and personality factors present in all Americans.

II. *Assumptions about product symbols, savers, and accumulations.*

American society is also characterized by social change, particularly technological change that moves in the direction of greater and greater production of more kinds and more numerous objects for consumption and accumulation.

Hypothesis: New varieties of objects will be most readily accepted by the accumulators, and most often opposed by the savers.

III. *Assumptions about the social values of accumulators and savers.*

American society is characterized by basic cultural differences, one of them being social status. Social class levels are occupied by people, some of whom are upward mobile by intent and fact. Others are non-mobile, by intent and fact. The values which dictate judgments about actions, such as the kinds of objects which are consumed and accumulated, will vary by class level and the presence or absence of vertical mobility.

IV. Assumptions about the personal values of accumulators and savers.

The personality components are distributed through the class levels and through the mobility types. By relating the social and personality components, it is possible to state a series of hypotheses about accumulators and savers as they are related to the object world around them, particularly to objects which are new and old to the culture, those which are imposing or not and those which are predominantly for display or for consumption.

At the direct, practical level, all of these theoretical questions can be summarized by one basic question: *What kinds of things are people likely to buy and not buy if they are in given class positions and if they are or are not socially mobile?* In other words, what is the effect on purchasing behavior of being in a particular social class, and being mobile or non-mobile?

If this is the crucial question, theoretically grounded, then a whole series of hypotheses can be laid out concerning values about money and values about buying various kinds of objects for consumption and for display. Some of these are:

1. *There will be a relationship between values held by a particular subject and the extent to which particular products exemplify those values.*
2. *There is a differential hierarchy of things for which it is worth spending money.*
3. *Veblen's theory that conspicuous expen-*

diture is largely applied to the Upper Class is erroneous. It runs all the way through our social system.

From these statements certain other hypotheses follow:

4. *At different class levels, symbols of mobility will differ.*

There is a differential hierarchy of things on which it is worth spending money. Class and mobility will be two of the dimensions that will differentiate—also personality and cultural background.

5. *The place in the home where these symbols will be displayed will shift at different class levels.*

The underlying assumption here is that there is a hierarchy of importance in the rooms of the house. This hierarchy varies with social class, mobility, age, ethnicity. The studies also revealed clear-cut patterns of taste for lamps, furnishings, house types, etc.

6. *The non-mobile people tend to rationalize purchases in terms of cost or economy.*

In other words, non-mobile people tend to be oriented more toward the pole of the accumulation of money. Purchases, then, are rationalized in terms of the savings involved.

The basic thesis of all the hypotheses on mobility is this: Whereas the stable individual would emphasize saving and security, the behavior of the mobile individual is characterized by spending for various symbols of upward movement. All of the evidence turned up indicates that this difference in values does exist, and furthermore that notable differences in personality dynamics are involved. For instance, the analysis of how families would make investments shows that stable people overwhelmingly prefer insurance, the symbol of security. By contrast, the mobile people at all levels prefer stocks, which are risk-taking. In Warner's words, the mobile individual acts as if he were free, white, and twenty-one, completely able to handle the world, and perfectly willing to gamble on himself as a sure bet to succeed.

CLASS PLACEMENT

Returning to the factor of social class, in this study class placement was based on a multi-state probability area sample of metropolitan Chicago, involving 3,880 households. It was found that the matter of placement could not be done by the relatively simple scoring sufficient for the smaller cities. To secure house typings, it was necessary to provide the field investigators with photographs covering a wide range of dwelling types, all the way from exclusive apartments to rooms over stores. Because of the very complexity of metropolitan life, occupations provided the biggest problem. To solve this operational problem, it was necessary to construct an exhaustive list of occupational types involving degree of responsibility and training required by each. The data finally used to calculate the Index of Status Characteristics (ISC) were:

> (weighted by 5)
>   Occupation (from 1 to 7 broad categories)
> (weighted by 4)
>   Sources of Income (from 1 to 7 types)
> (weighted by 3)
>   Housing Type (from 1 to 7 types)

The sum of the individual's weighted scores was used to predict his social class level as follows:[2]

ISC scores	Predicted social class placement
12–21	Upper class
22–37	Upper-middle class
38–51	Lower-middle class
52–66	Upper-lower class
67–84	Lower-lower class

[2] Dr. Bevode McCall helped to solve the ISC scoring problem for Metropolitan Chicago.

The study very clearly shows that there is a social-class system operative in a metropolitan area which can be delineated. Furthermore, class membership is an important determinant of the individual's economic behavior, even more so than in the smaller city. The one department store in the smaller city may satisfy almost everyone, whereas in the metropolitan city the stores become sharply differentiated.

This is the social-class structure of Metropolitan Chicago, typifying the transformation of the formerly agrarian Midwestern cities from Pittsburgh to Kansas City into a series of big mill-towns:

Upper and upper-middle	8.1%
Lower-middle	28.4%
Upper-lower	44.0%
Lower-lower	19.5%

While the Old Families and the Newly Arrived are still recognizable as types, they constitute less than 1 percent of the population. A similar study in Kansas City turned up so few that they could not be counted at all. On the other hand, we see the emergence of a seventh class, the Upper-Lower "Stars" or Light-Blue Collar Workers. They are the spokesmen of the Upper-Lower Class groups—high income individuals, who have the income for more ostentatious living than the average factory worker but who lack the personal skills or desire for high status by social mobility.

There is certainly a rough correlation between income and social class. But social class is a much richer dimension of meaning. There are so many facets of behavior which are explicable only on a basis of social class dynamics. For instance, this analysis of the purchase of household appliances in Chicago over a four-year period shows a very different picture by income and by class:

Nine appliance types—four-year period by income

Over $7,000	36.2%
4,000–6,999	46.0%
Under 4,000	17.8%

By social class

Upper and upper-middle	16.6%
Lower-middle	29.2%
Upper-lower	45.7%
Lower-lower	8.5%

Income analysis shows that the lowest income group represents an understandably smaller market, but nevertheless a market. Social-class analysis highlights a fundamental difference in attitudes toward the home between the two lower classes. The Upper-Lower Class man sees his home as his castle, his anchor to the world, and he loads it down with hardware—solid heavy appliances—as his symbols of security. The Lower-Lower Class individual is far less interested in his castle, and is more likely to spend his income for flashy clothes or an automobile. He is less property-minded, and he has less feeling about buying and maintaining a home.

Several *Tribune* studies have explored the way of life and the buying behavior in many new suburbs and communities. All of them quickly become stratified along social-class and mobility dimensions, and, therefore, differ tremendously among themselves. *Fortune* has reported on Park Forest, Illinois, a middle-class suburb of 30,000 and only ten years old. It is characterized by high degrees of both upward and geographical mobility. The people are overwhelmingly those who had moved from other parts of the United States, who had few local roots, and who consequently wanted to integrate themselves in friendship groups. But this was not typical of the new Lower-Status suburbs where the women did relatively little fraternizing. It was not typical of the new Upper-Middle Class

mobile suburbs where the people were preoccupied with status symbols, not in submerging themselves in the group.

One new community had crystallized as being for Higher-Status Negroes. This was a resettlement project with relatively high rents for Negroes. Eighty-five per cent of them had come from the South where social class was compressed. But, as soon as they came to Chicago, the class system opened up and they were anxious to establish a social distance between themselves and other Negroes. Almost all of them said they enjoyed the "peace and quiet" of their neighborhood, which was their way of insisting that they were not like the "noisy" lower-class Negroes. They deliberately avoided the stores patronized by other Negroes.

CHOICE OF STORE

All of these studies reveal the close relation between choice of store, patterns of spending, and class membership. In the probability sample delineating social class, such questions were asked in the total metropolitan area as:

> "If you were shopping for a good dress, at which store would you be most likely to find what you wanted?"
> "For an everyday dress?"
> "For living room furniture?"
> "At which store do you buy most of your groceries?"

To assume that all persons would wish to shop at the glamorous High-Status stores is utterly wrong. People are very realistic in the way they match their values and expectations with the status of the store. The woman shopper has a considerable range of ideas about department stores; but these generally become organized on a scale ranking from very High-Social Status to the Lowest-Status and prestige. The social status of the department

store becomes the primary basis for its definition by the shopper. This is also true of men's and women's apparel stores, and furniture stores, on the basis of customer profiles. The shopper is not going to take a chance feeling out of place by going to a store where she might not fit.

No matter what economics are involved, she asks herself who are the other customers in the store, what sort of treatment can she expect at the hands of the clerks, will the merchandise be the best of everything, or lower priced and hence lower quality? Stores are described as being for the rich, for the average ordinary people, or for those who have to stretch their pennies.

The most important function of retail advertising today, when prices and quality have become so standard, is to permit the shopper to make social-class identification. This she can do from the tone and physical character of the advertising. Of course, there is also the factor of psychological identification. Two people in the same social class may want different stores. One may prefer a conservative store, one may want the most advanced styling. But neither will go to stores where they do not "fit," in a social-class sense.

In contrast to the independent food retailer, who obviously adapts to the status of the neighborhood, the chain grocers generally invade many income areas with their stores. Nevertheless, customer profiles show that each chain acquires a status definition. The two largest grocery chains in the Chicago area are A&P and Jewel; yet they draw very different customer bodies. A&P is strong with the mass market, whereas Jewel has its strength among the Middle Class.

While the national brand can and often does cut across classes, one can think of many product types and services which do have social class labels. The Upper-Middle Class

person rarely travels by motor coach because none of his associates do so, even though there is certainly nothing wrong with this mode of transportation. On the other hand, even with low air-coach fares, one does not see many factory workers or day laborers on vacation around airports. Such sales successes as vodka and tonic water, and men's deodorants and foreign sports cars, were accomplished without benefit of much buying from this part of the market.

COMMUNICATION SKILLS

There is also a relation between class and communication abilities which has significance for marketing. The kind of super-sophisticated and clever advertising which appears in the *New Yorker* and *Esquire* is almost meaningless to Lower-Status people. They cannot comprehend the subtle humor; they are baffled by the bizarre art. They have a different symbol system, a very different approach to humor. In no sense does this imply that they lack intelligence or wit. Rather their communication skills have just been pressed into a different mold.

Here again, style of advertising helps the individual to make class identification. Most of the really big local television success stories in Chicago have been achieved by personalities who radiate to the mass that this is where they belong. These self-made businessmen who do the announcing for their own shows communicate wonderfully well with the mass audience. While many listeners switch off their lengthy and personal commercials, these same mannerisms tell the Lower-Status individual that here is someone just like himself, who understands him.

Social Research, Inc., has frequently discussed the class problem in marketing by dividing the population into Upper-Middle or quality market; the middle majority which combines both the Lower-Middle and Upper-Lower; and then the Lower-Lower. The distinction should be drawn between the Middle Classes and the Lower-Status groups. In several dozen of these store profiles, there is scarcely an instance where a store has appeal to the Lower-Middle and Upper-Lower classes with anything like the same strength.

It would be better to make the break between the Middle Class, representing one-third of the population and the Lower-Status or Working-Class or Wage-Earner group, representing two-thirds of metropolitan Chicago. This permits some psychological distinctions to be drawn between the Middle-Class individual and the individual who is not a part of the Middle-Class system of values. Even though this is the dominant American value system, even though Middle-Class Americans have been taught by their parents that it is the only value system, this Lower-Status individual does not necessarily subscribe to it.

WHO SAVES, WHO SPENDS?

Another important set of behavioral distinctions related to social class position was revealed in the "save-spend aspiration" study. The question was asked: "Suppose your income was doubled for the next ten years, what would you do with the increased income?" This is a fantasy question taken out of the realm of any pressing economic situation to reflect aspirations about money. The coding broke down the answers to this question into five general categories: (1) the mode of saving, (2) the purpose of saving, (3) spending which would consolidate past gains, meet present defensive needs, prepare for future self-advancement, (4) spending which

is "self-indulgent-centered," (5) spending which is "house-centered."

Here are some of our findings:[3] The higher the individual's class position, the more likely is he to express some saving aspirations. Conversely, the lower his class position, the more likely is he to mention spending only. Moreover, the higher the status, the more likely is the individual to specify *how* he will save his money, which is indicative of the more elaborate financial learning required of higher status.

Proceeding from the more general categories (such as saving versus spending only) to more specific categories (such as non-investment versus investment saving and the even more specific stock versus real estate investment, etc.) an increasingly sharper class differentiation is found. It is primarily *non-investment* saving which appeals to the Lower-Status person. Investment saving, on the other hand, appeals above all to the Upper-Status person.

Investors almost always specify how they will invest. And here in mode of investment are examples of the most sharply class-differentiated preferences. Intangible forms of investment like stock and insurance are very clearly distinguished as Upper-Status investments. Nearly four times as many Upper-Middles select insurance as would be expected by chance, whereas only one-fifth of the Lower-Lowers select it as would be expected by chance. By contrast, Lower-Status people have far greater preference for tangible investments, specifically ownership of real estate, a farm, or a business.

To sum up, Middle-Class people usually have a place in their aspirations for some form of saving. This saving is most often in the

---

[3] The saving-spending aspiration analysis was carried out by Roger Coup, graduate student at the University of Chicago.

form of investment, where there is a risk, long-term involvement, and the possibility of higher return. Saving, investment saving, and intangible investment saving—successively each of these become for them increasingly symbols of their higher status.

The aspirations of the Lower-Status person are just as often for spending as they are for saving. This saving is usually a non-investment saving where there is almost no risk, funds can be quickly converted to spendable cash, and returns are small. When the Lower-Status person does invest his savings, he will be specific about the mode of investment, and is very likely to prefer something tangible and concrete—something he can point at and readily display.

Turning from mode of saving to purpose of saving, very significant class relationships are likewise evident. Consider the verbalization of saving purpose. Lower-Status people typically explain why one should save—why the very act of saving is important. On the other hand, Middle-Class people do not, as if saving is an end-in-itself, the merits of which are obvious and need not be justified.

Spending is the other side of the coin. Analysis of what people say they will spend for shows similar class-related desires. All classes mention concrete, material artifacts such as a new car, some new appliance. But the Lower-Status people stop here. Their accumulations are artifact-centered, whereas Middle-Class spending mentions are experience-centered. This is spending where one is left typically with only a memory. It would include hobbies, recreation, self-education and travel. The wish to travel, and particularly foreign travel, is almost totally a Middle-Class aspiration.

Even in their fantasies, people are governed by class membership. In his day dreaming and wishful thinking, the Lower-Status individual will aspire in different patterns from the Middle-Class individual.

PSYCHOLOGICAL DIFFERENCES

This spending-saving analysis has very obvious psychological implications to differentiate between the classes. Saving itself generally suggests foresightedness, the ability to perceive long-term needs and goals. Non-investment saving has the characteristics of little risk-taking and of ready conversion, at no loss, into immediate expenditures—the money can be drawn out of the account whenever the bank is open. Investment spending, on the other hand, has the characteristics of risk-taking (a gamble for greater returns) and of delayed conversion, with possible loss, to expenditures on immediate needs.

Here are some psychological contrasts between two different social groups:

Middle-Class
1. Pointed to the future
2. His viewpoint embraces a long expanse of time
3. More urban identification
4. Stresses rationality
5. Has a well-structured sense of the universe
6. Horizons vastly extended or not limited
7. Greater sense of choice-making
8. Self-confident, willing to take risks
9. Immaterial and abstract in his thinking
10. Sees himself tied to national happenings

Lower-Status
1. Pointed to the present and past
2. Lives and thinks in a short expanse of time
3. More rural in identification
4. Non-rational essentially
5. Vague and unclear structuring of the world
6. Horizons sharply defined and limited
7. Limited sense of choice-making

8. Very much concerned with security and in-security
9. Concrete and perceptive in his thinking
10. World revolves around his family and body

CONCLUSIONS

The essential purpose of this article was to develop three basic premises which are highly significant for marketing:

I. *There is a social-class system operative in metropolitan markets, which can be isolated and described.*

II. *It is important to realize that there are far-reaching psychological differences between the various classes.* They do not handle the world in the same fashion. They tend not to think in the same way. As one tries to communicate with the Lower-Status group, it is imperative to sense that their goals and mental processes differ from the Middle-Class group.

III. *Consumption patterns operate as prestige symbols to define class membership, which is a more significant determinant of economic behavior than mere income.* Each major department store, furniture store, and chain-grocery store has a different "pulling power" on different status groups. The usual customers of a store gradually direct the store's merchandising policies into a pattern which works. The interaction between store policy and consumer acceptance results in the elimination of certain customer groups and the attraction of others, with a resulting equilibration around a reasonably stable core of specific customer groups who think of the store as appropriate for them.

Income has always been the marketer's handiest index to family consumption standards. But it is a far from accurate index. For instance, the bulk of the population in a metropolitan market today will fall in the middle-income ranges. This will comprise not only the traditional white collar worker, but the unionized craftsman and the semi-skilled worker with their tremendous income gains of the past decade. Income-wise, they may be in the same category. But their buying behavior, their tastes, their spending-saving aspirations can be poles apart. Social-class positions and mobility-stability dimensions will reflect in much greater depth each individual's style of life.

Questions

1. "A rich man is simply a poor man with more money." Discuss your views on this statement.
2. Summarize with an example the influence of social class in the choice of a store.
3. The Upper-Upper Class constitutes less than 1 percent of the population. Is it a viable market? Why or why not?

35. The Significance of Social Stratification in Selling

Richard P. Coleman

Dating back to the late 1940's, advertisers and marketers have alternately flirted with and cooled on the notion that W. Lloyd Warner's social class concept[1] is an important analytic tool for their profession. The Warnerian idea that six social classes constitute the basic division of American Society has offered many attractions to marketing analysts when they have grown dissatisfied with simple income categories or census-type occupational categories and felt a need for more meaningful classifications, for categorizations of the citizenry which could prove more relevant to advertising and marketing problems. However, in the course of their attempts to apply the class concept, marketers have not always found it immediately and obviously relevant. Sometimes it has seemed to shed light on advertising and merchandising problems and at other times it hasn't—with the result that many analysts have gone away disenchanted, deciding that social classes are not much more useful than income categories and procedurally far more difficult to employ.

It is the thesis of this writer that the role of social class has too often been misunderstood or oversimplified, and that if the concept is applied in a more sophisticated and realistic fashion, it will shed light on a great many problems to which, at first glance, it has not seemed particularly relevant. What we propose to do here, then, is discuss and illustrate a few of these more subtle, more refined and (it

must be acknowledged) more complicated ways of applying social class analyses to marketing and advertising problems. In other words, the purpose of this paper is to clarify *when* and *in what ways* social class concepts are significant in selling, and to suggest when they might not be as significant as other concepts, or at least need to be used in concert with other analytic categories.

THE WARNERIAN SOCIAL CLASSES

The six social classes which are referred to in this paper are those which W. Lloyd Warner and his associates have observed in their analyses of such diverse communities as Newburyport, Massachusetts,[2] Natchez, Mississippi,[3] Morris, Illinois,[4] Kansas City, Missouri,[5] and Chicago. These social classes are groups of people who are more or less equal to one another in prestige and community status; they are people who readily and regularly interact among themselves in both formal and informal ways; they form a "class" also to the extent that they share the

[1] See W. Lloyd Warner, Marchia Meeker, Kenneth Fells, *Social Class in America* (Chicago: Science Research Associates, 1949).

[2] See W. Lloyd Warner and Paul Lunt, *The Social Life of a Modern Community* (New Haven: Yale University Press, 1941).

[3] See Allison Davis, Burleigh B. Gardner and Mary R. Gardner, *Deep South* (Chicago: University of Chicago Press, 1941).

[4] See W. Lloyd Warner and Associates, *Democracy in Jonesville* (New York: Harper & Brothers, 1949).

[5] The writer's observation on the Kansas City social class system will be included in a forthcoming volume on middle age in Kansas City, currently being prepared for publication by the Committee on Human Development of the University of Chicago.

same goals and ways of looking at life. It is this latter fact about social classes which makes them significant to marketers and advertisers.

Briefly characterized, the six classes are as follows, starting from the highest one and going down.[6]

1. The Upper-Upper or "Social Register" Class is composed of locally prominent families, usually with at least second or third generation wealth. Almost inevitably, this is the smallest of the six classes—with probably no more than one-half of one per cent of the population able to claim membership in this class. The basic values of these people might be summarized in these phrases: living graciously, upholding the family reputation, reflecting the excellence of one's breeding, and displaying a sense of community responsibility.

2. The Lower-Upper or "Nouveau Riche" Class is made up of the more recently arrived and never-quite-accepted wealthy families. Included in this class are members of each city's "executive elite," as well as founders of large businesses and the newly well-to-do doctors and lawyers. At best only one and one-half per cent of Americans rank in this level—so that all told, no more than 2 per cent of the population can be counted as belonging to one layer or the other of our Upper Class. The goals of people at this particular level are a blend of the Upper-Upper pursuit of gracious living and the Upper-Middle Class's drive for success.

3. In the Upper-Middle Class are moderately successful professional men and women, owners of medium-sized businesses and "organization men" at the managerial level; also included are those younger people in their twenties or very early thirties who are expected to arrive at this occupational status level—and possibly higher—by their middle or late thirties (that is, they are today's

[6] Some of the phrases and ideas in this characterization have been borrowed from Joseph A. Kahl's excellent synthesizing textbook, *The American Class Structure* (New York: Rinehart & Company, Inc., 1957).

"junior executives" and "apprentice professionals" who grew up in such families and/or went to the "better" colleges). Ten per cent of Americans are part of this social class and the great majority of them are college educated.

The motivating concerns of people in this class are success at career (which is the husband's contribution to the family's status) and tastefully reflecting this success in social participation and home decor (which is the wife's primary responsibility). Cultivating charm and polish, plus a broad range of interests—either civic or cultural, or both—are also goals of the people in this class, just as in the Lower-Upper. For most marketing and advertising purposes, this class and the two above it can be linked together into a single category of "upper status people." The major differences between them—particularly between the Upper-Middle and the Lower-Upper—are in degree of "success" and the extent to which this has been translated into gracious living.

4. At the top of the "Average Man World" is the Lower-Middle Class. Approximately 30 per cent or 35 per cent of our citizenry can be considered members of this social class. For the most part they are drawn from the ranks of non-managerial office workers, small business owners, and those highly-paid blue-collar families who are concerned with being accepted and respected in white-collar dominated clubs, churches, and neighborhoods. The key word in understanding the motivations and goals of this class is Respectability, and a second important word is Striving. The men of this class are continually striving, within their limitations, to "do a good job" at their work, and both men and women are determined to be judged "respectable" in their personal behavior by their fellow citizens. Being "respectable" means that they live in well-maintained homes, neatly furnished, in neighborhoods which are more-or-less on the "right side of town." It also means that they will clothe themselves in coats, suits, and dresses from "nice stores" and save for a college education for their children.

5. At the lower half of the "Average Man World" is the Upper-Lower Class, some-

times referred to as "The Ordinary Working Class." Nearly 40 per cent of all Americans are in this class, making it the biggest. The proto-typical member of this class is a semi-skilled worker on one of the nation's assembly lines. Many of these "Ordinary Working Class" people make very good money, but do not bother with using it to become "respectable" in a middle-class way. Whether they just "get by" at work, or moonlight to make extra, Upper-Lowers are oriented more toward enjoying life and living well from day to day than saving for the future or caring what the middle class world thinks of them. They try to "keep in step with the times" (indeed, one might say the "times" are more important than the "Joneses" to this class), because they want to be at least Modern, if not Middle Class. That is, they try to take advantage of progress to live more comfortably and they work hard enough to keep themselves safely away from a slum level of existence.

6. The Lower-Lower Class of unskilled workers, unassimilated ethnics, and the sporadically employed comprises about 15 per cent of the population, but this class has less than 7 or 8 per cent of the purchasing power, and will not concern us further here. Apathy, fatalism, and a point of view which justifies "getting your kicks whenever you can" characterize the approach toward life, and toward spending money, found among the people of this class.

Now, we do not mean to imply by these characterizations that the members of each class are always homogeneous in behavior. To suggest such would be to exaggerate greatly the meaning of social classes. To properly understand them, it must be recognized that there is a considerable variation in the way individual members of a class realize these class goals and express these values.

For example, within the Upper Middle and Lower Upper Class, there is one group —called Upper Bohemians[7] by Russell Lynes

[7] See Russell Lynes, *A Surfeit of Honey* (New York: Harper & Brothers, 1957).

—for whom cultural pursuits are more important than belonging to a "good" country club. As a result, the tastes in furniture, housing accommodations, and recreations exhibited by the men and women of this "issues-and-culture set"—leaning toward the avant garde and eclectic, as they do—are apt to be very different from those practiced by the more conventional, bourgeois members of these status levels. Nevertheless, to both the Upper Bohemians and the Upper Conventionals, displaying "good taste" is quite important, with the differences between them not so much a question of good-versus-bad taste as one of whose form of good taste is preferred (though, to be sure, the Upper Bohemians are usually quite certain theirs is better).

Other sub-categories can be found in these higher classes and parallel kinds of sub-categories can be found in the Lower Middle and Upper Lower classes. Within the Upper Lower Class, for instance, there is a large number of people who are quite concerned with their respectability and spend much of their spare time in church trying to do something about it. Their respectability concerns are not quite like those of the Lower Middle Class, however, for they seem to care more about The Almighty's view of them than of their fellow man's. Thus, the Upper-Lower Class might, for certain analytic purposes, be sub-divided into Church-Going and Tavern-Hopping segments, although this would by no means exhaust all possibilities of sub-categorization here.

All of this is by way of indicating that the millions of individuals who compose each social class are not necessarily similar or identical in their consumption patterns, even though they are of equal status socially and share a set of goals and points of view which are class-wide. Thus far, the literature on social class in both marketing journals and sociological publications has emphasized the similarities of people within classes and rarely pointed out these variations. This has been necessary, of course, in order to properly introduce the concept and educate social scientists and marketers to its utility, but it has led on occasion to naive misuse of the concept and ultimate disillusion. In my view, is has come time for us to advance into a more sophisticated application of social class to marketing problems, which involves awareness of the differences as well as similarities within each class.

SOCIAL CLASS VERSUS INCOME

Let us proceed now to stating the basic significance of this class concept for people in the selling field. In the first place, it explains why income categories or divisions of Americans are quite often irrelevant in analyzing product markets, consumers' shopping habits and store preferences, and media consumption. For example, if you take three families, all earning around $8,000 a year, but each from a different social class, a radical difference in their ways of spending money will be observed.

An Upper-Middle Class family in this income bracket, which in this case might be a young lawyer and his wife or perhaps a college professor, is apt to be found spending a relatively large share of its resources on housing (in a "prestige" neighborhood), on rather expensive pieces of furniture, on clothing from quality stores, and on culture amusements or club memberships. Meanwhile, the Lower-Middle Class family—headed, we will say, by an insurance salesman or a fairly successful grocery store owner, perhaps even a Diesel engineer—probably has a better house, but in not so fancy a neighborhood; it is apt to have

as full a wardrobe though not so expensive, and probably more furniture though none by name designers. These people almost certainly have a much bigger savings account in the bank.

Finally, the Working Class family—with a cross-country truck driver or a highly-paid welder as its chief wage-earner—is apt to have less house and less neighborhood than the Lower-Middle or Upper-Middle family; but it will have a bigger, later model car, plus more expensive appliances in its kitchen and a bigger TV set in its living room. This family will spend less on clothing and furniture, but more on food if the number of children is greater, as is likely. One further difference: the man of the house probably spends much more on sports, attending baseball games (for example), going hunting and bowling, and perhaps owning a boat of some description.

The wives in these three families will be quite noticeably different in the kind of department stores they patronize, in the magazines they read, and in the advertising to which they pay attention. The clothing and furniture they select for themselves and their families will differ accordingly, and also because they are seeking quite different goals. This has become very clear in studies Social Research, Inc., has done for the *Chicago Tribune* on the clothing tastes of Chicagoan women, for the Kroehler Company on the place of furniture in American homes, and for MacFadden Publications on the purchasing patterns and motivations of their romance magazines' Working Class readers.[8] (These have been contrasted in turn with the motivations of Middle Class women who read service magazines.)

---

[8] This study has been published under the name *Workingman's Wife* (Oceana Press: New York City, 1959) by Lee Rainwater, Richard P. Coleman, and Gerald Handel.

The Upper-Middle Class wife—even of the struggling young lawyer—usually buys all her public-appearance clothes at specialty shops or in the specialty departments of her community's best department stores; she feels constrained to choose her wardrobe according to rather carefully prescribed standards of appropriateness. In furnishing her home, she thoughtfully considers whether a given piece or a combination of pieces will serve as adequate testament to her aesthetic sensitivities, plus doing credit in turn to her husband's taste in wife-choosing. She pays careful attention to the dictates of the best shelter magazines, the "smart" interior decorators in town, the homes of other women in her class, and maybe that of the boss's wife.

The Lower-Middle Class woman is more single-mindedly concerned with furnishing her home so that it will be "pretty" in a way that suits her and hopefully might win praise from her friends and neighbors. She tries to get ideas from the medium-level shelter and service magazines and is perpetually depressed because her home isn't furnished as much like a dream house as she would like it to be. In this she is quite different from the Upper-Lower wife who is apt to care more about having a full array of expensive, gleaming white appliances in her kitchen than a doll's house of a living room. Where the Lower-Middle housewife usually has a definite style in mind which she's striving to follow, the Upper-Lower woman simply follows the lead of newspaper furniture advertising (and what she sees when window shopping) toward furniture which is "modern-looking," by which she means the "latest thing" that has hit the mass market.

A great many more examples of differences in consumption patterns by class levels could be given, but the principal ones have been well reported already—facetiously by Vance Packard and seriously by Pierre Martineau;[9] for further amplification on this point the latter source is recommended. The significance to merchandisers and advertisers of these findings about motivational differences between classes is fairly obvious, the major idea being that for many products, advertising appeals and merchandising techniques must be differentially geared to the points of view reflected in these three main social classes. Advertising of brands or goods aimed at a specific class must take into account the motivations of that class, and not try to sell everything as if it were the Upper Class or Upper-Middle status symbol.

Up to now, we've been talking about product areas—clothing, furniture, and residential neighborhoods—where the relationship between social class and quality of goods purchased is highest. In these things the so-called "Quality Market" and the Upper Middle (and higher) markets coincide. That is, the purchasers of highest quality clothing and highest quality furniture are more nearly from the Upper-Middle and Upper social classes than from the highest income categories, and so on it goes down the hierarchy. The correlation between price of goods purchased and social class is relatively quite high in these product areas while the correlation between price paid and annual income is lower than one might expect.

There is another group of products which are not linked in such a direct way with social class, but neither are they linked with income categories in any obvious relationship. The current car market provides an instructive example of this situation, for the nature of the market cannot be grasped by using one or the other concept exclusively. What is happening

[9] See Pierre Martineau, *Motivation in Advertising* (New York: McGraw-Hill Book Company, 1957) and "Social Classes and Spending Behavior," *The Journal of Marketing,* Vol. 23, No. 2, October 1958, pp. 121–130.

in today's car market can only be understood when income categories are placed into a social class framework.

THE "OVERPRIVILEGED" AS "QUALITY MARKET"

Within each social class group there are families and individuals whose incomes are above average for their class. The Upper-Lower family with an income above $7,000 a year—sometimes a product of both husband and wife working, and sometimes not—is an example of this. So, too, is the Lower-Middle Class business owner or salesman who makes more than $10,000 a year, but has no interest in either the concerts or country clubs of Upper-Middledom and hence is still Lower Middle Class. The Upper Middle Class couple with more than $25,000 a year at its disposal but no desire to play the "society game" of subscription balls or private schools is also in this category. These are what might be called the "overprivileged" in the absolute sense, of course; they are "overprivileged," however, relative to what is required or needed by families in their class. After they have met the basic expectations and standards of their group in the housing, food, furnishing, and clothing areas, they have quite a bit of money left over which is their equivalent of "discretionary income."

In much the same way, each class has its "underprivileged" members; in the Upper-Middle Class these are the younger couples who haven't made the managerial ranks yet, the college professors, the genteel professionals, and a few downwardly mobile people from high-status backgrounds who are trying to hang on to what fragments of status they have left—for the most part these people are below the $12,000-a-year mark and they can barely meet some of the basic requirements of Upper-Middle life, much less experience any of its little luxuries; in the Lower-Middle Class these are the poorly paid bank tellers, the rows of bookkeepers in railroad offices, the school teachers with considerably more status aspiration than income; and in the Upper-Lower Class it is almost any family earning less than $4,500 or $5,000 a year, at today's rates of pay in metropolitan areas.

In the middle of each class's income range are its "average" members, families who are neither underprivileged nor overprivileged by the standards of their class. You might think of this as the Upper-Middle Class family between $12,000 and $20,000 a year, the Lower-Middle family in the $7,000–$9,000 range, and the Upper-Lower family near $6,000 per annum. However, this word of caution is necessary: a lot of people in the middle income range of their class see themselves as underprivileged because they are aspiring to become one of the "over-privileged" in their class or to move on up the ladder to a higher class.

The relevance of all this to the car market is that when you look at this particular market today, you find it is the "average" members of each class, whether Upper-Middle, Lower-Middle, or Upper-Lower, who constitute the heart of the Low-Priced Three's audience; these are the people who are buying Fords and Chevrolets this year and last, and probably next. No longer is the Ford and Chevrolet market just a lower-middle income market, or (in class terms) a Lower-Middle or a Lower Class market. Rather, it is recruited from the middle income group *within each* social class. Indeed, the $15,000-a-year Upper-Middle "organization man" is apt to choose a Ford or Chevy from the Impala-Galaxie level or else a top-price station wagon once he ventures into this market, whereas the average-income Lower-Middle man will settle for a middle-series Bel Air or Fairlane 500, and the "average-income" Upper Lower guy either splurges for an Impala or "sensibly" contents himself with the spartan Biscayne.

While this has been happening to the Low-Priced Three makes the heart of the medium-price car market has relocated in the "over-privileged" segments of each class. Today, rich blue-collar workers are joining pros-perous Lower-Middle Class salesmen and well-to-do Upper Middle Class business owners in buying Pontiacs, Buicks, Oldsmo-biles, Chryslers, and even Cadillacs. In fact, what there is left of big-car lust in our society is found at peak strength among the "over-privileged" Upper-Lowers or else among men who have achieved higher status, but grew up as kids in the Upper-Lower class and have not forgotten their wide-eyed envy of the big car owner.

Finally, as you may have guessed by now, the compact car market's heart is to be found in the "underprivileged" segments of each class (here we are speaking of the market for a compact as a first car). The overwhelming majority of Rambler purchasers, Falcon buyers, and foreign economy car owners come from this socio-economic territory. Thus, it is not the really poor who are buying these cheapest, most economical cars—rather it is those who think of themselves as poor relative to their status aspirations and to their needs for a certain level of clothing, furniture, and housing which they could not afford if they bought a more expensive car.

The market for compacts as second cars is somewhat more complicated in its socio-economic geography, being located in the middle range of the Upper-Middle Class, and the "overprivileged" segment of the Lower-Middle. The "overprivileged" Upper Middle may have one as a third car, but he prefers either a T-Bird, a foreign sports car, a Pontiac convertible, or a beat-up station wagon as his

second car, while the "overprivileged" Upper Lower is apt to go for a used standard if he wants a second car.

If marketers and advertisers had assumed that the market for compacts was going to be the lowest-income or lowest-status members of our society, they would have seriously miscalculated in their merchandising and advertising approach. Rambler, for one, did not make this mistake. American Motors advertised its cars as "bringing sense into the auto market" and thus enabled people who bought one to pride themselves on the high-minded rationality they had displayed. Rambler owners, as they drive down the street, are not ashamed that they couldn't af-ford better—instead, as the company has told them to be, they are proud that they did not yield, like their neighbors, to base emotional desires for a car bloated in size beyond necessity and loaded in gadgetry beyond reason. Compact car owners have their own form of snobbery—what might be called "sensibility snobbery"—with which to con-tent themselves and justify their purchase.

This analysis of the car market is one exam-ple of what I mean by the sophisticated ap-plication of social class concepts to marketing and advertising problems. There are many products and many brands which, like cars, are more nearly symbols of higher status class within class than symbols of higher status per se. A color television set is such a product, or at least it was two years ago when Social Research, Inc., studied its market. At the time color television manufacturers were puzzled because sales were thinly spread throughout the income scale, without any noticeable in-crease in concentration until an extremely high level was reached. Furthermore, they were unable to see any particular relationship between social class and color set ownership, since about as many Upper-Lower Class peo-ple owned them as did Upper-Middles. However, when the two factors of income and class were put together, in the manner described above, it became clear that the color television market was concentrated among high-income or "overprivileged" members of each social class. Other products which bear this complicated relationship to class and income are the more costly brands and larger sizes of home appliances. Fairly expensive recreational equipment like outboard motor boats also tend to be in this category.

In summary, today's market for quality goods and quality brands is not necessarily drawn from what has historically been described as the "Quality Market" of Upper-Middle and Upper Class people, nor even necessarily from the highest income categories. Rather, in many instances, it is drawn from those people within each social level who have the most discretionary income available for enjoying life's little extras above and beyond the requirements of their class. Every merchandiser and advertiser ought to take a good hard look at what he is selling and ask himself if it bears this particular relationship to the class and income picture. If his product does, and if his brand is one of the more expensive, then he should merchandise it not as if it were just for social climbers or for the upper classes, but rather as part of the Better Life, U.S.A. If, on the other hand, his brand is one of the least expensive, then he is not just selling to the poor, but rather to those in all classes who feel it is only sensible on their part to settle for a brand such as his and save the difference for other things which are more important in their statement of social class aspiration and identity.

SOCIAL CLASS ISN'T ALWAYS IMPORTANT

Now, to make the picture complete, it must be pointed out that Social Research, Inc., has found some products in which the income factor is all-important and the social class variable is relevant only to the extent that it is correlated with income. Perhaps the most perfect example of this is the market for air conditioners in Southwestern cities. There, everybody—except the sickly and the extremely old-fashioned—agree that air conditioning one's home is imperative if summer is to be survived with any degree of comfort. Consequently the expensiveness of a family's air conditioning equipment—whether centrally installed, or window units to the number of four, three, two, or one—is directly correlated with family income. It is not merely a function of discretionary income—as in our example about purchase of medium-priced cars; it is instead almost completely a function of total annual income. If more Upper-Middles than Upper-Lowers are fully air-conditioned it is only because more of them can afford to be; it is not because Upper-Middles as a group are placing higher priority on the air-conditioned existence.

Undoubtedly air conditioners are not alone in being classless—so that one more thing the marketer who uses social class in a truly sophisticated way needs to understand is that there can be occasions when it is an irrelevant variable. Realizing this, he will not become disenchanted with social class when he finds a marketing problem where it does not shed light or where it does not seem pertinent. Of course, he will want to make sure that in advertising such a product there is indeed no need to take class into account. After all, some apparently classless products are properly sold to the market in a segmental approach, appealing first on one ground to one class, then on other grounds to another.

There are other products—and probably air conditioning is one of them and children's play clothes may be another—where this is not necessary. For such products some factor, such as physical comfort (in the one case) or simple durability (in the other), is so basic in the consumer's consideration that all other motivations pale into insignificance beside it. There are even products, like beer, where the democratic approach—that is, a tone of "let's-all-be-good-fellows-together" is exactly right and segmental appeals or snob stories are all wrong.

Another aspect to the sophisticated employment of social class refers back to the point made earlier that social class groups are not always homogeneous. It must be recognized that at times a product's market is formed by "highbrows" from the Upper-Upper Class on down to the Lower-Middle, or by "suburbanites" and suburban-minded people of all classes—in which case the social class variable may confuse a market analysis more than clarify it.

Particularly must merchandisers and market analysts beware of equating "Class" with "Brow"; for they are not synonymous. For example, the Upper-Middle Class and those above it are mainly middle-brow in taste (veering toward an all-American lower-middle-brow level of preferences in television shows and advertising messages) even though the majority of highbrows are found at this level. At times advertisers have made the mistake of assuming that the Upper-Middle Class should be appealed to in a highly sophisticated fashion—and though this is just fine if the product itself is likely to appeal primarily to the Manhattanized type of Upper-Middle, it is not correct if it is expected to sell to the kind of doctor in Dubuque who enjoys a visit to New York every now and then but would never want to live there.

In short, not only must the sophisticated marketer abandon social class in favor of income categories on occasion in his analysis and interpretation of a market, he must recognize that at times both income and class

are superseded in importance by divisions of the public into brow levels, by divisions into "high mobiles" and "low mobiles," innovators and non-innovators, inner-directed and other-directed, urbanites, suburbanites, exurbanites, ruralites, and Floridians, or what have you. Usually, of course, fullest understanding of a market will require that social class be linked in with whichever subcategorization proves pertinent from among those in the catalogue just recited, much as income and class were linked together for fullest comprehension of the car market.

As a final point, let it be noted that the way of life and the goals of people in each social class are in perpetual flux. Neither the "who" of each class nor "what motivates them" are constants to be assumed without continual re-evaluation. Right now, particularly, it is very clear that our society is changing. Every year the collar-color line is breaking down further. More blue-collar workers are becoming Middle Class as well as middle income and Modern, and a white-collar position is less and less a guarantee of Lower-Middle status. As a consequence of this, the Lower-Middle Class is perhaps somewhat more "materialistic" in outlook and slightly less "respectability" conscious than it was 25 years ago, or even 8. Meanwhile, for men and women to achieve Upper-Middle status without college backgrounds is becoming more and more difficult, so that this class is turning much more worldly-wise and well-read, much less conventionally bourgeois than it was in the zenith of Babbitt's day.

In short, the form of our society and its division into social classes is not fixed as of Yankee City in 1931, Jonesville in 1944, Kansas City in 1952, or St. Louis in 1960. We won't be able to say exactly the same things about either the classes themselves or their relationships to specific markets by next year at this time. This fact about the American class structure, that it is not static, that it is in the process of change, is in itself important to merchandisers, to advertisers, to anyone in selling. Among other things, it means that undoubtedly they have played a part in past changes and can play a leading role in directing future changes. But of more direct concern here, to the marketing analyst it means that if he allows his stratification concept to become dated, his use of it will cease as of that moment to be sophisticated.

Questions

1. Briefly name and describe each of Warner's six social classes.
2. Is income class or social class a better predictor of a person's buying behavior? Explain.
3. Describe what is meant by the overprivileged and underprivileged segments. Relate this to their buying behavior.
4. How do you think the composition of the six social classes has changed since this article was written in 1958?

36. Extensions of the Basic Social Class Model Employed in Consumer Research

Terence A. Shimp

J. Thomas Yokum

This paper presents a critical analysis of the manner in which social class has been treated in consumer behavior and offers suggestions for improvement. These suggestions are predicated on the belief that the conceptual model of social class prevalent in consumer behavior is both inconsistent with major trends in American society and incompatible with the socialization perspective that represents a dominant orientation in studying consumer behavior.

SOCIAL CLASS IN CONSUMER BEHAVIOR

Consumer behavior interest in social class has waxed and waned over the past two decades. Martineau's (1958) seminal article provided the momentum for other solid works which appeared in the 1960s. Most notable were the writings of Coleman (1960), Carman (1965), and Levy (1966). Where Levy demonstrated that significant differences do exist among social classes with regard to various *general* behaviors, Coleman cautioned that the social class concept has been misunderstood and over-simplified. Carman, though critical of the overly simplistic manner in which researchers had applied the social class concept, presented a strong case supporting its potential usefulness.

The reflection and conceptualization personified by these works was followed by a period of empirical activity. Rich and Jain (1968) examined the relationship between social class and shopping behavior and concluded that social class *has* dubious usefulness in understanding this behavior.

Their skeptical perspective was countered by Wasson (1969), who argued, with a modicum of supportive evidence, that social class is superior to income as a predictor of consumer behavior. The social class vs. income debate was initiated, and a series of studies appeared (Hisrich and Peters 1974; Mathews and Slocum 1969; Myers, Stanton, and Haug 1971; Myers and Mount 1973; Slocum and Mathews 1970).

Empirical activity has been sporadic since then; exceptions are the store patronage research by Foxall (1975) and Prasad (1975) and Jain's (1975) novel application of conjoint analysis for delineating individuals' implicit social class concepts.

Interest in social class has not vanished, however. This is reflected in Nicosia and Mayer's (1976) writing on the sociology of consumption and in the provocative piece by Zaltman and Wallendorf (1977). These latter writers argue convincingly that a sociological perspective is needed to supplement the prevailing psychological orientation if a comprehensive understanding of consumer behavior is to be achieved. Their sentiments are echoed by Sheth (1977) who claims that demographic and SES variables, including social class, should not be discarded prema-turely; instead, more sophisticated measurement and application are needed. Carman (1978) arrives at a similar conclusion while asserting that social class research has ignored his earlier criticisms (Carman 1965).

CRITICAL ANALYSIS

A variety of reasons account for why social class has provided minimal explanation of consumption phenomena. In fact, there are nearly as many reasons as there are empirical studies (cf. Dominquez and Page 1978; Zaltman and Wallendorf 1979). This critical analysis will provide a useful framework for suggesting improvements in the application of social class to consumer behavior. First, however, it will be useful to examine the exact nature of social class and also explore the reason why social class should provide a useful explanation of consumption phenomena.

The Nature of Social Class

A fundamental difficulty in working with the social class concept is arriving at a clear understanding of its meaning. From a strict sociological perspective, social class is just one dimension of a more general social stratification construct. Class is a power-based concept, including both economic and political elements. But stratification also includes a prestige dimension, or what sociologists term "status."

Carman (1965) has argued that a third dimension, cultural class, is one of primary relevance to consumer behavior. Cultural classes are self-perpetuating subcultures which differ with respect to the value placed on education, solidarity of the family, religious involvement, media exposure, recreational activities, etc. Cultural class can be operationalized with real variables (e.g., values, attitudes, behaviors) or with such proxy variables as occupation and education (Carman 1965).

Viewed from the perspective that a particular social class is a group of individuals who share a common culture and manifest similar lifestyles, the concept of social class should be useful for understanding and predicting various consumption phenomena: Since human behavior is determined in large part by the particular elements of culture which are learned and transmitted from generation-to-generation, different social classes should exhibit differences in values, motives, and other precursors to consumption behavior.

Why Has It "Failed?"

Applications of social class in consumer behavior have not been extensive. The only sustained research has involved the social class vs. income controversy, and this research cannot be regarded as definitive since nonequivalent tests were employed, including different products, diverse data collection procedures, and different operationalizations of social class. The failure of social class rests more on the prevailing orientation that has guided the research.

The basic research approach has been to: administer a standard social class index (e.g., Warner's or Hollingshead's); use the household head's (typically husband's) score as the basis for determining the family's social class; and to statistically test whether different social classes differ with regard to product-, store-, or brand-choice behavior.

Three major assumptions are implicit in this "basic model." First, it is assumed that social class is capable, by itself, of explaining choice behavior, oftentimes without regard to whether or not the consumption behavior in question is subject to cultural influence. A second assumption is the tacit belief that a husband's social class by itself is the sole determinant of a household's class position. An additional assumption is that current consumption behavior can be explained by present social class, without regard to one's class standing during that period of primary socialization influence. These assumptions are now discussed in detail as the "choice behavior," "husband-only," and "present social class" fallacies.

The Choice Behavior Fallacy. The only substantive conclusion that can be drawn from empirical applications of social class is that neither social class nor income is an adequate explanation of consumer choice behavior. It is simplistic to expect a single variable to account for behavior that is caused by multiple determinants. Kassarjian (1971) has made this point cogently in his review of personality research, and it is equally applicable here.

A second aspect of the choice behavior fallacy stems from the fact that although social class is an indicator of lifestyle, different products can be used to fulfill the same lifestyle, and the same product can be consumed by different people, in different ways, for different reasons (cf. Kernan 1977). It is thus unreasonable to expect social class to explain and predict choice behavior. Its proper role should probably be to account for the values and motives that underlie this behavior rather than attempting to explain the behavior per se, especially when that behavior may not be subject to cultural influence (e.g., brand choice in a low-unit-value product category).

The Husband-Only Fallacy. Measurement of social class based exclusively on the class position of the household head, who is typically the husband in conventional American families, assumes that the husband's social class is the sole determinant of a household's class standing. In years past this assumption may have been tenable (in paternalistic societies the assumption still holds), but in contemporary America it is not. Indeed, nearly a third of all U.S. households include a wife who is working outside the home at least part-time (Pralle 1980). In addition to augmenting the family's purchasing power, this employment status, together with educational achievements, must have some effect on the family's class standing.

The social class categorization of households based exclusively on the husband's class indicators would be less unacceptable if there were a high degree of similarity (homogamy) in husbands' and wives' backgrounds and educations. Research performed by Blau and Duncan (1967) indeed reflects this. "For men 45 to 54 years of age, the correlation between husband's and wife's education is .580, and for men 55 to 64 years old it is no less than .632" (p. 190). These correlations, though apparently invalidating the above argument, actually suggest two reasons why a husband-only measure of social class is inadequate: (1) although husbands and wives share common backgrounds and educations in the majority of families-of-procreation, a large number of pairings are *not* homogamous; (2) assuming the lower correlation for the younger age cohort reflects a trend (Blau and Duncan did not suggest this), then American families are becoming even less homogamous.

The Present Social Class Fallacy. Operationalizing social class based on the husband's *present* class position assumes implicity that every household that is classified into the same social class will exhibit the same consumption behavior because they share this one commonality. The assumption would not be so limiting if American society were free of vertical mobility, but this is not the case. The father-son correlation for occupational status is of the order of .4 (Blau and Duncan 1967). Evidently, a very considerable amount of status modification does occur.

The consumer socialization literature (Moschis and Churchill 1978; Ward 1974; Ward, Wackman, and Wartealla 1977) affords an explanation of why this extensive status modification invalidates the assumption that current choice behavior is determined by one's present social class position alone. Basic consumption skills are acquired through a lifetime of information receipt and value inculcation. One's present values, beliefs, and attitudes are partially attributed to recent acculturation but, in addition, are in large part the result of the childhood enculturation process.

Since behavior is partly a function of deep-seated values, beliefs, etc., it follows that consumption behavior is largely determined by past social position in addition to present position. In short, people arrive at the same class position in different ways; just because they occupy the same class position at a particular point in time (the time at which a cross-sectional study is performed) is no reason why their consumption behavior should be the same.

This point takes on added significance when the nature of vertical mobility is examined. The greatest mobility occurs among the "sons" of skilled and semi-skilled workers, i.e., children from upper-lower and lower-middle class families are moving both up and down the class hierarchy. Since the mass market for most businesses (and researchers also) consists of the upper-lower, lower-middle, and upper-middle classes, the respondents in a social class study are the ones who are most likely to occupy a particular social class position that is different from the one in which they received their initial consumption socialization.

EXTENDED OPERATIONALIZATIONS OF SOCIAL CLASS

Revision and extension of the basic model that has dominated social class research in consumer behavior is long overdue. Previous extension efforts have achieved some success. Coleman's (1960) consumer privilege concept and Peter's (1970) relative occupational class income concept have both enhanced the ability of social class to predict select consumption phenomena. Neither extension goes far enough, however.

A number of extensions are possible. However, the present effort is not intended to provide an exhaustive treatment. The aim, instead, is merely to illustrate two extended concepts and to suggest the consumption conditions when each may augment the explanatory ability of the standard operationalization of social class. The logic of discovery rather than that of justification provides the philosophy of science rationale for these efforts (Hunt 1976).

A Husband-and-Wife Combined Measure of Social Class

The identification of a household's social class based exclusively on the husband's occupation, education, or other social class indicators has been criticized as a fundamental weakness of social class research in consumer behavior (Zaltman and Wallendorf 1979). Sociologists (e.g., DeJong et al. 1971) have also called for a re-examination of the use of husband-only indicators as the sole determinants of a family's social position. However, how husband's and wife's individual social class indicators should be combined to form an overall family social class score is an open issue.

One method would be to simply average husband's and wife's separate social classes (Haug 1973). This method, though computationally convenient, would be wrong conceptually. The United States is a "leveling-up" society: the marriage of an individual from an upper social class with one from a lower class would not produce a middle-class couple. An alternative would be to assign the higher social class of the husband or wife to the family as a whole (Haug 1973; Haug and Sussman 1971). Conceptual problems also plague this approach. In fact, it would yield results different from the husband-only approach only in those situations where a wife's social class exceeds her husband's.

Both methods ignore the joint influence of husband and wife in consumption-oriented decision making. They would structure a process wherein all consumption decisions would be predicted using the same set of spouse weightings. What is needed is a weighting scheme that assigns weights based on each spouse's relative influence in a specific decision process.

We propose a procedure that places weights on husbands' and wives' social classes proportionate to their relative influence in the consumption situation at issue. The procedure is based on two premises. First, it is assumed that much consumption behavior involves joint decision making. The foundation for this premise is solid (e.g., Davis 1976). A second premise is that the particular social class concept and corresponding operationalization used in consumer research should be situation-specific. To make an analogy, just as a single measure of IQ is inadequate across all cultures, a single social class measure is inadequate across all consumption situations.

For example, if the objective is to predict differences in product use for a product which involves a husband-dominant decision and whose use is not related to deep-seated enculturated values (say the purchase of a lawnmower), then the standard, husband-only concept may serve quite well. If, however, the objective is to account for the frequency of family vacation behavior, which is known to involve joint decision making (Davis and Rigaux 1974) and which likely is influenced greatly by childhood experience, then it is doubtful that the standard concept will account for much variance in vacation frequency.

Implementation of the proposed husband-and-wife-combined measure of social class necessitates two measurements. One would entail measurement of the relative influence of husband and wife in the consumption activity at issue; the other measure would involve indicators of husband's and wife's social class. Each is examined separately, and then we turn to the issue of indexing them into an overall family social class score.

Measurement of relative influence of husband and wife would require precise specification of the consumption situation, since the roles of husbands and wives are variable by decision process stage. Once this is done, it becomes a relatively simple matter of assigning influence to each partner. A common procedure would be to have husband and wife rate themselves on rating scales ranging from "husband decided" to "wife decided" (Davis 1976). Another method would be to have respondents divide a number of points between husband and wife, using a constant sum scale, to indicate each partner's influence (Haley and Overholser 1975).

The separate social classes of husbands and wives could be measured using traditional indices: Warner's Index of Status Character-istics, Hollingshead's Index of Social Position, and Carman's Index of Cultural Classes. Although the validity of these has been challenged in terms of both the choice and weighting of indicators (Dominquez and Page 1978; Haug 1977; Haug and Sussman 1971; Jackson and Curtis 1968), we will assume for simplification's sake that the indices are valid so that we can turn to the more fundamental concern of the paper.

The procedure for combining the separate social classes of husbands and wives is illustrated below. The discussion assumes that separate measures of social class have been obtained for both husband and wife, using for illustration Hollingshead's two-factor index. This procedure places each respondent into one of seven occupational and educational categories. The occupational score is weighted by seven, the educational score by four, and the indexed score is then assigned to one of five social classes (cf. Hawkins, Coney, and Best 1980). Using this procedure, the derived family social class would be a weighted sum of each spouse's social class:

$$F_{SC} = \sum_{i=1}^{2} w_i SC_i$$

where F_{SC} is the family's overall social class; w_i is the weight for each spouse, derived from the measure of relative role for the decision process at issue; and SC_i is each spouse's social class, ranging from class 1 (the highest) to class 5 (the lowest), following Hollingshead's convention.

A simple numerical example will illustrate the procedure. Consider a decision-making situation that varies from household to household in terms of relative influence of husband and wife. Assume for illustration that the decision involves the choice of vacation site. Data for four hypothetical families are presented.

	Decision process x weight: wife	Wife's + SC	Decision process x weight: husband	Husband's = SC	Family SC
Family 1	0.8	3	0.2	2	2.8 (2)*
Family 2	0.0	3	1.0	2	2.0 (2)
Family 3	0.3	2	0.7	3	2.7 (3)
Family 4	1.0	2	0.0	3	2.0 (3)

* Values in parentheses represent each family's social class based on the husband-only procedure.

These illustrations show how social class assignment for a family is weighted in the direction of the spouse who has a greater decision influence. Where the husband-only measure would have categorized Family 1 as class 2, the husband-and-wife-combined measure yields an indexed score that is closer to the wife's class position, since she plays the dominant role in the particular decision. The combined procedure has the opposite effect for Family 3, where the weighting emphasizes the husband's dominant influence. The illustration for Family 4 reflects a situation where the family would be assigned to the wife's social class because she has sole influence for this particular decision.

Family 2 reflects the only case where the husband-only index provides an equivalent result to our combined procedure. This occurs because the husband is the sole decision maker. Such a situation is the only occasion where it is theoretically appropriate and empirically prudent to designate a family's social class based exclusively on the husband's class position.

A Conjoint, Past-and-Present Measure of Social Class

The focus now turns to the issue of devising a social class index that extends beyond a family-of-procreation's present social class by incorporating the social classes of the families-of-orientation in which husband and wife received their early consumption socialization. In other words, what we are proposing is a social class index which combines "past" and "present" social classes. The considerable amount of intergenerational mobility of status modification provides the theoretical justification for such an index. It is unrealistic to expect to explain a household's current consumption behavior when this behavior in many instances is due to habits, choice rules, and other choice-determining factors that were acquired when family members occupied different (typically lower) class positions during childhood.

The rationale for combining past and present social classes is conceptually sound, but procedures for accomplishing this are not so obvious. For present purposes, we will simply conceptualize what the determining factors might be. Again, the premise is invoked that the amount of weight or influence that is assigned to the to-be-indexed components, past and present social classes, must vary by consumption situation, since there is also variability in the determinants of the particular behavior that the social class measure is attempting to explain. Vacationing behavior illustrates this point. While the decision to take a summer vacation may, for a particular family, be influenced greatly by what husband or wife were accustomed to doing as children, the decision concerning the particular vacation destination may be entirely independent of their past customs or experiences.

In a more general sense, we propose that the relative roles of past and present social position are a function of how "unique" the particular decision is. Where many decisions are highly habitual and based on past patterns (e.g., consumption decisions relating to child-rearing practices), other decisions are unique and require the construction or creation of choice procedures (e.g., the choice of whether to try an innovative birth control method).

This logic is similar to Bettman and Zin's (1977) distinction between stored rules and constructive mechanisms, where the latter is likely employed when a choice is made for the first time or when a changed situation is encountered. We hypothesize that the more unique or constructive the decision, the less the role of past social class as a determinant of current consumption activity. In such a situation, the indexing procedure should assign less weight to past social class. The proposition is portrayed in the Figure.

The empirical upshot is the need for a procedure to identify the relative influence of past and present social classes in context of the consumption decision at issue. Though

obviously not a simple task, it would be possible to devise a series of questions to get at the extent to which a family-of-procreation's decision is based on a constructive mechanism, or, instead, results from stored rules acquired during husband's and wife's respective families-of-orientation.

We close this section by suggesting that the empirical difficulties are not as insurmountable as might appear. This is predicated on our view that social class should in the first place be employed as an explanation only in those situations where the consumption activity is truly influenced by cultural class antecedents (Carman 1965). Provided that research is restricted to such situations, then adults in families-of-procreation should be capable of providing reasonably accurate responses concerning the types of behavior performed by their parents during the period of initial consumption socialization in their families-of-orientation.

DATA SUPPORTING THE NEED FOR EXTENDED CONCEPTUALIZATIONS OF SOCIAL CLASS

Implicit in the foregoing arguments are two crucial assumptions. One is that husbands'

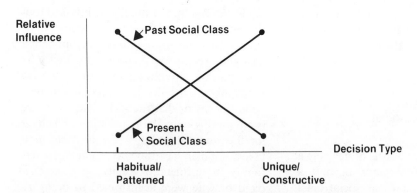

Type of decision and relative influence of past and present social class

and wives' social classes are indeed inconsistent in a relatively large number of households: If the amount of discrepancy were minimal, the combination of their separate classes would be moot, since the husband-only method would capture all the relevant information. A second assumption is that intergenerational mobility is sufficiently extensive to warrant the effort to devise a procedure for combining past and present classes.

A study was performed to test these assumptions. A statewide sample of approximately 800 South Carolina households received a questionnaire in 1979; measures of social class were included among many other questions. The initial mailing and a follow-up generated an 80% response rate. Respondents were somewhat upscale, mostly white, and predominantly from urban locales.

They were asked to describe as specifically as possible the occupation and education of: the husband, the wife, the husband's father, and wife's father. They were instructed to identify their fathers' occupations and highest educational achievement at that period when they (respondents) were "growing up," i.e., "when you were in elementary school." The intent was to capture fathers' social classes at the time of respondents' primary consumption socialization.

Hollingshead's two-factor index was used to assign each household's responses to four possible social classes associated with husband, husband's father, wife, and wife's father. Incomplete data were extensive due to such reasons as inability or unwillingness of respondents to designate their father's occupation or education; respondents were retired or had student status, and thus no current occupation could be assigned; a spouse was not employed outside the home; respondent was unmarried; etc.

One person coded all the questionnaires on two separate occasions, with a minimum separation of one month between recoding the same questionnaire. The agreement was substantial. When coding differences could not be reconciled, the questionnaire was removed from further analysis.

Congruity of Husbands' and Wives' Social Classes

The relationship between husbands' and wives' social classes is presented in Table 1. These data represent only those households where both husband and wife were employed outside the home. A total of 311 cases, or almost exactly one-half of the total responses, provided these data.

The main diagonal in Table 1 reflects in-

Table 1 / Congruency Between Husbands' and Wives' Social Classes

Husband's social class	Wife's social class given husband's class					
	1	2	3	4	5	Totals
1[a]	0	5	6	0	0	11
2	0	38	75	0	0	113
3	0	24	94	5	0	123
4	0	13	34	14	0	61
5	0	0	2	1	0	3
Totals	0	80	211	20	0	311

[a] In the Hollingshead two-factor procedure, lower numbers represent higher social classes.

stances of status congruency—a total of 29.3% of the 311 cases. Entries above the diagonal indicate instances where the husband's social class exceeds his wife's. There were 46.9% such cases. Though not surprising, it is noteworthy that the higher the husband's social class, the greater the probability that the wife's class was lower than his, with the obverse holding as well.

The most revealing result concerns the prevalence of cases where the wife's social class exceeds her husband's. There were a total of 23.8% entries, or nearly one-fourth of all cases, below the diagonal. Considering the upscale sample involved in this analysis, it is likely that much greater frequency of wife's-class-greater-than-husband's would be found in a more representative sample. The implication is clear: The traditional, husband-only measure of social class probably under-represents the true social class and purchasing power of a large percentage of families.

Intergenerational Mobility

Table 2 presents data indicating the relationship between the social class of husbands and wives in families-of-procreation with their respective fathers' social class. There was a total of 457 cases where data were available on husband's and husband's father's social classes, and a total of 325 cases of wife's and wife's father's social classes.

Entries on the main diagonal reflect the absence of intergenerational mobility, i.e., children in families-of-procreation possess the same social class as their fathers. The proportion of such cases is essentially equivalent for husbands and wives, 26.3% for the former and 24.9% for the latter. In other words, approximately three-fourths of all families-of-procreation have experienced status modification.

Upward mobility is indicated in the entries below the diagonal, which reflect fathers' social classes as lower than children's. In fact,

Table 2 / Relationship Between Family-of-Procreation and Family-of-Orientation Social Class

Father's social class		Husband's and wife's social class given their father's class										Totals	
		1		2		3		4		5			
		H	W	H	W	H	W	H	W	H	W	H	W
1	HF	1		14		4		0		0		19	
	WF		0		4		7		0		0		11
2	HF	11		36		9		2		0		58	
	WF		0		11		14		1		0		26
3	HF	7		59		46		6		1		119	
	WF		2		27		60		0		0		89
4	HF	6		59		92		37		3		197	
	WF		0		40		105		10		0		155
5	HF	1		19		21		23		0		64	
	WF		0		6		30		8		0		44
Totals	HF	26		187		172		68		4		457	
	WF		2		88		216		19		0			325

Note: H = Husband's social class: W = Wife's social class; HF = Husband's-father's class; WF = Wife's-father's class.

65.2% of all the husbands experienced upward mobility, while a slightly larger 67.1% of the wives experienced this mobility.

Entries above the diagonal reveal relatively few instances of downward mobility; there were only 8.5% cases of this nature for husbands, and 8% such cases for wives. These data are harmonious with previous results (e.g., Blau and Duncan 1967) indicating the extensive upward mobility in American society.

DISCUSSION

These data have obvious limitations; foremost, perhaps, is the nonrepresentative sample. However, the data are presented for illustration purposes only and are not intended as definitive. Limitations aside, the data clearly manifest extensive intergenerational mobility as well as significant discrepancies between the social classes of husbands and wives in those households where both partners have employment outside the home.

The upshot is that the traditional approach to social class research in consumer behavior is conceptually and empirically flawed. Measuring only the husband's social class and then attempting to predict choice behavior based on this information alone assumes that the husband's class is the sole indicator of a family's class standing. This assumption is untenable in view of the fact that women from approximately one-third of all households are in the work force, and many possess indicators of higher class than their husbands'. We have proposed a method which takes into consideration the social class of both husband and wife and combines the two by weighting each by the degree of influence each partner has in the particular decision process that is the subject of inquiry.

It is also unreasonable to assume that current behavior is solely a function of a household's present class standing. A present-only operationalization disregards past socialization influence. The empirical problem resulting from this is that a sample of households assigned to the same social class by a present-only measure may be quite heterogeneous with regard to values, motives, and other real determinants of consumption behavior.

It is one thing to recommend the indexing of past-and-present social classes into an overall conjoint scale. Doing so is another matter. We have conceptualized a general procedure for determining the relative weights of past and present classes, but specific procedures await future research.

The procedure for combining the separate social classes of husbands and wives is feasible, however; it is merely a matter of doing the research to ascertain whether a combined husband-and-wife index provides superior predictions to the simple, husband-only procedure that has dominated past research.

REFERENCES

Bettman, James R., and Michel A. Zins. (1977). "Constructive Processes in Consumer Choice." *Journal of Consumer Research* 4, 75–85.

Blau, Peter M., and Otis D. Duncan. (1967). *The American Occupational Structure,* New York: John Wiley & Sons.

Carman, James M. (1965). *The Application of Social Class in Market Segmentation.* Berkeley: Institute of Business and Economic Research.

———. (1978). "Values and Consumption Patterns, A Closed Loop." In *Advances in Consumer Research,* ed., H. Keith Hunt. Ann Arbor: Association for Consumer Research.

Coleman, Richard P. (1960). "The Significance of Social Stratification in Selling." In

Marketing: A Maturing Discipline, ed., Martin L. Bell. Chicago: A.M.A.

Davis, Harry L. (1976). "Decision Making within the Household." *Journal of Consumer Research* 2, 241-260.

——, and Benny P. Rigaux. (1974). "Perception of Marital Roles in Decision Processes." *Journal of Consumer Research* 1, 51-61.

DeJong, P. Y., M. J. Brewer, and S. S. Robin. (1971). "Patterns of Female Intergenerational Occupational Mobility." *American Sociological Review* 36, 1033-42.

Dominquez, Luis V., and Albert L. Page. (1978). "Stratification in Consumer Behavior Research: A Re-examination." Case Western Reserve University Working Paper.

Foxall, Gordon R. (1975). "Communication Note: Social Factors in Consumer Choice: Replication and Extension." *Journal of Consumer Research* 2, 60-64.

Haley, Russel, C.C. Overholser, and Associates (1975). "Purchase Influence: Measures of Husband/Wife Influence on Buying Decisions." New Canaan, Conn.: Haley, Overholser, and Associates, Inc.

Haug, Marie R. (1973). "Social Class Measurement and Women's Occupational Roles." *Social Forces* 52, 86-98.

——. (1977). "Measurement in Social Stratification." *Annual Review of Sociology* 3, 51-77.

——, and Marvin B. Sussman. (1971). "The Indiscriminate State of Social Class Measurement." *Social Forces* 48, 549-63.

Hawkins, Del I., Kenneth A. Coney, and Roger J. Best. (1980). *Consumer Behavior: Implications for Marketing Strategy.* Dallas: Business Publications, Inc.

Hisrich, Robert D., and Michael P. Peters. (1974). "Selecting the Superior Segmentation Correlate." *Journal of Marketing* 38, 60-63.

Hunt, Shelby D. (1976). *Marketing Theory: Conceptual Foundations of Research in Marketing.* Columbus, Ohio: Grid.

Jackson, E.F., and R.F. Curtis. (1968). "Conceptualization and Measurements in the Study of Social Stratification." In *Methodology in Social Research,* eds., H.M. Blalock and A.B. Blalock. New York: McGraw-Hill.

Jain, Arun K. (1975). "A Method for Investigating and Representing an Implicit Theory of Social Class." *Journal of Consumer Research* 2, 53-59.

Kassarjian, Harold H. (1971). "Personality and Consumer Behavior: A Review." *Journal of Marketing Research* 8, 409-19.

Kernan, Jerome B. (1977). "Retrospective Comment on Martineau's 'Social Classes and Spending Behavior." In *Classics in Consumer Behavior,* ed. Louis E. Boone. Tulsa, Oklahoma: The Petroleum Publishing Co.

Levy, Sidney J. (1966). "Social Class and Consumer Behavior." In *On Knowing the Consumer,* ed. Joseph W. Newman. New York: John Wiley & Sons.

Martineau, Pierre. (1958). "Social Classes and Spending Behavior." *Journal of Marketing* 23, 121-30.

Mathews, Herbert L., and John W. Slocum. (1969). "Social Class and Commercial Bank Credit Card Usage." *Journal of Marketing* 33, 71-78.

Moschis, George P., and Gilbert A. Churchill. (1978). "Consumer Socialization: A Theoretical and Empirical Analysis. *Journal of Marketing Research* 15, 599-609.

Myers, James H., and John F. Mount. (1973). "More on Social Classes Vs. Income as Correlates of Buying Behavior." *Journal of Marketing* 37, 71-73.

——, Stanton, Roger P., and Arne F. Haug. (1971). "Correlates of Buying Behavior: Social Class Vs. Income." *Journal of Marketing* 35, 8-15.

Nicosia, Francesco M., and Robert N. Mayer. (1976). "Toward a Sociology of Consumption." *Journal of Consumer Research* 3, 65-75.

Peters, William H. (1970). "Relative Occupational Class Income: A Significant Variable in the Marketing of Automobiles." *Journal of Marketing* 34, 74-77.

Pralle, Michael E. (1980). "Survey Dispels Myth About Growing Dual-Earner Market." *Marketing News,* May 16, 17-18.

Prasad, V. Kanti. (1975). "Socio-economic Product Risk and Patronage Preferences of Retail Shoppers." *Journal of Marketing* 39, 42-47.

Rich, Stuart U., and Subhash C. Jain. (1968). "Social Class as Predictor of Shopping Behavior." *Journal of Marketing Research* 5, 41-49.

Sheth, Jagdish N. (1977). "Demographics in Consumer Behavior." *Journal of Business Research* 5, 129-38.

Slocum, John W., and H. Lee Mathews. (1970).

"Social Class and Income as Indicators of Consumer Credit Behavior." *Journal of Marketing* 34, 69–73.

Ward, Scott. (1974). "Consumer Socialization." *Journal of Consumer Research* 2, 1–16.

———, Daniel B. Wackman, and Ellen Wartella. (1977). *How Children Learn to Buy.* Beverly Hills: Sage Publications.

Wasson, Chester R. (1969). "Is It Time to Quit Thinking of Income Classes?" *Journal of Marketing* 33, 54–57.

Zaltman, Gerald, and Melanie Wallendorf. (1977). "Sociology: The Missing Chunk or How We've Missed the Boat." *A.M.A. Educators' Proceedings,* Series #41, 235–38.

———. (1979). *Consumer Behavior: Basic Findings and Management Implications.* New York: John Wiley & Sons.

Questions

1. What are the three major assumptions implicit in the "basic model" of social class?

2. What are the problems with each of these assumptions?

3. Explain the authors' solutions to the problems with the basic social class model and how adopting these solutions in social class research will make future studies more accurate.

Part D

SUBCULTURES AND VALUES

37. Black Buyer Behavior

Donald E. Sexton, Jr.

Although black consumers are presently receiving increased attention from marketers, the marketplace in black neighborhoods is still beset with many difficulties. The selection of goods and services in these neighborhoods is still believed to be relatively limited in scope, lower in quality, and higher in price than in other neighborhoods.[1] These conditions may be traced to the lack of economies of scale, expertise, or honesty among retailers in black areas.[2] Also more experienced and reputable firms are often unwilling or unable to market to blacks. For example, chain supermarkets in Chicago are quite sparsely distributed in the city's black sections.[3]

Misconceptions or lack of information about black buyers often delay or prevent the entry of firms into the black market-place. Marketers have been challenged by leaders such as Senator Mondale to supply answers to such questions as how do black and poor consumers differ from others in their consumption attitudes and habits?[4] This article attempts to answer that broad question by examining and relating several comparative studies of black and white buying behavior. The insights provided by such an investigation may help firms to channel more of their marketing efforts to black areas either directly, or indirectly, by supporting black firms. Such activity could substantially improve the plight of the inner-city consumer.

DIFFERENCES IN BLACK AND WHITE BUYING BEHAVIOR

Studies of differences between black and white consumers have often been equivocal since they have frequently overlooked income's role in determining buyer behavior. Failure to consider income is a serious omis-

---

[1] David Caplovitz, *The Poor Pay More* (New York: The Free Press, 1967); Frederick Sturdivant, *The Ghetto Marketplace* (New York: The Free Press, 1969); and Donald E. Sexton, Jr., "Comparing the Cost of Food to Blacks and to Whites: A Survey," JOURNAL OF MARKETING, Vol. 35 (July, 1971), pp. 40–46.

[2] Frederick D. Sturdivant, "Better Deal for Ghetto Shoppers," *Harvard Business Review*, Vol. 46 (March-April, 1968), pp. 130–139.

[3] Donald E. Sexton, Jr., *Do Blacks Pay More?* Unpublished doctoral dissertation, University of Chicago, 1970.

[4] Walter F. Mondale, "The Challenge of the Ghetto to Marketing," in *A New Measure of Responsibility for Marketing,* Keith Cox and Ben M. Enis, eds. (Chicago: American Marketing Association, June, 1968), pp. 14–17.

sion, since the median annual family income of blacks is approximately half that of whites, even for those with the same level of education.[5] This article will show that the income differential is an important component in the explanation of apparent differences between blacks and whites with respect to shopping effort and selection of stores, products, and brands.

Motivation may provide a secondary explanation of black and white buyer behavior differences. Bullock, for example, concluded that blacks were motivated by a desire to become part of mainstream America, while whites wanted to obtain exclusiveness.[6] Bauer, Cunningham, and Wortzel hypothesized that Bullock's explanation was but one of the alternatives open to the black consumer. According to Bauer et al., "the basic dilemma of the Negro is whether to strive against odds for middle-class values as reflected in material goods or to give in and live more for the moment."[7] Such a choice may indeed be the dilemma of whites too. Unless it can be established that the proportions of strivers among whites and blacks are substantially different, motivation *alone* would not seem to offer an adequate explanation of overall buyer behavior differences between blacks and whites.

The underlying hypothesis of this article is that income differences can explain many of the overall buyer behavior differences between blacks and whites since it serves as the primary constraint on purchases. For families in a given income class, however, motivation differences can perhaps explain many of any remaining differences between black and white buying behavior. In short, it is hypothesized that although a family may decide to strive for material goods, it must have an income sufficient to afford such items before its motivations can substantially affect its buying actions.

Three aspects of buying behavior are examined: store shopping behavior, product buying behavior, and brand buying behavior. The studies cited were drawn from the marketing literature of the last decade.

STORE SHOPPING BEHAVIOR

For the general population, the most important criteria in food store selection appear to be the store's reputation concerning price level and quality of food.[8] A sample of black housewives, on the other hand, produced a quite different ordering—convenience of location and friendly atmosphere were found most important; low prices least important.[9] This difference may reflect the relative lack of spatial mobility among blacks due to their relatively lower incomes.

This rationale is partially supported by King and De Manche who found that among low-income families, store location and access to public transportation was more important to blacks than to whites.[10] Among

[5] Raymond O. Oladipupo, *How Distinct is the Negro Market?* (New York: Ogilvy and Mather, Inc., 1970).

[6] Henry A. Bullock, "Consumer Motivation in Black and White," *Harvard Business Review,* Vol. 39 (May-June, 1961), pp. 89–104, and (July-August, 1961), pp. 110–124.

[7] Raymond A. Bauer, Scott M. Cunningham, and Lawrence H. Wortzel, "The Marketing Dilemma of Negroes," JOURNAL OF MARKETING, Vol. 29 (July, 1965), p. 3.

[8] Burgoyne Index, Inc., *Twelfth Annual Study of Supermarket Shoppers* (Cincinnati: Burgoyne Index, Inc., 1965).

[9] *Consumer Dynamics in the Supermarket* (New York: *Progressive Grocer,* 1969), p. 196.

[10] Robert L. King and Earl R. De Manche, "Comparative Acceptance of Selected Private-Branded Food Products by Low-Income Negro and White

high-income families, urban blacks appeared to travel further to food stores than did urban whites.[11] This behavioral difference between high- and low-income blacks can be attributed largely to automobile ownership. Among the respondents in Goodman's study of a black neighborhood, 60% of those with incomes above $5,000 shopped for food by car, whereas only 25% of those with incomes below $2,000 used a car.[12]

With regard to nonfood shopping, a larger proportion of blacks than whites visited discount houses more often than department stores, as income differences would suggest. Perhaps due to housing patterns, high-income blacks tended to spend more time travelling to shopping areas and were more likely to drive than high-income whites.[13] Overall, these findings are generally similar to those found for food shopping.

Differing attitudes toward store personnel have been suggested to explain differences in store selection between blacks and whites. Bullock contended that blacks feel defensive in a store because of the belief that they must somehow prove themselves part of mainstream America by their action, while whites, on the other hand, aggressively expect courteous service.[14] Bauer and Cunningham found that within the same income group blacks rated themselves lower in status than did whites.[15] Feldman and Star provide evidence which supports Bullock's contention for one income group—proportionately more whites with incomes between $3,000 and $5,000 were found to visit large department stores than blacks in that income class; however, this difference disappeared among families with incomes above $5,000.[16]

These observations suggest that blacks recognize the generally lower quality of the selection of goods and services in their neighborhoods. Those with higher incomes who own an automobile typically drive to make their purchases somewhere else. Therefore, marketers who can offer economy and reasonable quality in black neighborhoods may find a profitable market. Food marketers, in particular, might consider the need for somewhat smaller supermarkets in the inner city that would be accessible by pedestrian shoppers, or perhaps special buses to bring low-income customers to large supermarkets.

PRODUCT BUYING BEHAVIOR

As the incomes of blacks have risen, their expenditure patterns have approached those of whites in categories such as housing, automobiles, and medical care.[17] However, in 1961 blacks and whites still had different expenditure patterns even after accounting for differences in income level. Blacks were

Families," in *Marketing Involvement in Society and the Economy,* Philip R. McDonald, ed. (Chicago: American Marketing Association, Fall, 1969), pp. 63–69.

[11] Donald E. Sexton, Jr., "Differences in Food Shopping Habits by Area of Residence, Race and Income," unpublished paper, Columbia University, December, 1971.

[12] Charles S. Goodman, "Do the Poor Pay More?" JOURNAL OF MARKETING, Vol. 32 (January, 1968), pp. 18–24.

[13] Lawrence P. Feldman and Alvin D. Star, "Racial Factors in Shopping Behavior," in *A New Measure of Responsibility for Marketing,* Keith Cox and Ben M. Enis, eds. (Chicago: American Marketing Association, June, 1968), pp. 216–226.

[14] Same reference as footnote 6, at p. 99.

[15] Raymond A. Bauer and Scott M. Cunningham, "The Negro Market," *Journal of Advertising Research,* Vol. 10 (April, 1970), p. 6.

[16] Same reference as footnote 13, at p. 222.

[17] Same reference as footnote 15. at p. 12.

found to spend proportionately more than whites for clothing, personal care, home furnishings, alcohol, and tobacco, and less for medical care, food, transportation, education, and utilities.[18] These differences suggest that blacks spend relatively more on socially than nonsocially visible items than do whites of the same income class.

Similar patterns have been observed with respect to new product adoption. Robertson, Dalrymple, and Yoshino found blacks to be more innovative with respect to clothing than whites. Furthermore, high-income blacks were more innovative than low-income blacks.[19] Another study reported that black women were at least as fashion conscious as white women at all income levels, and the higher the income level, the greater the porportion of fashion-conscious black women.[20] Fashion items may provide a visible way for blacks to achieve the middle-class style of life, as Robertson et al. have also noted. The higher their incomes, the easier it is for blacks to make purchases consistent with this goal.

Blacks were found to be less innovative than whites with regard to appliances which are not as socially visible as clothing. High-income blacks, however, were more similar to whites than were low-income blacks.[21]

Bullock suggested that many blacks "tend to view food basically as a means of sustenance," while many whites "conceive of eating as a self-indulgent and pleasurable experience."[22] If this is true, food is relatively a socially prominent product for whites, and one might expect to find whites more innovative regarding food than blacks. Overall, whites were found to be more innovative regarding food than blacks. High-income blacks were *less* innovative than high-income whites, but low-income blacks were *more* innovative than low-income whites.[23]

The limited evidence suggests that blacks are more likely to be innovators in product classes that are socially visible, such as clothing; however, income does limit the extent of their innovativeness. Socially visible product innovations may be one area where marketers may find race a useful basis for segmentation. This point is illustrated by a merchandising manager of Carson, Pirie, Scott, and Company who pointed out: "The Negro shopper is my guide. If I see him buying yellow shirts, I start to buy greater quantities of the color which will filter down to white men a little later."[24]

BRAND BUYING BEHAVIOR

Marketers have at times subscribed to either of two broad views of the brand selection process among black consumers. One states that blacks buy only on a price basis—as a group they are too poor to buy national brands. The second and more recent viewpoint involves status—blacks desire "the same brands, the same labels as they imagine the *best* white Americans have."[25] According to Johnson, the black consumer

---

[18] Same reference as footnote 15, at p. 10.

[19] Thomas S. Robertson, Douglas J. Dalrymple, and Michael Y. Yoshino, "Cultural Compatibility in New Product Adoption," in *Marketing Involvement in Society and the Economy,* Philip R. McDonald, ed. (Chicago: American Marketing Association, Fall, 1969), p. 72.

[20] Same reference as footnote 7, at p. 3.

[21] Same reference as footnote 19, at p. 72.

[22] Same reference as footnote 6, at p. 98.

[23] Same reference as footnote 19, at p. 73.

[24] *Men's Wear* (January 5, 1968), p. 3.

[25] W. L. Evans, "Ghetto Marketing—What Now?" in *Marketing and the New Science of Planning,* Robert L. King, ed. (Chicago: American Marketing Association, Fall, 1968), p. 528.

". . . often feels left out. . . Often the association of a name product with himself provides a lift."[26]

In a general sense, both theories may have some validity. While price does appear to be more important for low-income blacks, price *and* status both seem to be important for high-income blacks. For example, Feldman and Star found that blacks at all income levels considered price an important purchase consideration, but for blacks with incomes above $3,000 "living better" (status) increased in importance as income rose. On the other hand, price decreased in importance among whites as income increased.[27]

Studies of particular products corroborate the importance of status to high-income blacks. Aker found that, within a given income bracket, blacks generally owned higher priced automobiles than whites.[28] The visibility of an automobile makes it an ideal outlet for status aspirations, and since high-income families are more likely to own automobiles, Aker's results support those of Feldman and Star regarding high-income blacks' desire for "living better." Larson concluded that blacks did not tend to own higher priced cars, but he ignored the $4,000 difference in median incomes between the blacks and whites in his sample. Moreover, only Cadillac ownership was considered, and if all luxury cars in his study were aggregated, his conclusion is reversed.[29]

King and De Manche found low-income black families to be more concerned with prices for food than low-income white or middle-class families. The low-income blacks recalled more private brand names, stocked more private brands, and a larger percentage knew the prices of the six products studied.[30] On the other hand, based on a panel which likely consisted of families with higher incomes than those in the King and De Manche study, *Progressive Grocer* described the black housewife as being "particularly quality conscious" and leaning heavily toward nationally advertised brands. It added: "By purchasing well-known brands rather than house labels or secondary labels, she is purchasing a status symbol. . . . "[31]

High income level blacks, then, appear to be more status-conscious when buying brands than lower income blacks. A major reason for this difference may be that high income blacks can *afford* to make purchases which reflect this drive.

These findings should be of concern to many black businesses. Unless they can function efficiently and provide low prices, they will be unable to profitably market to low-income blacks. In any case, they may find it difficult to sell to high-income blacks. The substance of the following observation has been frequently repeated by blacks and black marketing consultants: The black consumer has a ". . . firmly established conviction that goods and services offered by white institutions are, on the average, better and more trustworthy than those offered by institutions operating within his own area."[32] However, the brand loyalties of blacks may be changing. Evans has recently reported that, "In the past four years, [among blacks

---

[26] Same reference as footnote 9, at p. 225.
[27] Same reference as footnote 13, at p. 200.
[28] Fred C. Aker, "Negro and White Automobile Buying Behavior: New Evidence," *Journal of Marketing Research,* Vol. 5 (August, 1968), pp. 285–286.
[29] C. M. Larson, "Racial Brand Usage and Media Exposure Differentials," in *A New Measure of Responsibility for Marketing*, Keith Cox and Ben M. Enis, eds. (Chicago: American Marketing Association, June, 1968), p. 210.

[30] Same reference as footnote 10, at pp. 67, 69.
[31] Same reference as footnote 9, at pp. 196, 215.
[32] Same reference as footnote 6, at p. 96.

there has been] strong evidence of a market revolution in brand disloyalty."[33] This increasing disloyalty may lead to improved chances of success for black business if black consumers increasingly patronize such enterprises.

CONCLUSIONS

The major conclusion marketers may draw from these studies is that the black market is a diverse one with at least two major segments: those consumers who are able to live a middle class life, and those who are not because they live at a subsistence income level. Income level is the primary determinant of these segments. Bauer et al.'s motivation hypothesis seems to explain some buyer behavior differences between blacks and whites, but mainly for the higher income classes. As Feldman and Star suggested in a narrower context, high-income blacks have sufficient income to give them the expectation of adopting the middle class

life, while the chances appear slim for the low-income blacks.[34]

This conclusion has several implications for marketers. First, as black income levels gradually rise, many of the apparent overall differences between "black" and "white" markets will substantially diminish. Second, in the interim period higher income blacks are likely to expend greater shopping effort to purchase the goods they want. In addition, they may become the innovators in numerous and diverse product classes. Third, a sizable proportion of blacks must buy at nearby stores and cannot afford to pay high prices. Marketers should consider increasing their efforts to reach them since these low-income consumers represent a large enough market to be potentially profitable to those marketers who can offer economy and reasonable quality to this segment. Moreover, the increased marketing activity would hasten the process of raising the income levels of blacks, and thus yield long-run economic and social rewards.

[33] Same reference as footnote 26, at p. 528.

[34] Same reference as footnote 13, at p. 226.

Questions

1. What part does income play in black buyer behavior?
2. Do blacks tend to spend more or less than whites on socially visible items? How can you explain this behavior? Give several examples.
3. Do blacks tend to be more or less innovative than whites in their buying behavior? How can you explain this? Give several examples.
4. What does the author contend is the main reason for differences in black and white buyer behavior? Why would this be the case? What does this say about trends currently and in the future?

38. What Every Marketer Should Know About Women

Rena Bartos

Marketing procedures and tools have never been more sophisticated and complex than they are today. Yet there is a curious gap between the realities of social change and the picture of society reflected in most marketing plans and advertising campaigns. Many marketing specialists who pride themselves on their pragmatism and realism have not related their day-to-day marketing activities to the facts of social change.

The potential contribution of these sophisticated marketing tools may be limited by the social perspective of the marketing specialists who use them.

Most marketing plans start with the definition of "target groups," that is, the type or types of consumers who represent the best prospects for the brand, the product, or the service. The more specifically the targets are defined, the more likely it is that any research study or market analysis that assesses them will reaffirm the assumptions of the definers. The reality gap cannot be closed after the marketing process is begun. We need to challenge the basic assumptions that underlie marketing planning before any planning gets under way.

The unspoken assumptions behind many marketing plans suggest that all of the United States lives in the kind of split-level pattern that emerged in the 1950s, with most women engaged in "home making," keeping house, shopping, drinking endless cups of coffee with their neighbors, critically eyeing the state of their laundry or the shine on their kitchen floors, and driving their kiddies to and from scout meetings, birthday parties, and Little League games.

Hubby, in the meantime, is off in the city striving for success—to get a bigger office (a Bigelow on the floor), a promotion, a title. Hubby's secretary is working only until she snags a beau who will propose ("she's lovely, she's engaged") and carry her off to her very own suburban ranch. There the pattern starts all over again.

When this view of society is expressed in marketing terms, the world is neatly divided into separate markets, one set for males and one set for females. Let us take a look at the familiar target groups that mirror these underlying assumptions about society. Most definitions of marketing targets are usually expressed in demographic terms. However, the attitudinal assumption about what motivates the demographic groups may be observed in the advertising that is often the visible end product of the marketing process. The advertising is beamed at these audiences:

Any housewife, 18 to 49: The key customer for all household products and foods is the housewife, who is the prime purchaser for the family. Her motivations are to win the husband's/children's approval of her competent, good housewifery; to do a better/faster job than her neighbor; to fool her husband/mother-in-law into thinking she's done something the hard way when she has taken a shortcut.

Any male head of household, 24 to 49: The key customer for all big-ticket items—cars, business travel, financial services—is a man (husband and father). His motivations?

Status, that is, keeping up with/ahead of the Joneses; achievement; and protection of his dependents.

Any girl, 18 to 25: The key customer for cosmetics, perfume, fashion is the young, single girl. Her motivation, naturally, is to get a man.

Any man, 18 to 34: The key customer for sports cars, beer, liquor, toiletries is the young bachelor before he settles down. His motivation? To have fun, to get girls.

The one characteristic that all these marketing targets have in common is that no one is ever over 49 years of age. In addition, marketers take for granted the conventional wisdom that brand choices are formed early and that younger families represent higher volume potential. Therefore, the most desirable customers are under 35, though in some cases the age target may go up as high as 49.

Is this set of assumptions an accurate reflection of the way most people live? If so, only in part. It is a static and monolithic view of our society that assumes that everyone is cut out of one of a few cookie-cutter patterns and that nothing really changes. Marketing programs built on this kind of perspective cannot reflect the diversity of different life-style groups in our country. Nor can they be responsive to the dynamics of changing attitudes and value systems, which, in turn, lead to changing behavior in the marketplace.

RECOGNIZING THE REALITIES OF THE WOMEN'S MARKET

Let's think of the different life-style groups in our country as representing a mosaic of targets that differ in their product wants and needs and in their value potential to the marketer. The key to unlocking this jigsaw puzzle lies in a combination of old and new demographic facts and in changing attitudes and value systems. This information provides clues to recognizing change and keeping up with it.

The demography is so basic it is almost simplistic. It consists of such straightforward facts as marital status, presence of children, age, sex, and occupation. These simple demographic facts are intertwined with changing attitudes and philosophies of life that influence the responsiveness of consumers to different products.

Most of the keys to keeping up with change are available to all. It is my contention that any practical-minded marketer can challenge the underlying assumptions on which past definitions of the market are based, learn whether the assumptions are out of date, and, if needed, bring his or her marketing procedures in step with the realities.

I have selected the traditional target group, "Any housewife, 18 to 49," to illustrate this discussion. However, this basic approach can be applied equally well to other kinds of ethnic or life-style groups, such as men, unmarrieds, and consumers over that cutoff age of 49.

What assumptions about the women's market are commonly reflected in marketing plans? Consider the following:

1. Most women in the United States are fulltime housewives, usually with a few children at home.
2. The number of women who work may be increasing, but they are usually unmarried women. They are mostly single girls working for a few years before they are married or some poor unfortunates who have to work because they are divorced or widowed.
3. If a married woman works, her husband

can't support her (and she probably isn't a very valuable customer).

4. No married woman would work if she could afford to stay at home.
5. Women with young children won't go to work.
6. All nonworking women are full-time housewives.
7. All homemakers are married.
8. Working women and housewives are sisters under the skin. They want the same things from products and they respond to the same strategies.

How valid are these assumptions? Let us look at the realities. Here are some simple demographic and attitudinal facts about women and the implications of those facts for marketers.

The Quiet Revolution

The number of working women is rising dramatically. The flood of women entering the work force is not only a demographic trend; it could be a manifestation of a profound social change. Eli Ginzberg, chaiman of the National Commission for Manpower Policy, calls it "the single most outstanding phenomenon of our century."

Even well-informed marketers tend to understate the number of women in the work force. They say: "It's around 30% to 40%, isn't it?" In 1970 and 1971 the number was actually 43%. Our most recent data from the Bureau of Labor Statistics show that in 1976 of all females in the United States 16 years of age and over, 47% were in the work force. And the preliminary figures in 1977 are mind boggling. In its June 1977 report, the Bureau of Labor Statistics tells us that 49% of all women 16 years of age and over are at work.

What are the other women doing? "Keeping house" would be the stock answer

of most marketers. Actually, in 1976 only 39% of U. S. women were fulltime housewives. This means that 8% more women are working out of the house than are staying home and keeping house. The remaining 14% were out of the mainstream. They were either still in school or they were retired and/or disabled (see *Exhibit I*). Once we remove the schoolgirls and the grandmothers from the picture, we see that the ratio of working women to housewives is 55% to 45%. This balance has shifted swiftly since the early 1970s. In each succeeding year the proportion of working women has increased and the proportion of housewives has decreased (see *Exhibit II*).

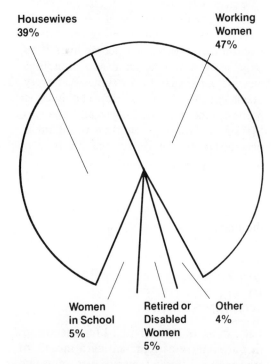

Housewives 39%

Working Women 47%

Women in School 5%

Retired or Disabled Women 5%

Other 4%

Exhibit I / Occupational profile of American women in 1976. *Source:* Bureau of Labor Statistics, January 1977. The base used is all women age 16 and over (81,198,000 women).

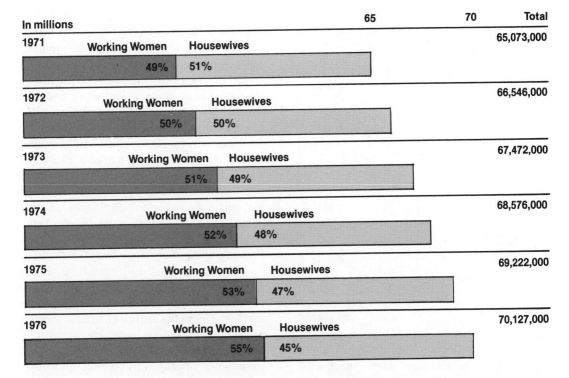

In millions		65	70	Total
1971 Working Women 49% Housewives 51%				**65,073,000**
1972 Working Women 50% Housewives 50%				**66,546,000**
1973 Working Women 51% Housewives 49%				**67,472,000**
1974 Working Women 52% Housewives 48%				**68,576,000**
1975 Working Women 53% Housewives 47%				**69,222,000**
1976 Working Women 55% Housewives 45%				**70,127,000**

Exhibit II / Ratio of working women to housewives, 1971 to 1976. *Source:* Bureau of Labor Statistics, *Employment and Earnings,* 1972 to 1977. These statistics include all women age 16 and over in the labor force or keeping house.

It is not enough for the marketer to say that the market for a product or service is housewives—or working women. Neither is a well enough defined target group. Approximately three out of five working women are married and, therefore, they are housewives as well as working women. We can no longer assume that every bride automatically becomes a full-time housewife. "Living happily ever after" does not necessarily mean staying barefoot and pregnant.

Another assumption to challenge is that married women are the only ones who keep house. Some 13% of all women are unmarried working women who are also heads of

their own households. While they may represent a smaller volume of buying because of the size of their households, they represent an additional increment to the "housewife" market.

Thus the housewife market is far greater than the size assumed by marketers who define housewives only as full-time housekeepers (45% of all women age 16 or more are housewives versus 55% who are working women). It includes another 31% of American women who are working and married; it also includes the 13% of women, unmarried and working, who are household heads (see *Exhibit III* on the next page).

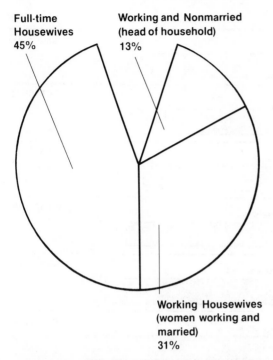

Full-time Housewives 45%

Working and Nonmarried (head of household) 13%

Working Housewives (women working and married) 31%

Exhibit III / The real size of the "housewife" market. *Source:* Bureau of Labor Statistics, *Employment and Earnings,* January 1977, and unpublished data, March 1976. Base used is all women age 16 and over who are in the labor force or keeping house (70,127,000 women).

The Changing Life Cycle

While recognizing the importance of working women as a market, we do not want to invent a new set of working women stereotypes to match those of housewives. One way to close the reality gap between women as they really are and cookie-cutter stereotypes is to recognize their diversity.

Women change as consumers as they move through different stages of life. The way they buy and use products and the way they read or watch or listen to media is affected by whom they live with or without. Is

there a man around the house? Are there any children at home? These two demographic facts are basic clues to women's marketplace behavior.

Exhibit IV shows the extent of the life cycle patterns of women who work and who do not. The patterns are remarkably similar. If we want to learn how working women differ from nonworking women as consumers, we should compare their marketing behavior *within* stages of the life cycle. This is a game that any number can play because the information is available to all. It just requires some straightforward crosstabs to decide how the targets differ from each other, how they are alike, and where to reach them.

The life cycle is also crucial to understanding the changes in the quality of the women who have flooded into the labor market. The major influx of women into the work force comes from an unexpected source: the married women we had assumed were happily engaged in keeping house. Apparently, marketers are not the only ones whose assumptions about life have colored their professional judgments. Earlier in the 1970s government forecasters underestimated the current rise of women in the work force because they assumed that women with very young children under six years of age would not go to work. If fact, as *Exhibit V* on page 390 shows, these young mothers have entered the labor force to a greater degree than any other group.

Why Women Work

What accounts for the exodus of wives from the kitchen to the work place? Are their husbands unable to support them? Are they driven to go to work out of sheer necessity?

There are no definitive answers to the question of why women work. Synthesizing observations from a number of sources,

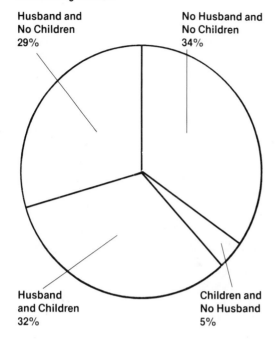

Nonworking Women

Husband and
No Children
29%

No Husband and
No Children
34%

Husband
and Children
32%

Children and
No Husband
5%

Working Women

Husband and
No Children
26%

No Husband and
No Children
35%

Husband
and Children
31%

Children and
No Husband
8%

however, reveals four basic motivations for women's employment. Two of them are economic, and two of them are attitudinal.

Economic Necessity. Some women must work if they or their families are to survive. Sheer economic necessity is a motivation that has always been with us, but one that tends to be ignored when we talk about the "new women" and their reasons for entering the work force. This group includes the unmarried women with no husbands or fathers to support them; some of them have never married and have always had to work for a living. Others have had their marriages interrupted by death or divorce and were suddenly thrust into the working world. Still others included are those married to men whose incomes simply cannot support their families.

The Second Paycheck. Another motivation is that a second paycheck, while not needed for survival, may enable a wife to maintain or improve her family's standard of living. Many women are working for conveniences of life that have begun to seem like necessities—the second car, the washing machine, the color TV set, the family vacation. They also appreciate the independence of having "my money, I earned it," which enables them to indulge their yearning for clothes, cosmetics, and personal luxuries.

"Something More Than the Kitchen Sink." The second paycheck motivation for working is intertwined with a craving for broader horizons. This is what might be called the "there must be more to life than the kitchen sink" reason for working. It is not so much a reaching out for professional achievement or personal fulfillment as it is a

Exhibit IV / Life cycle profiles of American women in 1976. *Source:* Bureau of Labor Statistics, March 1977.

Percentage of Each Group in Labor Force

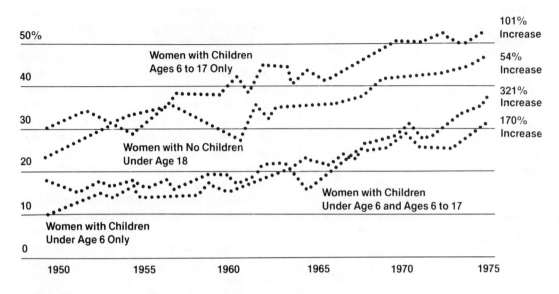

Exhibit V / Who the working wives are, 1950 to 1975. *Source: Employment and Training Report of the President, 1977.* Table B–4, published by the U.S. Government Printing Office. Base used is all civilian, noninstitutional married women, with a husband present, in the labor force.

yearning for the social stimulation and sense of identity that comes with going to work.

The evidence of this comes from several sources. In a study conducted by the Bureau of Advertising of the American Newspaper Publishers Association, with a national probability sample of 1,000 women, the working women were asked: "Suppose you could receive just as much money as you earn now without going to work?" A surprising six out of ten respondents indicate that they would rather go on working than receive their paychecks and stay at home. Obviously, something beyond economic necessity drives these women out of the house.

The Yankelovich Monitor reports that in answer to a question on the *primary* reason why women work, fewer than one in five cite income as their main motivation. More than half say that their main reason for working is a "source of enjoyment"; three in ten say a "desire for independence."

In an opinion poll conducted in the early 1970s, although economic motivation was the single most frequently cited reason for going to work, a constellation of "broader horizons" reasoning dominates the responses. These women say, "I need an interest outside the home," "I work for companionship during the day," "I prefer working to staying at home," or "Most of my friends are working."

Professional Achievement. The data also pinpoint the fourth reason for working. This is the motivation for personal fulfillment and professional achievement that career-minded men have always known. Although only 8% of the women say their reason for working is "my career," this motivation seems to be growing.

The Yankelovich Monitor has asked working women whether they think the work they do is "just a job" or "a career." These are not definitions of the kind of work they do, but rather how they feel about that work. In the six years since Yankelovich first asked this question, the proportion of working women who describe themselves as career-minded has risen steadily. A generation ago there were only a handful of women who carved out careers because they were really motivated to do so. Today, according to Yankelovich, about one in three women who work are strongly committed to careers. These women are motivated by the work itself. They equate working with an opportunity for self-realization, self-expression, and personal fulfillment.

Will this trend continue? Career-oriented working women are much more apt to be college educated than are women who perceive their work as just a job. Better educated women are more likely to work.

Of all women who have graduated from college, 65% go to work as compared with only 24% of the women who did not go past grade school. Therefore, it seems likely that achievement will become even more important as a motivation.

An increasing proportion of women go to college. More important, they seek training in professions that used to be considered the exclusive provinces of men. This is a far cry from the image of a coed going to college in order to major in catching a husband.

Changing Values

As we look to the future, it seems clear that we cannot assume that all young women will marry, settle down, and turn into traditional wives or mothers as their mothers did before them. Some may not marry at all. Many may live in a nontraditional life-style arrangement, which may not culminate in marriage. Indeed, according to the Yankelovich Monitor, more than half of the American public think there is "nothing wrong with a couple living together [without marriage] as long as they really care for each other." This new kind of household arrangement has a higher level of endorsement from men and unmarried adults.

Other women may decide against embarking on motherhood, even if they should get married eventually. While only a few years ago we might have assumed that all newly married couples were in a state of transition between the honeymoon and parenthood, there is a real possibility that, from now on, many of these women will not undertake the responsibility of bringing children into the world.

The acceptance of childlessness as an option is a major attitudinal change that presents a profound challenge to our assumptions about society. In turn, this could have a major impact on the way people live and their behavior in the marketplace. Almost nine out of every ten people in this country—89%, according to the Yankelovich Monitor—feel there is nothing wrong with a married couple deciding not to have any children. What is more, both men and women hold this opinion to the same extent.

The campus debates about marriage versus career that dominated our attention a generation ago would amaze these young women. They may marry later than their mothers, and they may opt to delay having children (or have no children at all), but for these women the question of whether to work is not even an issue.

MEANWHILE, BACK AT
THE RANCH HOUSE . . .

But what about the 39% of all adult women who are at home keeping house? Apparently, not all housewives are equally committed to the housewife's role. In 1971 the Yankelovich Monitor began asking housewives if they ever planned to go to work (or back to work). Obviously, answers to this kind of question in an interview situation are not predictive of behavior. However, the housewives who say "yes" would seem to have a different kind of "mind set" or predisposition than do those housewives who say they prefer to stay at home.

Yankelovich did a special analysis of the social values of these four types of women. The results are dramatic. "Plan to work" housewives have much more in common with working women (those who look at work as a career as well as those who consider it just a job) than with "stay at home" housewives. The stay at homes appear to be out of step with the majority of other women. This leads to some disquieting questions:

- Have we been building our marketing strategies and directing our advertising to only a limited segment of the female audience?
- Have all those marvelous marketing tools that aid decision makers been applied to a limited corner of the market?

Until recently there was no way to confirm or deny these questions. We at J. Walter Thompson could not tell which housewives in our research studies or in our audiences plan to work and which ones want to stay at home. Nor could we differentiate between just a job and career-minded working women.

In order to translate these attitudinal insights from Yankelovich into marketing actions, we asked our research organization,

Target Group Index, to add these "new demographic" questions to their questionnaire. (The index is an annual trend study of market and media behavior; it is produced by Axiom Market Research Bureau, a subsidiary of J. Walter Thompson.) The questions are simple. It's just that we had not thought of asking them before. The answers enable us to analyze working women and housewives from a new perspective.

What is the size of the four segments of American women (see *Exhibit VI*)? If we play a retrospective game here and apply the proportions of the new demographic groups reported by Yankelovich each year to the Bureau of Labor Statistics's ratios of working to nonworking women in each of those years, it becomes clear that the plan to work segment actually put their intentions into practice and swelled the ranks of working women as they departed from their homemaker roles.

Demographic Differences

What about the qualitative differences among the segments? An important one is education. The housewives who would rather stay at home than go to work have the lowest educational level of any of the four groups, while the career-oriented working women have the highest. The plan to work housewife is somewhat better educated than the working woman who says it's just a job.

Age is another important difference. The plan to work housewife is the youngest of the lot. There is not too much age difference between the just a job and career-oriented working women, but the stay at home housewives are the oldest of the groups by far.

What has been keeping the young, plan to work housewives at home? Not surprisingly, it is the children. The plan to work wives are

In Millions   65   70   Base

1971	Housewives		Working Women		65,073,000
	Stay at Home	Plan to Work	Just a Job	Career	
	27%	24%	35%	14%	

1972	Stay at Home	Plan to Work	Just a Job	Career	66,546,000
	26%	24%	34%	16%	

1973	Stay at Home	Plan to Work	Just a Job	Career	67,472,000
	25%	24%	35%	16%	

1974	Stay at Home	Plan to Work	Just a Job	Career	68,576,000
	28%	20%	33%	19%	

1975	Stay at Home	Plan to Work	Just a Job	Career	69,222,000
	27%	20%	34%	19%	

1976	Stay at Home	Plan to Work	Just a Job		70,127,000
	30%	15%	36%	19%	

Exhibit VI / Size of the segments. *Source:* Bureau of Labor Statistics, *Employment and Earnings,* 1972 to 1977, and Yankelovich Monitor, 1972 to 1977. The base used is all women age 16 and over in the labor force or keeping house.

most likely to have children under 18 years of age; also, they have more very young children in their households than do the other groups of women.

Some marketers might still assume that those housewives who want to go to work obviously need the money. Maybe so, but it is interesting that the plan to work housewife is more affluent than her stay at home neighbor. This checks with the fact that the housewives who do not want to go to work are the least educated and the oldest. Career-oriented working women live in the most affluent households of all.

Women's Self-concepts

You may say, "This is all very interesting, but they are really all sisters under the skin when it comes to how they look at life and how they buy products." Is this true? When one examines the self-perceptions of the group, they emerge as distinctly different. Specifically:

• Career women have the strongest positive self-images. They see themselves as more broad-minded, dominating, frank, efficient, and independent than the others. They are the only ones of the four types of women who describe themselves as self-assured and very amicable.

- The just a job working women are quite different from working women who perceive themselves as career-oriented. They are closer to the norm than any of the other three groups.
- The plan to work housewife is far different from her stay at home neighbor, towering above the others in being tense, stubborn, and feeling awkward. However, she echoes many of the self-perceptions of the career woman, describing herself as creative. Both career women and plan to work housewives are more apt than the others to think of themselves as affectionate.
- The stay at home housewife thinks of herself as kind, refined, and reserved. She is strikingly below the norm in feeling brave, stubborn, dominating, or egocentric. Incidentally, all women, including the supposedly self-assured career types, have a very low sense of ego when compared with the male population.

Media Behavior

When it comes to reaching women through the media, marketers tend to think they are a homogeneous audience. The unwritten assumption may be that "most of them watch the same programs" or that "women read magazines in such-and-such a way." However, the realities are quite different from these views.

Television. Both types of housewives watch more prime time TV than do the working women. The career-oriented working woman is least likely to watch TV during the evening. As for daytime TV, it is no surprise that both of the housewife groups watch it more than working women do. What is surprising is that the plan to work housewife has her set turned on even more than the stay at home housewife does.

Radio. Marketers have known that working women listen to radio more than house-

wives do. However, the new facts tell us that career women are the heaviest listeners. They use radio more intensely than do working women who say their work is just a job. The real insight is that the plan to work housewife has her radio turned on more than does her stay at home neighbor. The plan to work housewife seems to be a more active user of all media and a more active consumer. Actually, this is not surprising when we consider her age and educational level as compared with her stay at home neighbor.

Magazines and Newspapers. Marketers long have known that the habit of reading correlates closely with educational level. Therefore, it is no surprise that career-oriented working women are the heaviest users of magazines, and the plan to work housewives are second in magazine readership. Also, as might be expected, career women are more likely than are any of the other three groups to read newspapers.

However, the stay at home housewives are slightly more active in their use of newspapers than are their plan to work neighbors.

TRANSLATING THE DATA INTO MARKETING BEHAVIOR

How do the four groups of women compare as consumers and prospective consumers?

Buying Style

Career women are most likely to plan ahead, to be cautious, and to be brand loyal when they go marketing. On the other hand, they admit to being impulse buyers. I suspect that this apparent conflict between planning and impulse is a matter of the type of purchase to be made. Conversely, the just a job working woman says she is experimental when she goes shopping.

The stay at home housewife is the only one who is not an impulse buyer, and she describes herself as more persuasible than do the others. She is the only one who is above the norm in conformity. Both she and the plan to work housewife are more economy-minded than are working women. While all women are style conscious, the career woman is the most style conscious of all.

Assumptions about Purchasing

"The Traditional Housewife is House Proud; the Working Woman Wants Convenience." The realities of women's purchasing behavior challenge many of our assumptions about women. For example, many marketers assume that the stay at home housewife exemplifies traditional pride in housewifery and in housewifely skills. They are sure she is most "house proud" and most concerned with cleaning, polishing, and grooming her home. Also, they assume that to the extent that working women engage in housework, they give it minimal attention and are more concerned with product convenience than with any other considerations. The facts challenge such assumptions.

The data show that the stay at home housewife is slightly *below* the norm in her use of floor wax and rug shampoo and barely above the norm in her use of furniture polish. Surprisingly, it is the plan to work housewife who is the most active consumer of these products. The career-oriented working woman is also above the norm in her use of them.

When one examines frequency of use, the importance of the plan to work housewife begins to emerge. She is not only more likely

to buy these products, she also uses them far more often than do women in any of the other groups. An exception is that career women seem to shampoo their rugs almost as frequently as the plan to work housekeepers, while the stay at home is below the norm in the frequency with which she shampoos her rugs or waxes her floors.

Air fresheners are also a mass household product. There is very little difference in the extent to which the four types of women buy them. However, the stay at home housewife is the only one who is above the norm in using them *frequently*. She may not polish the floors much, but she apparently sprays the air a lot.

"Women May Pick the Color of the Upholstery, But Men Make the Car Purchase Decision." Is there anyone who still believes that the only role that women play in the car market is to pick the color of the upholstery? An examination of the facts shows that while women are not, as yet, equal to men in their importance to auto marketers, their importance is growing fast. They now account for about 40% of the automotive purchase decisions. However, not all women are equally valuable in this market. Life cycle and new demographic values should be considered if we are to identify the most promising female prospects for cars.

The households of married women, both working and not, are more likely to contain two or more cars than are those headed by unmarried women. Among married women with and without children, the career-oriented working woman is most likely to live in a two-car household. Where there are no kiddies at home, the plan to work housewife is far more likely to have two cars than her stay at home neighbor, and somewhat more likely to drive that second car than the just a job working woman.

Another cliche is exploded when it comes

to actual car use. The common assumption that women drivers are primarily housewives who drive the kiddies to the supermarket and to scout meetings is denied by the facts. Working women rack up more miles on their cars than do housewives. Among all life cycle groups, the career-oriented working woman—married or not, with or without children—does the most driving.

The role of life cycle becomes apparent when we consider the purchase decision. It is not surprising that married women are far more likely to share in the purchase decision than are unmarried women.

On the other hand, unmarried women are more likely to have made the decision themselves—but only if they are working.

The career-oriented working woman emerges as the heroine of the car advertiser. She is far more likely to have shared in the purchase decision than the average woman in any of the other three groups. Both types of unmarried working women are above the norm of the total population in having selected and purchased a car on their own. However, career-oriented working women without husbands tower above the other groups in making automotive purchase decisions for themselves.

"The Business Traveler Is a Man." Both their situation in the life cycle and new demographic dimensions affect women's travel behavior. For example, the data show that, in general, women who work are far more likely to travel than those who are fulltime housewives. As might be expected, women with children at home are far less likely to travel than are their childless neighbors. In addition, the career-oriented working woman is far more likely to own luggage, to use traveler's checks, to have a valid passport, and to have traveled outside the United States in the past year. She is also far more likely to have flown on a scheduled airline

and to have stayed in a hotel when she took her trip.

The career woman is not just a desirable customer when compared with other women. She is anywhere from 50% to 70% above the norm when compared with the total population. So, by any measure, she is a desirable customer for travel. Yet there is little evidence that her business has been cultivated by the travel marketer.

Travel marketers have always known that a small number of business people are heavy users of travel services. Most marketers have assumed that the business traveler is a man. This assumption holds up if business travel is analyzed on sex alone; for example, 17% of all men as compared with only 5% of women have traveled on business in the United States. But the assumption does not hold up if career women are distinguished from other women. As travel customers, career women are somewhere between 70% and 94% as important as men in their business travel activities (see *Exhibit VII* on the next page).

CHANGING ROLE FROM SUPERMOM TO PARTNER

These patterns suggest a redefinition of that traditional target, "Any housewife, 18 to 49." As we redefine the target, we also need to understand the context within which women use products and services. Do the traditional motivations of pleasing their husbands and competing with the neighbors still apply?

It is not enough to know what the consumers do; marketers need to know how they *feel* about what they do. Therefore, I have explored the life-style context within which the four groups buy and use products. One surprise is the shift in women's tone of

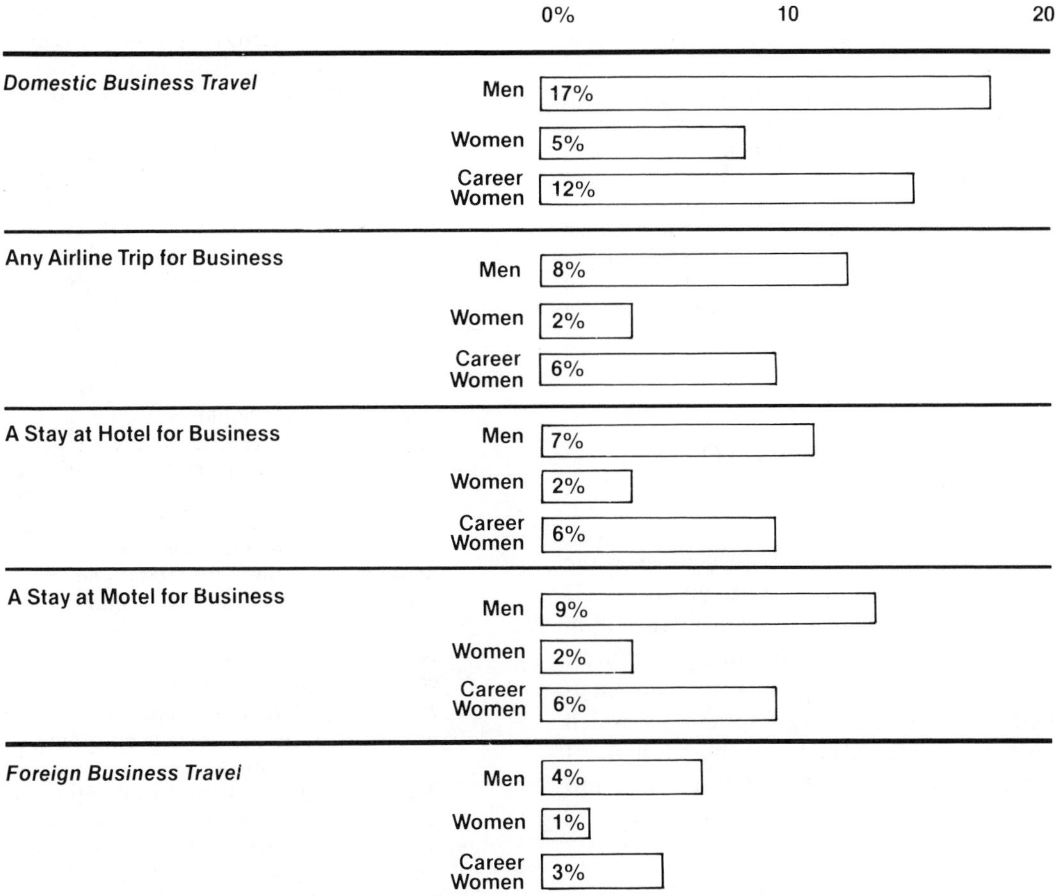

		0%	10	20

Domestic Business Travel

Men — 17%

Women — 5%

Career Women — 12%

Any Airline Trip for Business

Men — 8%

Women — 2%

Career Women — 6%

A Stay at Hotel for Business

Men — 7%

Women — 2%

Career Women — 6%

A Stay at Motel for Business

Men — 9%

Women — 2%

Career Women — 6%

Foreign Business Travel

Men — 4%

Women — 1%

Career Women — 3%

Exhibit VII / Business travelers. *Source:* TGI, Spring 1977.

voice toward their role as housewives—from "woman's work is never done" and "it's all on my shoulders" to a sense of partnership and family teamwork. This is particularly true of working women, both the job and career types. However, the attitude of partnership also is evident among the plan to work housewives. The stay at home women are least likely to expect to receive help from their husbands and children.

These attitudes are confirmed by new data on the extent to which husbands actually participate in household chores:

• More than half of the husbands in the United States are apt to participate in marketing chores, while three out of four men married to just a job working women are in the supermarket. This fact alone challenges our assumptions about who should be the target for household products.

• Caring for young children is the next level at which husbands are apt to participate. Here there is a strong difference among the men married to stay at home housewives and those whose wives plan to work. The latter are much more likely to have their husbands help with the children than are the stay at homes. Also, the career-oriented working women are far more likely to get help with the children than are their just a job counterparts.

- For almost every other chore, the husbands of working women are far more likely to help or participate than are husbands of housewives. However, the men who are married to the plan to work housewives are more likely to help around the house than are the husbands of the stay at home housewives. Machismo still lives in the houses of the stay at homes. Their husbands are far less likely to help with cooking, mopping floors, cleaning bathrooms, or ironing.

WE HAVE NOTHING TO LOSE BUT OUR ASSUMPTIONS

The keys to keeping up with change in the marketplace are available to all of us. If marketers use them, they can, in fact, link social change to their marketing procedures. Any practical-minded marketer can challenge the underlying assumptions on which past target definitions are based and, if needed, bring his marketing procedures into step with present realities. The process is simple:

1. *Reexamine the assumed target.* Examine the facts. The size and composition of particular groups or segments of consumers are available from the Census or Bureau of Labor Statistics. Professional journals, the daily newspapers, and the popular press are constantly full of reports on changing attitudes, values, and life-styles. Many companies have access to continuing sources of public opinion poll data that track social beliefs and attitudes. Does a review of both the hard and soft data suggest that some groups within our society are changing or represent departures from the monolithic norm? (In the case of women, as we have seen, the answer is a resounding "yes.")

2. *Evaluate the market potential of new target groups.* We can learn whether new or changing groups represent differing market opportunities by reanalyzing existing market data. An objective appraisal of the market behavior of newly identified consumer groups can tell us whether they buy or use products differently from their neighbors and whether their media behavior is distinctive. An equally objective appraisal of their incidence or volume of product use can tell us the kind of potential each group represents for a particular category or brand.

3. *Develop a fresh perspective.* The reanalysis of existing data is possible only if the key demographic questions are built in as a matter of course. When they are not, and when new insights suggest the need for new questions, these should be included in all ongoing and future studies. (As explained, a series of "new demographic" questions is necessary to keep up with changes among women customers.)

   If some of the life cycle groups are underrepresented in copy tests and other studies using small samples, it may be necessary to set quotas or "weight up the cells" in order to represent each constituency in its true proportion.

4. *Explore the attitudes and needs of the new groups.* It is classic research procedure to begin a study with a review of available data and to use qualitative explorations to develop general hypotheses that ultimately can be quantified. I suggest reversing this sequence. Hypotheses about potential targets are identified through a review of masses of data and verified through a reanalysis of existing data in order to determine whether their marketing and media behavior is unique. In order to understand why these redefined targets behave as they do, we need to return to qualitative exploration. The newly identified opportunity groups define the sample to be studied.

   This approach proceeds from quantified evidence of marketing behavior to seek qualitative understanding of the reasons for that behavior. Because marketers know the size of each group, exactly which products and brands it buys, and how much, the results are actionable. It will be clear how to reach the groups, whether women or other customers, through the media.

5. *Redefine marketing targets.* If the foregoing

examination of data suggests that the newly identified segments represent useful markets, it should be possible to revise planning readily to meet the need. No new tools or methodology are required. If the facts suggest untapped opportunities, the kinds of marketing procedures that have worked so well in the past can be put to work in approaching the new target groups.

The first marketers who meet the challenge and close the gap between the realities of social change and their procedures will reap the benefits of discovering new marketing opportunities. The tools are available to all.

There is a tide in the affairs of women,
Which, taken at the flood, leads—
God knows where.

From *Don Juan,* by George Gordon, Lord Byron, Chapter VI.

Questions

1. According to the author, name the four reasons why women work.
2. Name and briefly describe the four segments of women as defined by the author.
3. Name some of the ways in which the buying behavior of the "career" woman might differ from that of the "stay at home" woman.
4. What changes do you see occurring in the future in terms of the relative size of the four segments? What implications does this have for marketers?

39.   Children as Consumers: A Review

James U. McNeal

Son, next Friday is your birthday, and you will be eight years old. Your father and I have decided that you can have a birthday party Friday afternoon and invite all your friends. That is, you can invite all your friends eight or older. The reason why they have to be eight or older is that we are going to do something very special. After we have lots of cake and ice cream, we will all sit down in front of the TV and watch advertisements!

These statements may sound absurd now, but could be common within five years. The Federal Trade Commission issued a document in 1978 that recommended that children under eight be shielded from television advertising (*Advertising Age,* 1978). This is to be accomplished by eliminating all commercials from programs normally watched by this age group. The FTC reasoned that children under eight lack the judgment to grasp the selling intent of television commercials. The FTC report also requested a ban on commercials to children under 12 years of age if the commercials glamorized foods or food habits involving health risks, mainly dental health risks from sugared foods. The rationale was that youngsters under 12 do not have a good enough background in nutrition knowledge.

These issues presented by the FTC are major topics for debate, and no doubt will be targets for discussion by experts for a long time. Thus, they will not be argued here. An interesting and more basic issue that underlies the contents of the FTC document is the relationship of the child to the consumer role. The lengthy FTC document rarely refers to children as consumers. It offers no description of the child in the consumer role. In fact, the FTC's concern seems to be with the influence of the child on the parent consumer. The FTC is saying that deceptive advertising to the child is being passed on to his defenseless parents in the form of persuasion to buy the deceptively advertised products. The notion that children are actually consumers—not just users of what mom buys—is cast in a realm of remoteness and mystery.

The discussion surrounding the FTC effort to forbid advertised products to children under eight and to control advertising to children under twelve suggests that the child is not, or should not be a consumer. For example, the consumer advocate group, ACT, that supports the FTC's position recently stated in a direct mail campaign that the child is a child and not a consumer or market.

A dilemma is developing with the youngster as the pawn at the pivot. The parent is saying to the child. "You can be a consumer if you want to be." The businessman is saying to the child. "You are a consumer. Come buy from me." The Federal Trade Commission and consumer advocates are saying, "You are not a consumer until you reach puberty. It is an adult act."

It seems that there are several fundamental questions about the child being a consumer that need answers.

1. Is the youngster a consumer?
2. To what extent is the youngster a consumer?
3. If he is a consumer, what are his consumer behavior patterns like?
4. What is the cognitive status of the child relative to the consumer role?

By addressing these questions, information can be developed that might assist in determining regulations for the consumer behavior of children. Such an effort should also indicate the degree and type of information that exists about the youngster relative to the consumer role.

ARE CHILDREN CONSUMERS?

The literature that treats the topic of children as consumers is sparse. All of it, however, does say that children from approximately age four and on are consumers. From an economic standpoint, they have desires and the ability to buy. From a psychological view, they have needs and cognitive abilities to express these needs in the market place. Sociologically, children are consumers in the sense that they perform activities collectively termed the consumer role that are expected of them in the natural growth sequence characteristic of this society. From a business view, children are consumers in the sense that they plan purchases, obtain prepurchase information, perform the actual purchase, act often with their own money, and evaluate purchases.

At ages 4–7 the children are "consumer trainees" learning to understand the meaning of money and the intricacies of the exchange process (Riesman et al., 1953). By age nine they are "practicing consumers . . . participating frequently in buying activities'' (McNeal, 1964, p. 12).

There are around 30 million youngsters in our nation ages 4–12, spending an average of at least $1.50 per week of their own money for their personal satisfaction (Anderson, 1978; Ward et al., 1975; McNeal, 1969). Additionally, they spend much more than this for household purchases with household money. The annual expenditure by this group of its own money, thus, is between two and three billion dollars—enough for many businesses to consider it a market. Again, this money is their own that is derived from allowances, earnings and gifts.

There are no national studies to indicate which children have the most income or spend the most. One might expect youngsters of high income families to have more money and spend more, and youngsters from low income families to have and spend less. This is suggested by Ward et al. (1975). Also, youngsters' expenditures probably vary by age (Ward, et al., 1977; McNeal, 1964), with the older spending more. Perhaps, too, children who live closer to retail stores might spend more than those that live beyond walking or bicycling distance to stores.

It does appear, however, that children in most families are encouraged to become consumers (McNeal, 1964). Regardless of the characteristics of the household, parents seem to view being a consumer as a natural part of growing up. Children at age four (and under) are taken on shopping trips, talked to by the parents as potential consumers, and introduced to the main components of the market place—money, products and stores. There certainly does not appear to be an effort on the part of the parents to hide the market place from the youngster or to protect the youngster from effects of the market place.

Before discussing this subject further, it seems appropriate to point out an inconsis-tency. It already has been noted that studies of children's consumer behavior are relatively few, and none are extensive national studies. Yet, we also have said that most children are consumers to some extent, and that parents encourage them to participate in the consumer role. The inconsistency is that we usually make extensive studies of behavior patterns that are common in the society, but we have not done so with the consumer behavior of children. No doubt, some business firms have conducted capacious studies of children in the consumer role, but such studies are not offered to the public. University professors of business and behavioral sciences might be expected to conduct such extensive studies and publish their results, but they have not. Their studies have been limited types. There seems to be a posture in our nation that says that children may be consumers but they cannot be put under a microscope and studied. This posture, and the consequent dearth of facts about children as consumers, may cause difficulty for the development and implementation of regulations for consumer behavior by children such as that mentioned earlier.

TO WHAT EXTENT IS THE CHILD A CONSUMER?

This question is logical but difficult to handle because of a lack of standards for consumer behavior. For example, the Education Commission of the States (HEW) developed some tests of consumer behavior knowledge for youngsters of various ages. In pilot tests around the nation they scored poorly. Does this mean these youngsters were poor consumers? Perhaps, but the standards were developed by adults, and probably reflect what some experts would like for the youngsters to know. The FTC document mentioned earlier said that children interpret television advertising differently, and thus more incorrectly, than adults. Hence, there is no question about whose standards are used to interpret advertising. The standards, then, for the extent to which children are consumers are the consumer behavior patterns of adults. Whether or not such standards are correct can be questioned, but it is common to use adult behavior to judge the behavior of children. That generally is done here in utilizing information from McNeal (1964), Anderson (1978), and Saenz (1979) about the extent to which children are consumers.

At ages four and five the youngster is "trying out for the role" of consumer. He probably has made many trips to the store with parents, selected quite a few products with minimal parental guidance, and has purchased a number of items from vending machines. To call him a consumer at this point, though, is an overstatement.

Sometime during his fifth or sixth year the child consumer will solo. He will make his first unassisted purchase excursion, probably to a convenience store. It may be a "milk and bread" purchase or a purchase of a personal treat. In any case, the act seems to be viewed by the youngster as a major step toward maturity—one of the requirements for growing up.

From ages seven through twelve the young consumer is routinely and frequently making purchases. He does not consider consuming as a duty or a privilege, but a normal behavior of people—people his age or older. He buys products and services from many types of retailers. He shops from catalogs and magazines. He returns defective products. He complains about products that do not perform as advertised. He is critical of advertisers who, according to him, "lie to you." He buys for himself, but also buys things that "mom wants" as well as gifts for family members, relatives and friends. He attends new store openings, and often is puzzled about the requirements that contestants for door prizes must be eighteen and older. He also plays supermarket "games" in spite of his knowledge that he is too young to participate. He has brand preferences in most products he buys, but the preferences change with time and the influence of others.

He handles his own money, accumulates it for short periods of time, and enjoys handling and counting the accumulation. He plans purchases for his short-term savings, and usually forgets about sales tax in his planning. He is better at money arithmetic than school arithmetic, but both give him some trouble, particularly under age nine.

In short, he looks and acts like a consumer. He may not "pay the bills" or appreciate his savings account his parents keep for him. He may not be able to envision the monthly grocery bill, even though he buys some groceries for the household. He may not understand interest on time payment plans since he does not have one. But from about any point of view, including an adult's view, he is a consumer. He just happens to be a child, also.

WHAT ARE THE YOUNGSTER'S CONSUMER BEHAVIOR PATTERNS LIKE?

The previous statements give evidence that children are consumers, at least from age seven and on. They also briefly describe the extent of consuming. Now, we will describe what the youngster does when he is in the consumer role. The descriptions are limited to the available literature and thus are not organized on any basis.

What Do Children Spend Their Money On?

Using McNeal's (1964) study and Anderson's (1978), it is possible to generalize about what children purchase with their money. Both studies were conducted in the southwest with mainly middle social class children. Anderson studied children of ages eight to eleven; McNeal investigated the behavior of children five to nine years old. Thus, both studies together provide a good age spectrum.

Most children at all ages use their money to purchase items for immediate self-gratification. Their main purchases could be called "sweets." They buy candy, beverages, ice cream, frozen desserts, gum (mainly bubble gum), flavored gelatin (for eating in powdered form), and an occasional piece of fruit. These items "taste good," "are for children," and provide a mechanism for socializing just as some of them do for adults. These are the main items bought by the five-year-old. The five-year-old will occasionally buy a toy for himself or as a gift, and wants to buy "things for the house" but does not have the money as a rule.

In addition to "sweets," the seven, eight, and nine-year-olds spend their money on toys, crafts, games, entertainment, and school supplies. They buy some personal clothing items and gifts for others. The toys, crafts and games they buy are those also bought by their friends. Such purchases provide bonds for friendship groups. Clothing items are also group determined and include mainly tennis shoes (always by brandname) and T-shirts with special designs and messages printed on them.

Entertainment expenditures mainly include sporting events, movies and pinball machines. Some children reported spending much of their allowances and some money in-tended for school lunches in pinball machines. The pinball machines apparently meet a number of needs. They provide an element of competitiveness, togetherness, excitement, and adulthood. Very often the machines are located in convenience stores where the children can also enjoy beverages and snacks.

These older children make an occasional purchase for the home that combines into a symbol of responsibleness and thoughtfulness. They buy quite a few gifts for parents and friends. Buying for Mother's Day and Father's Day seems particularly important, even more important than Christmas.

Where Do Children Spend Their Money?

There are three types of stores in which youngsters make most of their purchases. They are convenience stores, discount stores, and supermarkets. The convenience store "has everything" for most children. It is close to home and school, it does offer many sweets and pinball machines, and "they usually like children." It appears that the smaller floor space of the convenience store and the presence of its store manager offers a more personal atmosphere. In contrast, "people are unfriendly" in supermarkets and discount stores.

The discount houses and the supermarkets do offer the youngsters a variety. "It's fun to look at things there," summarizes much of their feelings about these retail outlets. It is in these stores that the youngster buys toys, games, crafts, sacks of candy, and gifts for others such as mom and dad.

The children have welcomed the shopping mall. It is a place to meet, to spend hours "looking," and to get information for future purchases. The shopping mall is the main source of clothing items. Interestingly, the shopping mall "has a bunch of stores," while a shopping center is viewed as having one or two—mainly the anchor stores such as a supermarket, discount house, or department store. Department stores are "no-no's" in terms of a place to make purchases.

What Information Sources Do the Children Use?

The most trustworthy source of purchase information for children are parents. "They tell you the truth" said one youngster, emphasizing the dependence upon parents for purchase information. Parents confirm what is received from other information sources.

Television advertising and friends are the next most important sources of purchasing information. The reason the two are noted together here is that research has not been able to separate them well. Apparently there are two flows of information. One is from television which is confirmed with friends (and parents). The other is from friends and is confirmed by television advertising (and parents). There is substantial mistrust of television advertising even though it is an important information source. This mistrust may be the factor that causes it to be combined with another source.

The other major source of purchase information is the store. The store personnel usually are not the source; it is the products, their packages, brands and point-of-purchase advertising in the store that do the informing. Thus, children do some comparative shopping (they call it "looking") inside the store. They also "window shop" in shopping malls.

In sum, the youngsters seem to seek information about purchases just as adults do. The image of the child as an impulse purchaser is only slightly correct. They plan most purchases and seek purchase information for many. The length of their planning is usually relatively short, but it is fairly deliberative.

COGNITIVE STATUS OF THE CHILD CONSUMER

The term, cognitive status, is used here to refer to childrens' attitudes and knowledge relative to being a consumer. That is, what they know about the numerous components of the market place and what are their evaluations of them. The previous comments addressed mainly the consumer behavior of children. In this section of the paper we want to describe cognitions that direct or guide this behavior.

Descriptions of cognitions of young consumers are sparse just as are the descriptions of their behavior. What follows are some brief profiles of childrens' attitudes and knowledge regarding specific market place components that have been gleaned from the literature. No particular order of presentation is intended.

Money

Ward et al. (1975) and McNeal (1964) provide some information about childrens' knowledge and attitudes about money. Knowledge that money "buys things" exists by age four. While the four-year-olds are unable to count money, they know it can be exchanged for "good things." Five-year-olds have only vague knowledge about saving money, but by age nine or ten the children understand the notion of saving. They recognize by then that saving money provides a larger sum at a later date. Long-term savings is understood to some extent by the ten-year-old, but he does not fully appreciate the rationale for it.

The five to eight-year-olds find the ownership of money exciting. They enjoy counting it and handling it. But one senses that the joy from the money emanates from the coins symbolizing what they will buy. In fact, different coins are often associated with specific products, for example, "two quarters will buy two cokes [from a vending machine]." Money appears to lose some of its glamour by age ten. The youngster seems to feel assured that there is always some money available, perhaps from savings, but mainly from parents. Regardless of age, though, there is little question about the meaning of money to children. It is the basic requisite for obtaining the good things in life.

Stores

Stores, to children, are where you get the things that money buys. Products may be advertised on television, presented in a catalog, or owned by a friend, but you mainly get them at a store. Stores are collections of products for people with money.

According to McNeal (1964), even five-year-olds recognize that retailers put together collections of goods obtained from farms and factories. They believe that the stores are owned by a person (not a corporation), and they feel they know the person who owns them.

At age seven, the youngster holds some notion about profits, and by age ten profits are usually recognized as the raison d'etre of the store. The nine and ten-year-olds also understand that their expenditures contribute to the store's profit. However, they have no idea of how much profit is made, and they do not care.

Anderson (1978) has examined some of the feelings of children when they are in stores. Both third and fifth grade children experience positive and negative feelings in stores, and the negative feelings generally increased with age. Positive feelings include "exciting,"

"grown-up," "rich," "important," and "proud." The grown-up feeling declines with age while the feelings of proudness and importance increase.

Both groups of children noted that they felt "scared," "weird," "nervous," "not safe," "funny," and "embarrassed" in stores. Some of the older youngsters also felt crowded, small, that they were wasting their money, and that they just wanted to get out of the store.

The negative feelings may be explained in part by McNeal (1964) and Saenz (1979). Children feel more uncomfortable in large self-service stores than in convenience stores and specialty stores. The reason appears to be store personnel. In the smaller stores the children are aware of the store personnel and often are acquainted with them.

In general, children want to go to stores because "that is where you get things." They prefer to go with others, parents or friends. They prefer smaller personalized stores such as the convenience store.

Products, Brands, and Packages

It has already been noted that children are primarily interested in purchasing sweet goods. Their selection of stores is often related to quantity and types of sweet goods available. These sweets, like most other purchases, are for immediate gratification.

They view the sweets and certain other products as being offered mainly for children. Even if adults buy them, they are likely still viewed as children's products. Dry cereals are for children as are toys and games. Canned vegetables, for example, are adult products that are forced upon youngsters. Clothing is one of the few universal products they buy, from their point of view.

Children also perceive some products as

dangerous. For example, 97 percent of children in one study knew that they could get hurt using a toaster (Faber and Ward, 1977).

The brands of many products that children buy are important to them (Ward et al., 1975; McNeal, 1964, 1976). Brand recognition is high. Children who cannot yet read can recognize and pronounce a brand name when it is offered in its normal symbolic form, for example, on a package. Brand preference is rather high among children of all ages. It seems stronger among the younger, but that is apparently because the older youngsters have developed brand substitutes.

Brands have attributes. They can be cheap or expensive, high and low quality, and age oriented (for adults or for children).

Packages may influence the youngster's attitudes toward the product or brand (McNeal, 1976). They like wide mouths on jars of peanut butter and jellies, they like boxes of snacks better than sacks because the latter are difficult to open and close, they dislike the wrappers on some frozen desserts and candies, and in general, like canned beverages better than bottled beverages. They view aerosol containers as potentially hazardous (Faber and Ward, 1977) even though they enjoy using them.

Price

Since children have a relatively small amount of money to spend, it is logical to wonder about their concern with the price of goods they buy. According to Saenz (1979), children are not price conscious to any significant extent. Almost all children ages five through nine are aware that prices vary among stores. However, the amount of variance can not be described and does not seem to matter. They are aware that prices are rising. Their response to this is one of indifference.

Anderson (1977) found many children echoing their parents in terms of "getting a good buy" and "not wasting money." However, there was little evidence of implementation of the thinking. An exception seemed to be with more expensive items such as tennis shoes. In this case, price was important after brandname and style were decided.

The reason for the unimportance of price to the youngsters is not apparent. It may stem from a lack of understanding of money. Also, there is much preoccupation with the product and its benefits. Maybe, too, they do not feel that price variations among stores are great, and consequently believe variations in price not worth their concern.

Advertising

The youngster's involvement with advertising is of major concern to the Federal Trade Commission and consumer advocates. These groups feel that advertising, specifically television advertising, takes an unfair advantage of the child because of his inabilities to understand its purpose and influence. This issue will not be argued here. Instead, advertising is treated as another component of the market place that plays a part in the consumer behavior of children.

As early as 1964 the interaction between children and television advertising was examined (McNeal, 1964). Then, as now, children watched much television, and consequently, much television advertising. Half of the five, six, and seven-year-olds disliked television advertising. It was considered disruptive, annoying, untruthful, and ridiculous. Their positive feelings toward TV advertising were related mainly to the musical jingles and animations in some advertisements. The advertising did influence their purchases to the extent it informed them of new products. The nine-year-olds reacted more negatively to it, but still felt that it influenced their purchase of new products. For all the children, television advertising seemed to be a source of new ideas to be ratified by friends and parents.

Robertson and Rossiter (1974) found first graders to be generally trusting of television advertising, and thus responsive to its persuasiveness. However, third and fifth graders showed strong mistrust of television advertising and much defensiveness toward its persuasiveness. It appeared that not only was age a factor in attitudes and response to advertising, but also the degree of parental influence. Almost identical findings were presented by Ward et al. (1975).

The Anderson (1977) study showed children to depend upon parents as the main source of information and television advertising as a much lesser source. Her findings, like McNeal's, indicate that television advertising is a source of product ideas to be confirmed by parents and others.

Summing up, television advertising, according to three studies, is a major source of new product ideas for children, but it generally lacks credibility among them. Consequently, its information and persuasiveness is tempered considerably by the influence of others, mainly parents and friends.

SUMMARY AND CONCLUSIONS

There is a strong concern in government and among consumer advocate groups about the extent to which children should be participating in the consumer role. These bodies feel that the youngster lacks the skills to be a full-fledged consumer or they simply assume he is not a qualified consumer.

The findings presented here do not attempt to directly address this issue. They are meant to describe the child's involvement in the consumer role from both a behavioral and cognitive view. However, these descriptions may offer cues to those that are interested in regulations for consumer behavior by children.

The reports of studies of children's consumer behavior are relatively few. Their results are fragmented and do not allow for substantial conclusions. There are probably two main reasons for the paucity of investigations of children's consumer behavior. First, children are difficult to study. Wells (1966) has addressed this matter. He notes the difficulty in formulating questions, organizing the children for research and obtaining and holding their attention. His concern is confirmed when one examines the methodological quality of the studies mentioned here.

A second reason for the scarcity of studies of children's consumer behavior is the question of ethics. Is it proper to study the consumer behavior of children if the results benefit the businessman more than the child? Whether or not the question should be cast this way might be argued by some, but the fact is that it is the general view. The child is the embodiment of innocence in our society. To tamper with his innocence with profit as a motive is considered unforgivable. And, regrettably, studies of chidren's consumer behavior are always assumed to contribute to the profit motive either by intent or default. Consequently, neither government nor business, parent nor teacher, seems very willing to engage in research activities related to the child consumer unless such efforts are clearly labeled as public policy studies, for example, the Ward, et al. (1975) study or the numerous studies on television viewing. Adequate proof of this atmosphere was the large number of protest letters generated by an academic article that referred to children as a potential market (McNeal, 1969).

In spite of the paucity of information

about the consumer behavior of children, the few studies conducted have produced remarkable similarities in findings. They show the child at age four and five to be entering the consumer role with enthusiasm and "shaky legs." But by ages nine and ten he is performing as a consumer with at least as much confidence and expertise as he displays in any other societal roles. He sees consuming as a logical role to assume. He recognizes that basic needs such as affiliation and self esteem can be fulfilled in the market place with ease. Is he a naive consumer? Perhaps, but he can describe flaws in the Pepsi-Coke taste tests that are presented in advertisements. How does he differ from the average adult consumer? Mainly, he is younger.

REFERENCES

Anderson, C. J. 1978. "The Child Consumer: A Study of Purchasing Problems, Attitudes, and Decision-Making Skills." An unpublished research paper. Department of Marketing, Texas A&M University.

Faber, Ronald and Ward, Scott. 1977. "Children's Understanding of Using Products Safely." *Journal of Marketing* 41 (October), 39–46.

1978. "Federal Trade Commission Staff Report on TV Advertising to Children." *Advertising Age* 49 (February), 73–77.

McNeal, J. U. 1964. *Children As Consumers*. Austin: The University of Texas Bureau of Business Research.

———. 1969. "The Child Consumer: A New Market." *Journal of Retailing* 45 (Summer), 15–22.

———. 1976. "Packaging for the Young Consumer: A Descriptive Study." *Akron Business and Economic Review* 7 (Winter), 5–11.

Riesman, David, Glazer, Nathan and Denny, Reuel. 1953. *The Lonely Crowd*. Garden City, New York: Doubleday and Company, Inc., 1953.

Robertson, Thomas S. and Rossiter, John R. 1974. "Children and Commercial Persuasion: An Attribution Theory Analysis." *The Journal of Consumer Research* 1 (June), 13–20.

Saenz, S. L. 1979. "Children's Perceptions of Stores." An unpublished research paper. Department of Marketing, Texas A&M University.

Ward, Scott, Wackman, Daniel and Wartella, Ellen. 1975. *Children Learning to Buy: The Development of Consumer Information Processing Skills*. Cambridge, Mass.: Marketing Science Institute.

Wells, William D. 1966. "Children as Consumers." in Newman, Joseph W. Ed. *On Knowing the Consumer*. New York: John Wiley and Sons, Inc.

Questions

1. What does the author suggest are the four fundamental considerations in exploring the role of a child as a consumer?

2. Briefly summarize the extent to which a child carries out different consumer tasks at different ages.

3. If indeed the child is a consumer, should he or she be shielded from television commercials, considering the author's findings about advertising?

40. Exploring the Gray Market Segment

Betsy D. Gelb

Teen market, working-women's market, black market—why not a gray market, focusing special marketing effort on 65-and-over consumers? A recent review of business journals concludes that the 65-and-over consumer is neglected in the marketplace.[1] This indifference is attributed to the belief by business that "the elderly want pretty much the same things as adults generally." Others have linked the low interest in marketing to "seniors" (the term now in vogue) with a belief that this group lacks purchasing power as well as distinct market characteristics.[2]

Are these views out of date? To answer that question, or to examine any population segment as a potential market segment, a manager should evaluate whether it is feasible and profitable to market differently to these buyers and potential buyers. Ben M. Enis breaks this question down into a list of specific criteria for a useful market segment: identity, accessibility, responsiveness, and significance. In his terms, an organization would ask whether the members of a potential segment can be identified easily; whether the marketing organization can communicate with them; whether they will respond to special effort; and whether that response will generate enough extra revenue to exceed the extra cost of adapting some part of the marketing mix.[3]

This article is intended to help managers analyze retirement-age consumers within this framework. The objective will be to relate the gray market to all four of Enis's criteria, using data on population and buying power from published sources and data on buying-related preferences and behavior from a study of Houston-area seniors.

The first two criteria justifying a market segment—identification and accessibility—appear to be increasingly easy for the retirement-age population segment to meet. Finding seniors and communicating specifically to them has been simplified by the growth of retirement communities. Furthermore, even those elderly who do not move to Sun City or to Sunset Acres in their own hometown are more likely than in past decades to live in their own households, rather than with younger relatives. Fully 96 percent of those in this age bracket live outside institutions. Of those, 47 percent are in husband-wife units, 43 percent live alone, and only 10 percent live with children.[4] Thus, it can be expected that they make their own buying decisions and can be reached by segmentation strategies aimed at their age bracket.

Would they respond to such strategies or resent them? Here, data are needed before conclusions concerning responsiveness can be drawn. Furthermore, even if the "responsiveness" criterion is met, would the marginal profit justify extra effort? Here, one issue is buying power. Another is whether physical and life-style characteristics of this age segment require more age-tailored, but also more expensive, marketing strategies.

To judge the buying power issue, it should be noted that population trends point to an increase in the proportion of seniors among the nation's buyers. Unless the birth rate spurts in the last quarter of this decade, the 1971–1981 total U.S. increase in population will be 13 percent, but the increase in the over-65 segment will be 17 percent. By the year 2000, it is reasonable to expect that the combination of a decreasing birth rate and longer life expectancy will bring the proportion of those 65 and over to 15 percent of the U.S. population.

A second consideration in evaluating this age group's buying power is the money they have to spend per person. Previous discussions addressing the viability of the older market have stressed spending as the critical variable. Such discussions have led to the conclusion that the existence of a retirement-age market was questionable, except for a few goods and service categories such as hearing aids, nursing care, and the like.[5] More recently, however, it has been noted that the propensity of retirement-age consumers to spend, rather than to save, means that for many kinds of products they are a significant buying force. The principal argument advanced by those holding that view is that assets, not income alone, should be considered buying power for an age segment whose propensity is to "dis-save."[6]

It also has been pointed out that even the income picture is changing for older Americans. Pensions cover an increasing percentage of the work force, although their impact is reduced by inflation. A Conference Board report estimates that the per capita income of those 65 and over is only 5 percent less than the per capita figure for the population as a whole.[7] Furthermore, one writer calculates that an over-65 household with a $5,500 annual income actually does as well as a younger family with $7,200 or more. Older people need pay no Social Security tax if retired; can claim extra exemptions on their taxes; are more likely to have their home paid for; and have Medicare to reduce health costs.[8]

However, Enis's responsiveness and significance criteria for a market segment suggest that issues in addition to spending power be considered. Clearly, special efforts would rest not only on the segment's ability to buy, but also on two assumptions outside the economic realm. They are:

(1) that attitudes in this age segment offer support for age-oriented products, promotional appeals, pricing, or distribution strategies—a "pro-age" mind-set;[9]

(2) that such strategies will be more profitable than nonsegmented strategies because this market has different needs, related to physical and life-style characteristics. Here life-style characteristics refer primarily to smaller household size and increased leisure time.

THE HOUSTON STUDY

To test these assumptions, a study was undertaken in Houston. A third issue also was examined in relation to the other two: Are age-distinct preferences, if any, a function of age *per se*, or do they stem from other variables? This third consideration was based on the realization that a disproportionate number of older consumers are women and, despite high assets, members of low income households. Thus, it would be possible to find preferences and buying behavior in this age segment that upon examination would relate to sex or income category as well as to age.

Data were gathered from 403 Houston-area seniors, a convenience sample of individuals present at regular monthly meetings of four retirement-age groups. Groups selected were: American Association of Retired Persons (AARP), International Brotherhood of Electrical Workers Retired Members, Service Corps of Retired Executives (SCORE), and Retired Senior Volunteer Program (RSVP). The individuals were in no sense believed typical; active group members simply were assumed to represent those elderly consumers whose views would be of most interest to business.

The seniors filled out questionnaires handed to them as part of the business of the meeting and completed them on the spot. Exceptionally large type was used, and assistance was available from university personnel familiar with the questionnaire. Therefore, at least some part of the form was filled out by more than 99 percent of those present. Respondents were not asked to sign the forms and were assured anonymity.

The questionnaire asked for check-off responses to 56 items. Among these, respondents were asked to scale their degree of agreement ("agree strongly" to "disagree strongly") with statements focusing on age-group identity. The statements included:

"I would pay a little more to shop in a store that went after the business of retirement-age people."

"Stores that sell clothing should have a special department for people of retirement age."

"I prefer to deal with sales clerks who are younger than I am."

They also were asked to scale frequency of behavior ("always" to "never") relating physical or life-style changes to shopping behavior. The statements included:

"I cut short my shopping trips because I get tired."

"Getting to the store is a bigger problem to me than it was a year ago."

"Someone younger takes me shopping when I go."

Conventional demographic data also were collected.

RESULTS

Demographic data showed the convenience sample to be similar to the retirement-age population in several respects. Of the respondents, 31 percent were male, 69 percent female. They divided almost evenly between those 69 or younger and those 70 or older. About 45 percent were married; 45 percent were widowed; and 10 percent were single or divorced. One in five said he or she was employed. While 40 percent listed a household income of less than $400 per month, 30 percent checked categories between $400 and $699, and 30 percent listed household income of $700 or more.

The general notion that older buyers would welcome special treatment appeared to be supported by the majority of responses. Fifty-six percent agreed strongly or somewhat with the statement: "I would pay a little more to shop in a store that went after the business of retirement-age people." Fifty-six percent also agreed that clothing stores should have a special department for people of retirement age. The same percentage failed to agree even somewhat with the statement that "store owners are glad to see older people come in." Only 34 percent supported even somewhat the statement: "I prefer to deal with sales clerks who are younger than I am"—despite the fact that half the respondents were 70 or older. No relation was found between category of answer and either sex or income for any of these items.

The idea that special treatment would be appreciated was further supported by answers to a question asking what would attract the seniors to a hypothetical "new store in your neighborhood." Rating as high as a claim of low prices (Table 1) was the statement: "A sign in the window says 'Welcome, Seniors.'"

However, fewer than half the seniors reported buying behavior that could be attributed to the changes of retirement age. Concerning physical problems in shopping, for example, only 29 percent reported cutting

Table 1 / Factors Attracting Seniors to a Hypothetical New Store

Reason	Percentage selecting (N = 403)
Ads say the store is inexpensive	57
A sign in the window says "Welcome, Seniors"	57
The store has someone to carry packages outside	56
It's a new kind of store	51
Ads for the store show people your age	33
Someone your age works at the store	32
The store has benches outside	29
The store looks "Old-Fahioned" from the outside	15

Note: Multiple answers possible.

shopping trips short at least half the time because of getting tired. A preference for small stores rather than large for at least half their shopping was expressed by 44 percent and may be associated with physical difficulties. Also, 26 percent agreed that at least half the time they found it "more of a problem to get to the store than it was a year ago."

About one senior in four said that at least half the time "someone younger takes me shopping." Furthermore, 37 percent agreed strongly, and 27 percent agreed somewhat, that to "shop around" at different stores is more trouble than it is worth. In general, the answers were the same across income groups and for both sexes, and thus appeared related to age rather than these other factors.

Is buying behavior affected by the life-style adjustments of retirement, smaller households, and increased leisure time? Three items dealt specifically with the issue of package size and quantity, since a controversy exists on this topic. Some writers see in the senior's smaller household a need for one-serving containers, while others see in his or her increased free time and decreased income a market for

economy sizes or even case lots to be divided among households.

The Houston area seniors split on this issue. One-third replied that "always" or "most of the time" they bought in large amounts to save money, but 43 percent said they "hardly ever" or "never" did so, and low income correlated significantly with buying in small quantities. Also, 27 percent agreed "strongly" or "somewhat" that they would join a co-op buying group where members took turns shopping for the group and could buy in larger amounts. This percentage did not vary significantly between income categories but was significantly higher for men (53 percent) than for women (30 percent). On the other hand, 41 percent disagreed at least somewhat that they would participate in such a plan.

Limitations of the Houston study should be noted here: It involved only a convenience sample, was limited to one city at one point in time, and depended on self-reports of preferences and behavior. However, to the limited extent that its results and other population/buying power data can be used to draw conclusions, it may offer useful insights for evaluating the 65-and-over age segment as a distinct market segment.

At the outset of this discussion, such an evaluation was linked to four criteria: identity, accessibility, responsiveness, and significance. Published data suggest that the segment meets the first two criteria. Responsiveness, a criterion which will be met only if age-directed changes in the marketing mix of an organization are welcomed by the elderly, seems supported by the data. The fourth criterion, significance, appears more questionable: It can be met only if enough more sales result in sufficient extra revenue to offset the cost of the segmentation efforts.

The study reported here viewed significance as a function of two factors: buying power and the proportion of the elderly reporting buying behavior distinct to their age group.

The reasoning is that a segmentation strategy—for example, a special package size or an extra retail location close to a retirement community—entails extra cost. If the gray market cannot afford the extra cost, the significance criterion is unmet. However, if the gray market can afford the extra cost, but has no age-related need for special treatment, then one of two equally unattractive possibilities awaits the marketer:

1. To cover the extra cost, the retail price is raised. Since the seniors did not need the special package (or whatever), they reach instead for the lower priced ordinary version.
2. The retail price is not raised; volume increases are expected to provide the incremental revenue. Unfortunately, these increases are acccompanied by a volume decrease for the company's ordinary version, which seniors had been buying all along since no age-related characteristics precluded their doing so.

Therefore, the significance criterion can be met only if seniors report behavior suggesting a need for special treatment. The results of this study make that appear questionable for most seniors. It cannot be claimed that, by Enis's standards, the criteria to justify a market segment are met.

RECOMMENDATIONS

Nevertheless, several conclusions can be drawn from published data and from this study to assist marketers whose products are exceptionally sensitive to gray market purchase patterns. For such products, segmentation may pay off even if one-fourth or fewer of the elderly would respond differently to special marketing effort than to business as usual. These conclusions also lead to recommendations for the marketers of such products, to the extent that their particular markets make special action worthwhile:

1. The 65-and-over age segment is by no means homogeneous. Therefore, marketers will experience little success in learning the preferences of thousands of seniors by asking Great Aunt Jane.
2. To look at the 65-and-over group as low income shoppers can be misleading in two ways. First, it means overlooking the possibility that a senior with a $500-per-month income may be ready for a round-the-world trip. Assuming that income breaks down to $180 from Social Security and $320 from investments, the $320 may be a 5 percent return on about $77,000. Furthermore, the income may not be $500; it may, through a combination of pensions and transfer payments, be double that.
3. Surprisingly, perhaps, to feel valued as a *retirement-age shopper* has importance. The Houston respondents may not be typical in this respect, since they are members of retirement-age groups and thus have chosen

to identify themselves with their age segment. Nevertheless, such groups are growing in numbers and membership; there seems no reason to doubt that such identification is on the up-swing.

4. The majority of these seniors did not appear to need special treatment due to physical and life-style characteristics. More than one-third, however, do express agreement with statements indicating physical limitations.

Even such fragmentary conclusions as these can offer guidance for segmentation strategies directed to the gray market if a business expects the effort to be profitable. Such an effort may not be immediate, but managers who do not see seniors in their present customer mix should keep this age segment in mind; markets change. Therefore, the following recommendations can be seen either as examples that can be useful now, or as examples that will be useful if a marketing manager wakes up one morning to find that his or her buyers belong to "The Swingin' Sixties." From product design and promotion to the age of personnel employed, there are myriad marketing strategies available to those who see retirement-age buyers as a potential market segment.

PRODUCT PLANNING

For the senior market, physical and life-style changes point to an emphasis on services. Research shows car ownership for nearly 60 percent of households in this market segment, a high percentage of home ownership, and broad interest in health and gardening. Related services, then, may involve home security, auto maintenance and accessories, home remodeling, insurance, and perhaps lawn care services. The same homeowner who bought lawn fertilizer at 60 may be willing 10 years later to pay for a quarterly fertilizing service.

Based on some enthusiasm in the Houston study for buying co-ops and for economy, however, it appears that a substantial segment of the senior market seeks no-frills products and services. Perhaps after retirement the only way to "earn" money, with all the achievement that earning symbolizes, is to buy thriftily. Such an idea could be tested in further research by offering various product-service designs to buyers over a wide age range to see whether the demand for deluxe features drops off at retirement and to what extent the challenge of saving is significant for this age segment, independent of financial status.

PROMOTION

For promotion decisions, the findings of greatest interest appear to be those concerning physical limitations. Special events for seniors can include uncrowded Christmas shopping before a store's regular opening time. They can also include demonstrations, televised or in-store, on how to use products that the elderly might consider difficult to manage. Such demonstrations are not only useful, but also convey a message of corporate attention to the retirement-age consumer, a subtle but effective equivalent of the sign in the window that says "Welcome, Seniors." Furthermore, they are most effective when based on sound product research. Now being studied, for example, are kinds of doorknobs that are best for arthritic patients, and designs for cups, chairs, and mattresses.

PRICING

Conventional wisdom sees price as *the* salient feature in the senior marketing mix, but findings of this study suggest the possibility of interaction between pricing and a publicized effort to market to retirement-age customers.

A marketer who offers discounts to this age group simultaneously can convey the messages of saving and special attention—both powerful attractions. Further research is needed in this area to test the possibility, for example, that discounts as rewards for long-time buyers are more attractive than the same discounts given because of diminished income in retirement.

STORE LOCATION AND STAFFING

For retailers interested in elderly buyers or for manufacturers appraising a current or proposed channel structure, store location and staffing may be relevant factors. Proximity to public transportation and senior housing appears to be most critical. A location near a recreation center or a church with active retirement-age groups also may be desirable.

No clear-cut direction emerges from the Houston study for retail staffing decisions, but research in an individual community may yield different results. In this study, only one-third of the respondents said they preferred to deal with sales clerks younger than themselves. One-third said they would be attracted to a newly opened store in their neighborhood if someone their age worked there. This is a significant but hardly overwhelming percentage.

More relevant than rushing out to hire seniors as salespersons, however, may be the treatment that a firm gives to its own retirees, who will interact with potential 65-and-over consumers. In the present study, 56 percent of respondents failed to agree that store owners—representative of the marketing community—were glad to see them as customers. This perception suggests that more than staffing policies may be communicating indifference from marketers. Areas to be considered here include credit, support for public transportation, and the age mix of models used in advertising, in short, anything that represents the marketer to the retirement-age consumer.

In summary, the gray market may meet the three tests of identity, accessibility, and responsiveness as a market-segment, but it may not for most marketers meet the fourth test—enough extra profit. For those who choose to target efforts to this segment, however, opportunities range from product design to the context in which retirement discounts are presented. Clearly, this study offers only a beginning, and the marketing community has many opportunities for research to improve its strategies for serving the gray market.

FOOTNOTES

1. Joyanne Block, "The Aged Consumer and the Marketplace," *Marquette Business Review* 18 (Summer 1974): 73–80.

2. R. Eugene Klippel and Timothy W. Sweeney, "The Use of Information Sources by the Aged Consumer," *Gerontologist* 14 (April 1974): 163.

3. Ben M. Enis, *Marketing Principles: The Management Process,* 2d ed., (Santa Monica, Calif: Goodyear, 1977), pp. 243–46.

4. Fabian Linden, "Consumer Markets: Midlife and Beyond," excerpted from *Across the Board* 13 (December 1976): 2–3.

5. John A. Reinecke, "The 'Older' Market—Fact or Fiction?" *Journal of Marketing* 28 (January 1964): 60–64; and Sidney Goldstein, "The Aged Segment of the Market, 1950 and 1960," *Journal of Marketing* 35 (April 1968): 62–68.

6. Robert C. Atchley, *The Social Forces in Later Life* (Belmont, Calif.: Wadsworth Publishing Co., 1972), p. 123.

7. Linden, "Midlife and Beyond."

8. "The Over-65 Set: A Bonanza for Business?" *Nation's Business* 59 (November 1971): 34–35.

9. Betsy D. Gelb, "Gray Power: Next Challenge to Business?" *Business Horizons* 20 (April 1977): 38–45.

Questions

1. How would you describe the "gray market," and how different is it from other markets?
2. Based on the results of this study, do you see a potential in this market? Explain your answer.
3. How would you use the notion, "older buyers prefer special treatment," to attract more older people into a grocery store?

41. The Role of Personal Values in Marketing and Consumer Behavior

Donald E. Vinson

Jerome E. Scott

Lawrence M. Lamont

Marketers have long acknowledged the importance of attitudes and attitude change in the study of marketing and consumer behavior, but the role of values has received relatively little attention. Even though the marketing literature reflects an emerging interest in the topic,[1] personal values have not been widely used to investigate the underlying dimensions of consumer behavior. This is surprising considering the importance typically assigned to values by a wide variety of social observers and businessmen alike.[2]

While it seems that personal values have important implications for marketing practitioners and researchers, values and the ways in which they influence the behavior of consumers who look at and choose brands, product classes, and product attributes is not clear. In order to investigate these relationships, it is necessary to operationally define what values are, and to indicate empirical methods available for examining the connections between personal values and consumer behavior.

The purpose of this article is to address these issues. Specifically, attention will be focused on:

1. A discussion of the meaning of values and their relationship to behavior.
2. Presentation of an operational value paradigm suitable for studying consumer behavior.
3. Results of an empirical investigation of the

impact of value orientations on the importance of product attributes, the appeal of various consumer products, and a number of social issues.

4. The implications of value analysis for the practice of marketing.

PERSONAL VALUES

Conceptualization of the term "value" reflects the interest of several disciplines:

► Anthropology, with its interest in life styles and cultural patterns. (For example, Thomas and Zaraniecki define values as ". . . objective, social elements which impose themselves upon the individual as a given and provoke his reaction.")[3]

► Sociology, focusing on ideologies and customs. (For example, Bronowski suggests that "a value is a concept which groups together some modes of behavior in our society.")[4]

► Psychology, which examines values from the standpoint of attitudes and personal motives. (For example, Rokeach views ". . . a value as a centrally held, enduring belief which guides actions and judgments across specific situations and beyond immediate goals to more ultimate end-states of existence.")[5]

In this article, and in the study reported herein, we follow mostly the psychological definition, and in particular Rokeach's view.

Values and Behavior

The role of personal values as a standard or criterion for influencing evaluations or choices regarding persons, objects, and ideas suggests the relationship of values to behavior. Rokeach reports that "various combinations of values significantly differentiate men from women, hippies from non-hippies, hawks from doves, policemen from unemployed Negroes, good students from poor students, retail merchants from salesclerks,

Jews from Catholics, Democrats from Republicans, and so forth."[6] Williams has demonstrated that values relating to "cleanliness" have led to decisions concerning the choice of occupations,[7] while England used personal values to investigate behavioral differences among corporate managers.[8]

Values, then, are responsible for the selection and maintenance of the ends or goals toward which human beings strive and, at the same time, regulate the methods and manner in which this striving takes place.

Values and Consumer Behavior

Other than a few isolated studies discussing changes in national values, research in marketing has been in the context of expectancy-value analysis based on the models of Rosenberg and Fishbein.[9] Research interests have centered on predicting brand choice and assessing the relative importance of various product attributes in determining brand preference.

It is important to note that, with few exceptions,[10] "value" as used in the context of expectancy-value research has been taken to mean product attributes and thus has a meaning different from that developed in this article. The expectancy-value approach has been useful in predicting brand choice but does not explain *why* consumers differentially evaluate product attributes and thus prefer one brand to another.

In order to gain insight into this question and to understand *how* changing national values influence consumption patterns, it would be useful, both for students of consumer behavior and for those marketing executives responsible for the formulation of marketing strategy, to have a framework integrating:

- Deep-rooted personal values
- Generalized consumption values
- Beliefs relating to product attributes

A MODEL OF CONSUMERS' VALUE SYSTEMS

A review of existing value literature, recent empirical research, and the cultural conditioning viewpoint on value acquisition leads us to propose that values may be investigated at three mutually dependent and at least partially consistent levels of abstraction. These levels, arranged in a hierarchical network, are referred to as global or generalized personal values, domain-specific values, and evaluations of product attributes. Exhibit 1 shows each level of values and suggests the influence of the socio-cultural, economic, and familial environment on the formation and development on the individual's value system.

Global Values

Beliefs exist as the most elementary unit within this system. Very centrally held and enduring beliefs guide actions and judgments across specific situations and are referred to as global values. These global values are more abstract and generalizable than less centrally held beliefs. In our conception, these values form the central core of an individual's value system. They consist of closely held personal values which are of high salience in important evaluations and choices.

Domain-Specific Values

The second level of values, domain-specific values, reflects the belief that people acquire values through experiences in specific situations or domains of activity and that behavior cannot be understood or efficiently predicted except in the context of a specific environment. Thus, we contend that individuals

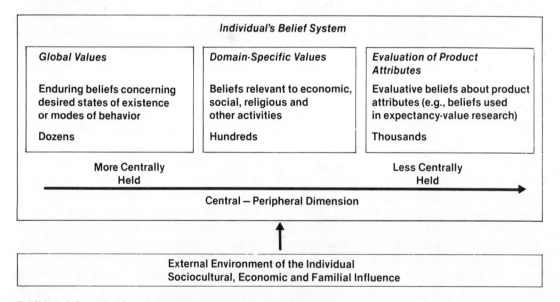

Exhibit 1 / Organization of the consumer's value-attitude system

arrive at values specific to economic transactions through economic exchange and consumption, at social values through familial and peer group interaction, at religious values through religious instruction and so on.

This intermediate value construct bridges the gap between the traditional conception of closely held, but very general, global values and the less closely held descriptive and evaluative beliefs about product attributes. Previous research has demonstrated this value construct to be cognitively separate but functionally related to an individual's system of global values and descriptive and evaluative beliefs.[11] A list of domain-specific values developed for consumption-related activities is shown in Exhibit 2.

This value set was developed from exploratory research with a large set of items and reduced through factor analysis. It includes statements about desirable modes of company behavior and desirable attributes of consumer products.

Evaluative Beliefs

The third category of values shown in Exhibit 1 is less abstract and consists of descriptive and evaluative beliefs. While such beliefs may be important, they are less centrally held. Among the many kinds of beliefs in this category are evaluative beliefs about the desirable attributes of product classes as well as specific brands. It is this category of values that most of the expectancy-value research has used in predicting brand appeal.

Manufacturers Should...	Manufacturers and Products Should Be...
Provide prompt service on complaints	Durable, long lasting
Guarantee products to work as advertised	Fairly, reasonably priced
Be responsive to true needs of consumers	Non-polluting
Supply clear, accurate information on products	Safe
Help eliminate environmental pollution	Inexpensive to use
Care about the needs of individual consumers	Exciting, stylish
Repair defective products free of charge	Easy to use
Locate stores for convenience to consumers	Dependable, trustworthy
Not lie or be deceptive in advertisements	Beautiful, attractive
Make products available nights and weekends	In a wide variety
Use courteous, helpful sales personnel	Health-promoting
Maintain the lowest prices possible	Easy to repair
Compete for the business of consumers	Resistant to environmental damage
Help solve urban decay and unemployment	Quiet
Work for legislation to protect consumers	Comfortable, secure
Not misrepresent a product	

Exhibit 2 / Domain-specific values (consumption-related)

Note that the conceptual model shown in Exhibit 1 suggests that people have many thousands of evaluative beliefs, hundreds of domain-specific values, but only dozens of global values. Those beliefs and values do not exist as sharply separated and unconnected elements; they coexist in an interconnected hierarchical structure with the more durable and closely held global values exerting influence on each other as well as affecting the more peripherally located domain-specific values. These domain-specific values, in turn, are inter-connected along the central-peripheral dimension and further influence the individual's evaluative beliefs associated with the attributes of products or brands.

COMPARATIVE ANALYSIS OF VALUES AND PRODUCT ATTRIBUTES

We have suggested that value acquisition represents a socio-cultural process and that differential value orientations will lead to variations in preferences for products and brands. To investigate these propositions, an exploratory research study was undertaken to investigate whether subjects from two culturally distinct regions of the United States would manifest different value orientations; and, if so, the extent to which these value differences may be related to attitudes toward automobiles and the importance of automobile attributes.

Additionally, measures were taken on attitudes toward a number of social issues to further explore attitudinal differences between the two groups. Information on related social issues such as air pollution and the energy problem can be of great importance in designing product and communications strategy for automobiles.

Subjects used in the research were selected from a sample of undergraduate marketing majors at two large state universities. Group I subjects consisted of 47 students from a western university well known for the liberal attitudes and viewpoints of its student body and faculty. The 80 subjects comprising Group II were selected from a conservative southern university known for its more traditional approach to education. Data collected on demographic variables indicated that subjects were equivalently matched in terms of age, sex, and family income.

Each group was administered an identical questionnaire, which included a number of seven point Likert-type scales designed to measure the importance of the Rokeach global values and the consumption-related values presented in Exhibit 1. In addition, data were also collected on the importance of 20 automobile attributes, the appeal of 10 consumer products and services, and the importance of 15 current social issues.

Significant Differences

The results, summarized in Exhibit 3, indicate a large number of differences relative to the number of items. Items included under Group I subjects are those for which subjects in the group scored significantly higher than Group II subjects. Likewise, the items shown with subjects in Group II are those for which these students scored significantly higher.

The differences between the two groups on values and attitudes toward social issues are striking and seem to identify two clear stereotypes. The first group seems to embrace more liberal, socially-motivated values and attitudes, while the second group seems more traditional or conservative in outlook. This confirms our prior hypotheses about these two groups. It should be noted, however, that we are describing the groups in a relative fashion, i.e., Group I relative to

Group I Subjects

Global Values	Domain-Specific Values	Automobile Attributes	Consumer Products	Social Issues
Exciting life[a] Equality Self-Respect Forgiving Intellectual Logical[a]	Durable Products Non-polluting Products[a] Health-promoting Products Products Easy to Repair Quiet Products[a] Help Eliminate Environmental Pollution	Operate on Unleaded Gas[a] High-speed Capabilities Handling Quality Workmanship[a] Advanced Engineering[a] Low-level Pollution Emission[a]	Compact Cars[a] Outdoor Recreation[a]	Air Pollution[a] Freedom of Press[a] Control of Housing Discrimination[a]

Group II Subjects

National Security[a] Salvation[a] Polite Social Recognition	Prompt Service on Complaints	Smooth Riding[a] Luxurious Interior[a] Prestige[a] Large Size Spacious[a]	Standard-size Cars Stylish Attractive Clothing Television	Crime Control The Drug Problem

[a]Significant at $p > .01$ level using "t" distribution. All others significant at $p < .05$ level.

Exhibit 3 / Summary of significant differences between groups I and II

Group II. It may be possible to find other segments of the population who, in absolute terms, would score higher or lower than either group on any of the items.

It is particularly interesting to the marketer to examine how these two groups rated the importance of the automobile attributes and their appeal for classes of automobiles and other products. Specifically, the data suggest that the automobile attributes evaluated as important to each group are related to the type of automobile more preferable to that group, and several of the global and consumption values seem logically related to the differentially evaluated automobile attributes and the appeal of various products or services:

► The *more liberal Group I* subjects had a higher preference for compact cars than

standard size cars, which is consistent with their global and domain-specific economic values. They also indicated a higher preference for automobile attributes which enhance their desire for an exciting life, yet with non-polluting, durable products.

► On the other hand, the *more traditional Group II* subjects preferred larger, more prestigious standard-size cars, which is consistent with their values.

IMPLICATIONS FOR MARKETING MANAGEMENT

While knowledge of personal values and changing value orientations has potential impact on all aspects of a marketing program, we believe some of the most promising avenues for research and application include market analysis and segmentation, product planning, promotional strategy, and public policy and society. Each of these application areas is discussed below.

Market Analysis and Segmentation

The research findings suggest that the basic value orientations of consumers can be expected to vary across geographical regions of the United States when various socio-cultural influences exist. Additionally, we might also expect the importance of personal values to vary by age, education, income, and other consumer demographics.

Knowledge of consumer value orientations provides an efficient, measurable set of variables closely related to needs which expand the marketer's knowledge beyond demographic and psychographic differences. If large market segments can be identified on the basis of value profiles, the marketing strategist could develop programs which would maximally enhance the important values of consumers in each market segment. Thus, in addition to the more traditional variables, values could be employed as a standard consideration in market analysis and as a tool to achieve greater precision and effectiveness in market segmentation.

Changing values in American society also have important implications for market analysis and segmentation. Business should be concerned with assessing changes in the size and composition of value segments and the implications of these changes for marketing. Here, professional marketing research organizations are useful in conducting broad based longitudinal research studies to identify changes in value orientations.[12] Marketing management would find this information of use in identifying new product opportunities

and in modifying existing products to be consistent with consumer value profiles.

Product Planning

Careful assessment of value orientations and emerging value trends will allow the identification of new product opportunities and the repositioning of existing products. Changing importance of global values such as *pleasure, an exciting life, a comfortable life,* and *self respect* may very well signal the need for products having brand names, colors, and designs which enhance these important values in their use and consumption. A furniture manufacturer, for example, might connect this value change with an increasing demand for contemporary styled furniture and design a new line having bright, bold colors, unique materials of construction, and unusual comfort features.

The existence of value segments containing significant numbers of consumers suggests that products can be positioned by designing products with the attributes which are connected to the global values distinguishing that particular market segment. For example, a value segment containing consumers who regard the values *imaginative, an exciting life,* and *independent* as important might be defined as a market segment of consumers concerned with individuality and self expression. Manufacturers might find this a viable market for products which are partially finished (furniture, pottery, homes, etc.) as well as for products which can be tailored to the individual needs of consumers through the use of accessories, styling, chemical formulation, etc. Manufacturers and marketers of homes, automobiles, clothing, cosmetics, and fast foods have successfully pursued this strategy.

Promotional Strategy

Since global and consumption values appear to be connected to the importance of product attributes and the appeal of different product classes, this suggests that a promotional strategy designed to create and reinforce a preference by appealing to centrally held values may be highly effective. Thus, the promotional messages for a product or service could be developed to not only refer to the desirable attributes of the product but also to enhance these global and consumption values associated with the product attributes.

Additionally, the appeal to closely held personal values might have the effect of making consumers even more aware of an attribute of a product which previously may not have been considered salient or of which an awareness may not have existed. A department store, for example, knowing that the consumers in its target market held the consumption values, *care about the needs of individual consumers* and *prompt service on complaints,* and that these were in turn connected to the global values *polite* and *cheerful,* might initiate an advertising campaign emphasizing courteous, helpful personnel, and the store as a pleasant, cheerful place to shop.

Values should also be connected to media readership and viewing habits. By knowing the preferences of large market segments, the promotional strategist will be better able to select media and design appeals which will reach and enhance the important value of consumers. *Gourmet Magazine,* for example, might be associated with the values *polite, true friendship,* and *imaginative.* This magazine would then be useful as a medium to advertise products which enhanced these same consumer values, thus allowing the medium to reinforce the advertising message.

Public Policy and Society

Value research also has important implications for public policy. Consumers holding truth in advertising and honesty in representing products as important values in the economic system, for example, might react favorably toward federal regulation of marketing programs. By monitoring changes in the importance of these values, and other values dealing with the ethics of marketing, marketers can assess the mood of consumers and take action to correct undesirable aspects of their marketing programs before adverse consumer reaction makes it a necessity. Additionally, knowledge of the global values which are connected to these consumption values might be of interest to business firms planning corporate image and corrective advertising.

CONCLUSION

It has been suggested that values are centrally held cognitive elements which stimulate motivation for behavioral response. They exist in an interconnected, hierarchical structure in which global values are related and connected to generalized consumption-related values which are, in turn, similarly associated with product attributes. It has been generally accepted in consumer behavior research that these product attributes represent the basic elements ordering an individual's attitude toward products and services. Hence, in our view, an individual's attributes are ultimately based upon his values, and changing values could have a profound impact upon these attitudes and upon behavior as well.

In order to test the proposition that values are culturally and socially learned, a study was conducted with subjects from two culturally distinct regions of the United States. The results indicated that the subjects were significantly different with respect to their basic value orientations and that each of the three constructs representing the value-attitude system were logically structured. That is, global values, consumption-related values and the evaluation of product attributes were consistent with preference for the consumer products or services as well as for the perceived importance of the selected social issues.

Finally, while values have been shown to be theoretically important for studying consumer behavior, we have attempted to describe their relevance to the businessman engaged in marketing management activities.

ENDNOTES

1. William Lazer, "Changing Societal Norms and Marketing Implications," in Reed Mayer, ed., *Changing Marketing Systems* (Chicago: American Marketing Association, 1967), pp. 156–60; Daniel Yankelovich, "What New Life Styles Mean to Market Planners," *Marketing Communication,* Vol. 299 (June 1971), pp. 38–45; "2nd Washington Social Indicators Conference to Explore the Response of Business to New Values," *The Marketing News,* Vol. VI (January 1, 1973), pg. 1.

2. Otto A. Bremer, "Is Business the Source of New Social Values," *Harvard Business Review,* Vol. 49 (November-December 1971), pp. 121–26; Arnold Mitchell, "Changing Values," *International Advertiser* (March 1971), pp. 5–9; Arnold Mitchell, "Changing Values and the Marketplace," in Fred C. Allvine, ed., *Marketing in Motion and Relevance in Marketing* (Chicago: American Marketing Association, 1971), pg. 614;

"The Squeeze on the Middle Class," *Business Week,* March 10, 1975, pg. 53.

3. W. I. Thomas and F. Zaraniecki, *The Polish Peasant in Europe and America* (New York: Alfred A. Knopf, 1927), pg. 1131.

4. J. Bronowski, "The Value of Science," in A. H. Maslow, ed., *New Knowledge in Human Values* (New York: Harper & Row, 1959), pg. 62.

5. M. J. Rokeach, *Beliefs, Attitudes, and Values* (San Francisco: Jossey Bass, 1968), pg. 161.

6. M. Rokeach, "The Role of Values in Public Opinion Research," *Public Opinion Quarterly,* Vol. 32 (Winter 1968–69), pg. 555.

7. R. M. Williams, *American Society: A Sociological Interpretation* (New York: Alfred A. Knopf, 1951).

8. G. W. England, "Personal Value Systems of American Managers," *Academy of Management Journal,* Vol. 10 (March 1967), pp. 53–68.

9. M. J. Rosenberg, "Cognitive Structure and Attitudinal Affect," *Journal of Abnormal and Social Psychology,* Vol. 53 (November 1956), pg. 330; M. Fishbein, "An Investigation of the Relationships Between Beliefs About an Object and the Attitude Toward That Object," *Human Relations,* Vol. 16 (1963), pp. 233–40.

10. S. W. Bither and S. Miller, "A Cognitive Theory of Brand Preference," in P. R. McDonald, ed., *Marketing Involvement in Society and the Economy* (Chicago: American Marketing Association, 1969).

11. J. E. Scott and L. M. Lamont, "Relating Consumer Values to Consumer Behavior: A Model and Method for Investigation," in Thomas W. Greer, ed., *Increasing Marketing Productivity* (Chicago: American Marketing Association, 1973), pp. 283–88.

12. Yankelovich, Same as reference 1.

Questions

1. Explain the relationship between values, attitudes, and consumer behavior.

2. Describe and give examples of the three levels of values.

3. According to the results of this study, what were some of the ways "Western liberal" individuals differed from "Southern conservative" individuals? How can you account for the fact that there were differences?

SECTION FOUR

Research Techniques in Consumer Behavior

Much information has been gathered about consumers in our economy. We possess reams of data on such characteristics as how much money is earned, spent, and saved; how much of each product is consumed by various types of families; and how much supposedly will be spent on products in the future. Yet we really know little about the causes behind consumer behavior. Far too much marketing research has concerned itself with what consumers are doing or will do, rather than why they are doing it or will do it. In medical terms, we have been concerned more with curing the disease than with determining its cause.

One only needs to note the excessive product mortality rate to know that there is something wrong somewhere. That "something," at least in great part, is our failure to understand why consumers behave as they do. It is folly to believe that we can deal millions of times daily with millions of customers spending billions of dollars without understanding clearly the causes of their spending patterns.

Recognition of this serious situation has brought a number of business practitioners and academicians to their feet—and they are doing something about it. First, they are changing their research approach from asking what and when to asking why. Second, they are realizing that their problems are behavioral in nature and are turning to the behavioral sciences for solutions.

In spite of a less than harmonious relationship with the behavioral scientist, business students have succeeded, to some extent, in borrowing a number of behavioral research tools and adapting them to the study of the consumer role. Numerous difficulties have been encountered in this undertaking and results have not always been desirable ones. Moreover, there have been a number of individuals, both in business and in academics, who have discouraged the innovation with various denouncements. Nevertheless, these "why" research procedures are paying off and show great promise of becoming the basic methodology of future market research.

Most of the behavioral research techniques that have been adapted to consumer behavior research have been those of the psychologist and psychiatrist—that is, techniques for examining individual behavior. Recognizing that individuals make up groups, or markets, we have used these research procedures to examine the behavior of a few individuals and then tested the results on larger groups. This course of action has proven to be a productive one.

The series of readings in this section discusses some research techniques and concepts that have been borrowed from the behavioral sciences in an effort to advance our understanding of the causes of consumer behavior patterns. The reader is reminded that a few brief discussions of behavioral research techniques also appear in some articles in the other sections of the book. Although these earlier comments are presented as incidental material, reexamination of them will broaden the value of the readings in this section.

Saul Sands opens this research section with the article "Motivation Research in Marketing: Fact and Fancy." In this very informative article, several motivation research techniques are reviewed, along with their application in consumer behavior studies. First Sands analyzes three basic motivation research techniques—depth interviews, focus interviews, and projective techniques. The most commonly used projective techniques are then reviewed —the Thematic Apperception Test, paired pictures, sentence completion tests, and word association tests. Sands concludes that the value of these tests depends heavily on the judgment and competence of the person using them. However, they have great applicability to consumer behavior research.

In the next article, "Focus Groups—Their Role in the Marketing Research Process," Carl McDaniel explains in detail how one particular kind of motivation research can be very beneficial to marketers and discusses some advantages of focus group studies over other motivation research methods. The results of a study that indicate that focus groups are more frequently being used by U.S. firms—especially consumer goods organizations—are also reported. McDaniel also reports that most focus group research objectives can be classified into three major classes, calling for three different categories of tests—exploratory groups (for pilot testing in order to help generate a hypothesis for testing or concepts for further research), clinical focus groups (for probing the consumers' subconscious), and the phenomenological focus groups (for experiencing a true emotional framework of a real experience).

The paper by William A. Mindak, "Fitting the Semantic Differential to the Marketing Problem," offers one way of solving the problem of obtaining a quantitative measure of consumers' reactions to the image of a brand or product. Mindak gives several advantages of the semantic differential, a research technique originated by the psychologist Charles Osgood. Particularly, the technique has a quick and efficient means to get direction and intensity of opinions; it gives a comprehensive image picture; it is standardized, repeatable, and reliable; it allows for individual frame of reference; and it eliminates the problems of phraseology in questioning. He suggests several improvements on the research technique and, as evidence of the value of this research method, discusses a study in which the semantic differential was used to compare the personalities (images) of three local brands of beer with three national brands.

The fourth article in this section is by Paul J. Watson and Robert J. Gatchel and is entitled "Autonomic Measures of Advertising." This review of 118 psychophysiological studies examines the findings of various attempts to relate such responses as pupil dilation, skin moisture, and heart rate to measuring advertising effectiveness. They conclude that advertising should use as many psychophysiological techniques as possible, because they have certain advantages, especially in the measurement of affective response, arousal, attention, and learning. Research shows that pupillary and electrodermal activity seem especially useful in making statements about the magnitude of a subject's responsiveness to an advertisement. Heart rate also may aid in determining a consumer's attention to an ad.

The final selection is an award-winning article by Jacob Jacoby, "Consumer Research: A State of the Art Review," in which this well-known consumer behaviorist evaluates the validity and usefulness of consumer behavior research findings. He points out some significant flaws in some of the research and offers some valuable insight into ways of correcting these errors in future studies. A concluding point made in the article, and one that all consumer behavior researchers should keep in mind in future research, is the danger of letting existing methods and tools work as constraints on our thinking and research. We can learn a great deal from these previous studies and find them very useful, but consumer behaviorists should always be open to new thoughts and new techniques for studying consumers.

42. Motivation Research in Marketing: Fact and Fancy

Saul Sands

During the past several decades, the increasing use of the phrase "motivation research" has given the impression of a new development in the marketing research field. However, until recently, the term referred to the study of buyers' motives. The present definition of motivation research includes the application of psychological techniques to obtain a better understanding of why people respond as they do to products, advertisements and other marketing situations.

For many years, marketing researchers have been delving into the question "why," using a variety of methods. However, asking consumers simple questions—why they like or dislike various products, what they intend to buy, why they did or did not buy a given product—has not always been satisfactory. In fact, the answers have frequently been misleading. People tend, for one reason or another, to give dishonest responses to questionnaires. Their dishonesty may be an attempt to satisfy the interviewer with a desired answer; a lack of thought or knowledge on the subject, or an inability to articulate an answer.

In order to surmount these obstacles, more subtle research techniques have been tried, including the psychological ones commonly referred to as motivation research techniques. A description of these techniques in an attempt to appraise their value and to indicate where and how they can best be used might be of value.

WHY MOTIVATION RESEARCH?

While examining consumer buying behavior, motivation researchers assume two things: first, the consumer has "certain strong drives or energies which, when stimulated, result in a response; and second, . . . the consumer is part of his culture and is in turn strongly influenced by his environment."[1]

In determining the stimulus to be used, the researcher must take into consideration drives and energies called "intervening variables." Intervening variables may be, for example, beliefs, attitudes, habits, feelings or assumptions. Once these variables are recognized and identified, the researcher must direct the correct stimulus to achieve the desired response. Conditions affecting respondents at the time the stimulus is applied must also be taken into consideration by the researcher when evaluating the responses. For example, an advertisement showing a hot day in the Virgin Islands would elicit different responses from a New Yorker sweltering in a heatwave and an Eskimo freezing in the dead of winter.

In using motivation techniques with the interaction of stimulus and intervening variables, the researcher assumes respondents are consciously aware of the motives for buying preferences and are willing to give an honest answer.

An opposing view suggests that respondents are consciously unaware of why they hold different buying preferences, that the reasons are imbedded in the preconscious mind somewhere, and that those reasons will come back to the memory of the respondents when activated by some slight association. Such knowledge leaves the conscious mind for at least two reasons: we have no immediate use for it and simply forget it or it is more comfortable not to remember it.[2]

In respect to the latter point, it is a fact that individuals like to make the best possible impression, particularly on themselves. What makes them feel good, they like to remember and exaggerate. What is painful is likely to be forgotten.

Women, for example, when asked what brands of shoes they buy, or even what brands of shoes they own, gave a list of prestigious advertised brands. When a physical inventory of their shoes was taken, the vast discrepancy between what was said and what was obtained by the inventory did not seem to worry the respondents. They had mentally rationalized their conduct to gain for themselves the greatest pride of ownership. On the other hand, the bargain counter shoes which gave them no such pride apparently had been forgotten.[3]

Actions such as the purchase of cheap cuts of meat or certain bargain counter clothing seem hard to remember because they generally do not enhance the consumers' egos. But the information goes into the preconscious mind, where it stays until it is recalled by an association. This tendency to forget things that may give individuals a poor impression of themselves has been a major handicap in the attempt to probe for marketing motives.

TECHNIQUES FOR MOTIVATION RESEARCH

Depth Interview

In terms of marketing research, depth interviewing is the practice of clinical psychology. It is an attempt to probe deeper into the unconscious mind of a consumer than the conventional methods of questionnaires can. However, unlike the psychologist who has long-term individual patients, the motivation researcher must work within shorter periods of time, in an attempt to define a common pattern for several respondents.

To establish good rapport between an interviewer and a respondent a nonstructured interview is employed. Open-ended questioning by an interviewer allows a respondent to direct the course of the interview, stimulating further revelation of buying motives. By this definition, depth interviewing connotes a tool wielded for a variety of purposes, some of which involve no more "depth" in the psychological sense than is yielded by the most conventional questionnaire.

Thus the depth interviewing of market research may barely scratch the surface of the unconscious mind, if it touches it at all. There simply is no precise definition because this interviewing is a research tool that is variously used and differently interpreted.

Focus Interview

A shift away from depth interviewing to focus group interviewing has occurred in motivation research. Focus group interview employs the use of a nonstructured discussion among several respondents. A discussion leader utilizes open-ended communication to allow development of free responses. He often may introduce or demonstrate products as an added stimulus to encourage discussion among respondents.

Focus group interviewing provides an interaction of many ideas, emotions and opinions but does not attempt to probe into the individual unconscious mind as does depth interviewing.

Projective Techniques

One group of methods borrowed by motivation researchers from clinical psychologists is called projective techniques. These techniques have a common purpose as merely varying methods of prying information from respondents. The following projective techniques are used in motivation research:

1. Thematic Apperception Test. The Thematic Apperception Test is quite popular with motivation researchers. Borrowed from the field of psychology, its original purpose was to explore the respondent's feelings, needs, worries, and outlook on life. Motivation researchers, applying the concept of the Thematic Apperception Test to the field of marketing research, have utilized it in obtaining data on consumer motivation.

Used in psychology, these test pictures form a series that do not induce a standardized form of response, with no standardized answers expected. When used in marketing, the test pictures do not necessarily form a series. In fact, pictures are carefully selected and organized in a way that induces responses related to the subject being researched without pushing the respondent along any specific line of thought. When interpreting the responses, the researcher then evaluates whether or not the responses given form any significant pattern.

Adaptations of the Thematic Apperception Test have wide applications in marketing research. Pictures like those in the Thematic

Apperception Test can easily be drawn. For example, a picture might show a woman taking a prepared cake mix from a supermarket shelf. When the respondent would be asked to tell the story portrayed by the picture, she may say: "This is a woman who works and she is buying a ready-mix cake because she does not have the time to bake one from scratch." This response would indicate that she feels that using ready-mix foods is a lazy way of cooking, only justified because the woman does not have enough time to cook with other family obligations.

Other responses to the same picture may reveal that those interviewed believe the use of ready-mixed cakes is smart, modern, thrifty or the sign of a poor cook. Because the respondent is talking about someone else (the woman in the picture), less personal involvement would be expected with a clearer portrayal of actual feelings emerging. These feelings then are projected into the picture by the respondent.[4]

2. Paired Pictures. In a derivation of the Thematic Apperception Test, paired pictures are used. A picture of a woman getting into one popular-priced automobile may be paired with a picture of a similarly dressed woman getting into another of the popular-priced cars. The pictures would be shown to respondents asked to tell a story about each one. They also may be asked to give their impressions of the woman getting into the car.

Some motivation researchers may show the two pictures to the same group of respondents at different points in the interview. Others may exhibit one of the pictures each to separate but similar samples of respondents. And in still other cases, the respondents' sample is divided into three groups: group A seeing one picture; group B, the other; and group C, both pictures. If the paired pictures are similar, any difference in their interpretation by the respondents may be assumed to arise from different attitudes toward the two cars. If sufficiently large groups of respondents are used and care is taken to see that there are no marked differences in average age, income level, racial background, etc., any differences in response would be held to reflect varying attitudes toward the two cars.

The marketing applications of the technique are almost limitless. Paired pictures may show a woman picking a package of butter from the market shelf, with the same or a similar woman choosing a package of margarine. Paired pictures may show the use of a pressure cooker as compared to a more conventional cooking utensil or an electric frying pan as compared to a more conventional frying pan. One picture may show a woman entering the supermarket and another, her twin, entering a small specialized food store. Respondents may observe a COD package being paid for by check in one picture and by cash in another. They may find a woman offering a child an apple in one picture and offering candy in another.[5]

Three instead of two situations also could be compared. But the importance of the technique is that respondents have a chance to comment on the behavior of consumers without being asked specifically to comment on the product or the purchase of it. They are given a chance to project their views into the pictures, and hopefully to reveal some hidden motivations that influence their own buying behavior. All these responses must then be interpreted by a skilled analyst.

3. Sentence Completion Tests. General tests like the Thematic Apperception Test possibly touch only thoughts that are close to the conscious mind. In making up a story about a picture, the respondent probably works with concepts he or she knows about, and there are only small influences from the preconscious or unconscious mind.

A more subtle type of probing is the sentence completion test. Here the respondents are asked to finish a series of incomplete sentences. In the motivational aspects of marketing research, its use is to uncover emotional responses to products or marketing situations. The sentence may be like the following:

A mother who belongs to the P.T.A. is _____.
A woman who buys at a discount house is __.

There is, of course, no right or wrong answer to any of these incomplete sentences. The respondent, in completing a series of these sentences, tells a little more about the emotional values that may motivate him or her. The woman who buys at a discount house may be "thrifty," she may be "progressive," she may be "foolish," or, in fact, she may be "a comparison shopper." The revealed sidelights of the respondent's mind are the goals of this test.

In developing a sentence completion test, it is necessary that the sentence order not lead the respondent to give biased answers.[6] Incomplete sentences not directly related to the intended subject matter should be inserted to obscure the real purpose of the test. If the respondent is aware of the researcher's purpose, the response may tend to be biased.

Here again the interpretation needed can be made only by a highly qualified and skilled interpreter because there is no performance criteria. There are no right or wrong answers. Any insight into the motivation is no greater than that made possible by the skills of the analyst. The sentences themselves must be prepared by someone with a lot of clinical experience. But the technique has the advantage of not requiring a trained psychologist. A good consumer interviewer can be trained to ask respondents to complete a series of sentences and to take the answers down on a blank without introducing any bias.

4. *Word Association Tests.* Akin to the sentence completion test is the word association test. A long list of words may be given to the respondent with a blank after each one. The respondent would fill in the blank with the first word that comes to mind. Sometimes the form may merely have numbered lines; then the interviewer would read the words, pausing long enough for the respondent to write the first association that comes to his or her mind. Sometimes the person administering the test may read the words and take down the first word that the respondent mentions. If a group of respondents is being tested simultaneously, the respondents obviously would write their own answers.

This test has had considerable clinical use. Its success depends upon the rapid reaction to each word for which an association is asked. If a respondent pauses at all, he is likely to think of a suitably appropriate word, blurring the desired associations.

An example will illustrate this point. If, for example, the phrase on the blank is department store, a respondent first may think of the word parking. A little later, after seeing the phrase shopping center, he or she may think of the word pleasure. There is the intimation that a respondent feels that shopping in the downtown department store is made difficult by parking problems, but that the shopping center is a pleasant place to shop. Word association tests would not ordinarily be used to obtain such information; it could have been elicited by straightforward questioning because the information was in a respondent's conscious mind. Where an attitude is lodged in the unconscious, then word associations may reveal it.

A single pair of associations of this sort does not prove anything, however. What such associations reveal must be substantiated by other ones in order to understand the individual respondent's attitudes. And they must be confirmed by similar reactions on the part of other respondents to be indicative of prevailing feelings.

The word association test focuses on the first word that comes to a respondent's mind. A similar test sometimes called free association or successive word association attempts to get at material consciously repressed by the respondent. This technique uses a list of words as in the word association test. In the successive word association test, however, the respondent is asked to give several successive responses to one word. The respondent is free to ramble on, giving all the words that come to mind after hearing the word.

APPLICATION OF MOTIVATION RESEARCH IN MARKETING

Success of the techniques used in marketing research depend to a considerable extent on the judgment of the market analyst who uses them. Motivation research that uses psychological methods, though highly judgmental, is valuable to the field of consumer behavior because it both supplements and compliments it.

Motivation research by means of psychological techniques can be carried out on a small enough scale to allow close observation. Its exploratory capacity makes it ideal for doing the preliminary work of designing a large-scale market study that uses more conventional survey methods.

In this exploratory phase, the psychological methods of motivation research can be put to excellent use. By their very nature, they are good for probing, for forming hypotheses and for helping to develop theories of market changes that can be supported or rejected by broader statistical research.

Questions concerning family relationships, the purchase and use of many types of pharmaceutical products, and a wide range of dietary and personal care items are often sensitive ones. More people believe that brushing teeth is socially acceptable than actually do brush their teeth. More people overeat and get heavy than believe becoming fat is a good thing. Admitting the use of drugstore aids to conceal gray hair is uncommon. Many persons are unwilling to admit that physical and health conditions impose restrictions on what they eat or drink. Direct interrogation on these lines is likely to meet refusal or evasion, while the penetrative approach of projective techniques may be highly useful.

It is important to remember that any buried associations are not necessarily important in influencing consumer behavior. The dominant influences still may reside in the conscious mind.[7]

Psychological motivation research has been used with major research problems. It has been applied to the difficulty of selling insurance, to the riddle of brand preference for bread, to consumer attitudes toward broadloom carpeting. Canned soup patronage motives have been studied, as have household cleaning preparation and detergent choices. Both coffee and tea have been objects of motivation research in the hope of increasing total demand; types and brands of coffee also have been studied. A great deal of effort has been made to determine why various makes of automobiles are purchased and whether or not new automobile brands should be marketed.[8]

The buying motives of correspondence school students have been analyzed. Brand loyalty motives for men's shoes have been sought. Factors possibly limiting the consumption of soft drinks have been studied; in fact, many kinds of food products and brands of food have been subjected to motivational research techniques. Why people fly and do not fly, what makes people turn to photography as a hobby all have been studied by these techniques. A considerable amount of advertising has been based on the findings of research that employed projective and depth interviewing techniques.[9]

Sometimes the interpretations of motivation research data result in conflicting claims. An example of this is motivation study of prunes made by two different organizations. Using projective techniques, one study indicated that most people considered prunes as shriveled, tasteless and ugly. They disliked prunes because they were symbolic of old age; prunes were devitalized and denatured; they were disliked as a symbol of parental authority; prunes did not have prestige; prunes were associated with peculiar people, and they were also associated with hospitals, boarding houses and the Army. Using other projective techniques, another study indicated that the principal hindrance to buying prunes was their use as a laxative.

From the first study, it was concluded the laxative attributes of prunes should not be emphasized in advertising them. To the contrary, the second study maintained the health factor and especially the laxative quality of prunes should be emphasized.[10]

In another example, two analysts were hired to determine consumer attitudes toward the advertising concepts of Dial soap. One analyst concluded that the emphasis on Dial's deodorant powers was all wrong because it made people subconsciously uneasy about losing their own distinctive body odors and scared them away. He recommended less emphasis on the soap's deodorizing features. The second analyst, on the other hand, found consumers well disposed to Dial's messages; because Dial's deodorizing agent was apparently winning the customers, he advised the company to continue the sales pitch.[11]

Contradictions of this kind, as they

become known in the business world, result in considerable skepticism about motivation research. But it is not too surprising to have different interpretations and recommendations from two different motivation research practitioners.

Success is not guaranteed in motivation research projects. Recently, for instance, the automobile market was seriously misjudged. Believing that consumers wanted larger automobiles, manufacturers have suffered declining sales due to misinterpreting the research results.[12]

Misinterpretations in findings do not mean that psychological techniques are unsound or cannot be safely used in marketing research. It does, however, serve as a reminder that the same data can be interpreted differently by various analysts. In effect, the analyst reads his or her beliefs into the data, with the findings reflecting a personal understanding of human motivation and a skill in interpreting the data's meaning in relation to the problem. Sometimes well trained analysts can, without doing any research, predict with considerable accuracy how people will react to given situations. Based on their knowledge of human behavior, they can predict that a given set of circumstances will probably evoke a certain reaction. They may simply use research to prove the validity of their hypotheses.

CONCLUSION

Motivation research, as it is applied to marketing research, can be summed up as an attempt to understand and forecast consumers' buying motives and decisions, using techniques that try to penetrate below the level of the conscious mind and uncover unconscious motives of consumers.

The techniques used are borrowed from clinical psychology and have been modified for application to marketing problems. Their value depends entirely upon the skill with which they are used and the competence of the person who interprets the results. Because it is virtually impossible to conduct reproducible experiments, it is almost impossible to prove or disprove the findings obtained by these techniques. There also is some question as to how applicable these techniques are in the new situations to which they are being applied. As a result, reliance must be placed on the integrity, competence, experience and past performance of the practitioner.

In summary, motivation research is not new. Marketing research, practiced for decades, has used a variety of techniques to determine what motivates people to buy. What is relatively new is the application of the techniques of psychiatry and other behavioral sciences to the study of why people react as they do to various marketing stimuli.

Many of these behavioral science techniques, particularly those employed by psychiatrists and psychologists, have proved valid in the study of emotional disorders. However, the success of these techniques as adopted to the study of marketing problems has not been established. At present, it can be said that these techniques are a valuable source of ideas regarding people's reactions to marketing situations.

The most advantageous uses of psychological motivational research are in developing ideas, exploring consumers' minds in search of motives that can be supported or rejected by further research, and perhaps in planning and pretesting advertising copy. Its use is necessary when people apparently can not give the reasons for their attitudes.

Viewed objectively, psychological techniques for motivation research are just one more set of techniques useful in marketing research, with distinct advantages and disadvantages. They supplement, not supplant, conventional marketing research.

NOTES

[1] Jerry Drake, *Marketing Research; Intelligence and Management.* Scranton, Penn. International Textbook Company, 1969.

[2] Robert Ferber, *Motivation and Market Behavior.* (N.Y.: Appleton-Century Crofts, 1970).

[3] Ernest Dichter, *The Strategy of Desire.* (N.Y.: Holt, Rinehart and Winston, Inc. 1971).

[4] Louis Cheskin, *How to Predict What People Will Buy.* (N.Y.: John Wiley & Sons, Inc. 1973).

[5] Edward Kirkpatrick, "New Methods of Measuring Consumer Motivation." *Journal of Marketing,* 25, 1972.

[6] Joseph Newman, *Motivation Research and Marketing Management.* (Glencoe, Ill.: The Free Press, 1970).

[7] Henry Paradise, "Depth Interviewing." *Psychology Abstracts,* LXXI, 1970.

[8] Paul Lazarfeld, "Consumer Motivation." *Handbook of Psychology,* XXXIV, 1971.

[9] Charles Klein, "Projective Techniques in Marketing." *Journal of Marketing,* 14, 1969.

[10] Lincoln Clark, *Consumer Behavior.* (N.Y.: Harper & Row, Inc. 1972).

[11] Perrin Stryker, "Motivation Research." *Journal of Marketing Research,* 29, 1971.

[12] Kenneth Brive, "The Strategy of Motivation Research," *Journal of Marketing,* 44, 1974.

Questions

1. What is motivation research? What is its importance in consumer behavior?
2. Name the four types of projective techniques and describe any one of them with an example.
3. The application of motivation research in marketing depends on the skills and competence of the user. Explain.
4. Briefly define the three types of interviews for motivation research.

43. Focus Groups—Their Role in the Marketing Research Process

Carl McDaniel

What Are Focus Groups?

Focus groups had their genesis in psychological group therapy. Today, a focus group consists of eight to twelve consumers who are led by a moderator in an in-depth discussion on one particular topic or concept.

Focus groups are much more than merely question and answer interviews. The distinction is made between "group dynamics" and "group interviewing." The interaction provided in group dynamics is essential to the success of focus group research. It is this interaction that is the reason for conducting group rather than individual research. One of the essential postulates of group session usage is the idea that a response from one group member may become a stimulus for another group member. The interplay of responses may yield more information than the same number of people would have independently contributed.

The idea for group dynamics research in marketing came from the field of social psychology where studies indicated that "unknown to themselves, people of all walks of life and in all occupations will tell us more about a topic and do so in greater depths if they are encouraged to act spontaneously instead of reacting to questions."[1] Normally, in group dynamics, direct questions are avoided. In their place are indirect inquiries that stimulate free and spontaneous discussions. The result is "more meaningful responses in place of forging answers that fit a prescribed form—yes, no; regularly, occasionally, never."[2]

The Popularity of Focus Groups

Qualitative research and focus groups are often used as synonyms by marketing research practitioners. Popular literature is replete with examples of researchers referring to qualitative research in one breath and focus groups in the next.[3] Focus groups are

but one aspect of qualitative research. Yet, the overwhelming popularity of the techniques has virtually overshadowed other qualitative tools.

How popular are focus groups? Most marketing research firms in the United States employ the technique.[4] Moreover, a recent survey of 1,200 large corporations found eighty-one percent of the consumer good organizations using focus groups. Only sixteen percent of the industrial good companies utilized the technique.[5] Consumer good companies have generally applied marketing research more extensively than industrial good firms. Also, industrial groups pose a host of problems not found in consumer research. For example, it is usually quite easy to assemble a group of twelve housewives. However, putting together a group of ten engineers, sales managers, or financial analysts is far more costly and time consuming.

Uses of Focus Groups

Despite the high cost of industrial focus groups, the technique can pay handsome dividends if it is properly employed. The use of focus groups is another hotly debated topic among research practitioners. A senior marketing analyst for Texize Chemicals Company noted that "focus groups may actually increase the marketing risk."[6] The researcher

[1] Dietz Leonhard, "Can Focus Group Interviews Survive?" *Marketing News* (October 10, 1975), pp. 6–7.

[2] *Ibid.*

[3] See for example: Myril Axelrod, "Marketers Get an Eyeful when Focus Groups Expose Products, Ideas, Images, Ad Copy, Etc., to Consumers," *Marketing News* (February 28, 1975), pp. 6–7; Eleanor Holtzman, "Use Groups for Parity Products, Those Meeting Psychological Needs," *Marketing News* (August 12, 1977), p. 6; Ann Schafer, "Schafer Answers Three Most Frequently Asked Focus Group Questions," *Marketing News* (November 21, 1975), p. 8; Melvin

Prince, "Focus Groups can Give Marketer Early Clues on Marketability of New Product," *Marketing News* (September 8, 1978), p. 12; and Samuel Hagler, "Group Interview not Hard, but Good One is Difficult," *Marketing News* (July 15, 1977), p. 8.

[4] Barnett Greenberg, Joe Goldstucker and Danny Bellenger, "What Techniques Are Used by Marketing Researchers in Business?" *Journal of Marketing* (April 1977). pp. 64–65.

[5] *Ibid.*

[6] "Approach Focus Group Use Cautiously, Meet Told," *Advertising Age* (June 13, 1977), p. 23.

goes on to say that he has seen instances in which marketing executives substituted focus groups' qualitative information for needed quantitative survey information. A well-known Chicago market researcher claims that, "in most cases, focus groups should be priced out as client entertainment rather than research."[7] This is overstating the case to say the least. Because of the relative newness of the technique, its low cost, and popularity, misuse does occur.

How should focus groups be employed? Bobby Calder cuts through the controversy by developing a classification system. The three major categories of focus groups are: exploratory, clinical, and phenomenological.[8]

Exploratory Groups. Exploratory focus groups can be viewed as pilot testing. They may be employed to test wording on a questionnaire, or product placement instructions. Exploratory groups may have a more lofty goal of attempting to generate hypotheses for testing or concepts for further research. In this instance, the groups are mainly used to stimulate the thinking of the marketing researchers. As Calder explains it, ". . . the rationale of exploratory focus groups is that considering a problem in terms of everyday explanation will somehow facilitate a subsequent scientific approach."[9]

Myril Axelrod, Vice President of Qualitative Research for Young and Rubicam Advertising, states the following about exploratory groups:

[Focus groups] can be used to provide insights into the reasons why something seems to be happening in a copy test or why a particularly unusual sales pattern seems to be turning up

on sales data. Talking to women, in a free-flowing way, about what they are doing in a category and what has been happening in a category can often start some very important thinking for the marketing minds of the client or the agency.

In our company, we often use group sessions for 'diagnostic' purposes when a commercial has performed in an unexpected way in an 'on-air' test. We expose the commercial in group sessions to learn what seems to have been happening which may have caused the poor score.

The use of qualitative research as a starting point for large-scale research like market segmentation is broadly accepted and its importance in this role cannot be minimized. One of my favorite clients is given to saying: 'Any segmentation study is only as good as the qualitative data that went into it.' He insists upon being personally involved in all of the group session work from which the basic questionnaire is developed and the indications of the qualitative phase must make sense to him before he will move on.

He believes that much of the 'direction' to be drawn from the study can be perceived at the completion of the qualitative phase (if, of course, the qualitative work is sound and professional) and that the rest of the research verifies and puts numbers on the data. This has, in fact, been our experience, too, in the segmentation work we have done.[10]

Clinical Focus Groups. Clinical groups are qualitative research in its purest form. The research is conducted as a scientific endeavor. It is based upon the premise that a person's true motivations and feelings are subliminal in nature. What consumers say cannot be taken at face value, but instead, the researcher must probe the subconscious.

Obviously clinical groups require a moderator highly trained in psychology and sociology. It is assumed that a person's real motives must be uncovered using clinical judgment. Thus, the focus group becomes the data input source for clinical judgment. The moderator

[7] "Focus Group Wrongs Include Construction, Analysis, and Price," *Marketing News* (November 21, 1975), p. 8.
[8] Bobby Calder, "Focus Groups and the Nature of Qualitative Marketing Research," *Journal of Marketing Research,* 14 (August, 1977), pp. 353–364.
[9] *Ibid.*
[10] Axelrod, "Marketers Get an Eyeful . . .," p. 7.

must be highly skilled to cause participants to reveal inner feelings and thoughts. An example of clinical focus group research for Muriel cigars is presented below.

> For many years, Edie Adams was effectively used as the brand spokeswoman. But sex symbols get old and fade. The question was how to advertise Muriel now. We did a great deal of group session work on cigar smokers.
>
> We found that cigars are a symbol of potency and a reinforcement of masculinity. The cigar symbolized dominance and strength. The kind of men who smoke cigars want to feel 'big' enough to smoke cigars.
>
> Edie Adams' sexuality excited smokers and made them feel more manly. But cigar smokers tend to be voyeurs rather than participants of sex.
>
> They daydream of the good time—but tell us that they don't really want to get too close to women. They could look at Edie and admire her—no need to actively participate.
>
> It was our interpretation and recommendation that Muriel continue to assert a sexy image: to draw on its original heritage as a brand built by a woman, but to give smokers new excitement and sexual pleasure.
>
> We ran a contest to find out which of three women should replace Edie Adams and Susan Anton won. The campaign using Susan Anton has been on the air since the fall. She has become a star.[11]

Because of the difficulty (if not impossibility) of validating findings from clinical groups and unskilled moderators attempting to conduct clinical groups, their popularity has markedly diminished.[12] Perhaps when new psychoanalytic tools are developed and certification standards are developed for moderators, clinical groups will enjoy a resurgence.

Phenomenological Focus Groups. When a researcher speaks of "doing a few groups" he is usually referring to phenomenological focus groups. The term is derived from the word phenomenology which means the representation of knowledge as conscious experience. As the President of Schafer Research puts it:

> Since quantitative research generally involves many intermediaries between the client and the consumer, a sense of isolation can develop. A client's decision makers need to be involved and feel close to the consumer, if results are to lead to meaningful action.
>
> Live and recorded observation of focus group discussions, coupled with client, agency, and moderator interaction at the debriefing session following each group, helps provide this sense of involvement and leaves clients with a better understanding of how these consumers feel, although these feelings may not be totally representative.[13]

Thus, a phenomenological approach represents an opportunity to "experience" a "flesh and blood" consumer. Reality in the corporate home office differs drastically from that of most kitchens or supermarkets. It allows the researcher to experience the emotional framework in which the product is being used—to, in a sense, go into her life and relive with her all of the satisfactions, dissatisfactions, rewards, and frustrations she experiences when she takes the product into her home.[14]

Phenomenological groups are often used by an advertising agency's creative staff. It allows the copy writers to express themselves in the consumer's own language. The experience may also spark ideas for entire campaigns or positioning themes.

CONDUCTING FOCUS GROUPS

Preparing for a Focus Group

Focus groups are usually conducted in a "group facility." The setting is normally con-

---

[11] Holtzman, "Use Groups for Parity . . .," p. 6.
[12] Calder, "Focus Groups . . .," p. 357.
[13] Schafer, "Schafer Answers Three . . .," p. 8.
[14] Axelrod, "Marketers Get an Eyeful . . .," p. 6.

ference room style with a large one-way mirror in one wall. Microphones are placed in an unobtrusive location (usually the ceiling) to record the discussion. Behind the mirror is the viewing room. It consists of chairs and note-taking benches or tables for the clients. The viewing room also houses the recording and/or videotape equipment.

Participants are recruited for focus groups from a variety of sources. Two common procedures are mail intercept interviews and random telephone screening. Researchers normally establish criteria for the group participants. For example, if Quaker Oats is researching a new cereal, they might request mothers with children ranging in age from seven to twelve years old that had served cold cereal (perhaps a specific brand) in the past three weeks.

The Critical Role of the Moderator

Having qualifed respondents and a good moderator are the keys to successful focus groups, regardless of the type of group conducted, a qualified moderator is essential. Qualifications, of course, depend upon the type of group the researcher is conducting. A moderator of clinical groups should have extensive training in psychology and social psychology. Not only is this individual responsible for conducting the group but interpreting it as well.

Considerable disagreement exists among researchers on educational requirements of exploratory and phenomenological group moderators.[15] One school of thought is that

these individuals should also be trained in psychology or sociology. It is believed that this background is important to understand the nuances of human behavior. Exploratory moderators, at the very least, need solid training in marketing research. How else, it is argued, can the moderator develop hypotheses and a framework for quantitative research?

The second school of thought on moderator training maintains a different posture. It emphasizes personality, empathy, sensitivity, and good instincts. It assumes that some people just have a "feel" for conducting groups. If individuals observe long enough and have the above innate abilities, they can become good group moderators.

Myril Axelrod, a veteran of almost 20 years in qualitative research exclusively, speaks for the "personality school" on moderators.

> Not everyone can be a moderator. It requires not only the kind of outward personality that encourages respondents to want to talk to you, but also an extreme degree of sensitivity, a genuine interest in people, an ability to listen 'with a third ear,' as the psychologists put it, a great deal of experience, and most of all, a serious concern with the importance of understanding this craft.[16]

A focus group tends to flow through three stages. In the first, rapport is established, the rules of group interaction are explained, and objectives are given. The second stage is characterized by the moderator attempting to provoke intensive discussion. The final stage is used for summarizing significant conclusions and testing limits of belief and commitment.[17]

[15] Thomas E. Caruso, "Moderators Focus on Groups: Session Yields 7 Hypotheses Covering Technology Trend, Professionalism, Training, Techniques, Reports, Etc.," *Marketing News* (September 10, 1976), pp. 12–16.

[16] Axelrod, "Marketers Get an Eyeful . . .," p. 11.
[17] Hagler, "Group Interview Not Hard . . .," p. 8.

STUDY OBJECTIVES

The objective of this research was exploratory in nature. Specifically, answers to several questions were sought:

1. Are focus groups as prevalent as the literature suggests?
2. What qualifications are required of the group moderator?
3. To what purposes or objectives are focus groups applied?
4. How are the groups structured?

This study also provides a basis for comparing Calder's normative classification scheme with real-world focus group applications.

METHODOLOGY

Data Collection Procedures

A questionnaire was sent to the director of qualitative research at marketing research firms throughout the United States. A cover letter was sent with the questionnaire to explain the nature of the study. Companies were selected on the basis of a brief description of services in a national listing of research firms.[18] Every firm that the researchers believed had any probability of conducting qualitative research was sent a questionnaire.

A total of 313 questionnaires were mailed. After five weeks, a second questionnaire was sent to nonrespondents. One hundred and fifteen usable questionnaires were returned for a response rate of thirty-seven percent.*

* Note: A binomial question with evenly divided responses (50 percent yes, 50 percent no) represents the highest level of divergence. In this case, the 95 confidence interval would be ±9.39.

[18] *The Green Book* (New York: American Marketing Association, New York Chapter, Inc., 1977).

Twenty-three additional questionnaires were not used due to incomplete data or not conducting qualitative research. It is also likely that many firms who did not engage in qualitative research simply discarded the questionnaires. Thus, the response rate among firms who conduct qualitative research in the United States is probably higher than the actual thirty-seven percent.

Dollar and Volume Impact of Focus Group Research

Respondents generally stated that focus group research accounted for a small portion of their research dollars, but a slightly larger portion of their projects (Table 1).

For almost half of the responding firms, focus group research represents less than ten percent of the total sales and total projects. However, focus groups comprise approximately fifty percent or more of total projects for twenty percent of the responding organizations. Similarly, fourteen percent of the

Table 1 / Financial and Workload Impact of Focus Groups

Percentage of firms	Focus groups as a percent of sales
51	Less than 10
22	10–25
13	26–50
6	51–75
8	76 and above

Percentage of firms	Focus groups as a percent of projects
40	Less than 10
29	10–25
11	26–50
9	51–75
11	76 and above

research firms stated that focus groups account for fifty percent or more of their total revenue. These latter organizations, of course, specialize in behavioral research.

Purposes of Focus Group Research

Respondents were given twelve different group objectives, as determined in a pretest, and asked to indicate how they use focus groups by responding (1) never, (2) rarely, (3) occasionally, (4) frequently, or (5) always. Table 2 shows how researchers are currently using focus group sessions. The percentage figures indicate the proportion of respondents who replied either "frequently" or "always."

The areas which are most frequently used are those which deal with broad topics, for example, testing new ideas and concepts, consumer attitudes and the development of hypotheses. It would seem then that focus groups are conducted most often to produce general conceptual data rather than evaluation of specific alternatives, i.e., pricing and packaging. This table supports the contention that a focus group is a broad qualitative research tool. Using Calder's terminology, it is apparent that most groups are either phenomenological or exploratory rather than clinical.

Cross-tabulation of the focus group objectives question by focus group research as a percentage of total sales was significant at .05 using the Chi Square test. As the proportion of focus groups to total sales increased, the variety of objectives covered by focus groups also increased. This suggests that firms which concentrate heavily in focus group research apply the technique more generally than other research organizations. Companies that indicated focus groups were a small percentage of their sales tended to utilize the technique only to generate ideas and concepts.

Table 2 / Objectives of Focus Group Research

Purpose of groups	Percent who replied "always" or "frequently"
Test new ideas	70
Identify consumer attitudes	70
Determine if concepts make sense	68
Development of hypotheses	68
Identify product problem areas	64
Determine consumer needs and wants	64
Stimulate creative design	53
Questionnaire design	49
Ads communicating the right message	47
Packaging evaluation	29
Ads targeted at the right audience	24
Pricing determination	13

MODERATOR QUALIFICATIONS

Academic Background

This study confirms earlier research that there is a wide divergence of opinion among researchers as to what qualifications moderators should possess (Table 3). This is perhaps due to the types of groups which they conduct. Most respondents (eighty-eight percent) recognized the need for a college education. Only twenty percent thought graduate work was necessary.

The specific degree mentioned most often was in psychology. Yet, some researchers commented that they would rather have anyone but a psychologist as a moderator. This response, no doubt, comes from a firm that is committed to phenomenological research. If a moderator must analyze a partici-

Table 3 / Moderator Academic
Qualifications

Academic background	Percent of respondents
Psychology	29
Social science	14
Marketing	3
Any degree	5
Bachelors	18
Graduate	12
Ph.D.	8
No degree required	12

pant's values and attitudes (clinical groups), a psychologist or someone with advanced training is necessary.

Group Analysis

Analysis of a session is a very important phase of any focus group project. The unstructured nature of the research and the plethora of concepts and ideas generated require unique analytical skills. This is particularly true in exploratory and clinical groups. Table 4 reveals who typically analyzes the group.

A significant relationship (.05) was found between moderator analysis and the percent-

Table 4 / Individual Responsible
for Group Analysis

Analysis by moderator	Percent
Yes	57
No	4
Sometimes	39

Non-moderator analysis	Percent
Project director	40
Company analyst	20
Client	15
Owner	13
Research assistant	7
Observer	5

age of focus groups to total sales. The larger the percent of sales constituted by focus groups, the more likely the moderator was to do the analysis. Perhaps this is because the more focus groups a research firm conducts, the higher the probability that the company will employ a highly trained moderator who can perform the analysis.

Increasing the Value of Focus Groups

Survey participants offered many suggestions on ways to increase the value and effectiveness of focus groups (Table 5). It was somewhat surprising to find that client education was mentioned most frequently. Further elaboration by some respondents indicated that education should include the advantages and disadvantages of focus groups, how they can and cannot be used, what they can and cannot accomplish, and the results to be expected from focus groups.

CONCLUSIONS

Although not widely recognized in academic journals, it is evident that focus group research is pervasive in the United States. Since qualitative research lacks statistical

Table 5 / Suggestions for Increasing the
Value of Focus Groups

Techniques to increase value	Percent
Educate clients	46
Qualified moderators	17
Use only as qualitative	10
Have clients observe the session	9
State objectives	8
Qualified respondents	4
Use with other research	3
Do not oversell	2
Do not be overstructured	1

validity, it may be that some academicians have chosen to deny its existence. This is unfortunate because it can only increase the chasm between the "real world" and academe.

Calder's classification system seems to fit stated focus group objectives. Goals such as testing new ideas, identifying product problem areas, and stimulating creative design are phenomenological in nature. Respondents who claimed that they conduct groups to test new ideas, aid in questionnaire design, or to develop hypotheses are using an exploratory approach. Finally, those who stated that their groups were used to identify consumer attitudes or to determine consumer needs and wants were probably conducting clinical focus groups.

The importance of training in psychology leads to several conclusions. Either a relatively large number of clinical focus groups are being conducted or exploratory and phenomenological groups are being needlessly analyzed on a clinical base. Another possibility is that researchers believe training in psychology will enable the moderator to better understand the group dynamic process. Hopefully, this would result in "better" exploratory and phenomenological groups.

The fact that only fifty-seven percent of the moderators do their own analysis is not surprising given Calder's classifications. Indeed, it is only necessary in a pure clinical group. If the moderator is not involved in exploratory group analysis, other qualified researchers must step in. On the other hand, a phenomenological group may be solely interpreted by the researcher's client, an advertising agency's creative director, or a product manager.

Evidently, a large communications education problem exists between research firm clients and research organizations. Focus groups tend to be less expensive than other forms of survey research, thus perhaps creating a client bias in favor of group interviewing. Overutilization and misapplication of focus groups seems to have created research user-supplier friction. Why else would such importance be placed upon the need to educate research clients? The marketing research community needs to develop standards for conducting and implementing group research. It also needs to explain the types of groups that can be conducted and the advantages and disadvantages of each. Until this is done, focus groups will continue to be a controversial research tool.

Questions

1. Name and define the three major categories of focus groups.
2. The author feels that the success of a focus group depends to a large extent on a good moderator. Explain.
3. Using this article as a basis, summarize the advantages and disadvantages of focus groups over other research techniques. In light of your discussion, evaluate the prospects for future use of focus groups.

44. Fitting the Semantic Differential to the Marketing Problem

William A. Mindak

Advertising and marketing men frequently are faced with the problem of quantifying highly subjective data, representing difficult-to-verbalize reactions of people to the "image" of a brand, product, or company.

Consistent with this attempt to define an "image" is the technique originated by Charles E. Osgood and his associates, called the semantic differential.[1] This technique attempts to measure what meaning a concept might have for people in terms of dimensions which have been empirically defined and factor-analyzed. Since this concept can indeed be something as abstract or nebulous as a company image, the semantic differential has seen increasing use in various ways.[2]

Osgood's semantic differential involved repeated judgments of a concept against a series of descriptive polar-adjectival scales on a 7-point equal-interval ordinal scale. These scales were usually selected from 50 pairs of polar adjectives, with heavy factor loadings labeled "evaluative" (on which are based the attitudinal measures), "activity," and "potency."

An example would be:

good __ : __ : __ : __ : __ : __ : __ :bad

Progressing from left to right on the scale, the positions are described to the subjects participating in the experiment as representing "extremely good," "very good," "slightly good," "being both good and bad," "slightly bad," "very bad," and "extremely bad." Subjects are encouraged to use the scales as quickly and as honestly as possible and not to puzzle over any particular concept.

In scoring the differential, weights can be assigned to each position; and these in turn can be converted to individual or group mean scores and presented in "profile" form. Reliability of the differential is reasonably high, and the measure has a high degree of face validity.

SEMANTIC DIFFERENTIAL IN MEASURING "IMAGES"

The semantic differential has a number of specific advantages for marketing researchers interested in measuring brand, product, or company images:

1. It is a quick, efficient means of getting in readily quantifiable form and for large samples not only the *direction* but *intensity* of opinions and attitudes toward a concept . . . be it brand, product, or company. If desired, these "profiles" can be used as a guide to indicate areas for more intensive research or interviewing.

[1]Charles E. Osgood, George J. Suci, and Percy H. Tannenbaum, *The Measurement of Meaning* (Urbana, Illinois: University of Illinois Free Press, 1957).

[2]William A. Mindak, "A New Technique for Measuring Advertising Effectiveness," *Journal of Marketing*, Vol. 20 (April, 1956), pp. 367–378. Mogul, Lewin, Williams & Saylor, Inc., "Product Semantic Indices," (private publication) (New York, 1958). John F. Bolger, Jr., "How to Evaluate Your Company Image," *Journal of Marketing*, Vol. 24 (October, 1959), pp. 7–10.

2. It provides a comprehensive picture of the "image" or meaning of a product or personality. Duncan Hines and Betty Crocker as corporate personalities might both be looked upon favorably, but reacted to differently in terms of "activity," "strength," "warmth," "helpfulness," etc.

3. It represents a standardized technique for getting at the multitude of factors which go to make up a brand or product "image." Comparison of one brand with another must take into consideration *specific brand attributes* (size, shape, price, ingredients, etc.) as well as *general product class characteristics* (including competition); the *sources* of the impressions (merchandising, packaging, advertising, media, etc.); the *company* that makes the product; and *types of consumers* associated with the product.

4. It is easily repeatable and quite reliable. Therefore, it can be used as a continuing measure sensitive enough to note changes in consumer reactions from year to year.

5. It avoids stereotyped responses and allows for individual frames of reference. The sheer number of scales and concepts and the speed of administration (both with groups and individuals), encourage quick "top-of-mind" responses. For this reason it has sometimes been called a "semantic projection" test.

6. It eliminates some of the problems of question phrasing, such as ambiguity and overlapping of statements. In addition, it facilitates the interviewing of respondents who may not be too articulate in describing their reactions to such abstruse factors as a brand, product, or company image.

MODIFICATIONS FOR ADVERTISING RESEARCH

To make the differential even more sensitive in evoking subtle distinctions in the images of physically similar products, researchers have suggested many modifications. The most important of these are:

1. *Descriptive nouns and phrases.* These are in addition to (and sometimes a substitute for) simple one-word adjectives. The original differential dealt primarily with single-word adjectives such as "good-bad," "weak-strong," "pleasant-unpleasant," etc. The "evaluation," "activity," and "potency" factors are still retained, but with increased shades of meaning provided by these longer, more involved scales.

Here is an example for a beer:

Happy-go-lucky—kind of serious
Something special—just another drink
Little after-taste—lots of after-taste
Really refreshing—not really refreshing
American flavor—foreign flavor

Here is an example for people who drink beer:

Live in average homes—live in expensive homes
Take life easy—always on the go
Drink just to be sociable—really enjoy it
Really know beer—can't tell one from another
Snobs—regular guys
Housewife—career girl

Edmund W. J. Faison, President of Visual Research Inc., in an attempt to match personality types with package designs, labels, colors, etc., has used these phrases as one end of a scale:

Stands out in a crowd
Self-made man
Likes to hunt and fish
Factory worker making $400 a month
Belongs to a higher social class than his parents

2. *Tailor-made scales.* In attempting to set up standardized scales, certain researchers have concentrated on the classic list of 50 word-pairs, factor-analyzed by Osgood. This direction offers comparative possibilities and a hope of generalized attitude scales. In rating TV commercials, Burleigh Gardner of Social Research, Inc., consistently uses 30 word-

pairs, with heavy factor loadings on evaluation, activity, strength, etc.

But for many researchers such a standardized list lacks flexibility and appropriateness to the specific problems at hand. They find it necessary to construct tailor-made word and phrase lists. Sources for these lists are content analyses of their own and competitive advertising, word association tests with consumers, individual or group interviews, and factor analyses.

In such exploratory or pretests, simple opposites are used, often without the 7-point scale. Once it is agreed that these adjectives and phrases cover the factors best delimiting the image, they are then scaled to permit profile comparisons.

3. *"Connotative" and "non-polar" opposites.* Although in theory every adjective or phrase should have a denotative opposite (true-untrue, good-bad, bright-dull), researchers have found that in practice respondents often refuse to "play the game," as it were. In an advertising context or in rating large well-known companies, subjects often balk at using negative sides of scales or to gradate a concept negatively.

Respondents can, and do, make sharp distinctions as to the level of believability of a company's advertising or of a particular claim. But they either hesitate to rate a concept as unbelievable (feeling that "if it is advertised, it must be true") or they are unable to gradate their feelings of unbelievability.

This failure frequently results in indiscriminate clustering about the middle of the scales, thus making it difficult to differentiate among concept profiles. Some researchers have attempted to circumvent this tendency either by "heightening" the level of the dimensions or by using phrases which, although not necessarily *denotatively* opposite, still seem to fit more logically and naturally into people's frame of reference. Scales such as these are used:

> Really modern—sort of old-fashioned
> High-quality product—so-so quality product
> Heavy beer drinker—a "sometimes" beer drinker
> Really peps you up—somehow doesn't pep you up

4. *Built-in control concepts.* As a realistic control, it is helpful to get ratings on such concepts as "the ideal company," or "my favorite brand," or "brand I would never use." These control profiles can be compared with test concepts or competitive concepts. Although one might expect respondents simply to use the extremes on all scales to represent their "ideal" or their "least-liked," such is not really the case.

5. *Personal interviews and mail questionnaires.* Early experiments with the differential usually were conducted with "captive" audiences, often students in class. In the main, though, the advertising researcher prefers to do field studies and depends on individual personal interviews. The differential has been used in these situations, and respondents show little reluctance in performing the task of checking several concepts on a variety of scales. The need for tailor-made scales is often quite apparent, however, in that certain age groups and certain socio-economic groups find it relatively difficult to think in terms of various continua and to deal with such abstractions as "concepts."

Other researchers have even experimented with the differential in mail questionnaires, although this means of delivery obviates most of the projective qualities of this test. Respondents have too much time to deliberate over their judgments and have too much control over their ratings. Personal supervision is necessary to assure speed and "top-of-mind" responses.

A BRAND–IMAGE STUDY

The following case study demonstrates the use of the differential, as well as some of the modifications discussed. This particular study's purpose was to determine beer drinkers' reactions to the personalities of three local brands of beer (and specifically Brand Y), compared with three competitive national brands in a large midwest city. Various facets of this image were to be explored, such as specific characteristics of each brand, the attitudes toward advertising, the image of the company, and feelings about various consumers who might be associated or not associated with each brand of beer.

Respondents were asked to rate these six beers on several dimensions. Scales were selected from content analyses of depth-interview responses, as well as from advertisements for the various brands. The mean ratings were converted into profiles for comparison purposes. Figures 1 through 4 illustrate certain critical scales for three local brands of beer.

Results

1. Looking at the profiles of products, company, and advertising image, (Figures 1, 2, and 3) it is apparent that Brands X and Y enjoy many more positive or favorable ratings than Brand Z. This reflects X and Y's domination of sales and their large market share. None of X's or Y's mean ratings fall on the negative side; and very few are in the neutral or indifferent area (3.5 to 4.5).

Brand X received essentially positive ratings in regard to specific *product* (it was quite refreshing, something special, relaxing, and had a distinctive flavor); *advertising* (it was outstanding, it was attention getting, and there was lots of it); and *company* (it was

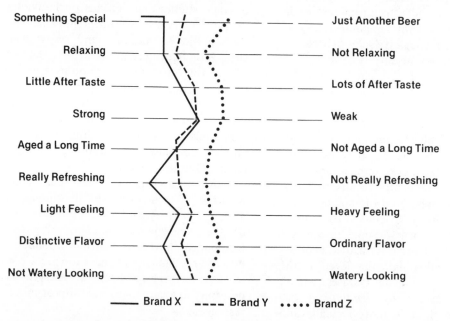

Figure 1 / Specific product image

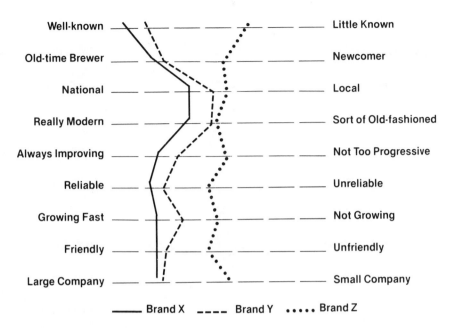

Figure 2 / Company image

friendly, large, well-known, and an old-time brewer who still manages to grow fast and always improve).

Although Brand Y's ratings usually were favorable, they were not as extreme as Brand X. The only two exceptions occurred in ratings of the specific products. Beer drinkers rated Y about the same as X on the "weak-strong" scale and the "aged-a-long-time" dimension. *Brand Z,* a relative newcomer to

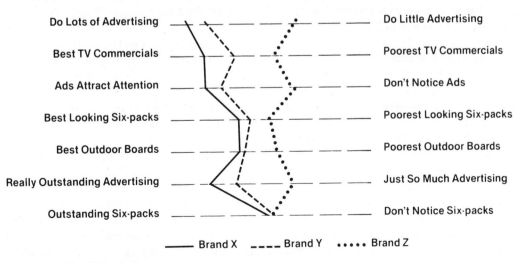

Figure 3 / Advertising image

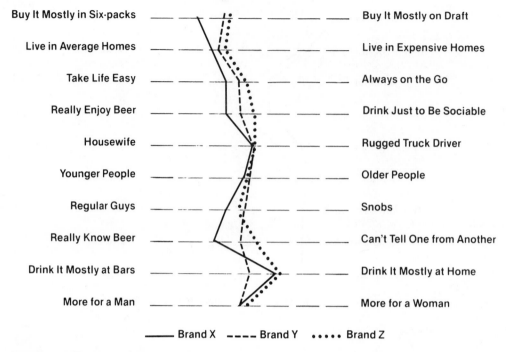

Buy It Mostly in Six-packs								Buy It Mostly on Draft
Live in Average Homes								Live in Expensive Homes
Take Life Easy								Always on the Go
Really Enjoy Beer								Drink Just to Be Sociable
Housewife								Rugged Truck Driver
Younger People								Older People
Regular Guys								Snobs
Really Know Beer								Can't Tell One from Another
Drink It Mostly at Bars								Drink It Mostly at Home
More for a Man								More for a Woman

——— Brand X ‒‒‒‒ Brand Y •••• Brand Z

Figure 4 / Consumer profile

the city, was reacted to quite neutrally—in this case, an indication of little consumer experience with, or knowledge of, the beer. In addition to its "militant indifference," Brand Z was thought to be less well-known than the other two brands, to do less advertising, and to be more of a local beer.

2. In products such as beer, advertising researchers are interested in determining the "types" of consumer most often associated with a particular brand. Social Research, Inc., the Psychological Corporation, the Institute for Motivational Research, Inc., and other organizations increasingly emphasize psychological typologies rather than conventional demographic characteristics.

In this case, Figure 4 shows that the consumer profile ratings, that is, the types of people considered likely to buy each of these beers, tend to cluster much more than for the other three factors. It might be advantageous for a beer *not* to be inordinately connected or identified with a particular type of consumer.

Beer drinkers thought Brands X and Y more "universal" than Z. They were "all things to all beer drinkers." Brand X was thought of as being consumed more at home and by average people who really enjoy and know beer. Brand Y was considered to be drunk more in bars. Brand Z's image tended toward home drinking and use by less discriminating beer drinkers.

The results of this study were interpreted by the management of Y company to be quite favorable, particularly when the advertising budgets of X and Y were compared. Management was pleased with reactions to the company which a few years back had not enjoyed the best of reputations. Possible weak areas which might need strengthening were Brand

Y's dealer displays (6-packs); the feeling that the company was not as modern as it could be; and the need of upgrading the image of the beer among "higher-class," sophisticated, home beer drinkers.

Implications

A great deal of controversy (some genuine, some "strawman") exists between the "quantifier" and the "qualifier" in attempting to delineate the image of a product, brand, or company. The semantic differential and techniques similar to it help to quantify what too often has been considered abstract, mysterious, and qualitative material regarding consumers' opinions, feeling tones, and emotional reactions. In addition, the modifications suggested by advertising researchers (phrases and nouns in addition to single adjectives, connotative as well as denotative opposites, tailor-made scales) add more scope and direction to what may be superficial quantitative information.

The differential serves as a two-edged tool: (1) It is a simple, large sample, nose-counting device which can be repeated from time to time to detect trends in consumer reactions, and to measure interaction between advertising and consumer attitudes. (2) In addition, the differential "profiles" serve as useful directional indicators for further and more intensive probing, using many of the qualitative projective techniques.

In either case, this knowledge can be quite useful in deciding on a possible advertising or marketing plan, in spotting weak areas which might need to be strengthened or strong areas which might need to be emphasized.

Questions

1. What is the semantic differential?
2. Summarize the main advantages of this technique, as suggested by the author.
3. Where do you see the use of this technique in marketing?

45. Autonomic Measures of Advertising

Paul J. Watson

Robert J. Gatchel

Advertising is a multibillion-dollar enterprise in which companies have turned to psychophysiological technology in fear of overlooking "any potentially valuable knowledge that could help them or their competitors" (Rice, 1974). This review examines what "potentially valuable knowledge," if any, psychophysiological approaches offer in the assessment of advertising effectiveness.

COMMON PSYCHOLOGICAL INTERESTS

Although not all psychological phenomena of concern to the psychophysiologist are relevant to advertising goals, there are common interests—for example, the affective impact of stimuli. Advertising tries, among other things, to add "more appeal to the product" (Krugman, 1964), but the fact that people may be unable to articulate their feelings makes it difficult to assess how well this goal is achieved. The use of psychophysiological techniques eliminates this verbal communication problem to some degree. Indeed, psychophysiologists have explored the emotional reactions, both pleasurable and unpleasurable, of their subjects. But Stern, Farr, and Ray (1975) have indicated that methodological considerations have led to a relative dominance of research into the correlates of unpleasant rather than pleasant psychological states. They suggest that three reasons may underlie this situation:

1. greater variability in what subjects may find pleasurable compared to what is perceived as unpleasurable;

2. difficulty in using pleasurable stimuli in a laboratory setting;

3. problems in quantifying the degree of pleasurableness.

Nevertheless, a considerable body of literature exists on the activity of physiological response systems during situations varying along a pleasurable-unpleasurable dimension.

The arousal concept, also of interest in advertising, is broadly used by psychophysiologists. When first formally conceptualized, psychophysiologists viewed arousal as a unidimensional continuum along which all behavior could be categorized (Lindsley, 1951; Malmo, 1959). The continuum extended from the lowest level of behavioral activation (sleep) to agitated behavioral states such as rage. An essential characteristic of the hypothesis was that the output of physiological systems varied directly in a stepwise function with behavioral activation. Subsequent evidence has revealed that behavioral and physiological arousal are not always directly related (Lacey, 1967), but psychophysiologists often use the term when discussing the vigor of a response.

Since the arousal concept is so broad, advertisers can use it in assessing affective impact in advertising. Research of sexual arousal provides an example of a psychophysiological investigation into what is a "pleasurable" affective state. This type of experimentation has attempted to discover the pattern of physiological responding during presentation of sexual stimuli. That marketing could be interested in this line of research is suggested by the fact that evaluating the emotional effects of sexual material in advertising has been important in the past (e.g., Morrison and Sherman, 1972). Unpleasurable arousal states such as anxiety, fear, and stress also have been examined by psychophysiologists. Advertising has been concerned with these emotional processes as well (e.g., Ray and Wilkie, 1970; Wheatley, 1971; Wheatley and Oshikawa, 1970).

It is impossible for a consumer to feel one way or another about a commercial if he or she does not pay attention to it. Thus, attention, awareness, and information processing, all of which interest psychophysiologists, also interest advertisers (Krugman, 1964). A key concept in understanding psychophysiological approaches to attention is the orienting response. Researchers conceptualize the orienting response as a system of unlearned motor, autonomic, and central responses elicited by noticed changes in the environment. It often occurs in response to stimulation of a low to moderate intensity. When a person is subjected to a stimulus of a relatively high magnitude, he or she usually displays a discriminably different reaction, the defensive response (Graham and Clifton, 1966). Given that one is familiar with the physiological correlates of the orienting and defensive responses, one may determine if a subject is attending to environmental input.

Finally, affective impact of and attention paid to advertising are necessary but insufficient marketing goals because advertisers want people to learn and remember the content of their advertisements. In fact, a usual method of evaluating advertising effectiveness consists of testing consumer recall of the advertisement (e.g., Clancy and Kweskin, 1971). Psychophysiologists also are interested in learning and memory and often break memory down into short-term memory (STM) and long-term memory (LTM). In theory, people place material attended to in an STM system that has limited capacity and that stores information only for a brief period of time. This information can be lost through a process of decay or of displacement. But it will enter the LTM system if it is rehearsed. Storage in LTM is relatively permanent (Craik and Blankstein, 1975). One could apply the physiological correlates of STM and LTM to advertising problems.

AUTONOMIC SYSTEMS AND PSYCHOLOGICAL PROCESSES

The autonomic nervous system (ANS), which exerts control over such bodily functions as glandular secretion and internal organ functioning, interests psychophysiologists. Traditional concepts of ANS physiology have stressed its involvement in involuntary psychological processes such as emotional reactivity. Although these ideas have been challenged (Miller, 1969), probably less voluntary control is exerted over autonomic functions than over functions controlled by the central nervous system. The two divisions of the ANS consist of sympathetic and parasympathetic systems. The sympathetic branch mobilizes the body for action while the parasympathetic branch involves itself in conserving energy.

THE PUPILLARY RESPONSE

The sympathetic system controls dilation of the pupils, while pupillary constriction reflects parasympathetic activity, and interactions of these two systems determine the size of the pupils at any one point in time. Changes in pupillary diameter occur in response to eyelid closure, environmental-lighting variation, and changes in the distance of viewed objects from the eye. The sympathetic influence also produces pupil-size fluctuations that are correlated with psychological processes.

Affective Response

Experimental interest in pupillary reflexes grew in the early 1960s, when it was demonstrated that pupil size seemed to vary directly with the hedonic value of observed stimuli. Hess and Polt (1960) photographed the pupils of six subjects, who watched pictures of varying appeal (a baby, a mother and child, a partially undressed male, a partially undressed female, and a landscape). The pupils of all these subjects usually dilated in response to the stimuli. In addition, the authors detected sex differences in responding. They interpreted their findings as demonstrating pupillary-sensitivity-to-pleasure reactions. Stimuli theoretically more pleasurable to females than males elicited greater dilation in females, and the same was true for males. Subsequent research by Hess also attempted to determine the pupillary response to unpleasant stimuli, and early results suggested that constriction followed this type of stimulus presentation. These data implied that the pupils could be used to objectively measure the valence and magnitude of emotional reactions. But even at this early stage, problems occurred. When Hess used unpleasant stimuli, pupillary dilation, not constriction, occurred. Hess concluded: "Our impression was that these were negative stimuli with an additional 'shock' content that prompted a strong emotional reaction" (Hess, 1965). Hess and his colleagues experienced further difficulties in using the pupillary response to determine emotional valence when they attempted to use the technique to determine reactions to nonvisual stimuli. The subjects' pupils dilated re-

gardless of emotional valence. The researchers obtained similar results when excerpts of music served as stimuli. Inconsistencies between self-report and pupillary data provided another difficulty for the Hess hypothesis (Hess, 1972). Despite these interpretative problems, Hess (1972) emphasized the consistent evidence and continued to espouse the use of "pupillometrics" to measure emotional valence.

Research from other laboratories produced both supportive and contradictory evidence. Hess (1972) reviewed some of this unpublished work. In one project, conducted at the Pupil Research Center at the University of Michigan, researchers used hypnotic suggestion to create affective reactions. Researchers told hypnotized subjects that they would be seeing a number of slides, some pleasant and some unpleasant. When the experimenters presented "pleasant" slides to the subjects, pupillary dilation occurred; constriction followed presentation of "unpleasant" slides. In actual fact, all slides were blank. The only difference between the different types of slides was the suggestion made by the experimenter to the subject.

To measure pupillary correlates of emotional responses, researchers often examine individuals with particular attitudes and present them with stimuli that conform or do not conform with their beliefs. Barlow (1969) recorded the pupillary responses of political conservatives and liberals who viewed slides of various political figures. His findings were consistent with Hess's because pupillary responses and verbally stated preferences agreed. Francis and Kelly (1969), on the other hand, were unable to obtain pupillary reactions that discriminated between the attitudes of choir members and physical-education students, but they did report some attitude effects when examining individuals with different religious convictions. Based on this finding, they suggested that the depth of one's beliefs may determine whether or not pupillary responses will appear.

Environmental situations also may influence the probability of obtaining consistent pupillary and self-report data. During the 1964 elections, Hess (1965) showed pictures of Barry Goldwater and Lyndon Johnson to students and employees of the University of Chicago. All subjects professed support for Johnson; however, a third of them displayed greater dilation responses for Goldwater. Hess suggested: "Certainly our data do not prove that a third of the subjects went on to vote for Goldwater. But the results do raise the interesting possibility that at least some of them did, and that in the liberal atmosphere of the university these people found it difficult to utter any pro-Goldwater sentiment." Hess thus assumed that environmental factors can inhibit valid self-report data but that pupillary responses can be used to determine the real situations. Another finding, however, indicates that environmental factors also can inhibit pupillary responsiveness. Chapman, Chapman, and Brelje (1969), for example, discovered that the personality of the experimenter conducting a study can affect the obtained pupillary data.

Finally, a number of additional studies have directly contradicted the Hess pleasantness-unpleasantness hypothesis. Paivio and Simpson (1966) were unable to detect differential changes in pupillary size when pleasant and unpleasant words were presented to their subjects, and Peavler and McLaughlin (1967) reported similar difficulties. Subjects presented with words of low, medium, and high importance also have failed to respond with differential pupillary responses (Vacchiano *et al.*, 1968). None of the eight subjects in Collins, Ellsworth, and Helmreich's (1967) study had pupillary responses that varied directly with the pleasantness of words. And

Bernick, Altman, and Mintz (1972) were unable to obtain differential pupillary activity in drug addicts' viewing control words and words having to do with drugs and sex. Work in Hess's laboratory also has revealed that it is difficult to obtain significant hedonic effects for a group of subjects when words serve as stimuli (Polt and Hess, 1968).

All these difficulties cannot be attributed to a peculiarity of word stimuli because negative findings have been reported in experiments using other pleasant and unpleasant cues (for example, Koff and Hawkes, 1968; Janisse, 1973, 1974; Hess and Polt, 1966; Hess, 1965). Janisse (1973) has argued: "For the present it appears that the most profitable avenue of future investigation lies along the continuum of intensity rather than the continuum of valence." And, as has already been pointed out, "the continuum of intensity" is what concerns psychologists when they talk about arousal or activation.

Arousal

Several researchers have examined pupillary responding in terms of arousal. Paivio and Simpson (1966) told their subjects to imagine an object or event related to various nouns. Not only did pupils dilate while this was being done, but dilation was greater for abstract than for concrete words. Based on the assumption that imagining material related to abstract words was demanding, they concluded that the pupillary reaction was "a general arousal effect" during the relatively more difficult cognitive task. In the Peavler and McLaughlin (1967) study, only slides judged capable of provoking arousal produced dilation. Bernick, Kling, and Borowitz (1971) also observed significant increases in pupil size prompted by arousal—watching an Alfred Hitchcock suspense movie.

The majority of experiments exploring

pupillary-arousal interactions have employed sexual material. Simms (1967) showed males and females slides of males and females, and pictures of the opposite sex elicited greater dilation. The responses of male homosexuals to same-sexed and to opposite-sexed visual stimuli were consistent with their sexual preferences in one study (Hess, Seltzer, and Shlien, 1965), but the reliability of this observation is questioned by the failure of Scott *et al.* (1967) to replicate. Atwood and Howell (1971) examined the pupillary responses of prison inmates convicted as female-aggressing pedophiliacs; convicts jailed for other reasons served as control subjects. The pedophiliacs displayed relatively more consistent dilation when viewing pictures of immature females than did the other convicts, who in turn responded more to slides of mature females. Male subjects in the Bernick, Kling, and Borowitz (1971) experiment responded to both homosexual and heterosexual movies with dilation. In addition, they found a correlation between pupil size and reports of penile erection by their subjects. This last observation led Zuckerman (1972) to interpret the study as a "hopeful note in the possibility of pupillographic response as a measure of sexual arousal"; but he stressed the need for replication because of the small sample size used and because of the lack of an objective measure of penile erection.

A few reports have been made of pupillary dilation during unpleasant or negative arousal states. Students fearing the firing of loud gunshots responded with dilation, and a painful loud tone produced the same effect (Nunnally *et al.,* 1967). Janisse (1974) found that subjects who experienced failure on a task dilated their pupils; but so did subjects who were successful. Janisse argued for the hypothesis of a curvilinear relationship between pupil size and affect valence and a linear relationship between size and affect intensity.

Attention

As Goldwater (1972) points out, Russian workers have included pupillary dilation as a component of the orienting response. The dilation observed by Nunnally *et al.* (1967) in subjects viewing novel stimuli supports this idea. Hutt and Anderson (1967) speculate that pupil size might be a mechanism used to shut out or to allow in environmental visual stimulation. Based on Hess's pleasantness-unpleasantness data, they argue that the dilation accompanying pleasant situations allows more light to reach the retina and therefore facilitates perception of stimuli, and the constriction associated with unpleasant situations reduces light input and therefore inhibits perception. Two conditions would have to be met before this hypothesis could be accepted. First, the pupillary response would have to precede perception of the stimulus because if perception occurred before the pupillary activity then that activity could hardly be a defense against a perception process that had already taken place. Second, it should be possible to manipulate recognition thresholds in the appropriate directions by experimentally altering pupil size. This latter requirement has received some support; but the occurrence of the first condition seems very unlikely (Stelmack and Leckett, 1974). Since the Hutt and Anderson suggestion rests on the Hess hypothesis, it too is challenged by the reported failures to obtain pupillary activity that was sensitive to affective valence. It should be noted that the correlation reported by Hutt and Anderson was small ($r = 0.18$).

If we extend the definition of attention to include attention to a particular task, the pupillary response may be a useful measure. A number of investigators have found that pupils dilate while subjects attend to such tasks as discriminating the pitch of auditory stimuli (Kahneman and Beatty, 1967), multiplying numbers (Hess and Polt, 1964), and generating mental images (Colman and Paivio, 1969). Further, the size of the dilation seems to vary directly with the difficulty of the task (Hess and Polt, 1964; Kahneman and Beatty, 1967; Kahneman *et al.,* 1969) until the task becomes too demanding; then, the pupils seem to remain at a constant level of dilation (Peavler, 1974) or to constrict below base-line values (Poock, 1973; Poock and Noel, 1975). Polt (1970) finds that punishing subjects with electric shock for missing a multiplication problem increases dilation during problem solving. He concludes that the shock contingency causes subjects to exert more "mental effort."

Learning and Memory

Kahneman and Beatty (1966), examining STM, first correlated pupillary responses with learning and memory. They orally presented a series of numbers and asked the subject to immediately repeat the numerical sequence. Pupils dilated as the subjects listened to the list of digits and constricted when the list was reported. The more demanding the task, the more the pupils dilated. Kahneman and Beatty concluded that dilation reflected a "loading function" and that constriction was associated with an "unloading function." They also noted that pupils dilated when people listened to sentences, but only after the sentence had been completed. Therefore sensory input alone does not cause dilation; apparently the cognitive processing of that input is required for the effect to occur.

Beatty and Kahneman (1966) extended these observations to LTM and discovered a linear relationship between diameter and amount of information stored in memory. They interpreted this finding as evidence "of pupil diameter as a measure of the momentary state of mental effort." This interpretation echoes the conclusions presented in the experiments exploring attention to tasks and is supported by other investigations involving memory (for example, Kahneman and Peavler, 1969; Kahneman, Onuska, and Wolman, 1968; Kahneman and Wright, 1971; Stanners and Headley, 1972; Wright and Kahneman, 1971; Craik and Blankstein, 1975; Colman and Paivio, 1970).

That pupillary size could be used to predict later recall is suggested in Peavler's study (1974), in which the researcher related various measures of pupil size to performance scores in remembering a sequence of numbers. But researchers may not always obtain this effect (for example, Kahneman and Peavler, 1969).

Pupillometrics in Advertising

When Hess reported on the correlation between pupillary responses and a subject's like and dislike of stimuli, the potential applications to advertising became apparent. Hess became a consultant first for the Interpublic and then for the Marplan communications research organizations. Advertisers employed pupillometrics to evaluate product and package design and to test advertisements, and a number of clients based their marketing decisions on these data (Hess, 1968). The experimental design often used to assess an advertisement or a commercial involved six phases:

1. a control period;
2. a picture of the product;
3. another control period;
4. the advertisement of the commercial;

5. another control period;

6. once again, a picture of the product.

According to Hess (1968), with this procedure, advertisers could determine the interest value of the advertisement or the commercial by examining pupillary response during its presentation relative to the preceding control period. They could also determine the relative change in attitude toward the product by looking at the difference between pupillary response during the first and second presentations of the picture of the product. If a choice between two different ads or commercials was involved, experimenters would present half the subjects with one ad or commercial while the other half viewed the remaining ad or commercial. Theoretically, the better of the two would elicit the greater dilation. The technique also made possible an assessment of viewer interest throughout various portions of a commercial because pupillary responses for each half-second interval were recorded. Also, experimenters often presented more than one showing of a commercial to subjects, since it was found that initial positive responses could become negative after a number of viewings.

Use of the pupillometric technique spread, and researchers in the field published a number of articles in trade journals on the subject (Krugman, 1964, 1965; Halpern, 1967; Coverdale and Leavitt, 1968; van Bortel, 1968; Stafford, Birdwell, and Von Tassel, 1970).

Rice (1974), having traced the history of pupillometrics in advertising, points out that its popularity declined as more empirical challenges to the Hess hypothesis appeared. But this does not mean that the measure is useless; it still can be used to determine if a consumer attends to a commercial. Others in the industry have come to believe that pupillometrics can present a picture of

arousal (Blackwell, Hansel, and Sternthal, 1970), but that caution is necessary in interpreting data. In short, more research is necessary before the psychological mechanisms underlying the response can be specified with certainty.

Summary

The pupillary response appears sensitive to psychological influences. Hess suggests that the measure can be used to detect affective valence, but the numerous empirical challenges to this interpretation suggest that we should give strong consideration to alternative explanations. The Janisse (1974) statement that "pupil size is linearly related to intensity of affect and curvilinearly related to its valence" perhaps handles the data better. Also, pupillary responses appear to accompany a number of other psychological processes, including arousal, attention, problem solving, learning, and memory; and the amount of "mental energy" demanded during these psychological processes may determine pupil size. Pupillometrics therefore may be useful in evaluating advertising even if it does not directly measure consumer like and dislike.

ELECTRODERMAL RESPONSES

Several measurements are available for studying electrical phenomena related to the skin. One measurement monitors the amount of resistance or conductance the skin offers to a small amount of current or voltage passed between two electrodes. Researchers have used skin-conductance or skin-resistance data in numerous psychophysiological investigations. Another measurement, skin potential, requires no externally applied current or voltage and records electrical activity intrinsic to the skin. The physical mechanisms underlying these responses remain the subject of considerable speculation (Edelberg, 1972), but they probably can be conceptualized most advantageously as indicants of sweat-gland activity.

Affective Response

Some evidence suggests that skin responses may be similar to pupillary responses in serving as indicators of affective magnitude but not valence. Stern, Farr, and Ray (1975) review evidence obtained earlier in this century that is consistent with this idea. Lanier (1941) finds that words with both positive and negative connotations elicit greater responses than words with only one connotation. He suggests that an "affective conflict" produced by these words creates a higher arousal state. Manning and Melchiori (1974) note that female college students displayed Galvanic Skin Responses (GSRs) to taboo (profane), illness, violence, and negatively valenced political words and that the greatest responses were for the taboo words. Students asked to discuss "the person they disliked the most" displayed greater sweat-gland activity than when they discussed a neutral topic (Baker, Sandman, and Pepinsky, 1975). Burstein *et al.* (1965) also demonstrate the sensitivity of both skin resistance and skin potential to emotionally charged words.

A number of studies have indicated that GSR measurements are sensitive to stimuli that either conform or are inconsistent with an individual's attitude (for example, Snoek and Dobbs, 1967; Clore and Gormley, 1974; Dickson and McGinnies, 1966; Cooper and Pollock, 1959; Cooper and Siegel, 1956). Overall, evidence dealing with the GSR and the affective impact of stimuli suggests that

1. the GSR is sensitive to these stimuli;
2. the GSR can measure magnitude but not valence of input;
3. the GSR may be more reactive to disagreeable material.

Arousal

A considerable amount of additional data dealing with the GSR and arousal, only a small sampling of which are examined here, indicates responsivity to affective input. Wilson (1966), examining the arousing properties of colors, tested the assumption that red is more arousing than green. He hypothesizes that by the process of natural selection or learning, extreme hues become associated with dangerous wave lengths such as ultraviolet and infrared and are more arousing than are hues in the middle, "safe" portion of the spectrum. Data collected by Nourse and Welch (1971) support this hypothesis, but not data collected by Hooke, Youell, and Etkin (1975).

Perhaps the greatest amount of work concerning GSR and arousal has focused on sexual stimuli. A study conducted by Thompson and Dixon (1974) suggests that researchers could use psychophysiological techniques to obtain objective measures of sexual arousal. Zuckerman (1972) reviews this literature and concludes that there are five generalizations about the relationship between skin responses and sexual stimuli:

1. Researchers almost invariably obtain GSRs when pictures of nude females are used as stimuli. These GSRs exceed those obtained for sexually neutral stimuli and pictures of clothed females.
2. Sweat-gland activity is enhanced while reading and fantasizing about material and while viewing erotic movies.
3. The use of male and female erotic stimuli does not produce differential GSRs.
4. The sexual preferences of subjects has little

effect on the GSR since males who are homo-sexual, heterosexual, or have a fetish all respond to pictures of nude females.

5. "Several authors have cautioned against interpreting electrodermal responses as specific measures of sexual arousal since they are known to be equally responsive in negative affective reactions. This caution is well taken. It is conceivable that a group of males might show equal electrodermal responsivity to male and female nudes because the former might elicit anxiety or surprise and the latter might elicit sexual arousal."

Thus, the evidence implies that autonomic measures may yield a picture of magnitude but not of valence.

Numerous studies could be cited to illustrate the responsivity of GSR to negative arousal states (for example, Ax, 1953; Learmonth, Ackerly, and Kaplan, 1959; Speisman, Osborn, and Lazarus, 1961; Wilson, 1967).

Attention

Electrodermal activity is a component of the orienting response and therefore is a measure of attention. The specific reaction is usually an increase in GSR amplitude in response to some stimulus presentation (e.g., Allen, Hill, and Wickens, 1963; Berlyne et al., 1963; Hetrick and Hartley, 1973; Velden, 1974). Fried, Korn, and Welch (1966) did not obtain the orienting response when they presented novel light stimuli. Nor did Fried et al. (1967) obtain the response when they used stimulus omission as the novel cue. Furedy (1968) collected data to suggest that these two failures were due to a concentration on the wrong measure of electrodermal activity. When he examined transient changes in skin response rather than long-term shifts, the GSR amplitude increase seemed to be a reliable part of the orienting response. Furthermore,

Jackson (1974) reports a direct relationship between GSR and stimulus magnitude.

Electrodermal alterations accompany attention to tasks also (for example, Tursky, Schwartz, and Crider, 1970; Kaiser and Sandman, 1975). As with the pupillary response, electrodermal activity tends to increase directly with the difficulty of the task (Kahneman et al., 1969).

Learning and Memory

With regard to the GSR during learning, Craik and Blankstein (1975) review the literature and conclude "that such autonomic measures as . . . GSR largely reflect the amount of effort or degree of attention the subject is giving to the material being learned." One of the major empirical findings linking GSR and memory has to do with the relationship between arousal and memory. Kleinsmith and Kaplan (1963) presented 48 subjects with eight words, each having an associated number. When recall sessions were conducted a short period of time after learning (e.g., two minutes), subjects displayed better recall for numbers associated with low-arousal words. At long intervals (e.g., one week), subjects displayed better recall with high-arousal words. But electrodermal activity at recall does not correlate with memory performance (Kaplan and Kaplan, 1968). This empirical demonstration led to a number of experimental explorations into and hypotheses about the effect. According to Craik and Blankstein (1975), researchers have replicated and generally accepted the relationship between arousal during learning and enhanced LTM. The effects of arousal on STM have remained confusing. The type of material learned may be an important variable, but it is not possible to make firm conclusions even when this influence is taken into consideration. But from a pragmatic point of view, the most important implications are that

1. arousal increases LTM;
2. GSR can measure arousal;
3. GSR may loosely predict recall performance;
4. monitoring electrodermal activity therefore may be useful in the assessment of how well an advertisement will make a long-term impression on consumers.

Electrodermal Responses in Advertising

We could locate only three published attempts at using skin responses to assess advertising. Caffyn (1964) suggests that researchers could use the GSR to monitor emotional reactivity to advertising, and he points out that it should be more difficult for consumers to misrepresent their feelings when it is used. He employed the GSR to examine responses to newspaper ads, posters, and television commercials. The dependent variable that proved most sensitive in this work was the sum of the amplitudes of each GSR during stimulus presentation. Once again, response magnitude, but not valence, could be predicted. GSR then could be combined with verbal reports of the direction of affective reaction to gain an assessment of the advertising material.

Kohan (1968) monitored the GSR of twenty subjects who were watching several commercials. He found that electrodermal activity increases as "interest in commercials builds up." Physiological and verbal indications of consumer reactions did not correlate well, and Kohan suggests that the physiological response was better because it was less biased.

Bose and Ghosh (1976) report significant correlations between GSR and advertising-preference data. They presented 10 magazine advertisements to postgraduate students, and the obtained association was between electrodermal activity and the rank order of advertisement preference.

Summary

In trying to apply electrodermal monitoring to advertising assessment, several points seem particularly salient.

1. GSRs are sensitive to affective stimuli; but they appear to be good measures only of response magnitude, not of valence.
2. As a component of the orienting response, electrodermal activity may help present a picture of ongoing attentional processes.
3. Arousal is an important facilitator of LTM. Since skin responses can be used to measure arousal, they may serve usefully as an indirect measure of long-term advertising recall.
4. Researchers have reported several successful attempts at using the GSR to judge advertising effectiveness.

HEART RATE

The electrocardiogram (EKG) registers the electrical discharges associated with the muscle contraction of the heart—it monitors heart rate. The EKG gives a readout of each beat. Rate is determined by counting the number of beats per unit period of time (usually one minute).

Affective Response

Not a great deal of data has been published concerning heart-rate responses to pleasurable and unpleasurable stimuli (Stern, Farr, and Ray, 1975). Research done in the early part of this century indicates that heart-rate acceleration is the response to unpleasant stimuli and that deceleration accompanies pleasant stimuli. But the measure is not always a sensitive indicant of the emotional reaction to stimuli. For example, Hooke, Youell, and Etkin (1975) find no relationship between heart rate and preference for different colors.

Even when cardiac sensitivity to emotionally valenced materials can be demonstrated, complex variables may influence the pattern of responsiveness. For example, Israel (1969) presented subjects with a number of slides and monitored heart rate. Later, each subject evaluated these stimuli according to preference, and the heart rate during presentation of the most preferred stimuli was compared to that during the least preferred stimuli. Cardiac deceleration accompanied all stimulus presentations, but personality characteristics were critical in determining cardiac-response patterning. Israel defined half the subjects as "sharpeners." This term refers to those individuals who utilize a particular cognitive style in relating to the environment, a style characterized by a tendency to examine all stimuli regardless of their interest value. "Levelers" attend only to those stimuli that are interesting and not too arousing. In Israel's experiment, sharpeners responded to both types of stimuli with equal amounts of deceleration. Levelers, in contrast, decelerated to both types, but the magnitude of deceleration was greater to the most preferred stimuli. These data therefore are consistent with the idea that levelers, not sharpeners, tend to respond differentially to some categories of stimulus input. These results can best be discussed as reflections of ongoing attentional processes. In terms of the practical implications of these findings, it appears that heart rate could be used to monitor degree of pleasantness only for individuals maintaining the leveling cognitive style.

Other data collected in early parts of this century suggest that if pleasure is thought of in terms of humor, then a direct relation exists between pleasure and heart rate. However, Stern, Farr, and Ray (1975), who review this evidence, also report on a study conducted by Sternbach in which eight-year-olds were shown the movie *Bambi* and were asked which portions were the "saddest, scariest, nicest, and funniest." No consistent relationship between autonomic activity and the pleasantness of stimuli was discovered. Averill's (1969) study is more consistent with the older work. He used movie stimuli to induce sadness and mirth. He noted that the maximal increase in heart rate was higher in the mirth film.

As this brief review indicates, the evidence relating heart rate to pleasant and unpleasant stimulus input is sketchy and often contradictory, and the cognitive style of the individual may exert a profound influence on the data obtained. Until more research has been conducted, heart-rate monitoring has little practical utility in assessing pleasantness and unpleasantness in advertising.

Arousal

Heart rate also is unlikely to be useful in measuring activation states such as sexual arousal, not because of a lack of evidence, but because of a demonstrated relative insensitivity to this psychological state. Zuckerman's (1972) review of the literature is again relevant. He states, "The research using heart rate as a measure of sexual arousal indicates that this measure is not very sensitive to sexual arousal. . . . Erotic motion pictures may stimulate a small increase in heart rate, but even these effects are not consistent across experiments. . . . Even with the highly erotic stimulus of a stag movie, heart rate changes were minimal in most subjects and, when pronounced, were not associated with a more direct measure of arousal, penile erection." Some studies even indicate that at least in females, cardiac deceleration may accompany presentation of erotic stimuli (Hamrick, 1974; Ray and Thompson, 1974).

Negative arousal states also seem to be accompanied by complex cardiac reactions. For example, Ax (1953) finds the response patterns for fear and anger discriminably different, one difference being a greater number of cardiac decelerations during anger. Physical stressors often elicit cardiac acceleration (e.g., Craig and Woods, 1969; Jennings *et al.*, 1970). But contradictory findings have been reported for cardiac activity during stimuli that predict aversive stimulation such as shock. During these anxiety situations, some report deceleration (e.g., Notterman, Schoenfeld, and Bersh, 1952), while others note acceleration (e.g., Lacey and Smith, 1954). Deane and Zeaman (1958) find accelerative responding during early aversive experience and decelerative responding later. Deane (1961) attempts to explain the contradictory data by claiming that acceleration accompanies anxiety or dread and that deceleration accompanies fear, which is experienced at times close to the aversive event. He reports data consistent with this hypothesis. Although some conflicting evidence has been reported (e.g., Bowers, 1971), subsequent research lends support to the idea of an anxiety-acceleration linkage. In regards to the fear-deceleration tie, Deane (1969) later concludes that heart-rate slowing reflects on orientation to stimulation of any kind rather than being a fear response. Observations outside the laboratory setting further indicate stress-related cardiac acceleration. Parachutists preparing to make a jump have displayed heart-rate increases that declined just before leaving the airplane (Fenz and Jones, 1974). Parachutists with poor ability,

who presumably would be more anxious, displayed greater acceleration and less prejump deceleration than jumpers with good ability. As another illustration of a direct relationship between anxiety and cardiac activity, Shapiro (1975) notes that children remaining calm while receiving an injection showed less cardiac acceleration than those who were obviously disturbed.

Overall, the best generalization about heart rate and arousal is that cardiac activity in some manner may be directly related to arousal magnitude, but deceleration produced by attentional processes may obscure the relationship. Deane's (1969) statement concerning deceleration as an orienting response to any type of stimulation was made in regard to negative arousal states, but it might be true for positive arousal states as well. For example, attention-produced deceleration may be a factor in the failure to find consistent acceleration during sexual arousal (Zuckerman, 1972).

Attention

Heart rate appears to be an important component of psychophysiological attention mechanisms. Generally, cardiac deceleration accompanies the orienting response and acceleration the defensive response (Graham and Clifton, 1966). Some researchers (e.g., Lang and Hnatiow, 1962) report a diphasic orienting response characterized by an initial acceleration followed by deceleration; but Graham and Clifton (1966), who review this evidence, conclude: "The acceleratory phase appeared to be relatively small, of questionable reliability, and relatively resistant to habituation." This last point is of interest because, by definition, the orienting response should decline in strength as a function of stimulus repetition. Graham and Clifton suggest alternative explanations of this initial acceleratory phase and argue that deceleration is in fact the true cardiac component of the orienting response.

Researchers (Lacey, 1967; Lacey and Lacey, 1970) argue that these cardiac events are not only of correlational significance, but have causational implications as well. Heart rate affects central-nervous-system structures via blood-pressure-induced alterations in the firing of cells located in the aortic arch and carotid sinuses. These central stuctures, in turn, serve as "gates" that facilitate or inhibit the flow of sensory input from the periphery to central stimulus-processing structures. When heart rate is high, these "gates" close, thereby reducing attention to environmental input; when heart rate is low, the "gates" open and increase the amount of sensory input to the brain.

Thus heart-rate acceleration theoretically becomes a means of reducing attention to the environment. In other circumstances in which attention to environmental stimuli is contraindicated, cardiac acceleration also apparently occurs. For example, problem solving that requires internal concentration and as little external disturbance as possible has been associated with tachycardia (heart-rate acceleration) in numerous experiments (e.g., Kahneman et al., 1969; Kaiser and Sandman, 1975; Tursky, Schwartz, and Crider, 1970). Cardiac deceleration operates in the opposite direction, according to Lacey, and situations or portions of tasks requiring attention to external stimulus events are associated with heart-rate slowing in a number of studies (e.g., Duncan-Johnson and Coles, 1974; Obrist et al., 1970).

The Lacey explanation of these data has been challenged, and alternative explanations have been formulated. The primary point of controversy seems to be whether or not the cardiac events are of causal significance, as Lacey claims, or of correlational significance, as suggested by others (e.g., Obrist et al., 1970). From a practical standpoint however the implication is that heart rate could be a useful tool in measuring attention to external stimuli.

Learning and Memory

Obrist (1962) measured heart rate during verbal learning tasks in five subjects across 28 to 36 sessions, and the within-subject relationships between heart rate and performance varied radically. Three subjects displayed a curvilinear relationship with maximal performance at medium heart-rate levels. Obrist obtained linear correlations, both positive and negative, with the other two. Spence, Lugo, and Youdin (1972) present a more consistent picture. They had their subjects listen to a 17-minute recording while heart rate was monitored. Subjects were aware of the critical materials to be learned in this recording, and the researchers noted cardiac deceleration when these important passages were presented. They interpreted these data in terms of the Lacey hypothesis, also remarking: "We would add that cubic change in rate is a good predictor of later recall; such a rate change seems to be a sign that the stimulus is being converted into long-term storage." Thus, there is some indication that EKG may be utilized to predict recall performance.

Summary

As this review suggests, heart rate is a complex measure. It is difficult to formulate with any certainty generalizations about this physiological response during a number of psychological processes. But cardiac activity seems to be a sensitive measure of attentional processes, and at least one study has suggested that it could be used to predict recall. The attention-cardiac relationship thus suggests that the EKG may have applied significance in assessing advertising.

CONCLUSIONS

We have tried in this report to review some psychophysiological response systems that could prove worthwhile in determining advertising effectiveness. Other systems and other techniques are available. We could not review all possible response systems; nor could we examine all the data collected on the three systems of interest. Nevertheless, the studies reviewed indicate that pupillary responses, electrodermal activity, and heart rate are sensitive to psychological processes of concern in advertising. Pupillary and electrodermal activity seem especially useful in making statements about the magnitude of a subject's responsiveness to advertisement content, and heart rate also may aid in determining a consumer's attention. A safe conclusion would be that as many physiological and psychological measures as possible should be used in trying to apply psychophysiological techniques to marketing decision making. As Hess (1972) has stated: "the simultaneous use of several different measures will certainly give us far more information than would any one of them alone. We cannot afford to be misled into thinking that any single dimension of measurement of behavioral response systems will provide complete information." Although Hess expresses this interest in exploring interrelationships between pupillary responses, electrodermal activity, and heart-rate changes in advertising research, apparently no such data have been published. Research is needed in this area.

REFERENCES

Allen, C. K., F. A. Hill, and D. D. Wickens. The Orienting Reflex as a Function of the Interstimulus Interval of Compound Stimuli. *Journal of Experimental Psychology,* Vol. 65, No. 3, March 1963, pp. 309–316.

Atwood, R. W., and R. J. Howell. Pupillometric and Personality Test Score Differences of Female Aggressing Pedophiliacs and Normals. *Psychonomic Science,* Vol. 22, No. 2, January 1971, pp. 115–116.

Averill, J. R. Autonomic Response Patterns during Sadness and Mirth. *Psychophysiology,* Vol. 5, No. 4, April 1969, pp. 399–414.

Ax, A. F. The Physiological Differentiation between Fear and Anger in Humans. *Psychosomatic Medicine,* Vol. 15, No. 5, September 1953, pp. 433–442.

Baker, W. M., C. A. Sandman, and H. B. Pepinsky. Affectivity of Task, Rehearsal Time, and Physiological Response. *Journal of Abnormal Psychology,* Vol. 84, No. 4, October 1975, pp. 539–544.

Barlow, J. D. Pupillary Size as an Index of Preference in Political Candidates. *Perceptual and Motor Skills.* Vol. 28, No. 2, April 1969, pp. 587–590.

Beatty, J., and D. Kahneman. Pupillary Changes in Two Memory Tasks. *Psychonomic Science,* Vol. 5, No. 10, August 1966, pp. 371–372.

Berlyne, D. E., *et al.* Novelty, Complexity, Incongruity, Extrinsic Motivation, and the GSR. *Journal of Experimental Psychology,* Vol. 66, No. 6, December 1963, pp. 560–567.

Bernick, N., F. Altman, and D. L. Mintz, Pupil Responses of Addicts in Treatment to Drug Culture Argot: II. Responses during Verbalization of Visually Presented Words. *Psychonomic Science,* Vol. 28, No. 2, July 1972, pp. 81–82.

Bernick, N., A. Kling, and G. Borowitz. Physiologic Differentiation of Sexual Arousal and Anxiety. *Psychosomatic Medicine,* Vol. 33, No. 4, July 1971, pp. 341–352.

Blackwell, R. D., J. S. Hansel, and B. Sternthal. Pupil Dilation: What Does It Measure? *Journal of Advertising Research,* Vol. 10, No. 4, August 1970, pp. 15–18.

Bose, S., and A. Ghosh. Efficacy of Psychogalvanoscopic Readings to Rank Appealing Advertisements Concurrent to Preferences of "Ad" Readers. *Indian Journal of Applied Psychology,* Vol. 11, No. 1, January 1974, pp. 7–11.

Bowers, K. S. The Effects of UCS Temporal Uncertainty on Heart Rate and Pain. *Psychophysiology,* Vol. 8, No. 3, May 1971, pp. 382–389.

Burstein, K. R., *et al.* A Comparison of Skin Potential and Skin Resistance Responses as Measures of Emotional Responsivity. *Psychophysiology,* Vol. 2, No. 1, July 1965, pp. 14–24.

Caffyn, J. M. Psychological Laboratory Techniques in Copy Research. *Journal of Advertising Research,* Vol. 4, No. 4, August 1964, pp. 45–50.

Chapman, L. J., J. P. Chapman, and T. Brelje. Influence of the Experimenter on Pupillary Dilation to Sexually Provocative Pictures. *Journal of Abnormal Psychology,* Vol. 74, No. 3, June 1969, pp. 396–400.

Clancy, K. J., and D. M. Kweskin. TV Commercial Recall Correlates. *Journal of Advertising Research,* Vol. 11, No. 2, April 1971, pp. 18–20.

Clore, G. L., and J. B. Gormly. Knowing, Feeling, and Liking: A Psychophysiological Study of Attraction. *Journal of Research in Personality,* Vol. 8, No. 3, October 1974, pp. 218–230.

Collins, B. E., P. C. Ellsworth, and R. L. Helmreich. Correlations between Pupil Size and Semantic Differential: An Experimental Paradigm and Pilot Study. *Psychonomic Science,* Vol. 9, No. 12, December 1967, pp. 627–628.

Colman, F. D., and A. Paivio. Pupillary Response and Galvanic Skin Response during an Imagery Task. *Psychonomic Science,* Vol. 16, No. 6, September 1969, pp. 296–297.

_____. Pupillary Dilation and Mediation Processes during Paired-Associate Learning. *Canadian Journal of Psychology,* Vol. 24, No. 4, August 1970, pp. 261–270.

Cooper, J. B., and D. Pollock. The Identification of Prejudicial Attitudes by the Galvanic Skin Response. *Journal of Social Psychology,* Vol. 50, No. 2, November 1959, pp. 241–245.

Cooper, J. B., and H. E. Siegel. The Galvanic Skin Response as a Measure of Emotion in Prejudice. *Journal of Psychology,* Vol. 42, No. 1, January 1956, pp. 149–155.

Coverdale, H. L., and C. Leavitt. Pupil Size as a Predictor of Coupon Return Performance: A Directional Trend Approach. In Al-

vin Rosenstein (Ed.). *Proceedings, Seventy-sixth Annual Convention, American Psychological Association.* Washington, D.C., 1968.

Craig, K., and K. Woods. Physiological Differentiation of Direct and Vicarious Affective Arousal. *Canadian Journal of Behavioral Science,* Vol. 1, No. 2, April 1969, pp. 98–105.

Craik, F. I. M., and K. R. Blankstein, Psychophysiology and Human Memory. In P. H. Venables and M. J. Christie (Eds.). *Research in Psychophysiology.* London: Wiley, 1975.

Deane, G. E. Human Heart Rate Responses during Experimentally Induced Anxiety. *Journal of Experimental Psychology,* Vol. 61, No. 6, June 1961, pp. 489–493.

_____. Cardiac Activity during Experimentally Induced Anxiety. *Psychophysiology,* Vol. 6, No. 1, July 1969, pp. 17–30.

Deane, G. E., and D. Zeaman. Human Heart Rate during Anxiety. *Perceptual and Motor Skills,* Vol. 8, No. 1, March 1958, pp. 103–106.

Dickson, H. W., and E. McGinnies. Affectivity in the Arousal of Attitude as Measured by Galvanic Skin Response. *American Journal of Psychology,* Vol. 79, No. 4, December 1966, pp. 584–589.

Duncan-Johnson, C. C., and M. G. Coles. Heart Rate and Disjunctive Reaction Time: The Effects of Discrimination Requirements. *Journal of Experimental Psychology,* Vol. 103, No. 6, December 1974, pp. 1160–1168.

Edelberg, R. Electrical Activity of the Skin: Its Measurement and Uses in Psychophysiology. In N. S. Greenfield and R. A. Steinbach (Eds.). *Handbook of Psychophysiology.* New York: Holt, Rinehart and Winston, 1972.

Elliott, R. Heart Rate in Anticipation of Shocks Which Have Different Probabilities of Occurrences. *Psychological Reports,* Vol. 36, No. 3, June 1975, pp. 923–931.

Fenz, W. D., and G. B. Jones. Cardiac Conditioning in a Reaction Time Task and Heart Rate Control during Real Life Stress. *Journal of Psychosomatic Research,* Vol. 18, No. 3, June 1974, pp. 199–203.

Francis, R. D., and M. R. Kelly. An Investigation of the Relationship between Word Stimuli and Optical Pupil Size. *Australian Journal of Psychology.* Vol. 21, No. 2, August 1969, pp. 117–125.

Fried, R., *et al.* Is No-Stimulus a Stimulus? *Journal*

of Experimental Psychology, Vol. 73, No. 1, January 1967, pp. 145–146.

Fried, R., S. Korn, and L. Welch. Effect of Change in Sequential Stimuli on GSR Adaptation. *Journal of Experimental Psychology,* Vol. 72, No. 3, September 1966, pp. 325–327.

Furedy, J. J. Novelty and the Measurement of GSR. *Journal of Experimental Psychology,* Vol. 76, No. 4, April 1968, pp. 501–503.

Goldwater, B. C. Psychological Significance of Pupillary Movements. *Psychological Bulletin,* Vol. 77, No. 5, May 1972, pp. 340–355.

Graham, F. K., and R. K. Clifton. Heart-Rate Change as a Component of the Orienting Response. *Psychological Bulletin,* Vol. 65, No. 5, May 1966, pp. 305–320.

Halpern, S. Application of Pupil Response to Before and After Experiments, *Journal of Marketing Research,* Vol. 4, No. 3, August 1967, pp. 320–321.

Hamrick, N. D. Physiological and Verbal Responses to Erotic Visual Stimuli in a Female Population. *Behavioral Engineering,* Vol. 2, No. 1, Summer-Fall 1974, pp. 9–16.

Hess, E. H. Attitude and Pupil Size, *Scientific American,* Vol. 212, No. 4, April 1965, pp. 46–54.

_____. Pupillometrics. In F. M. Bass, C. W. King, and E. A. Pessemier (Eds.). *Applications of the Sciences in Marketing Impact.* New York: Wiley, 1968.

_____. Pupillometrics: A Method of Studying Mental, Emotional, and Sensory Processes. In N. S. Greenfield and R. A. Sternbach (Eds.). *Handbook of Psychophysiology.* New York: Holt, Rinehart and Winston, 1972.

Hess, E. H., and J. M. Polt. Pupil Size as Related to Interest Value of Visual Stimuli. *Science,* Vol. 132, No. 3423, August 1960, pp. 349–350.

_____. Pupil size in Relation to Mental Activity during Simple Problem Solving. *Science.* Vol. 143, No. 3611, March 1964, pp. 1190–1192.

_____. Changes in Pupil Size as a Measure of Taste Difference. *Perceptual and Motor Skills,* Vol. 23, No. 2, October 1966, pp. 451–455.

Hess, E. H., A. L. Seltzer, and J. M. Shlien. Pupil Responses of Hetero- and Homosexual Males to Pictures of Men and Women: A Pilot Study. *Journal of Abnormal Psychology,* Vol. 70, No. 3, June 1965, pp. 165–168.

Hetrick, R. D., and H. V. Hartley. Multiple

Physiological Responses to Novel Acoustic Stimuli. *Journal of Auditory Research,* Vol. 13, No. 2, April 1973, pp. 93–96.

Hooke, J. F., K. J. Youell, and M. W. Etkin. Color Preference and Arousal. *Perceptual and Motor Skills,* Vol. 40, No. 3, June 1975, p. 710.

Hutt, L. D., and J. P. Anderson. The Relationship between Pupil Size and Recognition Threshold. *Psychonomic Science,* Vol. 9, No. 8, August 1967, pp. 477–479.

Israel, N. R. Leveling-Sharpening and Anticipatory Cardiac Response. *Psychosomatic Medicine,* Vol. 31, No. 6, November 1969, pp. 499–509.

Jackson, J. C. Amplitide and Habituation of the Orienting Reflex as a Function of Stimulus Intensity. *Psychophysiology,* Vol. 11, No. 6, November 1974, pp. 647–659.

Janisse, M. P. Pupil Size and Affect: A Critical Review of the Literature since 1960. *The Canadian Psychologist,* Vol. 14, No. 4, October 1973, pp. 311–329.

_____. Pupil Size, Affect, and Exposure Frequency, *Social Behavior and Personality,* Vol. 2, No. 2, July 1974, pp. 125–146.

Jennings, J. R., *et al.* Some Parameters of Heart Rate Change: Perceptual versus Motor Task Requirements, Noxiousness, and Uncertainty, *Psychophysiology,* Vol. 7, No. 2, September 1970, pp. 194–212.

Kahneman, D., and J. Beatty. Pupil Diameter and Load on Memory. *Science,* Vol. 154, No. 3756, December 1966, pp. 1583–1585.

_____. Pupillary Responses in a Pitch Discrimination Task. *Perception and Psychophysics,* Vol. 2, No. 3, March 1967, pp. 101–105.

Kahneman, D., *et al.* Pupillary, Heart Rate, and Skin Resistance during a Mental Task. *Journal of Experimental Psychology,* Vol. 79, No. 1, January 1969, pp. 164–167.

Kahneman, D., L. Onuska, and R. E. Wolman. Effect of Grouping on the Pupillary Response in a Short-Term Memory Task. *Quarterly Journal of Experimental Psychology,* Vol. 20, No. 3, August 1968, pp. 309–311.

Kahneman, D., and W. S. Peavler, Incentive Effects and Pupillary Changes in Association Learning. *Journal of Experimental Psychology,* Vol. 79, No. 2, February 1969, pp. 312–318.

Kahneman, D., and P. Wright. Changes of Pupil

Size and Rehearsal Strategies in a Short-Term Memory Task. *Quarterly Journal of Experimental Psychology,* Vol. 23, No. 2, May 1971, pp. 187–196.

Kaiser, D. N., and C. A. Sandman. Physiological Patterns Accompanying Complex Problem Solving during Warning and Nonwarning Conditions. *Journal of Comparative and Physiological Psychology,* Vol. 89, No. 4, June 1975, pp. 357–363.

Kaplan, S., and R. Kaplan. Arousal and Memory: A Comment. *Psychonomic Science,* Vol. 10, No. 8, March 1968, pp. 291–292.

Kleinsmith, L. J., and S. Kaplan. Paired-Associate Learning as a Function of Arousal and Interpolated Interval. *Journal of Experimental Psychology,* Vol. 65, No. 2, February 1963, pp. 190–193.

Koff, R. H., and T. H. Hawkes. Sociometric Choice: A Study in Pupillary Response. *Perceptual and Motor Skills,* Vol. 27, No. 2, October 1968, pp. 395–402.

Kohan, X. A Physiological Measure of Commercial Effectiveness. *Journal of Advertising Research.* Vol. 8, No. 4, August 1968, pp. 46–48.

Krugman, H. E. Some Applications of Pupil Measurement. *Journal of Marketing Research,* Vol. 1, No. 4, November 1964, pp. 15–19.

_____. A Comparison of Physical and Verbal Responses to Television Commercials. *Public Opinion Quarterly,* Vol. 29, No. 2, Summer 1965, pp. 323–325.

Lacey, J. I. Somatic Response Patterning and Stress: Some Revisions of Activation Theory. In M. H. Appley and R. Trumbull (Eds.). *Psychological Stress: Issues in Research.* New York: Appleton-Century-Crofts, 1967.

Lacey, J. I., and B. C. Lacey. Some Autonomic—Central Nervous System Interrelationships. In P. Black (Ed.). *Physiological Correlates of Emotion.* New York: Academic, 1970.

Lacey, J. I., and R. L. Smith. Conditioning and Generalization of Unconscious Anxiety. *Science.* Vol. 120, No. 3130, December 1954, pp. 1045–1052.

Lang, P. J., and M. Hnatiow. Stimulus Repetition and the Heart Rate Response. *Journal of Comparative and Physiological Psychology,* Vol. 55, No. 5, October 1962, pp. 781–785.

Lanier, L. H. An Experimental Study of "Affective Conflict." *Journal of Psychology,* Vol. 11, No. 1, January 1941, pp. 199–217.

Learmonth, G. J., W. Ackerly, and M. Kaplan. Relationship between Palmar Skin Potential during Stress and Personality Variables. *Psychosomatic Medicine,* Vol. 21, No. 2, April 1959, pp. 150–157.

Lindsley, D. B. Emotion. In S. S. Stevens (Ed.). *Handbook of Experimental Psychology.* New York: Wiley, 1951.

Malmo, R. B. Activation: A Neuropsychological Dimension. *Psychological Review,* Vol. 66, No. 6, November 1959, pp. 367–386.

Manning, S. K., and M. P. Melchiori. Words That Upset Urban College Students: Measured with GSR's and Rating Scales. *Journal of Social Psychology,* Vol. 94, No. 2, December 1974, pp. 305–306.

Miller, N. E. Learning of Visceral and Glandular Responses. *Science,* Vol. 163, No. 3866, January 1969, pp. 434–445.

Morrison, B. J., and R. C. Sherman. Who Responds to Sex in Advertising? *Journal of Advertising Research,* Vol. 12, No. 2, April 1972, pp. 15–19.

Notterman, J. M., W. N. Schoenfeld, and P. J. Bersh. Conditioned Heart Rate Response in Human Beings during Experimental Anxiety. *Journal of Comparative and Physiological Psychology.* Vol. 45, No. 1, January 1952, pp. 1–8.

Nourse, J. C., and R. B. Welch. Emotional Attributes of Color: A Comparison of Violet and Green. *Perceptual and Motor Skills.* Vol. 32, No. 2, April 1971, pp. 403–406.

Nunnally, J. C., *et al.* Pupillary Response as a General Measure of Activation. *Perception and Psychophysics,* Vol. 2, No. 4, April 1967, pp. 149–155.

Obrist, P. A. Some Autonomic Correlates of Serial Learning. *Journal of Verbal Learning and Verbal Behavior,* Vol. 1, No. 2, September 1962, pp. 100–104.

Obrist, P. A., *et al.* The Cardiac-Somatic Relationship: Some Reformulations. *Psychophysiology,* Vol. 6, No. 5, March 1970, pp. 569–587.

Paivio, A., and H. M. Simpson. The Effect of Word Abstractness and Pleasantness on Pupil Size during an Imaginary Test. *Psychonomic Science,* Vol. 5, No. 2, February 1966, pp. 55–56.

Peavler, W. S., Pupil Size, Information Overload,

and Performance Differences. *Psychophysiology,* Vol. 11, No. 5, September 1974, pp. 559–566.

Peavler, W. S., and J. P. McLaughlin. The Question of Stimulus Content and Pupil Size. *Psychonomic Science,* Vol. 8, No. 12, December 1967, pp. 505–506.

Peretti, P. O. Changes in Galvanic Skin Response as Affected by Music Selection, Sex, and Academic Discipline. *Journal of Psychology,* Vol. 89, No. 2, March 1975, pp. 183–187.

Poock, G. K. Information Processing vs. Pupil Diameter. *Perceptual and Motor Skills,* Vol. 37, No. 3, December 1973, pp. 1000–1002.

Poock, G. K., and C. E. Noel. Effects of Layout of Workplace on Pupillary Diameter. *Perceptual and Motor Skills,* Vol. 40, No. 1, February 1975, p. 304.

Polt, J. M. Effect of Threat of Shock on Pupillary Response in a Problem-solving Situation. *Perceptual and Motor Skills,* Vol. 31, No. 2, October 1970, pp. 587–593.

Polt, J. M., and E. H. Hess. Changes in Pupil Size to Visually Presented Words. *Psychonomic Science,* Vol. 42, No. 8, August 1968, pp. 389–390.

Ray, M. L., and W. L. Wilkie. Fear. The Potential of an Appeal Neglected by Marketing. *Journal of Marketing,* Vol. 34, No. 1, January 1970, pp. 54–62.

Ray, R. E., and W. D. Thompson. Autonomic Correlates of Female Guilt Responses to Erotic Visual Stimuli. *Psychological Reports,* Vol. 34, No. 3, June 1974, pp. 1299–1306.

Rice, B. Rattlesnakes, French Fries, and Pupillometric Oversell. *Psychology Today,* Vol. 7, No. 9, February 1974, pp. 55–59.

Scott, T. R., *et al.* Pupillary Response and Sexual Interest Reexamined. *Journal of Clinical Psychology,* Vol. 23, No. 4, October 1967, pp. 433–438.

Shapiro, A. H. Behavior of Kibbutz and Urban Children Receiving an Injection. *Psychophysiology,* Vol. 12, No. 1, January 1975, pp. 79–82.

Simms, T. M. Pupillary Response of Male and Female Subjects to Pupillary Difference in Male and Female Picture Stimuli. *Perception and Psychophysics,* Vol. 2, No. 11, November 1967, pp. 553–555.

Snoek, J.D., and M. F. Dobbs, Galvanic Skin Responses to Agreement and Disagreement in Relation to Dogmatism. *Psychological Re-*

ports, Vol. 20, No. 1, February 1967, pp. 195–198.

Speisman, J. C., J. Osborn, and R. S. Lazarus. Cluster Analysis of Skin Resistance and Heart Rate at Rest and Under Stress. *Psychosomatic Medicine,* Vol. 23, No. 4, July 1961, pp. 323–343.

Spence, D. P., M. Lugo, and R. Youdin. Cardiac Change as a Function of Attention to and Awareness of Continuous Verbal Text. *Science,* Vol. 176, No. 4041, June 1972, pp. 1344–1346.

Stafford, J. E., A. E. Birdwell, and C. E. Von Tassel. Integrated Advertising—White Backlash? *Journal of Advertising Research,* Vol. 10, No. 2, April 1970, pp. 15–20.

Stanners, R. F., and D. B. Headley. Pupil Size and Instructional Set in Recognition and Recall. *Psychophysiology,* Vol. 9, No. 5, September 1972, pp. 504–511.

Stelmack, R. M., and W. J. Leckett. Effect of Artificial Pupil Size on Recognition Threshold. *Perceptual and Motor Skills,* Vol. 39, No. 2, October 1974, pp. 739–742.

Stern, R. M., J. H. Farr, and W. J. Ray. Pleasure. In P. H. Venables and M. J. Christie (Eds.). *Research in Psychophysiology.* London: Wiley, 1975.

Thompson, J. J., P. W. Dixon. A Power Function between Ratings of Pornographic Stimuli and Psychophysical Responses in Young Normal Adult Women. *Perceptual and Motor Skills,* Vol. 38, No. 3, June 1974, pp. 1236–1238.

Tursky, B., G. E. Schwartz, and A. Crider. Differential Patterns of Heart Rate and Skin Resistance during a Digit-Transformation Task. *Journal of Experimental Psychology,* Vol. 8, No. 3, March 1970, pp. 451–457.

Vacchiano, R. B., *et al.* Pupillary Response to Value-linked Words. *Perceptual and Motor Skills,* Vol. 27, No. 1, August 1968, pp. 207–210.

van Bortel, F. J. Commercial Applications of Pupillometrics. In F. M. Bass, C. W. King, and E. A. Pessemier (Eds.). *Applications of the Sciences in Marketing Management.* New York: Wiley, 1968.

Velden, M. An Empirical Test of Sokolov's Entropy Model of the Orienting Response. *Psychophysiology,* Vol. 11, No. 6, November 1974, pp. 682–691.

Wheatley, J. J. Marketing and the Use of Fear- or Anxiety-arousing Appeals. *Journal of Mar-*

keting, Vol. 35, No. 2, April 1971, pp. 62–64.

Wheatley, J. J., and S. Oshikawa. The Relationship between Anxiety and Positive and Negative Advertising Appeals. *Journal of Marketing Research,* Vol. 7, No. 1, February 1970, pp. 85–89.

Wilson, G. D. Arousal Properties of Red versus Green, *Perceptual and Motor Skills,* Vol. 23, No. 3, December 1966, pp. 947–949.

_____. GSR Responses to Fear-related Stimuli. *Perceptual and Motor Skills,* Vol. 24, No. 2, March 1967, pp. 401–402.

Wright, P., and D. Kahneman. Evidence for Alternative Strategies of Sentence Retention. *Quarterly Journal of Experimental Psychology,* Vol 23, No. 2, May 1971, pp. 197–213.

Zuckerman, M. Physiological Measures of Sexual Arousal in the Human. In N. S. Greenfield and R. A. Sternbach (Eds.). *Handbook of Psychophysiology.* New York: Holt, Rinehart and Winston, 1972.

Questions

1. Describe the psychophysiological bases for using autonomic measures to determine the effectiveness of an advertisement.

2. Briefly describe the three autonomic measures of advertising discussed by the authors.

3. In what areas do the authors think these psychophysiological techniques could be most useful?

4. Can you think of any other similar techniques that might be useful in marketing research? Explain your ideas.

46. Consumer Research: A State of the Art Review[1]

Jacob Jacoby

Whether one does, sells, and/or buys consumer research, it stands to reason one should be able to critically evaluate and distinguish that which is acceptable from that which is junk. However, judging from papers which continue to be published in our most prestigious journals and from research reports which often form the basis for important marketing management and public policy decisions, it is all too apparent that *too large a proportion of the consumer (including marketing) research literature is not worth the paper it is printed on or the time it takes to read.*

Nearly a decade ago, Kollat et al. wrote:

The consumer behavior literature has doubled during the last five years. This constitutes a remarkable achievement by almost any standard. Unfortunately, however, it would not be surprising if 90% of the findings and lack of findings prove to be wrong . . .[2]

Unfortunately, the same frank evaluation can be made today. Unless we begin to take corrective measures soon, we stand to all drown in a mass of meaningless and potentially misleading junk! This assertion can be documented by considering five broad categories of problems: the contemporary *theories* (and comprehensive models), *methods, measures, statistical techniques,* and *subject matter* in consumer research. Before doing so, a brief digression is needed to make three points:

1. The evaluation of consumer research should logically be predicated upon a definition of consumer behavior. Such a definition has been presented and described at length elsewhere.[3] In essence, it holds that *consumer behavior* encompasses the acquisition, consumption, and disposition of goods, services, time, and ideas by decision-making units (e.g., individuals, families, organizations, etc.). *Consumer research,* then, is simply research addressed to studying some aspect of consumer behavior.
2. I shout at the outset: MEA CULPA! I have committed many of the sins about to be described. No doubt, I will continue to commit at least some of them long after this is published and forgotten. No one of us who is a researcher is without guilt. This does not mean, however, that we should passively accept the status quo and thereby stifle the impetus toward improvement.
3. Except in one instance, naming names and citing specific articles as illustrations of the problems being iterated would probably serve few, if any, positive ends. The interested reader has only to examine the articles in our leading journals to find numerous suitable examples. On the other hand,

because they may serve a guidance function for some, names are named and specific articles cited in order to illustrate *positive* examples addressed to the issue under consideration. However, citing an article as being positive in one respect does not mean that it is void of other deficiencies.

THEORIES, MODELS, AND CONCEPTS

Over the past decade, an increasing amount of attention has been devoted to the development, presentation, and discussion of relatively comprehensive theories and models of consumer behavior.[4] Five years ago, Kollat et al.[5] noted: "These models have had little influence on consumer behavior research during the last five years. Indeed, it is rare to find a published study that has utilized, been based on, or even influenced by, any of the models identified above." Unfortunately, not much has changed since then.

"Look Ma—No Theory"

Despite the availability of consumer behavior theories and models, the impetus and rationale underlying most consumer behavior research seems to rest on little more than the availability of easy-to-use measuring instruments, the existence of more or less willing subject populations, the convenience of the computer, and/or the almost toy-like nature of sophisticated quantitative techniques. Little reliance is placed on theory, either to suggest which variables and aspects of consumer behavior are of greatest importance and in need of research or as a foundation around which to organize and integrate findings. It is still true that nothing is so practical as a good theory. However, while researchers (particularly in academia) talk a good game about the value and need for theory, their actions loudly speak otherwise.

The Post Hoc, Atheoretic, Shotgun Approach

By neglecting theory, the researcher increases the likelihood of failure to understand his own data and/or be able to meaningfully interpret and integrate his findings with findings obtained by others. This problem has elsewhere been referred to as "the atheoretical shotgun approach" to conducting research.[6] These papers tried to illustrate the nature of this problem by considering empirical attempts to relate personality variables to consumer behavior. The most frequently quoted passage is as follows:[7]

> Investigators usually take a general, broad coverage personality inventory and a list of brands, products, or product categories, and attempt to correlate subjects' responses on the inventory with statements of product use or preference. Careful examination reveals that, in most cases, the investigators have operated without the benefit of theory and with no *a priori* thought directed to *how*, or especially *why*, personality should or should not be related to that aspect of consumer behavior being studied. Statistical techniques, usually simple correlation of variants thereof, are applied and anything that turns up looking halfway interesting furnishes the basis for the Discussion section. Skill at *post*-diction and post hoc interpretation has been demonstrated, but little real understanding has resulted.

These papers went on to illustrate why it was necessary to use theoretically derived hypotheses for specifying variables and relationships in advance. That is, they called on consumer researchers to (1) make specific predictions of both expected differences and *no* differences, (2) explain the reasoning underlying these predictions, and (3) do both *prior* to conducting their research. To illustrate:

> You're sitting with a friend watching Pete Rose at bat. Rose hits a home run and your

friend says: "I knew he was going to hit that home run. He always hits a home run off right-hand pitchers when he holds his feet at approximately a 70° angle to each other and his left foot pointing directly at the pitcher."

Think of how much greater confidence you would have had in your friend's forecast if he had made this as a *prediction* just as Pete Rose was stepping into the batter's box. (Anticipating another issue raised below, replication, think of how much greater confidence you would have if your friend had predicted Rose would hit home runs on two subsequent occasions just before Rose actually hit home runs, and also predicted Rose would *not* hit a home run on eight other instances, and he did not.

Although considered in the context of relating personality variables to consumer behavior, it is clear that almost every aspect of consumer research reflects the atheoretic shotgun approach, particularly when it comes to utilizing concepts borrowed from the behavioral sciences. Most consumer researchers are still pulling shotgun triggers in the dark.

"Whoops! Did You Happen to See Where My Concept Went?"

Even in those instances where consumer researchers seem to be sincerely interested in conducting research based upon a firm conceptual foundation, they sometimes manage to misplace their concepts when it gets down to the nitty gritty. For example, Gardner states:[8]

> It is imperative that any definition of deception in advertising recognizes the interaction of the advertisement with the accumulated beliefs and experience of the consumer.

Two paragraphs later he provides a definition which *ignores* this imperative, and subsequently goes on to propose procedures which completely disregard the fact that deception may occur as a function of the prior beliefs of the consumer and not as a function of the ad (or ad campaign) in question. The reason why we cite this paper here (and below) is because it has already been cited by others—receiving the 1975 Harold H. Maynard Award "for its contribution to marketing theory and marketing thought."[9]

Another equally frustrating example is provided by those who define brand loyalty as an hypothetical construct predicted upon the cognitive dynamics of the consumer—and then proceed to base their measure of brand loyalty *solely* on the buyers's overt behavior. The consumer behavior literature contains numerous such examples of our inability to have our measures of concepts correspond to these concepts.

The "Theory of the Month" Club

Interestingly, the failure to use existing models and theories has not discouraged some from proposing new models and theories, thereby generating a different kind of problem. Several of our most respected scholars seem to belong to a "theory of the month" club which somehow requires that they periodically burst forth with new theories and rarely, if ever, provide any data collected specifically to support their theories. Perhaps those with a new theory or model should treat it like a new product: either stand behind it and give it the support it needs (i.e., test and refine it as necessary)—or take it off the market!

Single-Shot vs. Programmatic Research

Another theory-related problem is the widespread avoidance of programmatic research. Judging from the published literature, there are fewer than a dozen individuals who have conducted five or more separate investigations in systematic and sequentially integrated fashion designed to provide incremental knowledge regarding a single issue. Instead, we have a tradition of single-shot studies conducted by what one scholar has termed "Zeitgeisters-Shysters."[10]

Rarely do single-shot investigations answer all questions that need to be answered or make definitive contributions on any subject of importance. Yet many consumer researchers seem to operate under the mistaken belief that such studies are capable of yielding payout of substance and duration. I am not advocating that we do *only* programmatic research. I appreciate the allure, excitement, and challenge often inherent in such studies and the potential that they *sometimes* have for providing resolution to a problem of immediate concern. However, to make contributions of substance, it is necessary that a greater proportion of our research efforts be programmatic.

PROCEDURES AND METHODS

The Ubiquitous Verbal Report

By far, the most prevalent approach to collecting consumer data involves eliciting verbal reports via interviews or through self-administered questionnaires.

Typically, verbal reports assess either (a) recall of past events, (b) current psychological states (including attitudes, preferences, beliefs, statements of intentions to behavior, likely reactions to hypothetical events), and/or (c) sociodemographic data. Of the 44 empirical studies in Schlinger,[11] 39 (87%) were based primarily or entirely on verbal report data. Of the 36 empirical studies in the first six issues of the *Journal of Consumer Research,* 31 (more than 85%) were also based primarily or solely on verbal reports. Given the numerous biases in verbal reports and the all-too-often demonstrated discrepancy between what people say and what they actually do, it is nothing short of amazing that we persist in our slavish reliance on verbal reports as the mainstay of our research.

The problems inherent in the ubiquitous verbal report approach can be organized into three categories: (1) interviewer error, (2) respondent error, and (3) instrument error.

Interviewer Error. We will disregard consideration of interviewer errors, since more than 75% of the published verbal report studies are based upon the self-administered questionnaires.

Respondent Error. Verbal report data are predicated upon many untested and, in some cases, invalid assumptions. Many of these concern the respondent. As examples, consider the following assumptions underlying attempts to elicit recall of factual information:

- ▶ Prior learning (and rehearsal) of the information has actually taken place; that is, something actually exists in memory to be recalled.
- ▶ Once information is stored in memory, it remains there in accurate and unmodified form.
- ▶ Said information remains equally accessible through time.
- ▶ There are no respondent differences in ability to recall which would be controlled or accounted for.
- ▶ Soliciting a verbal report is a non-reactive act; that is, asking questions of respondents is unlikely to have any impact on them and on their responses.

Analogous assumptions exist with respect to assessing psychological states (e.g., attitudes, preferences, intentions, etc.) via verbal reports. For example, Bogart noted that asking the respondent a question often "forces the crystallization and expression of opinions where (previously) there were no more than chaotic swirls of thought."[12] Actually, the assumptions underlying recall of factual material are few and simple relative to assumptions underlying verbal reports used as indicants of psychological states. Perhaps the most effective way to summarize the state of affairs is to say that many of the fundamental assumptions which underlie the use of verbal reports are completely invalid. The reader is asked to cogitate regarding the ramifications of this fact.

Instrument Error. Consider further the fact that instruments for collecting verbal reports often contribute as much error variance as do interviewers or respondents, or even *more.* In general, a large proportion of our questionnaires and interview schedules impair rather than enhance efforts to collect valid data. More often than not, we employ instruments which, from the respondent's perspective, are ambiguous, intimidating, confusing, and incomprehensible. Developing a self-administered questionnaire is one of the most difficult steps in the entire research process. Unfortunately, it is commonly the most neglected.

Formulating questions and questionnaires seems like such an easy thing to do that everyone is assumed to be an expert at it, or at least adequately capable. Yet many never become aware of the literally hundreds of details that should be attended to.[13] We assume that because *we* know what we mean by our questions and *we* are not confused by the lay-out and organization of our instrument, data collected using this instrument will naturally be valid; i.e., any errors which result are obviously a function of the respondent and not a function of our instrument. As a consequence, we are often left with what computer technicians refer to as GIGO—Garbage In,

Garbage Out. In most instances, the investigator is hardly even cognizant of the fact that this has occurred.

Please note that I am NOT proposing that we do away with verbal reports (i.e, interview and self-administered questionnaires). They are a valid and vital part of our methodological armamentarium. However, if we are to continue placing such great reliance on verbal reports, the least we ought to do is devote greater attention to the basics; i.e., learn how to formulate questions and structure questionnaires. What does it mean if a finding is significant, or that the ultimate in statistical analytical techniques have been applied, if the data collection instrument generated invalid data at the outset?

But do we actually have to place slavish reliance on the verbal report? Certainly not! One alternative is to devote less time to studying what people *say they do* and spend more time examining what it is that they *do do*. In other words, we can place greater emphasis on studying actual behavior relative to the amount of effort we place on studying verbal reports regarding behavior.

There have been several recent developments in this regard.[14] We would be well advised to begin using these as alternatives and/or supplements to the ubiquitous verbal report. As Platt notes: "Beware the man of one method or one instrument . . . he tends to become method oriented rather than problem oriented."[15]

Static Methods for Dynamic Process

We also need to begin studying consumer behavior in terms of the dynamic process that it is. Virtually all consumer researchers tend to consider consumer behavior as a dynamic, information processing, decision-making, behavioral process. Yet probably 99 + % of all

consumer research conducted to date examines consumer behavior via static methods administered either before or after the fact. Instead of being captured and studied, the dynamic nature of consumer decision making and behavior is squelched and the richness of the process ignored. Our static methods are inappropriate for studying our dynamic concepts. This issue is treated in greater detail elsewhere.[16]

Roosters Cause the Sun to Rise

Consider, also, the necessity for greater reliance on the experimental method, particularly in those instances where cause-effect assertions are made or alluded to. Examination reveals a surprising number of instances in which causation is implied or actually claimed on the basis of simple correlation. It bears repeating that no matter how highly correlated the rooster's crow is to the sun rising, the rooster does not cause the sun to rise.

More and Richer Variables

A final set of methodological issues concerns the need for research which (1) incorporates measures of a variety of dependent variables, (2) explores the combined and perhaps interacting impact of a variety of independent variables, and (3) uses multiple measures of the same dependent variable.

With respect to the former, it is often possible to measure a variety of different dependent variables at little additional cost (e.g., decision accuracy, decision time, and subjective states).[17] Unfortunately, opportunities for substantially enhancing understanding through the inclusion of a variety of dependent variables are generally ignored. Equally important, we live in a complex, multivariate world. Studying the impact of one or two variables in isolation would seem to be relatively artificial and inconsequential. In other words, we need more research which examines and is able to parcel out the impact of a variety of factors impinging in concert.

It is also too often true that conclusions are accepted on the basis of a single measure of our dependent or criterion variable. The costs involved in incorporating a second or third measure of that *same* variable are usually negligible, particularly when considered in terms of the increased confidence we could have in both our findings and our concepts if we routinely used a variety of indices and found that all (or substantially all) provided the same pattern of results.[18] This second issue (namely, using multiple measures of the same variable) relates more to the validity of our measure than to our methods, and is elaborated upon below.

MEASURES AND INDICES

Our Bewildering Array of Definitions

Kollat, Blackwell, and Engel[19] have referred to the "bewildering array of definitions" that we have for many of our core concepts.

As one example, at least 55 different and distinct measures of brand loyalty have been employed in the more than 300 studies comprising the brand loyalty literature.[20] Virtually no attempt has been made to identify the good measures and weed out the poor ones. Almost everyone has his own preferred measure and seems to blithely and naively assume that findings from one investigation can easily be compared and integrated with findings from investigations which use other definitions.

The same horrendous state of affairs exists with respect to many of our other core concepts. There are at least four different types of

"innovator" definitions[21] and three different categories of "opinion leadership" definitions (i.e., self-designating, sociometric, and key informant). Each one of these categories is usually broken out into several specific forms. As examples, Rogers and Catarno,[22] King and Summers,[23] and Jacoby[24] all provide different operationalizations of self-designating opinion leadership.

More stupefying than the sheer number of our measures is the ease with which they are proposed and the uncritical manner in which they are accepted. In point of fact, most of our measures are only measures because someone *says* that they are, not because they have been shown to satisfy standard measurement criteria (validity, reliability, and sensitivity). Stated somewhat differently, most of our measures are no more sophisticated than first asserting that the number of pebbles a person can count in a ten-minute period is a measure of that person's intelligence; next, conducting a study and finding that people who can count many pebbles in ten minutes also tend to eat more; and, finally, concluding from this: people with high intelligence tend to eat more.

Wanted Desperately: Validity

A core problem is the issue of validity: Just how valid are our measures? Little attention seems to be directed toward finding out. Like our theories and models, once proposed, our measures take on an almost sacred and inviolate existence all their own. They are rarely, if ever, examined or questioned.

Several basic types of validity exist, although often described with somewhat varying terminology.[25] In a highly readable and almost layman-like presentation of the subject, Nunnally writes of three basic types:[26] (1) content validity which is generally irrelevant in consumer research, (2) predictive validity, (3) construct validity. Face validity, a nonpsychometric variety, refers to whether a *measure looks like it is measuring what it is supposed to be measuring.* Examination of the core consumer behavior journals and conference proceedings since 1970—a body of literature consisting of approximately 1000 published articles—reveals the following:

Face Validity. First, there are numerous examples of face validity. The measures used almost always look like they are measuring that which they are supposed to be measuring. However, the overwhelming majority of studies go no further, i.e., provide no empirical support. Thus, face validity is often used as a substitute for construct validity.

Predictive Validity. There are also a sizable number of studies which suggest the existence of predictive validity, that is, the measure in question seems to correlate, as predicted, with measures of other variables. Unfortunately, many investigators do not seem to recognize that predictive validity provides little, if any, *understanding* of the relationship. One can have a predictive validity coefficient of .99 and still not know why or what it means—other than the fact that the scores on one variable are highly predictive of scores on a second variable. The relationship may even be meaningless. As one example, Heeler & Ray note that Kuehn in 1963 comments that he:[27]

> . . . improved the ability of the Edwards Personal Preference Schedule (EPPS) to predict car ownership. He did it with EPPS scores computed by subtracting 'affiliation' scores from 'dominance' scores. Such a difference really has no psychological or marketing significance; it is just a mathematical manipulation that happened to work in one situation.

Obviously, high predictive validity doesn't necessarily have to be meaningful.

Cross-Validity. One type of predictive validity, however, receives too little attention, namely, cross-validity. "Whereas predictive validity is concerned with a single sample, cross-validity requires that the effectiveness of the predictor composite be tested on a *separate* independent sample from the *same* population."[28] It should be obvious that unless we can cross-validate our findings, we may really have no findings at all. Again, examination of the literature reveals few cross-validation studies.[29]

Construct Validity. The most necessary type of validity in scientific research is construct validity.

Examination of the recent literature indicates that a negligible proportion of our productivity has been directed toward determining construct validity. A large part of the problem lies in the fact that many researchers appear to naively believe that scientific research is a game played by creating measures and then applying them directly to reality. Although guided by some implicit conceptualization of what it is he is trying to measure, the consumer researcher rarely makes his implicit concepts sufficiently explicit or uses them as a basis for developing operational measures. Yet virtually all contemporary scholars of science generally agree that the concept must precede the measure.[30]

It is not our intention to provide a lengthy dissertation of the nature of scientific research. We simply wish to point out here that many of our measures are developed at the whim of a researcher with nary a thought given to whether or not it is meaningfully related to an explicit conceptual statement of the phenomena or variable in question. In most instances, our concepts have no identity apart from the instrument or procedures used to measure them.

As a result, it is actually impossible to evaluate our measures. "To be able to judge the relative value of measurements or of operations requires criteria beyond the operations themselves. If a concept is nothing but an operation, how can we talk about being mistaken or about making errors?"[31] In other words, scientific research demands that clearly articulated concepts (i.e., abstractions regarding reality) intervene between reality and the measurement of reality.

Probably the most efficient means for establishing construct validity is the Campbell and Fiske *multi-method* × *multi-trait* approach.[32] Despite the fact that numerous papers refer to this approach as something that "could" or "should" be applied, considerably less than 1% of our published literature has actually systematically explored construct validity using this approach.[33] "Before one can test the relationship between a specific trait and other traits, one must have confidence in one's measure of that trait."[34] If we cannot demonstrate that our concepts are valid, how can we act as if the findings based upon measures of these concepts are valid?

Convergent Validity. A basic and relatively easy-to-establish component of construct validity is convergent validity. This refers to the degree to which attempts to measure the same concept using two or more different measures yield the same results. Even if few construct validity investigations are available, it seems reasonable to expect that, since many of our core concepts are characterized by numerous and varied operationalizations, we should find many studies to demonstrate convergent validity.

Surely there must be many investigations which have concurrently used two or more measures of these concepts, thereby permitting us to assess convergent validity. Examination of the literature reveals that such is not the case. Somewhat incredibly, only two (out of more than 300) published studies have administered three or more brand loyalty measures concurrently to the same group of subjects, thereby permitting an examination of how these measures interrelate.[35]

Our other core concepts fare equally poorly. Data that are available often indicate that different ways of measuring innovators are negligibly related to each other.[36] Given that we cannot demonstrate adequate convergent validity, it should be alarmingly obvious that we have no basis for comparing findings from different studies or making generalizations using such measures. More widespread use of multiple measures is urgently needed so that we can begin the relatively simple job of assessing convergent validity. We are being strangled by our bad measures. Let's identify and get rid of them.

Reliability and Replication

Another fundamental problem with our measures is that data regarding their reliability, particularly test-retest reliability, are rarely provided. As an illustration, only a single study appears in the entire brand loyalty literature which measures the test-retest reliability of a set of brand loyalty measures.[37] A similar state of affairs exists with respect to indices of other core constructs.

Consider also the case of the test-retest reliability of recall data. In the entire advertising literature, only two *published* articles can be found which provide data on the test-retest reliability of recall data.[38] Young notes that results obtained in ten retests were the same as those in the initial test *in only 50% of the cases.*[39] Assuming we were ill and actually had a body temperature of 103° Farenheit, how many of us would feel comfortable using a thermometer if, with no actual change in our body temperature, this thermometer gave us readings of 97.0°, 100.6°, 98.6°, and 104.4°, all within the space of one 15-minute period. Yet we persistently employ indices of unknown reliability to study consumer purchase decisions and behavior. More sobering, we often develop expensive nationwide promotional strategies and wide-ranging public policies based on findings derived from using such indices.

There is a strong necessity for replicating our findings using different subject populations, test products, etc. The name of the game is confidence in our findings.

Measurement Based on House-of-Cards Assumption

Another frequently appearing problem is the tendency to have one's measures (or proposed measures) rest on an intertwined series of untested and sometimes unverifiable assumptions so that the measures used are sometimes five or more steps removed from the phenomenon of interest. In such cases, if a single one of the many assumptions is rendered invalid, the entire measurement system must necessarily come cascading downward. Such is the case with the logic developed in the article on deceptive advertising noted above.[40]

The Folly of Single Indicants

A final measurement problem is easily illustrated by posing the following question: "How comfortable would we feel having our intelligence assessed on the basis of our response to a *single* question?" Yet that's exactly what we do in consumer research. Brand loyalty is often "definitively assessed" by the response to a single question; the same is true with respect to virtually all of our core concepts. The literature reveals hundreds of instances in which responses to a single question suffice to establish the person's level on the variable of interest and then serves as the basis for extensive analysis and entire articles.

Just as is true of such concepts as personality and intelligence, most of our core concepts (e.g., opinion leadership, brand loyalty, innovation proneness, perceived quality, perceived risk, etc.) are multi-faceted and complex. Intelligence and personality are generally measured through a battery of different test items and methods. Even single personality traits are typically assessed via 30 to 40 item inventories. Given the complexity of our subject matter, what makes us think that we can use responses to single items (or even to two or three items) as measures of these concepts, then relate these scores to a host of other variables, arrive at conclusions based on such an investigation, and get away calling what we have done "quality research"?

STATISTICS, STATISTICS

In general, our statistical techniques for analyzing data reflect the fewest number of problems and, in recent years, probably the greatest number of advances. However, at least four major problems remain.

Number Crunching

I have finally reached the point where I am no longer automatically impressed by the use of high-powered and sophisticated statistics. Why? Because too often the use of these statistics appears *not* to be accompanied by the use of another high-powered and sophisticated tool, namely, the brain. For example, what does it really mean when the fourteenth canonical root is highly significant and shows that a set of predictors including size of house, purchase frequency of cake mix, and number of times you brush your teeth per day is related to age of oldest child living at home, laundry detergent preference, and frequency of extra-marital relations? Examination of the recent consumer research literature reveals many more instances of such mindless applications.

Multi-Layered Madness

In its most sophisticated form, number crunching involves the multi-layering of statistical techniques so that the output from one analysis provides the input for the next analysis. Sometimes, this statistical version of musical chairs involves five to ten different techniques used in series. Again, given the nature of the data collected in the first place, what does the final output actually mean?

Measuring Giant Icebergs in Millimeters and Using Calipers to Measure Melting Marshmallows

Perhaps what is most surprising about this number crunching is the fact that the data being crunched are usually exceedingly crude and coarse to begin with. As already noted, the large majority of our data are collected using the self-administered questionnaire. Yet many researchers haven't the foggiest idea about the basic DOs and DON'Ts of questionnaire construction. Consider also the fact that the reliability and validity of the data we collect are often assumed, not demonstrated.

Finally, consider the fact that trying to measure diffuse, complex, and *dynamic* phenomena such as attitudes, information processing, decision-making, etc., may be like trying to measure melting marshmallows with Vernier calipers. In other words, what are we doing working three and four digits to the right of the decimal point? What kind of phenomena, measures, and data do we really have that we are being so precise in our statistical analyses?

Substantial developments in both our methodology (particularly in regard to questionnaire construction) and the psychometric quality of our measures (particularly in regard to validity and reliability) are needed before use of high-powered statistics can be justified in many of the instances where they are now being routinely applied.

Static State Statistics

There is one area, however, in which our statistics can use improvement. By and large, most of our statistics are appropriate only for data collection using traditional, cross-sectional, static methodologies. Just as we have a need for the further development of dynamic methodologies, we need further development of statistics for analyzing the data collected using such methods. That is, we need statistics which do not force dynamic process data to be reduced to static-state representations. Trend analysis and cross-lagged correlations can and have been used in this manner. However, our repertoire of statistical techniques for handling dynamic data needs to be expanded, either by borrowing from disciplines accustomed to dealing with dynamic data, or through the creative efforts of statisticians working within the consumer research domain.

SUBJECT MATTER

Many (including Cohen[41]) have called much consumer research "trivial." In all too many ways, they are right.

Systematically Exploring the Varieties of Acquisition

Most definitions of consumer behavior shackle us by confining attention to purchase. Aside from the fact that purchase can itself take a variety of forms (e.g., buying at list price, bargaining, bidding at auction), purchase is only one form of acquisition. There are others (e.g., receiving something as a gift, in trade, on loan, etc.), each of which can have important economic, sociological, and psychological consequences and dynamics different from purchase. For example, if one million more Americans this year than last suddenly decided to borrow their neighbor's rake to handle their fall leaf problems, the impact on the rake industry could be enormous.

What are the dynamics underlying being a borrower or being a lender? What are the dynamics underlying giving or receiving a gift?[42] Hardly any published data exist regarding these other forms of acquisition—or how they interact with and affect purchase behavior. Both for scholarly and practical reasons, we must begin to systematically explore the entire realm of consumer acquisition decisions and behavior.

Putting Consumption Back into Consumer Behavior

Although considerable research has focused on actual consumption, particularly by the home economists, this fact is not adequately reflected in the predominant theories and textbooks of consumer behavior. This is surprising inasmuch as what happens during consumption has a strong influence on subsequent acquisition (especially purchase) decisions. Consumption must be given greater salience and be more tightly integrated with the existing consumer behavior literature.

What About Disposition?

The third major facet of consumer behavior, disposition, appears to have been completely neglected. This neglect should be rectified for at least four reasons:[43]

1. Many disposition decisions have significant economic consequences for both the individual and society. Some (e.g., when and how to properly dispose of unused or outdated prescription drugs) even have important health and safety ramifications.
2. Since much purchase behavior is cyclical, a variety of marketing implications would most likely emanate from an understanding of the disposition subprocess.
3. We are entering an age of relative scarcity in which we can no longer afford the luxury of squandering resources. Understanding disposition decisions and behavior is a necessary (perhaps even logically prerequisite) element in any conservationist orientation.
4. There is some evidence that the study of consumer disposition could conceivably provide us with new "unobtrusive" macro-indicators[44]—both leading and trailing—of economic trends and the state of consumer attitudes and expectations.

Consumption and Production

Not only does our conception of what constitutes consumer behavior have to be expanded and its various facets studied, but the relationship between consumption and production should be explored. Consumption and production are integrally related. Studies are needed which examine this interrelationship by considering both domains simultaneously.

CONCLUSION

This compendium is by no means an exhaustive iteration of the problems in and confronting consumer research. It does, however, cover many of the most frequently occurring and severe problems.

Quite clearly, we think it is important to know that we don't know—important so that we don't delude ourselves and others about the *quality* of our research and validity of our findings as providing sound bases upon which to make decisions of consequence. One thing we most need to learn is that we must stop letting our existing methods and tools dictate and shackle our thinking and research. They are no substitute for using our heads. The brain is still the most important tool we have and its use should precede more than succeed the collection of data.

It is important to recognize that we are in the midst of a consumer research explosion; and unless we take corrective action soon, we stand to become immersed in a quagmire from which it is already becoming increasingly difficult to extricate ourselves. Fortunately, it is not yet too late.

ENDNOTES

1. This article is based on the following presidential address delivered in 1975 to the Association for Consumer Research: Jacob Jacoby, "Consumer Research: Telling It Like It Is," in *Advances in Consumer Research, Vol. 3,* B. B. Anderson, ed. (Atlanta: Georgia State U., 1976), pp. 1–11.

2. David T. Kollat, Roger D. Blackwell, and James F. Engel, "The Current Status of Consumer Behavior Research: Development During the 1968–1972 Period," in *Proceedings of the Third Annual Conference of the Association for Consumer Research,* M. Venkatesan, ed. (1972), pp. 576–85, at pg. 577.

3. Jacob Jacoby, "Consumer Psychology as a Social Psychological Sphere of Action," *American Psychologist,* Vol. 30 (October 1975), pp. 977–87; Jacob Jacoby, same as reference 1 above.

4. Alan R. Andreasen, "Attitudes and Consumer Behavior: A Decision Model," in *New Research in Marketing,* L. Preston, ed. (Berkeley, CA: Institute of Business and Economic Research, University of California, 1965), pp. 1–16; Francesco Nicosia, *Consumer Decision Processes* (Englewood Cliffs, NJ: Prentice-Hall, 1966); James F. Engel, David T. Kollat, and Roger D. Blackwell, *Consumer Behavior* (New York: Holt, Rinehart & Winston, 1968; 2nd ed., 1973); John A. Howard and Jagdish N. Sheth, *The Theory of Buyer Behavior* (New York: John Wiley & Sons,

1969); Flemming Hansen, *Consumer Choice Behavior: A Cognitive Theory* (New York: Free Press, 1972); Rom J. Markin, *Consumer Behavior: A Cognitive Orientation* (New York: Macmillan Publishing Co., 1974).

5. Kollat et al., same as reference 2 above, p. 577.

6. Jacob Jacoby, "Toward Defining Consumer Psychology: One Psychologist's Views," *Purdue Papers in Consumer Psychology,* No. 101, 1969. Paper presented at the 77th Annual Convention of the American Psychological Association, Washington, D.C. (1969); Jacob Jacoby, "Personality and Consumer Behavior: How NOT to Find Relationships," *Purdue Papers in Consumer Psychology,* No. 102 (1969).

7. Engel et al., same as reference 4 above, pp. 652–53; Harold H. Kassarjian, "Personality and Consumer Behavior: A Review," *Journal of Marketing Research,* Vol. VIII (November 1971), pp. 409–18.

8. David M. Gardner, "Deception in Advertising: A Conceptual Approach," *Journal of Marketing,* Vol. 39, No. 1 (January 1975), pp. 40–46.

9. Edward W. Cundiff, "Alpha Kappa Psi Foundation and Harold H. Maynard Awards for 1975," *Journal of Marketing,* Vol. 40, No. 2 (April 1975), pg. 2.

10. Victor H. Denenberg, "Polixities A. Zeitgeister, B.S., M.S., PhONY," *Psychology Today,* Vol. 3 (June 1969), pg. 50.

11. Mary Jane Schlinger, ed., *Advances in Consumer Research, Vol. 2,* Proceedings of the Association for Consumer Research, (Chicago: U. of Illinois, 1975).

12. Leo Bogart, "No Opinion, Don't Know, and Maybe No Answer," *Public Opinion Quarterly,* Vol. 31 (Fall 1967), pg. 335.

13. Paul Erdos, *Professional Mail Surveys* (New York: McGraw-Hill, 1970); Stanley L. Payne, *The Art of Asking Questions* (Princeton, NJ: Princeton University Press, 1951); Arthur Kornhauser and Paul B. Sheatsley, "Questionnaire Construction and Interview Procedure," in *Research Methods in Social Relations,* C. Selltiz, M. Jahoda, M. Deutsch, and S.W. Cook, eds. (New York: Henry Holt & Co., 1959), pp. 546–87.

14. Jacob Jacoby, Robert W. Chestnut, Karl Weigl, and William Fisher, "Pre-Purchase Information Acquisition: Description of a Process Methodology, Research Paradigm, and Pilot Investigation," in *Advances in Consumer Research:*

Vol. 3, B. B. Anderson, ed. (Atlanta: Georgia State U., 1976), pp. 306–14; John Payne, "Heuristic Search Processes in Decision-Making," in *Advances in Consumer Research: Vol. 3,* B. B. Anderson, ed., (Atlanta: Georgia State U., 1976).

15. John R. Platt, "Strong Inference," *Science,* Vol. 146 (1964), pg. 351.

16. Jacoby et al., same as reference 14 above; Peter L. Wright, "Research Orientations for Analyzing Consumer Judgment Processes," in *Advances in Consumer Research: Vol. 1,* S. Ward and P. L. Wright, eds. (Urbana, IL: Association for Consumer Research, 1974), pp. 268–79.

17. Jacob Jacoby, Donald E. Speller, and Carol A. Kohn Berning, "Brand Choice Behavior as a Function of Information Load: Replication and Extension," *Journal of Consumer Research,* Vol. 1 (June 1974), pp. 33–42.

18. Jacob Jacoby and David B. Kyner, "Brand Loyalty vs. Repeat Purchasing Behavior," *Journal of Marketing Research,* Vol. X (February 1973), pp. 1–9.

19. Kollat et al., same as reference 2 above.

20. Jacob Jacoby and Robert W. Chestnut, *Brand Loyalty: Measurement and Management* (New York: Wiley Interscience, in press).

21. Carol A. Kohn and Jacob Jacoby, "Operationally Defining the Consumer Innovator," *Proceedings, 81st Annual Convention of the American Psychological Association,* Vol. 8 (Issue 2, 1973), pp. 837–38; Thomas S. Robertson, *Innovative Behavior and Communication* (New York: Holt, Rinehart & Winston, 1971).

22. Everett M. Rogers and David G. Cartano, "Methods of Measuring Opinion Leadership," *Public Opinion Quarterly,* Vol. 26 (Fall 1962), pp. 435–41.

23. Charles W. King and John O. Summers, "Overlap of Opinion Leadership Across Consumer Product Categories," *Journal of Marketing Research,* Vol. VII (February 1970), pp. 43–50.

24. Jacob Jacoby, "Opinion Leadership and Innovativeness: Overlap and Validity," in *Proceedings of the Third Annual Conference of the Association for Consumer Research,* M. Venkatesan, ed. (1972), pp. 632–49.

25. American Psychological Association, *Standards for Educational and Psychological Tests and Manuals* (Washington: American Psychological Association, 1966); Reinhard Angelmar, Gerald Zaltman, and Christian Pinson, "An Examination of Concept Validity," in *Proceedings of the Third Annual Conference of the Association for Con-*

sumer Research, M. Venkatesan, ed. (1972), pp. 586–93; Lee Cronbach, *Essentials of Psychological Testing,* 2nd ed. (New York: Harper & Bros., 1960); Roger M. Heeler and Michael L. Ray, "Measure Validation in Marketing," *Journal of Marketing Research,* Vol. IX (November 1972), pp. 361–70; Jim C. Nunnally, *Psychometric Theory* (New York: McGraw-Hill, 1973).

26. Nunnally, ibid., pp. 75–102.

27. Alfred A. Kuehn, "Demonstration of a Relationship Between Psychological Factors and Brand Choice," *Journal of Business,* Vol. 36 (April 1963), pp. 237–41; Heeler and Ray, same as reference 25 above.

28. P. S. Raju, Rabi S. Bhagat, and Jagdish N. Sheth, "Predictive Validation and Cross-Validation of the Fishbein, Rosenberg, and Sheth Models of Attitudes," in *Advances in Consumer Research: Vol. 2,* M. J. Schlinger, ed. (Chicago: U. of Illinois, 1975), pp. 405–25, at pg. 407.

29. Leon B. Kaplan, George J. Szybillo, and Jacob Jacoby, "Components of Perceived Risk in Product Purchase: A Cross-Validation," *Journal of Applied Psychology,* Vol. 59 (June 1974), pp. 287–91; Raju et al., same as reference 28 above; Donald E. Speller, "Attitudes and Intentions as Predictors of Purchase: A Cross-Validation," *Proceedings, 81st Annual Convention of the American Psychological Association,* Vol. 8 (Issue 2, 1973), pp. 825–26; David T. Wilson, H. Lee Mathews, and James W. Harvey, "An Empirical Test of the Fishbein Behavioral Intention Model," *Journal of Consumer Research,* Vol. 1 (March 1975), pp. 39–48.

30. Dominic W. Massaro, *Experimental Psychology and Information Processing* (Chicago: Rand-McNally, 1975), pg. 23; Robert Plutchik, *Foundations of Experimental Research* (New York: Harper & Row, 1968), pg. 45; Selltiz et al., same as reference 13 above, pp. 146–47.

31. Plutchik, ibid., pg. 47.

32. Donald T. Campbell and Donald W. Fiske, "Convergent and Discriminant Validation by the Multitrait-Multimethod Matrix," *Psychological Bulletin,* Vol. 56 (1959), pp. 81–105.

33. Harry L. Davis, "Measurement of Husband-Wife Influence in Consumer Purchase Decisions," *Journal of Marketing Research,* Vol. VIII (August 1971), pp. 305–12; Jacob Jacoby, "The Construct Validity of Opinion Leadership," *Public Opinion Quarterly,* Vol. 38 (Spring 1974), pp. 81–89; Alvin J. Silk, "Response Set and the Measurement of Self-Designated Opinion Leader-

ship,'' *Public Opinion Quarterly,* Vol. 35 (Fall 1971), pp. 383–97.

34. Campbell et al., same as reference 32 above, pg. 100.

35. Jacoby et al. (in press), same as reference 20 above.

36. Kohn et al., same as reference 21 above.

37. Jerry Olson and Jacob Jacoby, ''A Construct Validation Study of Brand Loyalty,'' in *Proceedings, 79th Annual Convention of the American Psychological Association,* Vol. 6 (1971), pp. 657–58.

38. Kevin J. Clancy and David M. Kweskin, ''T.V. Commercial Recall Correlates,'' *Journal of Advertising Research,* Vol. 11 (April 1971), pp. 18–20; Shirley Young, ''Copy Testing Without Magic Numbers,'' *Journal of Advertising Research,* Vol. 12 (February 1972), pp. 3–12.

39. Young, ibid., pg. 7.

40. Gardner, same as reference 8 above, pp. 43–44.

41. Joel Cohen, Presidential Address, untitled, *Association for Consumer Research Newsletter,* Vol. 3 (January 1973), pp. 3–5.

42. Edward W. Hart, Jr., ''Consumer Risk-Taking for Self and for Spouse,'' unpublished Ph.D. dissertation (Purdue University, 1974); Karl Weigl, ''Perceived Risk and Information Search in a Gift Buying Situation,'' unpublished M. S. thesis (Purdue University, 1975).

43. Jacob Jacoby, Carol K. Berning, and Thomas Dietvorst, ''What about Disposition?'' *Journal of Marketing,* Vol. 41, No. 2 (April 1977), pp. 22–28.

44. Eugene J. Webb, Donald T. Campbell, Richard D. Schwartz, and Lee Sechrest, *Unobtrusive Measures: Non-Reactive Research in the Social Sciences* (Chicago: Rand-McNally, 1966).

Questions

1. Describe some of the major problems that exist in some of the consumer research studies.

2. Define the following terms:
   a. Theory
   b. Concept
   c. Instrument error
   d. Reliability

3. Explain the difference in predictive validity and convergent validity.

Cross-Reference Grid

Text Author(s), Title, Edition	Text Chapter Numbers										
	1	2	3	4	5	6	7	8	9	10	11
Assael, Henry. *Consumer Behavior and Marketing Action* (Boston, Mass.: Kent Publishing Co., 1981)		1 2 3 24 27 28 42 43 45 46	9 10 11 13		16 17	15 25	6 7 8 12 41 44			18 19 20 21 22	37 38 40
Berkman, Harold W., and Christopher Gilson. *Consumer Behavior: Concepts and Strategies,* 2nd ed. (Boston, Mass.: Kent Publishing Co., 1981)		1 2 3 26 43 44 46	38 20	21 22	32 33 37 40	34 35 36	23 39	9 10 11	14 15 16 17 25 41	12 13 18 19 42	6 7 8
Block, Carl E., and Kenneth J. Roering. *Essentials of Consumer Behavior,* 2nd ed. (Hinsdale, Ill.: The Dryden Press, 1979)		1 2 3	38	37 40 41	21 22 32 33 34 35 36	23 39	18 19 20	9 10 11 13 17		6 7 8	12 42 43 44 45 46
Engel, James F., Roger D. Blackwell, and David T. Kollat. *Consumer Behavior,* 3rd ed. (Hinsdale, Ill.: The Dryden Press, 1978)		24		37 40	34 35 36	21 22 23 32 33 38	18 19 20 41	5 12 13 14	15 16 17		30
Hawkins, Del I., Kenneth A. Coney, and Roger J. Best. *Consumer Behavior* (Dallas: Business Publications, Inc., 1980)		1 2 3	5	41	38	37 40	19 34 35 36	29 30 31 32 33	23	9 10 16 17 26	11 39
Loudon, David L., and Albert J. Della Bitta. *Consumer Behavior: Concepts and Applications* (New York: McGraw-Hill, 1979)		1 2 3	42 43 44 45 46		19 20	41	37	39 40	34 35 36	32 33	23 38
	1	2	3	4	5	6	7	8	9	10	11

Text Chapter Numbers

12	13	14	15	16	17	18	19	20	21	22	23	24	25	26	27
34 35 36	32 33	23 39	30	29 31	4 5	43	26	14							
30 45	5 24 27 28	29 31													
26	25	5	15 16 24 27 28	4 29 30 31		14									
29 31	7 9 10 11 26		8 44	6		4 27 28	14	1 2 3 25	42 43 45 46						
13 18	6 8	20 21 22	12 27 28	25		14 15	4 7 24	46							
29 30 31	5 12 13 14	15 16 17	9 10 11	18 21 22	6 7 8		24	26		4 27 28					
12	13	14	15	16	17	18	19	20	21	22	23	24	25	26	27

(continued)

Cross-Reference Grid (*continued*)

Text Author(s), Title, Edition	1	2	3	4	5	6	7	8	9	10	11
McNeal, James U. *Consumer Behavior: An Integrative Approach* (Boston: Little, Brown, 1982)		1 2 3	12	7 13	18 19 20	6 7 8	9 10 11 26	15	23 24 25	30 31 32 33	34 35 36
Runyon, Kenneth E. *Consumer Practice of Marketing,* 2nd ed. (Columbus, Ohio: Charles E. Merrill Publishing Co., 1980)			8	1 2 3	37 40 41	34 35 36	29 30 31 32 33	23 38 39	12 13	9 11	18 20
Schiffman, Leon G., and Leslie Lazar Kanuk. *Consumer Behavior* (Englewood Cliffs, N.J.: Prentice-Hall, Inc., 1978)		12 13 14 42 43 45 46	16 17 21 22 25	9 10 11	18 19 20	6 7 8 44	15 26	32 33	23 39	30	34 35 36
Walters, C. Glenn. *Consumer Behavior: Theory and Practice,* 3rd ed. (Homewood, Ill.: Richard Irwin, 1978)			1 2 3	24 25 27 28				4 5 14 16	21 22	12	13
Williams, Terrell G. *Consumer Behavior: Fundamentals and Strategies* (St. Paul, Minn.: West Publishing Co., 1982)	1 2	3 5 24	15 17 25	12 13 20 21 22	9 10 11 26	6 7 8 41	32 33 34 35 36 37	23 38 39 40	42 43 44 46	4 29 30 31	18
Zaltman, Gerald, and Melanie Wallendorf. *Consumer Behavior: Basic Findings and Management Implications* (New York: John Wiley & Sons, Inc., 1979)			5 37 38 39 40	24 34 35 36	19 32 33	23			30	9	10 11 15 16 17 21 22 25
	1	2	3	4	5	6	7	8	9	10	11

Text Chapter Numbers

12	13	14	15	16	17	18	19	20	21	22	23	24	25	26	27
21 22	4 29	16	17	5 14		37 38 39 40 41	27 28	42 43 44 45 46							
21 22	6 7 26	15 16 17	4 5 24 25	14 19	10	42 44 46	45								
	37 38 40 41	29 31	1 2 3 4 5 24												
15 17	6 7 8 44	9 11 26	18 19	29 30 31	20 23		38	32 33 34 35 36		37 39 40		42 43 44 45 46			10
16			45	14 19	27 28										
26	12	13 14	18 20 42	6 7 8 41 44		4 29 31			1 2 3 27 28 43 45 46						
12	13	14	15	16	17	18	19	20	21	22	23	24	25	26	27

AUTHOR INDEX

SUBJECT INDEX